Richelieu's
DESMARETS

I. Desmarests Seig.r de S.t Sorlin. Cons.r du Roy, Controlleur
Général de l'extraordinaire des guerres, et Secretaire
Général de la marine de leuant, celebre par vne infinité
de rares ouurages de prose et de vers &c.

Portrait of Jean Desmarets de Saint-Sorlin engraved by Pierre Lombard
after Henri Gascar: Bibliothèque Nationale, Cabinet des estampes,
58.20701 (*Phot. Bibl. Nat. Paris*)

Richelieu's

DESMARETS

and the Century of

Louis XIV

Hugh Gaston Hall

CLARENDON PRESS · OXFORD

1990

Oxford University Press, Walton Street, Oxford OX2 6DP

Oxford New York Toronto
Delhi Bombay Calcutta Madras Karachi
Petaling Jaya Singapore Hong Kong Tokyo
Nairobi Dar es Salaam Cape Town
Melbourne Auckland

and associated companies in
Beirut Berlin Ibadan Nicosia

Oxford is a trade mark of Oxford University Press

Published in the United States by
Oxford University Press (USA)

British Library Cataloguing in Publication Data
Hall, Hugh Gaston
Richelieu's Desmarets and the century of Louis XIV.
1. France. Social Life, 1613–1715—Biographies
I. Title
944'.033'0924
ISBN 0–19–815157–8

Library of Congress Cataloging in Publication Data
Hall, H. Gaston.
Richelieu's Desmarets and the century of Louis XIV/Hugh Gaston Hall.
p. cm.
Includes bibliographical references.
1. Desmarets de Saint-Sorlin, Jean, 1600?–1676. 2. Richelieu,
Armand Jean Du Plessis, duc de, 1585–1642—Friends and associates.
3. Authors, French—17th century—Biography. 4. France—Court and
courtiers—Biography. 5. France—History—Louis, XIV, 1643–1715.
6. Performing art—France—History—17th century. 7. Ancients and
moderns, Quarrel of. 8. Académie française—History. I. Title.
PQ1794.D6H35 1990 841'.4—dc20 89-16373
ISBN 0–19–815157–8

Typeset by Dobbie Typesetting Ltd.
Printed in Great Britain by
Biddles Ltd, Guildford and King's Lynn

To Gillian

Acknowledgements

I am grateful to the British Academy for a grant in aid of research, to the Institut Britannique for the use of its studio in Paris during research, to the University of Warwick for study leave, and to the Camargo Foundation, Cassis, for a Fellowship, during which the book was drafted. Some of the research was done a great deal earlier, for a Yale University Ph.D. thesis presented in 1958 and now superseded. Without encouragement at that time from Yale University and the Lewis-Farmington Trust, the research would not have been initiated. I have also to thank the associations which have provided a forum for presenting interim results of the sometimes lonely research on an unfashionable writer and his role in French literary culture, notably the Centre Méridional de Rencontres sur le XVIIe siècle, the Centre National de la Recherche Scientifique, the North American Society for Seventeenth-Century French Literature, the Société d'Études du XVIIe siècle, the Society for Seventeenth-Century French Studies, and the Society for French Studies. I am grateful to librarians, archivists, and colleagues—too numerous to mention individually—for generous assistance in a variety of ways.

Contents

List of Illustrations	ix
Introduction	1
1. Jean Desmarets and the Century of Louis XIV	19
2. Family	42
3. The 'Célèbre Marets' of Court Ballet	58
4. Missions and Offices	84
5. The Novels and the New Académie-Française	109
6. Richelieu, Desmarets, and Theatre	131
7. *Les Visionnaires*	154
8. The Historical Tragicomedies	162
9. Plays for the Grand'Salle of the Palais-Cardinal	179
10. *La Félicité* and *La Prospérité*	200
11. Short Poems and Games	212
12. Devotional Poetry	237
13. Devotional Prose	261
14. *Clovis, ou la France Chrestienne*	286
15. The Late Biblical and Heroic Poems	310
16. The Quarrel of the *Imaginaires*	319
Conclusion	343
Bibliography	357
A. *Corpus Maresianum*	357
1. Separately printed titles	358
2. Posthumous works	372
3. Manuscripts	372
B. Select Secondary Sources	373
Index	379

List of Illustrations

Portrait of Jean Desmarets de Saint-Sorlin engraved by
Pierre Lombard after Henri Gascar   ii

1. Dedicatory portrait of *Clovis*: Louis XIV on horseback
   engraved by Jean Couvay after Sébastien Bourdon   26

2. Signatures of Desmarets, Anne Fleury, René Fleury, and
   Marie Rousseau, 2 May 1634   43

3. Marets as the Grand Turk   74

4. Mélinte parachuting from a prison tower by the Tiber   112

5. Detail of the heart-sacrifice in *Ariane*   114

6. Ariane surprised in her bath   117

7. *Mirame*, perspective set   190

8. *Europe*, frontispiece   198

9. Louis XIII in *Cartes des Rois de France*   233

10. Louis XIV in *Cartes des Rois de France*   233

11. Anne of Austria in *Jeu des Reynes renommées*   235

12. Eusèbe and Philédon kneeling before Christ   276

13. The tauriform sea monster from *Clovis*   292

14. *Le Triomphe de Louis*, title-page   354

Introduction

Jean Desmarets, later Sieur de Saint-Sorlin (1600?–76), last jester of the royal Court of France and first Chancellor of the Académie-Française, is arguably one of the most versatile, and certainly one of the most prolific, French writers of the seventeenth century. He died the last surviving founder-member of the Académie-Française, having published in all the major literary genres: novels, lyric and heroic poetry, drama, letters, dialogues, essays, and treatises. The formats, reprints, and translations of his publications witness a writer far more successful with the contemporary reading public than might be judged from the literary history of the 'century of Louis XIV'. Indeed, he was one of the most successful writers of his time.

Desmarets's dedications

Dedications are a feature of his publications to which little attention has been given.[1] No other seventeenth-century French writer dedicated his books and poems to such a distinguished list of Court personalities—men and women at the very summit of French society and government, including: (for major books and plays) Louis XIII; Louis XIV; the Queen Regent, Anne of Austria; Louis XIV's Queen, Marie-Thérèse; the first ministers Cardinals Richelieu and Mazarin; the first Duchesse d'Aiguillon; the first Duchesse de Richelieu; and (for poems) the two Kings; Anne of Austria; Cardinal Richelieu, as well as Gaston d'Orléans, Lieutenant général de France; Chancellor Pierre Séguier; Nicolas Fouquet, Surintendant des Finances; Jean-Baptiste Colbert; Charles Perrault; Mme Du Vigean; the Duc and the Duchesse de Longueville; the second Duc de Richelieu, etc. In the third quarter of the century no one else dedicated so many titles to Louis XIV.

Such impressive dedications do not, of course, guarantee literary quality. They do imply unusual status, the background of which this

---

[1] W. Leiner, *Der Widmungsbrief in der französischen Literatur (1580–1715)* (Heidelberg, 1965), is a pioneering work in this area of scholarship but lists only thirteen titles for Desmarets; and these contain two wrong attributions. *Roxane* is misprinted as *Rosalie*. The repeated dedications of *Clovis* to Louis XIV and of *Les Délices de l'esprit* to Mazarin are among the omissions.

book seeks to explain. The dedication of *Clovis* (1657) 'Au Roy' escaped Wolfgang Leiner's normally careful notice. Yet it is one of the first prominent books—perhaps *the* first—advising the young King how to '*acquerir le nom de* **Louïs le Grand**'. It matters to an understanding of the Quarrel of the *Imaginaires* to add to Leiner's corpus of dedicatory epistles Desmarets's dedication to Louis XIV of his *Response à l'insolente Apologie des Religieuses de Port-Royal.* A copy in the Réserve des imprimés of the Bibliothèque Nationale bears Louis XIV's arms on the red morocco binding of his personal library.

In his poem *Au Roy, sur sa conqueste de la Franche-Comté* (1668), Desmarets recalls advice the young King had given him on the composition of *Clovis*: 'Des mensonges flateurs feroient tort à l'ouvrage'—a sentiment worthy of a *Louis-quatorziana*, and sound advice, not scrupulously followed by the poet. It is, however, personified France who, in Desmarets's 'Stances' dedicated during the Fronde to Louis XIV's mother, Anne of Austria, condemns flattery as a monstrous evil:

> Tay toy, Monstre infernal, dit la France en courroux,
> Peste des Souverains, boute-feu detestable,
> Qui portes à l'aigreur les esprits les plus doux,
> Et qui de mes malheurs es la seule coupable.
> Par toy l'on a perdu l'ordre avec l'équité,
> L'on a poussé mes maux jusqu'à l'extrêmité,
> Sans bornes, sans raison, sans pitié, sans prudence,
> Par toy les meilleurs Rois deviendroient des Tyrans.
> Que l'on fasse à la Cour taire ton impudence,
> Et l'on verra soudain finir nos differens.[2]

What he understood by 'l'ordre avec l'équité' differs sharply from current aspirations of pluralistic democracy, but he was never far from his rulers in expressing his own aspirations to a just political order.

A Court actor, dancer, musician, 'bouffon du Roi'

It has only recently come to light that the author of *Ariane* and *Les Visionnaires* was a star performer in Court ballets. The obvious

---

[2] 'La France à la Reine Régente, lors de la Guerre de Paris', in his *Comparaison de la langue et de la poësie françoise avec la grecque & la latine* (1670), 166. Compare the 'détestables flatteurs' topos in Racine's *Phèdre* (IV. VI).

explanation of Desmarets's Court connections is that, as an amateur actor, musician, celebrated dancer, favourite, and 'bouffon du Roi', he established access to Louis XIII as a youthful favourite two decades before entering Richelieu's personal service, in 1634. His personal contacts with members of the royal family, begun in the Regency of Marie de Médicis, continued into the personal reign of Louis XIV.

In this respect, Desmarets's experience contrasts with that of Charles Sorel (1600–74), an exact contemporary who had somewhat similar origins in the Parisian bourgeois gentry. Sorel, a talented writer, became Historiographe de France but never enjoyed at Court the familiarity evident throughout Desmarets's career. In *Artisans of Glory* Orest Ranum states:

It is impossible to determine why Sorel failed to gain attention at the court of Louis XIII, but his tendency to be farcical . . . may not have served him in good stead. The circle of gentlemen around Louis XIII, led by the first gentleman of the bedchamber, Claude de Rouvroy, first Duke of Saint-Simon, made it extremely difficult for men of Sorel's inferior social origins to do anything but bow before the King.[3]

Desmarets had aristocratic connections, as Chapter 2 explains. Undoubtedly such connections helped, but it may be equally important that he got in early. This first Duc de Saint-Simon, father of the memoirist, was not quite 6 years old when Desmarets (or Marets) was first noticed at Court. Saint-Simon did not become Premier Gentilhomme de la Chambre du Roi until 1628, nor a Duke before 1635. By then Desmarets no longer needed an introduction.

Why 'Richelieu's Desmarets'?

I have called him 'Richelieu's Desmarets' because of his close collaboration with Cardinal Richelieu from 1634 until Richelieu's death. 'Vingt fois,' notes Tallemant des Réaux, 'il a fait couvrir et asseoir Desmarestz dans un fauteuil comme luy, et vouloit qu'il ne l'appellast que *Monsieur*.'[4] Tallemant is not always a reliable witness, but the remark that Desmarets worked closely with Cardinal Richelieu is abundantly attested. It is difficult not to interpret as an

---

[3] O. Ranum, *Artisans of Glory. Writers and Historical Thought in Seventeenth-century France* (Chapel Hill, 1980), 130.

[4] G. Tallemant des Réaux, *Historiettes*, ed. A. Adam and G. Delassault (2 vols.; 1960–1), i. 274.

autobiographical reference to Desmarets's own relations with Richelieu the reminiscences of the Palais de la Fortune related by Eusèbe in *Les Délices de l'esprit*:

Donques auec l'ayde de quelques-vns sur lesquels ie m'appuyay pour arriuer iusqu'au haut, ie paruins à l'appartement de celuy qui dominoit en ce lieu éleué. Là ie goustay mille plaisirs rauissans, par l'estime qu'il fit de moy, par les caresses & particulieres & publiques dont il m'honora, par les applaudissemens que ie receuois de toutes parts, & par les victoires que ie remportois souuent sur mes enuieux.[5]

Of course Eusèbe (the pious discussant of the dialogues) is a literary invention. In the *Seconde Partie de la Response à l'insolente Apologie de Port-Royal*, Desmarets states with reference to the youthful debauchery admitted by Eusèbe:

Dans tout ce Livre je ne parle point de moy-mesme, ny en mon nom; mais j'introduis vn homme de pieté, qui s'appelle Eusebe, & qui traitte des choses humaines, & divines. Ie puis avoir recherché les Livres qui en parlent, sans que je doive pour cela estre accusé d'avoir voulu parler comme estant moy-mesme ce personnage . . . je n'ay point escrit que je suis Eusebe . . . je n'ay jamais écrit que ma vie ait esté semblable à mes livres, ny que j'aye esté dans le libertinage, n'ayant jamais esté dans l'impieté.[6]

However, it does not follow even from this pertinent warning about the dangers of literary biographism that Desmarets never alludes to himself in his imaginative works. On occasion he purports to do so.

Friends who assisted Desmarets's entry into Richelieu's personal service are mentioned by Tallemant, who also reports two of Desmarets's enemies as envious. In 1635 the Cardinal baptized and/or acted as godfather to Jean Desmarets's son, Armand-Jean.

After the Cardinal's death on 4 December 1642, Desmarets continued in the service of the Duchesse d'Aiguillon, Cardinal Richelieu's niece and executrix—one of the great ladies of the Court both before and after the death of Louis XIII. He is identified in a tax record of March 1649 as steward of the late Cardinal's estate: 'intendant des affaires de feu M. le Cardinal de Richelieu'.[7] He may

---

[5] *Les Délices de l'esprit* (1658), i. 5.

[6] *Seconde Partie de la Response à l'insolente Apologie de Port-Royal* (1666), 69, 73.

[7] F.-N. Baudot de Dubuisson-Aubenay, *Journal des guerres civiles 1648–1652*, ed. G. Saige (2 vols.; 1883–5), ii. 348. The document, an extract of taxes, indicates that during the siege of early 1649 Desmarets was living in Paris, in the rue Garancière near St-Sulpice.

have been the preceptor, and certainly became the steward, of the Cardinal's principal heir, the second Duc de Richelieu, in whose home in the Place-Royale in Paris he died on 28 October 1676. It was to that great-nephew of the Cardinal that Desmarets would in 1649 arrange—with the help of the Princes de Condé and de Conti and the Duc and Duchesse de Longueville—the clandestine marriage of his own cousin, Anne Poussart de Pons (née du Vigean).

It might be argued that for much longer than he was the Cardinal-Duc's Desmarets he was the second Duc de Richelieu's Desmarets: thirty-three years, from 1643 to 1676. But my title alludes to his association with the Cardinal's innovative cultural policies between 1634 and 1642, and to his fidelity to the Cardinal's vision for dynamic and coherent modernism in French literary culture, a vision which Desmarets carried into the quarrel of the ancients and moderns at the end of Louis XIV's long reign. The phrase 'Richelieu's Desmarets' also reminds us that he was not Sieur de Saint-Sorlin until past 50, and it separates this Jean Desmarets from the father of the unrelated minister Nicolas Desmarets, remembered in the eighteenth century as Louis XIV's Desmarets.

A late Renaissance universal man

Discussion of Desmarets's family connections, dancing, writing, other activities, and controversies will occupy the following pages. His now neglected books constitute the least inaccessible part of the record, but he was never solely, and seldom mainly, a writer. Indeed, he was scarcely a writer at all until past an age at which some famous authors are dead—though this last point is moderated by the discovery that he was evidently born some five years later than previously assumed.

The evidence that Desmarets was a talented performer is presented in Chapter 3. He was also a painter, an architect, and, from the age of 20, deputy Surintendant des fortifications, acting for the King in a divided Court. Sauval states that he had his family home reconstructed according to his own design—a reconstruction to which Jean Chapelain may refer in a letter to Boisrobert about an early meeting of the Académie-Française on 4 September 1634: 'la sale de M. Desmarest est, depuis six semaines, trois fois plus grande que d'ordinaire'.[8]

---

[8] H. Sauval, *Histoire et recherches des antiquités de Paris* (3 vols., 1733), ii. 260; J. Chapelain, *Lettres*, ed. P. Tamizey de Larroque (3 vols., 1883), i. 78. However, so

According to Tallemant des Réaux, François Sublet des Noyers, Surintendant des bâtiments (1638–43) and (from 1636) Secrétaire d'État de la Guerre, 'a nuy en tout ce qu'il a pu à Desmarestz, qui s'entend à tout et qui a beaucoup d'inclination pour l'Architecture, de peur que cet homme ne luy ostast quelque chose'.[9]

Architectural inspiration permeates Desmarets's literary works: *Ariane, Les Visionnaires, Les Amours du compas et de la règle, La Vérité des fables, Les Promenades de Richelieu, Clovis, Les Délices de l'esprit, Marie-Madeleine, Esther*, etc. The architectural inspiration is so strong that Jean-Pierre Lassalle has wondered whether Desmarets might have been an early Freemason, long before any formal Masonic organization is recorded in France.[10]

The universal erudition which the Desmarets brothers continued, in the mid-seventeenth century, to associate with the aspiration to excel in heroic poetry was recommended for architects by the Jesuit educationist Estienne Binet (1569–1639). The ideal epic poet would possess gifts similar to those of the ideal architect suggested in the chapter on architecture in Binet's *Essay des merveilles de nature*, first published in 1621: 'le parfait Architecte ne doit rien ignorer'; painting, skill with compass and rule, knowledge of perspective, arithmetic, history, medicine, and 'astrologie' (early astronomy in this case) are all required. Strikingly pertinent to Desmarets's published architectural descriptions and allegories, Binet's doctrine might also be taken as the metaphoric expression of the ideal 'architecture' in space, time, harmony, and symbolism of the Court ballets with which Jean Desmarets was long associated.[11] 'Poëtae autem,' Roland Desmarets writes to Antoine Godeau, 'nihil à se alienum putant, nullumque esse argumentum, quod non pro suo iure tractare possint'.[12] The spirituality of *Les Délices de l'esprit*, begun at the young second Duc de Richelieu's suggestion as a first French

---

soon after August, Chapelain may refer obliquely to poor attendance, of which there is mention elsewhere.

[9] Tallemant des Réaux, *Historiettes*, i. 298.

[10] J.-P. Lassalle, 'Un esprit supérieur passionné d'architecture: Jean Desmarets de Saint-Sorlin', *Cahiers de la Grande Loge provinciale d'Occitanie*, N S 3 (1986), 23-7.

[11] E. Binet, *Essay des merveilles de nature, et des plus nobles artifices*, ed. M. Fumaroli (Evreux, 1987), 438-70.

[12] *Rolandi Maresii Epistolarum philologicarum Libri II*, ii (1655), 38. Jean Desmarets shared this view, which would have been understood by Pierre de Ronsard (1524–85) or Victor Hugo (1802–85), but not by François de Malherbe (1555–1626) or Nicolas Boileau-Despréaux (1636–1711).

encyclopaedia, is based on a wide-ranging and detailed knowledge of the arts and sciences.

Jean Desmarets held other offices, with functions which, though not well understood, were clearly important. Chapter 4 provides details of previously overlooked missions by Desmarets. One is documented in *Le Voyage de Fontainebleau* (1623), a mission undertaken on behalf of the Paris Parlement to convey a *remontrance* to the King and made with Guillaume II Bautru, Comte de Serrant, whose friendship with Desmarets dates from that voyage. Desmarets was then already Député pour les fortifications, a commission he held from the siege of Caen in 1620 until he borrowed 10,000 *livres* to purchase the office of Surintendant des fortifications in 1634, shortly before France entered the Thirty Years War. Already Contrôleur de l'Extraordinaire des guerres for some time before 1634, he sold that office, having become, probably also in 1634, Contrôleur général de l'Extraordinaire des guerres, an office which may have been considerable, since (according to Charles Perrault) the annual budget of the Extraordinaire des guerres was raised *c.*1667 to 60,000,000 *livres*, a huge amount at the time.[13] Its supply became a major concern of government, as the Extraordinaire des guerres must have been to varying degrees throughout the years Desmarets was Contrôleur général, mostly during wartime. If we knew the functions of the Contrôleur général and the extent to which Desmarets actually exercised this *charge*, we could understand somewhat better the way in which the war with Spain (1635–59) was financed, for example the financial arrangements for the expansion of the French army between 1634 and 1635 to meet the Habsburg threat.[14] By 1634 Desmarets had already held the lesser office of Contrôleur de l'Extraordinaire des guerres for some time, and he was a Secrétaire du Roi in that department. There is evidence, disappointingly scant, that he actively exercised these *charges*. Signatures prove that between 1643 and 1661 he exercised the additional *charge* of Secrétaire-général de la Marine de Levant at the not inconsiderable annual salary of 3,000 (later 4,000) *livres*. A Conseiller du Roi, though apparently never in the Conseil d'en haut, Desmarets is said in the *Voyage de*

---

[13] Charles Perrault, *Mémoires*, ed. P. Lacroix (1878), 109.
[14] The recent work of R. Bonney, *The King's Debts: Finance and Politics in France 1589–1661* (Oxford, 1981), and of D. Parrot, 'French Military Organization in the 1630s: the failure of Richelieu's Ministry', *Seventeenth-Century French Studies*, 9 (1987), 151–67, sharpens the focus of the question.

Fontainebleau to have accompanied Louis XIII to meetings of the Conseil—years before Cardinal Richelieu's main ministry began in 1624.

A man of his century

It has been largely forgotten that Desmarets's acting delighted the French Court, that his prose and verse helped consolidate the modern French language, that he wrote the first inscription in French for a royal monument in Paris. It is recalled to his disadvantage that he wrote the deposition which helped convict the last man judicially burnt alive in Paris (Simon Morin, executed in March 1663) and that he caused the arrest of the Jansenist publicist Isaac Le Maistre de Sacy, in 1666.

Yet from well before 1620—when he wrote up the articles of surrender for the first triumph of Louis XIII, the surrender of the château de Caen—until he called upon Charles Perrault in 1675 to defend the literature of France from those who seemed to assume that it could never equal the letters of ancient Greece and Rome, Desmarets was involved in most of the major cultural events of his century: *Le Ballet de la délivrance de Renaud*, anticipating the *coup d'état* of 24 April 1617; the 'Guirlande de Julie', presented on 1 January 1634 to the daughter of the celebrated Marquise de Rambouillet (1588–1665); the foundation of the Académie française, which first met officially in his home; the Querelle du 'Cid', in which Desmarets was involved as one of the authors of the Académie's *Sentiments* on that play; the celebration of the birth of Louis XIV, in which Desmarets participated as author of, and dancer in, the *Ballet de la Félicité sur l'heureuse naissance de Monseigneur le Dauphin*; the opening of the first great theatre in France with a proscenium arch, and the rehabilitation of the acting profession in 1641; the quarrel of 'Job' and 'Uranie' on the eve of the Fronde; the clandestine marriage of the Duc de Richelieu, which precipitated the Fronde des Princes; the Quarrel of the *Imaginaires*; and a dispute over theatre involving Racine, Corneille, Molière, and the Prince de Conti. The Quarrel of the ancients and moderns is foreshadowed in the last two books he had published in his lifetime: *La Deffense du Poëme héroïque*, highly critical of Nicolas Boileau-Despréaux, and *La Defense de la poësie*, which appeals to Charles Perrault to take up the defence and illustration of modern French literature.

An officer-author in context

This book attempts to present Desmarets's cultural experience, activities, and achievements in context. Some of his attitudes, and many of his works, are more or less typical, not of French society as a whole—because the French fought and quarrelled amongst themselves and with other nations throughout most of his life—but typical of various groups, of changing groups, some of them dominant groups which subsequently lost influence. His less attractive activities —the prosecution of Morin and of the Jansenists, for example—are summarized long after his death by words inscribed on the last royal monument of Louis XIV's seventy-two-year reign, the triumphal arch erected in Montpellier in 1715: 'DISSOCIATIS REPRESSIS'— triumphal litotes, understating the savage persecutions which preceded and followed the revocation of the Edict of Nantes in 1685, the razing of Port-Royal-des-Champs in 1710, and other expressions of French national domestic policy.

Desmarets's attitudes, though not wholly consistent throughout his long life, mostly belong to an earlier period which did not survive to 1715 intact. He was like Richelieu and Richelieu's rivals in wishing to neutralize, marginalize, or eliminate groups and individuals perceived as a threat to the Crown and to the State. He seems to have shared Richelieu's cautious toleration of Protestantism, evidently enjoying good relations with individual Protestants (with Valentin Conrart, for example, and Abraham Bosse); and at the beginning of Louis XIV's reign he had favoured the example, later abandoned, of composing royal inscriptions not in Latin but in French.

It is not difficult to understand that Desmarets's late bout of witch-hunting when witch-hunting was going out of fashion, the spectacular execution of Simon Morin, and his persecution of Jansenists made enemies from the very moment first privileged by Perrault and Voltaire as beginning 'the century of Louis XIV'. In some ways he was the victim of a cultural revolution. F. L. Nussbaum begins a classic study with the observation that 'in 1660 Europe was in revolution. At no time in its brief history as a society had any generation stood to the future with an orientation so distinct from that of its ancestors.'[15] Attitudes were changing quickly. Nor is it

---

[15] F. L. Nussbaum, *The Triumph of Science and Reason 1660–1685* (New York, 1953), 1.

difficult to sympathize with Desmarets's enemies, ferociously intolerant though some of them were towards Court entertainments, theatre, fiction, and poetry—cultural activities all associated with a more positive affirmation of womanhood and less uneasiness about human sexuality than Desmarets's chief enemies managed to achieve.

These are all activities in which Desmarets had been deeply involved. The polemics in which he engaged after 1665, however interesting in themselves for French cultural history, have undoubtedly blighted the memory of his earlier, more original achievements. What has not been adequately grasped are firstly the links—religious, political, and aesthetic—between Desmarets's late heroic poetry and his other activities, and secondly the extent to which critical hostility towards Desmarets from the mid-1660s reflects not only a liberating concern for Cartesianism and the political interests of certain threatened religious minorities but also a rationalist arrogance with dangerous social and environmental consequences. In particular, critical rejection of Desmarets's imaginative work was to some extent inspired by the repressive sexual—and consequently sexist—attitudes of Jansenist publicists and their sympathizers.

Changing priorities

So much of Desmarets's great contemporary reputation was lost through late seventeenth-century quarrels and the changes in values and literary fashion which they reflect that much of the evidence concerning his position, his reputation, and the cultural world to which he belonged before 1661 has been overlooked or undervalued. One aim of this book is to revalue the career of this one man and, through him, the cultural experience of the 'century of Louis XIV'. Another is to scrutinize the historiography which makes the proposed revaluation exciting and necessary.

Is it not paradoxical that Desmarets, who invented the concept of a 'century of Louis XIV' and was once regarded as one of its ornaments, has all but disappeared from perception of the history of the period?[16]

---

[16] Early use of the concept by Desmarets, Perrault, and Voltaire is discussed in Chap. 1. Representative twentieth-century titles include the Bibliothèque nationale exhibition catalogue *Le Siècle de Louis XIV* (1927), H. Méthivier, *Le Siècle de Louis XIV* (1950), and O. and P. Ranum, *The Century of Louis XIV* (New York, 1972). In all the five hundred pages of this last book there does not appear to be a mention of Jean Desmarets.

Something of the spirit which once animated Egyptian Pharaohs to build new temples with stones pillaged from temples built by their predecessors, and something also of the French irreverence for the monuments of an undervalued past which led Napoleon's cannoneers to use the great Sphinx for target practice, has presided over the destruction of the great reputation which Desmarets once enjoyed. In Caen, the Place-Royale of the *ancien régime* has become the Place de la République. The Place-Royale in Paris—where before 1789 one could read Desmarets's sonnet in honour of the memory of Louis XIII—is now the Place des Vosges. The statue of Louis XIII has been replaced, but not Desmarets's sonnet advocating a new Crusade. Some of the French expeditionary force which set out to attack the Turks in Crete early in the personal reign of Louis XIV may have viewed their efforts in this light. When the French finally did conquer Egypt again, in circumstances different from those in which Saint Louis had set out from Aigues-Mortes in the thirteenth century, Napoleon's flagship, destroyed by Nelson in 1798, was operating under its third name, following recent changes in governmental fashion: *Le Sans-coulotte* of the First Republic had become *L'Orient*. Desmarets, who in 1639 had been entrusted with the main celebrations of the birth of the Dauphin (later Louis XIV) and soon afterwards became Secrétaire général de la Marine de Levant, would have preferred the name under which the ship had been launched in 1789: *Le Dauphin royal*. (Capital letters for such titles as 'Roi' and 'Duc' are here preferred to the decapitalization associated with the politics of the French republics that succeeded the *ancien régime*. On such points the typographical styles of a period reflect something of its values.)

Feeling for nature

An undervalued aspect of Desmarets's poetry is (in my view) his feeling for nature. Hill-climbing for pleasure is not commonly regarded as a theme of French seventeenth-century poetry, but it underlies the first edifying allegory of *Les Promenades de Richelieu*. The pleasures of swimming in the sea and the practical advantage for both men and women of knowing how to swim are evoked in *Clovis*, and this is another activity whose pursuit and poetization is seldom emphasized in literary histories of the 'century of Louis XIV'. In *Les Délices de l'esprit* Eusèbe expresses his pleasure in new scientific learning in a simile from swimming which Nicole found very strange: 'ie nage auec plaisir dans ce que i'y trouue d'vtile; comme si ie me laissois aller au courant d'vn grand fleuue'.[17] Or, if the sea is not to hand in a moment of discouragement, a tired hero may simply take refreshment in a cooling brook:

> Et sur l'herbe couché prés du bord d'vn ruisseau,
> Soulage sa chaleur dans la fraischeur de l'eau.[18]

Lines in *Clovis* implying the pleasure a war-horse might feel on awakening to the light of dawn may not stand comparison with the best of Shakespeare or Jean de La Fontaine (who in 1671 anthologized some of Desmarets's poems and was certainly well aware of others); but, in a French literary tradition undistinguished in sensitivity to animal welfare, they are not without interest. They may, for example, be compared with a contemporary account of the way Cartesian Jansenists used to crucify dogs (considered to have no feelings) in order to observe how moaning, whining, and howling could be produced mechanically by the repeated infliction of experimental wounds.[19]

Desmarets's feeling for nature was not hidden away in obscure publications but repeatedly reprinted in books of some considerable contemporary prominence.

Innovative illustrated books

Desmarets deserves revaluation not only in the history of French literature but in the history of the French book. The quarto *Ariane* (1639), the folio *Mirame* (1641), the quarto *Clovis* (1657), and the folio *Les Délices de l'esprit* (1658) are among the most outstanding illustrated books produced in France in the seventeenth century. *Ariane* contains seventeen engravings by Abraham Bosse after Claude Vignon and also an early use of Desmarets's special *privilège*—signed by his fellow Academician Valentin Conrart—for twenty years for any of his titles, published or to be published. *Mirame* contains six double-page illustrations of the stage of the Grand'Salle de Spectacle in the Palais-Cardinal, one with the proscenium curtain closed and

---

[17] *Les Délices de l'esprit*, i. 71.
[18] *Clovis* (1657, quarto), 73, 291.
[19] N. Fontaine, *Mémoires pour servir à l'histoire de Port-Royal* (Utrecht, 1736), ii. 52–3, in G. Delassault, *La Pensée janséniste en dehors de Pascal* (1963), 83–4.

one of a moment in the action of each act. It is the only French play separately published in folio in the seventeenth century. The first editions of *Clovis* and of *Les Délices de l'esprit* were innovative both in the technology with which the lavish illustrations were produced and in the commercial arrangements for their marketing. Cross-page woodcut ornaments above and below a copperplate engraving on the same page were used for the first time in France in these books, on the title-pages of which the printer's name occurs, most unusually, along with the names of the associated publishers in the Palais (on the Île-de-la-Cité) and in the rue Saint-Jacques in the Latin quarter.

In 1963 a copy of the folio *Les Délices de l'esprit* was displayed at the London exhibition Printing and the Mind of Man as one of the one hundred and ninety-four most beautiful books in the world. Quite apart from their texts, *Clovis* and *Les Délices de l'esprit* are of interest aesthetically. Their publication is an event in the history of the book in France. They also witness an interaction of technological and commercial innovation with the important underlying social and political structures in which such privileged publication could occur.

Les Délices de l'esprit is the first major apologia of the Christian religion in French. Its publication early in 1658 may well have prompted Blaise Pascal to begin the unfinished apologia, fragments of which became *Les Pensées* (1670). *Les Délices de l'esprit* is also of interest for Neoplatonic arguments that piety may be sought through graduated pleasures—a doctrine opposed to that of Pascal and of the Jansenists Pascal champions in the *Lettres provinciales* (1656–7) but already implicit in Desmarets's novels, in his plays, and in *Clovis*. Desmarets's debts in these dialogues to Erasmus, together with his exegeses in French of Genesis and of the Song of Solomon are also remarkable, since, like his earlier translation of liturgical and devotional works, vernacular exegesis is commonly associated with Protestantism and, in France, with Jansenism.

Despite the pioneering scholarship of Henri Bremond, the implications of such spirituality in books so conspicuously published and influentially dedicated is not widely appreciated.[20] This spirituality is rooted in Neoplatonism and in the optimism, feminism, and

---

[20] H. Bremond, *Histoire littéraire du sentiment religieux en France*, vi (1922), 445–581.

aspiration to fulfilment through progressively enhanced experience expressed in early seventeenth-century Jesuit doctrine and Court ballet. Desmarets's conversion was accompanied by scruples concerning worldly entertainments, as Anne of Austria's had been; but there is a balletic atmosphere in the decorative features and even in the texts of *Clovis* and *Les Délices de l'esprit*.

Together these two works contain many of the ideas, images, and arguments concerned with the Christian marvellous that were central to the literary preoccupations of Desmarets and his contemporaries in the early Académie-Française but which are better known as revived by Chateaubriand in *Le Génie du christianisme* (1802).

Energetic, redemptive women

From *Ariane*—dedicated 'Aux Dames' in 1632—until the late biblical epics *Marie-Madeleine* (1669) and the second version of *Esther* dedicated to the Duchesse de Richelieu in 1673, Desmarets's imaginative works present images of respected, energetic, independent, and redemptive women. They appear not only in imaginative works— for example the Amazons in *Clovis* (a feature of the epic genre)—but in texts like the exegesis of the Song of Solomon incorporated into *Les Délices de l'esprit*.

Consider in this light the heroines of those tragedies of Corneille which in the nineteenth century became the classical 'tetralogy'. Chimène in *Le Cid*, Sabine and Camille in *Horace*, Émilie in *Cinna*, and Pauline in *Polyeucte* are all hurt and humiliated and Camille is even killed by her warrior brother. Four of these vigorous heroines come to accept specifically male authority, and Pauline follows her husband's example of open Christian profession of faith. Contrast Desmarets's tragicomedies of the same period. Three out of four are named after their heroines: *Roxane*, *Mirame*, and *Érigone*; and *Scipion* is based on its hero's exemplary self-mastery in combining respect for a conquered princess with astute colonial (or provincial) politics. Respect for the women of these plays is clearly linked to the theory of idealist and exemplary literature proposed to the Duchesse d'Aiguillon by Desmarets in the dedication of *Rosane*, from an episode of which *Érigone* was adapted. This is a good standpoint from which to reconsider Nicole's assertion in the first *Visionnaire* letter that such plays poison souls.

The Corpus maresianum

Alexandre Cioranescu, *Bibliographie de la littérature française du XVIIe siècle* (1965–6), Avenir Tchemerzine, *Bibliographie des éditions originales et rares d'auteurs français des XVe, XVIIe et XVIIIe siècles* (10 vols., 1927–34), and/or the *Catalogue général des livres imprimés de la Bibliothèque Nationale* (1897–) have made a small number of unsound attributions. The 'Avis sur le Placard du Sr Desmarets' attributed to Desmarets by the Cambridge University Library catalogue is not by him but is simply about his lost wall-poster; the 'Avis' is probably by Nicole and/or Claude de Sainte-Marthe.[21] The 'Epitaphe de M. Arnauld' (whom Desmarets predeceased) is a French version of an epitaph by Jean-Baptiste Santeul (an early footnote was mistaken for a signature).[22] The *Livre de touttes sortes de chyffres par alphabets redoublés* (1664) was designed by Jean Desmarets's son, Armand-Jean Desmarets de Saint-Sorlin. *Les Morales d'Epictète, de Socrate, de Plutarque et de Séneque*, printed at the château de Richelieu in 1653, was compiled by Cardinal Alphonse de Richelieu, Archbishop of Lyons, brother of the Cardinal-Duc; it was probably seen through the press by Desmarets.[23] The tragicomedy *Roxelane* (1643) is by an otherwise unknown Desmares.[24] *Vénus et Adonis* (1697) is by Jean-Baptiste Rousseau, with a musical score by Henri Desmarets. Finally, the manuscript 'Discours sur les esprits' (Bibliothèque Nationale, Mss. ancien fds. fr. 645) is not the 'Discours de l'amour des esprits' read to the Académie-Française by Desmarets, although fols. 129–30 contain a reply by Boissat to Desmarets's lost discourse of that title.

Additions to the *Corpus maresianum* include six volumes of *Lettres spirituelles* (Paris, 1660–3), which the Bibliothèque nationale attributes to their editor, Jean de Lessot;[25] a printed version of the *Examen du livre, intitulé, L'Ancienne Nouveauté de l'Ecriture Sainte*,

---

[21] See H. G. Hall, 'A Polemical Parisian Wall Poster in 1666: Desmarets de Saint-Sorlin *vs.* Port-Royal', *Papers on French Seventeenth Century Literature*, 9 (16/2) (1982), 305–11.

[22] See 'Avis du Libraire' in Pinel de la Martelière (ed.), *Santeuilliana*, 6th edn. ('Cologne', 1742), for the 'démêlé que notre Poëte eut avec les Jésuites au sujet de la fameuse Epitaphe qu'il fit pour feu M. Arnauld'.

[23] M. Deloche, *Un Frère de Richelieu inconnu* (1935), 529–30.

[24] H. C. Lancaster, *A History of French Dramatic Literature in the Seventeenth Century* (9 vols.; New York, 1966), ii. 405.

[25] R. Briand, 'Sur la découverte des *Lettres spirituelles* de Desmarets de Saint-Sorlin', *XVIIe siècle*, 112 (1976), 41–6.

ou L'Eglise triomphante en terre (n.p., 1661); and a second small volume of *Maximes chrestiennes* (n.p., 1687). I also add three pamphlets in the Lb. 36 collection of the Bibliothèque Nationale. Two of them (1620 and 1625) are undoubtedly by Desmarets; *Le Voyage de Fontainebleau*, which concerns him, was probably written in collaboration with Guillaume Bautru. I have also located minor works in other libraries, assorted manuscripts, and archival documents. Agne Beijer's 'Une maquette de décor récemment retrouvée pour *Le Ballet de la Prospérité des armes de la France*' is fundamental. Previously unknown manuscript notes on Nicolas Faret's *Projet de L'Académie, pour servir de Préface à ses statuts* were published by Jean Rousselot in 1983.[26]

Desmarets's printed books present some serious bibliographical problems. More than one edition of *Ariane* was issued under the original engraved title of 1632, while the original sheets of three other books were reissued under new title-pages. Several titles were issued in different states by associated *libraires*. The *Œuvres poëtiques* is partly a collected edition, the contents of which vary somewhat from copy to copy. Some books were extensively revised between editions. The *Corpus maresianum* proposed in the Bibliography is a compromise between detailed description and a list of bare essentials, imposed by limitations of space.

I have not found the lost plays mentioned in Chapter 6, the lost poems and games noted in Chapter 11, the lost *Abrégé de la science universelle* mentioned in Chapter 12, nor the lost biblical epics recorded in Chapter 15.

Since 1963, when I edited *Les Visionnaires* for the Société des Textes Français Modernes (STFM) several of Desmarets's other books have been republished. Felix Freudmann's edition of *Clovis* (Louvain and Paris, 1972) combines a facsimile of the illustrated quarto with interleaved critical apparatus and further facsimiles; and there are Slatkine Reprints facsimiles of three late comparatist and polemical works: *La Comparaison de la langue et de la poësie françoise avec la grecque & la latine, La Deffense du poëme héroïque*, and *La Defense de la Poësie* (Geneva, 1972). Telecast on France Culture by the Comédie-Française on New Year's Day 1984, *Les Visionnaires* has now been reprinted in the Bibliothèque de la Pléiade's *Théâtre de XVIIᵉ siècle*, ii (1986).

---

[26] N. Faret, *Projet de l'Académie, pour servir à ses statuts*, ed. J. Rousselot (Saint-Étienne, 1983).

Perception of Desmarets is changing, but no comprehensive study has appeared taking into account new attributions, recent scholarship, necessary exclusions from the *Corpus maresianum*, his activities at the royal Court before 1630, and his offices.

Critical objectives

The myriad attitudes towards literature evident in current critical writing may be divided roughly into two types: one aesthetic and personal, in which all books are judged on the same criteria, irrespective of cultural differences or the context in which they were written, and are assessed simply according to their current imaginative appeal as literature—ostensibly *sub specie aeternitatis*, in fact subjectively and very much under the influence of literary fashion; the other historical, involved primarily with the interpretation of literature as an imaginative expression of the culture in which it is produced, however strange and foreign that culture may be. The present book would not have been written had it not seemed to me that a few of Desmarets's works could again give personal aesthetic pleasure (as *Les Visionnaires* has evidently done) to readers or listeners prepared to approach them without bias as poems, novels, or plays still pleasurable to read or hear.

I am, however, more concerned with the historical study of Desmarets in the context of his time and with the interpretation of cultural works and data formerly possessed of much more direct aesthetic appeal than most of them are ever likely to have again. No special indulgence is sought for Desmarets's religion, his politics, his theories or practice of literature; and it is often difficult to separate what is specifically personal and individual in his work from elements more generally representative of groups or factions in his time— or indeed of European baroque culture as a whole. Desmarets's nationalism—expressed in phrases like, 'France, ô ma chere patrie' (in an unpublished ode to Chancellor Séguier 'Sur le retour du Roy à Paris en l'année 1649')—is less rare in his generation than some have supposed and has a negative as well as a positive aspect, especially when viewed from outside France.[27] The same may be

---

[27] Bibliothèque Nationale, Mss. fr. 20,035. With reference to a text by Guillaume Du Vair (1556–1621), W. F. Church states that 'the key word *patrie* is used with sufficient frequency in the literature of the period to indicate widespread acceptance

said for his royalism and the less tolerant aspects of his Catholicism. But these are matters which can only be judged fairly in the context of a France that was either insecure within its frontiers or at war, or both, throughout most of Desmarets's life.

Although my approach is bio-bibliographical, the reader will soon discover that too few personal and family documents have been identified to support the writing of a detailed biography, while a full descriptive bibliography of Desmarets's numerous and varied publications would greatly exceed the scope of this book. This introduction and the first chapter are intended as an overview of his career and of the changing valuations of it. For the rest, discussion of selected aspects of Desmarets's background and works seemed less unsatisfactory than a strictly chronological account. However, the interconnection of his varied activities and the continuities in his career—both important for a proper understanding—make some repetition unavoidable.

Quotations and titles are taken from widely differing sources and are normally given as found, without normalization or modernization. Occasionally, editorial intervention is unavoidable. Where significant, it is indicated with brackets [ ], but not for the correction of obvious misprints nor for changes related to necessary adaptations within the norms of the text presented. Retention of the original spelling has the advantage of fidelity to sources, but it also has the disadvantage of making passages quoted from many nineteenth- and twentieth-century editions look more modern than texts of the same date quoted from early editions. 'V' capital and initial, 'u' internal, whether vowel or consonant, as retained until about 1660, soon becomes familiar as a convention but is modernized in recurrent titles such as the *Œuvres poëtiques*.

of the concept of the fatherland as applied to the realm at large', *Richelieu and the Reason of State* (Princeton, 1972), 21.

1

Jean Desmarets
and the Century of Louis XIV

Born with the century of Louis

Le Triomphe de Louis et de son siècle, dedicated to Louis XIV
in 1674 by Jean Desmarets, Sieur de Saint-Sorlin, opens out the
traditional celebration of French royal triumphs upon an ambitious
conception of the 'century of Louis XIV', relating contemporary
French success in all the arts to the personality of its monarch. The
poet's Génie in the poem associates him with the very origins of that
century:

> Tu nasquis lors que l'on vid naistre
> L'heureux & le premier instant
> De ce beau Siecle qui doit estre
> Des Siecles le plus eclatant.[1]

Desmarets's Génie speaks with less poetic licence than might be
assumed from consulting Desmarets's early biographers, who date
his birth around 1595–6.[2] On the basis of new evidence, Jean
Desmarets was probably the son of the Jean Marestz, 'marchand
bourgeois demeurant rue & paroisse S. Sauveur' in the St-Denis
quarter of Paris, who, on 29th July 1600, effected with his wife,
Marie Le Febvre, a 'donation mutuelle' of their property.[3] Such an
exchange might well have been associated with the birth of a son.
If these were indeed the poet's parents, we might take the Génie's
word for it that he really was born at the beginning of the calendar
century, *c.*1600.

---

[1] *Le Triomphe de Louis et de son siècle* (1674), 5.
[2] P. Bayle, *Dictionnaire historique et critique*, 5th edn. (Amsterdam, 1734),
'Marests'; J.-P. Niceron, *Mémoires*, xxxv (1736), 136; Beauchamps, *Recherches sur
les théâtres*, ii (1735), 149; L. Moréri, *Dictionnaire* (1759), 'Marets de S. Sorlin'.
[3] Archives Nationales, Insinuations du Châtelet, Y139, 6504, fol. 141. In moves
connected with the birth of his son Armand, our Jean Desmarets effects a lease with
a Denis Lefebvre on 3 Nov. 1635 (Minutier Central, xxxi' Guyon 1635 novembre 2).

Unlike *c.*1595, that date is consistent with an autobiographical statement in another late poem, the ode *Indignation. A Monseigneur le Duc de Richelieu*, which can be identified as Desmarets's ode read to the Académie-Française on St-Louis day (25 August) 1673:

> RICHELIEU, qui d'un nom illustre
> Soûtiens la sublime grandeur,
> Tu sçais qu'en mon quinzième lustre
> Ma veine n'est pas sans ardeur.[4]

A *lustre* or *lustrum* is five years. If Desmarets was not yet 75 in August 1673, he cannot have been over 80—as asserted in the early biographical notices—at the time of his death, on 28 October 1676. But anyone born *c.*1600 would have been in his fifteenth *lustrum* in 1673. No baptismal record has come to light. Indeed, no document of any sort dating from earlier than 1630 had been associated with Jean Desmarets before I renewed my research into his career in 1983. None of the early biographical notices was written by anyone so close to Desmarets as Louis XIV, the Duc de Richelieu, or the Academicians to whom the poems referring to his age were addressed. The notices are mainly by writers either hostile to Desmarets or sympathetic to his various opponents and enemies. There is more reason to doubt the early biographers' assertions that he was born *c.*1595 than to separate (on this issue) Jean Desmarets, the poet and Academician, from the poetic speakers of the cited poems. The meagre evidence related to the date of his birth points to *c.*1600.

If this conclusion is correct, it follows that at every recorded stage of his career Desmarets was some five years younger than previously assumed: five years younger, for example, than the founding Academician Jean Chapelain (1595–1674); only six years older than Pierre Corneille (1606–84); scarcely a year older than Louis XIII (1601–43), Louis XIV's father; and the same age as Anne of Austria and Marie de Rohan. (In 1617 the latter married Charles d'Albert de Luynes (1578–1621), Louis XIII's favourite; in December 1618 she became Surintendent de la Maison de la Reine and 'prenait une part active aux ballets dans lesquels la souveraine dansait'; in 1619

---

[4] Desmarets, *Indignation* (n.p., n.d.), 16. Dated by reference to *Le Mercure galant* for 1673 (1674), 64.

she became Duchesse de Luynes, and later she acquired fame as the Duchesse de Chevreuse of the Fronde.[5])

Desmarets's proposal that the century of Louis XIV also dates from the beginning of the seventeenth century, whether beginning in 1600 or 1601 with the birth of Louis XIII, has further fascinating implications. To begin with, it recognizes aspirations active throughout the calendar century. Elements of the concept of a 'century of Louis' date from the reign of Henri IV, to cite only Nicolas Bourbon's *Parallela Caesaris et Henrici Magni*, with its prophecy that the reign of the new-born future Louis XIII would bring a return of the Golden Age: 'le siècle d'or prendra sous son regne naissance'. The translation is by Henri IV's minister, Maximilien de Béthune, Duc de Sully (1560–1641).[6] When the future Louis XIV was born, on 5 September 1638, Desmarets—in some way related to Sully—was chosen to celebrate the 'miraculous' birth in the great *Ballet de la Félicité sur l'heureuse naissance de Monseigneur le Dauphin* (1639). *La Félicité* makes similar prophecies.

Desmarets's situation at the birth of Louis XIV

When the Court danced *La Félicité* in March 1639, Desmarets, ennobled as a Secrétaire du Roi, was still a star performer in Court ballet, he was still Conseiller du Roi, Contrôleur général de l'Extraordinaire des guerres, possibly still Surintendant des fortifications, and a founder-member of the Académie-Française. It was he—the poet, novelist, and playwright—who on 14 March 1639 obtained the most favourable *privilège* or copyright I have met in more than thirty years of research on seventeenth-century editions of French books: a general *privilège* for all his books, written or to be written, for twenty years from first publication.

There can be no doubt that at that time Desmarets enjoyed quite exceptional status as a writer and as a man of the theatre, especially Court theatre. It seems a reasonable deduction that Louis XIII's decree rehabilitating actors—the 'levée de l'infamie des comédiens' of 1641, making professional acting respectable—was prompted by a performance of Desmarets's *Mirame* at the opening, on 14 January 1641, of the Grand'Salle de spectacle in the Palais-Cardinal—later

[5] L. Battifol, *La Duchesse de Chevreuse* (1913), 11–13.
[6] N. Bourbon, *Opera omnia* (1651), i. 187.

the Palais-Royal theatre, used by Molière's troupe from 1661 to 1673 and, after Molière's death, as the Paris Opéra until destroyed by fire in 1763.

Mirame is an event of the first magnitude in the history of French theatre. Witness the folio edition illustrated by Stefano della Bella (1610–64): *Mirame* is, to my knowledge, the only French play to have been published separately in folio in the seventeenth century. 'L'honneur du format in-folio est une consécration', states Georges Couton with reference to an edition of Pierre Corneille's theatre published in 1663.[7] The implications for contemporary status must be the same for *Mirame*, dedicated to Louis XIII, and indeed for *Les Délices de l'esprit*.

Mirame opened the first great theatre in France known to have had a proscenium arch. Using new Italian stage machinery, with sets and lighting designed by Giovanni Bernini (1598–1680), Desmarets devised transformation scenes involving not only ships appearing or disappearing in the perspective point but the sun and moon moving across the set. His stagecraft is innovative not primarily because his *changements à vue* are four years earlier than those commissioned by Cardinal Mazarin for *La Finta Pazza* (generally associated with the introduction of such stagecraft to France). Transformation scenes had already been used in French Court ballets, and it was Mazarin who first brought the innovative stage machinery of the 1640s from Italy, not in the early years of his own ministry but in the last years of Richelieu's.[8] Desmarets's innovation lies in the solution he found to major contemporary problems of theatre-aesthetics by using transformation scenes in conjunction with a single unified type set. Movements of the sun and moon over a palace-garden by the sea not only symbolize the King and Queen, in whose presence the first performance took place, but mark the passage of time within the twenty-four hours of the classical unity of time, reconciling for the

---

[7] P. Corneille, *Œuvres complètes*, ed. G. Couton, (2 vols; 1980), vol. i, p. lxii. Of Molière's *Œuvres* (1663) Couton observes that, even as a collected edition of plays previously published separately, 'cela atteste l'importance qu'il prend dans le monde théâtral' (Molière, *Œuvres complètes*, ed. G. Couton (1971), vol. i, p. xlix). The contemporary implications of Desmarets's *Œuvres poëtiques* (1641), a partly collected edition of plays with a new edition of short poems, must be similar.

[8] A. Beijer, 'Une maquette de décor récemment retrouvée pour le "Ballet de la Prospérité des armes de la France" dansé à Paris le 7 février 1641', in J. Jacquot (ed.), *Le Lieu théâtral à la Renaissance* (1964), 377–403; M. Laurain-Portemer, 'Mazarin militant de l'art baroque (1634–1642)', in her *Études mazarines* (1981), 197–223.

first time in France the baroque taste for changing spectacle with a spectacular observance of the three dramatic unities. The *Gazette* for 19 January 1641, in its notice of the first performance of *Mirame*, certainly associates Desmarets with innovation: 'une pièce de theatre composée par le Sr Desmarets, esprit poli & fertile tout ensemble: laquelle n'a point eu sa pareille de nostre aage, si vous la considerez dans toute son estenduë'. Publication of Desmarets's *Œuvres poëtiques*, probably timed to coincide with the first performance of *Mirame*, provides further confirmation that towards the close of the reign of Louis XIII Desmarets was a writer of considerable standing.

Desmarets's reputation 1643–1661

What then happened to the great reputation Desmarets evidently enjoyed when Louis XIV was born? Fashions do change, especially in the modern world. The first French book on fashion, *La Mode* (1642) by François de Grenaille, dates from the last year of Richelieu's ministry. Desmarets's close association not only with extravagant Court spectacle but increasingly with Louis XIII's first minister, Armand-Jean du Plessis, Cardinal-Duc de Richelieu (1585–1642), must have made him enemies; and patronage for theatre declined abruptly after Richelieu's death. Desmarets was one of a number of playwrights who then ceased to write for the stage. Performers too were soon forgotten when lives generally were shorter and there were no films or recordings. Who, were it not for Molière's later successes, would remember that Madeleine Béjart was a famous actress at that time, or that Molière himself must have decided upon a career in theatre after the rehabilitation of the acting profession in 1641 but before patronage collapsed with the death of Cardinal Richelieu?

Yet that cannot be the whole story. Desmarets's reputations as office-holder, writer, and entertainer were not lost with the deaths of Richelieu and Louis XIII. His activities changed, but in the following decades he continued to be a prolific publisher of new titles, with three editions of *Europe* in 1643, including a pirated edition. A further pirated edition probably also dates from 1643. There were also new editions and translations of *Ariane*, revivals and new editions of several plays, a new section of *Odes, poëmes et autres œuvres* for the *Œuvres poëtiques*. In 1643 Desmarets became Secrétaire général de la Marine de Levant, at an annual salary of

3,000 (later 4,000) *livres*.[9] After the death of Louis XIII, a sonnet by Desmarets was engraved on the pedestal of his equestrian statue in the Place-Royale.[10] Only a reputable poet could have been entrusted with such an inscription, anticipating by nearly thirty years the debate over the relative merits of French versus Latin as the language for public inscriptions in France which helped fuel the Quarrel of ancients and moderns.[11]

No longer dancing or writing for the theatre, in 1644–5 Desmarets published four sets of educational card-games (originally suggested by Cardinal Richelieu) for the young Louis XIV on the themes of the kings of France, famous queens, mythology, and geography: his *Cartes des Rois de France* etc. Published correspondence on the games with an anonymous lady from Rennes suggests that he still enjoyed a reputation as a fashionable writer and entertainer. He dedicated to Anne of Austria the first translation into French verse of the *Officium parvum*—his *Office de la Vierge Marie* (1645)— and his third romance, *La Vérité des fables* (1648). During the civil wars of the Fronde, Desmarets was imprisoned for assisting his cousin, Anne Poussart de Pons (1622–84), in her clandestine marriage to the young Duc de Richelieu in December 1649; and Gui Patin reports that he was afterwards kept in prison for debts.[12] But these were troubled times; and the incident shows Desmarets still very well connected, because witnesses of the wedding included the Prince de Condé (1621–86), the Prince de Conti (1629–66), their sister the Duchesse de Longueville (1619–79), and her husband, Henri II d'Orléans, Duc de Longueville (1595–1663). Feared as frondeurs, the Princes and the Duke also went to prison.

Desmarets took the title Sieur de Saint-Sorlin in the year Louis XIV officially came of age. In October 1651 the young Duc de Richelieu transferred to Desmarets the marshes of Cosnac near the village of Saint-Sorlin de Cosnac, west of Mirambeau (Charente-Maritime), together with the title Sieur de Saint-Sorlin and confirmation of his appointment as 'Intendant Général des maisons et

[9] A. Jal, *Dictionnaire critique de biographie et d'histoire*, 2nd edn. (1872), 'Desmarestz' and 'Richelieu'; G. Patin, *Lettres*, ed. J.-H. Reveillé-Parise (3 vols., 1846), i. 522.

[10] Lefort de la Morinière (ed.), *Bibliothèque poétique*, (4 vols.; 1745), ii. 217.

[11] Compare F. Brunot, *Histoire de la langue française*, v (1917), 10–20.

[12] F. B. de Motteville, *Mémoires*, ed. A. Petitot (1824), iii. 422–3; F. de Montglat, *Mémoires*, ed. A. Petitot (1826), ii. 204; Dubuisson-Aubenay, *Journal des guerres civiles*, i. 236–9; Patin, *Lettres*, i. 522; *Gazette* for 6 Jan. and 24 Feb. 1650.

affaires du Duc de Richelieu'.[13] These arrangements were confirmed by the Duc de Richelieu as governor of Saintonge on 9 December 1653. Desmarets's mystic conversion occurred the following year; and, although he had written devotional poetry before 1640, conversion appears to follow the major religious poems written or begun in the early 1650s at the château de Richelieu in Poitou: *Les Promenades de Richelieu* (1653), his translation of *Les Quatre Livres de l'Imitation de Jésus-Christ* (1654), and his translation of Lorenzo Scupoli's *Le Combat spirituel* (1654).

Les Visionnaires and *Roxane* were in the repertoire of the Hôtel de Bourgogne in the 1640s. *Les Visionnaires* was reprinted five times between 1646 and 1659 and translated into Dutch; *Scipion* was reprinted in French in 1644 and twice in Dutch in the 1650s; *Roxane* was reprinted three times. Testimony in the Morin affair suggests that Desmarets accompanied the Court on the journey to meet the Spanish Infanta who married Louis XIV in 1660.

Among Desmarets's numerous publications of the 1640s and 1650s, two books in particular attest, through their dedications and the lavishness of their illustration, his special status as a writer in the late 1650s: *Clovis*, dedicated to Louis XIV and containing the earliest portrait of the adolescent king symbolically dominating a rearing horse (see Fig. 1), and *Les Délices de l'esprit*, dedicated to Cardinal Mazarin—books later mocked by Desmarets's enemies but, if judged by the standards applied to other authors at the time of publication, a 'consecration'.[14] In his *Mémoire des gens de lettres célèbres de France* (1655), Pierre Costar (1603–60) refers to Desmarets's recent conversion but none the less offers him as 'le plus ingénieux poète français, l'Ovide de son temps'.[15]

Desmarets's reputation 1661–1665

Aged about 61 when Cardinal Mazarin's death opened the way to Louis XIV's personal reign, Desmarets was not at the centre of the

[13] Information furnished by J. Coutura, discussed in my article 'Desmarets de Saint-Sorlin's Ennoblement and Conversion Reconsidered', *French Studies*, 27 (1973), 151–64.
[14] See J. Harthan, *The History of the Illustrated Book: the Western Tradition* (London, 1981), 114–15, and, more generally, H.-J. Martin, *Livre, pouvoirs et société à Paris au XVIIe siècle (1598–1701)* (2 vols.; Geneva, 1969).
[15] P. Costar, quoted by R. Kerviler, *Jean Desmaretz, Sieur de Saint-Sorlin, un des quarante fondateurs de l'Académie-Française* (1879), 107. Costar adds 'il s'est mis depuis peu à écrire sur l'Apocalypse'.

On verra par tout l'Vniuers
Ce Prince répandre sa gloire
Ce que Clovis est dans ces vers,
Louis le sera dans l'histoire.

FIG. 1 Portrait from *Clovis* (1657 quarto): Louis XIV on horseback engraved by Jean Couvay after Sébastien Bourdon (*Phot. Bibl. Nat. Paris*)

cultural activities of the Court as he had been twenty years earlier. However, he still held substantial offices, the best *privilège*, and a solid list of publications: three novels, seven plays, four card-games, five volumes of verse, devotional works and letters, pamphlets and *feuilles volantes*—including several of the most original and lavishly illustrated books yet published in France. Two kings and a queen regent of France, two Cardinal first ministers, and other eminent personages had accepted dedication of his books and plays. New editions of older works continued to be published: *Ariane, Europe,* and the *Imitation de Jésus-Christ* in 1661; a German translation of *Mirame* and the *Imitation* again in 1662; *Les Visionnaires* again in 1663; *Les Jeux de cartes des Roys de France, des Reines renommées, de la Géographie et des Fables* in 1664, *Clovis* again in 1666, etc. He was still associated with successful new publications: besides the six volumes of his *Lettres spirituelles*, his revision of *La Vie et les Œuvres de Sainte Catherine de Gênes*, first published in two volumes in 1661, was reprinted at least four times between 1661 and 1667, and again in 1695-7.[16]

In the *Liste de quelques gens de lettres français vivants en 1662* drawn up for the minister Jean-Baptiste Colbert (1619-83) by Jean Chapelain—Desmarets's influential fellow Academician, who had been invited to advise on matters of literary patronage—Desmarets has a relatively long, if now somewhat guarded, mention:

DESMARETS C'est un des esprits faciles de ce temps et qui, sans grand fonds, sait une plus grande quantité de choses et leur donne un meilleur jour. Son style de prose est pur mais sans élévation; en vers il est élevé ou abaissé selon qu'il le désire, et en l'un et l'autre genre il est inépuisable et rapide dans l'exécution, aimant mieux y laisser des taches et des négligences que de n'avoir pas bientôt fait. Son imagination est très fertile et souvent tient la place du jugement. Autrefois il s'en servait pour des romans et des comédies, non sans beaucoup de succès. Dans le retour de son âge il s'est tout entier tourné à la dévotion où il ne va pas moins vite qu'il allait dans les lettres profanes.[17]

---

[16] See Briand, *XVIIᵉ siècle*, 112 (1976), 41-6. The six volumes published in Paris by Florentin Lambert between 1660 and 1663 are attributed by the Bibliothèque Nationale Catalogue to Jean de Lessot, who collected the letters and obtained the *privilège*.

[17] J. Chapelain, *Opuscules critiques*, ed. A. C. Hunter (1936), 361.

The literary *pension* of 1,200 *livres* first paid to Desmarets in 1663 bore the more flattering official notation: 'Le plus fertile auteur et la plus belle imagination qui ait jamais été'.[18]

Due allowance must doubtless be made for the rhetoric appropriate to the official occasion, but Desmarets's major books are also treated with respect by Charles Sorel in his *Bibliothèque françoise* (1664).

The decline of Desmarets's reputation after 1665

Details of Desmarets's forgotten eminence, and even the respectability he still enjoyed as a writer in the early 1660s, have been spelt out in this first chapter because they are so remote from the 'image' he has (if he has one at all) in scholarly publications of the past three centuries. For by the end of 'the century of Louis XIV', as we have come to understand the redated concept and term we owe to Desmarets, most of his contemporary reputation had been lost. The eclipse was not total, but the occultation was severe. Only a handful of his books and poems were reprinted in the first half of the eighteenth century: *Ariane* in French (1724) and in German translations (1705, 1708, and 1714), *Aspasie*, his first comedy (1737), *Les Visionnaires* (seven editions and an Italian translation, 1705–57), and *Sainte Catherine* (1743). A few of his shorter poems, and extracts from longer ones, appeared in anthologies; but Voltaire and the few others who mention Desmarets seem to refer more often to *Clovis*—disobligingly. By 1750, when the last reprint of a book by Desmarets appeared under the *ancien régime* in France, no one seems to have remembered that the author of the despised *Clovis* had once been the 'célèbre Marets' of Court ballets.

It was, however, Isaac de Benserade (1612?–91) who (having been elected in 1674 to Jean Chapelain's seat in the Académie-Française) replied to the inaugural address delivered by Jean-Jacques III de Mesmes, on taking what had been Desmarets's seat. Benserade was the principal poet of Court ballets in the third quarter of the seventeenth century: his works comprised some twenty-three libretti (1651–69), including the *Ballet royal de la Nuit* (1653), in which Louis XIV first appeared as the sun-god Apollo, and most of the *comédies-ballets* involving Molière and Lully at Court in the 1660s.

---

[18] Quoted by Kerviler, *Jean Desmaretz*, 107. By way of comparison, Molière (five seasons after his return to Paris) received a mention of four lines and 1,000 *livres*.

There is a certain irony in Benserade's courtly eulogy of Desmarets to the Académie:

Feu M. Desmarets étoit un de ses premiers ornemens. Ce vaste et inépuisable génie a produit des ouvrages qui honorent son siècle, où l'on voit briller un feu qu'il a conservé jusqu'à l'extrême vieillesse, et qui éclairera sans doute bien loin dans la sçavante et juste postérité.[19]

It was Benserade's reputation in Court ballet which eclipsed Desmarets's.

From contemporary polemics to literary history

Doubtless Desmarets's reputation was vulnerable to the ephemeral nature of performing reputations, to changes of fashion in politics and literature, and to the unreasonable demands made on posterity by any writer who produces so many inventive books but polishes to perfection so few. But it suffered especially from the controversies in which he engaged during the last fifteen years of his life, from 1661 to 1676. Fifteen years can be a long time in literary history. Molière, for instance, owes his reputation almost exclusively to his activities between his return to Paris in 1658 and his death in 1673. Desmarets's prosecution of Simon Morin—a fanatic who threatened regicide and was burnt alive for lèse-majesté, heresy, and witchcraft— made him enemies, including apparently some of the Conseillers who were seeking at that time to save from execution the disgraced Surintendant des Finances, Nicolas Fouquet (1615–80).[20]

His controversy with Pierre Nicole (1625–95), his preparation for the arrest, on 16 May 1666, of Isaac Le Maistre de Sacy, and the enmity of the Jansenists proved to be even more damaging, and this is particularly true of Nicole's polemical Visionnaire letters (1665–6), which turned the Quarrel of the Imaginaires into a withering attack upon Desmarets. It seems more than a coincidence that Molière's troupe dropped Desmarets's Visionnaires from their repertoire soon after Nicole's Visionnaires began to appear. It is in a reference to that controversy that Desmarets is first mentioned by the hostile satirist Nicolas Boileau-Despréaux, in his 'Satire I' (1666): 'Saint-Sorlin

---

[19] I. de Benserade, quoted by Kerviler, Jean Desmaretz, 1.
[20] Hostility to Desmarets is evident in F. Ravaisson, 'Relation de la Découverte du faux Christ nommé Morin, chef des Illuminés, par Desmarets de Saint-Sorlin', in his Archives de la Bastille: Règne de Louis XIV (1661–1664), iii (1868), 1227–91.

janséniste', an oxymoron. The long-running dispute that developed between Desmarets and Boileau, who became a leader of the ancients in the Quarrel of the ancients and moderns and highly influential in matters of taste and reputation towards the end of Louis XIV's reign, was especially damaging to Desmarets's literary reputation. Desmarets's prosecution of Jansenists also upset Jean Chapelain, who, on 6 March 1666, replied to the Bishop of Angers as follows:

Il y a long temps que Mr Conrart et moy nous estions apperçeus des égaremens du pauvre visionnaire dont vous me parlés, mais nous n'eussions jamais pensé qu'il deust aller si loin qu'il a fait. Il est bien plus à plaindre que les personnes qu'il a entrepris de perdre et je vous puis assurer que les rieurs ne sont pas de son costé.[21]

It is difficult not to sympathize with Chapelain's unease. Jansenists preceded Protestants as targets of Louis XIV's intolerance. Valentin Conrart (1603–75), another founding member of the Académie-Française, was a Protestant; Chapelain's correspondent was a Jansenist; and Chapelain's patron, the Duchesse de Longueville, had been implicated in the papers found during the arrests of the so-called Villars on 10 February, and of Le Maistre de Sacy.[22] Chapelain may have considered her at risk not only for her Jansenist inclination but for having been a determined enemy of Mazarin during the Fronde. His was an awkward situation. Nothing indicates nostalgia for the early days of the Académie-Française and the glorious years of the Hôtel de Rambouillet thirty years before, when Desmarets had written for Mlle de Bourbon—the future Duchess—the ballet lyrics published in his Œuvres poëtiques. By mid-1665 Chapelain was entirely devoted to the new reign.[23]

The last use made by Desmarets of his general privilège of 14 March 1639 was for the second volume of Le Chemin de la paix et celuy de l'inquiétude (1665–6), 'achevé d'imprimer' on 30 April 1666. By 1667—if that is when he wrote his 'Ode à Colbert'—Desmarets was complaining

[21] Chapelain, Lettres, ii, no. 261.
[22] R. Rapin, Mémoires (1644–1669), ed. L. Aubineau (3 vols.; 1865), iii. 340–7, 360–5.
[23] See F. Wagert, 'Louis XIV par Chapelain: héros de la Renaissance et renaissance du héros'. Studi francesi, 30 (1986), 237–51.

Je languis, accablé de peines,
De soucis, de tristes succés,
D'Enfans, de dettes, de procés,
Et de poursuites inhumaines . . .[24]

At the beginning of 1666, however, Desmarets still had one distinguished laugher more on his side than literary historians commonly allow: Jean Racine, whose *petites lettres*, critical of Nicole's *Visionnaires*, are poorly understood evidence concerning Desmarets's standing at the outset of the Quarrel of the *Imaginaires*.

The only recorded portrait of Desmarets—by Henri Gascar (*c*.1634–1701) but known only through the engraving by Pierre Lombart (1612?–82) [see Frontispiece]—probably dates from 1667.[25] Its caption identifies the subject of 'I. Desmarests Seig[neu]r de S[ain]t Sorlin. Cons[eille]r du Roy, Controlleur General de lextraordinaire des guerres, et Secretaire General de la marine de leuant, celebre par vne infinité de rares ouurages de prose et de vers &c—'. I find no mention of this once famous engraver's work in Marianne Grivel's detailed thesis, *Le Commerce de l'estampe à Paris au XVIIe siècle* (1986).[26] Fame favours fame; neglect, neglect.

Pierre Nicole's fierce calumnies of Desmarets in his *Visionnaires* were crucial, because they were accepted by the authors of the early biographical notices on Desmarets. Adrien Baillet (1649–1706)— an ascetic of Jansenist inclination who from 1678 was librarian of the Hôtel de Lamoignon, frequented by Boileau—in his *Jugements des savants* (1685–6) takes from Nicole the notion that the author of the comedy *Les Visionnaires* must have been a mad *visionnaire* himself, presenting the comedy as 'le sceau du véritable caractère de

---

[24] In 'A Portrait of Desmarets de Saint-Sorlin . . . and Desmarets' "Ode" to Colbert (1668)', *Studi francesi*, 21 (1977), 40–9, I took the last stanza to refer to an examination success on 29 Aug. 1668 by Colbert's son Jean-Baptiste de Seigneley, later minister of the Marine. But the reference may be to another son, Jacques-Nicolas Colbert, later Archbishop of Rouen, who on 11 Aug. 1667 'soustint des thèses en philosophie dédiées au roi, dont le dessin était magnifique . . . Jamais père n'a été si aise que M. Colbert, et son fils a fort bien fait' (O. Le Fèvre d'Ormesson, *Journal*, ed. A. Chéruel (2 vols.; 1860–1), ii. 553–4). August 1667 is the *terminus a quo* for the 'Ode'.

[25] Bibliothèque Nationale, Cabinet des Estampes, 58. B. 20,717. See Note 24.

[26] Lombart's cut of the Duc de Gramont's portrait, for example, is inscribed 'Paris, 1663'. The Charpentier who cut the *Livre de touttes sortes de chyffres par alphabets redoublés* (1664), designed by Jean Desmarets's son Armand Desmarets, is also omitted—perhaps because neither he nor Lombart was technically a 'marchand-graveur'?

son esprit qu'il a gardé inviolablement dans tous ses autres Escrits et durant tout le reste de sa vie'.[27] Cervantes, Shakespeare, Charles Sorel, and Molière were allowed during Desmarets's lifetime to take an imaginative interest in obsessional characters without being considered insane, as Honoré de Balzac, Richard Strauss, and others have subsequently done to critical acclaim. In discussing Nicole's adoption of the title *Visionnaire*, Desmarets observes: 'par la mesme raison l'on pourroit donner le nom d'Avare à celuy qui auroit fait une Comedie où il auroit rendu les avares ridicules'.[28] But Nicole's ridiculous accusation not only stuck; it fostered disinformation concerning Desmarets and his relations with the numerous eminent contemporaries with whom he came in contact—not least in relation to Cardinal Richelieu as a patron of the theatre and of literature.

After Baillet, the Protestant Pierre Bayle (1647–1706) quotes as a matter of fact in the 'Marests' entry of his great *Dictionnaire historique et critique* (1697) Nicole's assertion that Desmarets was a *visionnaire*. Charles Perrault's admiration for writers of a Jansenist inclination may have kept him silent. In that same year, 1697, his *Eloges de Messieurs Arnauld et Pascal* appeared, with a 'Cologne' imprint. Former enemies of Jansenism such as Jacques-Bénigne Bossuet (1627–1704), Bishop of Meaux, had become enemies of the theatre. The author of the article 'Marets de S. Sorlin' in the ten-volume 1759 edition of Moréri's *Dictionnaire* cites Baillet as his authority for stating: 'pour connoître cet auteur, il faut lire *Les Visionnaires* de M. Nicole . . .' On that basis two of Desmarets's works are accepted unseen as containing 'les plus grandes extravagances, & le fanatisme le plus outré'. The damage was done. A partial and polemical contemporary attack had been promoted as if it were the last judgement of literary history.

Well into the twentieth century virtually every effort to reach an understanding of Desmarets's ideas, achievements, and personal relationships has been vitiated in whole or in part by the quite gratuitous assumption that Nicole, who had every reason for wishing to discredit his adversary, was correct in his accusation that Desmarets was a lunatic fanatic—or if not wholly correct,

---

[27] A. Baillet, *Jugemens des savants*, (9 vols.; 1685–6), iv. 292.
[28] *Seconde Partie de la Response*, 16.

then correct with respect to madness associated with Desmarets's controversial activities and publications from 1658 to 1668.[29] Nicole's polemics undoubtedly made it easier for Boileau to attack Desmarets's taste and judgement as a poet and theorist of literature and for Bossuet to suggest that theatre was unchristian.

It is unlikely that during the Quarrel of the *Imaginaires* Desmarets would have been the guest of the new Archbishop of Paris, Hardouin de Beaumont de Péréfixe (1605–70), a formidable enemy of the Jansenists, had he been as mad as Nicole alleges.[30] On the contrary, Desmarets's religious zeal seemed extravagant only to his adversaries. Consider the implications of Desmarets's rededication, in 1669, to Marie-Thérèse of Austria (1638–83), Louis XIV's Queen, of *Prières et Œuvres chrestiennes*—mainly a republication of his verse translation of the *Officium parvum*, which he had dedicated to Anne of Austria in 1645 as *Office de la Vierge Marie*. In its new 'Approbation' dated 1 July 1669, the University of Paris confirms its earlier 'Approbation' of 26 March 1645 covering Desmarets's versions of the offices, hymns which 'se chantent sur le chant de l'Eglise', and Psalms, reaffirming that 'le mesme Esprit qui parloit par la bouche de David, a animé ses paroles & ses pensées veritablement de Pieté'. Deserved or not, few translators since Saint Jerome (c.347–420) can have had such praise. If one looks beyond Nicole's *Visionnaires* and the testimony of those who had a political interest in its polemical efficacity, it is difficult to escape the conclusion that Desmarets, who first dedicated paraphrased Psalms to Louis XIII in 1640, possessed a reputation for piety before, during, and after the Quarrel of the *Imaginaires*.

With Anne of Austria's death in 1666 Desmarets lost, if not a friend, a queen uniquely placed to recall both his glorious days in Court ballet and his more recent devotional writings. Mme de Rambouillet had recently died. Numerous other people influential in earlier times, including Desmarets's friend Guillaume Bautru, had also disappeared. The influence of the Richelieu family had sharply declined. In 1661 the Duc de Richelieu was replaced as Général de la Marine de Levant; Desmarets must then have lost his office as

---

[29] A medical thesis of outstanding incompetence retrospectively diagnoses madness for Desmarets on the basis of traditional texts cited by Nicole: M.-A. Caillet, *Un Visionnaire du XVIIe siècle* (1935).

[30] See my note in *Papers on French Seventeenth Century Literature*, 9 (16/2) (1982), 305–11.

Secrétaire général, and probably other offices as well. The Duc's younger brothers—the influential Marquis de Richelieu, Lieutenant général des Armées du Roi, Governor of Le Havre, and Captain of the château of St-Germain-en-Laye and Versailles at the opening of the personal reign, and the Comte de Richelieu, Abbé de Marmoutier, Abbé de St-Ouen in Rouen, etc.—both died shortly afterwards, the Marquis in 1662, the Abbé in 1665. These young men must have shared something of the enthusiasm for theatre of their great-uncle the Cardinal-Duc: all three were patrons of Molière's troupe in the early 1660s.[31] Had Desmarets been luckier in the Cardinal's heirs, he might have received more help from that source during the Quarrel of the *Imaginaires*, which also concerned theatre and literary censorship. In any case, Colbert is said to have 'frequently annoyed Louis XIV by invoking precedents set under Richelieu'.[32]

After 1666 the occasional positive revaluations of various aspects of Desmarets's achievements had to be accommodated to the hostile Jansenist perspective, of which Boileau took early advantage. Even the most serious literary historians—the late Raymond Picard, for example—have felt authorized by this tradition to express damaging judgements on books by Desmarets which they have manifestly failed to examine. Picard's errors in this regard are revealing and only too typical.[33] The reader of later chapters may be persuaded that omissions by Picard and other literary historians are even more distorting to a balanced view of the Quarrels of the *Imaginaires* and of the ancients and moderns.

The century of Louis XIV redefined

Arguably none of the contemporary controversies would have damaged Desmarets's reputation so thoroughly but for redefinition of the concept and term 'century of Louis XIV'. Redefinition may be traced to *Le Siècle de Louis le Grand* (1687) by Charles Perrault (1628–1703), the fellow Academician to whom (as a potential leader of the moderns in the re-emerging Quarrel of the ancients and moderns) Desmarets had dedicated the last of his books published in his lifetime, *La Defense de la Poësie* (1675). A good generation

---

[31] *Le Registre de La Grange 1659–1685*, ed. B. E. and G. P. Young (1947), 36, 41, 53.
[32] R. Briggs, *Early Modern France* (London, 1977), 70.
[33] J. Racine, *Œuvres complètes*, ed. R. Picard (2 vols.; 1950–2), ii. 13, 1000.

younger than Desmarets, Perrault went on to adapt to Louis XIV's personal reign the courtly art of flattering parallels—an ancient tradition used throughout the seventeenth century to magnify the French monarchy—in the four volumes of his *Parallèles des Anciens et des Modernes* (1688–97). Quite apart from the mid-century Cartesian cultural revolution, the shift of focus to the beginning of the personal reign of Louis XIV was disastrous for Desmarets's reputation. Attacked by Jansenists, then by Boileau and other ancients in the Quarrel of the ancients and moderns, and also by Protestants, Desmarets's achievements and reputation were not defended by the moderns, whose cause he had done so much to promote.

If the disinformation still met in perfunctory references to Desmarets stems largely from Nicole, the neglect of a personage of such contemporary consequence derives in part from perception of a 'century of Louis XIV' beginning only with the personal reign in 1661: a focus on which Boileau and Perrault could agree.

Exactly a century after the proclamation of Louis XIV's majority, François-Marie Arouet (1694–1778), known as Voltaire, published his *Siècle de Louis XIV* (1751). Twenty-one years of age when Louis XIV died, Voltaire gives an account that is, of course, retrospective. Renewing and reinforcing the historiographical schema proposed by Perrault by adopting a similar focus extended to the personal reign as a whole, Voltaire passed this schema on to later historians, especially literary historians. In *Siècle de Louis XIV* the fifty-four years between 1661 and 1715 attract twenty-eight chapters, while the early years of the 'century'—which Voltaire does allow to have begun in some respects around 1635—are covered in only four.

The focus of Voltaire's complex and highly influential history is set in two catchy introductory chapters (first published separately in 1739, the centenary of Desmarets's *Ballet de la Félicité*). Voltaire declares at the outset that 'quiconque a du goût, ne compte que quatre siècles dans l'histoire de monde'—that is, four periods of supreme achievement in the arts, centuries forever exemplary to mankind. The earliest occurred in ancient Greece, the century of Alexander the Great and Pericles; the second in Rome, under Julius and Augustus Caesar; the third in Renaissance Italy, especially in Florence, under the Medici, in the fifteenth and sixteenth centuries; and the fourth was 'le siècle de Louis XIV, et c'est peut-être celui qui approche le plus de la perfection'. This still influential schema of privileged 'centuries' builds on familiar aspects of Perrault's *Parallèles des Anciens et des Modernes*. Voltaire's assumptions—his particular notions of perfection in political order, taste, and enlightenment—are of less interest here than the historiographical schema itself: the focus of its periodization, its devaluation of the tastes of disfavoured periods, its doubts about the latters' enlightenment, and the prize awarded to the 'siècle de Louis le Grand'. A reign which might have been remembered as revolutionary is consecrated as classicism.

Voltaire's schema assumes a cyclic conception of history, in which national renewal is linked to a transfer of cultural prestige and political authority: the well-established humanist concepts of *translatio studii* and *translatio imperii*. Voltaire's *Siècle de Louis XIV* continues in this respect the humanist historiography which proclaimed the Renaissance—or rather a succession of renascences. A period of 'enlightenment' is perceived and privileged, with the concomitant devaluation of the preceding period, reduced in status to a 'Dark Age' in which glimmers of enlightenment are glimpsed only selectively, and mainly as harbingers of the ensuing 'renascence'. Ignoring earlier renascences perceived in France by other scholars since the twelfth century, Voltaire extends the 'Dark Ages' right down to the last years of Cardinal Richelieu's ministry.

Thus in the opening chapter of *Siècle de Louis XIV* Voltaire sees a beginning of the privileged century in the 'dernières années du cardinal de Richelieu', commencing 'à peu près à l'établissement de l'Académie française', that is about three years before the birth of Louis XIV. But he shows little interest in Desmarets as a chief executant of Cardinal Richelieu's cultural renascence, or as the first Chancellor of the Académie-Française and the person in whose home it first met officially.

He might have noticed the historiography of Desmarets's *Triomphe de Louis et de son siècle*, seminal in extending to the arts and to the century as a whole the concept of royal triumphs commemorated by Charles Beys (1610?–59) and Pierre Corneille in *Les Triomphes de Louis le Juste* (1649). Or he might have acknowledged that the infant Louis XIV had been celebrated as successor to four conquering heroes, each symbolic of a privileged *imperium*, in the second *entrée* of Desmarets's *Ballet de la Félicité*. Cyrus, Alexander, Julius Caesar, and Tamerlane each in succession takes a globe representing the earth, holds and turns it at will, and then retires. Desmarets supposes four imperial centuries past, compared with three for Voltaire.

Of these, two coincide, despite differences in media and despite somewhat divergent aims. In the eighth *entrée* a chariot brings forth the Dauphin, with personified Justice at his feet, and the latter receives from current combatants both their submission and the orb representing the world. For Desmarets, prophetically, the century of Louis XIV would mark both a cyclic succession and a culmination, just as it would for Voltaire, but with this difference: Desmarets is conscious of building the 'century of Louis XIV', Voltaire is nostalgic for a perfection already past—'le siècle le plus éclairé qui *fut* jamais' (my italics).

Voltaire clearly retains the humanist historiographical schema that Perrault continued from Desmarets and others, accepting their preference for the century of Louis XIV over earlier privileged periods considered to offer parallels (in particular the Greece of Pericles and Alexander, and the Rome of the first Caesars). However, he also seems to have absorbed from the ancients in the Quarrel of ancients and moderns something of the curious doctrine—implicit in the notion of a renascence or rebirth—that perfection in the arts was attained at an identifiable period or periods in the past and was later lost, except to emulation. It also follows from Voltaire's assumption—in theory, though not in Voltaire's practice as a writer and critic—that anyone of good taste would prefer examples drawn from ancient Greece and Rome, or perhaps from the Italian renascence of classical culture. It is a reasonable simplification to suggest that this aspect of Voltaire's taste reflects that of the leader of the ancients in the Quarrel: Boileau, who was especially hostile to the medieval and biblical epic of the 1650s.

There is an implicit suggestion of a classical corpus in which the historical setting of imaginative works is privileged in terms of the historiographical schema currently considered in good taste. Events of the favoured 'century' are promoted to the status of mythic occurrences *in illo tempore*.[34] Obvious exceptions come to mind: Corneille's *Cid* (1637) and Racine's *Athalie* (1691), for example. Some neglected works of Desmarets's might indeed have benefited from such preferences, one example being the tragicomedies he dedicated to Cardinal Richelieu: *Scipion* (1638) and *Roxane* (1640), plays each suggesting a parallel between the Cardinal and the respective hero—Scipio Africanus and Alexander the Great. But there

---

[34] Compare M. Éliade, *Le Mythe de l'éternel retour* (1949).

is a clear prejudice against his two main late sources of inspiration: the French 'Middle Ages' and the Bible. Quite apart from questions of literary quality, fashion turned against Desmarets's parallel of Louis XIV and the Dark Age Frankish king Clovis I (466?–511), his exegesis of Old Testament books in *Les Délices de l'esprit*, and the late biblical epics *Marie-Madeleine* (1669) and *Esther* (1670).

Boileau's classical prejudice is explicit in his summary of theatre history in *L'Art poétique* (1674):

> Chez nos devots Ayeux le Theatre abhorré
> Fut long-temps dans la France un plaisir ignoré.
> De Pelerins, dit-on, une Troupe grossiere
> En public à Paris y monta la premiere,
> Et sottement zelée en sa simplicité
> Joua les Saints, la Vierge et Dieu, par pieté.
> Le sçàvoir à la fin dissipant l'ignorance,
> Fit voir de ce projet la devote imprudence.
> On chassa ces Docteurs preschans sans mission.
> On vit renaistre Hector, Andromaque, Ilion.

The same prejudice is equally apparent later in the same 'Chant III' in these lines on the poetics of classical mythology:

> La Fable offre à l'esprit mille agrémens divers.
> Là tous les noms heureux semblent nés pour les vers,
> Ulysse, Agamemnon, Oreste, Idoménée,
> Helene, Menelas, Paris, Hector, Enée,
> O le plaisant projet d'un Poëte ignorant,
> Qui de tant de Heros va choisir Childebrand!

Boileau's immediate target in this case is Jacques Carel de Sainte-Garde, author of the heroic poem *Les Sarrazins chassés de France* (1667). Its hero is the eighth-century warrior Childebrand, associated with his brother, Charles Martel, in the defeat of the Moors between Tours and Poitiers in 732 and himself the ancestor, through Hugues Capet, of the kings of France.

But the implications of Boileau's mockery go well beyond his immediate target, as Desmarets and his associates understood. Warriors who secured a basis for the French nation in a 'Dark Age' are subjects unworthy of serious literature, unimportant in comparison with pagan antiquity. Similarly, theatre directly expressive of the religious beliefs of the community is rejected in favour of subjects drawn from the alien religious traditions of antiquity generally regarded by Boileau and others in the 'century of Louis XIV' as false. In this respect *L'Art poétique* illustrates the aesthetic consecration of the alien, ancient, and pagan as the cultural norms for late seventeenth-century Catholic France, opening up a gap between national and personal religious experience and high literary expression. Independently of the failure of the heroic poets satirized by Boileau— Chapelain, Desmarets, Carel de Sainte-Garde, and others—to fulfil their own high literary ambitions, also steeped in veneration of ancient Graeco-Roman literary forms and norms, the classical perspective was itself damaging to Desmarets and to the aspiration he had once shared with Cardinal Richelieu for a culturally coherent modern French national literature grounded directly in Catholic religious experience.

Richelieu, for example, had not favoured plays from Greek religion, encouraging French and Catholic subjects. Louis XIV, on the other hand, was, as the new Sun King, deliberately associated, from early in his personal reign, with the pagan sun-god Apollo, to the exclusion of Apollo as a conventional metaphoric reference honouring other outstanding men: 'mythic inflation that was immediately given wide currency through medals, prints, and paintings'.[35] Although in *Le Triomphe de Louis et de son siècle* Desmarets can accept the Apollo imagery in the elaboration of Versailles, the new royal example favoured the literary aesthetics advanced by Boileau.

The Richelieu heritage

It is scarcely an exaggeration to suggest that the Quarrel of the ancients and moderns was a debate in which Desmarets defended the Richelieu heritage—policies promoting the French language, French heroic verse, and the Christian marvellous. *Clovis*, extensively revised for the 1673 edition in order to include references to Louis XIV's recent exploits, was of strategic importance for both sides in a long-running battle of the books. Hostilities were already well advanced when Desmarets's ode 'Indignation', 'contre le goust du siecle, & contre ceux dont la cabale fait réussir les Ouvrages', was read to the Académie-Française on St-Louis day 1673, reported in *Le Mercure galant*, and dedicated to the second Duc de Richelieu.

---

[35] N. T. Whitman, 'Myth and Politics: Versailles and the Fountain of Latona', in J. C. Rule (ed.), *Louis XIV and the Craft of Kingship* (Columbus, 1969), 294.

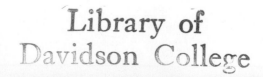

Explicitly linking the supremacy he claims for France in the arts and sciences to the enlightened patronage of Louis XIV, Desmarets traces that enlightenment to the earlier patronage of Cardinal Richelieu:

> La sçavante troupe choisie
> Par les soins du fameux ARMAND,
> En éloquence, en Poësie,
> Enseigne à juger justement.
> La docte & superbe Sculpture,
> Et l'Harmonie, & la Peinture,
> Donnent le prix à leurs Amans:
> Mais le Prince qui les anime,
> D'un goust delicat & sublime,
> Juge de tous les jugemens.

Through the arts of war and peace, through commerce and architecture, with the building of fountains at Versailles and the construction of the Canal du Midi, Louis XIV is said to have brought civilization in France beyond its previous cyclic summit under Augustus Caesar, whose

> siecle eut l'honneur de détruire
> L'éclat dont on avoit veu luire
> Les esprits jadis si vantez,
> Mais sur luy dans le cours des âges,
> LOUIS aura mille avantages,
> Si ses miracles sont comptez.

Typical of Desmarets's optimism concerning the century of Louis XIV, these lines update to the new reign the attitudes and values which he had brought into Cardinal Richelieu's personal service in 1634 as an *officier*, performing artist, novelist, poet, and founder-member of the Académie-Française. References in *Indignation* to the 'laches malices' of various 'Ennemis couverts', to a 'Muse, jeune écoliere', etc. are directed at Boileau and his sympathizers in the Hôtel de Lamoignon. When Boileau's collected works appeared in 1674, the book was assailed by Desmarets, Jacques Testu (1626–1706) (Aumônier du Roi, Abbé of Notre-Dame de Belval, and successor in 1665 to Bautru's seat in the Académie-Française—resident, like Desmarets, with the Duc de Richelieu), and Philippe-Julien Mazarini-Mancini, Duc de Nevers (1639–1707), in *La Deffense de poëme heroïque, avec quelques remarques sur les Œuvres satyriques de Sieur D[espréaux]* (1674)—dialogues in which even the ghost of the recently deceased Molière judges Boileau's satirical work severely. Then, in *La Defense de la Poësie* (1675), Desmarets appealed to Charles Perrault, Contrôleur général de la Surintendance des bâtiments and future leader of the moderns, for further help in combating writers regarded as excessively deferential to the ancients, deficient in invention, and incapable of sublimity.

Conflicts of personality and political rivalries between salons doubtless complicate the aesthetic issues. Boileau remained hostile to Desmarets's heroic verse, which Desmarets himself had brought to the centre of the quarrel. The Cartesian revolution, the Peace of the Church, and new literary fashions scarcely favoured him. Yet Desmarets might have received fuller recognition from Perrault, whose *Parallèles des Anciens et des Modernes* owe him unacknowledged debts of philosophic inspiration, method, form, atmosphere, and content. With the focus clearly on the personal reign of Louis XIV from 1661, Perrault chose not to defend in Desmarets what Nicole and Boileau had attacked.

2

Family

A *bourgeois gentilhomme*

On present evidence Iean, Jean, or Jehan Marets, Maretz, Marestz, Marests, Marais, Marays, or Des-marest, des Marets etc., or Desmarestz etc., was born in Paris *c*.1600. He was probably the son of the 'marchand bourgeois' Jean Marestz and his wife, Marie Le Febvre, living at that time in rue St-Sauveur in the St-Denis quarter of Paris, as indicated above on circumstantial evidence. Niceron refers to Desmarets's birth as 'honnête', which normally means respectable bourgeois.[1] Niceron also publishes a transcription of the epitaph which Jean shared with his brother Roland, establishing that Jean ('natu minore') was the younger and that he died on 28 October 1676. Kerviler surmises that they may be descended from an earlier Jehan Desmarets, the father of the poet Clément Marot (1496–1544), whose graceful verse our Jean Desmarets praises in *La Defense de la Poësie* (1675).[2] I wonder.

There is, however, good evidence to show that this young bourgeois had influential aristocratic relatives and family connections at Court; and some time before 1639 Jean Desmarets was ennobled by acquiring the ennobling office of Secrétaire du Roi in the Extraordinaire des guerres. Desmarets fits very well into the Paris described by George Huppert in *Les Bourgeois gentilshommes*.[3] He and members of his immediate family manifest upward mobility through education, professional activity, the acquisition of offices, writing, other cultural activities, and advantageous marriages. The *ancien régime*, observes Huppert, 'is characterized by the existence of families which deny that they are bourgeois', insist that they are 'living nobly', and complain about 'being treated as inferiors by the

---

[1] J.-P. Niceron, *Mémoires pour servir à l'histoire des hommes illustres dans la République des Lettres*, xxxv (1736), 136.

[2] Kerviler, *Jean Desmaretz*, 6. References to Kerviler are to this monograph unless otherwise stated.

[3] G. Huppert, *Les Bourgeois Gentilshommes. An Essay on the Definition of Elites in Renaissance France* (Chicago and London, 1977).

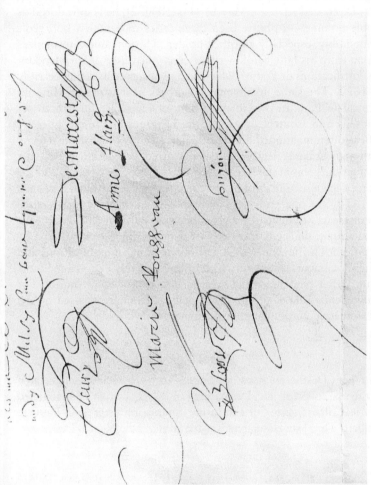

FIG. 2. Signatures of Desmarets, Anne Fleury, René Fleury, and Marie Rousseau, 2 May 1634. Photo enhanced by Walter Ritchie

gentilshommes.[4] From soon after the assassination of Henri IV until after he took the title Sieur de Saint-Sorlin in 1651, the talents of this bourgeois evidently made him very much a Court personality.

In the earliest indisputably pertinent archival document concerning Jean Desmarets, dated 2 May 1634 (see Fig. 2), he is introduced as 'noble homme'—a phrase used by notaries to denote a bourgeois living nobly, especially an office-holder. This document recognizes a loan from his father-in-law to purchase the office of Surintendant des fortifications de France, which he had exercised as deputy as early as 1620. The same document and others near it in the Minutier Central in Paris further identify him as Conseiller du Roi en ses Conseils and Contrôleur général de l'Extraordinaire des guerres, offices often mentioned on the title-pages of his books from 1639.[5] Although scarcely legible, these notarized acts confirm that the young bourgeois in the Regency Court of Marie de Médicis and the Academician recruited for his personal service by Cardinal Richelieu in 1634, are one and the same person. They are clearly signed 'Desmarestz', followed by a great baroque paraph. They may have been among the signatures seen by Auguste Jal but overlooked by Kerviler.[6] The name occurs in various spellings in publications and other documents, many of which unquestionably concern the same man. Other references may be argued to do so. Some do not. For convenience I have adopted the spelling 'Desmarets', used by the Bibliothèque Nationale and other major libraries.

Unrelated Desmarets families

Our Jean Desmarets does not appear to have been closely related to the tax-collector Jean Desmaretz (1608–82) who in 1646 married Marie Colbert, sister of the future finance minister Jean-Baptiste Colbert. That Jean Desmaretz was the father of the Nicolas Desmarets,

---

[4] Huppert, *Les Bourgeois Gentilshommes*, 2.

[5] Minutier central, xxx' Guyon 1634 mai 2; 1634 août 10; 1635 juin 12; 1635 novembre 4; xxxi' Guyon 1634 septembre 7; 1635 novembre 2.

[6] Jal, *Dictionnaire critique*, 'Desmarest'. Signatures 'Desmarestz' are recorded on a letter to Cardinal Richelieu's brother-in-law Maréchal Urbain du Maillé, Marquis de Brézé (1597–1650), dated 5 May 1638 from Paris, and on a receipt dated 10 Feb. 1667 (*L'Amateur d'autographes*, 38 (1905), 17–18). Kerviler claims to have possessed a document dated 3 Sept. 1668 signed 'Desmaretz' (p. 6). A. Auguste interprets as 'Desmarests' a signature of 12 Oct. 1668 reproduced opposite p. 13 in his *Sociétés secrètes catholiques du XVII* siècle et H. M. Boudon* (1913).

Desmaretz, or Des Marets, Seigneur de Maillebois (1648–1721), who became Contrôleur général des Finances (1708–15), made enemies for the name Desmarets, and was the first minister dismissed after Louis XIV's death.

Nor apparently did our Desmarets belong to the family of Paul Godet des Marais (1648–1709), the Bishop of Chartres who corresponded with Louis XIV's morganatic wife, Françoise d'Aubigné, Marquise de Maintenon (1635–1719). I can trace no connection with the family of the Protestant theologian Samuel Desmarets (or des Marets) (1599–1673). I do not know whether our Jean Desmarets was related to the earlier Des Marets (possibly Mme des Loges's third son) killed on 15 December 1637 at the siege of Breda, or to the Oratorian Charles Desmarets (1602–75), or to any of the minor seventeenth-century French writers whose names are commonly spelled Mares or Desmares, or to the minor writer of the 1660s Louis Marais, or to the barrister-biographer of Jean de La Fontaine, Mathieu Marais (1664–1737).[7]

The Dauvet–Desmaretz connection

It is plausibly suggested in *Le Voyage de Fontainebleau, faict par Monsieur Bautru & Desmarets. Par dialogue* (1623)—an anonymous pamphlet probably published by themselves—that the Desmarets of this dialogue is related to Gaspard Dauvet, Seigneur des Marets, 'ce brave Desmarets Cheualier de l'ordre' (p. 20). This is our Desmarets, whose friendship with Guillaume II Bautru, Comte de Serrant (1588–1665) is variously attested. The Dauvet-Desmaretz family had connections both in the Paris Parlement and at Court. A Charlotte Dauvet, daughter of a president of the Paris Chambre des comptes, was the mother of the Duc de Sully, who under Henri IV (1553–1610) was Grand Maître de l'artillerie (an office he retained without commission until 1634), Surintendant des fortifications (an office of which doubtless the same may now be said), and Surintendant des bâtiments du Roi. In 1606 a Claude Douet (i.e. Dauvet), Chevalier Des Maretz, was one of the knights of Malta recruited to the Marine de Levant.[8] The difference between 'Monsieur Bautru' for the son

---

[7] I am indebted for some of these exclusions to Gary McCallin, who is preparing a study of Nicolas Desmarets.

[8] D. Buisseret, *Sully and the Growth of the Centralized Government in France 1598–1610* (London, 1968), 163.

of a count and a minister and 'Desmarets' for his companion suggests
a social distinction to some extent borne out by the tone of the
dialogue, but perhaps it only reflects the twelve-year difference in
age and Desmarets's minority at that date.

In *Le Voyage de Fontainebleau* Desmarets seems fully conversant
with Court personalities, intrigues, and recent political events. A key
connection is doubtless that in 1601 Gaspard Dauvet had married
Jeanne-Isabelle Brûlart, the daughter of Nicolas Brûlart de Sillery,
who in 1623 was once again Chancelier de France and Garde des
Sceaux, offices previously held from 1607 to 1616 and 1604 to 1616
respectively. Mme Dauvet had an influential brother: the minister
Pierre Brûlart, Marquis de Puisieux, who had been sent as ambassador
extraordinary to Spain to conclude the marriage of Louis XIII to Anne
of Austria, and again to carry her back to France. Mme Dauvet also
had an influential brother-in-law, because in 1605 her sister Claude
Brûlart had married a Président à mortier in the Paris Parlement,
Nicolas de Bellièvre (1583–1650), son of Pomponne de Bellièvre, a
former Chancelier de France. In 1623 Cardinal Richelieu was still
far from out of the political wilderness into which he had been cast
by the fall of Concini. Sillery and Puisieux were as nearly in control
of the Grand Conseil as anyone, and they did not like Richelieu.

A useful cousin: Madame du Vigean

The Marquise de Puisieux was a particular friend of Anne de
Neubourg, Baronne du Vigean, a famous hostess of the period, also
born with the century, in 1600.[9] Mme du Vigean received guests
both at the château de la Barre at Deuil (Val-d'Oise) and in her Paris
homes: in the rue St-Antoine until 1634, when the house was sold
and became the Hôtel de Sully; thereafter in the rue St-Thomas-du-
Louvre, near the influential Hôtel de Rambouillet, with which she
enjoyed excellent relations.

That Desmarets was Mme du Vigean's first cousin once removed is
independently attested by Jean Chapelain, Gui Patin, and Dubuisson-
Aubenay.[10] She later became the intimate friend and 'comme la

---

[9] See A. Adam, *Histoire de la littérature française au XVIIe siècle* (5 vols.; 1956),
i. 271.

[10] In May 1638 Chapelain recommends to the Duc de Longueville a 'protégé de
M. Desmarests, cousin de Mme du Vigean' (*Lettres*, i. 233). See also Dubuisson-
Aubenay, *Journal des guerres civiles*, i. 326; and Patin, *Lettres*, i. 522.

femme de charge' of Cardinal Richelieu's favourite niece, Marie de Vignerot, who married Antoine du Roure, Sieur de Combalet, was widowed, and in 1638 became Duchesse d'Aiguillon.[11] In the last years of Cardinal Richelieu's ministry the Duchesse d'Aiguillon was mistress of his household. She was also his executrix. Edmond Chamaillard mentions her immediately after the Duchesse de Longueville in a short list of influential Court ladies of the Regency of Anne of Austria.[12] It was to the new first Duchesse d'Aiguillon that Desmarets dedicated his second novel, Rosane (1639), with a preface on exemplary fiction.

To his cousin Mme du Vigean, Desmarets addressed a sonnet on the second capture of her son, the Marquis de Fors, 'Mestre de camp du regiment de Navarre', at Thionville; and to his Œuvres poëtiques he added a sonnet and an elegy on the death, on 28 August 1640, of the Marquis de Fors, aged 19, from wounds received in front-line combat at the siege of Arras, 'regreté de toute la Cour; sa vie ayant esté pleine de gloire, & sa fin de pieté'.[13] A year earlier this Marquis de Fors had danced two entrées in Le Ballet de la Félicité.

The first Duchesse de Richelieu

It was to Mme du Vigean's widowed daughter, Anne Poussart de Pons, born in 1622 and one of Anne of Austria's Dames d'honneur, that Desmarets arranged the marriage in December 1649 of Mme d'Aiguillon's minor nephew and ward, Armand-Jean du Plessis (1629–1715). On his majority du Plessis became the second Duc de Richelieu, a person of consequence in Desmarets's life from 1643 until his death thirty-three years later in the Duc de Richelieu's home in the Place-Royale. The second Duc de Richelieu was the eldest son of François de Vignerot, Marquis du Pont-de-Courlai, who died in 1646. He had already been replaced as Général des galères by the 15-year-old future second Duc de Richelieu in January 1643, in

[11] A. Bonneau-Avenant, La Duchesse d'Aiguillon, 2nd edn. (1882), 405, after Mlle de Montpensier's Mémoires for 6 Nov. 1652. See also G. Mongrédien, 'Une Précieuse: Madame du Vigean (1600–1682)', Revue de France, 8/4 (15 Feb., 1928), 666–91; and V. Cousin, Madame de Longueville (1855), i, passim.

[12] E. Chamaillard, Le Chevalier de Méré (Niort, 1921), 28.

[13] Gazette, 1 Sept. 1640. This was the elder brother of the Marquis de Fors whose murder near Poitiers is mentioned by Jean de La Fontaine in a letter to his wife dated 19 Sept. 1663.

which connection Desmarets was (at the instance of Mme d'Aiguillon) appointed Secrétaire général de la Marine de Levant and steward of the late Cardinal's household. The marriage, for which Desmarets was sent to prison on 22 March 1650, at the instance of Mmes d'Aiguillon and du Vigean, is evoked in *Clovis*, at the end of Livre VIII, immediately after the prophecy of the young Duc de Richelieu's naval victory at Naples in 1647:

> Qu'il se rendra celebre en constance loyale!
> Pour conserver son cœur, & sa foy conjugale,
> A la chaste Beauté, dont l'auguste splendeur
> Et la grace & l'esprit l'auront remply d'ardeur
> De qui toute la Cour vantera la sagesse;
> D'vn courage & d'vn port dignes de sa noblesse . . .

Shortly before marrying the Duc de Richelieu, Anne Poussart de Pons had sought the privilege of the *tabouret*—a seat at Court in the presence of the Queen—normally reserved for duchesses or better.[14] When in 1673 Desmarets dedicated to her the second edition of *Esther*, she had become Première Dame d'honneur to Queen Marie-Thérèse.

The second Duc de Richelieu was the brother of Jean-Baptiste Vignerot, Marquis de Richelieu (1632–62), who in 1652 married the daughter of Catherine-Henriette Bellier, Première Femme de chambre and favourite of Anne of Austria. The Marquis de Richelieu was Lieutenant général des Armées du Roi and held other sensitive offices at the beginning of Louis XIV's personal reign, as indicated above. Another brother was Emmanuel-Joseph Vignerot, Comte de Richelieu, Abbé de Marmoutier, etc., the Abbé de Richelieu who died in Venice in January 1665, aged 25. Their sister Marie-Magdalène-Thérèse Vignerot became the second Duchesse d'Aiguillon (1675–1704) on the death of her aunt. The second Duc de Richelieu so important in Desmarets's life was the father, by a second marriage, of the third Duc de Richelieu, bŏrn in 1696 and illustrious in the eighteenth century as a member of the Académie-Française, Maréchal de France, and a close friend of Voltaire's. The third Duc de Richelieu would not appear to have cultivated the memory of relatives of his father's first wife.

---

[14] J.-P. Labatut, *Les Ducs et pairs de France au XVIIe siècle* (1972), 373.

The Duchesse de Richelieu had a younger sister, Marthe du Vigean, said by Victor Cousin also to have been born in 1622, equally celebrated by Vincent Voiture (1597–1648) and other poets who frequented the Hôtel de Rambouillet.[15] It was with Marthe du Vigean that the Duc d'Enghien (the future Grand Condé) was in love around 1640, not long before his marriage to Clémence de Maillé-Brézé, for which Desmarets's *Ballet de la Prospérité* was danced. In 1647 she entered the Carmelites and became Sœur Marthe de Jésus.

Roland Desmarets

Roland Desmarets's birth in 1593 or 1594 may be deduced from Niceron's transcription of his epitaph in the Paris church of St-Nicolas-des-Champs, which dates his death to 27 December 1653 'aetatis suae 60'. The *Vigneul-Marvilliana* states that Roland 'avoit été disciple du P. Petau, et conféroit souvent avec lui touchant la bonne latinité'.[16] So many aspects of the writings of the Desmarets brothers are compatible with a Jesuit education that I incline to accept this evidence.

In any case, I reject the view expressed by Lucette Sigaux in the introduction to her unpublished translation of Roland's *Lettres philologiques* that although Roland may well have been an admirer of Petau's 'il ne pouvait être l'élève des Jésuites', because the Collège de Clermont—closed when the Jesuits were expelled by the Parlement de Paris in 1595—did not reopen until 1618.[17] She fixes too narrowly on the one college. In the Edict of Rouen (1603) Henri IV recalled the Jesuits and founded new colleges, including La Flèche, where Denis Petau was teaching at the relevant time. According to the *Menagiana*, Petau's motto was: 'Nova quaerent alii, nil nisi prisca PETO.'[18] But, the pun apart, the motto does not really suit a classicist deeply concerned with rhetorical invention.

---

[15] Cousin, *Madame de Longueville*, i. 181 ff., 503–27. See also E. Magne, *Voiture et l'Hôtel de Rambouillet*, new edn. (2 vols.; 1930).

[16] *Vigneul-Marvilliana*, in *Ana, ou Collection de bons mots . . .*, ed. C. G. T. Garnier (Amsterdam, 1789), v. 162–3.

[17] R. Desmarets, '*Lettres philologiques I* (1650)' transl. and ed. L. Sigaux, thèse de 3ᵉ cycle (Sorbonne, 1978), iii. 4: the soundest work to date on Jean Desmarets's Latinist brother. See also P. Brun, 'La Critique littéraire et pédagogique: Roland Desmarets', in his *Autour du Dix-septième siècle* (1901), 73–103.

[18] *Menagiana*, new edn. (1729), ii. 44.

Roland became a barrister in the Paris Parlement. One of the most distinguished Latinists of the mid-century, he is remembered chiefly for the two volumes of his philological letters (1650 and 1655). Michel de Marolles, Abbé de Villeloin (1600–81), the art historian and translator of Virgil with whom Jean Desmarets quarrelled in 1673, states that Roland 'écrivoit aussi purement en latin, comme son frère s'est acquis de réputation par ses beaux ouvrages qu'il nous a donnés en notre langue en prose et en vers'.[19] It was to Roland that Cardinal Richelieu entrusted the Latin distichs in praise of illustrious Frenchmen whose portraits hung in the Galerie des hommes illustres of the Palais-Cardinal and (I conclude) a similar gallery in the château de Richelieu in Poitou, distichs published in 1636 as *Elogia illustrium Gallorum quorum imagines in tabellis depictae cernuntur in porticu Ricelianarum aedium*. These galleries constitute parallels of ancients and moderns, favouring the moderns.[20] Roland's poems were preferred to compositions already in preparation by Nicolas Bourbon, the laureate Latinist who had written the inscriptions for the equestrian statue of Henri IV erected beside the Pont-Neuf, opposite the Place-Dauphine, on the prow of the Île-de-la-Cité. Not without cause, Bourbon is reported to have feared criticism from a Desmarets more than that from any other source.[21]

Gilles Ménage (1613–92)—the distinguished scholar mocked by Molière as Vadius in *Les Femmes savantes*—wrote to P.-D. Huet on 9 May 1663 that he had known Roland 'très-particulièrement', adding that 'la pluspart de ses épîtres me sont adressées'. Ménage states: 'Je l'avois nommé Philadelphe, à cause qu'il étoit l'admirateur de son frère, et ne parloit jamais d'autre chose.'[22] Lucette Sigaux notes a similar impression on reading Roland's letters concerned with Jean's work: 'le plus âgé [Roland] est le disciple du plus jeune' ii. 6). When in the early 1650s Jean was resident at the château de Richelieu, Roland (who never married) was living in Paris with their sister, Marguerite Dupré. Jean mentions his 'chère sœur' in a letter

---

[19] M. de Marolles, *Mémoires* (Amsterdam, 1755), i. 331.

[20] See M. Vulson de la Colombière, *Les Portraits des hommes illustres françois qui sont peints dans la galerie du Palais Cardinal de Richelieu* (1650).

[21] P. Hallaeus, 'Roland Maresii elogium', in *Rolandi Maresii epistolarum philologicarum Libri II*. For a fuller account, see B. Dorival, 'art et politique en France au XVIIᵉ siècle: La Galerie des Hommes illustres du Palais-Cardinal', *Bulletin de la Société de l'histoire de l'art français* (1973), 43–60.

[22] *Menagiana*, iii. 198–9, 318.

from Richelieu dated 6 July 1652.[23] According to Pierre Hallé's
'Elogium', Roland was living with Jean at the time of his death: 'Insigni
vitae probitate et egregiâ in suum fratrem Joannem Maresium,
Gallicae Poëseos studiis, ingenio, & operum cultissimorum multi-
tudine clarissimum, pietate commendabilis extitit.'

Hallé's references to Jean's scholarship, wit, fame, and numerous
elegant literary works seem to go beyond the minimum requirements
of an elogium, if only as a reflection of Roland's admiration for his
brother, who is sometimes mentioned in the correspondence with
third parties. Nicholas Heinsius (1620–81) closes one letter, for
example: 'ut Poëtae summo fratri tuo me commendes'. Another letter,
written at Leyden on 14 September 1649, ends: 'Vale, clarissime
Maresi, cum fratre tuo, illibato illo flore Gallicae poeseos'. Once
again, phrases like 'supreme poet' and 'undiminished flower of French
poetry' would seem to express more than the minimal etiquette of
polite epistolary closing flourishes.

Roland Desmarets's philological letters—in effect structured essays
on matters of mutual interest and general importance addressed in
an elegant familiar style to respected correspondents—are exemplary
in their genre. They were sufficiently valued in their time for a
posthumous second volume to be added when the first volume (1650)
was republished in 1655; and they witness the respect in which, at
mid-century, Roland and his correspondents held his more versatile
younger brother. Roland's letters were reprinted in Leipzig in 1687.

Marguerite Desmarets

Kerviler is wrong to have assumed that Desmarets's sister Marguerite
died young (p. 7). She married Guillaume Dupré, identified by René
Rapin as 'médecin ordinaire du Roi' and in archival documents of
1669–70 as having been 'docteur régent en la Faculté de Médecine
à Paris'.[24] Gui Patin writes, on 1 April 1650, that Dupré attended
the Princes de Condé and Conti and the Duc de Longueville when

---

[23] J. Desmarets, 'Lettres datées de Richelieu', Bibliothèque de l'Arsenal, Mss.
3135, p. 38. Misled by Kerviler, Henri Bremond supposes the reference is to a non-
existent 'Mme Roland Desmarets' (Histoire littéraire du sentiment religieux en France,
vi (1922), 480 n.). They overlook P. Hallé's statement in 'Elogium Rolandi Maresii':
'Cœlibem vitam amplexus est.'

[24] Rapin, Mémoires, iii. 362 n.; Archives Nationales, Insinuations du Châtelet,
Y219, 966, 28 Feb. 1670, fol. 63.

they were imprisoned following the marriage of Anne de Pons (Dupré's cousin by marriage) to the Duc de Richelieu.[25] New documents show that, widowed before 1669, she proposed to marry Hilaire Avrie, Sieur de Brétigny. In January 1669, when she made a conditional gift to her fiancé, she lived in the rue St-Antoine, in the parish of St-Paul.[26] In April 1669 she witnessed the marriage-contract of Pierre Bautet, Seigneur de Marivatz, 'Contrôleur-général de la maison du Duc [Philippe] d'Orléans', Louis XIV's younger brother, who had married Henrietta, sister of King Charles II of England.[27] At the time of her proposed remarriage into the aristocracy, this widowed bourgeoise clearly had titled friends. She was living in the rue Beaubourg, in the parish of St-Merri, when, on 28 February 1670, she made a gift to her daughter Marie Dupré 'de terres à Louvres en Parisis, de vaisselle d'argent & de rentes'.[28]

Anne Fleury

In 1634 Desmarets married Anne Fleury, daughter of René Fleury, identified in notarized acts as Conseiller du Roi, Lieutenant au Grenier à sel de Sully, and Maître général des œuvres de maçonnerie des bâtiments du Roi, ponts et chaussées de France. Her mother was Marie Rousseau, who also signed the acts. Jal found in the registers of the St-Sulpice church in Paris an entry dated 21 December 1665 stating that Armand Desmarets, the son of Jean Desmarets and Anne Fleury, had been baptized there in July 1645 (*sic* for 1635), a few days after his birth 'dans la maison de son père, au faubourg St-Germain'.[29] The Minutier Central documents confirm that, by June 1635, with financial assistance from his father-in-law, Desmarets had moved from the rue Clocheperce in the Marais district to the rue des Saints-Pères in the parish of St-Germain-des-Prés, doubtless in anticipation of the child—Armand.[30] Related acts in the Minutier Central also show that in 1634–5 debts were incurred by the new

[25] G. Patin, *Lettres du temps de la Fronde* (1921), 185.

[26] Archives Nationales, Insinuations du Châtelet, Y215, 2864, 30 Jan. 1669, fol. 342.

[27] Archives Nationales, insinuations du Châtelet, Y207, 3318, 22 Apr. 1669, fol. 340.

[28] Archives Nationales, Insinuations du Châtelet, Y219, 966, 28 Feb. 1670, fol. 63.

[29] Jal, *Dictionnaire critique*, 'Additions', 'Marets, des'.

[30] Minutier Central, xxx' Guyon 1635 juin 12.

family. In February 1642 Desmarets and his wife were living with René Fleury in Paris, on the Quai de l'Arsenal, in the parish of St-Paul.[31] The act attests their joint purchase (with their notary André Guyon) from Claude Paris, Commissaire pour le Roi sur les mers de Levant, as 'procureur' of François [Jouvenel] des Ursins, 'Chevalier des deux ordres du Roi, trésorier de France & general des finances', of the Hôtel des Ursins on the Île-de-la-Cité, parish of St-Landry. A tax record shows that in March 1649 they were living in the rue Garancière near St-Sulpice, and his presence in Paris at that time is confirmed in correspondence with Roland.[32]

Desmarets's letter of 6 July 1652 from Richelieu indicates that his wife and daughters also formed part of the household which Roland shared with Marguerite Dupré. To Roland he reports himself in good health at that time, despite the separation: 'je vous diray que jamais je ne me portay mieux, et l'on dit souvent que je ne parois pas avoir 30. ans . . . jamais je n'eus le teint si frais. Je crois que cela me vient de vivre chastement.' But he is aware that for some time the same could not have been said for his wife, because the letter continues directly: 'car je l'ay promis ainsi à ma f[emme] à cause de maux horribles qu'elle a eues, afin de la laisser en repos; et ainsi nous nous separons avec moins de regret'.

The letter closes with greetings whose reference is not always clear, although 'M. Chap . . .' may indicate Jean Chapelain. The acknowledgement: 'J'ay receu la lettre de ma fille aisnée' following greetings for 'mes niepces et mes Enfans' confirms that Jean Desmarets had at least two daughters and two nieces. The only other reference I find to Desmarets's children collectively occurs in the 'Ode' to Colbert (c.1667). In July 1652 they would appear to have been in Paris with his wife, Anne Fleury, and Marguerite Dupré, and Roland Desmarets. Whether his son Armand-Jean was in Paris or with his father at the château de Richelieu is not clear.[33]

---

[31] Archives Nationales, Insinuations du Châtelet, Y181, 2648, fol. 404.

[32] Dubuisson-Aubenay, *Journal des guerres civiles*, ii. 348; Bibliothèque de l'Arsenal, Mss. 5422, fol. 32.

[33] An initial in the MS letter transcribed by Kerviler as N looks to me like an A, although it follows 'que': 'M . . . vous pourra dire que A[rmand?] a fait souvent cette remarque.' The second volume of Roland's letters contains a letter (no. 42) with a message in it for Armand, who presumably was with his father. Roland's letter is likely to have been written between publication of vol. i in 1650 and his death in December 1653.

Armand-Jean Desmarets de Saint-Sorlin

Armand-Jean Desmarets, baptized in the St-Sulpice church in 1635, is evidently his parents' first child and their only recorded son. He was named after Cardinal Richelieu, who either officiated at the baptism or was present as the boy's godfather. Roland refers to the occasion in a letter to Jean: 'Armandus tuus, vt glorioso isto nomine, quo vir inter homines eminentissimus, illum è sacro fonte susceptum insigniuit' (ii. 42). The same letter contains the avuncular advice that the boy should memorize the once-famous moralist *Quatrains* of Guy Du Faur, Seigneur de Pibrac (1529–84)—advice which, if followed, would certainly have helped Armand in the next decade to notice features of Molière's *Misanthrope* and of La Fontaine's *Fables* which escape the notice of most later readers. It is the form adopted by Molière for his quatrains 'La Confrérie de l'esclavage de Notre-Dame de la Charité' (1665) and by Jean Desmarets for his translation of *L'Imitation de Jésus-Christ* and his *Maximes chrestiennes*.

Armand was the designer of a *Livre de touttes sortes de chyffres par Alphabets redoublés* (1664), cut by an otherwise unknown Charpentier but published by Florentin Lambert in the rue St-Jacques, a major publisher of such artwork who in 1661 had acquired and reissued stocks of the quarto *Clovis* and of the folio *Les Délices de l'esprit*. Armand's *Alphabets redoublés* had some success. It was republished in 1695. The British Library printed Catalogue attributes to Armand certain designs it possesses for the illustration of *Clovis*, to the ornamental letters and woodcut bands of which Armand's *Alphabets redoublés* is clearly related, as they are to the similar decorative features of *Les Délices de l'esprit*. Whatever the relationship, it was close in both aesthetic invention and commercial distribution.

The designs contained in these three books appear to have had some appreciable influence upon the decorative arts—monograms, carpets, tapestries, marble tables, ornamental plasterwork, wrought iron, etc.—in the 'style Louis XIV'. In view of the mystical inspiration of *Les Délices de l'esprit* and the fervour of *Clovis, ou la France Chrestienne*, I doubt that their interlaced letters are purely decorative.

Though perhaps not possessing a precisely defined system of mystical significance, the designs do have a sacral atmosphere. They may relate to inscriptions on the tombs of early Christian martyrs rediscovered when *Clovis*, and Armand Desmarets, were first conceived. The *Gazette* for 1 January 1635 reports 'l'inuention des corps de quatre Saints Martyrs' in Rome in October 1634. The report details triumphs over Apollo, Diana, and Jupiter by the third-century martyred virgin Saint Martina, whose remains were identified by an inscription which also contained 'des charactères entrelassez, que nul n'a pû dechiffrer'.

Armand would appear to have collaborated in the design of the quarto *Clovis*, contributing to its decorative system the interlaced letters whose function may well be symbolic as well as ornamental. *Clovis* opens with an explicit rejection of Apollo in favour of the Christian marvellous and the magnification of the Christian kings of France:

> Quittons les vains concerts du profane Parnasse.
> Tout est auguste & saint au sujet que j'embrasse.
> A la gloire des Lis je consacre ces vers.
> J'entonne la trompette . . .

The vigorous metaphor of the fourth line may recall another event of 1635, when on 19 May Louis XIII's heralds rode into the Grand'Place in Brussels to sound the trumpet and (for the last time in European history in that style) declare war upon Spain—a war which had not yet ended when *Clovis* was first published.

Jean Desmarets's daughters

That Desmarets had at least two daughters is implied by his letter from Richelieu dated 6th July 1652 and closing with the acknowledgement of a letter from 'ma fille aisnée'. Either daughter may be the Mlle Desmarets identified in *La Clé du Grand Dictionnaire historique des Prétieuses* with the Doristhenie of Antoine Baudeau de Somaize's *Grand Dictionnaire des Prétieuses*, first published in 1660. If the identification is correct and one accepts the satirical verbal portrait as generally faithful, the daughter in question made little educational progress before the age of 14. She then began to devour a surfeit of imaginative literature—novels, poetry, and other books—until, in 1660-1, at the age of 19, she imagines that whatever man she has last met is her hero.[34] Either of the younger sisters of

---

[34] A. Baudeau de Somaize, *Le Grand Dictionnaire historique des Prétieuses*, (1661), ii. 112-5, and *La Clé du Grand Dictionnaire des Prétieuses* (1661), s.v.

Armand could have been 19 at the time; and I know of no other Mlle Desmarets likely to have caught Somaize's attention.

Marie Dupré

We know rather more about one of Jean Desmarets's nieces, mentioned in his letter from Richelieu: Marguerite Dupré's daughter Marie. She would appear to have been Roland's favourite niece, to whose education he devoted particular attention. In the 'Elogium Rolandi Maresii', Pierre Hallé states that because Marie appeared from an early age to be a gifted child Roland devoted his leisure hours to teaching her Greek and Latin. Reviewing her education in a letter addressed to her 'sub eodem mecum tecto', he argues from his experience with her and the example of the late Mlle Marie Le Jars de Gournay (1566–1645) that—prejudice and custom to the contrary notwithstanding—women are capable of a humanist education and that suitable women should receive one. The same letter makes it clear that her programme of study included Italian, rhetoric, and philosophy.

According to Kerviler (p. 7), Marie Dupré was admired by Mlle Madeleine de Scudéry (1608–1701), the novelist, and by Mlle Marie-Anne de La Vigne (1634–84), a minor poet, as 'la cartésienne', which suggests that Marie admired the publications of René Descartes (1596–1650). In Somaize's *Grand Dictionnaire historique des Prétieuses* she is identified with each of the two Diophanises, whom the author admits not knowing very well. Only the second Diophanise is given a detailed character, and it is impressive: 'elle fait profession ouuerte de Science, de Lettres, de Vers, de Romans & de toutes les choses qui seruent d'entretien à celles qui sont Pretieuses . . . Ses vers sont comparez à ceux de nos meilleurs Escrivains' (i. 111–12). *La Clé du Grand Dictionnaire historique des Prétieuses* (1661) states that Mlle Dupré was living in the cloister of St-Germain-l'Auxerrois, well placed to watch the demolition in that year of the Petit-Bourbon—the great hall where some of Jean Desmarets's greatest triumphs in Court ballet had taken place and which later had housed Molière's theatre (1658–61)—to make way for the great new colonnade, which still stands, designed by Claude Perrault (1613–88) for the east front of the Louvre.

According to René Rapin, Marie Dupré assisted her uncle in legal moves connected with the arrest in 1666 of Le Maistre de Sacy. After personal investigations, Desmarets brought suspicious activities to the notice of the Lieutenant civil, François Dreux d'Aubray, whom Marie Dupré 'gouvernoit un peu'. In order to act, d'Aubray required the assent of the Secrétaire d'État Michel Le Tellier (1603–85). 'Desmarets', Rapin continues, 'le fit prier par sa nièce de ne point faire mention de jansénistes s'il s'adressoit au Tellier, mais de gens dont la conduite paroissoit suspecte au voisinage et qui donnoient de la jalousie . . . L'ordre fut exécuté'.[35]

The gift to Marie from her mother of land at Louvres-en-Parisis, silver, and *rentes* on 28 February 1670 is noted above. It was she who placed in St-Nicolas-des-Champs the tombstone for her uncles bearing the epitaph transcribed by Niceron. The researcher who discovers the lost manuscripts of her poetry will be a fortunate individual indeed.

[35] Rapin, *Mémoires*, iii. 362.

3

The 'Célèbre Marets' of Court Ballet

First successes

The first contemporary reference to the future Sieur de Saint-Sorlin (long known, but not recognized as pertinent) occurs in a letter by the Court poet François de Malherbe (1555–1628) dated 28 February 1613. Referring to *Le Ballet de la courtisane appelée La Ronde*, danced at the Louvre, Malherbe states that its only redeeming feature 'fut un certain nommé Maret, habillé en berger, qui menoit un homme habillé en chien, et le fit danser avec des bouffoneries si agréables que je croy que jamais je ne vis rire personne comme je vis rire la Reyne'.[1] This was not a bad beginning at Court for a teenaged bourgeois. Marie de Médicis (1573–1642), Queen Regent of France since the assassination of Henri IV in 1610, was so fond of ballets, according to François de Bassompierre (1579–1646), that even during mourning she required them every Sunday.[2] The following year Desmarets appears to have played the 'fool' in the *Ballet de la Blanque*—the Premier Sot, dressed in a 'characteristic costume of cap with asses' ears, staff with bells, and parti-coloured dress' which (according to Grace Frank) characterized royal or Court fools well into the Renaissance.[3] Or so I interpret the contemporary account transcribed for me by Margaret McGowan on 17 March 1986: 'L'Asne fut représenté par Monsieur Marets avec vn autre incogneu qui emeuvent le combat pour avoir la preference de Prescheur ou Practicien à la joyeuse assemblée'. The young Marets would appear to have found a useful role: in the *historiette* 'Louis treiziesme', Tallemant des Réaux identifies him as 'le bouffon du

---

[1] F. de Malherbe, quoted in Tallemant des Réaux, *Historiettes*, i. 1012–13.
[2] F. de Bassompierre, *Mémoires* ('Cologne', 1665), i. 266–7, quoted by M. M. McGowan, *L'Art du ballet de cour en France (1581–1643)* (1963), 85. Unless otherwise stated, references to McGowan are to this book. For further illustrations, see her presentation of costume designs in the Victoria and Albert Museum, London: *The Court Ballet of Louis XIII: A Collection of Working Designs for Costumes 1615–33* (London, [1986]).
[3] G. Frank, *The Medieval French Drama* (Oxford, 1954), 244.

Roy'. 'Marais disoit au Roy: "il y a deux choses dans vostre mestier dont je ne me pourrois accommoder.—Hé, quoy?—De manger tout seul et de chier en compagnie." '[4]

It was on 2 October 1614 that Louis XIII was officially declared adult, and soon afterwards that the future Cardinal-Duc de Richelieu impressed with his closing speech the last Estates General before 1789.

In the *Ballet du Triomphe de Minerve* or *Ballet de Madame*, danced on 19 March 1615 in anticipation of the marriages of Louis XIII to Anne of Austria and of his sister to the Spanish Crown prince, participation of the Sieur Marais is noted—now as a recognized vocalist. This important occasion was organized by the poet Étienne Durand (1585–1618), the versatile librettist René Bordier, the once-famous machinist Tomaso Francïni, and three Court musicians: Pierre Guédron, Le Bailly, and Guédron's son-in-law Antoine Boësset (1585–1643), later 'Secrétaire ordinaire de la chambre du Roi' until appointed, on 3 September 1624, 'Surintendant de la musique du Roy, et Maistre de la musique de la Royne'. This Boësset—the father of Jean-Baptiste de Boësset (1614–85)—wrote music for numerous later ballets. Durand, 'poète ordinaire de Marie de Médicis', had collaborated on various ballets, including *La Félicité de l'âge doré*, danced on 6 December 1609 for the opening of the great Salle de fête in the Arsenal. *Le Triomphe de Minerve* was the first of many ballets for Bordier, who became the principal poet for Court ballets for two decades. On the title-page of his *Poème sur la levée du siège de Cazal et réduction en l'obéissance du Roy de toutes les villes de son royaume* (1630), he is described as 'ayant charge de la poésie près Sa Majesté'. This same ballet confirmed the reputation of the young Marets, who afterwards 'prend part à presque tous les ballets de cour'.[5] Two decades later, for example, Bordier supplied the verse and Antoine Boësset the music for *Le Ballet du Roy*, danced by Marets with Louis XIII in female costume, in 1635—an important source for *Les Visionnaires*.

La Délivrance de Renaud

On 29 January 1617, in *Le Ballet de la Délivrance de Renaud* by Durand and Bordier, one of a number of ballets based on episodes

---

[4] Tallemant des Réaux, *Historiettes*, i. 336, 339.
[5] McGowan, *L'Art du ballet*, 81, 87, 106.

of Torquato Tasso's *Gerusalemme liberata*, Marets danced the sorceress Armide. This spectacular narrative ballet in five acts was set in successive perspective settings based on a combination of painted canvas flats and mobile floats. Transformation-scene effects were achieved through the substitution of floats in conjunction with the rotation of a great turntable or revolve. Numerous illustrations from Durand's *livret* are reproduced by Boris Kochno and Maria Luz in *Le Ballet* (1954), and McGowan provides a detailed account (pp. 101–15).

Louis XIII danced first the Démon du feu, then the hero Godefroy. Charles d'Albert, Duc de Luynes (1578–1621), on the threshold of greatness, danced Renault, with other notables in other roles. The eighth illustration depicts a remarkably feminine Marets-Armide summoning her demons (McGowan, Pl. xi), which assume forms contradictory to her orders. In the ninth, a more masculine Armide conjures forth hags from animal costumes. Armide's vain attempts to maintain her magic powers in Act IV belong to a virtuoso role with scope for mime of bewilderment, grief, vexation, and rage at the destruction of her palace and garden (transformation scene) and the mockery as she is driven off. For the fifth tableau the musicians gather to sing the triumph of the youthful King, now in the role of the victorious Godefroy and seated on a throne 'accompagné des seigneurs, acteurs du ballet' before the final 'danse générale'. Marets and [Jacques de] Belleville, comments Durand in his *livret* (p. 19), 'tous les deux estans assez cognus, n'ont que d'estre nommez pour avoir des louanges' (quoted by McGowan, p. 106).

The political significance of *La délivrance de Renaud* as the first public affirmation of the majesty of Louis XIII as King of France has not escaped scholarly notice. In the *livret* Durand details an allegorical or moral significance. Armide-Marets represents concupiscence. Her flowers, shrubs, fountains, demons, and nymphs are voluptuous snares for youth, personified by Renaud-Luynes, who is only saved from himself by the wise Hermit (representing knowledge incarnate) acting for Godefroy-Louis XIII, representing divinely-inspired intelligence symbolically leading a crusading army.

This was Durand's last ballet, danced only three months before the *coup d'état* of 24 April 1617 broke the power of the Queen Regent with the death, 'resisting arrest', of her favourite Concino Concini, Maréchal d'Ancre, and gave the young King his epithet of Louis le Juste. Durand sided with the fallen Queen. In the succeeding trials which rocked Europe he was convicted of treason, and on 19 July 1618 he was broken on the wheel and burnt, just eleven days after Concini's widow, Léonora Galigai, had been convicted of witchcraft and burnt alive. These horrendous events are contextual to the judicial traditions continued in the trial and execution of Urbain Grandier (the Curé de Loudun burnt for sorcery on 18 August 1634, a few months after Desmarets entered Cardinal Richelieu's personal service) and the conviction and execution of Simon Morin at the beginning of Louis XIV's personal reign. They also suggest that the politico-religious symbolism of the Christian marvellous of Court ballets, inspired from, and inspiring, similar motifs in heroic poetry, were deeply-rooted in the beliefs and anxieties of the time—for some a crusade, but for others deeply disquietening repression.

Praise for Durand's poetry from contemporary poets—except, ironically, Théophile de Viau (1590–1626)—was boundless. In his *Vie d'Estienne Durand*, Guillaume Colletet (1598–1659) declares that in Durand, who 'chantoit et touchoit le luth à merveille', France lost 'l'une de ses lumières futures et l'un de ses plus grands ornements' (quoted by McGowan, p. 87). Durand's neglected verse has begun to attract the attention of academic critics.[6]

The Mother and Son Wars

Armand-Jean du Plessis, already Bishop of Luçon and recently made a minister, but not yet a Cardinal or the Duc de Richelieu, had followed Marie de Médicis in banishment to Blois, whence he was exiled from France and went to Avignon, which in 1617 was still a Papal State. In January 1619 Jean-Louis de Nogaret de La Valette, Duc d'Épernon (1554–1642), and his son the Archbishop of Toulouse helped Marie de Médicis to escape from Blois to Angoulême, precipitating the 'Mother and Son Wars' of 1619–20.[7] It is not always easy to understand exactly how loyalties of the culturally influential divided at this time, but it helps to know in which camp various writers were. Jean-Louis Guez de Balzac (1595–1654) and

[6] See A. Eustis's presentation of Durand's 'Stances à l'inconstance', in D. L. Rubin (ed.), *La Poésie française du premier 17ᵉ siècle* (Tübingen, 1986), 201–4; H. Rogers and R. Rosenstein, 'Late Renaissance Petrarchism: The Rhetorical Inconstance of Etienne Durand', *Papers on French Seventeenth Century Literature*, 14 (1987), 687–701.

[7] H. Méthivier, *Le Siècle de Louis XIII* (1971), 35.

François Le Métel de Boisrobert (1592–1662) were with Marie at Angoulême, whither Luynes despatched as negotiators Cardinal Pierre de Bérulle (1575–1628) and Cardinal François de La Rochefoucauld (1558–1645).[8] To avoid widespread armed conflict, Luynes also accepted an offer of mediation from Richelieu, who arranged the treaty of Angoulême on 30 April 1619. Under its terms Richelieu was allowed to remain with Marie, who was made governor of Anjou. The treaty also freed Henri II de Bourbon, Prince de Condé (1588–1646)—the 'Grand Condé's' father, whom Marie had sent to the Bastille in 1616.

However, the treaty brought neither stability nor lasting peace. Against the Duc d'Épernon and other notables holding fortified cities in defiance of the King in the summer of 1620, Louis XIII himself led a military campaign, beginning with the investment of the château de Caen and ending with the defeat, on 7 August at Pont-de-Cé, of the King's main armed domestic enemies. Secretly promised cardinalship, Richelieu then negotiated, on 10 August, the Peace of Angers', which allowed Marie de Médicis to return to Court; and Louis XIII moved his army to Bordeaux in preparation for settling (against Protestant interests) outstanding questions of religious observance and property rights in Béarn.

Notables of Court ballet were with Louis XIII at Pont-de-Cé, including Bassompierre (Maréchal de camp), the Duc de Luynes and his two brothers, and the poet Théophile de Viau. As Député pour les fortifications, known to have been with the Court at Caen, Desmarets is unlikely not to have been there too.

Ballet at Château-Trompette

Desmarets is not named in the published account, but he is likely to have been with the Court for the ballet danced on 27 September 1620 at the Château-Trompette, Bordeaux, celebrating 'la victoire des dernier[e]s armes de ce Ieune Vainqueur'. Drawing upon classical mythology and Italian Renaissance epic for metaphors expressive of recent political events, Fame personified—la Renommée—celebrates the victories of the King, portrayed as more powerful than Mars, Apollo, or Cupid. Two of the *entrées* suggest a Crusade, in which

---

[8] Méthivier, *Le Siècle de Louis XIII*, 35; Guez de Balzac, *Les Premières Lettres*, ed. H. Bibas and K.-T. Butler (1933), pp. x–xi.

the King's enemies are depicted as Turks, signifying diabolical evil. Louis XIII, his brother Gaston d'Orléans (1608–60), the Prince de Condé, the Ducs de Mayenne, de Luynes, and de Brantes (Luynes's brother), and other notables 'virent entrer douze jeunes enfans richement vestus à la Turque, couvers de Damars blanc, incarnad, & vert à grand floque, leurs turbans pendans'. When the children *exeunt*,

vn Rodomont entra auec des gestes merueilleusement naïfs, lequel apres auoir fait plusieurs tours & retours, dit ses paroles,

> Ie suis ce vaillant Capitaine
> Qui vainqueur de la race humaine
> Ay triomphé dans les Enfers:
> Maintenant ma force est perduë,
> LOVIS me l'a bien abbatue:
> C'est le plus grand de l'Vnivers.[9]

Rodomont was probably danced by Marets, who specialized in this type of virtuoso role.

Not only does Rodomont fit readily between Armide of *La Délivrance de Renaud* and Le Grand Turc danced by Marets in *La Douairière de Billebahaut* (1626); this overtly political ballet anticipates the themes and style of Jean Desmarets's later imaginative work. The initial self-praise of Rodomont's self-introduction, for example, may parody the self-presentation of pagan gods in Greek tragedies; it clearly anticipates the burlesque opening of Desmarets's balletic comedy *Les Visionnaires*, in which the braggart soldier Artabaze enters with a similar swagger: 'Je suis l'amour du Ciel, & l'effroy de la Terre.' Desmarets's last ballet, *La Prospérité des armes de la France*, is a grander celebration of French royal arms in the same political tradition; and throughout his career he reiterates calls for a new Crusade.

Le Ballet d'Apollon *and* Le Ballet du Soleil

Le Ballet d'Apollon, danced on 18 February 1621 in the Petit-Bourbon in Paris, does not focus directly upon the majesty of Louis XIII. The Duc de Luynes danced Apollo, resplendent in a golden costume and cast as the master of four arts: prophecy, healing, singing, and

---

[9] Bibliothèque Nationale, Imprimés, Lb. 36 1495, 5–6.

killing. Antoine Boësset composed the songs. Bordier calls attention
in his *livret* to 'changemens de theatre' for the four tableaux representing Apollo's four professions.

The allegorical identification of Apollo with Luynes is particularly
transparent when the latter appears with his own brothers, Cadenet
and Brantes, as Apollo's brothers Castor and Pollux. At the peak
of his influence, Luynes appears to have the best role, including three
poems by Théophile de Viau. However, in the lines written for 'Le
Forgeron', danced by Louis XIII, Théophile contrasts his King with
the cuckolded pagan god Vulcan, who in classical mythology forged
arms for others while, in company with Vulcan's wife, Venus, the
god Mars 'Faisoit des Fogerons pour luy'.

In a transparent allusion to the fall of Concini, Théophile's lines
for Vulcan-Louis XIII continue:

> Je suis un Forgeron nouveau,
> Qui sans enclume et sans marteau
> Forge un tonnerre à ma parole,
> Et du seul regard de mes yeux
> Fais partir un esclair qui vole,
> Plus puissant que celuy des Cieux.[10]

This new smith is cast as a Thunderer possessing a key attribute of
Jupiter, King of the gods. Later stanzas set him above Cupid (since
the dart he forges can generate love without inspiring hatred for the
archer), above warlike Mars, and even above the far-darting Apollo:

> Mais les fleches de mon courroux,
> Fatales qu'elles sont à tous,
> Font trembler le Dieu de la guerre,
> Et rien ne l'a fait habiter
> Dans un Ciel si loin de la terre,
> Que le soin de les eviter.[11]

The Artabaze of Desmarets's *Visionnaires* seems to parody this
conceit in the opening lines of the play when, claiming to be the son
of Mars, he states of the god of war that

> craignant ma valeur aux Dieux mesmes funeste,
> Il alla se sauver dans la voute celeste. (ll. 18–19)

---

[10] Théophile de Viau, *Œuvres poétiques*, ed. J. Streicher (2 vols., Geneva,
1951–8), i. 189–90.
[11] Ibid. 190–1.

Perhaps Louis XIII soon doubted the wisdom of allowing a mighty subject to appear as Apollo. Less than two weeks later Bordier's *Grand Ballet de la Reyne représentant le Soleil*, danced to music by Antoine Boësset, reaffirms the sun as an image of kingship—indeed the most frequent image of Louis XIII, states McGowan, and one long-used in royal entrances (p. 182). There was a sun king in France—as in other monarchies—before Louis XIV. But whereas the image-makers of Louis le Grand sought to identify him with Apollo—first in Benserade's *Ballet royal de la Nuit* and later through the Salon d'Apollon in the Louvre, the fountains of Versailles, and other metaphors of majesty—Apollo for Louis le Juste was not the sun.

In the preface to the *Ballet du Soleil* Bordier explains that the glory of the Duc de Luynes had, in the previous ballet, only momentarily eclipsed the majesty of the King, because in the earlier ballet the hero Luynes-Apollo, though a great man, is only a false god, a mortal mistaken for the sun. Bordier's two great ballets of 1621 draw upon quite different systems of imagery: the first is euhemerist and sceptical concerning the 'gods', considered mortals with an usurped title to divinity; the second is syncretistic and based on a perception of the pagan 'gods' as an imperfect manifestation of Christian truths. The syncretism evident in certain French ballets of this period does not seem to me to be radically different from the Spanish tradition whereby, for instance, the *musagetes* of Calderón's *auto*, *Sacro Parnaso*, is an allegory of Christ, considered 'el verdadero Apolo'.[12] Traditional perception of consonance or concordances between Graeco-Roman and Judaeo-Christian religious and philosophic systems does not disappear in France. Rather the divergent ways in which syncretistic systems are reaffirmed, denied, or prettified underlie the seventeenth-century literary quarrels concerning the Christian marvellous.

In *Le Ballet d'Apollon*, Apollo is presented as a mortal whose inventive genius caused him to be worshipped as a god by a grateful people. The Duc de Luynes danced Apollo, states Bordier, 'pour une infinité de belles actions qu'il fit jadis au monde' and because *in illo tempore* he had been 'plus honoré que le reste des hommes'. He prophesied, through Pythia, the birth of a Dauphin for France. With

---

[12] Compare E. R. Curtius, *European Literature and the Latin Middle Ages*, transl. W. R. Trask (London, 1953), 244–5.

Castor and Pollux he purged the world of brigands. He established the arts of medicine, poetry, and music; and as a warrior he slew the dragon Python (McGowan, p. 180). The allegory of Luynes-Apollo as victor over dissidence and sedition, as patron of the arts and exterminator of the monstrous Concini is euhemerist—one of the most striking seventeenth-century French interpretations of pagan gods as deified mortals before Desmarets's unfinished euhemerist romance *La Vérité des fables*, dedicated to Anne of Austria in 1648. Luynes is magnified as a hero through an allegory grounded in the same rationalist system used by Desmarets to discredit the pagan gods.

Rather than sun king imagery, *Le Ballet d'Apollon* proposes a parallel of ancients and moderns in which Luynes outshines Apollo, and Louis XIII eclipses Vulcan and other once-mighty mortals formerly considered gods. This analysis invites two conclusions. Firstly, Théophile's 'Le Forgeron' illustrates just how absurd it is to suppose (as Charles Perrault proposed and others repeat) that Benserade invented, in the reign of Louis XIV, the system of ambivalent ballet-verse applicable on one level to the character portrayed and on another to the dancer presenting the role. Secondly, *Le Ballet d'Apollon* provides the ideological point of departure not only for Desmarets's *Vérité des fables* but also for Guillaume Colletet's important *Ballet de l'Harmonie*, danced in 1632, when Richelieu was beginning seriously to develop his patronage of the performing arts. In *L'Harmonie* Apollo brings harmony into the world as a master of music, and without sun king symbolism.

Per contra, in *Le Ballet du Soleil* Louis XIII is presented as the true image of the sun, which is itself a manifestation of divinity: *lux visibilis* manifesting God, the *lux invisibilis*, in a syncretistic system found in the Fathers of the Church, especially Saint Augustine of Hippo (354–430). Contrast the image of Hell as 'darkness visible' in John Milton's *Paradise Lost*, I (1667). *Le Ballet du Soleil* symbolizes the power of the sun king to reach deep into the hearts of people anywhere throughout his kingdom. Contrasted with the darkness of night, light brings a beneficial dawn, regenerating hope after the nightmare horrors of civil disorder and Protestant rebellion. In his *Histoire du Roy Louis le Grand* (1691), C. F. Menestrier reproduces an image commemorating Louis XIII as 'Ortus Solis Gallici'. With the image of the glorious rising sun of France it combines the concept of the 'Prince ennemi de la fraude', familiar from the dénouement of Molière's *Tartuffe*, and the image of the sun as the all-seeing eye of conscience and justice, as found, blushing if not occulted, in Racine's *Phèdre*.

The image of the sun in relation to the King as a ballet dancer is presented in the *Gazette*'s account of *Le Ballet du Roy*, danced on 18 February 1635. Louis XIII danced three roles, including one in female costume and one in an *entrée* with Marets (of which more later). Just as the sun consorts with inferior bodies without descending from its sphere, the *Gazette* argues, so kings may 'se familiariser quand ils veulent auec leurs sujets, sans diminüer rien de leur authorité souueraine'. This assertion echoes the 'unsullied sun' topos of patristic literature, destined by St Augustine and others to suggest that the divinity of Christ was not impaired by the Incarnation. Tertullian declares, for instance, in *De spectaculis* (xx. ii) that, like the sun, God can gaze down upon the world without being contaminated by it. The sun's rays may fall even upon a sewer without being sullied.[13] Like the dance or measured movement of the King of stars—for the *Gazette* invokes the music or harmony of the spheres—the King of France's dancing communicates warmth and light. Even disguised in low costumes the King is recognizable, like the sun behind clouds. The enlightenment, conscience, and justice of Louis le Juste is implicit in the astronomical transformation scenes of *Mirame*, in which the movement of the sun and moon is properly interpreted as not only spectacular but also symbolic.

Contrast *La Vérité des fables*, in which pagan 'gods' are celebrated as innovative mortals. The frontispiece depicts personified Truth holding a torch of enlightenment aloft over the ruins of pagan religious statuary. The frontispiece of *Clovis*—in which pagan 'gods' are represented as diabolical evil through the syncretistic association of pagan 'gods' with Judaeo-Christian devils—shows the conversion of Clovis among the shattered shards of fallen idols.

Events of 1622–1624

New evidence related to the 'célèbre Marets' in these turbulent years of further civil war following the death of the Duc de Luynes later

---

[13] Tertullian's text 'Sol . . . immo ipse etiam deus de caelo spectat ne contaminatur. Plane, sol et in cloacum radios suos defert nec inquinatur' is quoted by A. Olivar, 'L'image du soleil non souillé dans la littérature patristique', *Didaskalia*, 5 (1975), 3–20.

in 1621, the return of Marie de Médicis to the Conseil étroit in 1622, the trials of Théophile de Viau, and the return of Cardinal Richelieu to the Conseil étroit in 1624, is difficult to separate from events to be discussed in the following chapter. It is a difficulty which to some extent confirms that the 'Marais, bouffon du Roy' cited on the fringes of the *libertinage* scandal which broke late in 1622 and led to the trials of Théophile is indeed the Desmarets chosen to accompany the minister's son Guillaume II Bautru, Comte de Serrant, on the mission attested by *Le Voyage de Fontainebleau* (1623). Bautru is thought to have been closely associated with Court hedonists around that time.[14]

I do not know whether Marets-Desmarets participated on 26 February 1623 in the *Ballet des Bacchanales*, to which Théophile contributed 'Bacchus' for Louis XIII and lines for Henri II, Duc de Montmorency (1595–1632), and which caused offence by suggesting that Montmorency was in love with the young Anne of Austria.[15] As Député pour les fortifications he is likely to have been—like Honorat de Bueil, Seigneur de Racan (1589–1670), poet of *Les Bergeries* and of verse for various ballets—at the siege of Montpellier the following summer. Before Louis XIII returned from Languedoc in the autumn of 1622, however, some libertine friends of Théophile had behaved with dangerous indiscretion. One of them, Jacques Vallée des Barreaux (1599–1673), appears to have taken a former favourite teacher too much into his confidence: the Jesuit André-Clément de Voisin, who had taught him (and probably the Desmarets brothers) at La Flèche.

Des Barreaux, who would become a Conseiller to the Parlement de Paris on 31 May 1625, is best remembered at a somewhat later date as a friend of the philosopher René Descartes, but also for his contacts with Méré, Damien Mitton, the Duc de Roannez, and other libertines frequented by Blaise Pascal before his conversion. In 1623 Des Barreaux appears to have sought in 'évocations diaboliques une preuve de fait, qui lui fît toucher au doigt la réalité du surnaturel'.[16] At that time Des Barreaux's sister Elisabeth Vallée is likely to have been Jean Desmarets's mistress. Frédéric Lachèvre notes that satirists

[14] C. J. Burckhardt, *Richelieu and his Age*, transl. B. Hoy (London, 1970), iii. 260–1.

[15] Théophile de Viau, *Œuvres poétiques*, vol. ii, p. xx. The incident is not mentioned by Ruth Kleinman, *Anne of Austria: Queen of France* (Columbus, 1985).

[16] Adam, *Histoire de la littérature française au XVIIe siècle* ii. 233.

of the manuscript *Roquentins de la Cour* 'lui prêtent une liaison avec Des Marets'.[17] On the basis of his other contacts at the time, our Desmarets (whom Lachèvre did not connect with Marais mentioned in the trial of Théophile) seems a much more likely lover for Mlle Des Barreaux than the third son of Mme des Loges, proposed rather tentatively by Lachèvre.

The trials of Théophile de Viau

In December 1622 a group of young men insulted the Jesuit François Garasse (1584–1631), then preaching the Advent sermons at the Paris church of St-Eustache. If connected with Théophile, their behaviour was indeed rash, because recent publication of *Le Parnasse des poëtes satyriques* had scandalized influential members of the Paris Parlement. Théophile was implicated. The volume opens with a 'Sonnet par le Sieur Théophile' deemed blasphemous and obscene. Garasse began to publish serious charges against Théophile in *La Doctrine curieuse des Beaux esprits de ce temps ou prétendus tels*, first published in the summer of 1623, with a second edition in 1624. Father Voisin set a converted Huguenot spy named Sageot upon Théophile, who obtained some protection from the Duc de Montmorency, as did the poet Marc-Antoine de Gérard, known as Saint-Amant (1594–1661). The Procureur général of the Paris Parlement, Mathieu Molé, none the less ordered the arrest, on 11 July 1623, of the presumed authors of the incriminated *Parnasse satyrique*: Théophile de Viau, Guillaume Colletet, Nicolas Frénicle (1600–1662?), and a certain Berthelot.

Like Théophile and Colletet, Frénicle was a poet of Court ballets. Like Saint-Amant, Berthelot was an admirer of the leader of the literary moderns in Italy and Savoy, Giambattista Marino or Marini (1569–1625), whose *Adone* had been published in Paris in 1622 and dedicated to Louis XIII. None of the four accused was arrested, because all four had gone into hiding—Théophile at Chantilly, Montmorency's property north of Paris. Although this was a plague-year in Paris, enough Conseillers were gathered on 18 August to convict Théophile of 'lèse-majesté divine' and sentence him to be burnt alive with his books—a sentence carried out in effigy the following day. Frénicle was sentenced to hang, and Colletet to exile

[17] F. Lachèvre, *Le Libertinage au XVIIᵉ siècle* (1911), 15 n.

for nine years (with remission, as it turned out). Before Théophile could escape abroad, he was arrested, brought back to prison in Paris, retried, from March 1624 to September 1625, and banished from France for life. However, it was in Paris, one year later, that Théophile died, his health broken by imprisonment. The failure of Louis XIII to intervene in the trials may be related to the discovery of a copy of the *Cabinet satyrique* (a predecessor of the offending *Parnasse satyrique* first published in 1618) in the possession of the young Anne of Austria, not long before her miscarriage in 1622.[18]

The dedication of *Les Délices de l'esprit*, containing as it does not only an homage to Cardinal Mazarin but also an apologia 'Aux Beaux Esprits du Monde', probably echoes Garasse's use of the term 'Beaux esprits'.

Desmarets and other Court musicians

Marets is mentioned in Théophile's deposition of 21 October 1624 as a witness to calumnies said to have been spoken and written against him by Voisin, 'ainsy que le Père Séguirant luy a advoué en présence de Marays, Molinier et Justice'.[19] Molinier or Moulinier and Justice were musicians of the King's Chapel whom Marets had assisted following the disgrace of Gaston d'Orléans's (and Richelieu's) adversary Charles, Duc de La Vieuville (1582–1653) in the *coup d'état* of 13 August 1624. According to Tallemant des Réaux, during La Vieuville's involuntary departure from the royal palace of St-Germain-en-Laye, 'on luy fit faire un charivary espouvantable par tous les marmitons, pour luy jouer . . . un bransle de sortie'. The King, 'rebutté des desbausches de Moulinier et de Justice', decided to reduce their salaries by half. However:

Marais, le bouffon du Roy, leur donna une invention pour les faire restablir. Ils allerent avec luy au petit coucher danser une mascarade demy-habillez; qui avoit un pourpoint n'avoit pas de haut-de-chausses. 'Que veut dire cela?' dit le Roy.—'C'est, Sire,' respondirent-ils, 'que gens qui n'ont que la moitié de leurs appointemens ne s'habillent aussy qu'à moitié.' Le Roy en rit et les reprit en grace.[20]

This is the Moulinier who, as master of music in Gaston d'Orléans' household, opened up a brilliant career for Michel Lambert (1611–96)

---

[18] Kleinman, *Anne of Austria*, 54–5.
[19] Tallemant des Réaux, *Historiettes*, i. 1013.   [20] Ibid. i. 336.

by making him Page de la musique de chambre de Monsieur. In another *historiette* Desmarets (identified this time as the writer) is said to have expedited Lambert's overdue wedding—which eventually took place on 13 May 1641— to Geneviève Dupuy, daughter of the publican of the Bel-Air cabaret near the Luxembourg Palace. On advice from the Duchesse d'Aiguillon, to whom the girl's mother had appealed for help with an expected child, Cardinal Richelieu asked Desmarets to compose a dialogue for the couple to learn, with this beginning and end:

TIRCIS

Filis, j'arreste enfin mon humeur vagabonde.

FILIS

Trop volage Tircis, pourquoy me fuyois-tu?

.   .   .

TOUS DEUX

Aymons-nous desormais,
Aymons-nous pour jamais.[21]

These were the parents, obliged by Cardinal Richelieu to marry, of Madeleine Lambert, born on 19 February 1642. Madeleine married Jean-Baptiste Lully (1632–87), Surintendant de la musique under Louis XIV, musical collaborator with Molière and Benserade on *comédies-ballets* (1661–71), and founder in 1672 of the Académie-Royale de musique (the Opéra). In 1653 Benserade and Lully collaborated with Lambert in *Le Ballet de la Nuit*, in which Louis XIV made his début in ballet as Apollo.

The music of the spheres

Desmarets addresses 'Au Sieur Lambert excellent musicien' the 'Stances' in his Œuvres poëtiques beginning:

Diuin Lambert, quand i'entend tes chansons,
Ie croy qu'Amour t'apprend les plus beaux sons
    De la douce harmonie
    Du roulement des cieux.

The importance of the music of the spheres for theorists and practitioners of Court ballet is shown, on the basis of other evidence, by McGowan.[22] This concept of universal harmony inspired the

---

[21] Ibid. ii. 524–5.   [22] McGowan, 16–24.

ideal of a synthesis of the arts capable, through their combined appeal to all the senses, of uplifting and refining corporeal experience, suffusing it in intellectuality, and linking mankind with the spirituality then associated with the sun, the planets, and the stars. It underlies a conception of Court ballet as a spiritualized form of 'total theatre', virtually a Court cult, with the King at its politico-religious centre. Desmarets is playing with this notion when in *Les Visionnaires* I. IV Amidor (combining two current metaphors) tells Filidan that he may glimpse ideal beauty:

> Quand la brunette nuict développant ses voiles
> Conduira par le ciel le grand bal des étoiles.

Jean-Antoine de Baïf (1532–89), founder of the first French academy of music and poetry, the Jesuit educationist Estienne Binet, Guillaume Colletet, and Charles Sorel, among others, reflect in their ballet-theory aspects of the Florentine Neoplatonism of Pico della Mirandola and of Marsilio Ficino's commentaries on Plato's *Timaeus*.

Perhaps the most ambitious allegory of universal harmony in this tradition is the trilogy of ballets devised by Guillaume Colletet for performance in the Jeu de Paume du Petit-Louvre in the winter of 1632–3: *Le Ballet de l'Harmonie*, *Le Ballet des Effets de la nature*, and *Le Ballet des Cinq sens*. Human nature is represented as a microcosm of the macrocosm, in which all parts of the body, all five senses, and the soul correspond harmoniously with the elements of the universe, physical and spiritual. The Neo-platonism of the ballets was reinforced in early seventeenth-century French courtly culture through theological treatises and Jesuit doctrine, through novels—especially *L'Astrée* of Honoré d'Urfé (1567–1625)—and through essays on *honnêteté*—such as *L'Honnête Homme* (1630) by Nicolas Faret (1596–1646). Faret, who was much involved with Desmarets's first association with the group who were forming the Académie-Française, is indebted, for instance, to Castiglione's *Il Corteggiano*, in which Pietro Bembo is allowed to reiterate Platonic theories of the soul and of love.

Neo-platonist idealism, debated in the early Académie, and the syncretism of recent Court ballets are of the greatest consequence for Cardinal Richelieu's patronage of the theatre. Neoplatonist idealism also provides a good guide to Desmarets's literary works, from *Ariane* through his dramatic works and *Rosane* to *Clovis*, and especially *Les Délices de l'esprit*, which invites mystic union with

God, not through asceticism but through the gradual elevation of the soul through a series of pleasures, first physical, then increasingly more intellectual, and finally mystical—a spiritual ascent reminiscent of the doctrine of the Jesuit Cardinal Roberto Bellarmini (1541–1621), author of *De ascentione mentis in Deum per scalas rerum creatarum* (1615), a work published in French as *L'Escalier spirituel portant l'âme à Dieu par les marches des créatures* (1616). The French theologians, Protestant and Catholic, who turned against the Neoplatonic immanence of Bellarmini were, of course, hostile also to its expression in dance, in fiction, and in Desmarets's own spiritual writings.

Le Grand Bal de la Douairière de Billebahaut

Marets retained his considerable reputation as a performer of ballets right up to the time when the first of his plays written for Cardinal Richelieu was performed in February 1636. Ten years earlier, in February 1626, he danced the role of Le Grand Turc in *Le Grand Bal de la Douairière de Billebahaut*—an important narrative ballet by Bordier, a certain Jombert, Claude de Lestoile (1597–1652), and Charles Sorel, danced by Louis XIII in the Salle du Louvre and at the Hôtel de Ville. Le Grand Turc is one of the representatives of many nations who arrive in emblematic national costumes to congratulate the Douairière on her marriage to Fanfan de Sotteville. Others include the Amerindian Roi des Américains, 'Baillifs de Groenland et Frisland' escorted by professional stuntmen on stilts ('car le costume du pays ne porte pas que les gens graves aillent à gambades'). Africans led by 'le Cacique' on an elephant (presumably a float), the Grand Can who 'pour s'accommoder de la caravane des chameaux suit la piste des Africains', and, lastly, Europeans—led in by musicians from Granada singing in Spanish.[23]

The *entrée* of Le Grand Turc came second; he was wearing a vast turban and was accompanied by two servants holding an umbrella. As illustrated in Kochno and Luz, he wears a greenish (turquoise?) coat lined in the yellow-orange then called 'aurore'—colours associated with the Levant and recurring in all three costumes later worn by Molière as M. Jourdain in *Le Bourgeois gentilhomme*, whose Turkish fantasy is to some extent anticipated in this burlesque ballet (see

---

[23] B. Kochno and M. Luz, *Le Ballet* (1954), 25.

Figure 3 Marets as the Grand Turk

Fig. 3). I wonder whether, aged 4 in 1626, he was taken to see it. Or, if not, then some revival of the *entrée*. The simulation and vertigo of his own Turkish masquerade suggest the children's games of 'dressing up' and 'whirling round'. If authentically reproduced, the colour-coding of the costumes may recall another childhood experience.

With its grotesque rendering of a pretentious Spanish-sounding dowager, this ballet is unlikely to have been devoid of political allegory. From an *entrée* in which La Douairière (who imagines that every man loves her) is teased in counter-Petrarchan imagery by Le Fanfan, Desmarets would appear to have developed the contrast in *Les Visionnaires* between Hesperie ('qui croit que chacun l'aime') and male roles based on the parody of Petrarchism: the extravagant poet Amidor, and Filidan, 'amoureux en idée'.[24]

Le Ballet du Château de Bicêtre

Marets appeared as a Magician in *Le Ballet du Château de Bicêtre*, danced on Sunday, 7 March 1632 at the Louvre, the Arsenal, and the Hôtel de Ville. The *Gazette* for 12 March gives a detailed account of his costume and performance:

Puis se presente vn Magicien auec la sotane de satin incarnat [et] la robbe de satin noir ouuerte de passement d'argent, tenant en sa main vne baguette d'ebene garnie d'vn bout d'argent, dont il frappoit en dançant son liure de Magie: c'estoit le Sieur Marais.

A ses charmes sautent en place quatre Lutins vestus de satin noir, & coiffez de plumes noires & grises, que dancerent les Ducs de Longueville, & de Candale, le Baron du Vigean, & le Comte de S. Germain Beau-Prê . . .

This was another important ballet. The *Gazette* estimates that there were four thousand spectators at the Louvre alone. The verse is by Pierre Corneille, who on 8 March obtained the *privilège* for his tragicomedy *Clitandre*—the first of his plays published. The ballet evokes events supposed to have occurred at a famous site near Gentilly, just south of Paris. Compare the pamphlet account published nine years earlier: *Histoire mémorable et espouvantable arrivée au chasteau de Bissestre près Paris, avec les apparitions des*

---

[24] *Le Grand Bal de la Douairière de Billebahaut* (1626), 67, quoted in *Les Visionnaires*, ed. H. G. Hall, Société des Textes Française Modernes (1963), p. L.

esprits et fantosmes qui ont esté veus aux caves et chambres du dit chasteau (1623).

The site had been redeveloped by Louis XIII as a home for war-wounded soldiers but retained a reputation as a haunted house. The ballet is something of a festival exorcism. In burlesque battle-*entrées* the war-wounded trounce the evil spirits and banish them from the site. After the ballet proper, Louis de Bourbon, Comte de Soissons (1604–41) and Anne of Austria opened the general dancing, which lasted from eight o'clock on the Sunday evening until eight the following morning. The Duc de Longueville who danced with Marets and the Baron du Vigean was the Comte de Soissons's brother-in-law by his first marriage.

This ballet is of special interest in stage history because it evokes the same site at different times of day, using successive stage sets (based on painted backdrops) to assure visual variety, while emphasizing strict unity of time and place. The *Gazette* makes this aspect of the spectacle quite clear:

> Le jour estoit figuré par vn grand tableau où ce chasteau estoit peint ayant le Soleil sur son horison, & autour de son faiste des grües, faizans, faucons, & autres oyseaux: comme au bas, toute sorte de bestes à quatre pieds . . . Deux Hiboux & quatre Corneilles en leur vraye forme, sous laquelle estoient cachez autant d'enfans, y vinrent apres danser leur bransle, & annoncer la nuict.
>
> Lors parut vn autre tableau au lieu du premier, où le mesme Chasteau de Bissestre estoit ombragé d'vne nuict qui n'auoit point d'autre clarté que celle d'vn Daemon qui sortoit tout en feu de la plus haute de ses fenestres . . .

Le Château de Bicêtre anticipates the blending of successive stage settings with emphasis on the unities of time and place as it appears in *Mirame*, where Desmarets could additionally assure the unity of illusion through *changements à vue* made possible by the new stage-machinery of Richelieu's Grand'Salle de spectacle. This ballet also anticipates an important aesthetic feature of *Les Promenades de Richelieu*, in which Desmarets evokes different aspects of that château under different lights, by night and by day. *Le Château de Bicêtre* may also anticipate the magical metamorphoses of the enchanted palace of the sorcerer Auberon in *Clovis*. In *Les Visionnaires* the braggart soldier's burlesque terror in taking the extravagant poet for a sorcerer may allude to this ballet.

As a site, Bicêtre would be better known had Louis XIII's home for 'estropiés de guerre' not been superseded by the present Hôtel des Invalides, built by Louis XIV in the Faubourg St-Germain.

Le Ballet du Roy *(1635)*

In the period between his entry into the personal service of Cardinal Richelieu in 1634 and the performance, on 12 February 1636, of *Aspasie*—his first play—with twelve ballet *entrées*, Desmarets danced with Louis XIII in at least three major Court ballets. One has been mentioned: *Le Balet du roy: où la vieille Cour & les habitans des riues de la Seine viennent danser pour les triomphes de Sa Majesté*, danced on 18 February 1635 in the Grand'Salle of the Louvre. This was a two-part ballet, contrasting the 'vieille Cour' with the new splendours beside the Seine. It was followed by a *Ballet de la Reine*. Together these made up a single entertainment in three main parts. There was an extraordinary cast—even for a great ballet—including Gaston d'Orléans, the Ducs de Beaufort, de Longueville, de Saint-Simon, de Mercœur, and de La Vallette, the Comtes de Brion, d'Harcourt, and de Soissons. The old problem of spectators' sight-lines was addressed through the provision of a raked stage:

Vn marche-pied insensiblement relevé par derriere au bout de cette sale, en forme de talus de 15. pieds [*c.*5 m.] de long, par où se deuoient faire les entrées, les rendoient si visibles aux spectateurs, qu'il n'y auoit rien à desirer de ce costé-là, le plus ordinaire defaut en telles actions.

The Marquis de Mortemart, a Sieur de Nyères, and the musician Moulinier, costumed as the Pléiade Court poets Pierre de Ronsard (1524–85), Étienne Jodelle (1532–73), and Rémy Belleau (1528–77), opened the ballet singing the King's praises.

In this triumphant ballet on the theme of the vicissitudes of human affairs the Court of Louis XIII seems confident, perhaps for the first time, of having eclipsed the splendour of the pre-civil-war Court of Henri II (1519–59). A year later Ronsard 'ressuscité' will assist the ghost of Remus, King of the ancient Gauls and legendary founder of the coronation-city of Rheims, in celebrating the erection of an equestrian statue of Louis XIII in Rheims—the first royal statue in France to my knowledge to have had its inscription in French and the most obvious precedent for Desmarets's inscription for the statue of Louis XIII in the Place-Royale in Paris.[25] Such events help explain the parody of Pléiade poets in *Les Visionnaires.*

Confidence in the growing architectural splendour of Paris is reflected in the staging of the second part. The Déesse de la Seine was depicted on a great backdrop, 'vn grand tableau, auec tous les ornemens qui paroissent sur ses deux riues'—a celebration of city sites comparable to that in contemporary plays such as Corneille's *La Galerie du Palais* and *La Place Royale*, of recent seasons, and *La Comédie des Tuileries* by Richelieu's Five Authors, which soon followed.

This ballet is important for Desmarets for another reason. His 'vers pour chanter' for Mlle de Bourbon (who would marry the Duc de Longueville on 2 June 1642) in the *Œuvres poëtiques* are probably for the third part of this ballet, the first in which she appeared. On temporary leave from the Carmelites and said to have been wearing a hair shirt beneath her elaborate costume, she greatly impressed the Court with her grace and beauty in an *entrée* with Anne of Austria, the first Mme de Longueville, and thirteen other illustrious beauties.[26] The experience is said to have changed her life. She lost her conventual vocation. To this great lady Desmarets would address in 1648 'Stances' siding with her and with the sonnet 'Uranie' in the 'Querelle de "Job" et d' "Uranie" ':

> Seule vous auez le pouuoir
> D'vnir l'amour et le deuoir,
> A vos appas rien n'est rebelle,
> Par vous la raison et les sens
> Terminent la grande querelle
> Qu'ils auoient depuis si long-temps.[27]

As Duchesse de Longueville she abetted and helped preserve the secret marriage in 1649 of Desmarets's cousin to the Duc de Richelieu. Her conversion and that of Desmarets occurred in the same year, 1654. A duel fought in defence of her honour in 1643 may be evoked at the end of the fifteenth book of *Clovis*.[28] She was undoubtedly embarrassed in Desmarets's campaign against Jansenism in the mid-1660s.

[25] See René de la Cheze, *Le Roy triomphant* (Rheims, 1637).
[26] Cousin, *Madame de Longueville*, i. 115–17.
[27] *Recueil Sercy* (1660), i. 435–6 (sixth stanza of twelve).
[28] See *Clovis*, ed. F. R. Freudmann (Louvain and Paris, 1972), 416.

Le Ballet de la Merlaizon *(1635)*

Louis XIII appeared in another (humble) role in female costume, as the wife of a bell and lure merchant, in a ballet he devised himself: *Le Ballet de la Merlaizon* (The Blackbird Hunt),[29] danced on 15 March 1635 at Chantilly, and two days later at Royaumont. The final *entrée* was 'le Chef de vol pour heron, representé par le Marests à cheval, suivi de six Fauconniers à pied, auec leurs cazaques'.[30]

This is one of the rare performances in which actual horsemanship is recorded on the seventeenth-century French stage.[31] A mounted performance for the Court suggests considerable confidence. When in *Clovis* XVII Clovis' mount Aquilon, refreshed by the moist coolness of the grass, neighs to greet the dawn, the lines suggest more than an echo of horses as epic convention.

Cardinal Richelieu, the Five Authors, and Desmarets

Le Ballet des Improvistes, danced by Louis XIII on 12 February 1636 in the Grand'Salle of the Louvre, was a celebration of dance, intended to show that 'la varieté merite absolument la qualité d'vne des plus agreables choses de la nature'. Each of the twenty-six *entrées*—except the twenty-fourth, where the mention 'Le Marais' is allowed to speak for itself—is described 'par l'vn des acteurs' in the *Gazette* for 19 February, the date when *Aspasie* was first performed.

It now seems scarcely surprising that Cardinal Richelieu, into whose personal service as a writer Desmarets had been introduced by Bautru in 1634, soon afterwards encouraged him (among others) to write for the theatre—especially for the theatre under construction in the Palais-Cardinal, where *Aspasie* was performed. He was one of the great performing artists of his time, advancing his career at Court through the exercise of talents which, in the commercial theatre, still legally dishonoured performers. In André Mareschal's comedy *Le Railleur* (1636), he is cited—with reference to a role evoking Anne of Austria's modish, more or less transvestite ladies-in-waiting—as a satirist performing in a new whistling mode:

---

[29] The thrush species *Turdus merula*, edible and an excellent songbird, not to be confused with any of the North American blackbirds.

[30] *Gazette* for 22 Mar 1635.

[31] H. C. Lancaster notes the use of a live horse only in one late performance of Corneille's *Andromède* in his *A History of French Dramatic Literature in the Seventeenth Century*, ii. 682.

> Dom Quichot la prendroit pour un jeune Amadis,
> Et Marays la sifflant à la mode nouvelle
> La diroit Damoiseau plustost que Damoiselle. (IV. III)

A decade earlier, in 'La Gazette du Pont-Neuf' addressed by Saint-Amant to Boisrobert, he is a byword in performing agility, given as an image of the 'souplesse' of a new mistress:

> Marais dançant la bergamasque,
> Le vray Harlequin sous le masque . . .[32]

Like Mareschal's parallel with Don Quixote (who figures in French Court ballets of the period, as does Harlequin somewhat later), the parallel with Harlequin is indicative. The allusion must be to Tristano Martinelli (1557?–1630), the Harlequin popular in Paris in the early seventeenth century and the likely originator of a theatrical persona compared by Allardyce Nicoll to Hamlet.[33] Comparable skills were required by amateurs and professionals; but the former were honoured, and the latter (except Italians as temporal subjects of the Pope) legally dishonoured in France before 1641.

Richelieu's patronage of the theatre became more active towards the end of 1634, after Desmarets's entry into his personal service. There is evidence that, ten years into his ministry, he was seeking not only to consolidate political control but to use it creatively in establishing new institutions and fostering deeper national consciousness. The capitulation of Gaston d'Orléans in 1634 provided an opportunity for taking a firmer grip on cultural patronage. For the triple marriage, on 28 November 1634, of three of his cousins to the Duc de La Valette, the Comte de Guiche, and the Sieur of Puylaurens (associated with the adventures of Monsieur), a grand spectacle of theatre and dance was organized in the Salle des fêtes of the Arsenal. Ballets were planned for performance with recent plays. Corneille's comedy *Mélite* and a play by Georges de Scudéry (1601–67) were performed—doubtless respectively—by the Théâtre du Marais troupe led by Guillaume Desguilbert, known as Montdory (1594–1651), and the Hôtel de Bourgogne company led by Pierre Le Messier, known as Bellerose. The collaboration of professional actors with the amateur performers of Court ballets had begun. The first play by the Five Authors, *La Comédie des Tuileries*, followed in March 1635.

[32] Saint-Amant, *Œuvres*, ed. J. Bailbé, i (1971), 248.
[33] See A. Nicoll, *The World of Harlequin* (Cambridge, 1963).

H. C. Lancaster was at a loss to explain Richelieu's choice of his Five Authors. He supposes that Richelieu chose Boisrobert because he liked him, Corneille and Jean Rotrou (1609–50) as two of the most successful writers of comedies, and Colletet and Lestoile (who had written no plays) as writers of verse and members of the Académie-Française, of which he was the protector.[34] R. A. Parker seems astonished that Lestoile was chosen before he had written his first play.[35] The choices are even more astonishing to historians of scripted theatre in the light of exclusions such as Scudéry and Jean Mairet (1604–86). Considering the tenuous connection which the latter may have had with the Five Authors, Philip Tomlinson comments:

Étant donné les mérites dramatiques de Mairet et de tant d'autres, il est étonnant que, lors de la constitution de cette équipe en automne 1634, Boisrobert ou Richelieu aient préféré des poètes si peu dramatiques que Colletet et l'Estoille.[36]

I disagree. Lancaster and Parker had not noticed that Desmarets (who soon replaced the Five Authors) was not imposed on the Académie-Française by Richelieu but recruited from it. No one since the seventeenth century had connected Desmarets with the Marets of Court ballet, a sphere which has generally been neglected in the history of seventeenth-century French theatre. The one criterion which the Five authors and Desmarets all meet is success in ballet. As writers of Court spectacle on either side of the Channel well knew to their cost and not infrequent complaint, the text was seldom, if ever, the most important aspect of masques and Court ballets. Stage settings, music, dance, and especially costume were of the greatest consequence. Richelieu's patronage of theatre—directed especially towards performances at Court, normally with ballet—has received harsh criticism from literary historians; but its effect must have been to enhance at Court the relative value of scripted drama. The striking thing is that in 1636 and 1641 he chose to open theatres in the Palais-Cardinal with a play. When Richelieu's selection of writers is considered in terms of the Court's taste in spectacle, it seems lucid and politically astute.

---

[34] Lancaster, *A History of French Dramatic Literature in the Seventeenth Century*, ii. 97.
[35] R. A. Parker, *Claude de l'Etoile, Poet and Dramatist* (Baltimore, 1930), 51.
[36] P. Tomlinson, *Jean Mairet et ses protecteurs: une œuvre dans son milieu* (Paris-Seattle-Tübingen, 1983), 241.

Experience in ballet is the key to the Five Authors. Having collaborated in *La Douairière de Billebahaut*, Lestoile was perhaps the most important poet of Court ballet after Bordier, whose inspiration seems to fail following *Le Ballet du Roy*. Colletet had devised the remarkable trilogy of 1632–3: *L'Harmonie*, *Les Effets de la nature*, and *Les Cinq Sens*. Boisrobert, already a playwright and author of one published novel, had established a reputation in Court ballet with *Le Grand Ballet de la Reine* (1623) and *Les Nymphes bocagères de la forêt sacrée* (1627), danced in the Grand'Salle of the Louvre. Corneille also fits into this pattern, being the poet not only of the early comedies but of *Le Ballet du Château de Bicêtre*. Rotrou is a little more difficult, but in his *Belle Alphrède* (1634) a ballet *entrée* is used to deliver a challenge-note. Thus, as the author of something very near (if not already) *comédie-ballet*, Rotrou too readily fits into the pattern of Richelieu's theatre-patronage between the Arsenal performances in November 1634, which was accompanied by ballet, and the première of *Aspasie*, which was followed by twelve *entrées*.

Comédie-ballet is claimed as a new genre for the French stage by Molière in the preface to *Les Fâcheux*, performed at Vaux-le-Vicomte in 1661, on the eve of Nicolas Fouquet's disgrace—an event illustrating Louis XIV's decision to govern personally. That is exactly the genre to which Richelieu's patronage was moving and which to some extent his milieu achieved in the mid-1630s, as Molière must have known. A poster fragment discovered in 1984 by Madeleine Jurgens announces that from 3 November [1644] at 2 p.m. in the Jeu de Paume du Mestayer, l'Illustre Théâtre will perform Lestoile's *Belle Esclave* with 'deux ou trois Entrées de BALET'. In anticipation of such performances, clearly associated with one of Richelieu's Five Authors, the dancer Daniel Mallet had been engaged on 28 June 1644; the contract bears Jean-Baptiste Poquelin's first recorded signature 'De Molière'.[37]

With the Five Authors and Desmarets, Cardinal Richelieu had established the conditions in which *comédie-ballet* could develop, if not the genre itself. Desmarets in particular is found at the beginning

---

[37] S. Chevalley, *Molière, sa vie, son œuvre* (1984), 31–3. If, against the arguments advanced in Chapter 6, a lost play by Balthasar Baro (1590–1650), novelist and playwright, is assumed to have honoured Mazarin in the small theatre in the Palais-Cardinal, he too fits the pattern as a dancer in, and organizer of, Court ballets.

and end of Richelieu's ministry in close association on the one hand with Court musicians and on the other with the King himself. To that extent I disagree with M.-C. Canova-Green, in whose view increasing politicization of the ballet in the last years of Richelieu's ministry ended the collaboration of ambitious young authors, leaving in their place 'un homme unique, sûr, dévoué, qui sait exécuter fidèlement les directives du maître: Desmarets, la créature du Cardinal'.[38]

Although such an assessment of Desmarets's importance for Court ballet in the last years of Richelieu's ministry is as welcome as it is overdue, the evidence does not support the notion that Richelieu imposed on the kingdom—and 'au roi comme aux autres'—the political images of King and State found in Desmarets's late ballets: *La Félicité sur l'heureuse naissance de Monseigneur le Dauphin* and *La Prospérité des armes de la France*. The birth of the Dauphin was an event of unusual political significance, and in the last years of Richelieu's ministry France was at war. But the images of King and State had been at the symbolic heart of Court ballet for many years. Nor can Richelieu have imposed Desmarets on the King. Apart from other considerations, Desmarets had been dancing in Court ballets for longer than Louis XIII himself, and with him for many years before he was recruited (doubtless partly for that reason) to Cardinal Richelieu's personal service. About a year before entering Richelieu's personal service—well before the official recognition of the Académie-Française and three years before the first Salle de Spectacle was built in the Palais-Cardinal—Desmarets had addressed to Richelieu a 'Discours de la poësie' containing these lines:

> Rends nostre siecle illustre en lettres comme en armes:
> Fay qu'vn esprit diuin descouure par ses vers
> Qu'vn LOVIS doit vn iour regir tout l'Vnivers . . .[39]

---

[38] M.-C. Canova-Green, 'Créatures et créateurs: les écrivains patronnés et le ballet de cour sous Louis XIII', *Papers on French Seventeenth Century Literature*, 15 (1988), 101–13.

[39] Desmarets's 'Discours de la poësie' is quoted from the *Œuvres poëtiques* (1641). It was first published (along with poems by Maynard, Racan, Lestoile, Malleville, Baro, Habert, Godeau, and Chapelain) in Boisrobert's anthology *Les Nouvelles Muses* (1633).

4

Missions and Offices

Desmarets held important offices, first as 'le bouffon du Roi', with access to the Conseil as a favourite perhaps as early as 1614. By 1620 he was Député pour les fortifications de l'Armée du Roi: the office of Surintendant des fortifications de France which he borrowed money to purchase in 1634, when Maître Jean Desmarets was already Conseiller du Roi, Contrôleur, Contrôleur général, and Proviseur général de l'Extraordinaire des guerres. However, in August 1634 he sold the linked offices of Conseiller du Roi and Contrôleur as incompatible with that of Proviseur général, which appears to have been compatible with the offices of Conseiller du Roi en ses Conseils and Contrôleur général de l'Extraordinaire des guerres, which he retained and complemented with the office of Secrétaire du Roi in the same department. In January 1643 (when the minor second duc de Richelieu was named Général des galères), Desmarets's became Secrétaire général de la Marine de Levant and Intendant de la maison et affaires of the late Cardinal Richelieu's household. It is not clear to what extent Desmarets retained his offices after 1661 or whether he was ever 'doyen' of the Conseil d'État. In 1673 (when he is last mentioned on a title-page as Conseiller du Roi) there are unlikely to have been any other Conseillers with such long first-hand experience of the Conseil.

Desmarets was also an active member of the Académie-Française for forty-five years, beginning with his introduction in 1631 to the group from which it developed. When it was incorporated in 1634, he became (by lot) its first Chancelier, an honorary office whose holder is responsible for keeping the seals and for presiding at meetings in the absence of the Directeur. On the death of Valentin Conrart in 1675, Desmarets, as the last surviving founder-member, became the Académie's 'doyen', and he remains its longest-serving Chancelier. Jean-Jacques III de Mesmes, Comte d'Avaux, Vicomte de Neufchâtel, who succeeded to his seat, was the grandson of Jean-Jacques I de Mesmes, 'doyen' of the Conseillers d'État in 1634 when Desmarets, already a Conseiller du Roi, entered Cardinal Richelieu's personal service.

Le bouffon du Roi

Of Desmarets's offices, the most curious is that of 'bouffon du Roi', which he held (officially or unofficially) from c.1614 until some time after 1624. He appears to have been the last holder of this 'office', not without counterparts in other early seventeenth-century Courts, to cite only Louis de Neufgermain (1574–1662). This 'poète hétéroclite de Monseigneur, frère unique du Roi', later something like 'master of revels' in the Court of Louis XIII, was, during the 1620s, jester in the Court of Gaston d'Orléans, who in 1630 secured the publication of Neufgermain's *Poësies et rencontres*. For its 'Éloges' Desmarets (among others) wrote an amusing epigram.[1] The first indication that Desmarets had political as well as artistic ambitions occurs in the *Contreveritez de la cour* of 1620: 'Vautray est chancelier, Marais garde des sceaux.'[2] The author of this satire envisages a topsy-turvy world in which Guillaume du Vair (1556–1621), Garde des Sceaux from 1615, keeps pigs, while François Vautray or Vautrel (who had been a professional actor, both in Paris and leading his own troupe on provincial tours) becomes Chancellor, and the 'bouffon du Roi' keeps the seals. In June 1620 Vautrel 'se fit réhabiliter' and 'acquit un office de fourrier de la Grande Ecurie, avec permission de tenir et exercer charges et dignités honorables'.[3] By July 1620 Desmarets (whom the King took with him to meetings of the Conseil) had been appointed Député pour les fortifications de l'Armée du Roi.

Député and Surintendant des fortifications

Important new evidence concerning Desmarets's offices is provided by the indemnity for 10,000 *livres* 'pour l'employer a sauoir . . . particulierement & solidairement au payement du prix de sa charge

[1] C. K. Abraham, *Gaston d'Orléans et sa cour* (Chapel Hill, 1964), 36–7. Anthologized in *Nouveau Recueil des plus belles poësies* (1654), the epigram is quoted by Magne, *Voiture*, i. 166.

[2] Tallemant des Réaux, *Historiettes*, ii. 1515. When, towards the end of *Le Voyage de Fontainebleau* (1623), Desmarets exclaims 'Pleust il à Dieu que le Roi se voulut seruir de mon espee' (p. 19), it is his companion Bautru who replies expressing the wish to be Chancelier. Bautru was known for his 'lardons' (in the sense of 'railleries piquantes'), and 'marotte' means the ironic sceptre of the Court jester (as well as an obsession or *idée fixe*). Does their continuation have a tinge of the *Contreveritez*: 'D. Tu serois vn braue Chancelier, & tu est [*sic*] fort à ta marotte. B. Et toy tu trancherois des lardons si tu estois Conestable' (p. 20)?

[3] Tallemant des Réaux, *Historiettes*, ii. 1515–16.

de Surintendant des fortifications de France' signed on 2 May 1634
by Desmarets, his wife, Anne Fleury, and his parents-in-law, René
Fleury and Marie Rousseau, and linking him to the author of
the pamphlet describing the surrender of the château de Caen in
1620.[4]

On 7 July 1620, in response to a revolt by Marie de Médicis (aided
and abetted by César, Duc de Vendôme, other members of the royal
family, and other notables), Louis XIII moved his Court and army
into Normandy, causing 'le Soleil de sa Iustice' to shine upon the
province by taking his seat in the *lit justicier* of the Parlement of
Rouen, and then moving on to Caen, where, on 15 July, he was
'fort honorablement receu de tous les habitans'.[5] But the King was
not admitted to the château, held by a M. Prudent for the Grand
Prieur, Alexandre de Vendôme, the Duke's brother—both bastard
sons of Henri IV by Gabrielle d'Estrées and thus the King's half-
brothers. Indeed, the garrison fired upon the King's army and
upon the city, and 'Prudent en tous ses discours se manifesta bien
imprudent.' There were numerous casualties. But enough of the
garrison were unwilling to fire upon the King when he appeared
in person in the newly dug trenches that Prudent was obliged to
negotiate. Then, after refusing various demands, 'Sa Majesté,
Flambeau de Iustice, Tableau de clemence, abondante en Pardons
. . . luy accorda & lettres d'Abolition, & remboursement des deniers
par ledict Sieur Prudent aduancés' in his commission. Prudent was
allowed to leave the château with his men, his sword at his side.
When the King and Court entered, with no other force than the
'auctorité de sa puissance Royalle', he was recognized as 'Maistre
Souuerain'. This was the first occasion on which Louis XIII personally
led his army under fire, the first triumph of Louis XIII, a precedent
for future royal acts of clemency, and the occasion of Desmarets's
first publication. The descriptive title-page of this pamphlet states: 'Le
tout Recueilli par le Sieur Des-Marest deputé pour les fortifications
de l'Armée du Roy, present en ladicte affaire.'

The office for which Desmarets was deputized in 1620 was still
held financially (but without commission) by the Duc de Sully, who
provided a precedent in so far as (according to Roland Mousnier)
he 'employa un grand nombre de commissaires pour exécuter ses

----

[4] Minutier Central, xxx' Guyon 1634 mai 2.
[5] *Articles accordez par la Clemence du Roy* (1620), 5.

décisions, autorisées par le Conseil: députés . . .'[6] The appointment
is compatible with Desmarets's well-attested competence in architecture and his familiarity in 1623 with the Conseil and with Court
personalities. There is a possible echo of the siege of the château
de Caen in the capture of Tigranocerte in *Ariane*, VI: held by
Parthians, 'le Chasteau ne se vouloit point rendre, bien que l'armée
fust dans la ville'.

The early seventeenth century was a period of intense cultural
activity for Caen, which produced Court poets well-known to
Desmarets, including Malherbe and Boisrobert. Caen had a strong
Protestant community. Samuel Bochart (1599–1667), the Protestant
minister who died during a dispute with Pierre-Daniel Huet (the
scholarly Bishop of Avranches) in the Académie de Caen, was in
various degrees related to Cardinal Richelieu, to François Sublet des
Noyers, and to Jean V Bochart, Seigneur de Champigny, who became
Contrôleur général on 23 January 1623 and later Premier Président
of the Parlement de Paris. Clemency in 1620 did not end dissent
in the province. In 1639 the Protestant Colonel Jean de Gassion
(1609–47), later Maréchal de France, led a force of 4,000 men and
1,200 horse against Caen, Rouen, and other Norman cities, savagely
repressing the *va-nu-pieds* rebellion.[7]

Caen was also the home of the mason-poet Guillaume Dubois,
'ouvrier du métier de maçon, maistre tailleur de pierre à la ville
de Caen', who in 1607 published his *Œuvres* in that city.[8] As
metaphor and motif of Dubois's verse, the compass takes on spiritual
connotations grounded in his confidence in the sanctity of construction:
'compassant tous mes vers', 'mon compas est ouvert', 'les escrits
loyaux/Mesurez par compas'. Dubois's is the most striking French
poetry of the compass before Desmarets's *Amours du Compas et de
la Règle*, dedicated to Cardinal Richelieu in 1637.

Le Voyage de Fontainebleau

*Le Voyage de Fontainebleau, faict par Monsieur Bautru et Des-
marets. Par dialogue* (1623) purports to be a conversation between

[6] R. Mousnier, *Les Institutions de le France sous la monarchie absolue* (2 vols.;
1974–80), ii. 566.
[7] Church, *Richelieu*, 336 ff.
[8] See J.-P. Lassalle, 'Guillaume Dubois, maçon opératif et poète', *Cahiers de la
Grande Loge provinciale d'Occitanie*, NS 1 (1985), 49–56.

Guillaume II Bautru, Comte de Serrant, and Desmarets. The Parlement de Paris had chosen Bautru, already a Conseiller, to convey a remonstrance to the King, who had returned from the Languedoc campaign late in 1622. Bautru is a colourful figure, later (like his father, Guillaume I) a Conseiller in the Conseil étroit (later 'd'en-haut') and (like Desmarets) a founder member of the Académie-Française. Remembered more for the clarity of his dispatches and the anecdotes in which he figures than for his scant publications, Bautru produced (probably in 1618) a memorable satire of the ill-educated but snobbish Duc de Montbazon,

> occupé à ne croire qu'un homme
> Qui sçait parler Latin puisse estre Gentil-homme.[9]

Bautru's friendship, which dates from this mission, served Desmarets well on future occasions. A poem in the Œuvres poëtiques is addressed to this Bautru, who in 1634 introduced Desmarets into Richelieu's personal service and later gave him the idea of Les Visionnaires. Bautru was also a close friend of Gilles Ménage, who knew Roland Desmarets 'très-particulièrement'.[10]

In his Mémoires Cardinal Richelieu (not yet returned to the Conseil in 1623) seems sympathetic to the Parlement's objectives:

Le Parlement, voyant que, sous l'administration des ministres, les affaires étoient dans un si honteux abaissement, crut être obligé d'en dire leurs sentiments au Roi. Leurs députés arrivèrent à Fontainebleau le 3e de mai, avec commission de représenter à S. M. la misère du peuple, la mauvaise conduite de ceux qui avoient la meilleure part au governement, le peu d'espérance de voir sa dignité relevée sous leur ministère et l'intérêt qu'il avoit de retrancher plutôt ses dépenses que de les soutenir par l'oppression de ses peuples.[11]

He also notes that at this time Marie de Médicis was living 'en grande familiarité avec le Roi'.[12]

Although Desmarets remarks, concerning the Court, 'ie ny cognois plus personne que le Pere, le Fils, & le Sainct Esprit', Le Voyage de Fontainebleau presents both Bautru and Desmarets as well-informed

[9] 'Onozandre, ou le Grossier', in F. Fleuret and L. Perceau (eds.), Les Satires françaises du XVIIe siècle (1923), i. 94–9.
[10] R. Kerviler, Guillaume Bautru, comte de Serrant (1876), 2; Menagiana, ii. 44.
[11] Richelieu, Mémoires, ed. Société de l'Histoire de France (10 vols.; 1908–31), iii. 298.
[12] Ibid. 301.

about current events and the numerous personal and political rivalries mentioned in the dialogue, in the course of which Desmarets expresses regret for earlier times (doubtless beginning before the *coup d'état* of 24 April 1617 and ending perhaps in October 1622), when, he says, 'j'auois accoustumé d'accompagner le Roi & la Roine quand il alloit au conseil'. The Father and the Son are the Brûlarts: Chancelier Sillery and the Marquis de Puisieux, whom Desmarets evidently distrusts. The 'Sainct Esprit' is the second Marquise de Puisieux (the first had died childless in 1613)—a particular friend of Desmarets's cousin Mme du Vigean. Bautru comments: 'Si tu prend [*sic*] la femme pour le S. Esprit tu vaut [*sic*] trop: car on dit qu'elle n'a pas moins d'esprit au fesse qu'a la teste.'

Bautru's unfinished remark 'au [*sic*] voyages que le Fils & le frere firent en Espagne' suggests that Gaspard Dauvet, Seigneur Des Marets (Jeanne Isabelle Brûlart's husband), accompanied Puisieux on the latter's missions as ambassador extraordinary to Spain to negotiate the Spanish marriages and to exchange the two queens in 1615: 'frère' may mean 'brother-in-law', and Puisieux's brothers Henri and Nicolas had died young. I do not know to what extent Dauvet, who was an ambassador to England, had been involved in the recent incognito visit to the French Court by the Prince of Wales—the future King Charles I, who two years later married Louis XIII's sister Henriette-Marie. On his way to what proved to be an abortive courtship of the Spanish Infanta in Madrid, Charles visited the French Court just long enough to see Boisrobert's *Le Grand Ballet de la Reine* danced at the Louvre on 5 March.

The two emissaries discuss far too many personalities and issues for comprehensive coverage here. On Puisieux's policies Desmarets comments:

Il fit pour lors le[s] Mariages[;] à present il ne veux [*sic*] pas qu'on aille à la Valtoline il ne trouue pas mauuais le voyage du Prince de Galles, il dit que le fort de Graueline n'est rien: mais si ne voudroit-il pas que le Royaume de France le perdist.

Everything after 'à present' must have seemed wrong to Richelieu. He took a serious view of the strategic implications of the revolt and Habsburg occupations of the Valteline in 1620–1, and in November 1624 he was to send in French troops. In his *Mémoires* Richelieu states that even the Queen Mother had warned the Conseil that with the Valteline the King of Spain might become 'maître absolu de l'Italie', adding that, since the advanced ages of the ministers made them fear travel, 'ils donnèrent des conseils conformes à la faiblesse de leur âge'.[13] He also states that Marie (doubtless already intent upon the marriage later arranged with her own daughter) opposed Charles's attempt at a Spanish alliance. Finally, on the river Aa between Calais and Dunkerque, Gravelines (strongly fortified by the Emperor Charles V in 1528) changed hands several times between the Spanish reconquest in 1558 and the French reconquest in 1658, following which it was annexed to France by the Peace of the Pyrenees (1659). It was not during Richelieu's ministry but following Gaston d'Orléans's most successful military venture as Lieutenant général de France in 1644 that Desmarets added to the *Œuvres poëtiques* his ode *A Son Altesse Royale Monseigneur le Duc d'Orléans, sur la prise de Graveline*.

Court personalities discussed in *Le Voyage de Fontainebleau* include Henri Schomberg, Comte de Nanteuil (1575–1632), replaced on 23 January 1623 by the Marquis de La Vieuville as Surintendant des Finances. That is also the date on which Sillery became Garde des Sceaux for the second time, and Bochart de Champigny Contrôleur général. Bautru explains how. Recovered from the 'rousseau'[14] at the beginning of the new year, Sillery approached the King with complaints about the conduct of the Finances—behind Schomberg's back and in the knowledge, states Bautru, that 'si les sceaux eussent vacqué lui estant en charge il eut prié le Roy d'en disposer autrement', continuing:

Le Roy qui ne se doutoit pas de cette ruse en laquelle estoit le Garde de sceaux condessandoit aux volontez de Nicolas le Platrier, & fist des ce iour le commandement au dict Conte de se retirer le lendemain, le garde des sceaux mourut il ne se trouue personne prés du Roy qui en fist parler, Maistre Nicolas les demande, le Roy les lui accorde . . .

On the basis of two contemporary sources, Schomberg's disgrace has been dated by Richard Bonney 20 or 21 January.[15] Bautru's statement that Schomberg was ordered to 'se retirer le lendemain' would appear to reconcile the double date. The Garde des Sceaux (Louis le Fèvre, Seigneur de Caumartin) is implicated in Sillery's plot by Bautru. According to the list of Chanceliers in Moréri's

---

[13] Richelieu, *Mémoires*, iii. 271–2.
[14] Measles? Shingles? Littré does not include a definition of 'rousseau' as a disease.
[15] Bonney, *The King's Debts*, 285–7, 108.

Dictionnaire, Caumartin died on 22 January, clearing the way for Sillery's reappointment as Chancelier and La Vieuville's appointment as Surintendant des Finances the next day. Sillery's nickname 'le Platrier' (another unusual word) suggests insincerity: compare 'plâtrer', in the figurative sense of concealing something wrong under specious appearances, 'platreur', and 'platreux'. Bautru declares that Sillery has spies everywhere, that on the eve of the day his son-in-law (Nicolas de Bellièvre, who had married Claude Brûlart in 1605) was made Procureur général he had seen a doctor at his door at midnight, and that the doors of the Louvre opened for him at 4 a.m. Bautru adds 'qu'il eut chassé Castille [Contrôleur général 1619–23] s'il n'eust esté bien asseuré que le bon-homme de President Ianin n'en pouuoit pas rechapper'. That must have been before the death of Pierre Jeannin, Baron de Montjeu, which Moréri's *Dictionnaire* dates 31 October 1622.[16] Jeannin's daughter Charlotte had married Pierre de Castille, 'conseiller d'État, contrôleur et intendant général des Finances'.[17] Their son, Nicolas Jeannin de Castille, Baron de Montjeu, was Trésorier de l'Épargne from 1644 to 1662—disgraced in the Fouquet affair.

Schomberg had replaced Jeannin as Surintendant des Finances in 1619 and in 1623 was still 'par commission' Grand Maître de l'artillerie. Returned to the Conseil in August 1624, he became Maréchal de France in June 1625. In 1620 he had led the King's army in the capture of Rouen, Caen, La Flèche, and Le Pont-de-Cé, ending—with the help of Richelieu's negotiating skills—the 'Mother and Son War' of that year. Tallemant des Réaux bases an anecdote on a visit by Desmarets to Schomberg's seat at Nanteuil.[18] The chronology of other political changes in 1624 includes the following: 1 January Étienne II d'Aligre, Seigneur de la Rivière (1592–1677), replaced Sillery as Garde des Sceaux; 4 April Sillery and Puisieux were dismissed from the Conseil; 29 April Richelieu re-entered the Conseil; 13 August La Vieuville was dismissed in a *coup d'état*

---

[16] L. Moréri, *Le Grand Dictionnaire historique* (10 vols., 1759), 'Chancelier'; other sources give '1622?'. Adam and Delassault mistakenly date his death 22 Mar. 1633 in their notes on Tallemant des Réaux's *historiette* 'Le Président Janin' (i. 537–9, 1163–4). Bonney states that according to André Lefèvre d'Ormesson a major ruling of the Conseil was drawn up against Sillery's advice on 12 October 1622: *Political Change in France under Richelieu and Mazarin 1624–1661* (Oxford, 1978), 11.

[17] Moréri, ii. 930.

[18] The incident, on an unspecified date, is indexed to Henri Schomberg's son, Charles, Duc d'Hallewin (1601–56) (ii. 807, 1541).

politically advantageous to Marie de Médicis and Gaston d'Orléans but leaving Richelieu as effective principal minister; in October d'Aligre became Chancelier following Sillery's death.[19]

Le Voyage de Fontainebleau alludes to unresolved constitutional flaws, areas of political stress, and financial ambiguities. On the personal level Bautru is unhappy about a recent lawsuit at la Tournelle where the judges 'n'ont faict non plus de compte de moi comme si ie n'eusse esté au Roy, & à la Royne sa mere', while Desmarets thinks he is seeing the Devil whenever he sees, at the Louvre, the Prévost des marchands de Paris (an important figure, loosely comparable to the Lord Mayor of London), who had prevented his obtaining 'quelque petit droict que le Roy m'auoit donné à prendre aux Halles'. Desmarets contrasts 'les Officiers de la Couronne & force noblesse' who used to attend the Conseil with attendance under Sillery, when 'n y va plus que quelques robes longues telles qu'il les choisist & chasse les autres', later stating 'on dit que les Parlements lui en veulent, & que à cause de ce il chasse du Conseil tous les Presidents [of the Parlements and other *cours souveraines*]'. Roland Mousnier confirms that from October 1622 members of the *cours souveraines* (courts functioning without even the theoretical presence of the King) who were also Conseillers d'État were expected to attend meetings only for specific functions and thus lost influence in comparison with Conseillers whose careers were based in the Conseil, a matter of resentment in the *cours souveraines*: the Parlements, the Grand Conseil (long since spun off as a *cour souveraine*), the Maîtres des requêtes, Cours des aides, and Chambres des comptes.[20] Desmarets's impression that even La Vieuville, the new Surintendant des Finances, 'n'est pas du Conseil' is confirmed by Bassompierre's statement that in the beginning La Vieuville 'ne fut point du conseil estroit'.[21]

According to Bautru, La Vieuville's appointment was:

vne ruze de maistre Nicolas, d'autant qu'il est gendre d'vn tresorier de l'espargne [Vincent Bouhier, Seigneur de Beaumarchais, Trésorier once again for 1623], & pour dire que dans l'espargne il ny a point de corruption n'a

---

[19] In addition to Bonney's books cited above and the 'Chancelier' article in Moréri's *Dictionnaire*, A. D. Lublinskaya, *French Absolutism: the Crucial Phase 1620–1629*, transl. B. Pearce (Cambridge, 1968), devotes ch. 5 to the two crucial years from autumn 1622 to autumn 1624.

[20] Mousnier, *Les Institutions*, ii. 575.

[21] Bassompierre, *Mémoires*, ed. Marquis de Chantérac (1875), iii. 180.

il pas faict donner aussi a vn autre tresorier de l'espargne vne charge de Secretaire d'estat [Raymond Phélypeaux, Seigneur d'Herbault].

Desmarets replies: 'Tellement qu'il a son fils Secretaire d'estat [the Marquis de Puisieux] qui signera les dons & mandements & acquits, partant lui qui a les sceaux les scellera.' Bautru does not like what he calls the 'reformation' of 23 January 1623 either: '& quoi le Marquis de la Vieu-ville ordonnera, & Beaumarchais son beau pere acquittera & payera, Derbault fera des ordonnance[s] comme Secretaire d'estat'. Even with the new Contrôleur général, it all seemed too cosy: 'Cest le plus pauure Prestre qui fut iamais[.] Maistre Nicolas la mis la, & le loge à sa porte toute expres, aussi bien que la Pissieux [les Puisieux?] Preaux, & Boulion sont tousiours enfermez ensemble.'

Preaux is Charles de l'Aubespine (1580–1653), Marquis de Châteauneuf, Abbé de Préaux, etc., who became Chancelier des ordres du Roi in 1620 and would later twice be Garde des Sceaux: from 1630 to 1633, after the disgrace of Marillac, and again during the Fronde, from 1650 to 1651. The other reference must be to Claude Bullion, Seigneur de Bonnelles (c.1580–1640), who in 1632 became joint Surintendant des Finances with Claude le Bouthillier.[22] I am not aware that their close association in 1623 is so clearly attested elsewhere.

Le Voyage de Fontainebleau confirms Richard Bonney's view 'that Schomberg's dismissal resulted less from clear-cut financial reasons than from a political coup'.[23] Desmarets goes as far as replying, 'Ce n'est donc pas le Conseil du Roy, c'est celuy de Maistre Nicolas', later commenting: 'Cela n'est pas bon que le premier Monarque du monde se laisse gouuerner par l'vn de ses Secretaires'—remarks typical of arguments favouring sedition in the seventeenth century, here strongly suggesting a concentration of governmental authority in the hands of a single principal minister during the months before the coup d'état of January 1623. The more one re-examines Desmarets's career in relation to Louis XIII and to Richelieu, the more apparent it becomes that Richelieu understood the implications of such comments. He also understood Desmarets's last remark in the

---

[22] The reference cannot plausibly be to either of the Ducs de Bouillon alive in part of 1623.

[23] Bonney, The King's Debts, 108.

dialogue: 'Mon ami tout va par compere, & commere, chacun fait pour les siens, & Dieu pour tous.'

Other early missions

Jean Desmarets must be the Sieur des Marests who on 26 August 1625 sent to M. de la Tisardiere, Gentilhomme ordinaire de la Chambre de sa Majesté, the memoir published as *L'Entreprise des Rochellois descouuerte* (1625). Another political pamphlet, this one combines the 'conspiracy discovered' and 'true narrative' topoi later adopted for fictional narration by César Vichard de Saint-Réal (1629–92). The incidents described belong to the 'rébellion des Rohan', Protestant leaders. In 1625 Benjamin de Soubise (1583–1642), the Duc de Rohan's brother, embarrassed Louis XIII and Richelieu (who were preoccupied with the Valteline) by seizing the islands of Ré and Oléron near the Protestant stronghold of La Rochelle, inciting open rebellion, and creating tensions between the French government and its recently acquired Protestant allies, the Netherlands and England. Secret purchases of provisions for La Rochelle were discovered: evidence that a siege was anticipated some six months before the temporary 'Peace of La Rochelle' and two years before the famous siege of 1627–8. Desmarets also reports the exposure of a group of Spaniards making undercover purchases of agricultural products for illegal export, and the execution of a Bordeaux merchant 'pour auoir traficqué auec lesdits Espagnols contre les Ordonnances de sa Majesté'. Desmarets may remember this incident when contrasting the short-lived Spanish affluence, based on gold from the New World, with French wealth, based on renewable agricultural production, in *Le Triomphe de Louis et de son siècle*, vi, where he asks Louis XIV:

> Que feroit l'Espagne sterile
> Avec tout son or inutile,
> Si ta France jamais ne luy donnoit ses fruits?[24]

The prose of this pamphlet, like that of the *Articles accordez*, betrays its background in Latin, in legal French, and in the style of Amyot's translations of Plutarch's *Parallel Lives*, from which examples of monarchy are drawn.

---

[24] *Le Triomphe de Louis*, 28.

On this mission the Député pour les fortifications must have been an *intendant* reporting not through the Conseil étroit but through an officer of the King's household, the Maison du Roi. According to Bonney, intendants were operating in this period in no more than seven of the French provinces.[25] Several provinces are mentioned in this pamphlet as having difficulties similar to those it describes. Whereas Desmarets's *Articles accordez* was published 'avec permission', no such declaration is made on the title-page of this pamphlet, despite the royal edict of 10 July 1624 forbidding publication without the express permission of the Secretary of State.[26] The number of political pamphlets published in France had greatly increased since 1610.[27]

W. F. Church notes that it was during the rebellion of 1625–6 that Richelieu's spokesmen first applied the doctrine of reason of State (echoes of which occur in Desmarets's tragicomedies) to the relations between Louis XIII and his subjects.[28] Reason of State is not invoked in this pamphlet, which opens with an apologia of the rule of law and of divine-right monarchy incarnate in kings, 'représentant icy bas la viue Image de Dieu . . . l'office desquels est de regir, & gouuerner toutes choses' as 'Vicaires & Ministres de ce Tout-puissant . . . lequel les appelle luy mesme Dieux'. Desmarets would thus appear to have considered himself the deputy of the agent of the Vicar of God.[29]

Seven years later Desmarets went to Trier, doubtless as Député pour les fortifications for the fortress at Koblenz, perhaps also as Conseiller du Roi and Contrôleur de l'Extraordinaire des guerres. On 18 September 1632, Jean Chapelain informs Antoine Godeau (1605–72), future Bishop of Grasse, that he is 'de retour de Trèves'.[30] The Elector of Trier controlled bishoprics of strategic importance for France. In August Trier had been occupied by two thousand French troops in a pre-emptive strike led by François Annibal d'Estrées,

---

[25] Bonney, *Political Change*, 34.   [26] Church, *Richelieu*, 113.
[27] Martin, *Livre, pouvoirs et société*, i. 268.
[28] Church, *Richelieu*, 189–90.
[29] Desmarets may have been one of the Cent Associés de la Nouvelle France, the company founded on 7 May 1627 to further the French dominion in Canada. One of the signatures on the contract, exhibited in November 1985 at the Sorbonne exhibition Richelieu et le monde de l'esprit (item 29), looks like Desmarets's, but is not so legible as the Minutier Central signatures of 1634–5. See *Richelieu et le monde de l'esprit* (1985), 323.
[30] Chapelain, *Lettres*, i. 3.

Marquis de Cœuvres (1573–1670), Maréchal de France, accompanied by François Sublet des Noyers as Intendant des Armées. An August issue of the *Gazette* reports the 'Archevesque de Tréves protegé par le Roy . . . tousiours victorieux de ses propres victoires'. In *Clovis* XIX Desmarets mentions Metz, Toul, and troops 'Que Treves fit sortir de ses portes antiques'.

I do not know whether or for how long Desmarets exercised the office of Surintendant des fortifications after 1634. The *Œuvres poëtiques* contains an epigram 'A M. De Ville sur son livre de l'art d'attaquer et deffendre les places'—*Les Fortifications du chevalier Antoine de Ville* [1596–1656] (Lyons, 1629), republished in 1640.

Conseiller du Roi

In 1632 Desmarets was not yet Contrôleur général de l'Extraordinaire des guerres, as Tamizey de Larroque supposes. On 11 August 1634, in order to avoid a conflict of interest, he resigned the offices of Conseiller du Roi and Contrôleur de l'Extraordinaire des guerres— which he may have acquired before going to Koblenz—in favour of Gallion Mandat, on receipt of 5,000 *livres*.[31] The earliest document identifying Desmarets as Conseiller du Roi en ses Conseils and Contrôleur général de l'Extraordinaire des guerres is the *indemnité* of 2 May 1634 to his parents-in-law for 10,000 *livres*, to be used for the purchase of his office of Surintendant des fortifications. Since Bautru had introduced Desmarets into Richelieu's personal service on 18 January 1634—to help revise for publication the speech the Cardinal-Duc had made that day to King and Parlement concerning the first decade of his ministry—Desmarets's promotion to Conseiller du Roi and Contrôleur général de l'Extraordinaire des guerres probably occurred between January and May 1634. Tallemant des Réaux indicates that the group into which Bautru introduced Desmarets 'de son chef' included three other members of the circle of friends (soon destined to form the Académie-Française) which Desmarets had frequented since 1631: Chapelain, Godeau, and Jean Ogier de Gombauld (1590–1666).[32] The date is compatible with Tallemant's explanation of Boisrobert's perfidy—described in Chapter 5—concerning the authorship of Desmarets's 'Discours de

---

[31] Minutier Central, xxx' Guyon 1634 août 10.
[32] Tallemant des Réaux, *Historiettes*, i. 269.

la poësie' (published by Boisrobert himself in 1633 and praised in critical commentary by Pierre Costar) when it was being read to Richelieu: 'Il craignoit des Marestz, que Bautru introduisoit chez le Cardinal et qui, ayant un esprit universel et plein d'inventions, estoit assez bien ce qu'il lui falloit.'[33] Desmarets's marriage, purchase of superior offices, sale of a lesser office, the establishment of the Académie-Française, and Richelieu's invitation to Desmarets to write for the theatre soon followed. In March 1637 he was lucky that Richelieu, annoyed with finance in the Extraordinaire des guerres, blamed defeat in the Valteline on Claude de Bullion and Sublet des Noyers.[34]

Le Voyage de Fontainebleau indicates that Desmarets had attended the Conseil some twenty years earlier, as an adolescent favourite of Louis XIII, but that at some time before May 1623 he had ceased to attend the Conseil étroit. I do not know when Desmarets officially became a Conseiller. Nor are the operations and structure of the Conseil in the seventeenth century easy to understand, especially before the 'revolution' of 1661. In 1634 the offices of both Contrôleur and Contrôleur général de l'Extraordinaire des guerres were evidently linked with an office as Conseiller du Roi.

The King (or, twice, a Queen Regent) was the head of government as well as (acting) head of state. A legal fiction preserved the unity of the Conseil. The Conseil étroit (later Conseil d'en haut) was concerned with matters of State and normally included only the Chancelier, the Garde des Sceaux (if different from the Chancelier), secretaries of state, the Surintendant des Finances, and sometimes others, especially the Queen Mother and princes of the blood, unless in disgrace. Desmarets does not appear to have belonged to the Conseil étroit.

Under the Conseil étroit were (a) the Conseil privé (later Conseil d'État, a consultative and deliberative body comprising the Chancelier, the Garde des Sceaux, all the Conseillers du Roi en ses Conseils, and some Maîtres des requêtes and (b) the Conseil d'État et des Finances, specializing in poorly understood matters of taxation and comprising the Chancelier, the Garde des Sceaux, princes of the blood (during the Regency of Anne of Austria), the Surintendant des Finances, the Intendants des Finances, the Conseillers du Roi, and some Maîtres

---

[33] Ibid. 399–400.
[34] Burckhardt, Richelieu and his Age, iii. 139.

des requêtes. Fictionally, the Conseil sitting for different purposes remained the same Conseil, and membership of the lesser councils overlapped. When sitting as an appeal court (*cour de cassation*), moreover, the Conseil privé was called the Conseil des Parties, which the Princes and *nobles d'épée* did not normally attend. Members of the Conseil could also meet as a Conseil de Conscience, but this and other divisions of the Conseil were in practice formalized with limited membership, especially after 1661.

The fictional unity of the Conseil meant that the lesser Conseils (which the King did not normally attend except on state occasions or for some matter of urgent policy) possessed the reserved powers (powers not conceded to the *cours souveraines*) as if the King were present. From around 1632 until 1648, states Roland Mousnier, the Conseil 'estime que, armé de l'autorité du roi, souverain justicier, il peut déclarer nul et casser tout arrêt donné contre les ordonnances, contre l'autorité royale, contre l'utilité publique et contre les droits de la couronne'.[35] Even in the Conseil, and especially during the Fronde, opinions about its authority in relation to the *cours souveraines* were divided; but generally Louis XIII used *lits de justice* in which he was personally and ceremonially present to transfer authority from the Parlements and other *cours souveraines* to the Conseil, notably in 1641 when separating retained legislative powers in matters of state from the judicial powers granted to the Parlements.[36] Until 1648 any section of the Conseil could set aside decisions of the *cours souveraines*.

A Conseiller du Roi en ses Conseils held an important office. There were only thirty-eight such Conseillers du Roi from 1633 to 1637, though the number rose considerably in the Regency of Anne of Austria: to one hundred and twenty-two by 30 April 1644 and perhaps higher still.[37] The title applies particularly to legists, i.e. appeal court judges: the 'longues robes' who in the seventeenth century dressed in long black gowns and were often selected from among the Maîtres des requêtes and the Présidents of the *cours souveraines*.[38] Maître Jean Desmarets (as he is named in various documents) was

---

[35] Mousnier, *Les Institutions*, ii. 583.

[36] S. Hanley, *The 'Lit de Justice' of the Kings of France* (Princeton, 1983), 294. Four earlier *lits de justice* (1632–5) had prepared the way.

[37] Bonney, *Political Change*, 19–21.

[38] H. Méthivier, *L'Ancien Régime* (1961), 57. See also Mousnier, *Les Institutions*, ii. 147 ff., and Bonney, *Political Change*, as indexed.

one of these. As Contrôleur général de l'Extraordinaire des guerres, Desmarets is unlikely not to have been active in the Conseil d'État et des Finances, devoted to contentious matters of government finance. The Conseil d'État et des Finances lost authority between 1631 and 1661 but was still meeting in 1674. Louis XIV may have been challenged in attempts c.1661 to call in offices and/or commissions. In the trial of Simon Morin the deposition of 'Jean Des Marests Sr de St Sorlin *cy devant* [my italics] Controlleur General de l'extraordinaire des Guerres, Intendant des affaires de M le Duc de Richelieu' is recorded under oath on 23 May 1662,[39] but the offices of Conseiller du Roi and Contrôleur général de l'Extraordinaire des guerres continue to figure on title-pages. He is last mentioned as Conseiller du Roi on the title-page of the revised edition of *Esther* (1673).

I do not know whether Desmarets's dedications of devotional works to Anne of Austria and Cardinal Mazarin imply attendance of the Conseil de Conscience. As explained below, *Les Délices de l'esprit* was vetted by Saint Vincent de Paul (1581–1660), Président of the Conseil de Conscience from 1643. For about a decade from c.1658 Desmarets took an active part in the prosecution of persons considered to hold unacceptable religious opinions, especially two fanatical secretaries in the Extraordinaire des guerres: Charpy de Sainte-Croix (1610–70) and Simon Morin. In the case of Charpy, who had been secretary to a seditious favourite of Louis XIII (the Marquis de Cinq-Mars, executed in 1642), Desmarets notified Mazarin that Charpy had caused to be printed without permission or *privilège* a book entitled *L'Ancienne Nouveauté de l'Ecriture Sainte ou l'Eglise triomphante en terre* (1657). Already on the way to the Spanish frontier for the royal marriage and the Peace of the Pyrenees, Mazarin requested further details through Colbert.

Desmarets obliged with an *examen* of Charpy's book, supplying either Bibliothèque nationale Mss. fr. 2436 or the privately printed *Examen du livre, intitulé, L'Ancienne Nouveauté de l'Ecriture sainte, ou, L'Eglise triomphante en terre*. But although Desmarets (who apparently accompanied the Court) met 'adorateurs' of Charpy in Bordeaux, ending the war with Spain, Louis XIV's marriage on 9 June 1660 to Marie-Thérèse d'Autriche, and Mazarin's subsequent long illness meant that nothing was done about the book before

---

[39] Ravaisson, *Archives de la Bastille*, (1868), 163.

Mazarin's death on 1 April 1661.[40] Then, Desmarets continues 'j'en portay l'Examen à Fontainebleau, et le mis avec le Livre entre les mains de M. de Rennes [Henri de La Mothe-Houdancourt, Bishop of Rennes, Grand Aumônier de France, later Archbishop of Auch] . . . qui en fit son rapport au Roy'.[41] La Mothe-Houdancourt, a member of the Conseil de Conscience, received the abjuration of Charpy, who had been sent to the Bastille; his book was burnt by the public executioner. Paul Émard quotes from the *Mémoriaux du Conseil* for 9 June:

le Roi a ordonné à Le Tellier d'écrire au sieur de Besmaux de [le] faire garder soigneusement en sorte qu'il n'ait communication avec qui que ce soit, de vive voix ni par écrit, ni qu'il permette qu'il puisse écrire en façon quelconque, empêchant pour cela qu'il n'ait du papier ni de l'encre . . .[42]

Besmaux or Baismaux (the officer in charge of the Bastille) was even ordered to select an appropriate valet for Sainte-Croix himself.

That Desmarets worked through the Conseil de Conscience is equally clear in the trial of the recidivist Simon Morin, considered a threat to the King's life. Suspecting that Morin's companion 'nommée Malherbe était sorcière et mariée au Diable', Desmarets deposes:

j'en donnai avis à MM. de Rhodez [the Bishop of Rodez, François Hardouin de Péréfixe, later Archbishop of Paris] et de Rennes [La Mothe-Houdancourt] et au R. P. Annat [François Annat (1590–1670), Louis XIV's Jesuit Confessor since 1654], lesquels m'exhortèrent de vérifier cette affaire par de bons témoignages.[43]

Desmarets consulted widely but throughout Morin's trial worked in the closest harmony with these three churchmen, who in 1661 were (with one other Conseiller, then unwell, and Louis XIV himself) the regular members of the Conseil de Conscience.[44] Morin had been under surveillance for a long time and was charged with threatening regicide, as well as with sorcery and heresy.[45] Convicted

---

[40] *Response à l'insolente Apologie des religieuses de Port-Royal* (1666), 45–6.
[41] Ibid. 46.
[42] P. Emard, *Tartuffe, sa vie, son milieu, et la comédie de Molière* (1932), 148–9.
[43] Ravaisson, *Archives de la Bastille*, 227.
[44] Mousnier, *Les Institutions*, ii. 157.
[45] See E. Bourgeois and L. André, *Les Sources de l'histoire de France. XVIIᵉ siècle (1610–1715)* (8 vols.; 1913–35), vii. 260–1. Morin was first charged with heresy some twenty years earlier, imprisoned, and released as lunatic. Imprisoned in the Bastille, and again released in 1644, he wrote and published his *Pensées*. Imprisoned again, he abjured and was released in 1649. After further disturbing prophecies, he

of the 'crime de Leze Majesté divine et humaine' and sentenced on 13 March 1663, Morin was the next day burnt alive in the Place de Grève. His followers, convicted of witchcraft and other offences, were severally whipped, branded, banished, or imprisoned.

In publishing Desmarets's 'Déposition' and other documents, Ravaisson stresses Desmarets's role as an *agent provocateur* and does his best to separate Desmarets from Louis XIV and from public opinion, quoting as the only evidence offered of public indignation at the sentence Jean Loret's letter in verse of 17 March 1663 to the Duchesse de Longueville, which, however, refers to Morin as

> Un Imposteur, un téméraire,
> Un mal-heureux Vizionnaire,
> Qui par des profanations
> Et sotes explications,
> A Dieu-mesme faizant injure . . .[46]

Ravaisson omits that Loret reports the execution of Morin

> Pour intimider tous infames
> Qui voudroient intimider les ames.

The capture of Morin is mentioned among 'bonnes œuvres particulieres' in the *Annales* of the Compagnie du Saint-Sacrement.[47]

Contrôleur, Proviseur général, and Contrôleur général de l'Extraordinaire des guerres

Desmarets is first identified as Contrôleur général de l'Extraordinaire des guerres on 2 May 1634, in a document which I have already mentioned indicating that he had been a Contrôleur in that department and that he had resigned the lesser office as incompatible with that of Proviseur général, no other mention of which has come to light. The Extraordinaire des guerres was a department of war-finance which included two or more Trésoriers (who received monies

---

was arrested a fourth time and sent to the Petites-Maisons in Charenton, then released in 1656. The arrest of Morin arranged by Desmarets was the fifth.

[46] Ravaisson, *Archives de la Bastille*, 1290–1; J. Loret, *La Muze historique, ou recueil des lettres en vers contenant les nouvelles du temps à S. A. Mlle de Longueville* [1650–65], ed. J. Ravenel and É. de La Pelouze, (4 vols; 1857–91).

[47] R. de Voyer d'Argenson, *Annales de la Compagnie du Saint-Sacrement*, ed. H. Beauchet-Filleau (Marseilles, 1900), 222.

monthly from the Épargne).[48] For each Trésorier there must have been a Contrôleur (like Desmarets before he resigned in August 1634), in principle to verify and countersign financial acts, under the general oversight of the Contrôleur général de l'Extraordinaire des guerres. But the functions of this office are not well understood. Perhaps it later incorporated that of Proviseur général, which is treated separately in at least two of the Guyon xxx' 1634 documents but not mentioned in Desmarets's general *privilège* of 14 March 1639, or elsewhere to my knowledge. Otherwise it is not clear why the office of Proviseur général was incompatible with that of Contrôleur, but not with that of Contrôleur général. Surprisingly few signatures have come to light. There are several reasons for this, beginning with poor record-keeping, especially after the arrest of Michel de Marillac on 12 November 1630.[49] Some transactions relating to war-finance were kept secret intentionally, and some documents were deliberately burnt as a matter of policy in the 1630s. Other papers related to Richelieu's financial affairs disappeared in fires at the Chambre des Comptes in 1737 and during the Commune of 1871. Desmarets evidently still held, or thought he held, some title to this office in 1673—perhaps without commission—because it appears on the title-pages of the revised versions of both *Clovis* (where he is no longer presented as Conseiller du Roi) and *Esther* published in that year. His deposition of 23 May 1662 as 'cy devant Controlleur General' is noted above.

Had Desmarets's career been the subject of more sympathetic study, we might be better informed in three areas of historical ignorance: French war-finance and expenditure, extraordinary revenues and expenditure, and the operations of the Contrôle général. That the office was important can be deduced not only from the very considerable budget of the Extraordinaire des guerres, mentioned in the Introduction, but from the fact that most of Desmarets's major publications between 1639 and 1673 identify him as the Contrôleur général in that department but not as its Secrétaire, which he also was in 1639, and never as Surintendant des fortifications (which by 1639 he may no longer have been).

A. D. Lublinskaya must be right in stating that extraordinary expenditures had greatly expanded from 1616, that in the period

[48] Mousnier, *Les Institutions*, ii. 190.

[49] One on a letter to Maréchal Urbain de Maillé, Marquis de Brézé, 5 May 1638, none the less seems diagnostic: *L'Amateur d'autographes*, 38 (1905), 17–18.

1620-9 war, internal and external, 'swallowed up the bulk of the government's resources', and that after the disgrace of Marillac the need (expressed by Schomberg) was felt to find extraordinary sources of new revenue to finance the reorganization of the army's systems of pay and supply.[50] That is, as Bonney explains in *The King's Debts*: revenues from sources other than the various indirect taxes gathered by tax farmers, such direct taxes as the *taille*, and the *droit annuel* or *parties casuelles*, by which numerous offices were taxed at one-sixtieth of their value—the *paulette* established by Sully and Charles Paulet in 1604. Extraordinary revenues involved new fiscal expedients including the sale of *rentes* and new offices, administered as separate contracts (*traités*) with fixed interest payments established at the time of the contract.

In *The King's Debts* Bonney republishes Mallet's figures for certain revenues payable to the French Treasury between 1600 and 1656, indicating that the *derniers extraordinaires* rose from 5,710,163 *livres* in 1631 to around 10.5 million in 1632-3, then to 66,687,431 in 1634, and 156,759,915 in 1635—much the highest figure for the whole period and just over 100 million higher than that for 1636. From less than 30 per cent of French royal income in 1630-4, the *deniers extraordinaires* rose, under Bullion, to over 52 per cent between 1635 and 1639, though the rise was achieved partly through fictitious accounting. Mallet's figures for sums payable by the Treasury do show war-expenditure (including the *extraordinaire des guerres*, but recorded separately from other extraordinary expenditure) rising from 16,836,676 *livres* in 1633 to 24,800,919 in 1634, and to 41,308,486 in 1635—a sum not exceeded until 1643, when it reached 48,550,314. The huge rise in 1634 of extraordinary expenditure (reimbursements, advance interest payments, etc.) to 84,376,898 *livres* would appear to reflect both concealed expenditure in preparation for war and the inefficiency of tax and loan systems which absorbed in collection and administration a high proportion of gross revenues.[51] Bonney shows both how close some proprietors were brought to bankruptcy by a sharp change of financial policy in 1634 and how little of the gross revenues raised through extraordinary affairs actually resulted in income net of interest charges and the salaries of office-holders. The financial reorganization of 1634 in

[50] Lublinskaya, *French Absolutism*, 299-310.
[51] Bonney, *The King's Debts*, 310-12, 175, 306-7.

preparation for the entry of France into the Thirty Years War, Minutier Central documents, and Tallemant des Réaux's *Historiettes* point to 1634 as the year in which Desmarets became Contrôleur général de l'Extraordinaire des guerres.

There was clearly some murky business connected with rearmament and state-building during Richelieu's ministry. William Beik suggests that during this time substantial sums were diverted into Richelieu's personal fortune.[52] The nature and huge scale of that fortune has now been critically re-examined on the basis of new documentation by Joseph Bergin, who notes that Richelieu's *ordonnances de comptant* (cash payments for unspecified purposes) were criticized during his ministry by Mathieu de Morgues, while Bullion claimed not to understand financial arrangements for the artillery and the navy (both controlled by Richelieu) or the finances of Richelieu's household.[53]

The Extraordinaire des guerres seems equally difficult to understand. David Parrot argues that despite advance preparation the war waged by France on an unprecedented scale from 1635 was 'beyond France's military capacity to bring to a successful conclusion'.[54] Actual forces must always have fallen well below the theoretical maximum within the agreed budget of 31.5 million *livres* suggested by the Bureau des Finances on 7 November 1634: 115,000 foot and 9,500 horse. Richelieu is well known to have quarrelled with Bullion and others over war-finance but never, as far as I know, with Desmarets, whom he encouraged to write for the theatre.

Secrétaire de l'Extraordinaire des guerres

Secrétaires du Roi, according to Mousnier, 'étaient chargés de rédiger et signer les lettres de justice et de grâces qui s'expédiaient de la Chancellerie', to which they were attached.[55] They began as a sacred order of one hundred and twenty scribes, established in 1351 in the monastery of the Célestins in Paris. There were also (at different times in the seventeenth century) various lay colleges comprising the original Collège des Six-Vingts plus others, created

---

[52] W. H. Beik, *Absolutism and Society in Seventeenth-century France. State Power and Provincial Aristocracy in Languedoc* (Cambridge, 1985).

[53] J. Bergin, *Cardinal Richelieu: Power and the Pursuit of Wealth* (New Haven and London, 1985), 78–9.

[54] Parrot, *Seventeenth-Century French Studies*, 9 (1987), 151–67.

[55] Mousnier, *Les Institutions*, i. 341 ff.; ii. 139 ff.

mainly by Henri IV. An edict of April 1672 merged the five colleges and established two hundred and forty Secrétaires du Roi (down from as many as five hundred and six in 1657). The office ennobled (usually after twenty years, in some cases at once). Carefully vetted through personal interviews, Secrétaires were required under oath to renounce all commerce and other forms of *dérogeance*, to attend Mass at the Célestins every 6 May and be present at the funerals of colleagues, and to purchase the office for 1,200 *livres* (plus 150 *livres* in donations to specified charities). The Compagnie and the Collège(s) des Secrétaires were legal entities, called upon to assist the State in time of need, especially through the purchase of offices. Desmarets is most likely to have been one of the Six-Vingts des Finances, evolved from the Secrétaires des Finances (twenty-six offices) founded by Henri IV in 1606. Increased by ten in 1625–6, this body became the Collège des Trente-Six, to which eighty-four new members were added in December 1635, with a corresponding change in title. Desmarets's general *privilège du Roi* of 14 March 1639 is granted to 'Nostre amé & feal Conseiller, Secretaire, & Contrôleur General de l'extraordinaire de nos guerres Maistre Iean Des-Marets'. In a notarized act of house-purchase dated 3 February 1642, Jean Desmaretz is identified as 'Conseiller du Roi, Secretaire & Contrôleur général de l'extraordinaire des guerres'.[56] It seems reasonable to suppose that he acquired the office of Secrétaire de l'Extraordinaire des Guerres in 1635 and thereafter held it in conjunction with his publicized office of Contrôleur-général de l'Extraordinaire des guerres. The Conseil may have considered that as a Secrétaire in this department Desmarets had a special responsibility for Charpy and Simon Morin, who were also employed there as Secrétaires. It certainly seems no accident that the library of the Célestins contained a number of Desmarets's books.[57]

Secrétaire général de la Marine de Levant

According to Bergin, Cardinal Richelieu as Grand Maître et Surinten-dant du Commerce had gained control of all appointments to Levant

[56] Archives Nationales, Insinuations du Châtelet, 1640–4. Y181, 2648, fol. 404.

[57] 'Mémoire des livres achetés pour la bibliothèque des Celestins du Couvent de Paris, 1661–1668', Bibliothèque de l'Arsenal, Mss. 5336, fol. 7.

offices by 1633,[58] that is, maritime matters in the Mediterranean (as distinct from the Ponant, the term used for Atlantic and Channel navigation) and especially the *galères* or galleys—the low, flat single-decked warships propelled both by the oars of prisoners and by sail, still used in the French Mediterranean fleet in the seventeenth century. In 1635 Richelieu bought the office of Général des galères for 500,000 *livres* from the Duc de Retz, then at odds with the Duc de Guise (disgraced and exiled in 1631). The latter had claimed, as governor of Provence, to be Admiral of the Levant. Thus Richelieu's nephew François II de Vignerot, Marquis du Pont-de-Courlai, became Général des galères until shortly after the death of the Cardinal-Duc on 4 December 1642.

The *Gazette* for 15 January 1643 states, in an item dated 9 January, from St-Germain, that in the past week the Duc de Richelieu (then aged 15) 'presta ici le serment au Roy pour la charge de General des Galeres, dont Sa Majesté l'a honoré'. From this time, and not 1637 as Kerviler guesses (p. 37), Desmarets became Secrétaire général de la Marine de Levant. In a letter dated 1 April 1650, Gui Patin writes:

Après la mort du cardinal, il [Desmarets] passa au service de Madame d'Aiguillon [the Cardinal-Duc's niece and executrix], laquelle lui donna enfin, pour le récompenser de toutes ses flatteries, la charge de secrétaire de général des galères, et est demeuré auprès du petit duc de Richelieu, pourvu de cette charge, et en a fait la fonction jusqu'ici.[59]

In his 'Discours' for the reception of Jean-Jacques III de Mesmes into the Académie-Française, Isaac de Benserade confirms that, on the death of the Cardinal-Duc, Desmarets was passed on to the second Duc de Richelieu 'comme un bien de la succession'.[60] Auguste Jal found documents showing that Desmarets began to receive an annual salary of 3,000 *livres* as Secrétaire général de la Marine de Levant on 4 January 1644, having served for some time (evidently one year) 'sans gages, estats, ny appointements'.[61] Jal adds that this was a 'charge assez considérable car le service des galères . . . était encore considérable à ce moment', that Desmarets's salary in this office was

[58] Bergin, *Cardinal Richelieu*, 113.
[59] Patin, *Lettres*, i. 522.
[60] I. de Benserade, in *Recueil des Harangues prononcées par Messieurs de l'Académie françoise* (1714), i. 492.
[61] Jal, *Dictionnaire critique*, s.vv. 'Desmarestz' and 'Richelieu'.

later increased to 4,000 *livres*, and that a number of *Estats des galères* in the Archives de la Marine are signed by Desmarets and (between 1647 and 1653) countersigned by the Duc de Richelieu. Desmarets may have taken up residence with the young Duc de Richelieu in the Place-Royale at this time, since it was customary for the Secrétaire to reside with the Général.

However, in March 1649, when identified in a tax document as 'intendant des affaires de feu M. le cardinal de Richelieu' Desmarets was living in Paris, in the rue Garancière.[62] I take this to mean that even before Desmarets was confirmed as the second Duc de Richelieu's steward between 1651 and 1653 he was steward of the Cardinal-Duc's estate, probably from January 1643. According to Tallemant des Réaux, Desmarets was also employed by Mme d'Aiguillon in the quest for an editor of Cardinal Richelieu's *Mémoires* and (with Jacques Lescot, Bishop of Chartres) in the revision of Richelieu's *La Perfection du chrestien*, published posthumously in 1646.[63] From 1643 may date also Desmarets's contacts with Saint Vincent de Paul, the Aumônier des galères who in 1643 became president of the Conseil de Conscience. In the *Response à l'insolente Apologie des religieuses de Port-Royal* (1666) Desmarets recalls that M. Vincent had repeated to him 'en presence d'vne personne de grande condition'—probably the Duchesse d'Aiguillon, who was particularly interested in M. Vincent's work in the galleys—that the Abbé de Saint-Cyran had declared the Church no longer to exist.[64] Vincent de Paul may be—if indeed the passage is referential—the Philosophe chrétien evoked by Eusèbe as responsible for his conversion in *Les Délices de l'esprit*.[65] In April 1655 M. Vincent reports to the Duchesse d'Aiguillon that he had been unable to see Desmarets on the charitable business in question but that he hoped to see him soon.[66] Further references may have been lost in the fire at Saint-Lazare which destroyed the *Registres* in 1792.[67] However, in the *Quatriesme Partie de la Response aux*

---

[62] Dubuisson-Aubenay, *Journal des guerres civiles*, ii. 348.

[63] Tallemant des Réaux, *Historiettes*, i. 270–1.

[64] *Response*, 126. The reference must be to Jean Duvergier du Hauranne, Abbé de Saint-Cyran (1581–1643), the director of conscience of Port-Royal imprisoned by Richelieu in 1638, and not to Martin de Barcos (1600–78), who became Abbé de Saint-Cyran in 1644. Barcos's denial (p. 273) in his *Défense de feu Monsieur Vincent de Paul* (1668) is merely a part of the quarrel of the *Imaginaires*.

[65] *Les Délices de l'esprit*, i. 5.

[66] Vincent de Paul, *Correspondance*, ed. P. Coste (1920–5), v. 361–2.

[67] A. Ménabrès, *Saint Vincent de Paul* (1944), 259–60.

insolentes Apologies de Port-Royal (1668), Desmarets gives this account of the relationship:

> Ceux qui gouvernent la maison de Saint-Lazare . . . sçavent que M. Vincent étoit mon bon Pere spirituel, que je le consultois souvent, qu'il a eu long-temps le Livre *des Délices de l'Esprit* avant qu'il fust imprimé, qu'il en lut beaucoup, bien qu'il fust si occupé, et qu'il en donna le reste à l'un des plus sçavants de sa maison . . .
>
> Et pour faire voir encore le soin charitable que M. Vincent prenoit de moy, il voulut alors me porter à prendre l'estat ecclesiastique, croyant que cela donneroit plus de poids à ce Livre; mais je luy répondis que j'en estois trop indigne . . . Depuis il ne m'en parla plus, mais il m'exhorta à détromper le monde de ses fausses maximes, sur lesquelles j'étois assez sçavant et dont il avoit plu à Dieu me détromper. Il me donnoit souvent de bons avis, et je remarquois qu'il ne donnoit jamais conseil qu'après s'être un moment recueilli en Dieu, le consultant plustost que son propre esprit et que sa science.[68]

The religious dimension retained in the seventeenth century by the office of Secrétaire du Roi should not be neglected.

The Duc de Richelieu resigned as Général des galères on 22 July 1661. The Secrétaire général must have had to resign at that time too. The whole French navy was in poor condition. It is just possible, however, that Desmarets continued to hold the office of Secrétaire général de la Marine de Levant (with or without commission) until August 1670, when (according to Jal) Colbert returned to him a copy of his original appointment to a salary of 3,000 *livres*. Desmarets is mentioned as Conseiller du Roi, Contrôleur général de l'Extraordinaire des guerres, and Secrétaire général de la Marine de Levant in the caption of his portrait, which probably dates from 1667, but (significantly?) not on the title-page of the *Response à l'insolente Apologie des religieuses de Port-Royal* (1666).

---

[68] *Quatriesme Partie de la Response*, 223.

5

The Novels and the
New Académie-française

Desmarets published three novels: *Ariane*, read from the manuscript in 1631 to the group of men who formed the Académie-française and dedicated 'Aux Dames' in 1632 under the pseudonym 'de Boisval'; *Rosane*, dedicated in his own name to the Duchesse d'Aiguillon in 1639; and *La Vérité des fables*, dedicated to Anne of Austria in 1647. Classified as 'romans héroïques' by Charles Sorel, they might equally well be described as historical romances with pastoral features.[1] All three are to some extent idealist and exemplary, involving extraordinary characters in extraordinary situations, although not to the total exclusion of episodes in the modes of contemporary 'histoires comiques' and 'nouvelles tragicomiques'. Desmarets's baroque comes with an occasional flavour of the burlesque. *Rosane* is said to be a 'roman à clé'. The other two may also allude to current events more obliquely.

Tranvestite disguises are a feature of these novels, as they are of *L'Astrée*, of Jean de Lannel's *Roman satyrique* (1624), of Court ballets, heroic poetry, and contemporary theatre. The transvestism sometimes occasions surprises. It generally permits female characters to function imaginatively in a male-dominated world, like the *mujeres varoniles* of Golden Age Spanish theatre, and gives male lovers familiar access to female company in circumstances permitting an evocation—discreet and oblique—of carnal heterosexual love, hermaphroditism, and homosexuality.

All three of Desmarets's novels are long. *Rosane*, the shortest, contains 550 octavo pages; the longest, *La Vérité des fables*, more than 1,300. Only *Ariane* was completed, and it had by far the greatest contemporary success in France and abroad. Rooted, like the novels of d'Urfé, Baro, and Marin Le Roy, Sieur de Gomberville (1600–74), in Milesian tales and in novels with 'Arcadia' and 'Amadis' in the title, they fall between the edifying allegorical novels

---

[1] C. Sorel, *La Bibliothèque françoise* (1664), 65–6.

of Jean-Pierre Camus, Bishop of Belley (1584–1652), and the heroic romances of Gautier de Coste, Sieur de la Calprenède (1614?–1663). Like the good Divine who had the cure of Arabella the Female Quixote's deranged mind, I presume to assert with great confidence that these writers of romances 'have instituted a world of their own, and that nothing is more different from a human Being, than Heroes and Heroines'.[2] Arabella supposes that 'the Empire of Love . . . like the Empire of Honour, is govern'd by Laws of its own, which have no Dependence upon, or relation to any other'.[3] In much the same way as it was supposed, in the century of Louis XIV, to occur with terrestrial realms, such empires flourish under a Providence that is at first hidden, but whose action becomes progressively more apparent as the narrative advances, especially in *Ariane*. It helps to remember that Desmarets's novels—indeed his entire career—fits, in both space and time, between Lope de Vega's *El Peregrino en su patria* (Madrid, 1601)—a long Milesian tale with a redemptive allegorical dimension in which the hero's travels represent the voyage of the soul, the return of the prodigal son, the restoration of the soul to its heavenly Father, and finally the redeemed soul's espousal of Christ in the Eucharist—and John Bunyan's *The Pilgrim's Progress from this World to that which is to Come* (London, 1678).

Ariane

Set in the reign of the Roman Emperor Nero (37–68), with veiled allusions to current events, *Ariane* is a virtuoso narrative in sixteen 'livres' in the manner of d'Urfé's more famous *Astrée*, to which it is indebted for themes, narrative techniques, atmosphere, and elements of characterization. With the confident authorial voice and hyperbole inherited from the epic tradition, Desmarets launches us *in medias res*:

Rome commençoit à sentir auec douleur les violences & les fureurs de Neron . . . Et ce peuple superbe des despoüilles de tout le monde, gemissoit sous les cruautez de ce Prince; Quand la Fortune voulut donner naissance aux accidens qui trauerserent les plus vertueuses affections de la terre . . .

---

[2] C. Lennox, *The Female Quixote*, ed. M. Dalziel (London, 1970) (first publ. London, 1752), 380.
[3] Ibid. 320.

Soon letters are exchanged, a flashback follows—the first of many in which a character tells his own tale. From now on, the author, hidden behind internal narrators, offers the reader not only episodes imaginative in themselves and pertinent to the polycentric main narrative but the effects produced as each story in the story is told. Unfolding episodes contextualize and characterize the two heroic couples on whose adventures and aspirations the main narrative is structured. Oracles, reported orations in the manner of ancient historians (or Corneille's *Cinna*, I. III), and what amounts to an anthology of lyric verse are deployed for suspense, surprise, variety, and enhanced moods. Through successive disguises and progressive discoveries the lovers of both sexes prove their constancy in good or adverse fortune, their heroism, prowess, and fidelity in love and friendship. At first concealed in the vicissitudes of fortune, Providence is revealed retrospectively through the relation of every episode of the novel to its triumphant denouement.

Introduced as the slave 'suivante' and 'confidente' of the beauteous and virtuous Ariane, Épicharis proves through her character, actions, providential encounters, and discoveries to be the long-lost sister of the constant hero-lover Mélinte, whose love for Ariane never —or hardly ever—falters. By way of contrast, Mélinte's devoted friend Palamède loves the apparent slave Épicharis with less resolve; but he proves to be Ariane's lost brother, entitled to marry Épicharis, whom he loved best all along. Struggles exalt the prowess of warrior heroes and heroines, symbolic of spiritual combat in which the virtuous are victorious. The progress of Ariane and Mélinte from tribulation to coronation, that of Épicharis from servitude to freedom and nobility, of all four principal characters from ignorance to recognition of their true identities, are allegories of redemption through love, constancy, and—when required—forgiveness.

Resurrection is a major theme. Thought dead after their escape from wrongful arrest in Rome, in Livre VII Palamède and Mélinte rescue first Ariane's uncle, then Ariane herself:

L'estonnement d'Ariane seroit difficile à représenter, tantost regardant Dicearque, tantost Mélinte, deux personnes qu'elle croyoit mortes; & ne sçachant si elle se deuoit estimer sauuée, ou entre les mains de quelques démons qui eussent pris ces figures pour l'abuser, elle chanceloit entre la ioye & la peur.

FIG.4. Mélinte parachuting from a prison tower by the Tiber, *Ariane* (1639),
Livre V. Engraved by Abraham Bosse after Claude Vignon (*Phot. Bibl.
Nat. Paris*)

Lepante, thought to have drowned himself in Livre VIII, is resurrected to love again in Livre X. As often in contemporary theatre (but not Racine's *Phèdre*), resurrection from a false report of death foreshadows felicity through recovered identity, enhanced status, forgiveness, and reconciliation. Pursued throughout the novel, the happiness symbolized by the coronations and marriages of the denouement seems also to signify redemption. Desmarets was well versed in a tradition of biblical exegesis in which themes like progress from slavery to freedom, from ignorance to knowledge, and from isolation to union with God figure—allegorically, morally, and anagogically—the soul's freeing itself from sin, from the body, and from time to eternity.

Thematically, *Ariane* is carefully crafted. Long before her coronation Ariane is crowned as a beauty queen—a popular competition, with older European roots than is sometimes assumed, and a striking use of the topos by which actions done in jest foreshadow denouements in earnest. In love with Épicharis in Livre V, Agilas 'ne sauoit par où faire sortir son cœur pour luy en faire present'. Much as furies or monsters latent in a Racinian tragedy may be exteriorized with baroque intensity in the denouement, that theme is hyperbolically recapitulated in the last peril of the novel. In Livre XVI, about to be sacrificed to the Gods, as he then supposes, Mélinte expresses this last gory wish to Ariane:

c'est que ce cœur qui vous a tant aimée, apres auoir esté tiré de mon estomac, soit pris de vos belles mains, & porté par vous pour estre bruslé sur ce bûcher ... & faites que n'ayant iamais bruslé que pour vous, il ne soit encore bruslé que par vous. Quelle joye pensez vous qu'il receura, lors qu'apres vous auoir tant adorée sans vous connoistre que par le desir, il se sentira porté par ces mains si belles & si aimées? Ariane, promettez moy cette grace: n'ayez point d'horreur de toucher vne chose qui vous a tant cherie ...

The anticipated *Liebestod* is the emotional climax of the romance, which ends in a festive finale. It is also the rhetorical climax of the hyperboles which Desmarets's readers—like those of Mme de La Fayette's *Princesse de Clèves* half a century later—seemed to have expected in a novel: Mélinte provides 'la plus belle image de vertu qui fust iamais' in Livre VI, where letters are addressed 'au plus genereux de tous les hommes', 'au plus audacieux qui viue', 'à la plus liberale princesse de la terre'. Virtue, charity, sacrifice, and passion meet in Mélinte's plea that Ariane fear not to handle the organ of his fierce affection.

FIG. 5. Detail of the heart sacrifice in *Ariane* (1643), Livre XVI. Engraved by Abraham Bosse after Claude Vignon (*Photo Walter Ritchie*)

The ritual heart-sacrifice from which Desmarets develops this scene (see Fig. 5) corresponds more closely to practices of the Aztecs, Toltecs, and other Indians encountered by Europeans in Mexico in the sixteenth century than it does to the imaginary setting of the chapter in first-century Scythia or the Palladian architectural frame of Vignon's illustration. In *The Conquest of New Spain*, for instance, Bernal Díaz del Castillo refers repeatedly to heart-sacrifices (transl. J. M. Cohen, Harmondsworth, 1963). As early as the expedition of Juan de Grijalva in 1518, the Spaniards named the Isla de Sacrificios after finding five Indians whose 'chests had been struck open and their arms and thighs cut off' (p. 37). Of the similar ritual practice encountered on the mainland by Hernando Cortés he states: 'They strike open the wretched Indian's chest with flint knives and hastily tear out the palpitating heart which, with the blood, they present to the idols' (p. 229). During the siege and conquest of Mexico City in 1520, he saw sixty-two of his comrades dragged up to altars, where priests laid them on their backs on sacrificial stones and, 'cutting open their chests, drew out their palpitating hearts which they offered to their idols' (pp. 387, 407). After 1596 the sacrifice of one of these famous Spanish victims was known from an imaginary scene illustrating Theodore de Bry's *America siue Noui Orbis*, a likely source of inspiration for Desmarets and for Vignon. The engraving is reproduced in Victor Wolfgang von Hagen, *The Ancient Sun Kingdoms of the Americas* (London, 1962, p. 56).

The American connection is worth stressing for several reasons. Cortés is a key figure in early modern European colonial triumphalism; and according to Díaz he was well aware 'that neither the Romans nor Alexander . . . had dared destroy their ships and attack vast populations and huge armies with a small force, as he had done' and 'that the most famous Roman captains never performed deeds equal to ours' (pp. 158–9). Desmarets and other French moderns conquered less, but shared that confidence. It is all the more curious, as background to Desmarets's modernism and to the Quarrel of the ancients and moderns discussed in other chapters of this book, that Cortés is said by Díaz to have told Montezuma's Caciques that Charles V's purpose in sending him 'to their lands was to abolish human sacrifices and the other evil rites they practised' (p. 96) and to have told Montezuma himself 'that these idols of yours are not gods but evil things, the proper name of which is devils' (p. 237). Since European conquerors justified their destruction of the sun kingdoms of the Americas as the eradication of devil worship in the name of Christ, it is strange that (unlike Louis XIII as a sun king) Louis XIV, 'Roi très-chrétien', came to rely so extensively on pre-Christian imagery in projecting himself as the Sun King. Early in the reign of Louis XIV Desmarets still judged the religion of the ancient Greeks and Romans very much as Cortés had judged Montezuma's beliefs, as the worship not of gods but of evil things and devils.

Lighter episodes include the disturbed night which Mélinte, Palamède, and Épicharis spend with Corinne and her husband in Livre VI, based on Boccaccio's tale of the two travellers and the innkeeper's daughter.[4] Frequent reference is made to musical and theatrical entertainments. Mélinte is a past champion of the Olympic games, in chariot-racing and the lyric poetry competion, which he is said in Livre VI to have contested costumed as Apollo.

An episode in Livre III seems strongly reminiscent of Court ballet. Tricked with Épicharis into ablutions in a temple of Diana, Ariane is discovered in her bath by Marcellin, accompanied by an actress disguised as Diana, who descends with him from the *trompe-l'œil* ceiling in a cloud-machine:

elle fut estonnée que les fenestres commencerent à deuenir plus obscures, comme si le Ciel se fust preparé pour vn orage: & aussi tost elle[s] sentirent tomber sur elles vne douce pluye d'eau de senteur. L'admiration qui les surprit, d'vn effet si merueilleux en vn lieu couuert, fut suiuie d'vne beaucoup plus grande, lors que tout à coup elles virent que le Ciel qui estoit representé au dessus de leurs testes, s'ouurit, & emplit la chambre de lumieres. Incontinent elles entendirent vn doux concert de voix qui chantoient les loüanges de Diane, & apres elles virent Diane mesme descendre peu à peu, ayant les cheveux troussez en chasseresse, vn croissant de diamans sur le front, vne robbe d'azur ceinte au dessous du sein, & qui ne la couuroit que iusques aux genoux, les jambes & les bras nuds, les pieds couuerts de brodequins dorez, le carquois en escharpe, & l'arc en la main: quand elle fut en terre la musique cessa . . . [see Fig. 6]

Cloud-machines like the one described were used in Court ballet as early as *Le Ballet comique de la Reine* (1581). Theatrical too are the illusionist décor and costumes. For the scene is an *entrée*, with the role of goddess played by an actress, as the priestess explains. Her brother, she admits,

---

[4] G. Boccaccio, *Decameron*, ix. 6.

FIG. 6. Ariane surprised in her bath, *Ariane* (1639), Livre III. Abraham Bosse
after Claude Vignon (*Phot. Bib. Nat. Paris*)

auoit paré la chambre des richesses qui luy appartenoient, & ayant choisi vn excellent Ingenieur pour dresser des Theatres magnifiques, & faire toutes sortes de representations, ils auoient ensemble aduisé de prendre la voûte de ce petit Temple, & en faire vn Ciel; que là dedans ils auoient mis vne Musique, auec quantité de flambeaux qui rendoient ceste lumiere & que l'obscurité auoit esté causée par le moyen de certain draps que l'on auoit abbatus deuant les fenestres, pour rendre puis apres le lieu mieux esclairé par les flambeaux. Que la Diane estoit la plus belle & la plus fameuse Comedienne qui fust alors dans Rome; les enfans estoient aussi accoustumez aux Theatres, & auoient leurs flesches frotées d'vne composition qui s'allumoit dans l'eau: que tout cela descendoit & montoit par le moyen de certaines machines en forme de nuages qui le soutenoient. Ariane estoit pleine d'estonnement d'entendre vne tromperie si bien conduitte . . .

How well Desmarets evokes the artificial lighting favoured in French indoor theatres (so different from the daylight theatres of London and Madrid), the illusionist set, the theatre music, machinery, and phosphorescent effects similar to phosphorescence in a nocturnal *entrée* of *Le Ballet du Château de Bicêtre*, danced the year in which *Ariane* was published.

Other pages in the novel point to unspoken parallels between imperial Rome and modern France, its architecture, arts, and aspirations. The post-Augustan setting of the novel is not without analogy in the political turmoil of France in the two decades following the assassination of Henry IV. To be sure, the narrative is laced with historical 'local colour' without obvious parallels, such as wax tablets for correspondence; and known historical events are sometimes given an imaginative interpretation. Nero's favourite is credited with starting the famous fire of Rome to facilitate his rape of Ariane as she escapes the flames. Since no influence of Agrippina is suggested in *Ariane*, no parallel is intended with Marie de Médicis. However, *Ariane* was written at a turning-point in French political history; and there is evidence that around 1630–2 Desmarets was not firmly allied to Richelieu. Indeed, persecution of the provincial heroes of *Ariane* by the Emperor's favourite may relate to current events of 1631–2, when the Duc de Guise was disgraced and the Duc de Montmorency was beheaded at Toulouse.

Desmarets, Richelieu, and the Académie-française

Kerviler's assumption that Desmarets was Richelieu's creature from 1626 has distracted attention from evidence that the company he kept in 1630–1 included Faret and Neufgermain, then more associated with Gaston d'Orléans and the Marquis de Rambouillet than with Richelieu's policies. Thus Émile Magne overlooked Desmarets's contribution to the famous 'Guirlande de Julie', presented on 1 January 1634 to Rambouillet's daughter Julie d'Angennes (later Duchesse de Montauzier). However, two madrigals by Desmarets are the first poems in the 'Recueils Conrart' manuscript, immediately after Chapelain's dedication.[5] Desmarets had contributed a letter to Faret's *Recueil de lettres* (1627), several of which praise Richelieu. The other contributors include Bautru, Boisrobert, a certain Colomby, Faret himself, Guez de Balzac, Malherbe, and Jean de Silhon (1596–1667). The example of Faret shows that unswerving loyalties to the new ministry cannot be assumed from the contributors. Indeed, Faret includes letters by François Molière d'Essertines, who was murdered aged about 24 in 1624, and these letters could not possibly reflect the new mood of Richelieu's ministry.[6] It is to Gaston d'Orléans that Faret dedicated *L'Honnête Homme*, 'achevé d'imprimer' just three days after the Day of Dupes.

The story of Desmarets's first association with the group destined to form the Académie-Française is worth retelling in this perspective In his *Histoire de l'Académie-Françoise* (1653) Paul Pellisson (1624–93) states that around 1629 a group of friends began to meet regularly at the conveniently situated home of Valentin Conrart. Along with Conrart himself, this group included Chapelain, Godeau, Jean Ogier de Gombauld (1590–1666), Louis Giry (1596–1666), Philippe Habert (1605–37) (Commissaire de l'artillerie), his brother Germain Habert, Abbé de Cérisy (1614–54), Claude Malleville (1597–1647), and Jacques de Sérisay (1598–1654). An obvious common denominator of this group is that it does not include the contributors to Faret's *Recueil de lettres*. Another is that, at this highly politicized moment, the group was not sufficiently close to Cardinal Richelieu to obtain authorization for the meetings.

According to Pellisson, the early meetings were neither formal nor exclusively linguistic and literary, rather something of a dining-club with cultural interests. They were also secret, until Malleville 'en dit quelque chose à M. Faret, qui venoit alors de faire imprimer

---

[5] Magne, *Voiture*, ii. 61; Bibliothèque de l'Arsenal, MSS. 3135, no. 63.

[6] See Adam, *Histoire de la littérature française au XVIIᵉ siècle*, i. 214–17, and J.-P. Collinet, 'La Polixène de Molière', in *Il Romanzo al tempo di Luigi XIII* (Quaderni del Seicento francese, 2; 1976), 39–67.

son *Honnête Homme*'.[7] Thus, soon after the Day of Dupes, and even sooner after publicly praising Gaston d'Orléans in the 'Epistre' of that book as one of those destined 'à commander aux autres hommes', Monsieur's 'tres-humble, tres-obeïssant, & tres-fidelle seruiteur' Nicolas Faret was admitted to Conrart's circle and took along a copy of his new book, which is said to have been admired but not to have been read to the group. Later, Pellisson continues:

M. des Marests, et M. de Boisrobert, eurent connoissance de ces assemblées, par le moyen de M. Faret. M. des Marests y vint plusieurs fois, et y lût le premier volume de l'*Ariane* qu'il composait alors. M. de Boisrobert desira aussi d'y assister . . .[8]

Desmarets's entry into the group is easily dated between the 'achevé d'imprimer' of *L'Honnête Homme* on 14 November 1630 and that of *Ariane* on 10 March 1632. Pellisson's commas (which I have verified in the first edition) are significant. Faret did not approach Desmarets and Boisrobert at the same time.

Pellisson does not mention the dedication of *L'Honnête Homme*. Nor does he explain that Malleville, whose initial indiscretion brought Faret into the group, was secretary to Maréchal François de Bassompierre, whom Richelieu sent to the Bastille on 25 February 1631.[9] Within a few weeks Gaston d'Orléans was again in open rebellion, his milieu suspect, and on 30 March his accomplices were charged with *lèse-majesté*.[10] When the Parlement de Paris refused, on 26 April, to register the charge, Louis XIII returned to Paris and in a *lit de justice* on 13 May forbade the Parlement to consider matters of State, exiling (until 30 May, in the event) several Présidents and Conseillers. After Marie de Médicis fled to Brussels in July, Louis XIII returned to the Parlement, on 22 August, to impose the charge of *lèse-majesté* on any who had followed her. Conrart's group was lucky that Boisrobert, who had been close to Richelieu for several years, did not discover its clandestine meetings until 1633—the moment corresponding to Pellisson's observation that he was then 'en sa plus haute faveur auprès du Cardinal de Richelieu'.

    [7] P. Pellisson and P.-J. d'Olivet, *Histoire de l'Académie-Françoise* (2 vols.; 1729), i. 6–7.
    [8] Ibid. 7.
    [9] Bonney, *The King's Debts*. I follow Bonney in dating the Day of Dupes 11 (not 10) Nov. 1630.
    [10] Mousnier, *Les Institutions*, ii. 577.

In 1633 Boisrobert published *Les Nouvelles Muses*, an anthology
of poems largely in praise of Cardinal Richelieu, including contributions from Chapelain, Desmarets, Godeau, the elder Habert,
Malleville (all members of Conrart's circle), together with contributions
from four other writers well known (like Boisrobert himself) as poets
of Court ballet: Baro, Lestoile, Françoise Maynard (1582–1646),
and Racan. Along with other members of Conrart's circle, Bautru,
Guez de Balzac, and new recruits, bringing the total to forty, these
men would be charter-members of the Académie-Française.

It must have been in the first quarter of 1634 that Boisrobert
attempted to block Desmarets's entry into Richelieu's personal service.
Reading to Richelieu the manuscript 'Remarques sur les odes de
Godeau et de Chapelain' by Pierre Costar, Boisrobert, according to
Tallemant des Réaux, uncharacteristically misrepresented Desmarets's
'Discours de la poësie'. At the point where Costar 'comparoit avec
les stances de ces messieurs dix ou douze vers d'une pièce au cardinal,
qu'il louoit fort', states Tallemant, 'Son Eminence ayant demandé
de qui elle estoit, il dit de [Pierre de] Marbeuf (1596?–1645]; et
elle estoit de des Marestz'—adding that Boisrobert 'craignoit des
Marestz, que Bautru introduisoit chez le Cardinal . . .'.[11]

From March 1634, when the *Registre* of the Académie-Française
was begun, it met 'chez M. des Marests, à l'Hôtel de Pellevé' in the
Marais district of Paris—a venue which Chapelain calls a 'réduit plein
d'honneur'.[12] The house was so named because it was on the site
of one formerly occupied by Cardinal Nicolas de Pellevé (1518–94),
the Archbishop of Rheims who became commander of the League
in Paris 1592–4. It stood in the rue Clocheperce (given as Desmarets's
address in an indemnity dated 2 May 1634) between the rue Tiron or
Tison and the rue du Roi-de-Sicile, near the place where Henri IV
was assassinated by Ravaillac in 1610.

The fortune of Ariane

As details of editions and translations in the *Corpus Maresianum*
witness, the fortune of *Ariane* was considerable, both in France and

---

[11] Tallemant des Réaux, *Historiettes*, i. 399–400. Details from the *Registre* of the
Académie-Française in Pellisson's *Histoire de l'Académie-Françoise* and another of
Tallemant's anecdotes (ibid., 269), confirm this sequence, which is entirely compatible
with documents relating to Desmarets's offices and with other events of 1634.

[12] Chapelain, *Lettres*, i. 75.

abroad until the end of the century of Louis XIV: there were some ten or more editions in French between 1632 and 1724 and a total of at least ten editions of the various translations into English, German, Dutch, and Flemish between 1636 and 1714. Early success is indicated by the six editions in French and six editions of translations by 1644. Such numbers are relatively high for editions of a long novel. The early success of *Ariane* is implicit also in the quarto editions of 1639 and 1643, firstly because authorship is acknowledged on the title-page by a serving office-holder of consequence: Jean Desmarets, Conseiller du Roi and Contrôleur général de l'Extraordinaire des guerres. The quality of the quarto editions further implies an enhanced status for the novelist, like the publication of new verse plays in quarto for a short period around that time. The lavish illustration of the quarto *Ariane* must have enhanced the status of the novel altogether: frontispiece and sixteen other full-page copperplate engravings by Abraham Bosse (1602–76), in his best manner, after Claude Vignon (1593–1670). Enlarged cartoons from Vignon's illustrations were woven into Aubusson tapestries.[13] Finally, the general *privilège* of 14 March 1639 under which *Ariane* was republished witnesses both a privileged status for Desmarets personally and an effort to enhance the status of the creative writer generally. Superseding any earlier transfers of *privilèges* for his works and available for twenty years from the 'achevé d'imprimer' of any of his works published or to be published, it is designed specifically to give the writer control of his intellectual work and the capacity to benefit from it commercially, without *dérogeance*.

Ariane was one of the three most popular sources in the French novel for new plays in the period 1635–51. Lancaster shows that Nicolas-Marc Desfontaines's tragicomedy *Eurémidon ou l'illustre pirate* (1637) is adapted from *Ariane* IX, XIV, and XVI.[14] Tallemant des Réaux correctly states that Gomberville secured a *privilège* protecting his novels from unauthorized adaptations

à cause que je ne sçay quel miserable rimailleur ayant fait une meschante piece qu'il appela *Ariane*, et qui estoit l'histoire d'Ariane de M. Desmarests,

[13] A. Deprecheins, 'La Tapisserie interprète et agent de diffusion de textes littéraires', in W. Leiner (ed.), *Horizons européens de la littérature française au XVIIe siècle* (Tübingen, 1988).

[14] Lancaster, *a History of French Dramatic Literature in the Seventeenth Century*, v. 32 and ii. 78–9.

le peuple crut, quoiqu'elle eust esté sifflée sur le théatre, que M. Desmarests l'avoit faite.[15]

The *privilège* obtained for *Polexandre* on 15 January 1637 confirms the anecdote.[16] Unlocated, the offending anonymous *Ariane* is unlikely to have been published.

Other plays from *Ariane* were more successful. Mairet's tragi-comedy *L'Illustre Corsaire* is based partly on the episodes dramatized by Desfontaines, but also on the episode in which Lepante is mistakenly supposed to have drowned himself for love, like Ariosto's Ariodante and d'Urfé's Céladon.[17] The Épicharis of *Ariane* is clearly echoed in the role of that name in Tristan L'Hermite's *La Mort de Sénèque*, performed in 1644 by the Illustre Théâtre and the role which Tallemant des Réaux regarded as Madeleine Béjart's 'chef d'œuvre'.[18] Maurice Magendie credits Émilie's ferocity when rejected by Mélinte with having inspired the character of Hermione in Racine's *Andromaque* (1667).[19] A lighter moment in *Ariane* is credited as the source of an anonymous Dutch 'biter bit' comedy, *De gewaande Ariane, of de Bedrieger door list dedrogen* (Amsterdam, 1718).

Mid-seventeenth-century critical opinion, moreover, is generally favourable to *Ariane*. In the preface to *Scanderbeg* (1644), Urbain Chevreau (1613–1701) cites it before Gomberville's *Polexandre* and Mlle de Scudéry's *Ibrahim* as 'oracles' of the genre. Around 1650 Roland Desmarets supposes that scarcely anyone in France can be unaware of it.[20] In March 1655 Pellisson recommends it as an 'opus lepidissimum', with *Astrée* and three other novels, to John Smith of Christ's College, Cambridge.[21] In 1664 Sorel declares that in *Ariane* 'les Mœurs des premiers Empereurs Romains sont bien dépeintes,

---

[15] Tallemant des Réaux, *Historiettes*, ii. 467.   [16] Ibid. 1304.

[17] Lancaster, *A History of French Dramatic Literature in the Seventeenth Century*, ii. 223–4.

[18] Ibid. 563.

[19] M. Magendie, *Le Roman français au XVIIe siècle de l'Astrée au Grand Cyrus* (1932), 413. That Racine draws upon *Ariane* for *Britannicus* seems equally likely, but both writers are likely to have remembered their classics, e.g. Dido's rage in *Aeneid*, iv and a similar fury in Heliodorus, *Aethiopica*, vii. xx. 5.

[20] 'Nec quisquam ferè est Gallus, qui de egretiâ tuâ Arianâ non inaudierit; adeò manibus omnium est trita, et idemtidem repetitis editionibus vulgata', *Rolandi Maresii Epistolarum philologicarum Libri II*, i. 74.

[21] P. Pellisson, quoted in W. H. Barber, 'A Seventeenth-century View of French Literature', *French Studies*, 2 (1948), 147.

avec beaucoup d'avantures agréables'.[22] A year later La Fontaine finds that 'le roman d'Ariane est très bien inventé'.[23] Chapelain gives it first place in the second order of French romances after *Astrée*, which he considers 'le premier roman en ordre et le premier en mérite propre à estre leu mesme par les sçavans', adding: 'Ceux qui occupent le second lieu sont l'*Ariane*, la *Cassandre*, la *Cléopatre*, le *Faramond*, le *Grand Cyrus* et la *Clélie*.'[24] Huet, who succeeded to Gomberville's seat in the Académie-Française in 1674, recalls that 'Marets had . . . written an elegant story in the walk of romance, under the title of "Ariadne," which was considered as one of the best after the "Astraea" of d'Urfé.'[25] Of course Pierre Nicole and other Jansenists did not appreciate it; and their judgement is reflected in adverse commentary by the barrister Gabriel Guéret (1641–88) in *Le Parnasse réformé*, 'achevé d'imprimer' on 7 February 1668. Ariane, suggests Guéret, inhabits 'lieux infames', so that to visit her is like visiting a brothel.[26] Written towards the end of the Quarrel of the *Imaginaires*, Guéret's remark is instructive: Desmarets went on to write *Marie-Madeleine* (1669), Guéret to publish *La Guerre des auteurs anciens et modernes* (1671).

Rosane

What proved to be the only volume of Desmarets's *Rosane* appeared in 1639. Another historical novel, the work has a title-page presenting itself as the first part of an 'histoire tirée de celles des Romains & des Perses'; and one of the contrasted heroines is loosely drawn from the account in the *Historia Augusta* of Zenobia, the third-century Queen of Palmyra famed—as Desmarets repeats in his *Jeu des Reynes renommées*—for virtue (whatever the modern evidence to the contrary) as well as for intelligence and beauty. Chapelain soon signalled two points of interest for contemporary readers in a letter to Guez de Balzac dated 4 December:

Mr Desmarets a fait un 1er volume de cinq qu'il a dessein de faire sous le titre de *Rosane*, dédié à Me d'Aiguillon et dont elle fait partie. Il

---

[22] Sorel, *Bibliothèque françoise*, 165.
[23] J. de La Fontaine, *Œuvres diverses*, ed. P. Clarac (1948), 586.
[24] Chapelain, in an undated letter to Gruterus, Moderator of the Erasmian College in Rotterdam, *Lettres*, ii. 542.
[25] P.-D. Huet, *Memoirs*, transl. J. Aiken (2 vols.; London, 1810), ii. 1–2.
[26] G. Guéret, *Le Parnasse réformé*, new edn. (1671), 171–2.

a fait beaucoup de bruit à cause de cela, et c'est une pièce qu'il faut lire.[27]

Heroic, pastoral, and exemplary like *Ariane*, *Rosane* more closely anticipates the *romans à clé* of the 1650s. Certain to be of interest in the Paris of 1639 was anything concerning the powerful Duchesse d'Aiguillon, idealized in the heroine Uranie. Dionée would appear to suggest Desmarets's cousin Mme du Vigean, whom he addresses under that name in an elegy added to the *Œuvres poëtiques* late in 1640. Léopold Lacour considers that Artémise represents the Princesse de Condé (mother of the 'Grand Condé') and 'la très élégante et courtoise Astérie, Mme de Rambouillet'.[28] Lacour, however, gives no proper evidence for his suggestion that publication of the novel was interrupted by Cardinal Richelieu, or Mme d'Aiguillon herself, because the relationship depicted between Uranie and Dionée was vulnerable to interpretation as a lesbian one, as suggested between Mmes d'Aiguillon and du Vigean in the *Milliade*. It seems more likely that, with so many other commitments in the late 1630s, Desmarets simply failed to find time to continue *Rosane*. Lacour was not aware that *Érigone*, Desmarets's prose tragicomedy which Mme de Rambouillet and her guests saw at the Palais-Cardinal on 19 January 1642, was adapted from Livre IV of *Rosane*—a third focus of interest, because it is unusual at that time for an author to adapt a play from one of his own novels.

For readers of *Rosane* unfamiliar with the personalities to whom it alludes Desmarets's preface may interest most. Stressing its allegorical dimensions, he makes a case for exemplary idealism in fiction. Thus Zénobie, the warlike heroine contrasted with Uranie, signifies 'la vie active', while Uranie herself—on an island of tranquillity, surrounded by friends who might have stepped out of Castiglione's *Il Corteggiano* or from the less contentious dialogues of Plato— represents the contemplative life. The purpose of *Rosane* (published soon after the birth of the Dauphin), he states, is to 'donner des preceptes aux ieunes Princes'. The novel represents a didactic instrument, making the useful agreeable, and the agreeable useful. Like other writers of his time, Desmarets adopts and adapts the Horatian notion of *utile dulci* later associated with La Fontaine and the frontispiece of Boileau's *Œuvres diverses* (1674) but already

---

[27] Chapelain, *Lettres*, i. 535.
[28] L. Lacour, *Richelieu dramaturge et ses collaborateurs* (1926), 64.

developed in the preface to *Rosane* into a theory of imaginative
literature in which the marvellous may serve didacticism:

> L'Esprit humain est de sa nature si curieux d'apprendre des histoires
> meslées d'auantures admirables, & s'y porte auec tant d'ardeur & de plaisir,
> que de tout temps ceux qui ont voulu luy imprimer quelque creance, & qui
> ont meslé des contes estranges parmy leurs discours, ont tousiours obtenu
> de luy ce qu'ils desiroient: pource que lors qu'il est charmé de ceste douceur
> qui l'amuse, il est conduit facilement à tout ce qu'on veut persuader. Quand
> l'Imagination est agreablement occupée à se representer de merueilleux
> euenemens, le Iugement qui ne manque iamais à venir considerer ce qui entre
> chez elle, se laisse aller à prendre part à son contentement; & si quelques
> preceptes sont addroitement meslez parmy les Histoires enrichies de feintes,
> il reçoit alors fauorablement les enseignemens qu'on luy donne.

Desmarets intends that the young princes for whom *Rosane* is
written 'admirent les exemples parfaits qu'on propose, & se portent
auec ardeur à les imiter; & pource que la nature produit rarement
des personnes parfaites, l'art de l'inuention supplée à ce defaut'. To
carry over into the world of fiction, where the writer is in control
of his material, the errors and impertinence of historical experience
would be folly. The novelist's art is like that of ancient philosophers
who were successful

> quand ils ont voulu apprendre aux hommes le culte de la diuinité, le reglement
> des mœurs, & la reuerence des loix: & en meslant la feinte auec la verité,
> & les instructions encore parmy ce meslange, ils ont composé par maniere
> de dire vn breuuage si vtile & si agreable tout ensemble, que les esprits l'ont
> gousté auec plaisir, & en ont receu en mesme temps leur guerison.

The Greek and Roman authors cited in support of this aspect of
his literary theory do not represent authority for Desmarets but
precedents. They are considered early successful practitioners. Fiction
understood in this way is not a falsification of the external world
but an independent act of the imagination:

> La Fiction ne doit pas estre considérée comme vn mensonge, mais comme
> vne belle imagination, & comme le plus grand effort de l'esprit; & bien
> que la Verité semble luy estre opposée toutefois elles s'accordent merueilleuse-
> ment bien ensemble. Ce sont deux lumieres qui au lieu de s'effacer l'vne l'autre
> & de se nuire, brillent par l'esclat d'vne de l'autre.

The more novels are 'pleins de feintes parmy la verité, plus ils
sont beaux & profitables', Desmarets adds, 'pource que la feinte

vraysemblable est fondée sur la bien-seance & sur la raison; & la
verité toute simple n'embrasse qu'vn recit d'accidens humains, qui
le plus souuent ne sont pleins que d'extravagances'.

In discussing fictional embellishment Desmarets quickly passes
over biblical examples, adduced thirty years later in the 'Epître' of
Marie Madeleine, here preferring to cite Xenophon's 'vie de Cyrus
[inventée] à sa fantaisie, pleine d'auantures guerrieres, entremeslées
d'amours', Plato's imaginary dialogues, Seneca's letters to Lucilius
(considered an at least partly fictitious correspondence), and Plutarch's
'belles œuvres morales'. However, his theory of embellished fiction
may have been adapted from the argument in Aristotle's *Poetics* ix
that poetry is more philosophical than history, since it deals in
universals. *Poetics* xxv suggests three categories of verisimilar
imitation or mimesis. Desmarets is not over-zealously concerned
with the first: 'things as they were or are', or the second: 'things
as they are said or thought to be'. His concept of verisimilitude
fits Aristotle's third category: 'things as they ought to be'. Indeed,
he writes:

L'Histoire simple a ses bornes bien plus estroites [que les romans]; & en
disant les choses comme elles ont esté, n'approche pas de la beauté d'vne
Histoire meslée de fiction, qui represente les choses comme elles ont deu
estre. L'vne est assuiettie à suiure le fil des reuolutions extrauagantes que
cause la fortune dans les Estats . . . [où l'on void] si souuent la Vertue
opprimée & le Vice triomphant: l'autre se promene dans les libres campagnes
d'vne inuention agreable, ayant touiours la Raison et les Graces à ses costez.
Là les plus accomplis des hommes maistrisent la fortune: & si quelquefois
ils en sont persecutez, ce n'est que pour faire esclatter dauantage leur vertu.
Là les vicieux sont detestez & punis; mille diuertissemens s'y rencontrent
à toute heure . . . narrations . . . discussions . . . dela on trouue des
descriptions plus belles que la nature mesme . . .

Desmarets understood the meaning of fiction.

Rosane was neither completed nor reprinted,[29] but the adaptation
of *Érigone* from one of its episodes confirms the initial success
reported by Chapelain. Cardinal Richelieu's death must have made
the 'applications' of *Rosane* less interesting. An Italian translation
was published in Venice in 1650.

[29] The Bibliothèque Nationale Catalogue entry misprints '1659' for '1639'. The
frontispiece is by Bosse after Vignon.

La Vérité des fables

Desmarets's third novel, *La Vérité des fables, ou l'Histoire des dieux de l'antiquité*, was 'achevé d'imprimer' on 16 November 1647 but dated 1648 on the title-page. In the preface Desmarets stresses 'sa hardiesse & son inuention', while the dedicatory epistle to Anne of Austria invokes the convention of the found manuscript—in this case a letter and book addressed by Euhemerus of Messene to the Cassander (suspected by some of having murdered Alexander the Great) whom Euhemerus served from 311 to 298 BC. The most obvious source of inspiration for *La Vérité des fables* is Bordier's euhemerist interpretation of *Le Ballet d'Apollon* in the *livret* of *Le Ballet du Soleil* (1621). Unfortunately, Desmarets did not really discover the lost travel-novel *Sacred Scripture*, in which Euhemerus claims to have journeyed to an island where he found that the gods of popular worship were only mortals deified in gratitude for their extraordinary achievements. He merely makes the anthropological interpretation of the pagan gods the point of departure for his own adventure novel, in which Apollo is the leading character. His sources include Cicero's *Tusculan Disputations* and St Augustine's *City of God* (which he also quotes in other contexts). He may have met euhemerism as a rationalist critique of pagan religious experience in Pliny and in Plutarch, in such other Church Fathers as Lactantius, Tertullian, and Jerome, and in Boccaccio, who gave euhemerism currency in the early Renaissance. It had in any case found its way into such seventeenth-century works as Petau's synchronization of pagan and biblical history and mythology *Rationarum temporum* (1633) from still standard historians: Diodorus Siculus (who seems to take Euhemerus lost fiction for fact), Eusebius, Paulus Orosius (for the identification of Jupiter with King Belus of Assyria), and Isidore of Seville. Euhemerism was also known to the medieval chronicler Ado of Vienne, to whom Desmarets refers in *Clovis*, where he resumes with altered emphasis his fictional critique of the pagan gods.[30]

Somewhat similar in atmosphere and theme to Desmarets's other novels, *La Vérité des fables* blends elements of Greek romance

---

[30] On euhemerism see J. Seznec, *The Survival of the Pagan Gods*, transl. B. Sessions (New York, 1953), 11–36; P. Decharme, *La Critique des traditions religieuses chez les Grecs* (1904), 372 ff. and ch. 12: and J. Dryhurst, 'Evhémère ressucité: *La Vérité des fables* de Desmarets', *Cahiers de l'Association internationale des études françaises*, 25 (1973), 281–93.

mediated by Diodorus Siculus with reminiscences of Ovid's *Meta-morphoses* and of *L'Astrée*. Apollo, for instance, is not an important subject for Diodorus; but Apollon is developed by Desmarets into a new, more heroic, inventive, and royal Céladon, permitting contrasts of constant with fleeting love, praise of progress in architecture and other arts, and disparagement of the credulity of ancient times, when exceptional men were mistaken for gods. The prince Apollon, who proves to be the long-lost son of Belus Jupiter and the brother of the less constant prince Mercure, owes his apotheosis to the invention of architecture, archery, and the lyre. Daedalus proves to have been an early engineer, imprisoned after the construction of the palace at Knossos—whose design was more elaborate than any previously devised—and having secured escape through the invention of a sailing vessel, which the ignorant Cretans mistook for wings. The legendary monocular vision of Polyphemus originates in his invention of a small target-shield in response to the far-darting Apollo's new archery, mistaken by passing seafarers for a single eye. In relation to the pagan gods as a theme in *Ariane*, there is a shift in emphasis from deliberate deception by criminals—the use of disguises and a cloud-machine in the temple of Diana, for example—to the self-deception of the credulous.

At the same time, *La Vérité des fables*—paradoxically introduced through the fiction of the 'found manuscript'—involves a more intricate play of mirrors than does *Ariane*. Through most of the two volumes it is not realized that the Ganymede loved by Jupiter Belus is a girl disguised as a boy. The *bienséance* apparently threatened by the avowal of what appears to be homosexual love is retrospectively restored—at least on the surface—not only in relation to Jupiter but also as regards the episode where Ganymede is taken into the service of the Queen of the Amazons and sleeps in her chamber. The extent to which the reader is allowed to misunderstand the sexuality of Ganymede is fully apparent when his story is contrasted with an episode (more closely inspired by a somewhat similar incident in the *Astrée*) in which Mercure, in a charming female disguise, of which the reader is clearly informed, kisses the nymph he loves in a silvan glade. The sexual ambiguities associated with Mercure's adolescent ruse are intensified through the narrative *trompe-l'œil* in which Ganymede is depicted.

Like *Rosane*, *La Vérité des fables* was not finished. Nor was it reprinted. Desmarets was obviously disappointed by the poor initial reception of this ingenious work, as he states in the preface to 'Les Amours de Protée et de Physis, ou l'Alliance de l'Art & de la Nature', a poem included in *La Comparaison de la langue et de la poësie françoise avec la grecque et la latine* (1670). Recalling similar initial hesitation over *Les Visionnaires*, he states that *La Vérité des fables* was neglected for two years:

enfin ceux de bon goust les lûrent; & ayant estimé cette invention, & la façon noble & delicate dont les apparentes origines des beaux Arts y avoient esté deduites, ils témoignerent à plusieurs l'estime qu'ils en faisoient: puis ceux cy les lûrent sur leur parole, & commencèrent à les aimer & les estimer à l'envy.

Put off by 'le méchant goust des esprits communs, & d'autres pensées plus solides' from completing the work, whose 'enjouëment' is more suited in any case to the age at which he began it than to the age he had reached in 1670, he would not complete it, being willing only to publish 'Les Amours de Protée et de Physis' as a verse sample of what might have followed and as an illustration of how much more invention is required 'à changer les Fables en veritez, qu'à changer les veritez en fables'.[31]

Not much wit is required to state metaphorically that a man in flight is transformed into a bird, or that a grieved and tearful woman is turned into a fountain. Far more 'force d'invention' is required 'pour donner de la vraysemblance à ce qui est fabuleux':

Car la noble invention est une espece de creation, sans qu'elle ait besoin d'aucun modele qui soit ou qui ait esté dans le monde; & dont la source est dans la seule fecondité de l'esprit, & non dans la memoire . . .

---

[31] *La Comparaison*, 268–9.

6

Richelieu, Desmarets, and Theatre

Desmarets's Plays and the Palais-Cardinal theatres

Desmarets's dramatic works, written at the request of Cardinal Richelieu and for his theatres, comprise seven plays, first performed between 19 February 1636, when or soon after the small theatre in the Palais-Cardinal opened, and 18 November 1642, less than three weeks before the Cardinal died. All but *Érigone* are in verse. The first four must have been written for the small theatre, the existence of which has curiously eluded literary historians. Antoine Adam, for instance, states that 'jusqu'en 1637, il [Richelieu] s'était contenté d'une installation de fortune', but then 'ordonna à l'architecte Mercier [*sic*] de bâtir une salle spécialement conçue pour les représentations dramatiques'.[1] Desmarets's last plays and *Le Ballet de la Prospérité* were written for that Grand'Salle, inaugurated on 14 January 1641 with *Mirame*.

The architect of the Grand'Salle was Jacques Lemercier (1585–1654), famed for the château and town of Richelieu, the Val-de-Grâce church, the horseshoe staircase at Fontainebleau, and the 'pavillon de l'Horloge' at the Louvre. According to Henri Sauval, the ancients possessed no comparable theatre. The Grand'Salle was a large rectangular room with a proscenium arch and raised stage at one end. The auditorium was fitted with twenty-seven stone steps, each about 6 in. (*c.*15 cm.) high and slightly less than 2 ft. (*c.*60 cm.) wide—about half the dimensions of a Roman theatre, but of course under cover. This arrangement allowed spectators to be seated on wooden forms on alternate steps. Both forms and steps are absent from the illustrations. The steps are said to have been relatively easy to climb, the forms not so cold as stone steps, and spectators less likely to 'gâter leurs habits et s'entrecrotter'.[2] Richelieu may have

---

[1] Adam, *Histoire de la littérature française au XVIIe siècle*, i. 468.
[2] H. Sauval, *Histoires et recherches des antiquités de Paris* (3 vols.; 1733), ii. 160–3.

been inspired by rivalry, not only with the ancients but with the Spanish Court. Nearly a decade earlier, on 25 November 1631, the *Gazette* had reported plans for an amphitheatre 'dans l'enclos du Palais pour tous les Seigneurs de Conseil, à leur despens, afin de les distinguer du peuple aux spectacles publics'. Spanning the roof of the Grand'Salle required oak beams 2 ft. in diameter and 10 *toises* long—*c*.19.5 m. or 21.3 yds. 'Jamais', states Sauval, 'on n'avoit vu, ni lu, ni ouï parler de poutres de chêne d'une longueur si extraordinaire et si prodigieuse'. This gives an interior width of *c*.9 *toises* (17.9 m.) There were two balconies on either side.

The interior decoration was entrusted to Jean Lemaire (1598–1659), Peintre du Roi. He was probably a pupil of Claude Vignon, the illustrator of *Ariane*. A specialist in perspective and architectural scenes, Lemaire had returned to Paris from Rome around 1637. Sauval describes the ceiling as follows:

Le tout est couronné d'un plat-fonds ou perspective, où le Maire a feint une longue ordonnance de colonnes Corinthiennes, qui portent une voute fort haute enrichie de rozons; et cela avec tant d'art, que non seulement cette voute et le plat-fonds semblent veritables, mais rehaussent de beaucoup le couvert de la salle, et lui donnent toute l'élevation qui lui manque.

Both the perspective sets of *Mirame* and the *trompe-l'œil* features of the plots of *Mirame* and *Érigone* were well suited to such a theatre. Although the new theatre is not well reported in the *Gazette*, its state-of-the-art stage-effects must have been startling, even if, being devoted to earlier styles, Michel de Marolles was not impressed at the 'faux-jours' or the perspective 'qui fait paroître les personnages, des Geans, à cause des éloignemens excessifs'.[3]

The illustration of the Grand'Salle in the folio *Mirame* was entrusted to the Florentine engraver Stefano della Bella (1610–64), who produced the six double-page plates familiar to theatre historians. Having arrived in France in 1640, della Bella was commissioned to engrave a perspective of the siege of Arras, elevations of other fortified towns, and other sieges. He may have met Desmarets as Surintendant des fortifications. His other commissions in France include the siege of Perpignan (1642), the battle of Rocroi (1643),

---

[3] M. de Marolles, quoted in Lancaster, *A History of French Dramatic Literature in the Seventeenth Century*, ii. 378.

the frontispiece of Desmarets's *Œuvres poëtiques*, and the four sets of Desmarets's educational card-games.[4]

Although only a few of the premières in Richelieu's theatres are securely documented, the available evidence indicates that such performances were staged by the main Parisian companies of professional actors, the Hôtel de Bourgogne and the Théâtre du Marais, who at the Palais-Cardinal performed at least once in collaboration with each other, and more than once in entertainments which included a banquet and a ball or a Court ballet. Further performances in royal palaces, on other less elaborate private stages, in the two commercial theatres of Paris, and doubtless in the provinces, must normally have been contemplated by both actors and authors. Performance of *Les Visionnaires*, for example, was assumed to have taken place at the Théâtre du Marais after a preliminary reading at the Hôtel de Rambouillet.[5] But the fact that Montdory played a role does not prove that 'it was originally acted at the Marais', as Lancaster concludes. It only indicates performance by the Marais company. The reference 'sur le theatre' in Chapelain's letter does not preclude previous performance. Any play written for Richelieu after 1636 must have been written for the Palais-Cardinal. Mme de Rambouillet's circle may have seen a preview or dress rehearsal of *Les Visionnaires* there— much as they later saw *Érigone*, though presumably on the later occasion in the Grand'Salle. Among other evidence, the arrogant quatrain closing the 'Argument' of *Les Visionnaires* becomes much easier to understand as written by a celebrity of Court spectacle whose second play was (like his first) especially written for private performance in the Palais-Cardinal:

> Ce n'est pas pour toy que j'escris,
> Indocte et stupide vulgaire:
> J'escris pour les nobles esprits.
> Je serois marry de te plaire.

No one ever expressed more succinctly the élitist character of Richelieu's patronage, destined to affect theatre in Paris until the end of the *ancien régime*. How could any of us have imagined that such

---

[4] See C.-A. Jombert, *Essai d'un catalogue de l'œuvre d'Etienne de la Belle* (1772), 16–7, 28, 90. Jombert misdates the plates for the cards 1646.

[5] *Les Visionnaires*, p. ix, after Chapelain, *Lettres*, i. 137–8; Magne, *Voiture*, ii. 61; Lancaster, *A History of French Dramatic Literature in the Seventeenth Century*, ii. 279.

lines were written about a play destined for first performance in a commercial theatre?

All seven of Desmarets's extant plays were published between 1636 and 1643, all but *Érigone* were reprinted, and several were translated. Pellisson reports a lost comedy 'toute comique en petits vers, appellée *le Sourd*' and two plays left unfinished at the death of Cardinal Richelieu, also lost: *Annibal* and *Le Charmeur charmé*.[6] Through all or most of this period Desmarets continued his activity in Court ballet and produced two of the most spectacular political ballets of the century.[7] TABLE 1 presents in simplified form Desmarets's extant plays and the two ballets.

TABLE 1. Genre and Dates of First Performance of Desmarets's Extant Dramatic Works

Title	Genre	Dates[a]	Place[b]
Aspasie	comedy	1636/36	PC
Les Visionnaires	comedy	1637/37	PC, Marais
Scipion	tragicomedy	1638/39	PC, Marais
La Félicité	ballet	1639/39	St-Germain, PC, Hôtel de Ville
Roxane	tragicomedy	1639/40	PC
Mirame	tragicomedy	1641/41	PC
La Prospérité	ballet	1641/41	PC
Érigone	tragicomedy	1642/42	PC
Europe	heroic comedy	1642/43	PC

[a] Performance/publication
[b] PC = Palais-Cardinal, small theatre 1636–40, Grand'Salle 1641–2; the commercial theatre of subsequent performances of plays is added, if recorded.

---

[6] Pellisson and d'Olivet, *Histoire de l'Académie-Françoise*, i. 283. Around 1650 Roland Desmarets, writing 'de comoediis priscis ac nostris', urges completion of the unfinished plays: 'quin potiùs duas, quas à longo tempore inchoatas habes fabulas . . . absolve', *Epistolarum philologicarum Libri II*, i. 119. Hannibal is a plausible subject for a playwright who had dramatized episodes in the lives of Scipio and Alexander. The title in publications least remote from that of *Le Charmeur charmé* is the Dutch comedy said to have been derived from *Ariane*: *De gewaande Ariane, of de Bedrieger door list bedrogen* (Amsterdam, 1718).

[7] Incidental verse for ballet by Desmarets is included in the *Œuvres poëtiques* and in the *Recueil des plus beaux vers* (1661) (four poems). Other poems attributed to Desmarets, published or in manuscript, may include verse for ballet, including several of the songs and verse associated with performance in *Ariane*. Desmarets seems likely to have written some of the verse unattributed in *livrets* and in the *Gazette* accounts of ballets in which he performed.

That the Desmarets invited by Richelieu to write plays was a celebrated performer of Court ballet is fundamental to reappraisal of Richelieu's poorly understood patronage of the theatre. In *La Dramaturgie classique en France*, for example, Jacques Scherer deals with problems arising from suppositions about *mise-en-scène* through the additional supposition that various playwrights (especially Desmarets) knew nothing about the stage.[8] In particular he limits available choices of decoration to either some adaptation of the medieval multiple setting (*décor simultané*), in which different, more or less distant, sites were signified as separate mansions or playing-areas through symbolic and/or representational stage decoration, or a new 'classical' unified decoration, in which the actual playing-space on stage corresponds more or less exactly with the poetic space of the play. The supposition is gratuitous, and the thesis not tenable with reference to certain plays by Desmarets, Baro, the Five Authors, La Calprenède, and Mareschal.[9] The late T. E. Lawrenson does correct the mistaken notion that the proscenium-arch curtain of the Grand'Salle 'opened in the middle and ran laterally', but he repeats the absurd assumption that the sets for *Mirame* were used again for *La Prospérité*.[10] Nor do the eminent authors of quatercentenary commemorative publications on 'Richelieu and the theatre' address the question of *mise-en-scène* in the smaller theatre, and both neglect evidence concerning the Grand'Salle.[11]

Lawrenson fails to notice, for instance, that the scene known as *Le Soir*—frequently reproduced from a painting in the Musée des Arts décoratifs, Paris, or from the engraving of it by Van Lochon—depicts the French royal family with a Cardinal watching a ballet *entrée*, presumed by Agne Beijer to be part of *La Prospérité*.[12] Beijer, however, does not allow for either of two other distinct

---

[8] J. Scherer, *La Dramaturgie classique en France* (1959), particularly the section 'Œuvre écrite et œuvre représentée' in the chapter on 'La Mise en scène et l'unité de lieu'.

[9] Even without some of the information about Richelieu's theatres now presented, G. Snaith demonstrates the extent to which La Calprenède, for example, worked with the stage and with actors in mind, 'Plaisir à La Calprenède', *Seventeenth-Century French Studies*, 9 (1987), 55–73.

[10] T. E. Lawrenson, *The French Stage and Playhouse in the XVIIth Century*, 2nd edn. (New York, 1986), 156, 220.

[11] G. Couton, *Richelieu et le théâtre* (Lyons, 1986), and J. Mesnard, 'Richelieu et le théâtre', in *Richelieu et le monde de l'esprit* (1985), 193–206.

[12] Beijer, in Jacquot (ed.), *Le Lieu théâtral*, 377–403, identifies the stage action depicted in *Le Soir* as an *entrée* from that ballet (not from *Mirame*, as Couton states in *Richelieu et le théâtre* in the caption opposite p. 58).

possibilities: (*a*) that it may be a rehearsal in the small theatre that is depicted, and (*b*) that the set may have been adapted to an *entrée* for the ballet-prologue to *Europe*, rehearsed just before Richelieu died but not performed (if fully performed at all) until some time afterwards. Lawrenson does not deal with the implications of my doubtless mistaken deduction (1978) that the performance (or rehearsal?) depicted is taking place in the smaller of the two theatres in the Palais-Cardinal, not the Grand'Salle, where *Mirame* was performed.[13] His untimely death prevented his seeing the more informed discussion in *Comedy in Context*, suggesting that *Le Soir*— which cannot simply depict the Grand'Salle, but does depict either *La Prospérité* or (more likely) a related moment in the ballet-prologue to *Europe*—represents a composite scene based on features of both theatres.[14] The implication of these suggestions remains the same, however, as far as the existence of a proscenium arch and the use of a front-stage curtain in Paris for drama before 1641 is concerned: both must have been features of the small theatre in the Palais-Cardinal from its inauguration, perhaps with *Aspasie*. Lawrenson himself gives a vital clue when he mentions the front-stage curtain drawn after the final act of Corneille's *L'Illusion comique* ('le théâtre se ferme avec la toile de devant'). He correctly argues—against persistent misconceptions—that this play was performed at the Palais-Cardinal, but he fails to grasp either (*a*) that it is the play (misattributed by the *Gazette* to Baro) used to celebrate Mazarin, or (*b*) that the Petite Salle must therefore anticipate the proscenium arch and the proscenium-arch curtain of the Grand'Salle.[15]

Valuations in the Cardinal-Duc's 'Inventaire après décès' suggest that both theatres had dressing-rooms, and they point to the considerable difference in scale, the smaller being built (according to Sauval) for about six hundred spectators, the Grand'Salle for perhaps as many as three or even four thousand (though modern theatre-historians

---

[13] Lawrenson, *The French Stage and Playhouse*, 241.

[14] H. G. Hall, *Comedy in Context: Essays on Molière* (Jackson, Miss., 1984), 38 ff. The double side-balconies, steps centre stage, and *trompe-l'œil* colonnade on the ceiling are all recognizable features of the Grand'Salle, unlikely to have replicated the small theatre in these respects. Other features, especially the flat auditorium floor, do not correspond to Sauval's description of the Grand'Salle. But the arms at the centre of the proscenium arch are not the same as in the plates for *Mirame*, suggesting (with the size of the royal infants) a date in 1642: a revival of *La Prospérité*? or (more likely) reuse of the monster effects in the ballet-prologue to *Europe*.

[15] Lawrenson, *The French Stage and Playhouse* 155, 207.

generally substitute a figure not above fourteen hundred). Valuing the machinery and other equipment of the Grand'Salle at 2,988 *livres*, the inventory must also put in doubt Henri Arnauld's statement of 18 November 1640 that the machinery for *Mirame* would cost 100,000 *livres*:

Dans la grande salle de la Comedye: Toutes les formes, chaires et sièges faitz de tripe de la chine et aussy plusieurs machines, le tout estimé deux mil neuf cens quatre vingtz huict livres . . . Dans la basse chambre derrière le téatre, tous les bancs, fasson d'armoire et une table, le tout montant environ à la somme de soixante unze livres. Dans la petite salle de la Comédye et dans les deux chambres de derrière, toutes les chaires, sièges et formes, le tout couvert de mocquette servant en ladicte salle, montant environ à la somme de quatre cens cinquante livres.[16]

During her Regency, Anne of Austria appears to have favoured entertainments in the small theatre. Mme de Motteville states that on Shrove Tuesday 1646, 'la Reine fit représenter une de ces comédies en musique dans la petite salle du Palais-Royal, où il n'y avoit que le Roi, la Reine, le cardinal et le familier de la cour, parce que la grosse troupe des courtisans étoit chez Monsieur', adding that since only twenty or thirty persons were present, 'nous pensâmes mourir d'ennui et de froid'.[17] None the less, she notes, the following year 'les soirs, la belle cour se rassembloit au Palais-Royal dans la petite salle des comédies'.[18] Even if the controversial performance on 2 March 1647 of *Orfeo*, said to have introduced Italian grand opera to Paris, took place in the Grand'Salle,[19] any painting or print purporting to represent the royal family 'le soir' in the early 1640s is likely to allude also to the smaller theatre.

Many of the difficulties that Scherer and others experience with the stagecraft of Richelieu's dramatists disappear in the light of evidence—published in the *Gazette*—that successive stage decorations were used in the small theatre and in the light of documentation showing that new sets, not those of *Mirame*, were used for *La Prospérité*. Antoine Adam should have realized that there was a

---

[16] 'Inventaire après décès', in Laurain-Portemer, *Études mazarines* (1981), 197–223. The figures for the capacity of the two theatres given by Sauval, *Antiquités de Paris*, ii, 160–3, are reviewed in detail by Lawrenson, *The French Stage and Playhouse*, 238–43; H. Arnauld, quoted by Lancaster, ii. 376.

[17] F. Bertaut, Dame Langlois de Motteville, *Mémoires*, i, ed. F. Riaux (1855), 265.

[18] Ibid. 303.

[19] Ibid. 312–13.

purpose-built theatre in the Palais-Cardinal when reporting that on 8 January 1637 *La Grande Pastorale* was given, 'avec changements variés et admirables de scène', in what he later, with reference to the performance there on 22 February 1637 of *L'Aveugle de Smyrne*, calls the 'salle des fêtes du palais de Richelieu'.[20]

Failure to realize that the great originality of *Mirame*, as far as the Paris stage is concerned, lay in transformation scenes permitting changing spectacle within unity of place, leads Scherer to stand well-observed evidence on its head:

L'insouciance des auteurs en ce qui concerne la détermination des lieux pose parfois des problèmes de mise en scène à peu près insolubles. Le cinquième acte de *Mirame* . . . est bien d'un écrivain qui n'a pas pensé au théâtre. L'héroïne . . . est absente des six premières scènes de l'acte . . . elle n'est pas en scène et n'a pu à aucun moment venir sur le lieu de l'action. Or, à la scène 7, les personnages décident de lui prodiguer leurs soins. Le roi s'écrie: 'Allons la secourir' et Azamor propose: 'Courons à son réveil'. Ils n'ont pas besoin de courir. Sans plus de transition, Mirame est là . . . Mais comment est-elle venue?'[21]

No good purpose would be served by quoting Scherer's further questions, all related to assumptions about Richelieu's theatre which have nothing to do with its capacity for a spectacular *changement à vue* at this crucial moment of the dramatic action. Paradoxically, it is Desmarets's use of a state-of-the-art *mise-en-scène* which leads Scherer to conclude: 'Ces problèmes regardent le metteur en scène. Qu'il s'arrange comme il peut! L'auteur n'y a pas pensé. Il n'a pas *vu* sa scène; il l'a simplement écrite.'

Scherer's reaction is cited as all too representative of critical commentary on Desmarets's stagecraft, except that few take the trouble to describe a scene so effectively, making it clear to readers aware of the capacity of Richelieu's theatre that a *changement à vue* must have occurred in conjunction with the symbolic resurrection of the heroine at this climactic moment of the action.[22] It helps,

---

[20] Adam, *Histoire de la littérature française au XVIIe siècle*, i. 467, 505.

[21] Scherer, *La Dramaturgie classique*, 159.

[22] Compare the transition from the comic or tragicomic to the Christian marvellous effected with a *changement à vue* in Molière's *Dom Juan*, performed on the same stage in 1665. Dom Juan's query, 'Mais quel est le superbe édifice que je vois entre ces arbres?' (III. v), alludes to a change in the perspective set effected at that moment of the action. See 'Marché de décors pour *Don Juan*', in M. Jurgens and E. Maxfield-Miller, *Cent ans de recherches sur Molière* (1963), 399–403.

even when handicapped by wrong dramatic theory, to respect the data given by the script.

Dismissive commentary has had disastrous consequences for the history of the Paris stage, because it implies firstly that Desmarets had little grasp of what he was doing as a playwright, secondly that Richelieu must have had a strange notion of theatre-patronage to encourage such a playwright and to select a play by him to open the grandest new theatre in France, and thirdly that technological innovation in the Palais-Cardinal theatres was unimportant in comparison with what took place a few years later, in the next reign. Comparison of the resurrection scenes in *Aspasie* with the resurrection of Mirame marks the difference in stagecraft between on the one hand a play written for performance in conjunction with stage decorations changed mainly behind a closed forestage-curtain and on the other a play in which new technology allows a 'miraculous' *changement à vue* to dramatize both the resurrection of Mirame and the transformation her miraculous resurrection produces.

Performance of Corneille's L'Illusion comique

Mazarin's involvement with Richelieu's theatres is worth stressing. The *Gazette* for 9 April 1636 reports that on the 5th of that month

Le Seigneur Mazarin Nonce extraordinaire de Sa Sainteté, eut son audience de congé de leurs Majestés . . . Le soir du mesme jour, fut représenté devant le Roy, la Reine, & toute la Cour dans l'Hostel de Richelieu, vne comédie dont la nouueauté du suiet qui estoit vne émulation plus réelle que feinte entre les troupes de Belle-roze & Montdori: l'ornement du théatre, la gentillesse de l'invention & la bonté des vers, ouvrage de Sieur Baro: le concert ravissant des luths, clavessins, & autres instrumens: l'élocution des acteurs, mirent l'honneur de la Scene en compromis entre tous les siécles passez & le nostre.

The performance required both major commercial troupes: collaboration which Richelieu arranged for grand occasions such as the triple marriages of November 1634 and the departure of the papal nuncio. The *Gazette* is again mistaken about the authorship of a play by Corneille, perhaps because Boisrobert again lied to disadvantage a rival.[23] If the play selected to open the new theatre was probably

---

[23] In reporting the ballets performed at the Arsenal with two comedies on 28 Nov. 1634, the *Gazette* for 30 Nov. mentions 'la Melite de Scuderi', a misattribution

Aspasie, the play performed for Mazarin's departure was almost certainly Corneille's *L'Illusion comique*, utterly appropriate and known to have been performed around that time. There is no doubt that, as one of the Five Authors, Corneille was writing spectacular theatre for Richelieu at the time. As a performer at Court and author of *Célinde* (1629), a 'play-within-a-play' play, Baro at first sight is a plausible author for the *Gazette* to suggest; and he may have had something to do with the production. At the same time, it seems as strange for a play performed so magnificently to have disappeared entirely as not to have any reference to the date and place of the première of *L'Illusion comique*, another theatrical occasion of consequence. Details of the play described in the *Gazette*—the 'nouveauté du sujet', the 'gentillesse de l'invention', 'la bonté des vers'—in no way indicate a play which its author would have wished to abandon. The machinery and front-stage curtain, the scene-changes, the deployment of a second troupe of actors, the theme of 'l'honneur de la scène', all point to *L'Illusion comique*.

Giovanni Bernini's stage-effects for Mirame

As indicated in Chapter 1, Laurain-Portemer has shown that on his return to Rome Cardinal Mazarin opened negotiations for the stage machinery, set designs, and lighting effects required for the Grand'Salle with Giovanni Bernini, who was not only a great sculptor and architect, but also a state-of-the-art specialist in perspective sets, theatrical lighting, and transformation scenes. Bernini's commission for the Grand'Salle has received little attention in comparison with his later projects in France: reconstruction of the Louvre (discarded in favour of plans by Claude Perrault) and the famous bust of Louis XIV. However, the correspondence of Mazarin's agents is sufficiently detailed to prove beyond reasonable doubt that Bernini was involved in the plans for Richelieu's Grand'Salle and for the major spectacles already envisaged for performance in it: *Mirame*, used at the inauguration, *Le Ballet de la Prospérité*, and probably *Europe*, long-planned like *Mirame*. In a letter dated 7 March 1640, Mazarin's

corrected on 10 Dec. For Boisrobert's deception concerning 'Le Discours de la poësie', see Chapter 5. Dating *L'Illusion comique* to the Petite Salle in April 1636 carries an implication that Mareschal's *Le Railleur* (which has an important braggart-soldier role and requires scene changes) was also performed on the same stage, not in 1635 but somewhat later, in 1636.

agent Benedetti writes that, unusually, Bernini had promised to explain for Mazarin's benefit the artificial simulation of day and night to his aide Nicolò Menghini.[24] Simulation of the change from day to night identifies with *Mirame* the further report in the same letter that 'Il s. caval. Bernino mi ha promesso i disegni per il teatro e l'invenzione di qualche nuova apparenza in modo che V. S. Ill. ma ha d'assecurarsi che il s. Nicolò verrà instruttissimo di tutto quello gli bisognerà per dar gusto al s. Card. e Duca e per farsi honore.' Mazarin's reliance on agents in these negotiations indicates that post-ponement of his own return to Paris until after the first performance of *Mirame* would not have prevented use of the machines and sets he had negotiated for it.

With the Grand'Salle, Richelieu must have hoped to eliminate the six causes preventing continued progress in the development of theatre in France identified by the Abbé d'Aubignac in his *Projet pour le rétablissement du théâtre françois* drawn up at his request in 1640: the common belief that theatre-going is sinful, 'l'infamie dont les loix ont noté ceux qui font profession de Comédiens publics', faulty performances, bad plays, poor stage sets, and 'les Desordres des Spectateurs'.[25] Whatever the immediate stimulus, Louis XIII's decree of 24 April 1641 rehabilitating actors and making acting a respectable profession is unlikely to be unrelated to his presence at the opening of the Grand'Salle and his acceptance of the dedication of the play performed on that occasion. The Grand'Salle represents a culmination of Richelieu's rehabilitation of theatre evoked by Alcandre in the final scene of Corneille's *L'Illusion*, published in 1639:

> à présent le Théâtre
> Est en un point si haut qu'un chacun l'idolâtre
> Et ce que votre temps voyait avec mespris
> Est aujourd'hui l'amour de tous les bons esprits . . .

Richelieu's theatre patronage and the rehabilitation of professional actors in 1641 must have helped the eighteen-year-old Jean-Baptiste Poquelin—the future Molière—in deciding shortly afterwards on a stage career. In the five years between the inauguration of the Petite

---

[24] Menghini, states Benedetti, 'verrà istrutto da s. caval. Bernino, il quale, perservire a V. S. Ill. ma mi ha promesso di farglie veder il modo conche si illumina e si fa quel sole et la notte, il che dice no haver voluto mai mostrare ad alcuno' (Rome 71, fol. 243), quoted by Laurain-Portemer, *Études mazarines*, 198.

[25] D'Aubignac, *Projet*, in his *La Pratique du théâtre*, ed. P. Martino (1927), 387.

Salle and that of the Grand'Salle, Richelieu came to depend on the collaboration of Desmarets perhaps more than on that of any other playwright, including Corneille (who left the Five Authors in a dispute over *Mirame*)[26] and even Boisrobert, finally disgraced for bringing doubtful company to a rehearsal of *Mirame* in the Petite Salle.[27]

Desmarets's recruitment as a playwright

Richelieu's recruitment of Desmarets as a playwright is well known. Having evoked in his *Histoire de l'Académie-Françoise* the pleasure Richelieu took in seeing new plays, discussing them with playwrights, suggesting dramatic subjects, and recruiting new writers for the stage, Pellisson adds:

Ainsi voyant que M. des Marests en étoit très-éloigné, il le pria d'inventer, du moins, un sujet de Comédie, qu'il vouloit donner, disoit-il, à quelqu'un d'autre, pour le mettre en vers. M. des Marests lui en porta quatre bien-tôt après. Celui d'Aspasie, qui en étoit l'un, lui plut infiniment; mais après avoir donné mille louanges, il ajouta, *Que celui-là seul qui avoit été capable de l'inventer, seroit capable de le traiter dignement*, et obligea M. des Marests à l'entreprendre lui-même, quelque chose qu'il pût alléguer. Ensuite ayant fait représenter solennellement cette Comédie devant le Duc de Parme, il pria M. des Marests de lui en faire tous les ans une semblable. Et lorsqu'il pensoit s'en excuser sur le travail de son Poëme héroïque de Clovis, dont il avoit déjà fait deux livres, et qui regardoit la gloire de la France, et celle du Cardinal même; le Cardinal répondit qu'il aimoit mieux joüir des fruits de sa Poësie, autant qu'il seroit possible, et que ne croyant pas vivre assez longtemps pour voir la fin d'un si long ouvrage, il le conjuroit de s'occuper pour l'amour de lui à des pièces de Théatre, dans lesquelles il pût se délasser agréablement des grandes affaires.[28]

This account anticipates Samuel Chappuzeau's suggestion that France as a whole should be disposed 'à vouloir du bien aux comédiens', thanks to

le plaisir qu'ils donnent au Roi pour le délasser quelques heures de ses grandes et héroïques occupations. Qui aime son Roi aime ses plaisirs; et qui aime

---

[26] Adam, *Histoire de la littérature française au XVIIe siècle*, i. 468.
[27] Tallemant des Réaux, *Historiettes*, i. 401–2.
[28] Pellisson and d'Olivet, *Histoire de l'Académie-Françoise*, i. 88–9.

ses plaisirs aime ceux qui les lui donnent, et qui ne sont pas des moins nécessaires à l'Etat.[29]

Pellisson's account is endorsed by Desmarets himself in the *Seconde Partie de la Response à l'insolente Apologie de Port-Royal*:

quand j'ay fait des comedies, qui n'ont esté que tres-honnestes, ç'a esté par le grand desir que m'en témoigna le Cardinal de Richelieu: Plusieurs sçavent quelle répugnance j'eus d'en faire; et M. Pelisson en a parlé dans son *Histoire de l'Académie*. Aussi apres la mort de ce grand soûtien de l'Eglise dans la France, je n'ay plus fait de Comedies; et mesme je ne croy pas en avoir vû représenter une seule.[30]

Aspasie

Pellisson's account of the first performance of *Aspasie* may be based on a notice in the *Gazette* dated 23 February 1636:

Le Mardy 19. Son Eminence receut en son Palais Son Altesse de Parme, & luy donna vne fort belle Comedie avec changement de Théatre & d'excellens concerts de luths, épignettes, violes & violons entre les actes. Cette Comédie fut suivie d'vn Balet, composé de douze entrées de fort bons danceurs richement vestus. L'assemblée estoit fort belle, & toute de personnes de condition. Ce divertissement dura trois heures: en suite duquel son Altesse de Parme fut menée en haut, où il trouva à son entrée vn excellemment beau buffet d'argent tout blanc, puis au lieu où il mangea, vn autre doré qui n'estoit pas moindre.

Thus the première of *Aspasie* was part of a grand occasion, with music between the acts, Court ballet, a grand collation, and (the *Gazette* continues) a concert by 'la Musique du Roy, du tout singuliere', given on the King's express instructions to entertain the Duke of Parma and Gaston d'Orléans in the Cardinal's private apartment. Since the performance fell in Lent, the *Gazette* takes pains to stress that 'toutes choses s'y passérent avec tant d'ordre & de règle que tous y soupérent fort bien sans rompre leur j[e]une'. There was nothing unusual about Court ballet in Lent at this period; but it is worth contrasting Anne of Austria's unease eleven years later about a performance of *Orfeo* during Lent, the difficulties involved, and the offence she caused Cardinal Mazarin by leaving the celebrations

---

[29] S. Chappuzeau, *Le Théâtre françois* (Lyons, 1674), 93.
[30] *Response*, 86.

at midnight on religious grounds.[31] Richelieu and Louis XIII have few discernible doubts about honouring the Duke of Parma in Lent with *Aspasie* and the attendant festivities.

Odoardo Farnese, Duke of Parma, of Piacenza, and of Castro (1612–46), by his marriage to Marguerita de' Medici Louis XIII's second cousin, was a strategic ally of France in the Thirty Years War. The *Gazette* for 27 September 1635 reports 'l'avantage obtenu par le Duc de Parme sur les Espagnols' at Valenza, where his artillery destroyed the bridge over the river Po. On the death of his father, Ranuccio I Farnese, in 1622, this Duke had inherited the magnificent theatre in Parma, the first in Europe built with a proscenium arch (1618).

The phrase 'avec changement de Théatre' linked to the mention in the *Gazette* of music performed between the acts is positive evidence that successive stage directions were used, probably depicting the same street-scene with houses and a temple in Acts I to IV and a garden in Act V. Access to the stage in the first décor is through practicable doors in the houses of Aspasie and Lysis (presumably represented by angle wings), through the door of the temple at the beginning of Act III, and by streets to either side of the temple. Contrary to Jacques Truchet, I conclude that in *Les Visionnaires* II. IV, the word 'rideau' in Sestiane's lines on the unity of place can really only refer to the front-stage curtain clearly in use at the Palais-Cardinal:

> Vous avez beau chanter, et tirer le rideau,
> Vous ne m'y trompez pas, je n'ai point passé l'eau.[32]

Interlude music—implying delay—must relate to scene changes more substantial than any required by the *tapisseries* used as backdrops or for discovery scenes in Parisian commercial theatres. The *tapisserie* is associated with visual *coups de théâtre*. It is often used as a discovery curtain, whereas Sestiane has complained about interruptions in the action which break up the unity of illusion:

> il faut poser le jour, le lieu qu'on veut choisir;
> Ce qui vous interrompt ôte tout le plaisir,

---

[31] Motteville, *Mémoires*, i. 312–13.
[32] J. Scherer and J. Truchet (eds.), *Théâtre du XVIIe siècle* (2 vols.; 1975–86), ii. 430, 1369. This is the first recorded use of the phrase 'tirer le rideau' in its most obvious and still current sense.

Tout changement détruit cette agréable idée
Et le fil délicat dont votre âme est guidée.

Sestiane rejects scene changes even within a notional unity of place
defined merely as sites reachable within the time taken by the
imaginary action of the play—including such 'changement de théâtre'
as that used for *Aspasie*. The delay of which she complains ('ce qui
vous interrompt') does not rule out partial scene changes effected
by means of small *tapisseries*, but it implies something more.

The 'changement de théâtre' of *Aspasie* is in line with theoretical
requirements outlined in *La Poëtique* of Jules de la Mesnardière. His
chapter on 'l'Appareil ou la disposition du theatre' admits successive
stage decoration while rejecting *décor simultané*:

il faut de nécessité qu'elle [la scène] change d'autant de faces qu'elle marque
d'endroits divers[.] Qu'elle ne découvre pas vn Iardin, ni vne Forest, pour
la Scene d'vne Action qui s'est passée dans le Palais; & que mesme en ce
Palais elle ne fasse pas voir dans l'Appartement du Roy ce qui doit auoir
été dans le Cabinet de la Reine.[33]

Although still used successfully in 1637 for *Le Cid*, multiple sets no
longer fully satisfied the new realist requirement for stage decoration
to represent the imaginary scene of the action. Chapelain addresses
the problem in a letter dated 7 May 1670 to Girolamo Graziani,
concerning the latter's new tragedy *Cromwell*:

Je suis encore en peine de l'unité de la scène qui est tantost la place publique
devant le palais, tantost la prison où le roy est estroittement gardé, tantost
la place intérieure de la tour où Arturo parle. Cela ne peut passer, à moins
qu'à tous ces changemens vous ne faciés changer la scène par machine.[34]

The stagecraft of *Aspasie* corresponds to an experimental period during
which, in the Petite Salle of the Palais-Cardinal, such scene changes
within a general unity of place were effected with stage machinery
inadequate for *changements à vue* and damaging to the unity of
dramatic illusion. *Les Visionnaires*, by way of contrast, supposes
the strictest observation of the unities of time, place, and action.
None of the brief published commentary on *Aspasie* does much
to explain the quality of this comedy as symbolic drama, or its

---

[33] J. de la Mesnardière, *La Poëtique* (1639–40), 412.
[34] J. Chapelain, *Lettere inedite a corrispondenti italiani*, ed. P. Ciureanu (Genoa, 1964), 237.

importance for Molière's stagecraft. *Aspasie* is a domestic obstacle-comedy of reciprocated love, unmatched fortune, and father–son rivalry which lends itself readily to figurative interpretation. Lysis loves the less wealthy Aspasie, whom his father recklessly marries. Through apparently almost culpable submissiveness, in which there may well be an element of parody, fierce conflicts of love and duty are resolved by the lovers in terms of the honour due to their parents. The young couple do not reject their parents, and elope to a wild place, like Pyramus and Thisbe in Ovid's tale or in Théophile's tragedy *Pyrame et Thisbé* (1626). Overcome by emotion, they eventually swoon in the walled garden in which they are inadvertently confined together—*hortus conclusus* and *locus amoenus*, symbolic in Renaissance pastoral of grace and redemption, the symbolic point of the scene change, and perhaps the earliest French set requiring three walls with a fourth supposed invisible to the audience. Believing the young couple dishonoured and dead for love, and then dead but not dishonoured, Lysis' father comes to repent his selfishness and hasty marriage. When the sleepers awaken (another metaphor of redemption), the marriage, contracted without genuine consent, is annulled, permitting the union of Lysis and Aspasie.

If a figurative interpretation is attempted, anagogic meaning may be perceived in the lovers' ultimately successful struggle against despair and other sinful temptations and towards their new life, begun when born again in paradise: denouement and threshold to lasting happiness. Moral meaning would lie in the couple's exemplarity, converting by their example Lysis' father and others to a more generous attitude towards life, much as the example of Mélinte's constancy in *Ariane* finally provokes a generous response in Émilie. More unusually, however, *Aspasie* may be read as an allegory of the love of eloquence, personified in a heroine whose material fortune does not match her beauty, charm, and virtue. Such an allegorical interpretation is entirely consistent with Desmarets's experience in Court ballet, recent activity in the Académie-Française, the allegorical poem *Les Amours du compas et de la règle* dedicated to Cardinal Richelieu in 1637, *Clovis* (interrupted to write *Aspasie*), and other allegorical works published by Desmarets in the 1650s, especially *Le Combat spirituel* and *Les Délices de l'esprit*.

A striking feature of *Aspasie* is the Neo-platonism of its inspiration, stamping Lysis as a lover of ideal beauty in the very first lines of the soliloquy with which he opens the play:

Que ton pouuoir est grand, Beauté, present des Cieux!
Doux charme de nos cœurs, delices de nos yeux;
Et dont la chere Idee auec vn trait de flame
Penetre par nos sens, & se graue en nostre ame.
Soit que dedans les eaux tombe l'Astre qui luit,
Soit qu'il chasse les feux & l'ombre de la nuict,
Incessamment paroist deuant ma fantaisie
L'adorable portrait de la belle Aspasie.

Lysis' speech is a heightened form of Mélinte's soliloquy in *Ariane* III:

Ah! divine Ariane, que ta veuë m'est chere . . . Il semble que . . . tu veuilles former en [mon âme] vne nouvelle idée, plus belle encor que celle qu'elle cherissoit. Beautez qui n'aurez iamais d'egales, puis-je assez vous aimer? Ah! Ariane, que les esclats de ta beauté remplissent mon ame de lumiere! & que mon imagination te recevant ressent de ioyes! Mais confesse aussi, chere Idée, que tu es receuë en vn lieu bien pur, & regarde avec combien d'ardeur, & de respect tu y es adorée.

Lysis' swooning for love (III. III and V. VI) also recalls a passage in *Ariane* (Livre VIII) where Mélinte faints for love, and the contrasting disastrous swoon in which the reawakened Thisbe discovers Pyramus.

Idealism and Neoplatonism are more concentrated in *Aspasie* than in *Ariane*. Lysis would appear to have been named in allusion to Plato's dialogue *Lysis*, in which a boy of that name is considered to approach the ideal in beauty. Themes of *Lysis* include love, friendship, and paternal love. Plato's Lysis is told, for instance, that his father will come to rely upon him not through age alone but 'le jour où il estimera que tu t'y entends mieux que lui, et pour ce qui est de ses propres affaires'. Something like a realization of this prediction occurs in the denouement of *Aspasie*, in which Lysis' father finally resembles the ideal father of *Lysis* by showing himself capable 'de mettre au-dessus de tout l'intérêt de son fils'.[35] But there is also a Christian symbolism in Lysis' role. His opening soliloquy ends:

Mais ie voy mon Aurore.
Le Ciel vient de s'ouvrir. Quelle douce clarté
De mon ame a soudain le nuage escarté!

Dawn is a figure of the Virgin Mary; light a figure of Christ; and both are figures of redemption through love from the *tenebrae* imaged

---

[35] Plato, *Œuvres complètes*, ed. L. Robin and M.-J. Moreau (1950), i. 329, 344.

in the parted cloud. Comic hyperbole perhaps, but serious symbolism in a Cardinal's theatre.

Aspasie must be named in allusion to the fifth-century BC Milesian courtesan Aspasia attached to (among others) the Athenian statesman Pericles.[36] Aspasia has particular associations with rhetoric and with Platonism, both of concern to the new Académie-Française and to Cardinal Richelieu. J. H. Elliott stresses the importance of eloquence not only for Richelieu but for his mighty Spanish opposite.[37] As with Ariane, the known historical (or mythological) name retains attention while the writer idealizes his fiction, embellishing history by creating an ideal heroine of the same name. In his life of Pericles, Plutarch states that Aspasia 'avait le bruit d'être hantée par plusieurs Athéniens pour apprendre d'elle l'art de rhétorique'.[38] It is to Pericles' Aspasia that Plato entrusts an important speech on the eloquence of funeral oratory in the dialogue *Menexenus*, which takes its title from a principal discussant of *Lysis*:

l'éloquence d'un beau discours qui . . . vaut aux actions accomplies le souvenir et la glorification d'œuvres excellemment réalisées. Il y a donc besoin d'un discours capable, et de louer convenablement ceux qui sont morts, et, d'autre part, de donner avec bienveillance des conseils à ceux qui vivent, en exhortant et les fils commes les frères, à imiter la vaillance de ces hommes-là.[39]

Aspasia's rhetorical doctrine corresponds *mutatis mutandis* to the first objective of the Académie-Française as set out in the 'Projet de l'Académie', revised by Desmarets and here quoted from Pellisson's summary:

Que de tout temps le païs que nous habitons avoit porté de trés-vaillans hommes, mais que leur valeur estoit demeurée sans reputation, au prix de celle des Romains, & des Grecs, parce qu'ils n'avoient pas possedé l'art de la rendre illustre par leurs escrits. Qu'aujourd'huy pourtant les Grecs, & les Romains ayant esté rendus esclaves des autres nations, & leurs langues mesme si riches & si agreables, estant contées entre les choses mortes; il se rencontroit heureusement pour la France, que non seulement nous estions

---

[36] Other allusions are possible, including an Aspasie mentioned in *Ariane* IV as 'l'vne des plus belles de Syracuse' and Artaxerxes' concubine Aspasia, the mother of Darius of Persia said to have been enamoured of her even as an old woman—a particularly incestuous form of father–son rivalry not developed in Desmarets's comedy.

[37] J. H. Elliott, *Richelieu and Olivares* (Cambridge, 1984), 30–1.

[38] Plutarch, *Les Vies des hommes illustres*, transl. J. Amyot, ed. G. Walter (1959), i. 361.

[39] Plato, *Œuvres complètes*, i. 494.

demeurez en possession de la valeur de nos ancestres; mais encore en estat de faire revivre l'Eloquence, qui sembloit estre ensevelie avec ceux qui en avoient esté les inventeurs, & les maistres.[40]

Desmarets's 'Discours de la poësie' (1633) challenges Cardinal Richelieu: 'Rends nostre siecle illustre en lettres comme en armes.' In the *lettres patentes* establishing the Académie that idea is blended with concerns just quoted from the 'Projet'. Louis XIII states that Richelieu

nous a représenté qu'une des plus glorieuses marques de la felicité d'un Estat, estoit que les Sciences & les Arts y fleurissent, & que les lettres y fussent en honneur, aussi bien que les armes, puisqu'elles sont un des principaux instrumens de la vertu. Qu'aprés avoir fait tant d'exploits memorables, nous n'avions plus qu'à adjouster les choses agreables aux necessaires, & l'ornement à l'utilité, & qu'il jugeoit que nous ne pouvions mieux commencer que par le plus noble de tous les Arts, qui est l'Eloquence.[41]

Eloquence was indeed a favourite theme of the founding Academicians. The first 'discours' formally delivered in the Académie-Française, on 5 February 1635, was 'sur l'Eloquence Françoise', given by Hay du Châtelet.[42] Although Godeau spoke on 22 February 'contre l'Eloquence', Pierre Cureau de La Chambre argued on 19 March 'que les François sont les plus capables de tous les peuples, de la perfection de l'Eloquence'; and Gomberville on 7 May 'que lorsqu'un siecle a produit un excellent Heros, il s'est trouvé des personnes pour le loüer'. Desmarets's allusion to Pericles' Aspasia may also be interpreted in terms of his own first preoccupation in the mid-1630s with *Clovis*, reluctantly abandoned to write for the stage.

In content and atmosphere, however, *Aspasie* more nearly reflects discourses 13 to 16 in the Académie-Française, beginning on 25 July 1635 with Honorat Laugier de Porchères's 'Des differences, & des conformitez qui sont entre l'Amour & l'Amitié'. Chapelain spoke on 6 August 'contre l'Amour', seeking to 'oster à cette passion la divinité que les Poëtes luy ont attribuée'.[43] He was answered on 13 August by Desmarets, 'De l'Amour des esprits', seeking to show that, 'si l'amour dont Monsieur Chapelain a parlé doit estre blasmé & mesprisé, celuy-cy est non seulement estimable, mais encore a quelque chose de divin'. Finally, in 'De l'Amour des Corps' Pierre de Boissat

---

[40] P. Pellisson, *Histoire de l'Académie-Françoise*, (1701), 21–2.
[41] Ibid. 40–1.   [42] Ibid. 100.   [43] Ibid. 103.

argued, on 2 September, 'par des raisons physiques prises des sympathies, & des antipathies, & de la conduite du monde . . . que l'Amour des Corps n'est pas moins divin que celuy des esprits'.[44] The love of Lysis and Aspasie, which certainly includes chaste sensual love, is depicted in Desmarets's comedy as divine. Links with Aspasia's doctrine of exemplary rhetoric are provided on two levels, firstly by the exemplarity of the action in *Aspasie*, in which Lysis' father is inspired to generosity by the quality of his son's love, and secondly by the allegorical tradition of spiritual combat in which virtue is associated not only with the manliness of warriors and statesmen but with any sort of ethical behaviour achieved through inner struggle. Reminiscent of *Ariane*, the sententious line with which Aspasie closes I. II of Desmarets's first comedy fits securely between the concept of literature as 'un des principaux instrumens de la vertu' expressed in the *lettres patentes* of the Académie-Française and the exemplary idealism of the theory of fiction advanced by Desmarets in the preface to *Rosane*: 'La Vertu n'a iamais vn succez malheureux.'

There may well be a Neoplatonist dimension in the shift to a garden scene for Act V. The garden described in Plato's *Phaedo* was interpreted by Pontus de Tyard as an allegory of Eden:

non simplement un jardin terrestre; mais bien un celeste & divin vergier, planté par un celeste & divin Jardinier, non point en ceste terre corruptible & fangeuse, mais en celle eternelle terre des vivans, figurée aussi par la mesme histoire souz le nom de terre de promission, vray heritage des enfans du Seigneur . . .[45]

Lysis and Aspasie are depicted as such children of the Lord. Against love, instinct, and apparent self-interest, they honour father and mother—a thing for which, along with loving another as oneself, Christ in Matt. 19 promises eternal life. Desmarets seems to have remembered the scene and its symbolism in *Clovis* X, where first

---

[44] Desmarets's discourse is lost. Bibliothèque Nationale, Mss. ancien fds. fr. 645, contains (along with a false attribution to Desmarets) what appears to be Boissat's discourse. It may be the discourse of the same title which Boissat gave earlier in the circle of Gaston d'Orléans. See Moréri, *Dictionnaire* (1759), 'Boissat'.

[45] J. C. Lapp, *The Universe of Pontus de Tyard* (Ithaca, NY, 1950), 112. Desmarets was closely involved with Pléiade poetics from the *Ballet de la vieille cour* (1635) to the parody of the Pléiade (and of Lysis) in *Les Visionnaires*. Compare 'Agréable Jardin . . . / Que tu marques bien cét heureux changement / Que fait la grace en un moment', in B. Vignier, *La Morale de la nature*, dedicated to the Duchesse de Richelieu (1676), 2.

Argilane faints and then Aurèle. The reawakening of Aurèle and Argilane is associated with baptism, marriage, redemption through suffering, constancy, love, chastity, and observance of the word of God. The action of *Aspasie* links the Christian theme of immortality through redemption to the theme of literary immortality, introduced through the allusion to Pericles' Aspasia.

Allegory of devotion to eloquence in *Aspasie* would not appear to exclude reference—often through literary allusion—to current events and policies, though these are no easier to interpret than corresponding aspects of contemporary ballets and novels. The plot is reminiscent of a somewhat similar episode in Plutarch's life of Demetrius (chs. 51–3). Antiochus, son of Seleucus, falls in love with his mother-in-law, Stratonice, who had already borne Seleucus a son, but 'étant jeune et singulièrement belle, il en fut si vivement épris et atteint, que combien qu'il essayât et fît tout ce qui lui était possible pour vaincre sa passion, si se trouvait-il toujours le plus faible'.[46] The languishing Antiochus was revived by marriage to his mother-in-law, which Seleucus decided in favour of on the basis of medical advice and the national interest, convincing Stratonice 'qu'elle devait trouver bon et honnête tout ce qui plaisait au roi, et qui était pour le bien universel du royaume et l'utilité de la chose publique'.[47] The story was well known in the seventeenth century. In her edition of Philippe Quinault's tragicomedy *Stratonice*, Elfrieda Dubois notes dramatic use of the story by Gillet de la Tessonnerie (1642), Brosse (1644), and L. Du Fayot (1657), together with the appeal it had in 1659 for Thomas Corneille and for Quinault.[48] The story challenges proprieties. Other earlier father–son rivalries before Molière's *L'Avare* and Racine's *Mithridate* are even more pertinent to *Aspasie*, especially Mairet's *Chryséide et Arimant* (1630) and Auvray's *Dorinde* (1631).

Plutarch's story is more concerned with a father's sacrifice for his son and with the annulment of a marriage for reasons of State than it is with father–son rivalry. Desmarets idealizes that aspect of the story by avoiding consummation of Aspasie's marriage to Lysis' father while giving unusual prominence to the first marriage and its annulment. Why?

---

[46] Plutarch, *Vies*, ii. 841.
[47] Ibid. 842.
[48] P. Quinault, *Stratonice*, ed. E. Dubois (Exeter, 1987).

The theme was of political interest. It was common knowledge that Henri IV's marriage to Marie de Médicis was only possible through annulment of his previous marriage to Marguerite de Valois, daughter of Henri II and Catherine de Médicis. Similarly, the marriage between Louis XII and Jeanne de France had been annulled in 1498 after twenty-two years. Henry VIII of England, whose sister Mary was Louis XII's last wife, later himself procured the annulment of his own childless marriage to a Spanish Infanta—Catherine of Aragon. None of these examples can have been encouraging to Anne of Austria, still childless in 1636 after twenty years of marriage to Louis XIII and rumoured to have inspired love in hearts as different as those belonging to the Duke of Buckingham, the Duc de Montmorency, and the Cardinal-Duc de Richelieu. Tallemant des Réaux reports that Richelieu 'vouloit la faire répudier'.[49] Tallemant also states that in 1635 Richelieu sent his brother Cardinal Alphonse de Richelieu, later Archbishop of Lyons, to Rome 'pour la poursuitte de la dissolution du mariage de M. d'Orléans'—Monsieur's unauthorized love-marriage on 31 January 1632 to Marguerite de Lorraine, a matter of fierce controversy in the royal family.

Annulment, however, is also a novelistic theme. Néron annuls Émilie's marriage to Tuberon in *Ariane* I. Not the least interesting aspect of *Aspasie* is the way in which Desmarets combines the theatrical fantasy of a love-match with the politically fraught theme of annulment. Desmarets's idealism is evident in any comparison with the divorce and love-match which conclude Monteverdi's *L'Incoronazione di Poppea*, performed in Venice in 1642.

Aspasie is thematically coherent. Lysis's apparent death and resurrection is well prepared in an earlier scene in which he faints for love (III. iii), a scene already requiring the mime of lunacy through thwarted love written into such lines as Lysis' apostrophe: 'Rages, & desespoirs à vous ie m'abandonne', and Aspasie's appeal:

> Lysis, consolez-vous; & faites pour le moins
> Que de si grands transports se passent sans tesmoins.

Indeed, it is the quality of the stagecraft as much as the misunderstood symbolism of this first play by a great French actor that has led me to give it so much attention.

---

[49] Tallemant des Réaux, *Historiettes*, i. 237.

Aspasie, Molière, and Mozart

With the possible exception of *Les Visionnaires*, I know of no single comedy from which Molière might have derived so many characteristic aspects of his stagecraft: the recurrent comic theme of false death rehearsed (as it were) and later fully exploited in *L'Avare* and *Le Malade imaginaire*, for example, and the idealized, submissive, and not universally admired lovers of the obstacle comedies, which are generally closer in dramatic structure to *Aspasie* than they are to better-known comedies by Corneille, Rotrou, and Scarron. *Aspasie* is not mentioned in La Grange's *Registre* but would seem to me unlikely not to have been in Molière's repertoire at some time before 1658. Argiléon's soliloquy (IV. I) beginning 'Que d'hommes importuns se trouuent par la ville' and his impatience on meeting Telephe contain the dramatic idea of *Les Fâcheux*. Argiléon's reaction to unwelcome news about a rival ('Contraignons-nous') anticipates Arnolphe's feigned responses to Horace's confidences in *L'École des femmes*, and Argiléon's impatience to learn from Telephe distressing news of a rival—suffering at his own interrogation—anticipates the famous 'ruban' scene of that comedy (I. V). Even Aspasie's apostrophe 'O deuoir de nature expliqué faussement', concluding 'Car suivre son desir c'est suivre la nature', anticipates the characterization of Agnès.

Telephe's unsuccessful attempt to intercede for the young lovers anticipates Cléante's role in *Tartuffe*, especially before the amplification in 1667 of I. V. The *quiproquo* by which Aspasie supposes that the marriage arranged for her is to Lysis, when it is to be with his father, Argiléon, anticipates similar scenes in *L'École des femmes*, *Tartuffe*, and *Le Malade imaginaire*. Lysis' lines to Aspasie (considered at the time unfaithful) 'Beauté de trop de vœux pour mon bien desirée' (V. V) anticipate Alceste's reproaches to Célimène in *Le Misanthrope*. Space precludes fuller consideration, which must await a separate study or the edition of *Aspasie* in preparation by Philip Tomlinson.

Aspasie was published anonymously by Jean Camusat, Libraire to the Académie-Française, with a *privilège* dated 14 February 1636. Republication in the eighteenth century indicates that it could, directly or indirectly, have inspired a curious change in the cast of W. A. Mozart's opera *Mitridate* (1770): the work is based on Racine's tragedy, but the heroine's name is nothing like that of Racine's Monime—she is called Aspasia. No historical Aspasia seems to me so close to the inspiration of the role as Desmarets's Aspasie.

7

Les Visionnaires

First performed by the Marais troupe probably just before 15 February, and in any case before 6 March 1637, Desmarets's second comedy is his most successful work. According to the *Menagiana*, Bautru told Ménage that he had given to Desmarets 'le dessein de la comédie des *Visionnaires*, à laquelle il a si bien réussi, que l'on peut dire que c'est une pièce inimitable'.[1] The plot is simple. Alcidon, a complaisant father, has promised a daughter in marriage to each of four obsessional male suitors; but he has only three daughters, each with her own obsession. These seven characters and the imprudent father are the *visionnaires*: Artabaze, the braggart Capitan, played by Bellemore (a specialist in braggart soldier roles); the 'poète extravagant' Amidor, played by Montdory; the 'amoureux en idée' Filidan; the 'riche imaginaire' Phalante, who describes in detail the new château de Richelieu; Melisse 'amoureuse d'Alexandre le Grand'; Hesperie 'qui croit que chacun l'aime'; and Sestiane, 'amoureuse de la comédie'. All are contrasted with Alcidon's relative Lysandre, a *raisonneur*. The norms of obstacle comedy, tragicomedy, and pastoral are reversed, as the multiple hasty matches must be unmade in the denouement. No marriage takes place, because each of the *visionnaires* is, as Artabaze puts it in his last speech, 'seulement amoureux de moy-mesme' (V. IX)—too self-absorbed to make a match. This denouement anticipates that of Molière's *Le Misanthrope*, where none of the rival self-absorbed obsessional characters (including the Misanthrope himself and Célimène) can agree to marry, contrasted by Molière with the *honnêteté* of Philinte and Éliante, who can.

The 'Argument' to *Les Visionnaires* makes it clear that the play presents

plusieurs sortes d'esprits Chimeriques ou Visionnaires, attaints chacun de quelque folie particuliere, mais c'est seulement de ces folies pour lesquelles on ne renferme personne; et tous les jours nous voyons parmy nous des

---

[1] *Menagiana*, in *Ana, ou Collection de bons mots*, iii. 39. A 'key' proposed by the *Segraisiana* (1721) is discussed and rejected in the STFM edition (1963), p. xxx.

esprits semblables, qui pensent pour le moins d'aussi grandes extravagances, s'ils ne les disent.

Comedy of obsessional types made artistically articulate through rhetoric at once erudite and hyperbolical invites aesthetic response on the basis of what such roles signify, and not on the basis of what they may or may not depict naturalistically.[2] For this concept of comedy Desmarets was almost certainly indebted to Charles Beys's adaptation of Lope de Vega's *Los Locos de Valencia* (or *El Hospital de los locos*), a tragicomedy first entitled *L'Hospital des fous* (1636). Indeed, his comment that *Les Visionnaires* presents 'seulement de ces folies pour lesquelles on ne renferme personne' reads like an implicit acknowledgement of a conceptual debt to Beys's comedy, an episode of which contrasts six lunatics: a philosopher, a musician, a litigant, an astrologer, a braggart soldier, and an alchemist, with passing reference to the madness of poets and lovers.

Specifically, Beys advises the reader of *L'Hospital des fous*:

Si les Fous que je mets dans cét Hospital te semblent sçavans, tu diras qu'il s'en trouve de pareils, et que j'ay voulu prendre les meilleurs. Toutes leurs images ne sont pas broüillées, ils ne sont blessez qu'en un endroit. Ils sont fous, en ce qu'ils s'estiment plus qu'ils ne sont, et dans cette opinion ils parlent d'eux, comme tu voudrois parler des choses qu'ils estiment estre.

Developed in *Les Visionnaires*, Beys's concept is pertinent to the analysis of the rhetoric of French comedy for over a century, beginning with Corneille's *Le Menteur* and the comedies of Scarron. In particular the concept that the rhetoric of comedy selectively focuses, exaggerates, and enhances ordinary discourse is fundamental.

Desmarets's braggart soldier and his poet are inspired from comic types fashionable in the mid-1630s; and the 'Argument' offers a sound guide for interpretation. The poet is used to satirize surviving admirers of Pléiade poetics, in particular their reliance on pagan mythology,

---

[2] However, Tallemant des Réaux, mentions inspiration from life for Hesperie: Mme d'Anguittard, i.e., Anne Arnould de Saint-Simon, who on 3 Apr. 1618 married Jean Poussart, Sieur d'Anguittard, younger brother of the François Poussart, Baron de Fors, Sieur du Vigean, who himself married Desmarets's cousin, and cites 'une fille qui faisoit fort le bel esprit' whom he met at Nanteuil as the inspiration of the 'Stances' (*Historiettes*, ii, 582, 807). There are also said to have been some strange people in Cardinal Richelieu's family, e.g. his brother Cardinal Alphonse de Richelieu (who sometimes thought of himself as God) and his sister, the Marquise de Maillé-Brézé, who thought she was made of glass and dared not sit down. See P. Erlanger, 'Le Roi et son ministre', in *Richelieu* (1972), 155, cited by Elliott, *Richelieu and Olivares*, 17.

a theme developed by Desmarets in *La Vérité des fables* and numerous later works. Filidan caricatures an enthusiast for such poetry who has no real understanding of it. Filidan also parodies the Lysis of *Aspasie*. This character seems mad, not systematically but (like other *visionnaires*) mainly in the misapplication of his obsession, 'estant une chose ordinaire que chacun est serieux dans sa folie'. Melisse is a female Quixote, an early 'précieuse ridicule' representing 'beaucoup de filles, qui par la lecture des Histoires et des Romans, se sont esprises de certains Heros, dont elles rebattoient les oreilles à tout le monde'. In believing that every man she meets falls in love with her, Hesperie only differs from many girls in so far as 'peut-estre elles ne disent pas si naïvement leurs sentimens'. Through Sestiane, Desmarets satirizes indiscriminate enthusiasts of theatre, newly fashionable in high society; but she is much more ridiculous in her endless outline of a complicated tragicomedy than in her echoes of critical doctrine, which are well reported.

Written as 'un honeste divertissement' and seeking 'l'estime des honestes gens', *Les Visionnaires* develops comedy through pastiche, parody, and hyperbole. The characters depict themselves very much in the same terms used for flattery in recently fashionable encomiastic verse. The *visionnaires* are brought together in a sequence of situations in which they show each other off and show each other up, as the poet's jargon frightens Artabaze, enthralls Filidan, attracts Sestiane, etc. Hesperie naturally supposes that Filidan is mad for the love of her. When Artabaze is cast as Alexander in the rehearsal of a play within the play, Melisse mistakes him for the historical Alexander. In Quintus Curtius—one of Desmarets's sources for her reply—an Artabazus is mentioned as a follower of Alexander formerly faithful to Darius (iv. 2).[3] In some other respects Artabaze continues satirical associations with Spanish warriors evident in Bellemore's earlier roles, especially the braggart Spaniard of Mareschal's *Le Railleur* and Matamore in Corneille's *L'Illusion comique*, each a *miles gloriosus* created by Bellemore and performed in the Petite Salle of the Palais-Cardinal.

In such interplay of roles the coherence of the comic idea is as striking as the virtuosity with which the sequence of situations unfolds. Two other allusions suggest a neglected allegorical dimension to *Les Visionnaires* and a tighter coherence in the internal structure

---

[3] Quintus Curtius, *L'Histoire des faicts d'Alexandre le Grand* (1614), 246.

of this comedy and with Desmarets's other plays. Hesperie suggests Hesperia, which signifies not Italy as in the *Aeneid* (Desmarets personifies Italy as Ausonie in *Europe*) but the Iberian peninsula, united under Spanish rule from 1580 to 1640, the westernmost part of continental Europe, with its vast western empire in the Americas. The *Gazette* which reports performance in the Palais-Cardinal of the Five Authors' *L'Aveugle de Smyrne* on 22 February 1637 publishes a Latin poem about the Spanish war with this line: 'Hinc scripta Hesperiae mendacia pura loquuntur'—Spanish publications contain nothing but lies.[4] Hesperie may have been understood politically at Court—a role between the pretentious Douairière de Billebahaut (Bilbao) danced by Desmarets in 1626 and the deceitful Ibère personifying Spain in *Europe*. Melisse may be named in allusion to Guillaume Colletet's *Amours de Mélisse* (1625), which also contains an Alcidon. In the 'Au lecteur' Colletet presents his book as out of fashion, 'car l'autheur . . . mesprisant de propos délibéré l'inepte composition qui est aujourd'huy en crédit, tient le party des Anciens et fait profession de Poésie'.[5]

Colletet may be important not only in what Desmarets rejects in sixteenth-century poetics but for the high claims he continues—against the Malherbian current—to make for the mission of the poet in society. In particular, Filidan and Lysis of *Aspasie* are likely to have been characterized in relation to Colletet's interpretation of Maurice Scève's *Delie objet de plus haute vertu* (Lyons, 1544). 'Délie' is taken by Colletet as an anagram of 'l'Idée', expressing 'sous ce nom feint . . . l'idée véritable de la vertu dont il était amoureux'. Much in Desmarets's literary theory in this period seems close to Scève's *dizain* beginning:

> Le Naturant par ses hautes idées
> Rendit de soy la nature admirable
> Par les Vertus de sa Vertu guidées
> S'esvertua en œuvre esmerveillable.[6]

Like Don Quixote and a number of Molière's comic enthusiasts, however, the *visionnaires* are depicted with appreciation of the charm

---

[4] *Gazette* no. 27 (1637), 122. Compare Horace, *Odes*, i. 36.

[5] G. Colletet, quoted by Adam, *Histoire de la littérature française au XVIIe siècle*, i. 342.

[6] M. Scève, quoted in G. Colletet, *Vie de Maurice Scève*, ed. A. S. Armani (Fasano, 1988), 56–7.

such folly may have for its victims. Filidan's ideal (a travesty of
Petrarchan love imagery) may be ridiculous, and his swoon at the
end of I. V, may parody the collapse of Lysis and other lovers, but
he is an idealist as well as a fool. Such lines as

> J'adore en mon esprit ceste beauté divine
> Qui sans doute du ciel tire son origine (I. IV),

and

> O Dieux! qu'une beauté parfaictement descrite
> De desirs amoureux en nos ames excite!
> Et que la Poësie a des charmes puissans
> Pour gagner nos esprits et captiver nos sens! (I. V),

are not ridiculous in themselves but only in the context of Filidan's
particular delusion. Otherwise they express the Neoplatonic exemplary
idealism evident in Desmarets's writings from *Ariane* to *Les Délices
de l'esprit*. Such lines not only parody Lysis but may help in any
interpretation of the allegory of *Aspasie*. It is not difficult to identify
in *Les Visionnaires* the four forms of ecstasy associated by Platonism
with the lunatic, the lover, the poet, and the mystic. Although not
certifiable, and tending merely to express the sorts of things that
others think without saying them outright, all the *visionnaires* must
qualify as lunatics. Filidan, Melisse, and possibly Hesperie qualify
as lovers. Nor is Amidor the only poet. Other characters create their
own worlds in words. Artabaze, Filidan, Phalante, Hesperie, and
Sestiane all may to a certain extent qualify as poets, even if—unlike
Amidor—they do not write down the figments of their visionary
imaginations. Amidor's poetic 'fureur' or fury

> Prophane, esloigne toy, j'entre dans ma fureur.
> Jach Iach Evoé (I. II)

associates the poet also with the mystic frenzy of bacchanals.

I do not know whether in February 1623 Desmarets had danced
Le Grand Balet des Bachanales with 'Princes & Grands . . . en
Cour'.[7] Bacchanals were, however, a theme of the new château de
Richelieu in Poitou described by Phalante in this comedy. The first
important commission from a French patron for work by Nicolas

---

[7] *Mercure françois* (1623), ix. 427. Some of the verse is by Malleville. Not
entirely by coincidence, a folio edition of Ronsard's collected works appeared in 1623.

Poussin (1594–1665) was the *Bacchanals*, painted in 1635–6 for that château: the *Triumph of Pan*, now owned by the Morrison Trustees, and the *Triumph of Bachhus*, now in Kansas City.[8] Phalante's description of the château de Richelieu (III. v) does not refer to those pictures. But his lines pay much attention to sculpture, particularly to representations of the pagan gods associated with the fountains of Richelieu. Estienne Binet, in his *Essay des merveilles de nature, et des plus nobles artifices* (Rouen, 1627), provides the link in his chapter on 'La Sculpture': 'L'ame des Poëtes, et les mains des Ouvriers sont ravies d'enthousiasme pour représenter les choses divines.'[9] In *Les Visionnaires* Desmarets is playing with serious symbolism. His *Ballet de la Félicité* contains, in the bacchanals *entrée* 16, a 'Chanson à boire' by Hay du Chastelet in which the Dauphin is symbolically linked to Bacchus and to Christ, syncretistically linked:

> Beuuons à ce mignon, il est du sang des Dieux . . .
> Que le goust est diuin du breuuage vermeil . . .
> Sa source vient des Cieux . . .[10]

Other allusions—and references in an early version of the comedy to *Aspasie*, to Corneille's *Le Cid*, and to Georges de Scudéry's *L'Amant libéral* not retained by Desmarets—are discussed in the STFM edition.

Finally, the *visionnaires* are all happy in their various delusions. In Livre IX of *Ariane* Desmarets had observed:

Il n'a y que les insensez qui puissent estre heureux par fantaisie; pource que leur iugement n'agissant point, & ne pouvant discerner le faux d'avec le vray, ils reçoivent & ressentent leur biens imaginaires comme veritables.

In this reflection Desmarets anticipates Pascal's famous amplification of the topos on the tyranny of the imagination: 'Les habiles par imagination se plaisent tout autrement à eux-mêmes que les prudents ne se peuvent raisonnablement plaire.'[11]

---

[8] See *Poussin: Sacraments and Bacchanals*, a catalogue compiled by H. Macandrew and H. Brigstocke (Edinburgh, 1981), reviewed by A. Blunt in *French Studies*, 36 (1982), 327–9.

[9] Binet, *Essay*, 373. Binet's immediate reference is to a sculptural representation of a metamorphosis, 'Callistrate en la Bacchante'.

[10] *Gazette* no. 30, 12 Mar. 1639.

[11] Pascal, *Pensées*, ed. L. Lafuma (1960), no. 81. The passage also brings to mind the opening of Descartes's *Discours de la méthode* (Leiden, 1637): 'Le bon sens est

That is the nature of the *visionnaire*, defined in P. C. Richelet's *Dictionnaire français* (1680) as 'Qui a de fausses ou de folles visions, qui a des imaginations extravagantes', and described by Nicolas de Malebranche (1638–1715) as 'un homme dont l'attention détermine . . . le cours des esprits, mais elle n'en peut mesurer la force, ou retenir le mouvement. Ainsi le visionnaire pense à ce qu'il veut: mais il ne voit rien tel qu'il est.'[12]

Contrary to the assertion of various lexicographers, 'visionnaire' is not a neologism in Desmarets's comedy. Henriette Lucius dates first use of the term from a work by the Genevan theologian Antoine de la Faye:

Le Traditionneur [Constantin] amena puis apres une autre vision, recitée par Crille Hierosolymitain. A ce conte sa Theologie ne sera pas seulement imaginaire, mais aussi visionnaire.[13]

By a strange coincidence, the great Dutch Tulip Mania of 1634–7 collapsed in February 1637. It had taken the price of a single Semper Augustus bulb to 5,500 guilders—roughly equivalent 350 years later to something over £25,000, more than four times the 1,200 guilders for which Rembrandt was commissioned in 1638 to paint the *Night Watch*.[14]

Les Visionnaires was published in quarto by Camusat with a *privilège* for seven years dated 20 July 1637. It had a considerable success in France. There were four editions between 1637 and 1640, seven more between 1647 and 1676, eight editions between 1705 and 1750, and a separate edition in 1800. It was also translated into Dutch (Amsterdam, 1658) and into Italian (Venice, 1737). Little is known of its early acting-history apart from Bellemore's creation of Artabaze and Tallemant des Réaux' comment that 'le personnage du poëte, *des Visionnaires*, a bien fait voir ce que c'estoit que Mondory; personne n'en a approché'.[15] It was probably revived at

la chose du monde la mieux partagée'. 'Bon sens' is promptly identified as 'la puissance de bien juger, et distinguer le vrai d'avec le faux'.

[12] N. de Malebranche, *Traité de morale* (Amsterdam, 1684), i. 211.

[13] A. de la Faye, *Replique chrestienne* (Geneva, 1604), 110, quoted by H. Lucius, *La Littérature 'visionnaire' en France du début du XVIe siècle au début du XIXe siècle* (Bienne, 1970), 118. In the Quarrel of the *Imaginaires* Nicole returns the terms *imaginaire* and *visionnaire* from Desmarets's more general application to something nearer their original range of reference in theological debate.

[14] P. M. Garber, 'Speculation Flowers', *The Wall Street Journal Europe*, 8 Jan. 1988.

[15] Tallemant des Réaux, *Historiettes*, ii. 775.

the Hôtel de Bourgogne around 1646-7: it is mentioned in the *Mémoire de Mahelot*, and the *Ballet de la Boutade des comédiens* (also dated to or near that season) contains an *entrée* featuring Amidor and Artabaze. La Grange's *Registre* shows that Molière's troupe performed *Les Visionnaires* twenty-one times between 1659 and 1666. It had sixteen performances at the Théâtre Guénégaud from 1677 to 1679, followed at the Comédie-Française by twenty-nine performances between 1680 and 1695, three in 1710, and two in 1716. Reprints in the repertories suggest performances on other stages until around 1750, but none is documented to my knowledge until the France Culture telecast by the Comédie-Française on 1 January 1984.[16]

Molière's inspiration from *Les Visionnaires*, in works ranging from *Les Précieuses ridicules* and *Sganarelle, ou le Cocu imaginaire* to *Le Malade imaginaire*, is discussed in the STFM edition, with particular reference to *L'École des femmes*, *Le Misanthrope*, and *Les Femmes savantes*. Mention is also made of appreciation of the comedy by Mme de Sévigné and by Bussy-Rabutin, who found Bélise in *Les Femmes savantes* 'une foible copie d'une des femmes de la comédie des *Visionnaires*', together with the Abbé d'Aubignac's critical incomprehension of the dramatic structure of the play, succinctly expressed in *La Pratique du théâtre* (1657). Various details, especially in the role of the Comtesse de Pimbêche, suggest reminiscences of *Les Visionnaires* in Racine's comedy *Les Plaideurs* (1668). More recently I have argued that Alexis Piron's comedy *La Métromanie* (1738), one of the most successful new comedies produced in eighteenth-century France, includes substantial adaptation from *Les Visionnaires*.[17] In *Filosofia nova*, Henri Beyle, known as Stendhal (1783-1842), cites *Les Visionnaires* as an example of comedy no longer pertinent as satire.[18] He seems nearer to Desmarets when remarking somewhere in *Le Vie de Henri Brulard*: 'toute ma vie j'ai vu mon idée et non la réalité'.

---

[16] Production by G. Gravier with G. Descrières (Phalante), Y. Gaudeau (Sestiane), B. Dhéran (Amidor), P. Noëlle (Hesperie), S. Eine (Filidan), A. Pralon (Artabaze), C. Murillo (Melisse), L. Arbessier (Alcidon), and G. Michel (Lysandre).

[17] H. G. Hall, 'From Extravagant Poet to the Writer as Hero', *Studies on Voltaire and the Eighteenth Century*, 183 (1980), 117-32.

[18] Stendhal, *Pensées. Filosofia nova* (1931), ii. 263-4 (7 fructidor XII = 4 Aug. 1804): 'toute comédie étant un plaidoyer contre une mauvaise manière d'agir, elle cesse d'avoir de l'intérêt pour nous dès que nous sommes d'accord que la manière d'agir est mauvaise: Ex. *les Visionnaires* de Desmarets.'

8

The Historical Tragicomedies

Prompted perhaps by Corneille's success with *Le Cid*, Desmarets abandoned comedy for tragicomedy. Corneille and Scudéry had been offended by what Sestiane said about *Le Cid* and (apparently) *L'Amant libéral* in a first version of *Les Visionnaires*, although—as Desmarets is reported to have explained to Chapelain 'en riant' on or before 15 February 1637—the offence was caused by 'ce qu'il avoit mis dans la bouche d'une folle, comme le sens d'une folle, et non pas comme le sien'.[1] Desmarets was elected on 16 June, with Chapelain and the Abbé de Bourzeis, by the Académie-Française to the committee of three entrusted with general appreciation of *Le Cid*. Then on 30 June he was charged with editing the observations of the separate committee—comprising Cérisy, Gombauld, Baro, and Lestoile—elected to consider its versification.[2] Not surprisingly, in view of the success of *Le Cid*, Desmarets turned to tragicomedy and to an episode in the career of another virtuous conqueror of Spain, Scipio Africanus (235–183 BC). It is a tragicomedy, he explains 'Aux Lecteurs', because 'les principaux personnages sont Princes, et les accidens graues et funestes, mais . . . la fin est heureuse, encore qu'il n'y ait rien de Comique qui y soit meslé'.

From his first battle to rescue his father from the Carthaginian army descending on Rome from the north, the adolescent Scipio was perceived as a *dux fatalis*. The situation of the Romans, encircled by the Carthaginians and with Hannibal marching from the north to the walls of Rome, is roughly comparable in the mid-1630s to that of France, encircled by Spanish forces, one section of which

---

[1] Chapelain wrote on 15 Feb. 1637 to Mlle Paulet (daughter of the revenue farmer Charles Paulet) that Desmarets 'se garderoit bien, en cette matiere de préférence du *Cid* à l'*Aspasie*, de donner un arrest contre soy mesme' and that the offending passage 'seroit biffé et annullé et qu'il n'en seroit jamais fait mention sur le theatre ni dans l'imprimerie', Chapelain, *Lettres*, i. 137–8.

[2] Pellisson, *Histoire de l'Académie-Françoise* (1701 edn.), 123–4. In the event it was Chapelain who prepared the final draft of the *Sentiments de l'Académie Françoise sur la tragi-comédie du Cid*. Unlike the Academicians at this time, Corneille was in receipt of a gratification from Richelieu, who also ennobled his father.

advanced in 1636 from what is now Belgium to Corbie, dangerously near Paris. In the Roman emergency the young Scipio rallied a routed army, saved Rome, and went on to deliver his country from further threat by carrying the war to Spain and seizing Carthago Nova (now Cartagena)—key to Carthaginian domination in Iberia and to communications between Carthage and Hannibal's army in Italy.

Scipion

Scipion, the first of Desmarets's two historical tragicomedies dedicated to Cardinal Richelieu, shares with *Ariane* and *Le Cid* a conquering hero of noble origins and royal aspirations: 'le cœur magnanime . . . excellent en toutes vertus . . . d'une singuliere beauté & belle proportion de tout le corps, la face joyeuse', as Scipio is described in a life often appended to Plutarch's *Les Vies des Hommes illustres*.[3] For in that source Scipio bears himself with 'maiesté souueraine', exemplifying at home and abroad the civil and military virtues. *Scipion* also shares with *Le Cid* the specific themes of self-mastery and of marriage for reasons of State. These are well summarized by Urbain Chevreau, at least seven and probably all eight of whose published plays were (like Desmarets's) inspired by Richelieu's patronage and first performed between 1636 and 1642, notably *La Suite et le mariage du Cid* (1638):

Tous les Historiens ont vanté la continence de Scipion; et la voici. Aprés avoir soûmis Carthagene, parmi les ôtages qui étoient enfermez dans cette ville de l'Espagne Tarraconnoise, il se trouva une fille parfaitement belle [Olinde in the play]. Quand il sçut qu'elle étoit de naissance illustre, et fiancée à un grand Seigneur de Portugal [the Celtiberian prince Allucius in Livy, Lucidan in the play], il le fit venir avec les parens de cette Dame; et sans avoir eu la pensée de la toucher, il la rendit aux uns et aux autres. Il luy donna même pour sa dot, la somme qu'on luy avoit apportée pour sa rançon; et l'augmenta d'une autre somme fort considerable. Cela est beau pour un General de vingt-quatre ou vingt-cinq ans, qui étoit bien fait; et qui, sans recourir à la violence, ou au droit de guerre, renvoya fort honnêtement sa prisonniere dans le même état qu'il l'avoit trouvée.[4]

---

[3] Plutarch, *Les Vies des Hommes illustres grecs et romains translatées par Jacques Amyot* (2 vols.; 1606), ii. 698.

[4] *Chaevræana* (1697–1700), i. 7. Compare B. Vignier's quatrain on the bust of Scipio at the château de Richelieu in *Le Chasteau de Richelieu ou l'Histoire des Dieux et des Héros de l'antiquité avec des Réflexions morales*, dedicated to the Duc de Richelieu (Saumur, 1676), 17:

Desmarets probably takes the story (to which he adds a contrasting sub-plot of faithless love and treachery) not only from the life of Scipio appended to Plutarch but also (as Lancaster suggests)[5] from Livy's history of Rome, Bk. xxvi of which illustrates Scipio's astute leadership in siege warfare (doubtless of special interest to a Surintendant des fortifications), self-mastery during the capture of Carthago Nova, and diplomatic use of magnanimity in furthering—in the interests of Rome and against his own amorous inclinations—the marriage of his fair captive to a Celtiberian prince. Desmarets may also have known Petrarch's life of Scipio and/or the interpretative tradition which it represents.[6] He must also have known Cicero's *Dream of Scipio*, which follows the hero's soul into a future life.

Scipion has a sub-plot in which the Numidian Garamante, still loved by Hyanisbe, whom he had abandoned in the 'Îles fortunées' and who pursues him in male attire like the Epicharis of *Ariane*—or the Rosaura of Calderón's *La Vida es sueño* (1636)—contests Olinde's betrothal to Lucidan. Indeed, he betrays the city to the Romans between Acts I and II in the hope of taking Olinde as his reward, which he very nearly succeeds in doing: novelistic themes which may be more than simply novelistic. From his practical experience of French fortifications, Desmarets is likely to have been suspicious of Livy's account of Scipio's surprise capture of Carthago Nova following a lagoon-crossing at a low tide. Such a tide would have been an event (if indeed there was such an event) not only unnecessary in terms of the local topography as assessed by a more recent historian but visible from the city and quite unpredictable by the Romans.[7] The sub-plot also provides scope for dramatic

Le plaisir de la gloire est un plaisir bien doux,
Plusieurs l'ont merité par leur valeur extrême;
Mais peu goûtent celuy de se vaincre soy-même,
Quoy qu'il soit le plus grand de tous.

[5] Lancaster, *A History of French Dramatic Literature in the Seventeenth Century*, ii. 218.

[6] See F. Petrarch, *La Vita di Scipione l'Africano*, ed. G. Martellotti (Milan and Naples, 1964). Petrarch highlights particularly well the implications of Scipio's *coup d'essai*, the rescue of his father at Ticino: 'Scipio id etatis servati ducis et civis et patris, publice scilicet ac private pietatis, triplicem meruit coronam, iam dum clarum magni futuri ducis initium' (p. 35), and the political reward for his magnanimity in dealing with the captive princess at Carthago Nova (p. 39).

[7] R. Vera Tornell, *Un Enigma histórico: la tome de Cartagena por Escipión* (Alicante, 1953) discusses with reference to local topographical conditions various implausibilities in Livy's account, suggesting (though not claiming to demonstrate)

contrasts in attitudes towards love as Olinde resists Garamante's attempt to abduct her: (III.I)

> Detestable fureur de feux illegitimes!
> Va, ne me pretens pas pour le prix de tes crimes.
> Considere, insensé, l'honneur que tu me fais,
> D'espérer mon amour à force de forfaits.
> A la seule vertu la vertu s'abandonne.

It also provides opportunities for Desmarets to embellish an historical account through inventive retelling, as he does in *Roxane*, *Rosane* and *La Vérité des fables*.

Scipion's self-mastery is not automatic. Smitten by Olinde's great beauty in IV. VII, he almost swoons:

> Helas! quel nouueau mal est celuy que ie sens,
> Qui surprend ma raison, & qui trouble mes sens?
> Ie rougis, je paslis; je brusle, & je frissonne;
> Mon courage s'esteint, la force m'abandonne.

A rich baroque amplification of the *amore captivae victor captus* topos which *Scipion* shares with *Roxane* follows scenes of agonizing bewilderment and indecision until—alone in IV. IX—Scipion apostrophizes Olinde's eyes:

> Ô! Regards penetrans, Ô! triomphantes larmes,
> Captiue, qui domptez nos glorieuses armes,
> Beaux astres, mais plustost deux miracles nouueaux,
> Qui respandez ensemble & des feux & des eaux.

Recovering himself, Scipion apostrophizes Roman duty:

> Dur frein de mes desirs, vertu triste & farouche,
> Que sans le bien public nul interest ne touche . . .

He debates the contrasting calls of love and virtue and (mistaking the situation) supposes that by giving Olinde to Garamante (who claimed her as a prize) he would make virtue victorious.

---

that elements of the garrison may well have opened a gate to the Romans and that Scipio had an obvious interest in suppressing any mention of such treason. It is not clear to what extent Tornell allows for the possibility that, following deforestation in ancient and modern times, silt levels were lower than now around the then new city, founded in 223 BC.

In V. II, however, a now jealous Scipion threatens to execute Lucidan or take him captive to Rome for a triumph unless Olinde accepts his love (the blackmail through a threatened hostage topos used by Shakespeare in *Measure for Measure*, by Corneille in *Pertharite*, and by Racine in *Andromaque*): 'Donnez-moy vostre amour, je luy donne la vie.' Olinde refuses, advising:

> Fay, sans me regarder, ce que veut la vertu.
> Comme de mon honneur, il y va de ta gloire.
> A ne me vaincre pas mets toute ta victoire.

When Scipion asks ambivalently: 'Donques dans Cartagene il reste à vaincre vn cœur?', Olinde replies: 'A se vaincre soy-mesme est le plus grand honneur.' Compare Shakespeare's Marina. Touched by the virtue of this redemptive woman, Scipion at last declares:

> Ie me rends à moy-mesme, en me rendant à vous;
> Et je vous rends encor ce bien-heureux espoux.
> Mesme je veux qu'il m'ayme; & l'ombre de mon Pere,
> Veut bien qu'à vos vertus j'immole ma colere.

Such triumphs over vengeance and passion attract Olinde's benediction, which is political as well as personal: 'Loin s'estende par vous l'Empire des Romains.' Garamante's return, and Scipion's pledge, delay the union of Olinde and Lucidan until Garamante is first claimed and then rejected as unworthy by Hyanisbe. Scipion can at last unite the lovers, while (like the chaste Amazons in *Clovis*) Hyanisbe now prefers celibacy to marriage—a socially significant aspect of the denouement. In 1639 François de Grenailles began to publish *L'Honneste Fille*, expressing a new social aspiration for women who wished to be neither wives nor nuns.

Scipion was performed before 18 May 1638, when Chapelain wrote to Jean-Jacques Bouchard (1606–41):

Une place d'Académicien en France n'est pas un bénéfice, et son Eminence est assiégé de tant d'affaires qui attendent depuis si longtemps, que jusqu'ici nous n'avons vu aucun de nostre troupe gratifié de pareil bienfait, si vous exceptés M. de Bois-Robert . . . Il n'y a de nouvelle comédie que le *Scipion* de Desmarests.[8]

Léopold Lacour concludes that it was the first performance of *Scipion* that Chapelain had tried unsuccessfully to see at the Marais theatre on

---

[8] Chapelain, *Lettres*, i. 236.

13 February, dating, on the same assumptions, another performance to 24 April.[9] Or, if we believe Émile Magne, Chapelain might have heard an earlier reading of the play at the Hôtel de Rambouillet.[10] Both seem to reckon without the Palais-Cardinal theatre.

Of the Marais theatre around this time Georges Forestier asserts: 'il n'est pas question d'imaginer des "balcons" '.[11] Contrast *Scipion* I. III, which opens with Garamante before Olinde's door and contains the rubrics 'OLINDE PARLANT DV BALCON' and 'OLINDE DEHORS'; the contrasting scene IV. II, with Lucidan instead of Garamante, mentions 'OLINDE DV BALCON' and then, after the lover's complaint:

> Mais soudain ce bel astre, autrefois secourable,
> Refuse ses rayons à mon sort miserable,

'OLINDE SORTANT'.[12] If Forestier is correct in what he writes about the Marais theatre, these scenes, evidently written for a set with a balcony, must indicate that such a set was available as a special feature of the Petite Salle of the Palais-Cardinal. As a frequent feature of Spanish Golden Age theatre, the balcony may even have been intended to rival facilities in Olivares' Madrid and to add a touch of Spanish local colour, like the role of Hyanisbe disguised as a *mujer varonil* and Garamante's treachery with the scarf presented by Olinde to Lucidan on his departure for battle (II. I).[13] Note that *Roxane* V. V also almost certainly requires a balcony (or at least an upper window), when officers seek the heroine's assistance in rescuing Alexandre from his remorse, i.e. before she enters through a practicable door in V. VI.

Perhaps Olinde's balcony overlooks the urban square in which the action of Act I takes place, where the Roman herald makes his proclamation (II. V), and Scipion evokes 'Ce superbe arcenal, de

---

[9] Lacour, *Richelieu dramaturge*, 75-7.

[10] Magne, *Voiture*, ii. 118.

[11] G. Forestier, review of Daniel Guérin de Bouscal, *Le Gouvernement de Sanche Pansa*, ed. C. E. J. Caldicott (Geneva, 1981), *Papers on French Seventeenth Century Literature*, 9 (16) (1982), 383-5. Forestier is the author of *Le Théâtre dans le théâtre sur la scène française du XVIIe siècle* (Geneva, 1981).

[12] *Scipion* (1639), 4to edn., 38, 40, 54.

[13] For instance, Don Juan takes Mota's cape to deceive Doña Ana in Tirso de Molina's *El Burlador de Sevilla* (II. X); in Lope de Vega's *El Caballero de Olmedo* (II) the unwelcome lover Rodrigo steals the ribbon Doña Ana had intended for Alsonso and presents himself to her wearing it.

tant d'armes fourny' (II. VI). The temple with a practicable door required in II. VII ('Orcade sortant du Temple, soldats romains, Olinde
aussi sortant du Temple') may have been discovered; but it could also
have formed part of one unified set, used also for Scipion's deliberations
in Acts IV and V. The evidence of the text is not conclusive.

Desmarets's dedication to Cardinal Richelieu of this 'suiet plein de
vertu, estant asseuré que vous seriez pour le moins charmé par la
matiere de l'ouurage' invites a comparison readily confirmed externally
by the plates for prints depicting such a parallel, ordered by the
Cardinal in 1631 when he was created Duc de Richelieu,[14] and by
Puget de la Serre's great two-volume folio *Portrait de Scipion l'Africain
ou l'image de la gloire et de la vertu représentée dans celle de
Monseigneur le Cardinal-Duc de Richelieu* (Bordeaux, 1641). Intended
parallels are unlikely to involve personal qualities only; they will also
involve achievements and policies such as the successful siege of La
Rochelle, where the clemency of the 'Articles accordés' by the King
on 28 October 1628 are no less striking than those written up by
Desmarets for the surrender of the château de Caen in 1620: 'pour
apprécier sa modération dans le triomphe, il faut lire les "articles
accordés par le roi" à cette cité qu'il trouva pleine de mourants. Libre
exercice du culte, rétablissement de chacun en tous ses biens, amnistie
générale'.[15] Since sieges were the standard form of warfare in the
seventeenth century, these lines of Aspar's (II. V) must have had
special significance for a contemporary public:

> De toutes les horreurs de Mars impitoyable
> La prise d'une ville est la plus effroyable.

According to Livy, Scipio allowed his troops to pillage Carthago
Nova until the citadel surrendered. By way of contrast, Scipion's
immediate concern in the play is to control his troops, as well as
the conquered city, idealizing the historical hero and through him
allegorically idealizing the hero to whom the play is dedicated.

There is a further parallel in Richelieu's bids to relieve military
pressure on Paris by striking directly at Spain, as in the French strike
that had recently been made at Fuenterrabia and the successful efforts
to dismember the Spanish dominion in Iberia—splitting off Portugal

---

[14] Lacour, *Richelieu dramaturge*, 77.
[15] See E. Lavisse and A. Rambaud, *Histoire générale du IVe siècle à nos jours*, v
(1893–1901), 341.

(and Roussillon) and nearly spinning off Catalonia. Other implicit parallels are more difficult to illustrate succinctly. Note, however, that Scipio cultivated parallels between himself and Alexander, victor of a famous siege at Tyre and reported in Plutarch's life (xxxviii) to have considered—after the capture of Darius' wife and daughters—that it was 'chose plus royale, se vaincre soi-même, que surmonter ses ennemis' and not to have touched any of them, or any other woman 'excepté Barsine' without a form of marriage.[16] Alexander would be Desmarets's next parallel with Richelieu.

Writing to Balzac on 7 May 1639 Chapelain reports:

Le *Scipion* de Mr Desmarests a eu le succès à Paris qu'en vos quartiers, c'est-à-dire médiocre et bien au dessous du *Cid*. Cependant comme il faut avouer que le point de tendresse luy manque et que partout où ce point joue dans le *Cid*, l'avantage est tout entier de son costé, il faut aussy tomber d'accord que, dans les autres parties, le *Scipion* a tous les avantages, soit pour la bienséance, soit pour la beauté des vers et des sentimens.[17]

Chapelain dislikes Hyanisbe, however, since she acts for herself and not through one of her knights or her army. In *La Pratique du théâtre* François d'Aubignac criticizes the lack of verisimilitude of Hyanisbe's long recognition scene.[18] Compare Shakespeare's *Pericles*, V. i.

'Achevé d'imprimer' in quarto on 18 March 1639 by Henri Le Gras, with a title-page engraved by Abraham Bosse after Claude Vignon, *Scipion* is the first book published under Desmarets's general *privilège* of 14 March 1639. Its publishing history confirms Chapelain's assessment of its reception. Details of Dutch translations (1651 and 1657) are given in the *Corpus maresianum*, but I know of only one further edition in French (1644). However, the *Scipion* which Dr Janet Clarke informs me was briefly in the repertoire of the Théâtre Guénégaud (1673–80) was probably Desmarets's.

Scholars have noticed aspects of *Scipion* echoed in later plays, beginning with Corneille's *Horace* and *Cinna*. Nicolas Pradon's tragedy *Scipion l'Africain* (1697) is not an adaptation of Desmarets's tragicomedy. The action is transferred to Scipio's camp near Zama,

---

[16] S. de Priézac, *Le Chemin de la gloire* (1660), recalls that Scipio also 'forma son courage sur le model du Cyrus de Xenophon' (p. 3)—another link between Scipio and models of French kingship.

[17] Chapelain, *Lettres*, i. 420–1.

[18] F. d'Aubignac, *La Pratique du théâtre* (1657), 303. Chapelain and d'Aubignac are quoted at length by Lancaster, ii. 218.

the time is nearer the fall of Carthage, and the cast includes Hannibal himself. But Pradon cannot conceal a debt to Desmarets. Scipion is in love with Ispérie, loved by and betrothed to the Celtiberian Prince Lucéjus, whom she loves. Scipion's struggle for self-mastery following Lucéjus' unsuccessful bid to rescue Ispérie is more reminiscent of Desmarets's *Scipion* than of any strictly historical source.

Roxane

Desmarets's second tragicomedy, *Roxane*, was first performed on an unknown date in 1639. It is sometimes confused with his second novel, *Rosane*, published the same year.[19] Chapelain informs Guez de Balzac on 28 October 1640: '*Roxane* est une tragicomédie de Mr Desmarests qui fut repŕesentée l'année passée, avec assés d'applaudissement et qui est imprimée depuis trois mois'.[20] It appeared between 12 June 1640, when the *privilège* was transferred to Henri Le Gras, and 4 July, when Chapelain wrote to Conrart: 'M. Desmarests est un de ceux à qui il a esté bien fascheux de ne pas vous présenter sa *Roxane* entre les premiers depuis qu'elle a receu la lumiere de l'impression.'[21] Chapelain informs Balzac on 8 July that d'Aubignac's candidacy for the Académie-Française had been rejected 'à cause d'un libelle qu'il avoit fait contre la *Roxane* de Mr Desmarests qui avoit charmé les puissances'—a judgement reaffirmed to Balzac on 29 July:

L'une des plus fortes ambitions [de d'Aubignac] a esté d'entrer dans l'Académie et il y avoit grande apparence qu'il eust esté le premier receu, s'il n'eust point fait un libelle contre la *Roxane* de Mr Desmarests où il blasmoit le goust de son Em[inen]ce et de Me d'Aiguillon qui l'avoient estimée.[22]

Per contra, on or about 1 September Vincent Voiture praises *Roxane* extravagantly in a letter to Léon Bouthillier, Comte de Chavigny: 'Nihil meherculè usquàm elegantius, nihil ornatiùs, nihil sublimiùs, dignum denique Alexandro, et Armando.'[23] But there are doubts about Voiture's sincerity. In a further letter to Balzac,

---

[19] For instance, by Balzac in correspondence with Chapelain in 1640; by the Bibliothèque Nationale Catalogue, which dates the novel 1659 and lists a 'n.p., n.d.' 12mo edn. of the play as 8vo 1639; by A. Blum, *L'Œuvre gravé d'Abraham Bosse* (1924), which notes Bosse's engraved title-page for *Rosane* while overlooking his vignette for the title-pages of the 4to and 12mo *Roxane* (1640).

[20] Chapelain, *Lettres*, i. 712.   [21] Ibid., 656.

[22] Ibid., 659, 664.   [23] V. Voiture, *Œuvres*, 7th edn. (1665), 405.

Chapelain expresses surprise that Balzac still has not realized that *Roxane* is by Desmarets, suggests that he may be pretending not to know in order to enhance his praise, and states that, in the belief that the letter to Chavigny would be shown to Richelieu, Voiture 'y a mis cet éloge contre son sentiment, et cela je le sçay de sa propre bouche'—adding ironically, 'après quoy on se pourra fier aux louanges de telles gens'.[24] Balzac denies any such intention. On 6 November, Achille de Harlay de Sancy, then Bishop of Lavaur, later ambassador to Constantinople and Bishop of Saint-Malo, lists *Roxane* and Du Ryer's *Alcionnée* among 'pièces nouvelles des poëtes académiques', confirming that they were 'grandement approuvées par S[on] Em[inence]' but not altogether to his own taste.[25] La Mesnardière calls Alexandre a 'muguet'—a sighing lover, as Scipion too becomes in the last act of *Scipion*.[26] Like Scudéry in his *Eudoxe* (1639), Desmarets introduces and develops a romantic love story within the historical plot of these tragicomedies—a dramatic formula fully exploited in the tragedies of Racine, as Adam remarks without showing the importance of redemptive heroines for the idealization of Desmarets's heroes.[27]

Like the 'amoureuse d'Alexandre' in *Les Visionnaires* (II. I), Desmarets might have stated:

> Un tome de Plutarque
> M'a fourny le portraict de ce divin monarque.

An emblem published in Amyot's translation of Plutarch's *Lives* (1606) shows Alexander with this caption:

> Ta vertu, qui remplit toute la terre ronde,
> O Grand entre les grands, te surhausse invaincu:
> Tu serois le Tres grand si tu eusses vaincu
> Ton cœur: car qui le vainc est le plus grand du monde.[28]

Desmarets embellishes the portrait by allowing Alexander to master his passions in a play based on the marriage of Alexander to Roxana, Cohortanus' submission, Phradates' treacherous ambition, and the

---

[24] Chapelain, *Lettres*, i. 698.

[25] Richelieu, *Lettres, instructions diplomatiques* . . . , vi (1638–42), ed. G. d'Avenel (1857), 727.

[26] La Mesnardière, quoted by Adam, *Histoire de la littérature française au XVIIᵉ siècle*, i (1956), 552.

[27] Adam, *Histoire de la littérature française au XVIIᵉ siècle*, i. 552.

[28] Plutarch, *Les Vies* ii. 96.

murder (or execution) of Clitus, successor to Artabazus' position in Alexander's camp and Court. Lancaster is correct in stating that Desmarets could have found the subject of this play in Quintus Curtius' *Alexander*, Bks. vi, viii, and x, and that Clitus' fidelity to Alexander, his protest at receiving a difficult land to subdue, and his criticism of Alexander are historical.[29] But it is misleading to add that Clitus' objection to Alexander's marriage with Roxana, 'though in keeping with his character, is fictitious, for he died before Alexander met Roxana'. Quintus Curtius' chronology may be correct; but Plutarch narrates the events in the order in which they are dramatized by Desmarets, relating the marriage in paragraph 81 and the killing of Clitus in paragraphs 86-8. The tragicomedy highlights Clitus' objections to Alexander's marriage to Roxana, symbolic of the fusion of Greek and Persian civilisation. To Clitus it meant the 'barbarization' of Alexander's camp. For an audience concerned with relations between the Estates, between the provinces, and between Catholics and Protestants, this seems a legitimate use of historical data for symbolic drama. Lancaster is again misleading in his observation that *Roxane* contains 'no substantial account of the conflict between the Greek and Oriental civilizations with its large historical consequences'.[30] Alluding to an historical context which he assumes to be familiar, Desmarets stresses issues with a particular resonance for his audience. For instance, Plutarch and Quintus Curtius make it clear that, though prompted by immediate sexual desire, Alexander married Roxana for reasons of State consistent with his controversial policy of cultural fusion. In the play, Clyte complains (IV. II):

> Le Roy nous abandonne & les mœurs de la Grece.
> En domptant les Persans, il a pris leur foiblesse:
> Il a pris auec eux l'orgueil, la volupté,
> Et s'est laissé dompter, parce qu'il a dompté.

---

[29] Lancaster, *A History of French Dramatic Literature in the Seventeenth Century*, ii. 220-1. Desmarets is likely to have used a French translation of Quintus Curtius dedicated to Louis XIII: *Histoire des faicts d'Alexandre le Grand*, transl. N. Seguier (1622), first published Geneva, 1614. He may also have known the Latin text and also *L'Alexandre françois*, transl. N. de Soulfour (1629). Desmarets's play seems unrelated to the Latin tragedy *Roxana* (London, 1632) acted at Trinity College, Cambridge.

[30] Lancaster, *A History of French Dramatic Literature in the Seventeenth Century*, ii. 221.

Quoy? nous perdons nos mœurs, nos vertus, nostre gloire.
Nous avons plus perdu qu'acquis par la victoire.
Il respand ses faueurs sur les peuples domptez.
Il mesprise les Grecs qui les ont surmontez.
Il se faict adorer comme les Roys de Perse.
Quand la vertu se perd, tout ordre se renverse.

Clyte is cast in the spirit of Quintus Curtius' observation that, after Alexander had established in his palace a harem with three hundred and sixty concubines, eunuchs, etc., like that of Darius,

Les vieux soldats de Philippe accoustumez à vne vie austere, ayant à contre cœur tout luxe, & toutes façons de faire estrangeres, detestoient tous d'vn commun accord par le camp que la victoire auoit apporté plus de ruïne que la guerre: qu'ils s'estimoyent eux-mesmes alors estre vaincus, puis qu'ils estoyent assuiettis aux meurs & façons de faire des estrangers . . .[31]

The historical Clitus had been one of Philip's officers. He had saved Alexander's life at the crossing of the river Granicus in Asia Minor. In the play Clyte's dislike of Alexander's policies—cultural fusion and magnification of the monarchy on the Persian model—must echo resistance to the rise of absolutism in France. For the men in Richelieu's entourage Alexander and the Persian kings provided models of kingship, cited by Desmarets himself as early as *L'Entreprise des Rochellois descouuerte*. Protestant officers who had assisted Henri IV's succession to the throne may well have thought that the French royal Court had come to imitate too much of the ritual splendour of the Spanish and of certain Italian Courts. Clyte may be taken to voice the French equivalent to Puritan opposition in England in 1640 to similar aspects of the Court of King Charles I— who owned a copy of Desmarets's *Ariana*.

Quintus Curtius states that, having fallen in love with Roxana, the daughter of a 'tres-illustre Satrape' and thus noble, but not royal, Alexander

dit que pour affermir son royaume il falloit ioindre par marriage les Perses, & les Macedoniens ensemble, & que c'estoit l'vnique moyen pour oster la honte aux vaincus & l'orgueil aux victorieux . . .[32]

Citing Achilles, who had taken an Asian wife, Alexander caused a loaf to be brought to him, in accordance with Macedonian custom,

---

[31] Quintus Curtius, *L'Histoire des faicts d'Alexandre*, fol. 151.
[32] Ibid. fos. 227-8.

then cut and shared it with Roxana. Thus, continues Quintus Curtius,

le Roy d'Europe et d'Asie, prist à femme vne jeune fille, qu'on auoit amenée pour passetemps en vn festin, & alloit engendrer en vne prisonniere vn Roy pour commander à sa victorieuse nation

—a marriage shaming to Alexander's companions.[33] For 'prisonniere' Seguier gives 'esclave'.[34] Plutarch confirms the background of the marriage in a feast but not the loss of Greek liberties with the death of Clitus, nor the acute sense of shame. Indeed, Plutarch states that Alexander's marriage with Roxana came

aussi à propos pour le bien de ses affaires, que s'il eust esté fait par meure deliberation de conseil: car les Barbares en prirent asseurance de luy dauantage quant ils virent qu'il contractoit alliance de mariage auec eux, & l'en aimoient beaucoup mieux que devant . . .[35]

Plutarch even mentions Alexander's continence on such occasions: specifically that he had not wished to 'toucher cette jeune dame, de l'amour de laquelle seule il s'était trouvé vaincu, sinon en légitime mariage'.[36] Such self-mastery was a further triumph for Alexander.

It was also a triumph for Roxana, the ace of diamonds in Desmarets's *Jeu des Reynes renommées* (1644):

Roxane, Femme d'Alexandre le Grand. Heureuse. Elle fut si heureuse, n'estant fille que d'vn Satrape Persien, que d'espouser par sa beauté cet admirable Conquerant.

When an anonymous lady of Rennes wrote that her circle only considered 'Roxane heureuse . . . pour s'être acquis tant de reputation par la Poësie de Monsieur Demarests', the latter replied:

Pour Roxane il suffit de dire pour prouuer son bon heur extreme, qu'estant fille d'vn simple Satrape, elle eut l'honneur d'épouser ce grand Alexandre, apres la mort duquel ce luy estoit plutost vn bon heur qu'vn mal heur de mourir, pour ne suruiure pas à vne telle perte. Ie croy que le Roman que vous aymez [La Calprenède's *Cassandre* (1642–5)], & qui l'a depeinte si cruelle, est bien plus beau que la Comedie où ie l'ay dépeinte si courageuse

---

[33] Quintus Curtius, *L'Alexandre François*, 557.
[34] Id., *L'Histoire des faicts d'Alexandre*, fol. 228.
[35] Plutarch, *Les Vies*, ii. 130.
[36] Plutarch, *Les Vies des hommes illustres*, transl. J. Amyot, ed. G. Walter (1959).

& si sage: mais vous n'auez pas plus le droit de croire l'vn que l'autre; & ie m'estonne comment vous m'alleguez des Romans, apres m'auoir reproché les histoires fabuleuses.[37]

Desmarets seems to know 'the meaning of fiction'—and that fictitious characters must be distinguished from the historical personages to whom writers pay the compliment of borrowing a name. For Desmarets ignores Alexander's harem and makes Roxana comparable to the Old Testament Esther, since both of these 'simples filles épousèrent de si grands Empereurs'.[38]

In the dedicatory epistle, Desmarets ventures to suggest that Richelieu appreciates

cette ardeur auec laquelle ie tasche de m'eslever, pour conceuoir des pensées qui ne soient pas indignes d'estre considerées par vous; & de voir que vous ayant pour objet, j'essaye à ne rien produire qui soit bas . . . j'iray puiser iusques dans la source de vostre grand esprit, & vous admirerez en moy des lumieres, sans cognoistre qu'elles viennent de vous-mesme.

A passage in the play to which these remarks may relate occurs in Alexandre's long soliloquy (IV. VI) after the attempted murder of Roxane. *Pace* Lancaster, Alexandre's reflections on his enemies within the ranks of the Greeks do suggest the repeated conspiracies against Richelieu:

> Legitime courroux dont ie me sens bruler,
> Que la prudence icy m'a fait dissimuler.
> Esclatte maintenant contre ces infidelles,
> Ces jaloux de mon bien, ces traistres, ces rebelles,
> Qui par seditions & par lasches discours
> Touiours de ma fortune interrompent le cours.
> Dans mes plus beaux desseins sans cesse ils m'abandonnent?
> Ma peine la plus grande est celle qu'ils me donnent.
> Rien sans double travail à moy ne s'est soumis.
> Il faut que ie les vainque auant les ennemis.

Lancaster condemns Lacour's 'puerilities' in seeking to establish not only contemporary references for incidents in the play but aspects

---

[37] 'Lettre d'vne Dame de Rennes à M. Desmarests, sur le Ieu des Reines renommées' (1644), cited from his *Jeux de cartes* (1664), 26, 57–8.
[38] Ibid. 58. Similarly, in *Alexandre le Grand* Racine ignores Alexander's harem; and in *Andromaque*, Hector's notorious polygamy.

of the play attributable to Richelieu.[39] Had he read the 'Epistre'? Some of Lacour's judgements do seem far-fetched, but Richelieu was as familiar as anyone with parallels of ancients and moderns. Visitors to his theatre, like those to his gallery, must have been versed in the art of understanding current events through loosely parallel historical examples. Witness another work, by the royal historiographer Puget de la Serre: *Le Portrait d'Alexandre le Grand* (1641).

In *Roxane* the jealous Phradate's conspiracy (V. I) to murder Alexander as well as Roxane is novelistic but may also evoke the Montrésor affair of 1636. During the crisis of the Spanish invasion, the Comte de Montrésor and the Comte de Soissons arranged with Gaston d'Orléans to assassinate Richelieu following a council of war at Amiens; but Gaston failed to make the agreed signal and afterwards disclosed the conspiracy. Desmarets's historical sources mention various threats to the life of Alexander, including one in which a man is condemned to death for failing to denounce a conspiracy—a judgement revived on French precedent for the execution of François de Thou (1607–42).

Phradate's conspiracy is no more a documentary of the Montrésor affair and other recent French conspiracies than of plots against Alexander. Desmarets embellishes history, playing on analogies. It is not so much the analogies themselves which assist in the interpretation of Desmarets's stagecraft as the way in which he reorganizes a blend of ancient and recent historical data to associate the murder of Clyte, for example, with resistance to royal policy, with a challenge to royal prerogatives, and with the crime of *lèse-majesté*.

As so often elsewhere in Desmarets's imaginative works, the catalyst of this reorganization is the divine beauty of a redemptive woman: Roxane. As early as II. II, Alexandre states that she can, 'Inspirant les desirs inspirer la vertu'; and in his last speech at the end of the play, recovering with her help from his suicidal remorse at his murder of Clyte, her virtue removes his shame. Alexandre's remorse (V. III) brings the dramatic climax of the play:

> O trop prompte colere! ô bras trop violent!
> Quoy? punir par la mort vn propos insolent?

---

[39] Lancaster, *A History of French Dramatic Literature in the Seventeenth Century*, ii. 221.

Ah! puisse pour jamais s'esteindre ma memoire.
Ce sang, ce sang versé tache toute ma gloire . . .
Non, non, ie dois mourir: quel crime as-tu commis,
Detestable assassin, bourreau de tes amis?
Comment pourras-tu viure, horrible à tout le monde?
Crois-tu qu'aucun des tiens t'abborde ou te responde?
Nul ne peut plus te voir, ny souffrir tes regards:
Tu verras vn desert pour toy de toutes parts.
Chacun t'éuitera comme vne beste affreuse,
Que tout craint, qui craint tout, farouche & malheureuse.
D'vn coup irreuocable inutile remords.
Helas! par ce seul coup tous mes amis sont morts.

Such lines mark limits to Alexander's exemplarity: neither in the *coup d'état* of 24 April 1617 nor in response to later conspiracies did Louis XIII (or Richelieu) act personally as executioner. Clovis did. Desmarets comments, in the 'Au Roy' of *Clovis* (1657), on the anachronism of those who 'jugent legerement de ce temp-là selon le nostre'. Enumerating the cases in which Clovis 'porta luy mesme à son costé l'espée de sa Iustice'—he personally despatched the thief of the sacred vessels, two kings who betrayed him, and a man who had killed his own father—Desmarets declares: 'Ces actions sont plustost dignes de loüanges que de blâme, & ne témoignent qu'vn prompt & ardent amour de la Iustice.' In any case, deficiency in an ancient is a warning to moderns. The Erasmian tradition of encomium, in which praise of rulers also exhorts to conformity with ideal standards, is pertinent in assessing such parallels. Finally, in Alexandre's remorse there are already tears of magnanimity, like those shed by Alexander in Plutarch and Quintus Curtius—and later by the hero of *Clovis* and by Titus in Racine's *Bérénice*. Self-mastery in the style of Corneille's heroes was not a universal aspiration in 1640.

The success of *Roxane* is witnessed by at least five editions, four certainly, and perhaps all five, within ten years—about half the number achieved in comparable time by *Le Cid*, but far above the norm for new plays. In 1647, when *Roxane* was probably revived at the Hôtel de Bourgogne, there was a second quarto-edition introducing a few variants, notably eight lines added to Roxane's last speech in IV. IV.

After Richelieu's death, parallels with Alexander in the reign of Louis XIV were directed first to the Duc d'Enghien, who became the

Grand Condé—for example by that sometime celebrant of Richelieu, Puget de la Serre, in *L'Alexandre, ou les parallèles de Monseigneur le Duc d'Anguien avec ce fameux monarque* (1645)—and then to Louis XIV himself, as in the dedication of Racine's *Alexandre le Grand*, first performed by Molière's troupe in 1665.[40]

---

[40] See J. Grimm, 'Alexander Darstellungen zur Zeit Ludwigs XIV', *Romanistisches Jahrbuch*, 23 (1972), 74–102; R. W. Hartle, 'The Image of Alexander the Great in Seventeenth Century France', in *Ancient Macedonia* (2 vols.; Thessalonica, 1970-7), i. 387–406, ii. 517–30; and E. Schwarzenberg, 'From the *Alessandro morente* to the Alexandre Richelieu: the Portraiture of Alexander in Seventeenth-Century Italy and France', *Journal of the Warburg and Courtauld Institutes*, 22 (1969), 398–405.

9

Plays for the Grand'Salle of the Palais-Cardinal

As early as 1638 Desmarets began working on plays for performance in the planned Grand'Salle de spectacle in the Palais-Cardinal. His last three plays are experimental and innovative, especially *Mirame*, with stagecraft adapted to show off the technical capacity of the new theatre and initiate (as Desmarets remarks in the dedicatory epistle 'Au Roy') a series of triumphs for Louis in theatre:

> Bien que l'vsage des triomphes publics semble estre aboly par toute la terre, la France a maintenant vn lieu où j'espere que vostre Majesté triomphera souuent, par les vers & par les beaux spectacles que vostre grand Ministre y fera faire pour celebrer vos conquestes.

Although the ministry had less than two years to run, Richelieu's Grand'Salle helped to make acting more respectable and nudged French theatre further toward élitist productions, dominated by its great framing proscenium arch. *Europe*, an allegory of Richelieu's plans for a settlement of the Thirty Years War, must also have been written to benefit in performance from the new theatre's special characteristics, as I have argued elsewhere.[1] The stagecraft of *Érigone* is innovative as one of several serious plays in prose written for Richelieu around 1640–2 not only by Desmarets but by d'Aubignac, La Calprenède, and Puget de la Serre. *Mirame* and *Europe* are the first and last plays performed for Richelieu in his new theatre. As might be supposed in the light of the occasion of *Mirame* and the subject-matter of *Europe*, both met with considerable contemporary success as well as with criticism. In some ways they represent the apex of Desmarets's career in theatre, though neither play achieved so much lasting success as *Les Visionnaires*.

---

[1] '*Europe*, allégorie théâtrale de propagande politique', in J. Mesnard and R. Mousnier (eds.), *L'Age d'or du mécénat, 1598–1661* (1985), 319–27.

Mirame

The first performance of *Mirame*, on 14 January 1641, was a grand occasion, with the Cardinal and Court in attendance. Bishops and priests acted as ushers.[2] Admission was by special invitation only, and the performance was followed by a banquet and a ball. As early as 2 January, Henri Arnauld, who had more than once commented in correspondence on preparations for the new theatre and for the performance of *Mirame*, reports that Richelieu 'veut que tous les honnêtes gens de Paris la voient, et pour cela on la jouera quatre fois'.[3] Rehearsals of *Mirame* took place (according to Tallemant) in the small theatre. The first performance, originally scheduled for 12 January, was postponed to avoid conflict with a royal hunting-party. Unlike more recent commentators, the *Gazette* notes the excellence of the dramatic subject,

traité avec vne telle abondance de pensées delicates, fortes & sublimes, qu'il seroit mal-aisé de trouver dans tout l'amas des plus belles tragédies de l'antiquité, les raisonnemens qui sont dans cette seule piece, ornée des plus nobles sentimens & des tendresses les plus grandes de l'amour.

Doubtless the *Gazette* is partial, and not all of the original spectators were so enthusiastic about spectacular theatre and this play—or about churchmen as ushers. Marolles, for example, did not find 'l'action beaucoup meilleure pour toutes ces belles machines, et grandes perspectives'. Henri de Campion (1613–63) confirms Richelieu's enthusiasm but also found 'quantité de defauts' in the performance.[4] Yet considered in its own terms and as a reflection of the aspirations of the Parisian élite around 1640, *Mirame* is not lacking in delicacy, wit, nobility of feeling, and the elevated expression of ideal love.

As in several of Corneille's early comedies, the quality of the dialogue often depends upon equivoques, especially those by which Mirame attempts to win time, conciliate conflicting loyalties, and reconcile passion with reason. Such equivoques were approved for statesmen in contemporary moralist literature and used by Desmarets

---

[2] *Gazette* for 19 Jan. 1641; Tallemant des Réaux, *Historiettes*, i. 401. The occasion is also evoked in the memoirs of Marolles, Montchal, Montglas, and of A. Arnauld de Pomponne.

[3] H. Arnauld, quoted by Lancaster, *A History of French Dramatic Literature in the Seventeenth Century*, ii. 376.

[4] Marolles and Campion, both quoted ibid. ii. 378.

in dealing with Simon Morin. Considered as a personality, and not simply as a prize related to the fortunes of diplomacy and war, Mirame herself may be thought to dispose of few ways other than equivoques for asserting her own aspirations, represented by her attachment to Arimant. Language economical of the truth and capable of misleading without actual lying probably has a topical resonance and is best judged not simply in terms of literary fashions and styles but also in relation to the options available to a princess in Mirame's situation. The plot, incidents, and atmosphere of *Mirame* are reminiscent of *Ariane*, of *Aspasie*, and of other plays of the 1630s. The Grand'Salle permitted new operatic stage-effects.

Mirame was probably performed by the actors of the Hôtel de Bourgogne: it was in the repertoire of that troupe in 1646-7.[5] There is no basis for Pierre de Beauchamps's anecdote that the play was generally ill received or that Desmarets persuaded the disappointed Cardinal that the actors had been too drunk to perform it properly.[6]

Here briefly is the plot. Mirame, daughter of the King of Bithynia, falls in love with Arimant, a favourite sent to woo her for the son of the King of Colchos. That prince having died, Arimant allies himself with the King of Galata, at war with Bithynia, to secure the release of his captured lieutenant Arbas and the hand of Mirame for himself. The latter's confidante Almire arranges for Arimant to meet Mirame by night in a garden by the sea, where—torn between love and duty—Mirame reassures him of her love and allows him to continue the war as long as her father is not killed. But Arimant, defeated in the ensuing naval battle, is captured swimming away by his rival Azamor, King of Phrygia, to whom Mirame is now promised by her father. After another meeting with Arimant, Mirame receives news of his despairing death at the hand of a slave and, with Almire, takes poison. When news of their death reaches the Court, Azamor too contemplates suicide. But Almire discovers that the potion shared with Mirame was only a soporific, while Arimant had not expired but swooned. An ambassador from the King of Colchos reveals that Arimant and Azamor are brothers. Fraternal feelings prompt Azamor to cede his claim to the hand of Mirame, who is at last permitted to marry Arimant, now recognized as royal.

[5] Ibid. ii. 379.
[6] P. F. de Beauchamps, *Recherches sur les theatres de France*, ii (1735), 148-55.

The *Gazette*'s account of theatre, stage, and performance is invaluable, despite the absence of commentary on the music and on the acting, which probably involved less novelty:

La France, ni possible les païs étrangers, n'ont jamais veu vn si magnifique theatre, & dont la perspective apportast plus de ravissement aux yeux des spectateurs. La beauté de la grand'salle où se passoit l'action s'accordoit merveilleusement bien auec les majestueux ornemens de ce superbe theatre: sur lequel, avec vn transport difficile à exprimer & qui fut suiuy d'vne acclamation vniverselle d'estonnement, paroissoient de fort delicieux jardins, ornez de grottes, de statuës, de fontaines & de grands parterres en terrace sur la mer, avec des agitations qui sembloient naturelles aux vagues de ce vaste élement, & deux grandes flottes dont l'vne paroissoit éloignée de deux lieuës, qui passèrent toutes deux à la veuë des spectateurs. La nuit sembla arriver en suitte par l'obscurcissement imperceptible tant du jardin que de la mer & du ciel qui se trouva éclairé de la Lune. A cette nuit succéda le jour, qui vint aussi insensiblement avec l'aurore & le Soleil qui fit son tour d'vne si agreable tromperie qu'elle duroit trop peu aux yeux & au jugement d'vn chacun. Apres la comedie circonscrite par les loix de la poësie dans les bornes de ce jour naturel: les nüages d'vne toile abaissée cachérent entierement le theatre.

The perspective sets, garden, fountains, statues, sea, vanishing-points, and mobile sun and moon evident in della Bella's illustrations (which must have been sketched and etched some time before the actual performance) are here confirmed, along with changes in stage lighting, shown by Madeleine Laurain-Portemer to have been negotiated in Rome with Bernini by Mazarin's agents, as indicated in Chapter 6. There must also have been a wave-machine, like one still in use at the Drottningholm Theatre in Sweden, the museum of which holds details of the multiple sets for *Le Ballet de la Prospérité des armes de la France*, announced in the dedicatory epistle of *Mirame* and danced in the Grand'Salle on 7 February 1641.[7] The wave-machine is likely to have been used to exteriorize states of mind symbolically, like mood music in opera or film. Thus the troubled Mirame says to Almire in her suicide speech (IV, V): 'Au pied de ces iardins voy la mer agitée.'

The proscenium-arch curtain depicted by della Bella may have been used only for an initial discovery of the whole stage. Note the tense in 'vn transport . . . qui *fut* suiuy d'vne acclamation vniverselle

---

[7] See Beijer, in Jacquot (ed.), *Le Lieu théâtral*, 377–403.

d'estonnement'. *Per contra*, the imperfect tense used in '*paroissoient de fort delicieux jardins* [etc.]' has iterative implications readily identifiable with *changements à vue* not adequately recorded by della Bella, whose plates in any case depict only five moments in the action and not the continuity of a complete performance. In particular, the proscenium-arch curtain depicted in the frontispiece does not correspond to the way in which the *Gazette* reports the performance was terminated: 'les nüages d'une toile abaissée cachérent entierement le theatre'.

The main curtain was not drawn at curtain-down because the entertainment was not finished and the audience needed access to the stage. 'Alors', continues the *Gazette*:

trente-deux Pages vinrent apporter vne collation magnifique à la Reine & à toutes les Dames, & peu apres sortit de dessous cette toile vn pont doré conduit par deux grands paons qui fut roulé depuis le theatre jusques sur le bord de l'eschafault de la Reine, & aussi tost la toile se leva, & au lieu de tout ce qui avoit esté veu sur le theatre, y parut vne grande sale en perspective, dorée & enrichie des plus magnifiques ornemens, éclairée de seize chandeliers de cristal; Au fonds de laquelle estoit vn throsne pour la Reine, des sieges pour les Princesses, & aux deux costez de la salle des formes pour les Dames; tout ce meuble de gris de lin & argent. La Reine passa sur ce pont pour s'aller asseoir en son throsne, conduite par Monsieur: comme les Princesses, les Dames et Damoiselles de la Cour, par les Princes & Seigneurs: lesquelles ne furent pas plustost placées que la Reine dança dans cette belle sale vn grand branle avec les Princes, les Princesses, les Seigneurs & les Dames: tout le reste de l'assemblée regardant à son aize ce bal si bien ordonné . . .

Thereafter the Queen watched other accomplished dancers, who were richly dressed for the occasion but not, on this occasion, exotically costumed. Nor, according to the *Gazette*, were French guests the only spectators 'enchantez par les yeux & par les oreilles': 'Les Generaux Iean de Werth, Enkenfort & Dom Pedro de Leon prisonniers de guerre en eùrent leur part, y ayant esté conduis du Bois de Vincennes.'

According to Marolles, it was Léonor d'Estampes, Seigneur de Valençai (1588–1651), then Bishop of Chartres but soon afterwards Archbishop of Rheims, who 'aidant à faire les honneurs de la maison, parut en habit court sur la fin de l'action' and stepped down from the stage to present the collation to the Queen, followed by officers holding twenty dishes of oranges and confections. To various details which confirm the *Gazette*'s account of arrangements for opening the ball Marolles adds that Richelieu walked behind the Queen wearing 'un manteau long de tafetas couleur de feu, sur une cimarre de petite étoffe noire, aïant le colet et le rebord d'en-bas fourré d'hermine' and that 'le Roi se retira aussi-tôt que la Comédie fut finie'.[8]

Among numerous faults found with the play by Lancaster are the *préciosité* of the dialogue, violations of the unity of action, occasional failure to link scenes, and the 'puerile idea of selecting for all the names in the play, with the exception of the heroine's, those that begin with the letter *A*: Almire, Alcine, Arimant, Azamor, Acaste, Adraste, Antenor . . . Arbas, and Arcas'.[9] Perhaps Desmarets intended compliments to the Cardinal (Armand) and the Queen (Anne). *Préciosité* seems in any case to extend to the two principal names. That of Mirame, for instance, contains such anagrams as 'ma rime' and 'à rimer' and vocabulary linked to themes of the play: 'aimer', 'âme', 'mire' (a goal), and 'mirer' (which may mean to gaze, as into a mirror or a lover's eyes). Thus Arimant's orders his own execution (IV. I):

> Frape, garde pourtant de toucher à mon cœur,
> A ce cœur inuincible, à ce cœur tout de flame,
> De crainte de fraper l'image de Mirame.

Compare Almire's remonstrance to the suicidal Mirame (I. III):

> Si l'ame d'Arimant en vostre ame est viuante,
> C'est le tuer encor que tuer son amante.

Such verbal associations are unlikely to be accidental, compatible as they are with themes of the play, the taste for word-play in salon verse, the emphasis given to invention in Desmarets's poetics. Whereas the historical tragicomedies suggest parallels of ancients and moderns, *Mirame* is offered as invention entirely modern. Arimant's name correspondingly contains 'rimant', 'aimant', and 'amant', as well as 'riant' and 'Armant' for 'Armand'.

Lancaster further mocks Mirame's 'silly decision to approve of her lover's making war upon her father, provided he limit the slaughter so that it would not include her relatives'. One might have corresponding doubts about decisions taken by Racine's Hermione or Shakespeare's

---

[8] Marolles, *Mémoires* (Amsterdam, 1755), i. 235–7, quoted by Lancaster, *A History of French Dramatic Literature in the Seventeenth Century*, ii. 376.
[9] Ibid., ii. 221.

Juliet. Mirame's decision arises from the dilemma confronted by any young Christian deeply in love against her parents' will while mindful of Christ's advice (Matt. 19: 19) that honouring one's father and mother is a prerequisite to immortality—a consideration pertinent also in *Aspasie* and *Érigone*. It can be further interpreted in two contrasted, but not mutually exclusive, ways: firstly as reflecting the situation of any early modern European princess betrothed to a potentially hostile dynasty, and secondly as marking the measure of her love by the extent to which other considerations are subordinated to it, as in the novels of La Calprenède and in Thomas Corneille's immensely popular *Timocrate* (1656).

One need only contrast Camille in Corneille's *Horace*, murdered because outspoken about the slaughter of her brothers and her fiancé, to mark the difference between the atmosphere of tragic theatre (an ancient form revived) and that of *Mirame*—intended as a new form of idealized tragicomic theatre reflecting the ethos of the modern pastoral romance. The difference is not absolute: In *Cinna* (V. III) and *Polyeucte* (I. V) characters considered dead—Maxime and Sévère—are restored to life, like Arimant in *Mirame*; and in *Les Sentiments de l'Académie françoise sur la tragicomédie du Cid*, in which Chimène's father is killed by Rodrigue in his first duel, Chapelain suggests that the proprieties might be better served if his wound proved not to have been fatal. In 1648 *Le Cid* was reclassified as a 'tragédie'. *Mirame*, though not a parody of *Le Cid*, as suggested by Lacour, was not intended as tragic drama. Tragedy is inappropriate both to the symbolism of the play and to the mood of the occasion, for which performance of *Le Ballet de la Prospérité* along with the play may have been originally planned.

The symbolism of *Mirame* is pertinent not only to the inner coherence of the play but to the vexed question of what it may have implied with respect to the Queen. Antoine Arnauld de Pomponne (1616–98), for one, was astonished

avec beaucoup d'autres, qu'on eût eu l'audace d'inviter Sa Majesté à estre spectatrice d'une intrigue qui sans doute ne devoit pas lui plaire, et que par respect je n'expliqueray point. Mais il luy fallut souffrir cette injure qu'on dit qu'elle s'estoit attirée par le mépris qu'elle avoit fait des recherches du Cardinal.[10]

---

[10] A. Arnauld de Pomponne, quoted in Tallemant des Réaux, *Historiettes*, i. 906.

The same story is given in more detail in the *historiette* 'Le Cardinal de Richelieu', where Tallemant relates that, in love with Anne and anxious about the succession, Richelieu wished to father an heir to the throne himself, was refused, discovered her secret correspondence with the Spanish Court, persecuted her,

et pour la faire enrager . . . fit jouer une piece appellée *Mirame*, où on voit Boucquinquant [George Villiers, first Duke of Buckingham (1592-1628), admiral and ambassador to the French Court in the 1620s] plus aymé que luy, et le héros, qui est Boucquinquant, battu par le Cardinal. (Desmaretz fit tout cela par son ordre et contre les regles.) Il la força de venir voir cette piece.[11]

Similarly, the Archbishop of Toulouse, Charles de Montchal (1589-1651) refers in his *Mémoires* to 'la grande comédie de l'histoire de Buckingham'.[12] For anyone who enjoyed theatre as much as Anne of Austria, seeing *Mirame* should have been a great pleasure, as Ruth Kleinman observes; but the 'subject of the play . . . made court gossips wonder whether Richelieu had intended to insult the queen rather than compliment her'.[13] Those gossips were almost certainly wrong. Richelieu and Anne had had their differences, and both had enemies; but no one reporting this particular bit of gossip has attempted to explain why, if Desmarets's play, with its signed dedication to the King, had in any way insulted the Queen, she accepted from that same pen so many dedications after the deaths of Richelieu and Louis XIII: odes following the battle of Rocroi at the beginning of her Regency and during the Fronde, his *Jeux de cartes*, *L'Office de la Vierge Marie*, and *La Vérité des fables*.

That some lines in *Mirame* allude to contemporary circumstances is not in question—these lines of Le Roy, for example (I. I):

> On sappe mon Estat & dedans & dehors;
> On corrompt mes sujets, on conspire ma perte,
> Tantost couuertement, tantost à force ouuerte.

Like Kleinman, however, I find it 'difficult to imagine that Richelieu could have meant to humiliate the queen in such a setting, not only before the court but also in the presence of distinguished foreigners'.[14] Comparison with the idealized Mirame, which might

---

[11] Tallemant des Réaux, *Historiettes*, i. 237.
[12] C. de Montchal, quoted ibid. 906.
[13] Kleinman, *Anne of Austria*, 116.   [14] Ibid. 117.

make some sense as indirect flattery, is scarcely credible as a mode of vengeance; and the proposed allusions are all seriously out of date by January 1641. As Lancaster and Kleinman both observe, the situation of the princess Mirame is quite different from that of Anne at any time after her marriage to Louis, especially after the reconciliation which produced the Dauphin and a second son. Anne's Porte-manteau Pierre de la Porte had indeed been arrested in connection with her Spanish correspondence of 10 August 1637, but that was some months before their reconciliation. The proposed allusions to Buckingham go back much further—to the scandal of his attempt to kiss the Queen in a riverside garden in Amiens in June 1625 and to his abortive efforts to relieve the siege of La Rochelle. As for Richelieu's alleged proposition, any worries he had had around 1630 about the conception of an heir were substantially lessened with the birth of the Dauphin on 5 September 1638.

Work on *Mirame* was begun a few months before, probably in the spring, by the Five Authors, reduced to four around June 1638 by the departure of Corneille.[15] In other words, *Mirame* was written in anticipation not only of the Grand'Salle but of the birth of the Dauphin, an event which profoundly altered Anne's position at Court. For *Mirame* must have been thoroughly planned, if not completed in its final form, by 16 March 1639, when Desmarets transferred to Henri Le Gras his general *privilège* of 14 March 1639 with respect to *Mirame*: that is, two days before the 'achevé d'imprimer' of *Scipion* and four days after the *Gazette* had published a detailed account of *Le Ballet de la Félicité*, the third 'récit' of which—containing verse by Desmarets reprinted in his *Œuvres poëtiques*—celebrates the happiness 'que l'on espere par vne paix generale; A l'imitation des belles Tragicomedies, qui de l'infortune & du milieu mesme du desespoir, font naistre agreablement la joye & le repos'. It would be difficult to find a phrase more suggestive of the stagecraft of *Mirame*, especially if 'agreablement' is interpreted as applicable not only in terms of plot (the fate of the characters) and themes (love, including filial and fraternal love, light/darkness, reconciliation, redemption, resurrection), but to stage decoration at once innovative, spectacular, and symbolic.

The astronomical symbolism of *Mirame*, preparations for which figure conspicuously in Mazarin's negotiations with Bernini from as

[15] Adam, *Histoire de la littérature française au* XVIIe *siècle*, i. 468, 505.

early as March 1640, draws upon symbols used in Paris to celebrate the birth of the Dauphin. The *Gazette* for 17 September 1638 records that among the fireworks there was a display organized on 7 September by the Jesuit college in Paris entrusted with the education of the Prince de Conti: 'ils firent paroistre vn Soleil communiquant ses rayons à la Lune, & produisant vn Daufin couronné par deux Anges'. At the very least it seems limiting to suppose that Desmarets, associated with so many Court ballets involving sun-king symbolism, developed in *Mirame* movements of the sun and moon merely to show off machinery and mark the unity of time, which of course they also do. He may have noticed in Cardinal Bellarmini's *De ascentione* (1615) that there is 'grand plaisir à considérer l'esclat admirable des Astres, & particulierement du Soleil, lors qu'à son leuer il nous apporte la ioye auec la lumiere'—a topos recurrent in Desmarets's theatre from the first scene of *Aspasie*.[16] Inverted, it is used in conjunction with marvellous stage effects to heighten the mood of a dawn separation in *Mirame* II. IV.

For Bellarmini, divine light does not reach the subject only through the sun, visible image of God. The first step in *De ascentione* involves recognition that one's own soul, modelled on God, 'vive source de lumiere exempte de tenebres, & vne beauté infinie' (1 John, 1), reflects divine light, 'dont l'esclat efface celuy des Astres & les rauit d'admiration'.[17] The 'Second Degré' recognizes that nothing 'nous emporte à l'esgal de nôtre propre beauté'.[18] Citing the admonition of Ecclesiastes that 'pour la beauté de la femme plusieurs se sont perdus', Bellarmini none the less maintains that feminine beauty remains a powerful image of ultimate beauty in God.

Mirame gains if taken as an allegory of happiness successfully pursued at the dawn of a new era in the realm of the King and Queen of France, represented by the sun and moon. Arimant's fidelity to the image of Mirame's beauty in his own heart and his resurrection to enhanced royal status may be argued to imply anagogically the redemptive quality of feminine beauty for men capable of perceiving the divine nature of its appeal. Probably the most important allusions in *Mirame* are contained in the names of the chief protagonists. Unless the word-play of *préciosité* is strangely devoid of social and religious meaning, the best clue to the meaning of *Mirame* is suggested

[16] St R. Bellarmini, quoted from the French translation: *Les Degrez mystiques pour eslever l'Ame à Dieu, par la considération des créatures* (1655), 52–3.
[17] Ibid. 16.   [18] Ibid. 53

in the title: 'Mire âme', a Modern form of γνῶθι σεαυτόν—'Know thyself'—modified to the values of dramatic pastoral, a modern genre. Unlike the famous admonition inscribed over the entrance to the sun-god Apollo's shrine at Delphi and adopted by Socrates, chief spokesman of Plato's dialogues, Desmarets's play recognizes a redemptive role for feminine beauty (spiritual and physical) in male self-knowledge.

The six plates engraved for the folio *Mirame* by della Bella include the frontispiece, with proscenium-arch curtain drawn, and a plate for each of the five acts. Thus each print depicts a different moment of the action within the same architectural frame: Act I in broad daylight with the noonday sun assumed to be overhead (see Fig. 8); II by night with a moon; III with the sun rising through mist; IV in the morning with the sun again out of sight, but with fewer clouds; and V again at high noon. Della Bella could not, of course, etch either movement on stage or transformation-scenes.

There were three editions of *Mirame* (1641–2) besides the folio, one of them pirated—a sure sign of curiosity, in the event short-lived. However, a German translation appeared in 1662. Stage history after 1647 is limited to a revival in 1872 at the Théâtre de la Gaieté in Paris.[19]

Érigone

The 'comédie en prose' by Desmarets which the guests of Mme de Rambouillet saw at the Palais-Cardinal on 19 January 1642 was his tragicomedy *Érigone*.[20] Lancaster, who always gives a summary of plots, finds it 'a rather cleverly constructed play that should have been made into a comedy or farce'.[21] Adapted from *Rosane*, the plot has nothing to do with the mythological Érigone seduced by Dionysus in the form of a bunch of grapes. Eurydice, Queen of Taprobania, has promised her daughter Érigone to Cléomène, Prince of Carmania, despite Érigone's preference for Ptolomée, Prince of Arabia. Érigone refuses to elope with him. Ptolomée departs. Supposed to have drowned himself, he captures and imprisons Cléomène, the

[19] C. Hippeau, 'Conférence faite en 1872 au Théâtre de la Gaieté avant la reprise archéologique de *Mirame*' (Bibliothèque Nationale pamphlet, n.d.).

[20] Magne, *Voiture*, ii. 223, and J. H. Stellwagen, *The Drama of Jean Desmarests, Sieur de Saint-Sorlin* (Chicago, 1944), 9.

[21] Lancaster, *A History of French Dramatic Literature in the Seventeenth Century*, ii. 379.

FIG. 7. *Mirame* (1641 folio), illustration of Act I. Engraved by Stefano della Bella from his own drawing (*Phot. Bib. Nat. Paris*)

Carmanian ambassador, and returns disguised in that role. Thereupon Eurydice offers to marry Ptolomée herself because she had been promised happiness in a second marriage by an oracle if she would marry the man who comes to marry Érigone in place of a king. None the less married by the high priest to the equivocal Ptolomée 'sous le nom du Roy de Carmanie', Érigone consents with the phrase 'Ie vous prens pour espoux' (III. IV). Whereupon Cléomène arrives. Denounced as a pirate by Ptolomée, he is sent to prison, despite the interest taken in him by Eurydice, who now insists that Ptolomée must marry her. The elopement of the newly-weds is prevented when Astérie betrays their confidence to Eurydice, who imprisons them and frees Cléomène. Ptolomée apologizes. Érigone reminds her mother of her own marriage to Ptolomée. Offering to marry Eurydice, Cléomène removes the last obstacle by revealing that he is himself the King of Carmania whose ambassador he had pretended to be.

Érigone is rich in the novelistic devices of tragicomedy, in moral dilemmas, provocative situations, suspense, surprise, and ambivalent language. It is hard to imagine that the suspense and dialogue arising from the double disguises and mistaken identities is not intended to include comic effects, especially the mother–daughter rivalry for Ptolomée, disguised as Cléomène (who is imprisoned as a pirate) and thought by Eurydice to be a new husband for herself rather than for Érigone (III. VI):

PTOLOMÉE

Cleomene a trouué icy vne prison.

EVRYDICE

Ne luy parlons point de nostre affection, ie vous prie.

PTOLOMÉE

Pourquoy cacher cette verité? chacun la void, il m'est impossible de la celer. Cleomene est captif, & semble estre destiné à l'estre toute sa vie.

ÉRIGONE

Voulez-vous me perdre, en descouurant qui est Cleomene?

EVRYDICE

Ie vous prie de ne luy rien dire encore. Vous voulez parler de ce feint Cleomene.

PTOLOMÉE

Et le feint & le veritable sont tous deux prisonniers: mais bien differemment: l'vn dans une prison d'où il voudroit bien sortir; & l'autre dans vne qui luy est fort agreable.

EVRYDICE
Elle entendra ce que vous voulez dire.

ÉRIGONE
Pourquoy luy découurir nostre affection?

Ptolomée's virtuosity in deceiving with the truth may be the outstanding feature of these equivoques; and the reader may recall that 'el engañar con la verdad' is an invention particularly admired by Lope de Vega in his discourse on modern theatre, *El Arte nuevo de hacer comedias* (1608). This is the theatre of a modern. The scene has irony, suspense, and the contrasted anxieties seldom admired by literary critics of theatre but characteristic of European tragicomic drama and of the libretti of *opera seria* well into the eighteenth century.

There are also moments of what would be known in the eighteenth century as 'comédie larmoyante' or sentimental comedy, as when Ptolomée attempts to console Érigone (I. III):

Quoy? vous pleurez, ma belle Princesse, & vous daignez bien fauoriser de vos larmes vn malheureux amant, que vous obligez à s'esloigner de vous pour quelque temps? Ah! que ces pleurs me donnent de contentement . . .

These lovers are readily identified as lovers because they speak like the lovers in romances, a characterization adapted to domestic comedy by Molière in the novelistic opening scene of *L'Avare*. For Desmarets, however, there were few examples of drama in French prose, which he handles inventively, as in this later passage from the same scene. Érigone is attempting to inform Ptolomée that Eurydice has promised her to Cléomène:

PTOLOMÉE
Quel mal me peut-il arriver?

ÉRIGONE
Il n'arrivera pas, il est desia tout arrivé.

PTOLOMÉE
Quel mal?

ÉRIGONE
Je n'ay pas.

PTOLOMÉE
Hélas!

ÉRIGONE
La force.

PTOLOMÉE
O Dieux!

ÉRIGONE
De vous dire.

PTOLOMÉE
Ma princesse.

ÉRIGONE
Qu'elle m'a.

PTOLOMÉE
Hé quoy?

ÉRIGONE
Promise au roy de Carmanie.

Perhaps Desmarets's use of prose resulted from Chapelain's theory of *vraisemblance*, as suggested by Stellwagen.[22] It can be imitated in verse, as in the famous 'ruban' scene of Molière's *L'École des femmes* (I. V).

Desmarets's *privilège* was transferred for *Érigone* on 16 March 1642 to Henri Le Gras, who published it in duodecimo. As far as I know it was not revived or reprinted.

Europe

Desmarets's last extant play and only 'comédie héroïque', *Europe* is a five-act political allegory in verse plus a 'Prologue', presenting Richelieu's proposals for a settlement of the Thirty Years War. Like the origins of *Mirame* and *Érigone*, those of *Europe* take us back to the period around the birth of the Dauphin. The 'Prologue' is a third Court ballet in the series begun with *La Félicité* and continued with *La Prospérité*. Consider these opening lines of 'La Paix descendant du ciel':

> Du tranquille séjour de la voûte azurée
> Ie reuiens aux climats des mortels habitez,
> > Pour combler de félicitez
> > Ces lieux où ie suis desirée.

Europe must have been almost complete when, on 24 December 1638, Chapelain wrote as follows to Godeau:

---

[22] Stellwagen, *Drama of Jean Desmarests*, 10.

Je ne voy point de nos amis qui aye sur le mestier aucun ouvrage, si ce n'est Mr Desmarests qui doit donner à nostre théâtre une pièce allégorique de la grande querelle qui agite l'Europe et dont l'ambition espagnole fait le principal sujet. Je souhaitte qu'elle réussisse et peut estre qu'elle réussira, encore que je voye assés de lieu d'en douter. Il ouvre bien et son imagination luy présente tousjours de beaux commencemens, je ne trouve pas qu'il les pousse de mesme et ses fins, qui devroient estre les plus parfaittes, clochent et tombent le plus souvent.[23]

The 'Prologue' (whether or not already in the form published) was complete by 31 January 1639, when according to the *Registre* it was examined by the Académie-Française.[24] Written and discussed while Desmarets was working on *Le Ballet de la Félicité*, the 'Prologue' must be verse for Court ballet intended as part of a spectacular performance.

Europe was rushed into performance on 17 or 18 November 1642, following Richelieu's return to the Palais-Cardinal, desperately ill, from the trial and execution at Lyons of Cinq-Mars and de Thou. Two letters from Henri Arnauld leave the exact date in doubt. In the first, dated 16 November from Pomponne, he writes: 'Demain on représente au Palais-Cardinal *l'Europe*, comédie nouvelle, en grande magnificence. On ne sait si la Reine n'y sera point; car l'on prépare une grande collation.' Then in a letter dated 19 November from Paris he reports: 'Hier se représenta au Palais-Cardinal la comédie de *l'Europe*. Ce n'était qu'une répétition. S. E. [Richelieu] n'y assista point. Il y avoit pourtant grand monde.'[25] Tallemant des Réaux states also that when *Europe* was performed, Richelieu 'n'y estoit point; il l'avoit bien veu repéter plusieurs fois avec les habits qu'il fit faire à ses despens; son bras [severely abscessed] ne luy permit pas d'y aller'.[26]

I find no evidence that Richelieu himself wrote any of *Europe*. There is evidence that the play was his idea and that he was, not surprisingly, consulted about its content. According to Tallemant des Réaux, when Richelieu

fut de retour à Paris [17 October 1642], il fit adjouster à *l'Europe* la prise de Sedan [29 September], qu'il appelloit dans la pièce: *l'Antre des monstres*.

[23] Chapelain, *Lettres*, i. 341.
[24] Pellisson and d'Olivet, *Histoire de l'Académie-Françoise* i. 133.
[25] H. Arnauld, quoted in Lacour, *Richelieu dramaturge*, 142–3.
[26] Tallemant des Réaux, *Historiettes*, i. 288.

Cette vision luy estoit venue dans le dessein qu'il avoit de destruire la monarchie d'Espagne. C'estoit une sorte de manifeste. M. Desmarestz en fit les vers et en disposa le sujet.[27]

Europe does indeed contain a reference to the seizure of Sedan, although nothing corresponding exactly to *l'Antre des monstres* occurs in the published text. Tallemant may indicate a moment in the ballet-prologue related to a cave representing the mouth of hell, beginning 'Fuyez, detestables Fureurs, / Allez dans les Enfers'. This scene, which may well have been revived from *La Prospérité*, is arguably the scene depicted in the painting of *Le Soir*. The mouth of hell is a feature of medieval stage sets which survived as a topos of baroque stage-decoration, e.g. in a Monteverdi fragment related to *Orfeo*. Mathieu de Morgues confirms that *Europe* was Richelieu's idea: 'Excogitatam a se . . . fabulam quam Europam triomphatam vocabit'.[28]

A main interest of the allegory lies in the new ideas it airs for an honourable settlement of the Thirty Years War, for which Spanish imperialism is blamed. *Europe* is the most ambitious political allegory staged in France in the seventeenth century. Desmarets evokes the main incidents of Richelieu's ministry and celebrates Louis XIII's triumphs, from the capture of La Rochelle to the more recent French victories at Monaco, Perpignan, Tortona, and Sedan. He points to political troubles in Spain: the separatist movements of 1640, which succeeded in Portugal but eventually failed in Catalonia, except for the cession to France of Roussillon.

A key published with the play interprets the allegory. The hero Francion is, of course, the Frenchman who succeeds in putting his own house in order while sheltering Queen Europe, the heroïne, from the advances of Ibère, the Spaniard trying to enslave her. Francion succeeds in separating Ibère from Germanique, Ibère's relative, interpreted as 'l'Allemand'—the Habsburgs of Vienna. Francion also alters the relations of Ausonie (= Italy) with Ibère's partners, Parthénope (= Naples) and Melanie (= Milan), then under Spanish control. The inconstancy of Austrasie (= Lorraine) provides peripeties and pretexts for intervention by Francion. Three locks of hair taken from the fair Austrasie represent the strategic towns of Clermont, Stenay, and Jamets; the 'boite de diamans' the seizure of Nancy.

---

[27] Ibid. 287.   [28] M. de Morgues, quoted ibid. i. 955.

Sedan is the place indicated in Francion's triumphant speech in the last scene of the play:

> J'ay dissipé des miens les entreprises noires
> Qu'Ibère nourrissoit pour borner mes victoires;
> Et pour comble d'honneur la place est en mes mains,
> Par où pouvoient un iour s'esclore leurs desseins.

More than most plays, *Europe* is a period piece firmly linked to the political situation at the end of Richelieu's ministry.

Despite various adverse critical assessments related to its political content, it possesses outstanding theatrical qualities: a majestic (though of course nationalistic) conception, provocative ideas on matters of the greatest national and international consequence, great scope for audio-visual effects, well-scripted peripeties, and well-wrought verse. Combining an allegorical play that might be transferred to any theatre with a balletic prologue designed to exploit the unique capacities of the Grand'Salle, the stagecraft of *Europe* reflects an intention to combine the appeal of prestigious Court celebrations with a script that could be widely distributed in Europe—an intention frustrated by the death of Cardinal Richelieu.

Europe was published by Henri Le Gras in quarto and duodecimo, 'achevé d'imprimer' on 16 January 1643. A special *privilège* of twenty years for *Europe* was issued to Le Gras on 2 December 1642 specifically and unusually granting the rights for publishing the play not only in French but in Latin, German, and any other language. No such translation has come to light. Four editions in French within a year or so of publication, if both pirated editions are included, followed by an edition in 1661, do witness a substantial success. In 1954, *Europe* was revived by the remarkable company of actors of the Société des Chemins de Fer Français directed by Henri Demay in the theatre at 1, place Valhubert, Paris, which now bears Demay's name.[29]

Another interest attaches to this play. As far as I know, *Europe* is the first occurrence in French of the word 'Europe' in the geographical sense in the title of a separate publication—anticipating Puget de la Serre's *Tableau de l'Europe* and Samuel Chappuzeau's *Europe*

---

[29] See E. W. Najam, '*Europe*: Richelieu's Blueprint for Unity and Peace', *Studies in Philology*, 53 (1956), 25–34.

vivante.[30] This reflects a change of consequence to Desmarets's ambition for a new Crusade. In the 1630s the *Gazette*, for example, tends to use the term '*Chrétienté*'. Desmarets may have been playing with mythological expectations, as he does in *Ariane* and *Érigone*. Contrast Daniel Rampalle's *L'Europe ravie* (1641), an idyll about Jupiter loving in the form of a bull, written in imitation of Marino. Any such *préciosité* is subordinated in this, his last play, to a new vision for the theatre and for peace in Europe.

Richelieu's ambitions for French theatre

The prophecy for the French stage made in this last performance for Richelieu in the Grand'Salle reflects his too often disappointed ambitions for French theatre and for French culture. In the Regency of Anne of Austria the Grand'Salle would see the introduction of Italian opera to Paris. From the beginning of the personal reign of Louis XIV it would, though partly fallen into ruin, house Molière's troupe. In 1674 it was refurbished to house the Paris Opéra, which it did for ninety years, until France lost dominion of the world in the Seven Years War and the Opéra was burnt down (1763). In the 'Prologue' to *Europe*, Desmarets imagines a modern form of total theatre, linked on the one hand to the music of the spheres long symbolized by the Court ballets and on the other to dramatic poetry, comic and tragic. Richelieu and Desmarets had a vision for the performing arts in which the performers have a dignity that is well understood in the twentieth century but which, in the decades following the death of a great prince of the Church who cherished theatre, was begrudged by churchmen such as Pierre Nicole, Jacques-Bénigne Bossuet, and the obscure clergymen who sought to deny Molière Christian burial and persecuted the corpse of the great actress Adrienne Lecouvreur (1692–1730). Here is their prophecy:

> La troupe des neuf sœurs, de la terre bannie,
> Va descendre du Ciel, pour former des accens,

---

[30] There is some doubt about the date of the first edn. of Puget de la Serre's *Tableau*, a 2nd edn. of which '1651' is listed in A. Cioranescu, *Bibliographie de la littérature française du* XVIIe *siècle* (1965–6), no. 55785). See J.-D. Candaux, 'Samuel Chappuzeau et son *Europe vivante*' (1666–73), *Genava*, NS 14 (1966), 57–80, and D. Hay, *Europe: the Emergence of an Idea* (Edinburgh, 1957).

FIG. 8. *Europe*, (1643 quarto), allegorical frontispiece: Francion (France) rescues Europe from Ibère (Spain) while Austrasie (the Duchy of Lorraine), Germanique (the Austrian empire), and Parthénope (the Kingdom of Naples) look on. Engraved by (?) Abraham Bosse (*Phot. Bib. Nat. Paris*)

> Pareils aux accords rauissans
> Que rendent la celeste harmonie.
> Elles n'auront pas à mespris
> De monter sur la scene, & de plaire aux esprits
> Par vn vers, ou comique, ou digne du cothurne.
> Elles charmeront tous les sens
> A chanter la douceur d'vn siècle de Saturne
> Auec la pompe & l'art des siècles plus recens.

The frontispiece, engraved probably by Abraham Bosse, is in keeping with the final stanza of the 'Prologue' (see Fig. 8). The sun is shining on the side of Francion, the valiant warrior rescuing Europe from the chains held by Ibère, depicted as a dusky Spanish grandee (and not of course as the King of Spain) under lowering storm-clouds which Francion will disperse. No scene in the play itself is depicted, but the frontispiece suggests the sorts of meteorological and lighting effects for which the Grand'Salle was designed.

The 'Prologue' also outlines Richelieu's plans for the economic development of France, for patronage of the arts, and for future performances in the Grand'Salle. La Paix announces a *translatio studii* and a new Augustan age superior to the ancient one:

> Ie vay faire fleurir les arts;
> Et le siecle fameux du second des Cesars
> N'eut rien de comparable à celuy qui va naistre.

The century predicted to the Académie-Française just after the birth of the Dauphin and to the Court just before the death of Cardinal Richelieu is the century of Louis XIV.

10

La Félicité *and* La Prospérité

Desmarets's work as an office-holder, novelist, and playwright did not preclude continued activities in Court ballet to the end of the reign of Louis XIII. Indeed, as the chapters on theatre indicate, his first and last plays for the Palais-Cardinal theatres were intended for performance with ballet, as some of his other plays may also have been. Before the ballet-prologue for *Europe* he was associated with two other great celebratory political ballets—*La Félicité* and *La Prospérité*—as principal poet, dancer (in the former, if not in both), and choreograph (probably of both, certainly of the latter). Nor were these the only ballets in which he participated. Some time before 20 November 1640, when the *Œuvres poëtiques* was 'achevé d'imprimer', he had written the verse, included in the 'Autres Œuvres poëtiques', 'Pour vne mascarade Des Graces & des Amours s'adressans à Mme la Duchesse d'Aiguillon, sous le nom de Syluie. En presence de Mme la Princesse [de Condé] et de Mlle de Bourbon [the future Duchesse de Longueville]'. This Princesse de Condé was Louis XIV's godmother. In another song, written for Louis XIII and published in the *Recueil des plus beaux vers* (1661):

> Du plus doux de ses traits, Amour blesse mon cœur,
>   Pour l'aimable Sylvie.
> Je l'ayme sans désirs . . .

set to a tune by Antoine Boësset and probably also ballet verse, 'Sylvie' indicates Marie de Hautefort, later Maréchale de Schomberg. Two of the other poems in that anthology are from *La Prospérité*, while the fourth (set to a saraband by a certain Verpré) is probably also from a ballet.[1] Lyrics for song and dance are a feature, apparently unusual, in both *La Félicité* and *La Prospérité*.[2]

---

[1] See F. Lachèvre, *Bibliographie des recueils collectifs de poésie publiés de 1597 à 1700* (5 vols.; 1901–22), ii. s.v. and Tallemant des Réaux, *Historiettes*, i. 1014–15.

[2] McGowan (189–90), notes a madrigal for *La Prospérité*—included in F. de Chancy, *Airs à quatre parties* (1644)—as an exception to the rule that music scarcely has an independent role in political ballet, in which case *La Félicité* in this respect is also exceptional.

Tallemant des Réaux illustrates Boisrobert's malice toward Desmarets with an anecdote in which Boisrobert is said first to have complained to Richelieu about the behaviour of his guards at the theatre and then to have told the guards that 'des Marestz avoit dit telle et telle chose contre eux. Depuis cela', Tallemant continues, 'les Gardes poussoient le valet de des Maretz aux ballets et aux comedies mesmes qu'il avoit faittes, et disoient que c'estoit à cause qu'il estoit à M. des Marestz'.[3] Elsewhere Tallemant states that Honorat Laugier, Sieur de Porchères (1572–1653), Academician and Intendant des plaisirs nocturnes, 'voulut se formalizer de ce que Desmaretz avoit fait le dessein du ballet qui fut dansé au mariage du duc d'Anghien'—*La Prospérité*, unlikely on such an occasion to have been his *coup d'essai* in choreography.[4]

First celebrations of the birth of the Dauphin

Soon after the 'miraculous' and long-awaited birth of Louis Dieu-donné on 5 September 1638 symbolic celebrations began in Paris, in the provinces, and abroad. Reviewing the immediate firework displays, other 'magnificences' performed in Paris, the 'liesse publique', and 'extréme réjouissance' at the birth of a Dauphin, issue 127 of the *Gazette* begins an expanded despatch dated 17 September by reporting signals agreed for the Seine at Neuilly, where the recent collapse of the bridge might otherwise have delayed receipt in Paris of the news of the royal birth at St-Germain-en-Laye. For the birth of a girl (excluded from the succession by Salic law) the signalman was to remain 'morne sur la gréve les bras croisez'; but for the birth of a Dauphin he would raise his hat, 'entre nous le signal & l'embléme des masles, comme il l'estoit autrefois à Rome de la liberté'.

At the Hôtel de Ville 'le lendemain de cette heureuse naissance' there was a spectacular display:

---

[3] Tallemant des Réaux, *Historiettes*, i. 400. The agreement of 'faittes' with 'comédies' need not exclude reference to the earlier plural 'ballets'. Tallemant adds that Desmarets discovered the calumny through a complaint made to 'Manse, lieutenant des Gardes', doubtless (I suggest) the Sieur de Manse who in the 2nd and 14th *entrées* of *La Félicité* danced with the Marquis de Fors, Desmarets's cousin, and the Sieur de Sillery: that is, Louis Brûlart (1619–91), who in May 1638 had married Marie-Catherine de La Rochefoucauld (sister of Duc François VI, the author of the *Maximes*) and in 1640 would become Marquis de Sillery, on the death of his father, Pierre IV Brûlart.

[4] Ibid. ii. 154–5. For information on other ballets see McGowan, *L'Art du ballet*.

au milieu d'vn theatre de quinze pieds [16.2 ft., almost 5 m.] de haut &
vingt de face en quarré [6.6 m. × 6.6 m., an area of nearly 470 sq. ft.], [on]
fit paroistre vn rocher: sur le sommet duquel estoit vn Soleil naissant; à
ses deux costez la Prudence & la France. L'enceinte de ce rocher estoit
vne balustrade à quatre faces, avec autant de figures assavoir la Paix,
l'Abondance, la Science & l'Harmonie.

These are important themes not only of La Félicité but also of La
Prospérité and of the 'Prologue' to Europe, on which Desmarets is
known to have been working around this time.

On successive days the Venetian ambassador arranged festivities
suggestive of those taking place in Italian states sympathetic to
France: 'tours & cercles en l'air, formez de lumieres sans nombre',
'vn char de triomphe à six chevaux, rempli de bergers & de violons,
suivis de tambours & trompettes', and 'vn grand chasteau tout de
lumieres ardentes, accompagné des armes de France, de celles de la
Republique', etc. Another source records the celebrations in Italy,
especially in Venice. Displays included an emblem that depicted the
Dauphin on a globe, dominant over parts of the world, evoked the
triumph of Louis at La Rochelle, and suggested a Crusade against
the Turks.[5]

In Paris, Jesuits arranged spectacular festivities, including one in
which an artificial sun, by shedding light on a moon, produced a
dolphin crowned by two angels, on a background of royal insignia
in lights. Opposite, they had built 'vn theatre de 40 pieds de long sur
20 de large' (13.2 m. × 6.6 m. or 43.3 ft. × 21.7 ft.) with colonnades,
pyramids, and vases of fleur-de-lis. In a courtyard 'sur vn eschafault
de 16 pieds en quarré, & cinq de haut' (5.28 m. square, 1.65 m.
high = 17.3 ft. square, 5.4 ft. high) 'estoit vn globe transparent
de dix pieds [3.3 m. or 10.8 ft.] de diametre: la statüe du Roy
soustenant vn monde, & autour de luy l'Europe, l'Asie, l'Afrique
& l'Amérique'. Nearby a 'scelet [scellé, an imprinted seal, doubtless
a much-enlarged model] représentant l'envie' motivated struggles of
Mars and Pallas (war and peace)—a conflict settled when 'des amours
amenérent vn Daufin dans vne petite gondole en forme de berceau'.
When all nature had gathered for this new Nativity, conflict again
broke out among the four elements (Earth, Air, Water, and Fire),

    [5] F. Siguret, 'Venezia festiva per la nascita del real delfino di Francia', an account
of celebrations in Venice and other Italian cities in autumn 1638, in Leiner (ed.),
Horizons européens.

with Fire finally victorious. Fire then 'despecha vers le Ciel ses fusées, fit courir vn comete, briller vne Lune, éclater & tourner vn Soleil, & ayant tout dompté, s'assujettit soi-mesme au Daufin'. The Dauphin in turn 'fit crever l'envie & en fit sortir mille serpenteaux, fut receu du Roy & des quatre parties du monde'.

Issue 143 of the *Gazette* carries an article dated 14 October describing celebrations in other French cities. At the Jesuit college in Rheims there were symbolic decorations including a horoscope, huge firework maxims in Latin, and a mythological ballet in five *entrées*, festivities partly sponsored by one of the *pensionnaires*: Roger de Thibaud, son of the 'Mareschal de Camp & Gouverneur des Villes & Citadelles de Stenay, Dun & Iametz'—strategic towns evoked in *Europe*.

Thibaud had provided a lighthouse capable of spouting fire through the top and showers of golden rain all around. Diana, Flora, and Thetis, invited to a feast and wishing to fulfil the terms of an oracle 'Date optimum optimae', respectively present the nymph Galatea ('Amazone Gauloise') with a lion, a lily, and a dolphin. But which gift could be considered the best? The inventive god Proteus explains:

nostre bonne & incomparable Reine, que ces trois Deesses representent en vn mesme fils, a donné à la France deguizé[e] sous le nom de Galathée vn lion, vn lys & vn Dauphin: Vn lion, qui par la force de son courage se rendra redoutable à tout l'vnivers: vn lys, dont la blancheur sera vne pure expression de l'innocence & de la vertu: & vn Dauphin, qui calmera les vents & les orages de la guerre, & ramenera avec la paix la saison des beaux jours & la serenité que toute l'Europe souhaite avec passion.

That the occasion was sacral as well as political is borne out by the inscriptions 'Delphino Gallico', one of which reads: 'Divi Ludovici abnepoti primogeniti Ecclesiae primogenito, Dei & Deiparae dono recèns per miraculum nato Theologia Deum scire, Deiparam colere, Ecclesiam tueri, avitam pietatem emulari.'[6] Beliefs, aspirations, and symbolism expressed in celebrations of the birth of the Dauphin, including the requirement that he set a high example of personal conduct. The call for an example to suppress *libertinage* and heresy

---

[6] 'To the Dauphin of France, first-born son of the divine Louis great-great-grandson of the eldest son of the Church, lately miraculously born as the gift of God and the Mother of God—to know God through Theology, worship Mary, protect the Church, [and] emulate ancestral piety.'

in France and to unite Europe in a new Crusade against the Turks is echoed not only in Desmarets's late ballets but in dedications well into the personal reign of Louis XIV. In the 'Epistre au Roy' rededicating the second official edition of *Clovis* he still professes misplaced confidence in the King's example, 'puisque Dieu . . . par vn miracle visible vous a donné à la France'.

Finally, on 17 February 1639 Louis XIII himself danced 'son balet' at St-Germain and again at Richelieu's nearby château at Rueil: *Le Ballet des réjouissances faites à Paris à la naissance de Monseigneur le Dauphin*, 'où Sa Majesté tesmoigna par son adresse & agilité . . . qu'elle ne sçait pas moins donner le prix à toutes les actions, que le remporter'.[7]

La Félicité

Le Ballet de la Félicité sur l'heureuse naissance de Monseigneur le Dauphin, probably the grandest of these celebrations, was danced on 5 March 1639 at St-Germain for the King and Queen, on 8 March at the Palais-Cardinal 'en presence de la Reine, de Monsieur, de Mademoiselle [Gaston d'Orléans's daughter, Marie-Louise d'Orléans, Duchesse of Montpensier (1627–93)], des Prince et Princesse de Condé', etc., and on 17 March (apparently a week late) at the Paris Hôtel de Ville. The *Gazette* for 19 March states that on the 17th:

Le Marquis de Brézé dansa son balet de la Felicité dans la maison de ville: d'où la fleur de nos Dames, & la pluspart des autres personnes de condition de cette ville, remportérent la satisfaction qu'elles avoient eüe Dimanche dernier: la foule des survenans ayant empesché qu'il n'y pûst estre dansé des lors.

Presumably Urbain de Maillé, Marquis de Brézé, Maréchal de France, governor of Anjou, and later viceroy of Catalonia, had sponsored at least this third performance, in which he himself danced more than one conspicuous role. In 1617 he had married Nicole du Plessis-Richelieu, Cardinal Richelieu's younger sister.

The *Gazette* for 12 March had carried a detailed account of *La Félicité*, explaining that the expression of extraordinary joy requires 'de nouvelles inventions, pour rendre la naissance de nostre jeune Prince autant celebre, comme l'on se promet que le cours de sa vie

---

[7] *Gazette* for 25 Feb. 1639.

sera glorieux'. Readers mindful of the horrors of the War of the Spanish Succession (1701–14) may see irony where none was intended in the *Gazette*'s declaration that Louis-Dieudonné was 'né parmi les vœux de tant de peuples pour l'obtenir de la Divinité avec la Paix'—and to suspend disbelief at the prediction 'que ce Royal Enfant doit servir à l'vnion de tous les Princes de l'Europe, puisque desia le sang de deux grands Roys est vny en sa personne'.

La Félicité is in three parts, each part a *récit* comprised of ballet *entrées* and music, including solo and ensemble vocal parts. The first part represents misfortunes past; the second 'le bon heur présent de cette naissance'; and the third happiness desired 'par vne paix generale'. The first part opens with an aria which Ambition personified, responsible for past misfortunes, addresses to the King. Ambition admits that Louis's moderation and 'esprit magnanime' exempt him from the passion which she represents. The *entrées* then present (1) Discord, who casts a globe (likened to the golden apple of Greek mythology) to foster dissension among princes;[8] (2) Bellona (personified war) on a cannon drawn by Gold and Silver personified, accompanied by four conquerors (Cyrus, Alexander, Caesar, and Tamerlane) who in turn take the world and then retire. Further struggles for world dominion follow until the Chariot of Felicity enters for the eighth and final *entrée*. Drawn by two Cupids and accompanied by four lutanists representing 'les contentemens', it contained the Dauphin with personified Justice at his feet. The combatants cease combat, bow, 'puis se sousmettent à sa iustice':

laquelle prenant le globe du monde, & le touchant de son espée, il se divise en quatre parts. Vn François en donne vne aux Espagnols, vne aux Allemands, vne aux Suedois, & en retient vne autre pour luy & pour son compagnon, & se touchant tous dans la main, ils se retirent.

The second part opens with a lute-accompanied allegorical ensemble sung by La Félicité, La Justice, and Les Amours. La Justice begins: 'Ie suis l'adorable Equité, / Qui conduis la Felicité', followed by

---

[8] It was in this *entrée* that Manse and Sillery danced Gold and Silver, while the four conquerors were danced respectively by Brézé, by Gaston, Marquis (later Duc) de Roquelaure (1615–83), by the Marquis de Fors, and the 'Comte de Roussillon', whom I take to be Charles-Amedée, Comte de Rossillion, (later?) Duc de Bernex, father of Michel-Gabriel de Rossillion de Bernex, Bishop and Prince of Geneva. Roquelaure, whose career included numerous important offices and commissions, was an important combatant in victories celebrated in Desmarets's odes from Thionville (1644) to Mastricht (1673).

La Felicité: 'Apres tant de malheurs, enfin je viens parestre / Avec ce noble Enfant' and Les Amours: 'Et nous l'avons fait naistre / D'vn grand Roy triomphant'. Other *entrées* respectively represent festivities, the hommage of three French rivers, 'Vne machine representant vn feu de joye pour la naissance', the pleasures of the hunt, the pleasures of playing-cards, 'La machine d'vne Table sur laquelle est vne fontaine de vin, & des beuueurs allentour, chantans & dançans', etc. The *Gazette* records a drinking-song by Hay du Châtelet and an *entrée* by Marais and Molinier representing 'vn Soldat estroppié & son Goujat' returning from the siege of Brissac—a fortified town on the Rhine taken in December 1638 by Bernard of Saxony, Duke of Weimar, with the assistance of French troops commanded by Jean-Baptiste Budes, Comte de Guébriant, Maréchal de France. 'On y trouva de grandes richesses, & plus de deux cens piéces de canon.'[9] Doubtless loot and not war-wounds were the source of rejoicing in this *entrée*, danced by Desmarets.

The third part opens with an aria for La Renommée, winged and trumpet in hand:

> Ie vay sur la terre & sur l'onde,
> Avec toutes mes voix,
> Publier les exploicts
> Du plus grand Roy du Monde:
> De ce Roy qui s'est fait, par vne iuste guerre,
> L'Arbitre de la Terre.

This and the two following stanzas are republished in Desmarets's *Œuvres poëtiques*, along with the 'Chanson à dancer', sung in the final *entrée* by a Basque shepherd positioned on a float depicting the Pyrenees, who invites three Basque couples to sing and dance on the mountains 'En l'honneur du Dauphin qui doit vnir les Roys'.[10]

Three *entrées* are *turqueries*, featuring the Grand Turk etc. Against the Turks the third of these (21) presents two dancers in half-French, half-Spanish costume, another in half-German, half-Swedish costume, and a fourth in half-Flemish, half-Dutch costume, swords in hand and presenting to the Turks their Spanish, German, and Flemish sides. When the Turks attack,

---

[9] Moréri, *Dictionnaire*, 'Brisach ou Brissac' and 'Guébriant'.
[10] Compare *Œuvres poëtiques*, 'Autres Œuvres poëtiques', 64–5.

ils se retournent & presentent le costé François, Suedois, & Hollandois,
ayant aussi l'espée à la main. Les Turcs considerans ceste vnion de François
& d'Espagnols, d'Allemans & Suedois & de Flamans & Hollandois, se
retirent, & l'Europe demeure garentie.

European union against the Turks, not new to Court ballet, remained
a theme of Desmarets's poems and 'Avis'.

La Prospérité

Le Ballet de la Prospérité des armes de la France was danced on
7 and 14 February 1641 in the Grand'Salle of the Palais-Cardinal
in anticipation of the marriage of Clémence de Maillé-Brézé (daughter
of the Marquis de Brézé who danced in *La Félicité*, and the Cardinal's
niece) to the Duc d'Enghien in the chapel of the Palais-Cardinal on
11 February. Tallemant associates Desmarets with 'le dessein du
ballet qui fut dansé au mariage du duc d'Anghien', as noted above.
In the 'Epitre au Roy' of *Mirame*, Desmarets remarks

si mon trauail [*Mirame*] a esté suiui de quelque heureux succès en vn sujet
inuenté, elle [vostre Majesté] iugera, s'il luy plaist, de ce que je pourray
faire en parlant de ses exploits veritables. Dés-jà les Ballets que l'on a veus
depuis sa representation n'ont eu pour sujet que les victoires de vostre
Majesté, & tous leur recits n'ont parlé que des merveilles de sa vie.

The plural 'Ballets' is presumably intended to take into account the
second performance of *La Prospérité*. The *Gazette* for 13 February
states that the first performance was danced 'en presence du Roy,
de la Reine, de Monsieur, de son Eminence, des Princes, Princesses,
Seigneurs & Dames de cette Cour, qui en demeura grandement
satisfaite'. It was repeated on the 14th 'pour le faire voir au Duc
Charles de Lorraine'.[11]

La Prospérité deploys allegorical and mythological characters in
praise of recent French victories. It is in five parts—compared in the
preface to the acts of plays, since ballets are 'des comedies muettes',
while the 'entrées de danseurs sont autant de scenes'.[12] In comparison
with French scripted theatre in the century of Louis XIV, however,
the *entrées* are visually more important as scenes, firstly because
the decorations for ballets were normally more lavish and secondly

---

[11] *Gazette* for 20 Mar. 1641.
[12] Quoted by McGowan, *L'Art du ballet*, 187.

because the scene might actually be changed for a new *entrée*. Nor does the concept of mute ballet then extend to the *récits*, which in *La Prospérité* were sung, as in *La Félicité*.

When a 'grande toile' depicting 'un beau palais' is raised for Act I, 'la terre ornée de bocages' is revealed, with Harmonie suspended on a cloud machine, surrounded by birds and singing 'Je suis l'agréable Harmonie'. When she exits, 'le théâtre s'ouvre' [that is, shutters open laterally], et l'Enfer paroist dans l'enfoncement'. At the fourth *entrée* an eagle descends from a cloud, and two lions come forth from their dens. The Furies smite them with serpents to arouse their wrath. 'L'Enfer se referme [the shutters close] et la Terre paroist comme auparavant.'[13] Mars and Bellona dance the fifth *entrée*, followed by Fame and Victory. Finally 'Monsieur le Comte d'Harcourt,[14] representant Hercule Gaulois [who represents Louis XIII], vient au milieu de Mars, Bellone, la Ronommée et la Victoire', frightens off the eagle (Spain) with an arrow and the two lions (Sweden) with his club, then leaves the stage with Pallas and Bellona. Harcourt had defeated the Spanish army besieging Casale Monferrato on 29 April 1640, inflicting heavy casualties, taking numerous prisoners, and seizing their standards, artillery, and baggage.

At the opening of Act II the stage depicts the snow-covered Alps. Personified Italy on a mountain sings her *récit* 'A mon secours, Monarque des François' and retires; 'les Alpes s'ouvrent et Cazal paroist dans l'éloignement, les tentes et le retranchement des Espagnols et le camp des François'. The allusion to Casale is more than a boast of victories past. Cardinal Mazarin, who had first risen to fame by negotiating an end to an earlier siege of Casale 1629–30 and had more recently negotiated with Bernini the machinery for *Mirame* and *La Prospérité*, was on another crucial diplomatic mission to Turin in February 1641. After the fourth *entrée* 'Le théâtre se change et resprésente Arras', the setting for the final *entrée*, in which Pallas Athena, 'déesse de la Prudence', enters on a chariot decorated with fleur-de-lis and drawn by heraldic dolphins (the arms of the Dauphin) and persuades some of Spain's allies to side instead with the French.[15] Contrary to Beijer, I think here 'le théâtre se change'

---

[13] Quoted by Beijer, in Jacquot (ed.), *Le Lieu théâtral*, 378–403.

[14] Henri de Lorraine, Comte d'Harcourt, d'Armagnac, and de Brionne (1601–66), second son of Charles de Lorraine, Duc d'Elbeuf.

[15] Pallas was danced by François-Christophe de Levis-Ventadour, Comte de Brion and later Duc de Damville (1603–61), member of a family claiming kinship with the

implies the use of shutters, while 'le théâtre s'ouvre' indicates that a painted curtain (comparable to a backdrop, but downstage) is raised, as in Act I. Can he be correct in supposing that the change of scene from Casale Monferrato to Arras did not involve a shift of the *chassis latéraux*? In both scenes the French are involved in a siege—at Casale they are being besieged, at Arras besieging. Since Stefano della Bella, who sketched and engraved the plates for *Mirame*, had also sketched and engraved elevations of the siege of Arras in 1640, and Desmarets was or had been Surintendant des fortifications, obtaining sets of Arras convincing to combatants—however imaginatively enhanced—cannot have presented much difficulty.

Shutters and *chassis latéraux* only may figure in Act III, in which 'le théâtre représente la Mer environnée de rochers, et les Syrenes viennent sur le bord faire le récit'. In the fifth *entrée* 'les Gallions françois paraissent, combattent et brûlent ceux d'Espagne'. The marvellous of Act IV is based on cloud-machines: first the nine Muses are lowered from an open sky; they and a series of gods and goddesses do hommage to the Gallic Hercules; then in the seventh *entrée* 'Monsieur le Duc d'Anghien, représentant Jupiter, descend du Ciel dans un throsne lumineux, environné et sousenu de nuages.'[16] After placing Hercules' club on his shoulder to show he has done enough, Jupiter completes his dance and is hoisted heavenward.

Act V has the most spectacular effects of all:

Le théâtre représente la Terre pleine de fleurs et de fruits, et la Concorde paroist sur un char doré, orné d'une abondance de fleurs et de fruits, sousenu par des nues. Dans la dernière entrée le Sieur de La Force,[17] représentant la Gloire, après avoir dansé parmi les admirations, s'esleve dans les nues, et se perd dans le ciel, ce qui fait une admirable confusion de toutes les entrées.

Virgin Mary. Once Premier Écuyer in the household of Gaston d'Orléans, he became governor of Limousin, captain of Fontainebleau, and Viceroi de l'Amérique (1655).

[16] A principal star in this most lavish Court ballet at the beginning of his illustrious career—which would include the victory at Rocroi (1643) and the conquest of Franche-Comté (1668) celebrated in odes by Desmarets—Louis II de Bourbon, Prince de Condé was destined to have, on 10 Mar. 1687 in Notre-Dame Cathedral on Louis XIV's orders, the most theatrical funeral yet seen in France. See J.-B. Bossuet, *Oraisons funèbres*, ed. J. Truchet (1961), 353.

[17] Armand-Nompar de Caumont, a seasoned combatant who in 1637 had resigned as Grand Maître de la Garderobe and in 1652 became Duc de la Force and Maréchal de France. He was the brother of Jean de Caumont, Seigneur de Montpouillon, a favourite of Louis XIII and the father of Charlotte de Caumont, who in 1653 married Henri de la Tour, Vicomte de Turenne and Maréchal de France.

This is a grand finale in which personified Concord and Abundance return to France in gilded triumphal chariot-cloud machines, followed by *entrées* reminiscent of *La Félicité*—games, feasts, and virtuoso dancing by one Cardelin, 'dont les sauts périlleux et admirables font retirer les autres confus'. The celebrations include burlesque *entrées*, notably seven marquis doing 'tours et dispositions sur des [pantomime] Rinocerots'—an *entrée* perhaps repeated in *Le Ballet du Rhinocéros*, also danced in 1641. Finally, the great curtain came down. When it was lifted a few moments later, the stage sets had given way to a gilded throne-room:

au lieu des Theatres . . . il se void une grande salle dorée et ornée de toutes sortes de peintures et embellissemens esclairée de quantité de chandeliers de cristal, au fonds de laquelle est un throsne pour le Roy et pour la Reyne.

Then, as after *Mirame*, 'du dessous du Theatre il sort un pont imperceptiblement, qui va s'appuyer sur l'eschaffaud du Roy et de la Reyne, pour les faire passer dans la salle du Bal'—an apotheosis of the French monarchy in all its splendour.

As political ballet, *La Prospérité* functions in several ways: as a celebration of French military victories, as a celebration of diplomatic successes obtained by Richelieu and Mazarin, as a celebration of the French monarchy, and as a celebration of a marriage uniting Cardinal Richelieu's family to the French royal family. In Desmarets's stagecraft it is closely related not only to *La Félicité* but to *Mirame*, exploiting sets, machines, and lighting commissioned from Bernini by Mazarin, and to *Europe*. Indeed, after mentioning *La Prospérité* in the 'Epistre au Roy' of *Mirame*, Desmarets links it to *Europe*, assuring the King:

je prepare vn ouurage sur le sujet de la justice de ses armes, et de la moderation d'vn si grand Roy dans ses glorieux succés, qui auec l'ayde de la renommée de vostre Majesté volera, comme j'espere, par tout le monde.

McGowan stresses continuities in the use of cloud-machines and other devices in occasional use since *Le Ballet du Triomphe de Minerve*, danced by Marais in 1614, and other ballets discussed in Chapter 3. At the same time she notes important changes related to the proscenium arch and raised stage of the Grand'Salle, which distance spectators from performers in a manner later taken for granted in proscenium-arch theatres throughout Europe. Even if these changes were anticipated in Richelieu's small theatre, they are of great aesthetic consequence. She is mistaken, however, to state that no staircase or ramp linked raised stage to auditorium: both *Le Soir* and the illustrations of *Mirame* show a flight of five stone steps which do just that, and she herself notes the mechanical bridge deployed after *Mirame* and *La Prospérité* and used by the royal party in progressing to the stage.[18] Nor in this case is it quite correct to conclude that 'la musique n'a pas de rôle indépendant, elle ne sert guère que d'accompagnement aux danses'. Doubtless the spectacular effects received special attention; but with five sung *récits* in addition to the dances, *La Prospérité* must qualify as music theatre. McGowan's conclusion that the greater dimensions of the Grand'Salle 'permettent au machiniste (inconnu) de réaliser une mise en scène dont la magnificence ne semble pas avoir été atteinte auparavant' remains convincing, except that the machinist has now been identified as Bernini.

By identifying the 'maquette de décor' of *La Prospérité* and by meticulous analysis of known sources, including the historiography of the first performances in the Grand'Salle and of important performances later in the 1640s, Beijer has shown the extent to which Torelli's 'admirables changemens de scene, jusques à présent inconnus en France'—the terms in which the *Gazette* reviews *La Finta Pazza* on 14 December 1645—are anticipated by *La Prospérité*. This was a grand event, recalled in the memoirs of Marolles, Montglat, Montpensier, and others—an event which would certainly have received more sympathetic attention from theatre historians had they taken into account Marolles's preference for an earlier style of Court ballet and the probable absence from the performance of *La Prospérité* of Théophraste Renaudot (1584–1653), principal author of the *Gazette*. As Madeleine Laurain-Portemer has now documented, in Bernini Mazarin had found for Richelieu's Grand'Salle a machinist comparable to Inigo Jones and Torelli and worthy of the French Court.[19]

---

[18] McGowan, *L'Art du ballet*, 188–9.
[19] Laurain-Portemer, *Études mazarines*, 197–223.

11

Short Poems and Games

Like a number of his contemporaries in Court circles, the salons, and the early Académie-Française, Desmarets wrote numerous short poems: ambitious poems on poetics, serious odes, a burlesque allegory, elegies, sonnets, inscriptions, lyrics, epitaphs, epigrams, enigmas, and other forms of occasional and society verse. In the first years of the Regency of Anne of Austria he also devised educational card-games for Louis XIV.

With early ambitions as an epic poet, Desmarets did not achieve in lyric poetry the great reputation of such rival practitioners as Malherbe and Théophile de Viau in the early seventeenth century, Voiture and Benserade at mid-century, or Boileau and La Fontaine by the end of his career. Given his multiple associations with Court poets, he is unlikely not to have written verse before the trials of Durand and Théophile—some of the poems of *Ariane*, perhaps. Yet the earliest verse positively identified as Desmarets's was not published until 1630. He wrote other poems from 1633 for anthologies or inscriptions.[1] Several of his poems were printed as fugitive pieces between 1637 and 1674. Others were published with ballet *livrets*, doubtless including unidentified verse, because many of the poems and lyrics for ballet are anonymous. A few are known only from manuscripts in the Bibliothèque Nationale and the 'Recueils Conrart' in the Bibliothèque de l'Arsenal. Some poems are lost. I have not found 'une ode de M. Desmarests sur les mouvements de Naples', which Conrart mentions to André Félibien (1619–95) in a letter from Paris dated 27 December 1647.[2] Nor have I found the sonnet

---

[1] Lachèvre, *Bibliographie des recueils* attributes only twelve anthologized poems to Desmarets between 1633 and 1661, including two identified in a 1661 *Recueil* as having already appeared in an extralimital musical publication: F. de Chancy, *Airs à quatre parties* (1644).

[2] V. Conrart, in R. Kerviler and É. de Barthélemy, *Valentin Conrart. Sa Vie et sa correspondance* (1881), 416. In 1646 and 1647 there had been a massive uprising in Naples under the popular leader Masaniello, of special interest to Desmarets as Secrétaire général de la Marine de Levant. An abortive French effort to exploit the situation led to the capture of Henri II Duc de Guise by the Spanish, who regained control of the kingdom.

mentioned in a letter from Paul Scarron (1610–60) to Nicolas Fouquet. Scarron writes:

Monsieur *des Marés*, who yesterday honour'd me with a Visit, will, if he please, assure you of the affliction it was for me, that I should be ignorant of what all the world knew ['the great loss that has happened to you']. He put me into the confidence of writing an extempore Sonnet, which I made some difficulty to send you, out of a fear of renewing your grief. But, at last, I chose rather to run the hazard of doing a thing unseasonably, than that of seeming indifferent in an affliction . . .[3]

Fouquet's 'great loss' must be the death of his eldest son François in late 1656.[4]

Desmarets published three collections of his verse: a section of his *Œuvres poëtiques*, a further section of *Odes, poëmes & autres œuvres* added to the *Œuvres poëtiques* in 1643, and *La Comparaison de la langue et de la poësie Françoise avec la Grecque & la Latine*. *La Comparaison* includes a few uncollected pieces, poems reprinted from the *Œuvres poëtiques*, and extracts from *Les Promenades de Richelieu* and *Clovis*.

Desmarets was, however, a reputable poet in the minor genres, particularly in the 1630s and 1640s; and his reputation lasted into the third quarter of the century. That it was owed partly to his fame as a performer, novelist, and playwright—and doubtless partly also to his connections at Court and in the Richelieu family—seems likely. Most of these poems are now mainly of biographical and period interest, but some retain considerable charm.

Œuvres poëtiques

Many of Desmarets's early poems may be found in his *Œuvres poëtiques*, a partly collected quarto edition 'achevé d'imprimer' on 20 November 1640, to which various additions were later made. Published by Henri Le Gras, with a title-page engraved by Stefano della Bella and dated 1641, it contains Desmarets's first four plays and an eighty-page fifth section entitled 'Autres Œuvres poëtiques'. The most important poems in this section are probably the first two:

[3] *Monsieur Scarron's Letters, to Persons of the Greatest Eminency and Quality*, transl. J. Davies, of Kidwelley (London, 1677), 76–7.
[4] J. A. Lair, *Nicolas Foucquet* (1890), i. 392–3. It seems reasonable to date Desmarets's lost sonnet and visit to Scarron soon after François Fouquet's death.

the 'Discours de la poësie', dedicated to Cardinal Richelieu and reprinted from *Les Nouvelles Muses* (1633), and *Les Amours du Compas et de la Règle*, also dedicated to Richelieu and said by d'Olivet to have been separately published in quarto in 1637.[5] The elegy 'A Elle mesme, sur la mort de son fils, sous les noms de Dionée et d'Agis' occupies most of six leaves intended to follow the stanzas 'A Madame du Vigean, sur la seconde prise du Marquis de Fors son fils par les Espagnols' and to precede the section entitled 'Amours', for which it includes a half-title.[6] Other occasional poems are also related to siege warfare at Arras and elsewhere, including a sonnet to Cardinal Richelieu 'Sur la prise d'Arras' and stanzas 'A Monsieur de Bautru, sur la mort de Messieurs de Lamet, de Charnacé, & de Rambures'.[7] An epigram 'A Monsieur de Ville sur son livre de l'art d'attaquer & deffendre les places' acknowledges *Les Fortifications* (Lyons, 1629 and 1640), a folio volume by Antoine de Ville (1596–1656), a Maréchal de camp and military engineer from Toulouse who by 1640 had published several other books on sieges and fortifications.

The 'Amours' are reprinted mainly from *Ariane*. The 'diverses poësies' for ballet include *récits* for *La Félicité*, 'Pour vne mascarade des Graces & des Amours', mentioned in Chapter 10, and two songs 'Pour Mademoiselle de Bourbon' mentioned in Chapter 3. 'Pour vne Beauté grotesque', on the same air as the preceding song, is a *récit*

---

[5] Pellisson and d'Olivet, *Histoire de l'Académie-Françoise*, s.v.

[6] The half-title is misplaced before the elegy in several copies through wrong folding of the half-sheet. Mistaking this binder's error for the poet's intention, Kerviler (*Jean Desmaretz*, 10) cites the supposed inclusion of the elegy among the 'Amours' as evidence of poor literary judgement on the part of the poet. See my description in *The Yale University Library Gazette*, 33 (1958), 18–23. A sonnet on the death of the Marquis de Fors found with the elegy in one Bibliothèque Nationale copy was probably not normally bound with the *Œuvres poëtiques*, although in the early 1640s Desmarets several times added a sonnet to a longer poem, elegy, or ode on the same occasional subject.

[7] Hercule-Girard, Baron de Charnacé, who around 1618 married Jeanne de Maillé de Brézé (Urbain de Maillé-Brézé's great-aunt) and distinguished himself in diplomatic missions to Sweden, the Netherlands, etc. was killed at the siege of Breda in 1637. Jean V, Sire de Rambures, Maréchal de camp des Armées du Roi, Gouverneur de Dourlens (now Doullens, Somme), etc. (the son of Charles, 'le brave Rambures' who died of war wounds in 1633), was killed in the siege of La Capelle in 1637. Unable to trace Lamet, I wonder whether L is a misprint for Z. The banker Sébastien Zamet, governor of Fontainebleau and very much the sort of man that Desmarets and Bautru would have known, died before 1640. His son Jean Zamet had died at the siege of Montpellier in 1622. See Tallemant des Réaux, *Historiettes*, i. 606, 1016.

for an unidentified burlesque ballet or perhaps *Le Ballet du Triomphe de la beauté*, danced on 19 February 1640.

'La Guirlande de Julie'

These lyrics are followed by 'La Violette, s'offrant pour seruir à la Guirlande de fleurs de Mademoiselle de Ramboüillet qui luy a esté faite sous le nom de Iulie', the first flower of the original 'Guirlande de Julie', the 'Couronne impériale' presented to Julie d'Angennes, daughter of the famous hostess of the Hôtel de Rambouillet and future Duchesse de Montausier, on New Year's Day 1634:

> Franche d'ambition ie me cache sous l'herbe,
> Modeste en ma couleur, modeste en mon sejour,
> Mais si sur vostre front ie me puis voir vn iour,
> La plus humble des fleurs sera la plus superbe.

This once-famous madrigal—the first two lines are sometimes inverted—is published between lyrics for ballet and stanzas 'Au Sieur Lambert excellent musicien' in the 'Autres Œuvres poëtiques'. The 'Couronne impériale' must have begun as a performance for Julie, which probably commenced with this madrigal. In stating that 'Julie trouva le présent sur sa toilette le 1ᵉʳ janvier de 1633 ou 1634, et non en 1641, comme on le dit dans le recueil de ces vers, à la suite de la vie de Montausier,' Huet appears to have conflated the birthday presentation of 1641 (which certainly occurred) with the original event, which he correctly dates earlier.[8] Chapelain mentions preparations as early as 9 September 1633. Scudéry published his contributions in 1635. The presentation copy was made later.

In terms of Court and salon priorities, the famous manuscript with calligraphy by Nicolas Jarry, illuminated by Nicolas Robert, bound by Le Gascon, and presented by the Duc de Montausier in 1641 is easier to interpret as a keepsake of a memorable performance than simply as a superior copy of a seven-year old manuscript.[9]

---

[8] P.-D. Huet, quoted in Adam, *Histoire de la littérature française au XVIIᵉ siècle*, i. 266.

[9] 'La Couronne imperiale à la Princesse Julie', Bibliothèque de l'Arsenal, MSS. 3135. I have not seen Bibliothèque Nationale MSS. f fr. 19,142, the MS in the National Trust collection at Waddesdon Manor, Bucks., or the presentation copy which in 1930 was in the Duchesse d'Uzès' collection. 'La Guirlande de Julie' was first published in the anthology known as the *Recueil de Sercy*, 2nd edn. (1653). For a history of the MS calligraphed by N. Jarry, illuminated by N. Robert, bound by Le Gascon,

In the Conrart manuscript, 'La Violette' is placed first, immediately after Chapelain's dedication and before 'Les Lys'—also by Desmarets but not included in his *Œuvres poëtiques*. This was a place of honour. Gilles Ménage recalls that 'M. Desmarests choisit la violette, & fit ces vers auxquels je donnai le prix par dessus les autres: Modeste en ma couleur . . .'.[10] There can be no reasonable doubt that Desmarets was involved in the original presentation; and madrigals are written for four-part performance, e.g. Desmarets's madrigals collected in Chancy's *Airs à quatre parties*. Their resemblance to lyrics for ballets and masquerades has received less attention than well-observed analogies between Robert's illuminated title-page and the garland as a painterly motif in seventeenth-century portraits. 'Les Lys', written before the capitulation of Gaston d'Orléans in 1634, may have been dropped from the *Œuvres poëtiques* because by 1640 the hyperbole no longer seemed quite appropriate:

> Belle[,] ces lys que Ie vous donne
> Auront plus d'honneur mille fois
> De seruir a vostre couronne
> Que d'estre couronnez aux armes de noz Roys.

'Autres Œuvres poëtiques'

The 'Autres Œuvres poëtiques' includes other poems very much in keeping with the lighter literary fashions of the Hôtel de Rambouillet: six verse 'énigmes' with solutions on a separate page and an inscription 'Pour vne Amphitrite de bronze, qui doit verser le grand ruisseau de la cascade de Rueil' (the château de Rueil, in which Cardinal Richelieu sometimes resided in the 1630s). I cannot date this inscription precisely, but any date between 1634 and 1640 is early for (*a*) an ornamental cascade in France and (*b*) an inscription in the French language.

Second only to the 'Amours' in length is 'Œuvres chrestiennes', for which see Chapter 12.

---

and presented by the Duc de Montausier, see P. de Cossé-Brissac, 'La Guirlande de Julie', *Revue des deux mondes* (15 Jul. 1937), 420–32, and C. E. J. Caldicott, 'The Drawings of Nicolas Robert in Trinity College Library: a Seventeenth-century View of Nature', *Lang Roam* (special no., summer 1981), 6–15. Poems were also contributed by Arnauld d'Andilly, Colletet, Conrart, Godeau, Gombauld, Le Moyne, Malleville, Ménage, the Marquis de Rambouillet, and Georges de Scudéry.

[10] *Menagiana* (1729), iii. 318.

'Discours de la poësie'

The opening poems of 'Autres Œuvres poëtiques', dedicated to Cardinal Richelieu, are of special interest. Neither fits into received categories of French literary history. Discussing the reaction against the ambitious poetics of the sixteenth-century Pléiade during the Counter-Reformation, Antoine Adam stresses the cultural impoverishment of Malherbe's famous reform of poetic diction. Hostile to imaginative hyperbole, Malherbe could no longer find a place for the poet as visionary, prophet, or conscience of society, suggesting instead that in a nation governed by a King and guided by the Church the poet is a mere arranger of syllables, 'pas plus utile à la société qu'un bon joueur de quilles'.[11] For Adam, Counter-Reformation rejection of Pléiade poetics implies a cultural collapse, which he contrasts with a Renaissance climate of intellectual liberty,

un affranchissement des traditions, le droit pour l'individu de courir tous les risques et d'oser toutes les audaces. La monarchie, l'Église, l'aristocratie ont repris la situation en main, étouffé les efforts de l'esprit pour se libérer. La poésie paie le prix de sa liberté perdue.

Something of what Adam describes undoubtedly occurred; but it did not occur all at once, and it did not take place without a struggle within the Church of the Counter-Reformation. Nor, as far as I can see, does it characterize Cardinal Richelieu's relations with Desmarets. The triumph of triviality was not secure before the publication in 1674 of Boileau's Art poétique, with its catchy clichés, myopic historiography, and partisan promotions: 'Enfin Malherbe vint . . .' and all that. High ambitions in the epic and the Christian marvellous were not the only victims of Boileau's censure. Perception of a whole range of imaginative minor genres still vigorous in the reign of Louis XIII—lyrics and airs for ballets, paraphrased Psalms, etc.—was marginalized.[12] By way of contrast, in La Defense de la Poësie Desmarets admires both Malherbe's style and Ronsard's 'genie élevé', with reservations mainly concerned with Ronsard's imitations of 'enflures antiques',[13] that is, Ronsard's alleged subservience to the

---

[11] F. de Malherbe, quoted in Adam, Histoire de la littérature française au XVIIᵉ siècle, i. 32.

[12] See F. Nies, 'Les Silences de Boileau. Genres poétiques déconsidérés du Grand Siècle', Cahiers de littérature du XVIIᵉ siècle, 8 (1986), 35–50.

[13] La Defense de la Poësie (1675), 25 praises: 'le vers si doux et si superbe, / De

ancients and the 'termes empoullez & obscurs' mocked in *Les Visionnaires*.

In his 'Discours de la poësie', Desmarets is already modern, imaginative, and selectively anti-Malherbian:

> Mais ceux qui d'vn genie au labeur indompté
> Feront ce beau present à la posterité,
> Ne suiuront pas l'erreur de ces nouueaux critiques,
> Qui retranchent le champ de nos Muses antiques,
> Qui veulent qu'on les suiue, & qu'adorant leurs pas
> On evite les lieux qu'ils ne cognoissent pas.
> Leur Muse cependant de foiblesse & de crainte
> Pensant se soustenir affecte la contrainte,
> N'ose aller à l'escart de peur de s'esgarer;
> Et parlant simplement croit se faire admirer:
> Elle a peur d'eschauffer le fard qui la rend vaine,
> Et la moindre fureur la mettroit hors d'haleine.
> Imbecille troupeau, sans art & sans sçauoir,
> Dont les esprits rampans ne sçauroient concevoir
> Vne Muse sublime, actiue & vigoureuse,
> Qui rompt auec mespris ceste loy rigoureuse,
> Qui sent dedans son sein vn cœur ambitieux,
> Qui d'vn superbe vol s'emporte vers les Cieux,
> Et void auec orgueil, marchant dessus la nuë,
> La terre dont le globe à ses yeux diminuë:
> Le Ciel qu'elle apperçoit & plus vaste & plus pur,
> Qui de l'or du Soleil enrichit son azur,
> Luy paroist vn seiour digne de son courage:
> Iamais dans vn destroit sa grandeur ne s'engage . . .
> Elle descrit des champs la diverse peinture,
> Et se sert, pour suiet, de toute la Nature.
> De celeste fureur quelquefois s'animant,
> Elle se sent rauir iusques au firmament,
> Et laissant quelquefois sa verve & son caprice,
> Sous la naïueté cache vn bel artifice.

First published by Boisrobert, who resented the interest in it shown by Cardinal Richelieu, this 'Discours' was admired by Mlle Marie Le Jars de Gournay, Montaigne's adoptive daughter, who added a page to *L'Advis* quoting from it extensively and professing not to

---

Malherbe dont l'art nous apprit à chanter / Avec pompe, avec élégance, / Sans affecter la docte extravagance'.

know whether to praise 'plus en ce Royal present . . . l'excellence de son Poëme, ou celle de son jugement'.[14] Thirty years later Sorel states that the poems in *Les Nouvelles Muses* by Chapelain, Godeau, and Desmarets 'furent estimées de tout le monde'.[15] It is the first poem reprinted in *La Comparaison*, ii.

'L'Art de la poésie'

The 'celeste fureur' of the Neoplatonists is very much a part of Desmarets's poetics, more directly applicable to *Clovis* (which he began *c.*1634) than to the short poems of the *Œuvres poëtiques*. The 'Discours' is complemented by an 'Art de la poésie', probably written around 1642 and also dedicated to Cardinal Richelieu, but only published with 'L'Excellence et les plaintes de la poésie héroïque' prefaced to the first edition of *Esther* (1670). In 'L'Art de la poésie' Desmarets reiterates his ambitions for French poetry and poetics, developing notions previously expressed in the 'Discours' and in the 'Epistre' of *Rosane* in terms of imitation theory. Depicting 'toute la Nature' never means for Desmarets 'the representation of reality' warts and all. He relies more than many later writers on the Aristotelian notion that mimesis involves not only things as they are, or are said to be, but things as they ought to be. He can scarcely have failed to notice Ronsard's defence of the rhetoric of mimesis in the second preface to *La Franciade* published in the folio *Œuvres* (1623) and detailing the figures, metaphors, and other tropes required 'tant pour representer la chose, que pour l'ornement et splendeur des vers'.[16] Understood in this way, representation clearly involves imitation not only of the thing represented but of a rhetorical tradition independent of that thing. In 'L'Art de la poésie' Desmarets proclaims the writer's autonomy: imitation may be independent of the subject, thing, or 'reality' represented, because the inventive Muse may imitate the Creator rather than His creatures:

---

[14] Mlle de Gournay, *L'Advis* (1634), 420–1, her major work revised from *L'Ombre* (1626). Her thanks are evidence that Desmarets was in touch with her around 1633, not 1623 as (doubtless a misprint) in R. Pintard, *Le Libertinage érudit dans la première moitié du XVIIᵉ siècle* (2 vols.; 1943), i. 135.

[15] Sorel, *Bibliothèque françoise*, 183.

[16] Ronsard, quoted in F. Vial and L. Denise, *Idées et doctrines littéraires du XVIIᵉ siècle* (1922), 27.

> Mais alors qu'elle invente vne belle aventure
> Glorieuse elle suit l'autheur de la Nature;
> Et produisant au jour ce qui ne fut jamais,
> Imite du grand Dieu les admirables faits.[17]

It is on this basis that in the 'Epistre au Roy' of *Mirame* Desmarets distinguishes the 'sujet inventé' of that play from his historical tragicomedies and from *Europe*, which represents recent historical events. Imitation of the Creator is invention. The poet is a 'maker' in the fullest sense, an author in his own right, a creative writer—a concept sometimes said to originate in the eighteenth century, but clearly fundamental to Desmarets's poetics.

Les Amours du Compas et de la Règle

Presented to Cardinal Richelieu in the first years of their close association, *Les Amours du Compas et de la Règle* illustrates a conception of literature in which wit, invention, and symbolic meaning are more important than the representation of phenomena: 'jeux' and 'contes enfantez d'une riante Muse' to distract the great minister in moments he could spare from affairs of state, framed in conversational verse fully compatible with the story by which Tallemant des Réaux illustrates Richelieu's passion for verse:

Un jour qu'il estoit enfermé avec Desmarestz, que Bautru avoit introduit chez luy, il luy demanda: 'A quoy pensez-vous que je prenne le plus de plaisir?—A faire le bonheur de la France,' luy respondit Desmarestz. 'Point du tout,' respliqua-t-il, 'c'est à faire des vers.'[18]

From Ovid's tale of Daedalus, interpreted euhemeristically, Desmarets develops a grotesque allegory of the birth of architecture: a modern metamorphosis in which the Compass and the Rule are personified and animated as if to dance in a burlesque ballet. The action opens heroi-comically:

---

[17] 'Art de la poésie', Bibliothèque de l'Arsenal, Mss. 4116. For the full text and more detailed commentary, see 'Desmarets de Saint-Sorlin's "Art de la poésie": poetics or politics?', in D. L. Rubin (ed.) *Convergences: Rhetoric and Poetic in Seventeenth-century France* (Columbus, 1989).

[18] Tallemant des Réaux, *Historiettes*, i. 272. Desmarets shared with Richelieu a passion not only for verse but also for architecture. In *Les Visionnaires* (III. v) a brief amplification in Phalante's evocation of the château de Richelieu contextualizes this poem architecturally and stylistically: 'cet art qu'ont produit la regle et le compas, / (J'entens cette mignarde et noble architecture)'.

> Dédale n'avoit pas de ses rames plumeuses
> Encore traversé les ondes écumeuses;
> Et d'un art merveilleux, par le vague des airs,
> Evité de Minos la colere et les fers:
> Il n'avoit pas encor pour un honteux usage
> Fait servir au taureau l'incestueux ouvrage,
> Qui fut du lit royal le reproche éternel,
> Et rendit l'Artisan célèbre et criminel;
> Quand sa sœur qui vit l'art surpasser la nature,
> Lui présenta Perdix sa chere nourriture;
> Afin qu'un jour instruit par ses doctes leçons,
> Il se rendît fameux entre ses nourrissons.[19]

Guided by his uncle, Perdix made such progress that on the threshold of a temple of Pallas Athena:

> Soudain, qui le croira! comme de sa cervelle
> Jupiter fit sortir la sçavante Pucelle,
> Nâquirent du cerveau du jeune vertueux
> La Scie et le Compas, deux enfans monstrueux . . .

Envious of Perdix's fame, Daedalus cast him down from the temple; but his life was saved by metamorphosis into a partridge, allowing Desmarets to carry his invention beyond Ovid to Perdix's prodigious offspring.

Along came Compass:

>   pourvû seulement
> De jambes et de tête, et marcha justement,
> Tournant de tous côtez par ordre et par mesure;
> Et de cercles divers traçant quelque figure.

Forewarned in a dream that he would marry the daughter of a god, Compass soon meets Rule, presented as:

> Droite, d'un grave port, pleine de majesté,
> Inflexible, et sur.tout observant l'équité . . .

Impressed,

> Il l'aborde, et rempli d'une honnête assurance,
> Tournant la jambe en arc lui fait la révérence.
> Pour rendre le salut à ce grotesque amant,
> La Règle ne daigna se courber seulement.

---

[19] Quoted from last printing, Lefort de la Morinière (ed.), *Bibliothèque poëtique*, ii. 207–14.

On learning Compass's genealogy, however, Rule tells her own tale, the 'Amours du Soleil et de l'Ombre', explaining: 'Je nâquis des baisers du Soleil et de l'Ombre.' It all began, according to Rule, when Jupiter asked the Sun:

> As-tu vû l'Ombre en tous tes longs voyages?
> Cette brune agréable, et de qui les douceurs
> Sont les plus chers plaisirs des doctes, des chasseurs,
> Et de tant de mortels qui la trouvent plus belle
> Que tes plus beaux rayons que l'on quitte pour elle?

The smitten Sun sought Shade:

> Mais l'Ombre habilement évitoit ses regards:
> Cette froide Beauté fuyoit de toutes parts:
> Sa course s'avançoit d'une invisible adresse:
> Il la suit; elle fuit d'une égale vitesse;
> Il double en son ardeur ses efforts vainement;
> Tous les corps s'opposoient à son contentement.
> Il pense la tenir; sans la voir il la touche;
> De ses rayons aigus il joint cette farouche:
> Enfin ne pouvant mieux soulager sa langueur,
> En courant il la baise en toute sa longueur;
> Et parmi les baisers de cette douce guerre,
> De leur droite union je nâquis sur la terre.

The rekindled ardour of Compass is again spurned by Rule:

> Va présenter ailleurs tes impuissantes flammes,
> Trop difforme galand pour pouvoir plaire aux Dames.

But he woos and wins her with the children they might have:

> Toutefois nos amours, répliqua le Compas,
> Produiront des enfans qui vaincront le trépas:
> De nous deux sortira la belle Architecture,
> Et mille nobles arts pour polir la Nature.
> Ne pense pas, dit-elle, ébranler mon repos;
> Ou pour autoriser tes fabuleux propos,
> Tâche à charmer mes yeux par quelques gentillesses;
> Et montre tes effets pareils à tes promesses.
> Le Compas aussi-tôt sur un pied se dressa,
> Et de l'autre en tournant un grand cercle traça.
> La Règle en fut ravie, et soudain se vint mettre
> Dans le milieu du cercle, et fit le diametre.

Son amant l'embrassa l'ayant à sa merci,
Tantôt s'élargissant, et tantôt racourci;
Et l'on vit naître alors par leurs justes mesures,
Triangles et carrez et mille autres figures.

There is a point to these 'jeux' not limited to affirmative attitudes towards sexual love (reminiscent of the novels and plays) and the arts (anticipating *Les Délices de l'esprit*). Desmarets's euhemerism is more than a negative interpretation of ancient religions. It invites a positive interpretation of history, of human accomplishment, of invention in the arts and technologies through which the moderns have come to surpass the ancients. Positive euhemerism, developed in *La Vérité des fables* and in the verse continuation published in *La Comparaison*, underlies Desmarets's claim to superiority over the ancients both in this poem and in later polemics. Whereas Ovid accounts wittily for what is or was believed, this poem proposes superior future achievements through an allegory of past invention. Desmarets's poem 'Les Amours de Protée et de Physis, ou l'Alliance de l'Art et de la Nature', which he claims in the 'Préface' as 'd'une invention particuliere, & toute nouvelle, & sans exemple dans l'antiquité', is as much a continuation of *Les Amours du Compas et de la Règle* as it is of *La Vérité des fables*. Indeed, from the former he quotes four lines which illustrate the extent to which the modern position adopted by Desmarets in the last decade of his life was developed from his literary association with Cardinal Richelieu:

Animé d'un beau feu, plein d'une noble audace,
D'un pied libre je cours aux vallons du Parnasse;
Et la Muse en riant me conduit par la main
Où ne marcha iamais le Grec ni le Romain.[20]

Four years later in *Le Triomphe de Louis et de son siècle*, Desmarets's Génie appears as if in a cloud-machine of Court ballet and offers to show him not only how the greatness of the century of Louis XIV had been prepared in the reign of Louis XIII, but also a 'route inconnuë', declaring:

Loin des chemins tracez par les esprits antiques,
Nous sçavons des détours ignorez des critiques.
Pour les sentiers battus j'eus toûjours du mépris.[21]

---

[20] *La Comparaison*, 274.
[21] *Le Triomphe de Louis*, 6.

Not the least disgraceful aspect of French literary history is the way in which Desmarets's collaboration with Cardinal Richelieu has been marginalized and his reiterated cry for literary invention forgotten. Omitted from *La Comparaison*, *Les Amours du Compas et de la Règle* was included in La Fontaine's *Recueil de poésies chrestiennes et diverses* (1671), dedicated to the Prince de Conti the following year.

Odes, poëmes & autres œuvres

Soon after May 1643 Desmarets added to the *Œuvres poëtiques* a twenty-eight-page section of *Odes, poëmes & autres œuvres*, beginning with an ode *A la Reyne Regente, sur la bataille de Rocroy gagnée par Monseigneur le duc d'Enghien*:

> Rends graces au Dieu Tout-puissant,
> Mets à ses pieds toute ta gloire,
> Anne, dont le regne naissant,
> Commence par vne victoire . . .

That ode is followed by a sonnet to the Queen on her two sons, 'Reyne, dont les ayeulx domptèrent tant de mers'; an elegy *Sur la maladie de Monseigneur le Cardinal* [de Richelieu];[22] a sonnet on the same subject: *Tombeau du Grand Cardinal Duc de Richelieu*; a sonnet on that subject; a sonnet and a 'Plainte' 'A Monseigneur le Cardinal Mazarin'; an epigram 'Pour le portraict de Madame la Princesse [de Condé]', assumed to speak for itself; and a sonnet 'A Monsieur le Comte de Saint Agnan—François VII de Beauvillier, Comte (and from 1663 first Duc) de Saint-Aignan (1608?–87). He had spent part of 1639–40 in the Bastille for lack of success at Thionville, would enter Gaston d'Orléans's services in 1644, and in 1649 become Premier Gentilhomme de la Chambre du Roi. To some copies of the *Œuvres poëtiques* was added an ode *A son Altesse Royale Monseigneur le Duc d'Orléans, sur la prise de Graveline* in 1644. In one Bibliothèque Nationale copy *Odes, poëmes & autres œuvres* are substituted for gatherings of 'Autres Œuvres poëtiques'

---

[22] Previously issued separately with the sonnet as a *Récit des vers presentez à Monseigneur le Cardinal sur sa maladie* (n.p., n.d. [1642]) and not to be confused with the earlier poem 'Sur la santé de Monseigneur le Cardinal de Richelieu' published in the anthology entitled *Le Sacrifice des Muses* (1635), beginning: 'O Cieux ne nous ravissez pas'.

before the 'Amours', and no two copies of the *Œuvres poëtiques* are exactly alike. These poems reflect both Desmarets's loyalty to the memory of Cardinal Richelieu and his interest in new patronage. The ode *Tombeau du Grand Cardinal de Richelieu*, addressed to Louis XIII ('Rare modele des Princes, / Loüis, juste Conquerant'), is the most striking. Issued separately before May 1643 by Henri Le Gras and reprinted in *La Comparaison*, its sculptural allegory evokes in vigorous heptasyllabic verse both a tomb for the Cardinal in the Sorbonne chapel and the political allegories of *Europe* and *Clovis*:

> Place aux Muses immortelles,
> O! troupe de médisans,
> Detestables partisans
> D'Ennemis, ou de Rebelles.
> Fuyez, elles vont parestre,
> Pour couvrir de lauriers verds
> Richelieu qui fit son Maistre
> L'Arbitre de l'Univers.[23]

The *Tombeau de Richelieu* sharply contrasts with verse written after Richelieu's death by several other poets formerly eager for his patronage:

> Quand la Parque inexorable,
> Par un cruel accident,
> Fit voir le triste occident
> De cét Astre incomparable,
> Le Chœur des divines Sœurs,
> Dont il aimoit les douceurs,
> Et la majesté sublime,
> Sentit à ce grand malheur
> Que le seul silence exprime
> Une profonde douleur.

Another stanza may be contrasted with the more familiar scepticism of the frondeur Duc de La Rochefoucauld in his famous *Maximes*, or that of Jacques Esprit in *La Fausseté des vertus humaines* (1677–8)—moralists for whom the virtues are, if not actually vices dissembled,

---

[23] First of twenty-five stanzas, quoted from *La Comparaison*, 253–65, where a preliminary note (p. 252) supposes 'que les Lecteurs équitables reconnoistront qu'il faut estre Architecte, & Peintre, & Poëte, pour avoir pû imaginer & representer un tombeau aussi magnifique & aussi surprenant que celuy qui suit'.

tinged with vice. Theirs is the sort of analysis attributed by Desmarets to the late Cardinal's detractors:

> Soudain de noires malices
> Ses beaux faits sont combatus.
> On déguise ses vertus
> De l'affreux masque des vices.
> Sa justice est cruauté:
> Son courage une fierté
> Funeste à l'heur de la terre;
> Et tous, d'une ingrate voix,
> Font un crime de la guerre
> Qui mit l'Espagne aux abois.

Desmarets's sonnet 'Si tu pouvois, Armand, du tombeau qui t'enserre' treats the themes of the ode with similar vigour.[24]

In the 'Plainte' addressed to Cardinal Mazarin, Desmarets asks for a continuation of the special relationship he had enjoyed with Richelieu:

> laisse en ton palais entrer pour vn moment
> Vne muse, autrefois les délices d'Armand,
> Autrefois éclatante, heureuse, caressée,
> Des louanges d'Armand cent fois récompensée
> Et que tu vis cent fois venir à ton secours
> Pour t'alleger du poids de tes sages discours.

Then, reminding Mazarin that one of Richelieu's last requests had been:

> 'A tout ce qui m'ayma sois vn autre moy-mesme,
> Et comme je t'aymois, ayme ce que j'ayme',

Desmarets adds:

> Jules, des Grands Romains le véritable sang,
> Je dirai sans orgueil que j'eus place en ce rang.
> Car tu sçais qu'il m'aymoit, que cet esprit sublime
> Eut pour moy des momens de tendresse & d'estime,
> Et que tu fus tesmoin dans ces temps glorieux,
> Que cent fois cet honneur me fit des envieux . . .

---

[24] *La Comparison*, 266. Apparently first published as a fugitive piece, its first line in *Odes, poëmes & autres œuvres* is more immediate: 'Si tu pouuois Armand hors du plomb qui t'enserre'.

Other poems on politics and war

When, on 14 May, less than six months after Richelieu's death, Louis XIII himself died, the Duchesse d'Aiguillon arranged for a sonnet by Desmarets 'Pour Louis le Juste' to be engraved on the pedestal of the equestrian statue of Louis XIII which Cardinal Richelieu had placed in the Place-Royale on 27 September 1639. Like the original statue, the pedestal and its inscriptions—two in Latin and two in French—were destroyed in the Revolution of 1789. The late King, supposed to be speaking for himself, reiterates policies expressed in *La Prospérité* and in *Europe*:

> Que ne peut la vertu? Que ne peut le courage?
> J'ai dompté pour jamais l'Hérésie en son fort.
> Du Tage impérieux j'ai fait trembler le bord,
> Et du Rhin jusqu'à l'Ebre accru mon héritage.
>
> J'ai tiré par mon bras l'Europe d'esclavage;
> Et si tant de travaux n'eussent hâté mon sort,
> J'eusse attaqué l'Asie, et d'un pieux effort,
> J'eusse du Saint Tombeau vengé le long servage.
>
> ARMAND, ce grand génie, ame de mes exploits,
> Porta de toutes parts mes armes et mes lois,
> Et rehaussa l'éclat des rayons de ma gloire.
>
> Enfin il m'éleva ce pompeux monument
> Où pour rendre à son nom mémoire pour mémoire,
> Je veux qu'avec le mien il vive incessamment.[25]

This earliest recorded inscription in French on a royal monument in Paris, anticipated only by the French inscription for the statue of Louis XIII erected in Rheims in 1636, is as much a tribute to Richelieu's policies for the French language and for French verse as an endorsement of his military policies, internal and external—including the notion of a new Crusade.

Of the poems which Desmarets continued to write in the Regency of Anne of Austria and afterwards, two of the more attractive are included in *La Comparaison*: the ode 'Détestation de la guerre' and the stanzas 'La France à la Reine Régente lors de la guerre de Paris'. His ode 'A Monseigneur le Chancelier [Séguier] sur le retour du Roy

---

[25] 'Pour Louis le Juste', in Lefort de la Morinière, (ed.), *Bibliothèque poétique*, ii. 217; previously published e.g. in *Nouveau Recueil des épigrammatistes français, anciens et modernes* (Amsterdam, 1720), i. 165, with 'La Violette' and other poems.

à Paris en l'année 1649' is known only from a manuscript copy.[26] For his odes to Colbert, written around 1667, and his 'Indignation. A Monseigneur le Duc de Richelieu', read to the Académie française on 25 August 1673, see Chapter 1. Other short poems celebrate victories of Louis XIV: *Au Roy sur sa conqueste de la Franche-Comté*, 'permis et achevé d'imprimer' on 14 March 1668; and *Au Roy, sur la prise de Mastrich. Ode* (1673); *Au Roy sur sa seconde conqueste de la Franche-Comté. Stances* (1674).

Other secular poems

The earliest of Desmarets's poems, one of the 'Eloges' published with *Les Poësies et rencontres du sieur de Neufgermain, poète hétéroclite de Monseigneur, frère unique du Roy* (1630), is also one of the wittiest, anticipating the peculiar blend of burlesque and *précieux* of *Les Visionnaires* and *Les Amours du Compas et de la Règle*:

> Un jour, les Muses débauchées
> Voulant mettre un poëte au jour
> Prièrent Apollon d'Amour
> Qui les eut bientost despechées;
> Dans huit mois [et] quatre semaines,
> L'une un pied, l'autre fit sa main,
> Bref fut fait de neuf sœurs germaines
> L'incomparable Neufgermain.[27]

Another anthologized poem omitted from the *Œuvres poëtiques* is an epitaph for the Zaga(or Gaza)-Christ, who arrived in Paris in 1635 claiming to be the Prince of Ethiopia and—though 'tousiours assisté par les gens de son Eminence'[28]—died at Rueil on 22 April 1638, aged about 21:

> Cy gist du Roy d'Etiopie
> L'original, ou la Copie.[29]

---

[26] Bibliothèque Nationale, Mss. fr. 20,035.

[27] Quoted by Magne, *Voiture*, ii. 61, from *Nouveau Recueil des plus belles poésies* (1654), 224.

[28] *Gazette* for 24 Apr. 1638.

[29] 'Epitaphe du Zaga Christ qui se disoit Roy d'Etiopie', Bibliothèque de l'Arsenal, Mss. 4129; published in *Jardin d'Epitaphes* (1648). In *Les Visionnaires* (II. II) Hesperie boasts: 'C'est pour moy qu'est venu le Roy d'Ethiopie'. See J. de Giffre de Rechac, *Les Estranges Evenemens du voyage de son Altesse, le Serenissime Prince Zaga-Christ d'Ethiopie* (1635).

The 'Recueils Conrart' also contain a sonnet, 'Vers de Monsieur des Marestz sur vn beau sein':

> Beau sein d'un si beau corps la pompeuse merueille,
> Monts sur qui les regards s'égarent doucement;
> Rempars fermes, et fiers d'vn cœur de diamant,
> Qui gardez ses dehors d'vne audace pareille.
>
> Globes blancs dont se cache vne pointe vermeille,
> Neiges, qui repoussez les ardeurs d'vn amant
> Sur qui l[e] traistre amour repose molement,
> Et d'où sans cesse il blesse en feignant qu'il sommeille.
>
> De mille libertez agreables tombeaux,
> Mon ame m'abandonne en vous voyant si beaux,
> Pleine d'vn doux transport vous aproche, et vous touche
>
> D'inuisibles baisers caresse vos apas,
> Et perdant le respect qu'elle impose à ma bouche
> Se rit de ce qu'elle ose, et qu'on ne la void pas.[30]

Adapted directly or indirectly from Torquato Tasso's *Gerusalemme liberata* (4.31), this sonnet was probably omitted from the *Œuvres poëtiques* because (*a*) literary fashion had moved against such echoes of earlier 'blasons du corps féminin' and (*b*) the fashion in apparel supposed in the sonnet had begun to attract criticism. Behind the pleasure expressed in the sonnet lies a fashion of *décolletage* with which Desmarets must have been familiar from his earliest days at Court but which in the 1630s began to be imitated beyond Court circles. Around 1634 the Compagnie du Saint-Sacrement reacted against 'la mode . . . de porter la gorge découverte jusqu'à l'excés'.[31] Three years later Pierre Juvernay published a tract against *décolletage*: his 'Discours particulier contre les femmes desbraillées de ce temps'.[32] The line 'Globes blancs dont se cache vne pointe vermeille' and the tone of the sonnet suggest that the *décolletage* evoked would not have seemed excessive at Court around 1638–42 (the period to which other poems in the manuscript can be dated), while Juvernay's Tract helps to explain why the sonnet was not published.

---

[30] Bibliothèque de l'Arsenal, Mss. 4129.

[31] René II de Voyer de Paulmy, Seigneur d'Argenson, Comte de Rouffiac (1623–1700), *Annales de la Compagnie du Saint-Sacrement*, ed. H. Beauchet-Filleau (Marseilles, 1900), 51–2, quoted by H. P. Salomon, *Tartuffe devant l'opinion française* (1962), 21.

[32] According to Salomon (22), three editions of P. Juvernay's 'Discours particulier' were published by P. Le Mur in 1637, which suggests a certain concern.

Jeux de cartes

Towards the end of 1644 Desmarets's *Cartes des Rois de France* appeared—thirty-nine cards plus frontispiece, probably for old French piquet, although Orest Ranum mentions with the title *Histoire de France* a series of sixty-five cards for the game of goose—by which he presumably means a form of the *jeu de l'oie*, usually played with dice.[33] The *Cartes des Rois* were the first published by Desmarets as part of an ambitious system of educational cards whose publication was never completed. The *Jeu des Reynes renommées*, *Jeu de la Géographie*, and *Jeu de la Fable*—each a set of fifty-two playing cards—soon followed. Every card has a brief caption in prose and a vignette engraved by Stefano della Bella—'une suite de près de deux cens planches extrêmement intéressantes et du meilleur temps de la Belle'.[34]

According to Paul Pellisson, the games had been commissioned by Cardinal Richelieu before his death, 'pour l'instruction du Roi Louis XIV, en son enfance, et lorsqu'il n'étoit que Dauphin'.[35] This suggests a time around 1640–1, when della Bella was working on elevations of Arras, the frontispiece for the *Œuvres poëtiques*, and the plates for *Mirame*. Desmarets's intention in the *Jeux* is to 'deguiser en forme de jeux les sciences les plus necessaires aux princes, comme l'Histoire . . . la Géographie', an aim reminiscent of the dedication of *Rosane*, a novel in which he purports to combine knowledge with pleasure and 'donner des preceptes aux ieunes Princes'. Like Desmarets's novels and plays, these *Jeux* are rooted in Neoplatonism: in *Laws* i and vii Plato proposes that children can be taught useful things through play and that teaching is more effective when pupils are not vexed.

In dedicating the *Jeux* to Anne of Austria, Desmarets explains that he intends to encapsulate the principles of the most useful arts and sciences in his games and to convey useful knowledge to princes in

---

[33] O. Ranum, 'Jeux de cartes, pédagogie et enfance de Louis XIV', in *Les Jeux à la Renaissance* (Tours, 1982), 553–62. I have seen only the undated mounted set in the Bibliothèque Nationale and the cards reprinted in book form with one hundred and ninety-five engravings (two edns., 1664 and 1698, both Bibliothèque Nationale, plus partial sets in the Library of Congress.) For a reproduction of the cards, see P. D. Massar, *Stefano della Bella* (New York, 1971). Ranum furnishes further useful references.

[34] Jombert, *Essai d'un catalogue*, 28. Jombert misdates the plates 1646.

[35] Pellisson and d'Olivet, *Histoire de l'Académie-Françoise*, i. 282–3.

a new art-form—notably to the child Louis XIV, whose 'généreuses inclinations' are duly noted. Kings of France are ranked 'par classes d'un costé les Roys Illustres et les bons, et de l'autre les faineans et les mauvais, avec avantage pour les premiers, & desadvantage pour les autres', so that 'vn jeune Prince en passant le temps à ce Ieu, imprimeroit en son ame vn extreme desir d'imiter les vns, et vne grande horreur pour les deffauts des autres'. Desmarets's theory is that the child, 'ne devant ces connoissances qu'à sa propre meditation', may form his own precepts and cherish them more than precepts 'donnez par ses Gouverneurs'. After the *Cartes des Rois*, he continues:

J'inventay les Ieux des autres Histoires, comme des Empires, des autres Royaumes, des Reynes renommées et des hommes Illustres, avec le Ieu des Dieux de l'Antiquité, et celuy des Fables, et de la Geographie. Puis le courage me croissant, j'ay mesme refait en Ieux la Logique, la Morale, la Politique, et la Physique, avec un tel succès que l'on pourra s'estonner de l'heur avec lequel j'ay mélé tout ensemble la science, la breveté, la clarté et le plaisir.

The title of one of the lost games suggests a latent affinity with Cardinal Richelieu's Galerie(s) des hommes illustres, parallel portraits for which Roland Desmarets had provided Latin couplets: exemplars with captions as *aides-mémoire*, as Ranum remarks. It was easy to adapt for playing-cards the sort of captioned portraits found in various historical works: Aymot's version of Plutarch's *Lives*, for example (*Les Vies des hommes illustres*, 1606) and later the *Histoire de France depuis Faramond jusqu'à maintenant* (1643–51) by François Eudes de Mézerai (1610–83), the Historiographe de France elected in 1648 to Voiture's seat in the Académie-Française. Even the 'Guirlande de Julie' provides precedents: the poems provide the image of each flower not only with a compliment but also with a caption recalling the main associations of the violet, the lily, etc. Indeed, Desmarets scarcely needed to look beyond the tradition of the emblem book to imagine detached illustrated cards on which a single prose caption replaced both verse caption and prose explanation: a tradition exemplified by Gomberville's *La Doctrine des mœurs tirée de la philosophie des stoïques, représentée en cent tableaux et expliquée* (1646), dedicated to the young Louis XIV but published with additional letters to Anne of Austria and Cardinal Mazarin.

Perhaps only the *Cartes des Rois de France* and the *Cartes des Reynes renommées* were published by December 1644. In a letter from Rennes dated 27 December 1644 a lady signing herself

M. D. B. writes to Desmarets that when she attempted to purchase from her bookseller a second copy of the *Cartes des Rois*, 'le bonheur commun de toutes vos pieces, et nostre mal-heur voulurent que ce Libraire n'en auoit plus. Toutes ces cartes estoient venduës presqu'aussi-tost arriuées.'[36] Instead he supplied a copy of the *Jeu des Reynes renommées*, the absence from which of Anne of Brittany (the duchess whose marriage to Louis XII in 1499 added Brittany to France) prompted her letter. Desmarets's reply on 10 January 1645 indicates that the *Jeu de la Géographie* and the *Jeu des Fables* had not yet appeared, permitting their publication to be dated 1645. His reply does raise a few doubts about the educational value of his cards and of the courtly attitude he affects: 'J'ay composé ce jeu de Reines de ma pure memoire, sans le secours d'aucuns livres.'[37] Writers, he explains, often cannot be troubled to look for a book to verify their historic sources and draw instead upon memory and imagination. Another critic of Desmarets's *Jeux*, Charles Sorel, rejects the very notion of learning through play and points out that reliance on 'ces cartes d'inventions' might 'embrouiller l'esprit des enfants', so that when proper instruction is later provided, 'ils croiroient toujours jouer, et parleroient plustot de jeu que de science . . . il me semble indigne de la majesté des sciences de les traitter si bassement'.[38]

Correspondence with the lady from Rennes, criticism by Sorel, and two reprints in book form witness success for the *Jeux*. Unaware of just how closely Desmarets had been associated for three decades with royal entertainments for adolescents and adults, Ranum doubts whether the young Louis XIV was actually allowed to try them. I doubt, on the contrary, that Anne of Austria would have permitted such a dedication without being satisfied with the content of this and other works addressed to her during her Regency by Desmarets. The main thing about the *Cartes des Rois de France* is that, however conventionally, they do bring into sharp focus characteristics associated with individual kings. Good kings all have an entire card to themselves, with a positive iconography: on a chariot, on horseback,

[36] *Lettre d'une Dame de Rennes à M. des Marests sur le Jeu des reines renommées, avec la réponse de M. des Marests*, in *Les Jeux de cartes*, 2–3: letters first published, according to d'Olivet, in 1645. Bibliothèque de l'Arsenal, Mss. 4119, contains under that title six letters exchanged between Dec. 1644 and Jan. 1645.

[37] *Jeux de cartes*, 37.

[38] C. Sorel, *De la perfection de l'homme* (1655), 376, quoted by Ranum, *Les Jeux à la Renaissance*, 558. Sorel had, however, published *La Maison des jeux* (1642).

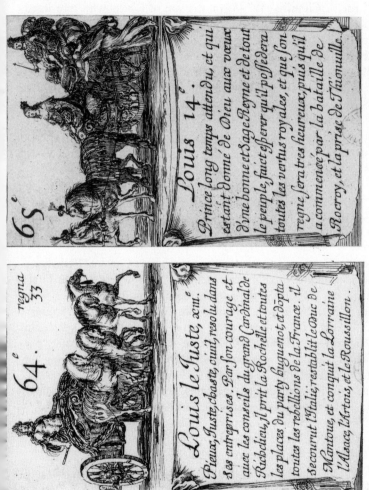

64.

regna 33

Louis le Juste, xIII.

Pieux, Iuste, chaste, ciuil, resolu dans
Ses entreprises. Par son courage et
auec les conseils du grand Cardinal de
Richelieu, il prit la Rochelle et toutes
les places du party huguenot, et dōpta
toutes les rebellions de la France. Il
Secourut l'Italie, restablit le Duc de
Mantouë, et conquit la Lorraine
l'Alsace, l'Artois, et le Roussillon.

65.

Louis 14.

Prince long temps attendu, et qui
estant Donné De Dieu aux vœux
D'une bonne et Sage Reyne et De tout
le peuple, faict esperer qu'il possedera
toutes les vertus royales, et que son
regne sera tres heureux, puis qu'il
a commencé par la bataille De
Rocroy, et la prise De Thionuille.

FIG. 9. Louis le Juste (Louis XIII). 64th King of France, in triumph, from *Cartes des Rois de France* (1644), and FIG. 10. Louis XIV, 65th King of France, in triumph, with Anne of Austria holding the reins, from *Cartes des Rois de France* (1644). Engravings by Stefano della Bella *(Phot. Bib. Nat. Paris)*

Saint Louis with a fleet in the background suggesting the Crusades, etc. (see Figs. 9 and 10). The 'Rois fainéants' look lazy, in attitudes not normally associated with French royal image-making. Among the 'Cruels', Clotaire (497–561), the son of Clovis who murdered his nephews—a French counterpart to Richard III, about whom Desmarets expresses no historic doubts—is depicted sword in hand with a caption to match. Other negative categories are the 'Malheureux', 'Simples', 'Ny Bons ny Mauvais', 'Meslez', and 'Sans Foy'. Kings representing models that are not to be followed share cards in no dynastic order, have smaller depictions and shorter captions, because Desmarets (as Ranum says so well) 'estime que les histoires exemplaires sont considérées plus importantes que l'ordre dynastique'.[39]

Pierre de La Porte (1603–80), later Premier Valet de chambre du Roi, states that Louis XIV was 'incensed over the behavior of the early *fainéant* kings, and determined not to be Louis, the *Fainéant*'.[40] I know of no channel through which he could have met 'rois fainéants' more graphically than in the *Cartes des Rois de France*.

Georges Couton states that in the years before Cardinal Richelieu's death Desmarets was 'le précepteur du petit-neveu du Cardinal, Armand de Vignerot'—the future second Duc de Richelieu with whom Desmarets was in any case closely connected from January 1643.[41] This relationship may be pertinent to Desmarets's *Jeux*. In his *Histoire de l'Académie-Françoise* Pellison mentions that 'par l'ordre du Duc de Richelieu son maître' Desmarets was preparing 'un ouvrage considérable, qu'il appelle l'*Abrégé de la science universelle*, et qui contient en près de mille chapitres, des connoissances sommaires, sur la plus-part des choses qui tombent dans l'entretien ordinaire.[42] Such a work probably incorporated the lost *Jeux*. It must also have provided much of the material for the conversational progression through the arts and sciences in *Les Délices de l'esprit*.

Only limited commentary on the other *Jeux* is possible. The *Jeu des Reynes renommées* reflects the feminism also evident in Jacques Du Bosc's *La Femme héroïque, ou les héroïnes comparées avec les*

---

[39] Ranum, *Les Jeux à la Renaissance*, 557.

[40] J. B. Wolf, 'The Formation of a King', in Rule (ed.), *Louis XIV and the Craft of Kingship*, 102–31.

[41] Couton, *Richelieu et le théâtre*, 34.

[42] Pellison and d'Olivet, *Histoire de l'Académie-Françoise*, i. 283.

Saincte

Anne d'Austriche

Reyne de France, Saincte, Sage, d'vne bonté merueilleuse, et d'vne modestie pareille a sa grandeur. Petite fille d'Empereurs, fille et sœur de deux grands Roys, femme d'vn plus grand encore et tous jours victorieux, et mere d'vn Roy donné du Ciel a ses vœux, qui surpassera tous les Roys du monde.

FIG. 11. Anne of Austria, from *Jeu des Reynes renommées* (enlarged) (*Phot. Bib. Nat. Paris*)

héros en toute sorte de vertus (1645). Like Du Bosc, Desmarets had
been sympathetic to feminism throughout the 1630s. Married from
humbler origins to Alexander the Great (one of the official models
for Louis XIV), Roxana is 'heureuse'. Eleanor of Aquitaine is
'capricieuse'. Elizabeth I of England and Catherine de Médicis are
'habiles'. Marie de Médicis is omitted. Anne of Austria (see Fig. 11)
and Blanche of Castille, mother of the Crusading King, Saint Louis,
are both 'sainctes'—a fashionable parallel at the time, well suited
to the theme of *Clovis*.

   The *Jeu de la Géographie* deploys iconology long used in Court
ballet, together with assessments—France is fertile, Spain sterile—
reflected in *Europe* and other contemporary works. The *Jeu des Fables*
relates most obviously to *La Vérité des fables*, also dedicated to Anne
of Austria. The *Jeux* belong to a moment of French cultural history
in which (*a*) the images of kings, queens, and knaves were coming
to be styled in something like their current common forms and (*b*)
educational sets were invented by various writers, including René
Descartes, whose *Geometric and Mechanick Powers Represented
in a Pack of Playing Cards* (designed for quite serious study) is
preserved, as far as I know, in a unique copy in the Yale University
Library.[43] All Desmarets's *Jeux* fit well into the cultural climate
reflected also in works of his fellow Academician Jean Baudoin
(1564–1650) concerned with mythology, iconology, and emblems:
Mythologie ou explication des fables (1627), *Iconologie, ou explication
de plusieurs images, emblèmes et autres figures hiéroglyphiques,
tirée de César Ripa* (1636), *Recueil d'emblèmes divers* (1638), etc.
Desmarets's *Jeux* are all the more valuable in interpreting the use
of such symbols and images in the Regency Court for his having
been (in my view) a very much less marginal figure than assumed
by Ranum.

   Ranum contrasts with Desmarets's *Jeux* Louis XIV's 'plus grand
jeu' in the garden of the Palais-Royal—a superb miniature fortress
which he could take with his miniature army several times a day.
I do not know whether Desmarets as (a former?) Surintendant des
fortifications had anything to do with its design.

---

[43] The British Library holds a copy of the accompanying book, *The Use of the
Geometrical Playing-cards* (London, 1697), and other related material.

12

Devotional Poetry

Religious experience was such an important part of life in Desmarets's time that it is somewhat arbitrary to separate his devotional poetry from his other verse. Nor does what he wrote before his mystic conversion in 1654 always contrast with what he wrote thereafter. Following the death of Cardinal Richelieu he had abandoned writing for the theatre; and before *Aspasie* he had begun writing *Clovis*—a poem whose royalism and nationalism are steeped in once-dominant French Catholic ideology, as are his late biblical epics. Works dedicated to the Queen Regent in the 1640s show that no sharp break occurs in 1645 between *Les Jeux de cartes* and *L'Office de la Vierge Marie*: the ode 'Sur la bataille de Rocroy' (1643) could be considered a devotional poem, drawing upon the 'Exultemus Domino' and 'Jubilemus Deo' of matins; and his next dedication after *L'Office de la Vierge Marie* is a novel with a doctrinal subtext, *La Vérité des fables*.

Desmarets's earliest devotional poems—the 'Œuvres chrestiennes' collected in the *Œuvres poëtiques*—date from the final years of the reign of Louis XIII, to whom they are dedicated. According to Desmarets himself, *Les Promenades de Richelieu*, *L'Imitation de Jésus-Christ*, and *Le Combat spirituel* precede rather than follow his conversion. His two small volumes of posthumous *Maximes chrestiennes* were probably written after 1654, perhaps long after; but the time (or times) of their composition is not known.

'Œuvres chrestiennes'

The first of the published poems may be dated between 1635, when the arrival of the Zaga-Christ in Paris aroused interest in a Christian kingdom beyond Egypt, and the birth of the Dauphin. One is a sonnet 'Pour vn grand tableau de Sainct Philippe baptisant l'Ethiopien, Présenté deuant l'Autel de la Vierge à Nostre Dame', beginning:

> Voy le Ciel, ô Passant, que t'ouvre le baptesme,
> Voy l'esclat rayonnant de l'immortelle Cour;

Et brûle de desir d'estre en ce beau sejour,
Qui brille du grand Dieu la Majesté suprême.

This sonnet on a sacred painting is cited not as Desmarets's most accomplished devotional verse but for the light it sheds on Desmarets's reputation as a poet and closeness to the throne. Significantly, it is followed by a 'Vœu à la Vierge, pour le Roy et la Reyne', written in anticipation of the Dauphin. The second of the two quatrains concludes with the prayer:

Conserve le plus iuste, & le plus sainct des Rois;
Et que des chastes flancs de sa moitié fidele
Sorte vn Prince qui fasse à l'Orient rebelle
Sentir son bras vangeur ou reuerer la Croix.

Desmarets's poem—thematically close to *Clovis*, on which he was already working at that time—can scarcely be unrelated to the votive offering repeatedly made by Louis XIII during Anne's pregnancy with the Dauphin. By *lettres patentes* recorded in the Parlement de Paris on 11 December 1637 and 10 February 1638 he dedicated his crown and his kingdom to the Virgin in hope of peace in the war with Spain.

Hubert Méthivier states that the idea of the 'vœu' occurred to Louis XIII—long devoted to Mary—on 15 November 1636 at a *Te Deum* following French victories at Corbie and Saint-Jean de Losne.[1] He reaffirmed the 'vœu' at Abbeville (Somme) on Assumption Day 1638. An annual procession each 15 August was instituted and a statue of the Virgin placed at the high altar of Notre-Dame Cathedral.

According to Goujet, *Psaumes de Davide paraphrasés, et accommo-dés au Règne de Louis le Juste*, a major subsection of the *Œuvres chrestiennes*, was also separately published by Le Gras in 1640.[2] In the epistle 'Au Roy' republished here, Desmarets dares to hope that his Psalms will rise to heaven, 's'il sont si heureux que d'estre agreez de Vostre Majesté, & prononcez de sa bouche sacrée, dont les prieres trouuent vn accez si facile deuant Dieu'. Whether or not they had that success, they were reprinted not only in the *Œuvres poëtiques*, but in the *Office de la Vierge Marie* (at least three editions dedicated to two queens) and in *Prières chrétiennes* (1680). Desmarets's dedication implies that his Psalms are best read aloud.

---

[1] Méthivier, *Le Siècle de Louis XIII* (1971), 48.
[2] C.-P. Goujet, *Bibliothèque françoise* (1756), vol. 17, s.v.

Translation of any biblical text presents special problems of style in relation both to fashion and to interpretation, astutely analysed for French paraphrased Psalms of this period by Paulette Leblanc.[3] Indeed, the Council of Trent (1545–63) had forbidden vernacular translations of the Bible and discouraged translation of the Church Fathers, insisting on the use of Latin for the Eucharist and other sacraments of the Church.[4] Some of Desmarets's Psalms appear to have a political subtext analogous to the imperial themes of *Scipion*, *Roxane*, and of Corneille's tragedies performed in this period. Consider this fifth stanza of Psalm 71, 'Deus iudicium tuum':

> Il verra courber deuant soy
> Les Rois qui commandent l'Afrique;
> Et les rebelles à sa Loy
> Sentiront le fer de sa pique.
> Mille presens de tous costez,
> Soit des hommages volontaires,
> Soit des Prouinces tributaires,
>   Luy seront apportez.

The political subtext of other Psalms is more closely related to internal matters. Consider this stanza from Psalm 96, 'Dominus regnavit':

> Deuant l'ire de Dieu les monts s'humilierent,
> Et leurs chefs orgueilleux, de crainte se plierent;
> Iusques à s'abbaisser au creux de leurs vallons:
> Les riuages des mers se cacherent sous l'onde
>   Deuant l'Autheur du monde,
> Comme font les roseaux deuant les Aquilons.

Desmarets begins his selection with Psalm 19, 'Coeli enarrant gloriam Dei', a Psalm important in the seventeenth century not only as a Psalm of praise, but as a scriptural authorization of the natural world as a second revelation. He includes Psalms of degrees.

The longest subsection is Desmarets's version of 'Les Préceptes de mariage de Saint Grégoire de Naziance'—a fourth-century Church Father admired by Desmarets for having introduced poetic fictions into his tragedy *Suffering Christ* and Virginity as an allegorical

---

[3] P. Leblanc, *Les Paraphrases françaises des psaumes à la fin de la période baroque, 1610–1660* (Clermont-Ferrand, 1961).

[4] Martin, *Livre, pouvoirs et société*, i. 114.

personage in another play. Although 'trop abondant en discours, comme tous les Grecs,' Desmarets observes, 'il est excellent pour ce qui regarde les sentimens, les mœurs, les comparaisons, les figures, & la diction'.[5] This St Gregory was particularly hostile to Arians, who denied the consubstantiality of Christ. The 'Préceptes de mariage' are addressed to wives. Here are two of them:

> Aymez Dieu le premier, puis d'vne amour feconde
> > Honorez vostre espoux;
> C'est l'oeil de vostre vie, & luy seul dans le monde
> > Doit estre aymé de vous.

.   .   .   .   .

> De l'espoux honoré gardez-vous de pretendre
> > Ny l'employ, ny le rang,
> Et ne vous vantez point par orgueil de descendre
> > D'ayeux de noble sang.

Such precepts mark the cultural limits of Desmarets's feminism and suggest a way in which the religious doctrine he supports interacts with social structures. These are the precepts parodied in Molière's *L'École des femmes*, III. II.

L'Office de la Vierge Marie

L'Office de la Vierge Marie is remarkable for its dedication to the Queen Regent and the 'Approbation' of the Sorbonne on 25 March 1645, signed by A. L'Escuyer and N. Le Mayre.[6] The work is given warm support:

L'Autheur de ces Psaumes mis en vers, aussi bien que de ces Hymnes et Prieres de l'Eglise, a ioint auec tant d'heur et d'adresse la politesse de son style à la pureté du langage du S. Esprit, la nouuauté industrieuse de ses traductions

---

[5] 'Traité pour juger des Poetes Grecs, Latins, et François', in *Clovis*, 3rd edn. (1673), 38. Although by the end of the sixteenth century Parisian theologians had published numerous French translations from the Patrology, not many were published in the period 1598–1643. Martin (*Livre, pouvoirs et société*, i. 114, 493–5), finds works by St Gregory of Naziamzus in considerably fewer 'petites et moyennes bibliothèques'—only 17—than works by St Augustine (78) and St Bernard (51), but better represented than Sts Clement of Alexandria (15), Cyril (15), Hilary (12), and Denys of Alexandria (11).

[6] This must be the Nicolas Le Maire, at some time Chanoine de Soissons, who published *Le Sanctuaire fermé aux profanes, ou la Bible défendue au vulgaire* (1651) and (more in line with Desmarets's work in translation) *Le Sacre du Roy, avec la version des prières en françois* (Rheims, 1654). This 'Approbation' was reaffirmed by the Sorbonne on 1 July 1669.

à la richesse et fecondité de ses diuins enseignemens, et la grace et majesté de sa Poësie à la dignité et saincteté de ses mysteres, qu'il est facile de iuger que le mesme Esprit qui parloit par la bouche de Dauid, a animé ses paroles et ses pensées dans cét ouurage veritablement de Pieté. Ce qui est cause que bien loin d'y trouuer à redire . . . Nous le iugeons plustost tres-vtile au salut des ames . . .[7]

In his 'Epistre' to Anne of Austria, Desmarets relates his translation to the modern position on several issues:

C'estoit, Madame, vne honte et vn deffaut considerable à nostre siecle, que ce bel art [de la poësie] ne seruit qu'à loüer les creatures, et que les loüanges du Createur fussent si negligées, que les dames n'eussent dans leurs liures de Prieres que des traductions rudes et obscures, plus capables de rebuter la deuotion que de la satisfaire.

In other words, a translation should convey a sense of the literary quality of the original as well as its literal meaning; poets should not avoid the major doctrinal themes of national faith, which may be expressed in French as well as in Latin or Greek; women should be allowed to worship decently in the vernacular;[8] and the art of poetry should be used to propagate the faith 'reuestue . . . des graces et de la magnificence de la Poësie'—an intention echoed many times in the seventeenth century.[9] Desmarets allows that other writers might have been more successful in what he undertook but claims the merit 'd'auoir monstré le chemin aux autres, et de leur auoir fait sentir, que c'est à loüer Dieu qu'ils deuroient employer le talent qu'il leur a donné'. When men of genius come to treat the subject, he continues, not only will the pious be satisfied, but even those of little zeal who read the prayers through curiosity 'connoistront sans y penser ce qu'ils n'auoient peut estre encore iamais consideré: c'est à dire, les merueilles de Dieu'. L'Office de la Vierge Marie thus incorporates the Psalms translated for Louis XIII and anticipates both Desmarets's later emphasis on the Christian marvellous and the apologetic aims of Les Délices de l'esprit.

---

[7] Office de la Vierge Marie, mis en vers auec plusieurs autres prieres par I. Desmarests (1647).

[8] Education for women typically included Italian and Spanish rather than Latin and Greek.

[9] Compare the College of Propaganda established by Urban VIII, Pope from 1623 to 1644.

Only minimal illustration of this aspect of Desmarets's work is possible. First a poem easy to compare with other versions, the Lord's Prayer, 'Pater Noster':

> Nostre Pere, qui des hauts Cieux
> Habites l'heureuse demeure,
> Que ton nom par tous à toute heure
> Soit sanctifié dans ces lieux.
>> Ton regne ainsi que ton pouvoir
> Par toute la terre s'épande.
> Qu'icy bas comme au ciel s'entende,
> Et s'accomplisse ton vouloir.
>> Qu'en toutes mes necessitez
> Ton soin ce jour ne m'abandonne;
> Et tout ainsi que je pardonne,
> Pardonne mes iniquitez.
>> Empesche l'Esprit infernal
> De tenter mon ame fragile:
> Sois mon secour & mon asile,
> Et me garanty de tout mal.[10]

In some poems Desmarets seeks simplicity—'In manus tuas', for example:

> O Dieu du ciel que je reclame,
> En tes mains je remets mon ame.

Others allow more invention through amplification—by way of contrast, this 'Oraison':

> Seigneur, entend nos voix, de ton sejour heureux
>> Regarde ta troupe soûmise,
>> Pere Eternel, reçoy nos vœux,
>> Et les devoirs de ton Eglise.
> Le Prestre est nostre organe, & va te les offrir,
>> Daigne, Seigneur, nous secourir.
>> Verse nous tes graces immenses,
> Ne nous épargne pas tes celestes tresors.
> Donne nous le pardon de toutes nos offenses,
> Et la santé de l'ame avec celle du corps.
>> Seigneur, uny les cœurs par unité de foy:

---

[10] 'Pater noster', quoted from *Prières chrétiennes* (n.p. 'la sphère', 1680), 4. The following illustrations are also taken from this edition.

> Dissipe les erreurs diverses,
> Tous les ennemis de ta Loy,
> Les conseils des ames perverses.
> Estend pour ton honneur ta creance en tous lieux:
> Fay que ton nom victorieux
> Retentisse par tout le monde.
> Mets sous un seul Pasteur tant de peuples divers,
> Qui vivent sur la terre, ou qui voguent sur l'onde:
> Que tous aiment ton Fils, qui sauva l'Univers . . .

An elegant expression of aspiration towards Christian unity, this 'Oraison' may carry a subtext of religious intolerance. Its form is interesting, emulating the sonorities of odes and paraphrased Psalms in the grand stanzaic manner of Malherbe and Racan, but in *vers mêlés* of the sort adapted to burlesque and *précieux* verse by La Fontaine in his *Fables* and by Molière in *Amphitryon*. *L'Office de la Vierge Marie* is not intended for silent reading but for recitation and song. The 'Approbation' mentions hymns 'qui se chantent sur le chant de l'Eglise'. It makes no critical sense to expect from lyrics conceived as an element of a work for performance the sort of verbal density appropriate for silent reading.

Les Promenades de Richelieu

The Fronde appears to have brought the most important changes in Desmarets's life since the death of Cardinal Richelieu, mainly because he helped to arrange the clandestine marriage of his cousin Anne de Pons to the young Duc de Richelieu. Imprisoned on 22 March 1650 for his part in that marriage, and still held a week later for debts said to amount to 60,000 *livres*, he was probably released through the intercession of the Duc de Richelieu, who was himself detained by the Duchesse d'Aiguillon until 27 June.[11]

Exiled to Sainte-Mesme, between Rochefort (Charente-Maritime) and Dourdan, the Duc and Duchesse de Richelieu escaped to Brouage.[12] In May 1651 the Duc attempted unsuccessfully to take possession of the château de Richelieu.[13] Rumoured in June to have

[11] Dubuisson-Aubenay, *Journal des guerres civiles*, i. 236–9, 274–81.
[12] They had been 'en la maison de l'un de leurs amis', Anne-Alexandre de l'Hôpital, Comte de Sainte-Mesme (1624–1701), Premier Écuyer of Gaston d'Orléans, from whose guards they escaped.
[13] Dubuisson-Aubenay, *Journal des guerres civiles*, ii. 63.

tried to abduct the Duchesse d'Aiguillon with the help of Desmarets's cousin the Marquis de Fors, the Duc's brother-in-law, he was confined to Paris by Anne of Austria and expressly forbidden either to go to Richelieu or to molest the Duchesse d'Aiguillon.[14] Dubuisson-Aubenay mentions that in October the Duc de Richelieu was rumoured dead.[15] In fact he was in Saintonge (of which he was governor) borrowing 600,000 *livres*, raising troops for the Princes, making the new duchess pregnant, appointing Desmarets his steward, and erecting 'en fief les marais de Cosnac en faveur de Jean des Marais'—the 'fief et seigneurie de Saint-Sorlin' whose cession he confirmed on 9 December 1653. By that time Desmarets had been at Richelieu for at least eighteen months.[16] The Marquis de Richelieu having also married without permission in October 1652, Mme d'Aiguillon rendered her accounts as guardian of both Duc and Marquis on 19 December 1652.[17] Shortly thereafter the Duc ordered the completion of the château de Richelieu.[18]

Les Promenades de Richelieu, ou les Vertus chrestiennes, dedicated to the new Duchesse de Richelieu, is an allegory of the seven Christian virtues: faith, hope, charity, humility, obedience, patience, and mansuetude or meekness. It also celebrates a site which (to judge from Phalante's description in *Les Visionnaires*) Desmarets had known for many years, now with its park more mature, a château more nearly complete, and an even grander collection of paintings and sculpture, as passages in the poem and an eighth promenade within doors confirm. The verse epistle opens with an allusion to the horrors of the Fronde:

> Pendant que la Discorde espouuante les loix,
> Seme ses noirs serpens dans le sein des François . . .

and to the 'naufrage heureux' by which he had found a port in such a lovely place.

Aspects of *Les Promenades de Richelieu* belong not to devotional poetry but to travel literature and 'la découverte de la France au XVIIᵉ siècle', especially lines concerning the interior and collections, where the eye of the beholder is that of the new steward. It is

---

[14] Dubuisson-Aubenay, *Journal des guerres civiles*, 82.   [15] Ibid. 125.

[16] For further references, see my article 'Desmarets de Saint-Sorlin's Ennoblement and Conversion Reconsidered', *French Studies*, 27 (1973), 151–64.

[17] Bonneau-Avenant, *La Duchesse d'Aiguillon*, 407.

[18] E. Bonnaffé, *Recherches sur les collections des Richelieu* (1883), 150.

somewhat surprising that art historians have not made more of the eighth promenade, which evokes the major themes of Richelieu's collections (the Christian marvellous, exemplary lives of illustrious men and women, parallels of ancients and moderns, allegories of virtues and vices, of the arts and ignorance, etc.) For instance, Anthony Blunt mentions (but does not appear to use) Desmarets's account of the 'chambre royale' or Cabinet du Roi, which suggests an arrangement of the pictures different from later descriptions.[19] To begin with, Desmarets makes it clear that the canvasses, more numerous than Blunt deduces, were not 'all set into panelling above a high dado'. Twenty 'quadres dorez' with the maritime scenes mentioned by Blunt were, according to Desmarets, below 'les bords de la corniche', while the Poussins, the Mantegnas, the Perugino, etc. Desmarets mentions as positioned 'plus haut', beginning with the Poussins:

> Que de douces beautez! que d'aimables figures!
> Voyez le riche amas de diuerses postures,
> Le char orné de pampre où triomphe Baccus
> Des peuples du Matin par son tyrse vaincus.
> Voyez la fureur gaye, & les folles boutades
> Des Satyres cornus, & des belles Menades.

That these two Poussins, the *Triumph of Bacchus* and the *Triumph of Pan*, are smaller than Mantegna's *Minerva Driving out the Vices*, 'en l'autre quadre', presents no real problem when the implication is grasped that they were displayed as a pair, while the Mantegna was hung separately. Over the fireplace Pyrrhus 'Immole Polyxene aux Manes de son pere'.

Whether or not always to be taken literally, gold is much more prominent in Desmarets's description than in Blunt's account: 'desja de tous costez / L'or bruny nous respand ses brillantes clartez, / Et laisse peu d'espace à la douce peinture', gold in the embroidered bed-coverings, a tapestry of the Trojan War 'plus plein d'or que de soie', and finally 'La pompe luit partout: sur l'or doux l'or brillant. / D'or les riches plafonds, d'or les lambris éclattent.'

Between devotional poetry and travel literature, the allegorical promenades often witness a feeling for nature unusual in French

---

[19] A. Blunt, *The Paintings of Nicolas Poussin, a Critical Catalogue* (London, 1966), 95-9.

poetry in the century of Louis XIV—an aspect of *Les Promenades* stressed in *La Comparaison de la langue et de la poësie Françoise, avec la Grecque & la Latine*, where Desmarets reprints extracts entitled 'Les Beautez et les douceurs de la campagne, ou la Journée du solitaire' for comparison with Virgil's *Georgics* and the *Odes* of Horace. These same promenades are entitled *Les Sept Vertus chrétiennes* when posthumously reprinted (1680).

The 'voice' of the poetic speaker shifts with changes of place, time, theme, and mood; and a good modern edition could bring out the various traditions on which Desmarets draws for different effects— the Psalms, Virgil, Horace, Ovid, Du Bellay, Du Bartas, etc. The epistle suggests a relative ranking of his intentions, placing awe at the wonder of natural beauty just after worship of the greatness and goodness of God, but before moral meditation:

> Adorons ses grandeurs, benissons ses bontez,
> Admirons la Nature & ses viues beautez,
> Meditons les Vertus diuines . . .

The first promenade 'De la foy' begins by rejecting works of art, especially ancient statuary of pagan gods, but dismissing too the formal gardens, canals, and fountains of Richelieu which anticipate the reconstruction of Versailles:

> Dédaignons des mortels les ouurages superbes,
> Pour les œuvres de Dieu, pour la moindre des herbes.
> Mesmes de ce chasteau laissons les enuirons,
> Ces parterres dont l'art a formé les fleurons,
> Et ces eaux auec l'art dans les airs élancécs,
> Et ces routes de bois que la ligne a dressées,
> Ces canaux estendus, & ces sables vnis,
> Et par les soins humains tous ces lieux applanis.

With these works of man Desmarets contrasts a nearby mountain,

> Eluant dans les airs son sommet sourcilleux,
> Et portant jusqu'au Ciel ses sapins orgueilleux,

witnesses to 'la grandeur de Dieu dans ses moindres ouurages'. I am struck less by the Psalmist's theme that 'the firmament showeth His handiwork', or by the effort of climbing as a metaphor for faith, than by climbing as a metaphor for the exhilaration found in faith:

Montons sur cette croupe, & de là sur la cime.
L'ardeur d'aller au Ciel est noble & legitime.
C'est là nostre patrie . . .
Ie sens vn air plus pur en quittant les lieux bas;
Et mon cœur est plus gay, plus j'auance mes pas.

Dawn is the opening metaphor of the second promenade, 'De l'espérance':

Ie te saluë, Aurore, esperance du jour,
Qui de l'astre brillant annonces le retour.
Au dernier de mes jours sois plus brillante encore,
Et d'vn jour eternel sois l'agreable Aurore.

A metaphor for hope as a Christian virtue in *Aspasie* and *Mirame*, the dawn theme in *Les Promenades* does not preclude temporal pleasures:

Allons gouster aux champs vn plaisir innocent,
Voir les astres mourans, & le jour renaissant.

But temporal fulfilment fails to satisfy:

Tousjours sur le bon-heur l'Esperance fondée
Nous peint du temps futur vne agreable idée.
Le present seul desplaist, & cherche l'auenir.
Le passé deuient doux dans nostre souuenir:
Mais le sort que l'on gouste, & tant soit-il prospere,
N'est point si doux encor que le sort qu'on espere.

This account of what might be termed the pessimism of hope might help define the temperament of Molière's Misanthrope, a caricature of the malcontent who looks before and after and pines for what is not because (as Desmarets puts it), 'Le plaisir plaist tousjours moins que son esperance.' Clearly such feelings do not begin with Romanticism.

The third promenade 'De la charité' evokes the relative cool of summer days, 'quand les volantes nuës / Estendent sur nos chefs leurs ombres continuës'—days when the flowers in the formal gardens of the château 'ont leur beauté plus viue'. An apostrophe to flowers is readdressed after various metaphors to butterflies as images (traditional in devotional poetry) of death and transfiguration:

Doux astres de la terre, esbloüissantes fleurs,
Qui brillez à l'enuy de diverses couleurs,

> Beaux jeux de la Nature, vn doux Zephir vous flate,
> Baisant de vostre teint la beauté delicate;
> Et vous souffrez l'amour de ces chastes Zephirs,
> Qui n'osent vous baiser qu'auecque leurs soûpirs.
> L'amour pour la beauté deuroit estre innocente,
> Comme de ces doux vents l'haleine fremissante.
> O papillons legers qui sur les fleurs errez!
> D'vn agreable esmail comme elles bigarrez,
> Autrefois humbles vers rampans dessus les herbes,
> Maintenant fendans l'air de vos ailes superbes,
> L'homme, de vostre sort doit bien estre jaloux . . .

Not surprisingly, perhaps, the fourth promenade 'De l'humilité' seems most effective when, in heroic verse, Desmarets attacks the countrary vice, which is pride:

> L'Orgueil a de malheurs remply tout l'Vnivers.
> L'Orgueil a de Demons peuplé les creux Enfers.
> Le detestable Orgueil, par vne seule audace,
> Dans le premier mortel perdit toute sa race.

Following restatement of man's first disobedience, Desmarets evokes the history of oracles, anticipating *Paradise Lost* i and Bernard Le Bovier de Fontenelle's *Histoire des oracles* (1687):

> L'abominable Orgueil, en flattant les mortels,
> Pour eux-mesmes bastit des temples, des autels,
> Fit allumer l'encens, inuenta les Idoles,
> A fleschir les genoux força les troupes folles . . .

This promenade begins in the 'Pantheon pompeux' of pagan statuary in the great court, notices winged Fame on the dome but moves down towards the beauties of the valley below the artificial reflecting pools. The paradoxes used to express the Incarnation as a triumph of humility involve contradictions by no means limited to this promenade:

> L'homme par son orgueil aux cieux osoit pretendre:
> Dieu par l'humilité des cieux voulut descendre;
> Fit son entrée au monde auec l'Humilité,
> Porté dans le pur char de la Virginité,
> Traisna l'Orgueil captif, la Pompe, & l'Opulence;
> Aux oracles trompeurs imposa le silence,
> Pour chantres, pour herauts, eut les Anges legers,
> Eut pour ses spectateurs des Rois & des bergers,

> Les astres pour flambeaux, & sur de pauures gerbes
> Triompha de la terre, & des Demons superbes.

What seems personal is the extent to which, despite strain on 'le pur char de la Virginité' as a conceit, this 'Triumph of Humility' has been imagined as an allegorical *entrée* in Court ballet. Like the *Triumphs* of Poussin described by Desmarets in the eighth promenade, such ballet *entrées* have literary sources in Latin historians, in Ovid, Petrarch, and other poets; and the point of the allegory is the implicit contrast with the worldly triumphs of Caesar and other conquerors. But Desmarets, who uses the word 'entrée' metaphorically, presents a continued action in terms of a performance, with musicians ('chantres'), an on-stage audience ('pour ses spectateurs des Rois & des bergers'), successive visits (evoked in reverse order), and the stars as metaphorical theatre-lighting ('les astres pour flambeaux'). Other personifications in *Les Promenades*, such as La Discorde in the epistle and La Renommée in this promenade, though doubtless also of literary inspiration,[20] are typical allegorical figures of Court ballet.

The fifth promenade 'De l'obeyssance' ends, after meditation on universal harmony as a model for humanity, in the riding-school, 'en cette escole sage / Où pages & cheuaux font leur apprentissage' with an admonition to the pages: 'noble jeunesse' instructed to model their behaviour on that of the master and mistress of the château and reminded 'qu'il faut obeïr, pour sçauoir commander'.

'De la patience', the sixth promenade, opens with a celebration of formal landscape-gardening:

> O! parterres, ô! prez, où les heureux regards
> Estendent leurs plaisirs si loin de toutes parts;
> O! routes, ô! canaux, ô! larges auenuës,
> Dont se traisnent si loin les longueurs continuës;
> O! champs non limitez, qui montrez à nos yeux
> L'azur des lieux lointains joint à celuy des cieux . . .

Aware that a wide, open view 'Dissipe trop d'esprits à qui veut mediter' (but expressing no notion that a limited view may be enhanced as if by being framed), Desmarets makes an ancient oak-wood an image of patience. The contrary vice, anger, is illustrated from the Old Testament and ancient history: Cain murderer of Abel,

---

[20] Fama in *Aeneid* iv, Discordia and Silenzio in Ariosto, *Orlando furioso*, xiv. 76 ff., etc.

Absalom avenger of Tamar, and especially Alexander, remorseful
executioner of Clitus, evoked in lines with tragic hints beyond
Roxane (V. III):

> Il fuyoit le Soleil, pleurant le mal commis,
> Refusoit du manger le secours necessaire,
> Et s'imposoit luy-mesme vn supplice exemplaire.

Finally, perhaps the most suggestive of Desmarets's many architectural descriptions is the evocation of the château de Richelieu by
moonlight at the opening of the seventh promenade, 'De la mansué-
tude'. The moon illustrates meekness through willingness to shine
only by reflected light, effects of which include chiaroscuro and the
illusion of three châteaux: the structure itself, its shadow, and its
reversed image in the reflecting pools:

> Que j'aime la nuit fraische, & ses lumieres sombres,
> Lors que l'astre des mois en adoucit les ombres!
> Que ce palais pompeux me paroist bien plus beau,
> Quand il n'est éclairé que du second flambeau,
> Dont la douce clarté d'autres graces apporte,
> Rechauffant les reliefs par vne ombre plus forte.
> Sous la corniche aiguë, vne longue noirceur
> Sur le mur qui la porte en marque l'espaisseur;
> Et chaque niche creuse a de chaque statuë
> La figure imprimée, obscure & rabbatuë . . .
> Lorsque sur ce chasteau la Lune se fait voir;
> En éclaire vne part, & peint l'autre de noir,
> Ie pense voir deux temps que confond la Nature.
> Le jour est d'vn costé, d'autre la nuit obscure . . .
> Desja du grand Palais si clair, si bien dressé,
> I'en voy sortir vn autre obscur & renuersé,
> Noircissant le parterre; & ses superbes domes
> Sur la terre couchez comme de longs fantômes.

Walking further he seems to see a second moon in the calm waters
of the canals:

> Icy le palais mesme, & si clair, & si beau,
> A chef precipité se renuerse dans l'eau.
> O! tromperie aimable, ô! jeu de la Nature.
> Est-ce vne verité? n'est-ce qu'vne peinture?
> Ensemble en trois façons ce palais se fait voir,
> En soy-mesme, en son ombre, & dans ce grand miroir,

Ou tout est à l'enuers, ou tout change d'office,
Ou les combles pointus portent tout l'edifice.
Les astres petillans y sont encor plus bas,
Et semblent dans vn lac prendre leurs doux esbas.

The eighth promenade, mainly within the château itself, begins with an evocation of autumn. The sun having withdrawn, 'Tout pleure son départ, l'air, les toits & les murs.' 'Adieu, beaux promenoirs', Desmarets continues, regretting finished flowers, fallen and dying leaves:

Ie ne voy qu'à regret ces couleurs differentes
Dont l'Automne sans art[21] peint les feüilles mourantes.
Leur beau verd si riant tout à coup s'est changé
En jaune, en amarante, en ´rouge, en orangé.

Even if Petit de Julleville exaggerates in suggesting that such passages constitute 'une peinture . . . de la nature unique peut-être en ce siècle',[22] in the development of aspects of French poetry from Racan to La Fontaine and Racine, or indeed from Du Bellay to Victor Hugo, *Les Promenades de Richelieu* deserves more in the way of critical attention than it has received.

Doubtless it illustrates as well as *Paradise Lost* the famous dictum in Edgar Allan Poe's 'The Poetic Principle' that 'a long poem does not exist', because 'that degree of excitement which would entitle a poem to be so called at all, cannot be sustained throughout a composition of any great length'. At the same time it is a work of considerable distinction, and not simply as devotional poetry. I have tried to suggest something of how Desmarets combines an account of actual promenades with the allegorical celebration of the Christian virtues, including rejection of contrary vices. He does not appear to have sought a high 'degree of excitement' throughout *Les Promenades*: numerous lines are literally pedestrian, narrative in verse concerned primarily with informing the reader of walks about the château and park, linking-lines comparable to recitative in opera, lines whose

---

[21] 'Sans art' means 'naturally, without consciously acquired skill or human endeavour' not 'crudely': compare 'icy sans art s'éleue vne montagne' in the first promenade.

[22] L. Petit de Julleville, *Histoire de la langue et de la littérature française* (1895–1903), iv. 392. 'L'Adieu aux champs à la fin de l'Automne' is one of the passages anthologized in *La Comparaison* and also in Lefort de la Morinière (ed.), *Bibliothèque poétique*, ii. 206–7.

function is to set the scene for passages intended to edify or transport. Some passages are much more distinguished.

Desmarets did not introduce the promenade to French literature. That distinction may belong to a certain Rayssiguier, author of *La Bourgeoise, ou la Promenade de Saint-Cloud* (1633), although Desmarets is more directly indebted to Salomon de Priézac, author of a caprice entitled *Les Promenades de Saint-Clou* [*sic*] (1643), the last page of which contains lines which may have been Desmarets's point of departure. Priézac desires his muse to sketch

> Non les sacrez Palais des Princes & des Roys,
> Mais la sombre espaisseur de ces superbes bois . . .
> Ces parterres diuers, ces riches broderies,
> Ces tranquilles canaux, & ces vertes prairies,
> Dont les tapis tremblans & parsemez de fleurs
> Estallent à nos yeux tant de viues couleurs.

Desmarets begins his first promenade somewhat like Priézac in this passage: 'Ie te laisse, Palais de pompeuse structure', but of course repeatedly returns to the château. Unlike Priézac, for whom the myriad beauties of Saint-Cloud are offered simply as 'autant d'appas & d'attrais pour les yeux', Desmarets constructs an allegory which invites not only an aesthetic response to aspects of the site selected but moral meditation and worship of a hidden Creator through the perceptible beauty of His creatures. Some of the lines seem less pedestrian when read for allegorical, moral, and anagogical as well as literal meaning.

Les Promenades de Richelieu would almost certainly be better known had the great château itself survived the Revolution of 1789. Indeed the eighth promenade follows the tourist route:

> Suiuons des Estrangers la bande curieuse,
> Qui de leur cher païs ont laissé les climats,
> Pour voir de raretez vn si splendide amas,
> Attirez par le nom du Ministre de France . . .
> Desja d'estonnement cette troupe est muette;
> Et je peux leur seruir de guide & d'interprete.[23]

---

[23] It is, of course, a nonsense to suppose that touring only began in the eighteenth century, when the scale of the activity no doubt increased. In the dedicatory epistle of *The State of France* (London, 1652), John Evelyn develops a theory of (grand) touring, contrasting the man 'that would travel rationally, & like a Philosopher' with such men as travel simply to acquire 'the flourish & Tongue of a Place' and those who go about merely 'counting Steeples, & make Tours'.

A letter to his young wife dated 12 September 1663 shows that
La Fontaine, for instance, used *Les Promenades* as a guide on his
visit to the château on the way to exile in Limousin following
his implication in the disgrace of Nicolas Fouquet, though not
as a guide to his manner of writing about it.[24] I see no irony in
his comment, 'Ce qui s'en peut dire de beau, M. Desmarets l'a
dit . . .'.[25] Michel de Marolles refers to the château de Richelieu,
'dont nous voions une si noble description en vers, dans les agréables
promenades de M. des Marais', whose moral sentiments please
him.[26]

Les Promenades de Richelieu met perhaps its most positive response
from a young poet not often associated with lyrical landscape poetry,
Jean Racine. Yet it almost certainly inspired Racine's *Le Paysage,
ou les Promenades de Port-Royal*, a series of seven odes written
*c.*1656–8 whose poetic architecture, moods, and sometimes phrasing
seem strongly reminiscent of *Les Promenades de Richelieu* despite
obvious differences related to the young Racine's choice of a form
with shorter lines. Consider, for instance, 'Que je me plais sur ces
montagnes' at the opening of 'Ode 2', the 'vivantes fleurs, / Les
papillons, dont les couleurs / Sont si frêles et si superbes' in 'Ode
5', and the first lines of 'Ode 7':

> Mes yeux, pourrai-je bien vous croire?
> Suis-je éveillé? Vois-je un jardin?
> N'est-ce point quelque songe vain
> Qui me place en ce lieu de gloire?

In replying to Nicole's attack on Desmarets in the first *Visionnaire*
letter, the poet of *Le Paysage* is unlikely to have forgotten such
adolescent inspiration from *Les Promenades de Richelieu*.

From Madeleine de Scudéry's *La Promenade de Versailles*, dedicated
to Louis XIV in 1669, the promenade is more commonly associated
with a secular point of view and with prose rather than verse.
Desmarets may be said to have established the promenade as a genre,
later illustrated in different ways by Jean-Jacques Rousseau and by
Stendhal.

---

[24] See my commentary 'Reflections on Rival Claims in La Fontaine's "Le Songe
de Vaux"', in *Voyages: récits et imaginaire*, ed. B. Beugnot (Montreal, 1984),
337–49.
[25] La Fontaine, *Œuvres diverses*, 555.
[26] Marolles, *Mémoires*, i. 186.

L'Imitation de Jesus Christ

Desmarets's next book, *Les Quatre liures de l'Imitation de Jesus Christ*, is the first French verse-translation of all four books, published in duodecimo by Pierre Le Petit (Libraire to the Académie-Française) and Henry Le Gras, and 'achevé d'imprimer' on 6 July 1654.[27] Pierre Corneille had begun to publish piecemeal and republish his better-known verse translation: the first twenty chapters of the first book 'achevé d'imprimer' on 15 November 1651, followed by I, 1–25, and II, 1–6 on 31 October 1652; Bks. I and II on 30 June 1653 (reprinted three times before the end of the year); and Bk. III some time in 1654—a very considerable publishing success for the time. The work itself was greatly esteemed. H.-J. Martin mentions it as a mystical work popular in the sixteenth century which actually gained readership in the seventeenth.[28] René de Voyer d'Argenson states that for a number of meetings of the Compagnie du Saint-Sacrement after the desecration of the Paris church of St-Nicolas-des-Champs in 1632 'on lisoit le *Combat spirituel* ou l'*Imitation de Jésus-Christ*'.[29] It was the first book published in a luxury edition by the Imprimerie Royale, established in 1640, with a frontispiece depicting Louis XIII kneeling before a crucifix. In the first two decades of the reign of Louis XIV, Martin remarks, 'un vaste public suit avec passion les querelles concernant l'attribution' of the *Imitation*.'[30] Roughly, Cardinal Bellarmini and various Benedictines attributed the work to the French theologian Jean Charlier, known as Gerson (1363–1429), while Cardinal Mazarin's librarian Gabriel Naudé (1600–53) favoured the now generally accepted attribution to the German mystic Thomas Merken, known as Thomas à Kempis (1380?–1471).[31]

---

[27] Desmarets had, on 2 June, transferred to them his *privilège* of 14 Mar. 1639.

[28] Martin, *Livre, pouvoirs et société*, i. 132.

[29] Voyer d'Argenson, *Annales*, 36.

[30] Ibid. 604. For instance, a second edn. of Jean de Launoy's *Dissertatio continens judicium de auctore librorum de Imitatione Christi* (1650) was followed by his *Remarques sommaires sur un livre intitulé 'La Contestation touchant l'auteur de "L'Imitation de Jésus-Christ" '* (1652).

[31] In 1641 Maître Naudé had published his *Raisons péremptoires* for rejecting the attribution to Gerson and accusing three Benedictines (D. Placide Roussel, Robert Quatremaires, and D. François Valgrave) of using falsified documents in their attribution. In 1650 he published a 'Requête servant de factum au procès' between himself and D. Placide Roussel, then Prior of St-German-des-Prés, and the other named Benedictines. These were followed in 1651 by his *Bibliographia Kempensis Causae* and *Kempensis conjectio*. But the quarrel was by no means ended. The Benedictine François Delfau (1637–76) renews the attribution to Gerson in his edition *I. Gerseni de Imitatione*

Accepted even by Jansenists, it was also translated by Le Maistre de Sacy.[32]

Arrested at a meeting of the Conseil on 18 January 1650 and imprisoned in the château de Vincennes, along with his brother the Prince de Condé and brother-in-law the Duc de Longueville, for his part in the clandestine marriage of the Duc de Richelieu, the Prince de Conti is said to have wept each night whilst reading the *Imitation* in bed.[33] Meanwhile the Duchesse de Longueville—said by Mme de Motteville to have planned the clandestine marriage in order to bring Le Havre (administered by the Duchesse d'Aiguillon for the Duc de Richelieu) into the interests of her husband, governor of Normandy—attempted to rouse that province for the Princes; but she was ordered out of Rouen by its Parlement and later refused entry into Le Havre by the Duc de Richelieu himself, who had prematurely taken up command of perhaps the strongest citadel in France, only to lose the governorship of Le Havre soon afterwards.[34] When the Court moved to Rouen, the Procureur des États de Normandie (a Longueville supporter) was deprived of his office and, on 12 February, was replaced by Pierre Corneille.[35] However, in 'La Poésie à la peinture' (1653) Corneille affects to believe that as far as literature is concerned, 'le Siècle . . . n'a qu'un Mécène'—the Duc de Longueville, Chapelain's patron.

Corneille was mistaken. Desmarets had the Duc de Richelieu. In the 'Advertisement' of *L'Imitation* Desmarets states:

je n'eusse jamais eu la pensée de faire cette traduction en vers, sçachant qu'elle avoit esté entreprise, & déja fort advancée, par vn homme de rare merite

---

Christi et contemptu omnium vanitatum mundi libri IV (1674), contested by Philibert Testelette, *Vincidiae Kempenses* (1677), and defended by the Benedictine Jean Mabillon (1632–1707) in his *Animadversiones in 'Vindicias Kempenses'* (1677). It was N. Lenglet du Frenoy (1674–1755) who published the first French translation of the *Imitation* including i. 26 (Amsterdam, 1735), after an earlier version without the missing chapter (1698).

[32] *De l'imitation de Jésus-Christ*, transl. 'le Sieur de Beuil, Prieur de Saint-Val', 3rd edn. (1662).

[33] Patin, *Lettres du temps de la Fronde*, 1 Apr. 1650, p. 185. Condé is said to have asked for the 'imitation de M. de Beaufort, afin que je me puisse sauver d'ici, comme il fit il y a tantôt deux ans' (ibid., 1 Mar. 1650, pp. 179–80). Desmarets is likely to have heard the story, since the doctor in attendance on the princes was his brother-in-law, Guillaume Dupré.

[34] Motteville, *Mémoires*, iii. 422–3; Montglat, *Mémoires*, ii. 204; J.-F.-P. de Gondi, Cardinal de Retz, *Mémoires*, ed. A. Petitot (1825), ii. 102.

[35] Corneille, *Œuvres complètes*, i. lviii.

& de grande reputation. Mais il a pleu à Dieu de m'y engager insensiblement . . . pour me faire gouster la merveilleuse doctrine de ce Livre . . .

It was the Duc de Richelieu, he continues, who asked for a chapter in verse

en style pressé & naïf comme celuy de l'Auteur: puis il eut impatience d'avoir en vers le quatriesme Livre qui traitte du saint Sacrement; & . . . me fit entreprendre celle des autres Livres.

Desmarets must have been working on *L'Imitation* when his brother Roland died on 27 December 1653.

In the 'Advertisement' Desmarets justifies the choice of quatrains for his translation, grateful to God for the grace which permitted him to 'achever èn peu de temps la traduction difficile, naïve & fidele d'vn si vtile & excellent ouvrage, qui dans plusieurs ames pourra produire des biens eternels'. The four books contain about sixteen hundred quatrains altogether. These first three of i. 1, are a small but not unrepresentative sample:

> Celuy qui suit mes pas, dit le Verbe adorable,
> Ne chemine jamais dedans l'obscurité.
> Soyons imitateurs de sa vie admirable,
> Pour estre illuminez de sa sainte clarté.
>
>   De ses dits, de ses faits, meditons les merveilles;
> Et jamais nostre cœur n'aura d'aveuglement.
> Que ce soit l'entretien de nos jours, de nos veilles,
> Il faut que le fidele y songe incessamment.
>
>   La doctrine de Christ, que luy-mesme a preschée,
> Surpasse tout sçavoir; son auteur l'anoblit.
> Et chacun y savoure vne manne cachée,
> Lors que d'vn esprit humble il l'escoute ou la lit.

The maxims of *L'Imitation* often coincide with major literary themes of the century of Louis XIV or suggest an ideal in relation to which characterization, comic or tragic, may have been imagined. Consider this maxim in iii. 27, 'L'amour propre te nuit plus que toute autre chose', and the quatrain which follows it:

>   Si ton amour est pur, simple, & plein de justice,
> De toute folle amour tu sera destaché.
> Iamais d'aucun desir ne te fais vn supplice.
> Ne souhaitte nul bien dont tu sois empesché.

The 'Approbation' dated 2 July 1654 is signed by two Sorbonne doctors of theology: De Breda (probably Antoine de Bréda, who on 17 June 1643 delivered the *Oraison funèbre* for Louis XIII in the church of St-André-des-Arts, closely linked with the Sorbonne) and Quatrhommes. *L'Imitation* was reprinted with *Le Combat spirituel* on the press at Richelieu, 'achevé d'imprimer' on 6 October 1654; and there were at least two further editions (1661–2). In his *Bibliothèque françoise* Sorel states only that French prose versions of *L'Imitation* may be well received, adding 'on verra aussi celles qui ont esté faites en Vers François, par Messieurs Desmarets & Corneille'.[36]

Le Combat spirituel

'Après avoir mis en vers françois le Livre d'Or de l'*Imitation de Jésus-Christ*, j'ay esté obligé par des commandements auxquels je ne puis resister, de traduire de mesme celuy du *Combat spirituel*': thus Desmarets in the 'Notice' of his verse version of *Le Combat spirituel ou de la perfection de la vie chrestienne*, 'achevé d'imprimer' at the new press at the château de Richelieu on 24 August 1654 but published in Paris by Le Gras and Le Petit.[37] It is a book which, in Desmarets's words, 'va presque de pair avec celuy de l'*Imitation*'. The order for the translation must have come again from the Duc de Richelieu.

As was the case for *L'Imitation*, attribution of *Le Combat spirituel* was disputed. Now firmly attributed to Lorenzo Scupoli (b. 1610), it was claimed in the seventeenth century by certain Benedictines as the work of one of their own members, Juan de Castagniza, while some Jesuits assigned it to A. Gagliardo. *Le Combat spirituel* was twice reprinted: in 1654 with, as noted, *L'Imitation*, and again in 1680. Like *L'Imitation*, it is a poem about union with God, partly mystical, partly moral. For his translation Desmarets once more selects quatrains, linking them throughout each chapter and shortening the even-numbered lines to the equivalent of an Alexandrine hemistich, like Malherbe in 'Consolation à Monsieur Du Périer'. Witness these closing lines of ch. VI, 'Des deux volontez qui sont en l'homme':

[36] Sorel, *Bibliothèque françoise*, 43–4.
[37] 'Notice', quoted from Kerviler, *Jean Desmaretz*, 72, and P. Corneille, *Œuvres*, ed. C. Marty-Lavaux (12 vols.; 1862–8), viii. 13.

> Le devot est trompé, qui veut dans la priere
> Chercher de saints plaisirs,
> Auant qu'auoir acquis vne victoire entiere
> Sur ses propres desirs.

In the 'Au lecteur' prefaced to his version of *L'Imitation*, first published complete in 1656, Corneille states that he had 'promis à quelques personnes dévotes de joindre à cette traduction celle du *Combat spirituel*'. He begs, however, to be relieved of that obligation, 'puisque j'ai été prévenu dans ce dessein par une des plus belles plumes de la cour'.[38] Doubtless there was an element of 'fraternal correction' in the compliment, because Corneille adds that, although such books are in the public domain, a first translator makes a sort of moral acquisition, 'et on ne peut plus s'y engager sans lui faire un secret reproche de n'y avoir pas bien réussi, et de promettre de s'en acquitter plus dignement'.[39] This observation was not reprinted in later editions, and it did not prevent Corneille from publishing his verse version of *L'Office de la Sainte Vierge* late in 1669—just after republication of Desmarets's *L'Office de la Vierge Marie* under the new title *Prières et Œuvres chrestiennes*.

Desmarets's conversion

In 1666 Desmarets links his conversion to the devotional poems just considered:

Avant ma separation des conversations du monde, j'avois fait le Poëme *des Promenades de Richelieu, ou des Vertus Chrestiennes* ; & j'avois traduit en Vers les Livres de *L'Imitation de Jésus-Christ* ; & *du Combat Spirituel*, desquels Dieu se servit pour m'émouvoir à changer de vie. Puis je quittay toute volontaire production d'esprit, et je demeuray quatre ou cinq ans ayant l'ame bien éloignée de penser de faire des livres.[40]

Unless the translations had been prepared long before publication, this would place Desmarets's conversion in 1654, perhaps influenced by the death of his brother, Roland. The word 'volontaire' is crucial with respect to major publications in preparation: *Clovis* and

---

[38] Corneille, *Œuvres*, viii. 13.

[39] 'En attendant que Dieu m'inspire quelque autre dessein,' Corneille continues, 'je me contenterai de m'appliquer à une revue de mes pièces de théâtre'—a decision resulting in the three-volume edition of his *Théâtre* (1660) with the 'examens' announced in the 'Au lecteur' of *L'Imitation*.

[40] *Seconde Partie de la Response*, 66-7.

Les Délices de l'esprit. The 'Epistre aux Beaux Esprits' published with the latter states that, after much hesitation, 'Dieu me fit connoistre, par la bouche de ceux qui luy sont agreables, que i'achevasse le Poëme.' It is impossible otherwise to find four or five years without new publications. It is not unusual for devout persons (Corneille, for example) to feel obliged by their faith to undertake certain actions. Desmarets's conversion is part of a general movement. H.-J. Martin refers to an 'élan [spirituel] général submergeant toute la société' in the years 1655–60.[41] Desmarets's conversion, and that of the Duchesse de Longueville, also in 1654, anticipate the fashion. So does Pascal's, leading to the famous 'Mémorial' of 23 November 1654.

More is involved than mere coincidence. These not untypical examples arise not from an accident of history but from a conception of its time-scale based on premisses including Ptolemaic cosmology (queried but still widely accepted) and millenary eschatology. In 1666 astrology was excluded from the new Académie des Sciences under the terms of its charter. Twelve years earlier it still enjoyed an enormous vogue throughout Europe, and astrologers were concerned with the possible baleful implications of the solar eclipse of 12 August 1654, at the entry of Saturn into Leo.[42] Many serious people seem to have believed that the end of time and the Last Judgement were nigh.

Chronologists and historians dated the Creation around 4004 BC. On a cosmic scale in which a thousand years are as a day, the millennium—the seventh day in the cosmic week—could not be thought far away. More precisely, since the Flood was generally dated to exactly 1656 BC, many assumed that the Last Judgement might take place in AD 1656.

Maximes Chrestiennes

Two small volumes of *Maximes Chrestiennes* were printed after Desmarets's death on the press at (or once at) Richelieu (1680 and 1687). Attribution of the first to Desmarets by Tchemerzine seems

---

[41] Martin, *Livre, pouvoirs et société*, ii. 620.
[42] See E. Labrousse, *L'Entrée de Saturne au Lion: l'éclipse de soleil du 12 août 1654* (The Hague, 1974), and *Time and the Classical Writer*, special no. of *Australian Journal of French Studies*, 13/2 (1976).

to me entirely reasonable, since it fits readily into a series of reprints of Desmarets's known devotional works 'à la sphère'. A second, shorter volume of *Maximes Chrestiennes* from the same press, unknown to bibliographers, would also appear to be by Desmarets and not previously published in the volume of *Vertus, maximes, instructions, & meditations Chrestiennes* (1678) mentioned as 'à la Sphère' by Tchemerzine. The posthumous volumes of *Maximes Chrestiennes* are comprised of quatrains in the tradition of Pibrac and Matthieu, although several chapters are devotional poems of which the quatrains are stanzas, rather than independent maxims. These quatrains must be related to Desmarets's translation of *L'Imitation*, with which there are affinities in thought, mood, and style. They are represented fairly by the first and last quatrain of ch. 21 of the second volume, the last new work by Desmarets published in the seventeenth century:

> Eclaire-moy, Seigneur, d'une vive lumiere,
> Et du fond de mon cœur chasse l'obscurité.
> De mes distractions vien borner la carriere,
> Ecarte les objets dont je me voy tenté . . .

> Preste-moy ton secours, ô Verité suprême,
> Que je ne sois épris de nulle vanité.
> Vien, celeste douceur, vien, seul amour que j'aime,
> Vien garantir mon cœur de toute impureté.

13

Devotional Prose

The works to be considered in this chapter include a book by each of the two Cardinals de Richelieu revised by Desmarets, together with over a dozen volumes of his own new works, translations, and revisions first published between 1656 and 1666, including scriptural exegesis and works of apologetics, mysticism, and spiritual guidance. Most of these new works were reprinted at least once; the dialogues of *Les Délices de l'esprit* at least nine times; and another work five times—altogether a considerable publishing success. Indeed, the publishing history of Desmarets's devotional works witnesses a substantial contribution to the religious experience of the century of Louis XIV.

Richelieu's La Perfection du chrestien

After describing the way in which Desmarets was recruited by Bautru to assist in revising a speech which the Cardinal-Duc made to the King and Parlement on 18 January 1634,[1] Tallemant des Réaux adds that Bautru did not want Richelieu to see how much revision there had been:

Elle estoit pleine de fautes contre la langue, aussi bien que son Cathéchisme ou Instruction chrétienne. Il voyoit bien les choses, mais il ne les estendoit pas bien. A parler succinctement, il estois admirable et délicat.[2]

Tallemant then proceeds to give a somewhat garbled account of the editing of Richelieu's devotional works, the ghosting and revision of which he attributes to several writers in Richelieu's entourage:

Il n'y a que l'*Instruction des Curez* qui soit de luy; encore a-t-il pris des uns et des autres; pour le reste, la matiere est de [Jacques] Lescot [Bishop of Chartres], et le françois de Desmarestz . . . Le Catéchisme a esté corrigé depuis par Desmarestz, qui l'a mis en l'estat où on le voit aujourd'huy.

---

[1] *Harangue de M. le cardinal duc de Richelieu, faite au Parlement, Sa Majesté y étant présent* (n.p., 1634).
[2] Tallemant des Réaux, *Historiettes*, i. 269.

Il y a encore deux autres livres de luy; le premier s'appelle *la Perfection du Chrétien* . . . M. Desmaretz, par l'ordre de Mme d'Aiguillon, et M. de Chartres, Lescot, qui avoit esté son confesseur, ont un peu reveû cet ouvrage.[3]

The anecdotes make sense if Tallemant is assumed to have given two accounts of the same arrangements, but the titles are incorrect. No published work by Richelieu is entitled *Instruction des curés*. Adam and Delassault suggest that Tallemant means the *Ordonnances synodales*, published by Richelieu as Bishop of Luçon for the instruction of priests in his diocese in 1613—a work lost until the late nineteenth century.[4] I wonder. The Duchesse d'Aiguillon would appear to have involved Desmarets with Lescot in the posthumous revision not of that work but of Richelieu's better-known *Instruction du chrestien* (Poitiers, 1620). She may have felt that the French style of the latter— begun during Richelieu's exile in Avignon in 1618 and frequently reprinted during his ministry, notably by the Imprimerie royale in 1642—had gone out of fashion. The *privilège* which she obtained for works of the late Cardinal-Duc on 2 June 1646 relates to the publication of the *Traitté de la perfection du chrestien par l'éminent Cardinal Duc de Richelieu* (n.p., 1646).[5] If the assertions made twice by Tallemant are basically sound, Desmarets and Lescot must have revised the *Instruction du chrestien* for republication as *La Perfection du chrestien*. Desmarets cannot on this evidence have been involved, as Kerviler implies, in editing such texts for Richelieu in the 1620s.[6]

Les Morales d'Epictete, de Socrate, de Plutarque et de Séneque

Apparently the first book from the new press at the château de Richelieu, *Les Morales d'Epictete, de Socrate, de Plutarque et de Séneque* (1653) is said by Maximin Deloche to have been compiled

---

[3] Tallemant des Réaux, *Historiettes*, i. 269–70. Revision of the other book, *Traité enseignant la methode la plus aisée et la plus asseurée pour convertir ceux qui se sont sesparez de l'Eglise* (1651), is said to have been entrusted by the Duchesse d'Aiguillon to Lescot and Amable de Bourzeis. Tallemant adds that she did not accept Chapelain's revision of an *Invocation à la Vierge*. He also states that Desmarets assisted Mme d'Aiguillon's search for an editor of Richelieu's *Mémoires* (ibid., 271).

[4] Ibid. 941.

[5] Bonneau-Avenant, *La Duchesse d'Aiguillon*, 354.

[6] Kerviler, *Jean Desmaretz*, 11–12.

by Cardinal Alphonse de Richelieu, Archbishop of Lyons, and edited by Desmarets, probably soon after the Archbishop's death on 23 March 1653.[7] *Les Morales* as first published include a section containing aphorisms drawn from the Stoic philosopher Epictetus, eleven of the *Moralia* of Plutarch, extracts from Seneca's letters, and a section representing the wisdom of Socrates—made up of anecdotes and aphorisms drawn more often from Xenophon than from Plato.

Antoine de Sommaville obtained a nine-year *privilège* for this title on 30 April 1655, in association with Henri Le Gras and Jean-Baptiste Loyson; but the volume they published under the new title *Les Morales de Plutarque, Seneque, Socrate et Epictete* is considerably longer, containing also Arrian's *Manual* of Epictetus. Reprinted in 1659 and 1667, these volumes indicate that scholars— through neglect of such evidence as this book and Poussin's Stoic landscape-paintings—have been somewhat hasty in assuming that Neostoicism abruptly declined after 1650. The frontispiece of editions of La Rochefoucauld's *Maximes ou sentences et maximes morales* of 1665, for instance, show a Cupid unmasking a bust of Seneca. Why unmask a philosopher already out of fashion? Many of La Rochefoucauld's maxims seem to function as contradictions of Stoic maxims. For example, ch. 16 in 'La Morale d'Epictete' states: 'Si tu veux profiter en sagesse, ne te mets pas en peine, si pour les choses qui sont estrangeres, tu es estimé fou ou sot.'[8] La Rochefoucauld's maxim 231 (in editions of the *Maximes* from 1666) contradicts this advice: 'C'est une grande folie de vouloir être sage tout seul.' The duality of comic vision in Molière's *Le Misanthrope* invites perception of Alceste in both perspectives.

I have not researched the extent to which the translations in *Les Morales* are genuinely new, except to note that the selection from Seneca's letters does not really amount to a new translation. The extracts are edited, with occasional stylistic changes, from Malherbe's translation of *Les Epitres de Seneque* (1637), posthumously published by Malherbe's nephew J.-B. de Boyer, with a dedicatory epistle 'A Monseigneur l'éminentissime Cardinal Duc de Richelieu', an

---

[7] Deloche, *Un frère de Richelieu inconnu* 529–30. For several decades this private press was distinguished for the clarity of its type but may not have remained at Richelieu. The posthumous editions of devotional works by Desmarets 'à la sphère' are from this press. J. Brunet (*Manuel du libraire* (1878–80), 'Desmarets de Saint-Sorlin') denies that its font was silver.

[8] *Les Morales de Plutarque, Seneque, Socrate et Epictete* (1659), 14.

'Au lecteur' by Jean Baudoin, and praise by Guillaume Colletet and others.

Les Délices de l'esprit

Desmarets's most ambitious publication in devotional prose, *Les Délices de l'esprit: dialogues dediez aux Beaux Esprits du Monde*, four parts in one substantial and lavishly illustrated folio volume, was 'achevé d'imprimer' on 15 April 1658. It is also dedicated to Cardinal Mazarin, a particular dedication not intended as excluding Mazarin from the general one. The first three parts comprise thirty dialogues between Eusèbe ('le Pieux') and Philédon ('qui aime la volupté'), each dialogue generally representing an imaginary day's conversation in a sequence structured as a pilgrim's progress into the deeps of the mind. Part iv (printed in two sections) consists of an 'Explication allégorique de la Genese', followed by exegeses of the Psalms of degrees and the Song of Solomon. 'Instructions pour l'Oraison', a treatise on elevation to the knowledge of the perfection of God, and the 'Approbations des Docteurs'.[9] The prayers and instruction for prayer are generally in keeping with doctrine already propagated in *L'Imitation*, *Le Combat spirituel*, and other devotional aids discussed in Chapter 12, but more ascetic and mystic in emphasis, especially in Parts iii and iv.

At least two of the exegetical sections had been previously published with titles providing a useful summary of their contents: *Le Cantique des Cantiques, représentant le Mystére des Mystéres. Dialogue amoureux de Jésus-Christ avec la Volonté son Epouse, qui s'unit à lui en la réception du Saint Sacrement* (1656) and *Le Cantique de*

---

[9] 'Approbations' for *Le Cantique des cantiques* and *Le Cantique des degrez* from the Sorbonne are dated respectively 18 Mar. 1656 and 5 July 1657—during the controversies reflected in Pascal's *Provinciales*. The 'Approbation' of the Faculty of Theology of Aix-en-Provence for *Les Délices de l'esprit* is dated 10 April 1658, seven months after the papal decree of 6 Sept. 1657 condemning the *Provinciales*. To the dedication of *Les Délices de l'esprit* Desmarets adds a 'Protestation de l'Autheur à sa sainteté': 'Ie proteste deuant Dieu, & deuant ses Anges, que bien que j'aye soumis ce liure . . . au iugement & à la correction de plusieurs sauans & pieux Theologiens, experts en la science des choses de l'Interieur: Ie le soûmets encore à tousiours à Nostre Saint Pere le Pape unique Chef visible de sa Ste Eglise Catholique, Apostolique & Romaine . . . de laquelle je veux mourir fils tres-obeissant, & hors de laquelle je reconnois qu'il n'y a ny mérite ny salut' (dated Paris, 10 Apr. 1658 and signed 'Desmarests'). For Desmarets's statement that the manuscript was read by St Vincent de Paul, see the last section of Chapter 4.

degrez, ou les quinze Psaumes Graduels, contenant les quinze degrez par lesquels l'Ame s'élève à Dieu (1657).[10] These sections indicate the methods and aims of the work as a whole: elevation of the soul, through progressively heightened experience of creation, to mystic union with the Creator. The system is reminiscent of Cardinal Bellarmini's *De ascentione mentis in Deum per scalas rerum creatarum* (1615), a work translated three times into French between 1616 and 1655, beginning with *L'Escalier spirituel portant l'âme à Dieu par les marches des créatures* (Vienne, 1616).

Desmarets draws inspiration from many writers, including the Benedictine Blosius[11] and earlier masters of the dialogue: Saint Catherine of Genoa (discussed in the next section), Desiderius Erasmus (*c.*1469–1536, author of the colloquy 'The Epicurean'), and Plato. In the *Symposium* Plato points to a rising scale of perception from first youthful response to physical beauty. Love of one beautiful body may inspire beautiful language, followed by response to beauty in whatever bodies. Next comes response to beauty residing in souls, judged to be of greater worth. This response is followed by a response to knowledge, and thereafter to beauty discovered in knowledge. Finally the lover 'contemplant les beaux objets dans l'ordre correct de leur gradation . . . aura la soudaine vision d'une beauté dont la nature est merveilleuse'.[12] In adapting this system, Neoplatonists such as Desmarets needed only to associate the marvellous with the divine, which they interpreted in terms of Christian beliefs—an association fundamental to the poetics of the Christian marvellous which Desmarets vigorously championed as practitioner and theorist in the last two decades of his life.

Les Délices de l'esprit involves architectural allegory more centrally and more systematically than *Les Promenades de Richelieu*, in which responses to nature and to the park, gardens, architecture, and collections at Richelieu in the course of solitary promenades are shared with the reader. These are the responses of an unusually imaginative member of the urban gentry temporarily—and somewhat

[10] Pellisson and d'Olivet, *Histoire de l'Académie-Françoise*, s.v.

[11] i.e., Louis de Blois (1506–66?), author of *Opera Blosii* in ten volumes (Antwerp, 1632–3), mentioned by Desmarets as a source in *Seconde Partie de la Response*, 'addition', p. 19. Blosius' *Institutio spiritualis* was translated into French under various titles, notably by the Jesuit Antoine Girard (1603–79) as *Institution spirituelle et consolation des pusillanimes* (1642). H.-J. Martin mentions reprints of Girard's version in 1650, 1658, and 1673 in *Livre, pouvoirs et société*, i. 131–2; ii. 614.

[12] Plato, *Œuvres complètes*, ed. L. Robin and M.-J. Moreau (1950), i. 745–7.

self-consciously—at home in the provinces. In contrast, *Les Délices de l'esprit* supposes discussion, opposed points of view, developing perspectives, the different responses of the recently converted Eusèbe and his old friend Philédon, a hedonist whose enjoyment is enhanced by progress through the graded pleasures of their promenades before and after Philédon's conversion on the eleventh day. There are other notable differences; but the most striking one is that in *Les Délices de l'esprit* the allegory is based not on an actual country-château, evoked or rejected according to theme, but on fictitious progress into a city along a route permitting sojourns in a series of ever more sumptuous imaginary homes and palaces. These imaginary buildings possess features which often allude to châteaux known to Desmarets and to his first readers—the Palais d'Orléans in Paris (now the Luxembourg) in the first illustration, for example—but they represent activities such as the arts, 'Sciences humaines', fame, fortune, moral philosophy, and theology, and the sojourns in these buildings correspond to degrees of elevation from carnal and sensual pleasures to intellectual and, finally, spiritual delights in mystic union with God in the celestial city, here named the Ville de la vraye Volupté, ou de l'Intérieur. For the new Jerusalem towards which the pilgrims progress is, of course, within.

Though rooted, like Bunyan's 'celestial city', in religious traditions, Desmarets's urban image of mystic union doubtless reflects in an easily overlooked way the readership targeted in the dialogues at a particular historical moment. The 'Beaux Esprits' are aristocratic courtiers, drawn from anywhere in France and its sphere of influence, and the urban gentry, particularly of Paris—'la Cour et la Ville', still close in 1658. Desmarets addresses *libertins*, hedonists, gamblers—like those for whom Pascal devised the famous wager argument in *Les Pensées* (begun as an apologia in 1658)—and fops capable of assuming, if not asserting, that 'hors de Paris, il n'y a point de salut pour les honnêtes gens'.[13] After the reconstruction of Versailles undertaken in the next decade, when the Court began to be less closely identified with the city of Paris, a French apologist addressing a fashionable readership whose ambitions centred on Versailles might have hesitated to subordinate châteaux on the way into a city to the city itself.

On first meeting Philédon after his own conversion, Eusèbe is reminded of the Bacchus and Venus—the tavern where, as Philédon

---

[13] Mascarille in Molière, *Les Précieuses ridicules* (1659), sc. IX.

recalls, they had once spent 'de si delicieuses journées'.[14] But Eusèbe has put behind him the 'plaisirs charnels & grossiers' of that 'cabane' which, he states, 'ne me satisfaisoient point, & ruinoient mon corps & ma fortune', and he now wants to persuade Philédon to do so too.[15] They spend three days in preparatory discussions, that is, in double dialogues entitled 'D'vn Dieu, & d'vne Religion', 'Qu'il faut gouster Dieu pour le connoistre, Et qu'il y a des choses surnaturelles', and 'De l'immortalité de l'âme, Et des plaisirs du corps et de ceux de l'esprit'. In the first dialogue Eusèbe explains that the mystic Ville de la vraye Volupté is like a city surrounded by suburbs which provide other, lesser delights. When Philédon demands proofs 'par raisons demonstratiues qu'il y a vn Dieu', Eusèbe likens God to an excellent wine which, once tasted, is never forgotten, adding:

Si tu auois gousté Dieu vne fois, tu sentirois bien que ce n'est pas vne chose imaginaire; mais vn estre reel, tres-parfait, & tres-delicieux; & pour ce goust, tu quitterais bien tost tous les gousts des plaisirs de la terre.[16]

On the third day Eusèbe assures Philédon: 'par les delices de l'esprit ie te conduiray jusques à Dieu'.[17] After this preparation, Eusèbe relates his own progress along that way.

Eusèbe first encountered 'vne grande et agreable maison, aussi grande qu'vne ville'—'le sejour des Arts'—entering which he was charmed by 'la Musique, par la Peinture, par l'Architecture, par la Perspectiue, & par plusieurs autres Arts' among which he remained a long time 'iouïssant de grands plaisirs':

Ie me suis veu quelquesfois composant vn air de Musique, ou faisant vn dessein de Portraiture, ou d'Architecture, ou de Perspectiue, que i'en quittois les meilleurs repas; & qu'il estoit impossible de m'arracher de là pour me faire manger, quoy que i'eusse alors grande faim: Mais ie ne la sentois point, tant i'estois attaché à mon ouurage, par la douceur du charme de l'art qui m'occupait.[18]

It was not a matter of study, Eusèbe explains, but 'vne inclination naturelle':

---

[14] *Les Délices de l'esprit*, i. 5. Bacchus and Venus of the tavern-sign serve not only as allegories of gluttony and lust but also as reminders of the corrupt behaviour of the pagan gods.
[15] Ibid. 3.   [16] Ibid. 4–8.   [17] Ibid. 38.   [18] Ibid. 55.

dans mon enfance ie composois des airs, sans maistre de Musique, ny estude quelconque; & ie faisois toutes sortes de desseins sur le papier, sans aucun maistre ny de Portraiture, n'y d'Architecture, ny de Perspectiue.[19]

Finally, music is presented as an extension of divine order—the harmony or music of the spheres—in language foreshadowing the ecstasy of mystical union:

La Musique a quelque chose de surnaturel & de diuin; & est incomprehensible dans ses diuers sons . . . La Musique a la force d'attendrir & de faire fondre & liquifier les passions; comme la chaleur fait fondre la cire . . .[20]

The musical scale provides Eusèbe with another metaphor of graded pleasures: the octave, neglecting sharps and flats. The base-note represents the receptivity of the human soul in its natural state, and the same note an octave higher God. The six tones between correspond to delights judged in relation to the base-note and its octave: the second, carnal pleasure, is discordant; the third, the arts, is harmonious, because 'les Arts sont agreables à Dieu & à l'homme, parce que l'Art est l'ouurage de l'homme sur l'ouurage de Dieu'; the fourth, 'Sciences humaines', are discordant as 'vaines sciences'; the fifth, honour and fame, is harmonious, 'parce que l'honneur et la Renommée accompagnent legitimement les vertus, la sainteté, & les bonnes œuvres'; the sixth, the pleasures of fortune, is discordant, because 'la Fortune nous égare & de Dieu & de nous mesmes'; and the seventh, the pleasures of ancient moral philosophy, is all the more discordant since the pride of pagan philosophers appears to bring them nearer to divinity.[21] The six interoctaval tones correspond to days and dialogues 3 to 8 of Les Délices de l'esprit i.

The apartments of painting, architecture, and perspective need not detain us, except to remark that each of these arts relates to important aspects of Desmarets's literary works (including their illustration), theatre, and other activities. This is particularly true of architecture, the literary response to which in Desmarets's works often takes the form of word-painting or 'peintures parlantes', inspired by the tradition of descriptions of paintings in literary texts and by Horace's advice in the Ars poetica, 'Ut pictura poesis . . .'. Perspective for

---

[19] Les Délices de l'esprit, i. 56. Molière mocks this sort of pretence, if not this passage, in Les Précieuses ridicules, where Cathos is surprised that Mascarille has composed an air without having studied music and Mascarille explains: 'Les gens de qualité savent tout sans avoir jamais rien appris' (sc. IX).

[20] Les Délices de l'esprit, i. 59–60.   [21] Ibid. 63–4.

its part is the basis of illusionist baroque stage-decoration and of the architectural features in *trompe-l'œil* favoured by Cardinal Richelieu's decorators.[22] Painting for Eusèbe is above all an illusionist art: 'plus elle imite parfaitement, plus elle donne de plaisir'.[23]

Eusèbe next stopped for several years in the Palace of the 'Sciences humaines', where he found:

L'Eloquence, la Poësie, l'Histoire, la Logique, la Physique, la Morale, la Politique, la Geometrie, l'Astrologie, la Geographie, la Medecine, la Chymie, & plusieurs autres Sciences curieuses.[24]

Discussion elicits a fuller account, with grammar as the first science, followed by rhetoric and eloquence, then law, logic, philosophy (speculative and practical), physics, metaphysics, mathematics (geometry and arithmetic), cosmography (astrology/astronomy, geography, and hydrographics), medicine (anatomy and surgery), chemistry, history, and finally poetry, where, Eusèbe recalls, 'i'ay pris mes plus cheres delices'.[25]

Philédon is surprised to find poetry classified among the sciences. Indeed, the classification does represent a change since Desmarets's 'Art de la poésie', which outlined his ambitions for French heroic poetry. Eusèbe explains that the arts include all inventions for the senses and the body, such as music for hearing, painting for sight, agriculture for nourishing the body, and architecture 'pour le logement', while he classifies as sciences 'toutes les inuentions dont on a fait des regles, & dont l'esprit seul est le iuge'.[26] Thus 'science' is used in a general way to cover organized activities of the mind; and the classification reflects a mind–body dichotomy often associated with Descartes, although there is an ample independent basis for it in scholasticism. The lower status of the arts reflects not only their connection with the senses and the body but also associations with

---

[22] The ceiling of the Grand'Salle de spectacle in the Palais-Cardinal, for example, and the painted replica of the Arch of Constantine at Rueil, which swallows are said to have tried to fly through. Compare Eusèbe's comment with this passage by the illustrator of *Ariane*: 'il n'a a guieres que ceux qui ont déjà quelque dauant-goust de la Portraicture & de l'Architecture, & qui ont consequemment quelque espece de commencement de la Geometrie au moins pratique à qui l'enuie naisse d'apprendre les pratiques de la perspectiue . . . & encore moins de prendre quelque diuertissement à les mettre eux mesmes à execution', A. Bosse, *La Pratique de trait à preuues, de Mr [G.] Desargues [1593–1662] Lyonnois* (1643), 12–13.

[23] *Les Délices de l'esprit*, i. 66.   [24] Ibid. 4.

[25] Ibid. 81.   [26] Ibid. 88–9.

manual work, as in the phrase 'arts et métiers'. The classification of poetic genres is itself hierarchical, beginning with 'fables' (mythology, as in Ovid's *Metamorphoses*), eclogues, lyrics (that is, songs etc.), elegies, and other short forms (satires, rondeaux, enigmas, sonnets, madrigals, and epigrams), and ending with comedy, tragedy, and heroic poetry.

Eusèbe then progressed to the 'charmante demeure de la Reputation', the door to which was crowded by the many people all trying to enter at the same time and bumping into one another in their efforts to occupy the main apartment. 'Mais quoy que i'y receusse assez de plaisir, tant par moy-mesme, qui m'estimois beaucoup, que par ceux qui m'estimoient, afin que ie les estimasse,' he states, 'i'en voulus chercher ailleurs vn plus grand et plus solide.'[27] It was thus that closer to the City he discovered the great Palace of Fortune where he might find the honour and wealth missing in the dwellings of the Arts, the Sciences, and Fame. It had an imposing entrance, but actually getting in proved even more difficult than at the House of Fame, 'estant gardée par des hommes, qui repoussoient auec rudesse & insolence la foule qui se presentoit pour y entrer'. But Eusèbe managed to enter 'par la faueur de mes amis qui me presterent la main, & qui me rendirent ces gardes fauorables', and soon afterwards he was admitted 'à la conversation familiere de celuy qui estoit logé au plus haut estage de ce Palais de la Fortune'. 'Là', he continues, in a passage interpreted as probably autobiographical in Chapter 1,

ie goustay mille plaisirs rauissans, par l'estime qu'il fit de moy, par les caresses & particulieres & publiques dont il m'honora, par les applaudissemens que ie receuois de toutes parts, & par les victoires que ie remportois souuent sur mes enuieux.[28]

The dialogues of the eighth day, 'Des délices de la Philosophie, ou de la Sagesse morale', brings the discussants from a 'chambre des liures' into the 'beaux & riches appartemens des grandes Vertus', below which lie 'les prisons des Passions; & plus bas encore . . . les cachots des Vices'—a reminder to Eusèbe 'que nous n'auons dans le monde autre guerre à soutenir, que celle des Passions & des Vices'.[29] The vices are caged like a collection of wild animals in a

---

[27] *Les Délices de l'esprit*, i. 5.
[28] Ibid. 5. One may suspect an autobiographical element in this reminiscence pertinent to Desmarets's apologetics.
[29] Ibid. 112–13.

menagerie or in the cellar cages of the imperial Roman Coliseum.
Intemperance is one of them: 'fort fiere, pour les triomphes qu'elle
a remportez sur les plus grands hommes de la Terre . . . Alexandre,
le vainqueur de tout le monde . . . toute l'armée de Cyrus . . .
Annibal . . .'.[30] But intemperance can be defeated by temper-
ance . . .

This allegorical struggle of virtues against vices is easy to interpret
in terms of Le Combat spirituel and to relate to Desmarets's historical
tragicomedies and other plays in which spiritual combat is a theme.
It is equally easy to relate the vices of this menagerie to the beasts
and monsters of La Délivrance de Renaud and other allegorical Court
ballets in which the youthful Desmarets danced some forty years
earlier. More importantly, perhaps, the historical examples through
which he personifies the allegory imply the historical succession
depicted in Le Ballet de la Félicité, in which successive rulers first
seize and later lose world dominion: not just Cyrus, Alexander, and
Hannibal in these examples, but imperial Rome, with the monstrous
cruelty of its perverted entertainments. There is often an historico-
political subtext to Desmarets's promenades towards the mystic
depths of the mind. Past declines in the imperial succession are
implicitly linked to defeats in the sort of spiritual combat in which
Desmarets sought to make the century of Louis XIV victorious.

As Eusèbe and Philédon continue their progress, the dialogues
become more ascetic, more spiritual, more mystical. They also
become more specialized and more difficult to relate directly to
Desmarets's other activities. The religious issues discussed are of the
greatest consequence for the century of Louis XIV, characterized as
it was by religious fervour and religious controversy. Religious
fervour was itself controversial, often focalizing variants of belief
and expression which may seem to involve minor or even trivial
points of interpretation, regarding them as fundamental. For most
readers, however, Henri Bremond's treatment of Les Délices de
l'esprit will be sufficiently detailed.[31]

The five dialogues of Part ii deal respectively with: (9) belief in
the Trinity and Jesus; (10) the implicit belief of blasphemers in Jesus;
(11) the conversion of Philédon and his entry into the Ville de la

---

[30] Ibid. 114–15.
[31] Bremond, Histoire littéraire, vi. 445–581.

vraye Volupté; (12) 'Des Vertus ou Filles de la Charité'—humility, obedience, benevolence, purity, patience, prayer, and mortification (virtues on the whole more ascetic than the seven basic Christian virtues celebrated in *Les Promenades de Richelieu*); and (13) charity, including the love of God and of one's neighbour.

Recognizing the difficulties of Parts iii and iv, Desmarets provides a further 'Advis aux Beaux Esprits du Monde', warning that they are not for grosser readers: 'Vir insipiens non cognoscet, et stultus non intelliget haec.'[32] The seventeen dialogues of part iii begin with a lesson in the language of mysticism: (14) 'Instruction pour apprendre le langage des choses de l'Interieur dans les saintes Escritures', a dialogue which shows Desmarets conversant with figurative interpretation—both the tradition by which the Holy Spirit 'donne souuent diuers sens à vne mesme chose', as Eusèbe remarks, and the particular system for interpreting Revelation which he elaborates here.[33] What he calls the interior is like a new world whose upper part is figured in the heavens and lower part in the earth. The kings of the earth indicate the senses, the princes sensual pleasures. The four corners of the earth stand for the natural passions: desire, fear, joy, and sorrow. The peoples of the earth are the affections. 'God's temple' means the interior. The whore of Babylon prostituted with the kings of the earth is human nature corrupted by original sin. Gog and Magog stand for the senses of taste and touch. Holy Jerusalem signifies 'l'âme pleinement en grace', and its twelve gates represent twelve modes of prayer.

The precepts of this dialogue are followed by (15) 'Exemples comment Dauid s'est seruy des termes de ce langage particulier . . . afin de cacher sa Theologie mystique [in Psalms]; & comment Nostre Seigneur s'en est seruy luy-mesme'. Day 16 interprets the first chapters of Revelation, with an exhortation to conversion and preparation for 'l'Vnion parfaite auec Dieu', followed by (17) 'La magnifique entrée dans la basse ville de l'Interieur' with 'L'ouuerture du Liure de Vie, qui est la connoïssance de Dieu le Createur, & de Dieu le Redempteur'. Dialogue 18 outlines the subjugation of the promptings of sensuality to the kingdom of God, shows in 'De

---

[32] *Les Délices de l'esprit*, ii. 91. Front matter for Part iii was printed with Part ii. Source not identified.

[33] Desmarets mentions Gaston-Jean-Baptiste, Baron de Renty (1611–48) and Antoine Yvan (1576–1653), both connected with the Oratoire and founders of religious establishments for the needy, as knowledgeable in the mysteries of Revelation (ibid., 2).

l'oraison interieure' the benefits of silent prayer (one of the striking features of Desmarets's spirituality), benefits especially evident in spiritual combat against 'la concupiscence des yeux pour les choses exterieures, qui sont les possessions, & les vanitez'. Dialogues 19 and 20, which deal respectively with (19) the struggles against the flesh and against pride and (20) the sacrament of repentance, are followed by a more relaxed atmospheric and personal evening dialogue, apparently intended at one time to follow the eighteenth day.[34]

Dialogue 21, 'De ne priser que les choses de l'Interieur, & de mépriser toutes les choses exterieures. Et de l'Oraison, & de la Mortification', is followed by (22) 'Du Combat du Demon contre la Volonté' and by a dialogue (23) particularly pertinent to doctrine concerning absolution and redemption: 'De la dangereuse Beste du Chimere de pechez passez & pardonnez. Et d'vne autre dangereuse Beste ou Chimere, qui est la fausse mortification'. The way to victory over those two chimeras is more fully outlined in (24), 'Le Triomphe des fideles Sentimens, qui ont surmonté la vaine-crainte des pechez pardonnez. Et le Triomphe de Dieu mesme dans l'Interieur'. Dialogues 25 and 26 deal with 'La Mortification ou destruction entiere de la Chair, ou de la Nature corrompue en Adam', represented in variants of the whore of Babylon. Dialogue 27 is an allegorical presentation of the Eucharist as the marriage of the soul to Christ. In dialogue 28 Philédon and Eusèbe discuss, after communion, the power of grace and the problem of temptations related to the senses of taste and touch. The dialogues are then concluded by (29) 'La riche & admirable description de l'Ame vnie à Dieu, representée sous le nom de la sainte Cité, ou de la nouuelle Ieruselem' and (30) 'Les admirables delices de la ville de la vraye Volupté'—the mystic experience.

The title of this volume and its general dedication 'aux Beaux Esprits du monde' are rooted in literary traditions and social activities pertinent to the author's purpose. An anthology of libertine verse in the fashion that led to the trials of Théophile de Viau in 1623–5 is entitled *Les Délices satyrique[s]* (1620). Desmarets probably alludes to that period both in the dedication and in the allegory of the tavern of Bacchus and Venus.[35] On a more respectable level, a

---

[34] Ibid. iii. 85.

[35] The best-known polemical use of this phrase probably remained F. Garasse, *La Doctrine curieuse des beaux esprits de ce temps ou prétendus tels* (1624). It was c.1624 that Saint-Amant's *La Musique de la taverne et les prophéties du cabaret* was printed.

French translation of Lope de Vega's *Arcadia* is entitled *Les Délices de la vie pastorale* (Lyons, 1624). Then 'délices' is deployed in the titles of spiritual books by Puget de la Serre: *Le Tombeau des délices du monde* (1630) and *Les Délices de la mort* (1631). But *Les Délices de l'esprit* gives more emphasis than Puget de la Serre does in those volumes to temporal pleasures associated with the mystic experience.[36]

Desmarets's dedication and strategy may also reflect the activities disclosed in a 'Manifeste aux beaux esprits de ce siècle', thus summarized by F. L. Marcou:

> Une société anonyme institue par souscription, à l'hôtel d'Anjou, rue de Béthisy [in Paris], siège ordinaire des établissements de loterie . . . des bals, concerts, comédies, conférences, conversations, leçons de philosophie par [Louis de] Lesclache [1620?–71], qui durèrent du 1er janvier à la mi-carême de 1655. Le manifeste contient le programme de l'emploi de chaque jour de la semaine. La société a pour but de propager le goût des plaisirs honnêtes de l'esprit, afin de détourner 'du vice, des débauches et des méchantes habitudes, qui ne sont que trop fréquentes'.[37]

Whether or not Desmarets was directly associated with this venture is not known, but he can scarcely have failed to be aware of it. Preservation of the 'Manifeste' in the 'Recueils Conrart' of the Bibliothèque de l'Arsenal indicates that it was known to members of the Académie-Française. It involved the sort of activity to arouse interest in, if not originate from, the salon of the Duchesse de Richelieu, cited as a model in the 1650s 'de la politesse des mœurs'.[38]

In his dedication 'Aux Beaux Esprits du monde' Desmarets discusses the reactions of some who had seen part of his new work in the hands of friends but who themselves 'n'ont aucun goust pour les matieres spirituelles et hautes qui sont dans les dernieres parties'. When he interrupted work on *Les Délices de l'esprit* to complete *Clovis*, they hoped that he had decided not to complete the final parts. But he was impatient

> de satisfaire à Dieu, & de publier les choses qu'il luy a pleû m'inspirer, pour le salut de plusieurs ames égarées; & pour ramener les personnes d'esprit à ce qui doit estre leur plus noble entretien, & leur plus solide nourriture.

---

[36] Illustrations of *Les Délices de l'esprit* were crudely copied to illustrate several posthumous edns. of Puget de la Serre's *La Vie heureuse* (or *L'Homme content*) (1695 etc.).

[37] F. L. Marcou, *Étude sur la vie et les œuvres de Pellisson* (1859), 98.

[38] Ibid. 99.

His concern is with both the 'voluptueux charnels', whose debauchery leads to impiety, insolence, public disorder, and shameless conduct, and who 'vomissent par tout leurs impuretez & leurs blasphemes, & les font éclater iusques dans les Temples', and also with the 'voluptueux spirituels', 'personnes dont la sensualité leur semble spirituelle, parce qu'elle est plus ouuerte & plus raffinée, & comme detachée des sens'—professed Christians who suppose that 'il leur est permis de gouster, au moins par l'esprit, les choses les plus sensuelles'. Desmarets now expresses regret at having formerly written so much for the pleasure and vanities of the latter, but his apologia will only be effective if the habits of the voluptuous are taken into consideration:

Puisque les voluptueux charnels, & les voluptueux spirituels, ne cherchent que le plaisir; il leur faut des liures qui les attirent par le plaisir mesme, & qui les conuainquent encore par le plaisir . . .

Libertines must not be the only ones who appeal through pleasure. Others need to be encouraged in the practice of 'l'oraison interieure' and in awareness that they can do 'ce que font les ames les plus détachées & les plus simples; & qu'ils peuuent estre attirez à la douce quietude des jouissances de l'ame, & à la delicieuse vnion auec Dieu'.

Desmarets's general *privilège* was transferred for *Les Délices de l'esprit* to Augustin Courbé, Henry Le Gras, and Jacques Roger, the original publishers and printer, on 12 April 1658, and they in turn transferred it to Florentin Lambert on 12 September 1659. This great folio volume, lavishly illustrated in the original way (to which attention is drawn in the 'Introduction') contains scenes drawn, signed, and engraved by François Chauveau, set between exceptionally large and distinguished woodcut headbands and tailpieces in the form of monograms or interlaced initials on the same page (see Fig. 12).[39] These ornaments, similar in style, execution, and disposition to those used a year earlier in the quarto *Clovis*, were probably designed by Armand-Jean Desmarets de Saint-Sorlin. In terms of its printing and illustration, it is one of the finest books produced in France in the seventeenth century. The folio edition was not reprinted, but it was reissued by Lambert with a new title-page in 1659 and again in 1661, when Lambert also reissued the quarto

---

[39] J. Duportail, in 'Les Livres à gravures du XVIIe siècle', in H. Martin, A. Blum, *et al.*, eds., *Le Livre français* (1924), 78.

FIG. 12. Eusèbe and Philédon kneeling before Christ in the company of martyrs and Old Testament prophets and kings, from *Les Délices de l'esprit* (1658 folio). Above the plate: 'There will be joy in heaven over the repentance of one sinner among the people.' Below the plate: 'The Lord is compassionate and merciful, long-suffering and merciful.' Plate engraved by François Chauveau from his own drawing. Headband and tailpiece cut by (?) Jean Le Pautre or Charpentier after (?) Armand Jean Desmarets de Saint-Sorlin (*Phot. Bib. Nat. Paris*)

Clovis.[40] Reissue of such expensive books need not indicate that they were not read. The dialogues of *Les Délices de l'esprit* without Part iv were reprinted at least nine times, including eight editions between 1677 and 1691. I have not located the Spanish translation which Desmarets mentions in the course of the Quarrel of the *Imaginaires*.[41]

Critical reception of *Les Délices de l'esprit* was mixed, as the author anticipated. The Quarrel of the *Imaginaires* in particular has cast a shadow over it. For the *Menagiana*, the errata slip could have been reduced to a single correction: '*Délices*. lisez *délires*'.[42] The *Vigneul-Marvilliana* notes that Christina of Sweden (1626–89), who was in France in early 1658, regretted that Desmarets 'se fût jetté dans le stile dévot', while others said that 'Desmarets encore jeune avoit perdu som ame en écrivant des romans; & que vieux il avoit perdu l'esprit à écrire de la *mystiquerie*'—adding, in terms reflecting the hostilities of both Nicole and Boileau:

En effet, sa theologie mystique est un galimatias incompréhensible; & ses *Les Délices de l'esprit* qui n'ont rien de beau que le titre & les chiffres, ne lui ont pas fait plus d'honneur que son *Clovis* . . .[43]

Before the Quarrel of the *Imaginaires*, however, Charles Sorel mentions *Les Délices de l'esprit* as a work

où l'incrédulité est combattuë par des raisons aisées à comprendre, et on y trouve des explications ingenieuses de quelques Livres de la Bible, autant remplie de pieté que d'érudition.[44]

Henri Bremond attests not only the strangeness of Desmarets's work on the basis of contemporary judgements but the soundness of his knowledge of the states of prayer.[45]

Much of the information in the earlier dialogues must have been taken from an unfinished earlier work, the *Abrégé de la science universelle*, an 'ouvrage de prose considerable', on which, according to Paul Pellisson, Desmarets

---

[40] A discussant in 'Le Libraire du Palais', a dialogue in the *Carpenteriana* (1724), 93, notes that 'sans réimprimer un livre une seconde fois, vous en pouvez faire six éditions consécutives; il n'y faut changer que le premier feuillet'.

[41] *Seconde Partie de la Response*, 31.

[42] *Menagiana*, ii. 396.

[43] *Vigneul-Marvilliana*, in *Ana, ou collection de bons mots*, v. 162–3.

[44] Sorel, *La Bibliothèque françoise*, 41.

[45] Bremond, *Histoire littéraire*, vi. 446.

a aussi travaillé par l'ordre du Duc de Richelieu son Maistre . . . & qui contient en prés de mille chapitres, des connoissances sommaires, sur la pluspart des choses qui tombent dans l'entretien ordinaire.[46]

Some of the information collected in that project must have gone into the *Jeux de cartes*. Some of the rest appears to have been subordinated to apologetics in *Les Délices de l'esprit*, a shift of priorities in which Desmarets is found in distinguished company in the century of Louis XIV. The literary fortune of this great book would doubtless have been greater had he persevered in the original intention, anticipating the *Dictionnaires* of Moréri and of Bayle and the great eighteenth-century *Encyclopédie*.

Lettres spirituelles

Lettres spirituelles, recueillies par vn Ecclesiastique, some three hundred letters grouped in five parts in six volumes, were published by Florentin Lambert (1660–3), with a *privilège* for ten years dated 19 December 1659. The 'achevés d'imprimer' for the six volumes are dated from 20 December 1659 to 15 September 1663. The first three volumes are dated 1660; volumes iv and v, 1661; and volume vi, 1663. The 'Ecclésiastique' of the title is Jean de Lessot, 'prêtre du diocèse de Poitier', to whom the volumes are attributed by the Bibliothèque Nationale. The letters were identified as Desmarets's lost letters by René Briand from controversy over them and from passages quoted during the Quarrel of the *Imaginaires*.[47] The attribution seems generally secure on grounds of style and content. Desmarets himself refers to his 'saintes lettres'; and Charles Sorel states categorically: 'Il y a plusieurs Volumes de Lettres spirituelles de *M. Desmarests* qui sont fort estimées des personnes adonnées à la devotion.'[48] Lessot states at the beginning of the first volume that he collected the letters from the recipients, adding 'ie me suis trouué émeu par elles à me conuertir à Dieu, & à l'aimer; d'autres le pourront faire aussi'. The 'Approbation des Docteurs' for all six volumes, dated 17 December 1659, finds in the letters nothing

qui ne soit conforme à la Foy Catholique, Apostolique & Romaine, & qui ne serue aux bonnes mœurs; comme aussi à porter le Lecteur à vne haute

---

[46] Pellisson, *Histoire de l'Académie-Françoise*, 344.
[47] Briand, XVIIe *siècle*, 112 (1976), 41–6.
[48] *Seconde Partie de la Response*, 74; Sorel, *La Bibliothèque françoise*, 94.

perfection & deuotion; n'étant remplies que de tres-saintes pensées, & de tres-bons aduis pour la vie spirituelle.[49]

This favourable judgement, like those of Lessot and Sorel, is pertinent to Desmarets's reputation for piety at the time of the Morin affair, shortly before the Quarrel of the *Imaginaires*.

Letter i. 1, to the daughter of a friend, reads like authentic Desmarets, though its theme is a commonplace: 'I'ay esté au Monde bien plus longtemps que vous; & i'ay creu longtemps que le Monde me pourroit satisfaire: mais ie ne songeois qu'à le satisfaire', an approach which led to disappointment. Later in the same letter he states: 'I'aime la solitude, le silence, l'exercice des vertus contraires aux passions & aux vices, & l'heureuse tranquillité de l'ame, qui s'appelle la paix de Dieu, laquelle surpasse tous les plaisirs des sens: Et ie hay la curiosité des sens.'[50]

Letter ii. 2, 'Quel auantage on reçoit à aimer la retraite & le silence . . . Que l'Oraison consiste à faire l'amour à Dieu', is also characteristic of Desmarets's spirituality in this period. It concludes that 'nous n'auons point de foy, si nous n'auons point d'amour pour Dieu, qui nous a faits de rien, & nous a rachetez; & qui veut encore continuellement s'vnir à nous par pur amour'.[51] So is letter i. 16, 'Comment il faut faire mourir l'amour propre': 'Ie croy qu'vn amour ne peut iamais estre dompté ny détruit que par vn autre amour.'[52] The maxim sums up the psychological basis of Desmarets's strategy in *Les Délices de l'esprit*. It is also pertinent to the 'psychology' of other contemporary writers, to cite only Corneille, La Rochefoucauld, and Mme de Lafayette. Other letters advise on questions recurrent in contemporary secular literature and theatre. For instance, letter i. 17, on the dangers of casuists, considered 'd'ordinaire des hommes sensuels qui donnent ces Liures à des filles, afin de leur apprendre le mal qu'elles ne sçauent pas'; i. 30, 'De la fréquente communion'; and i. 34, 'Sur la cónduite d'vne Superieure, & sur les diuertissemens honnestes', recommending 'que vous ayez toutes vne deuotion gaye,

---

[49] The 'Approbation' is signed 'N[icolas] de Lestocq [?–1662], Curé de Saint Laurens lez Paris', himself the author of *Pieux Entretiens* (1644) and *La Voie de l'aigle au Ciel, ou l'intention chrestienne dirigée à la gloire de Dieu par les règles et pratiques tirées de l'Ecriture Sainte* (1664), and 'I. (*sic*) Gosset, Curé de Sainte Opportune [in Paris]', probably the same as Nicolas Gosset, author of *La Vie et miracles de Sainte Opportune* (1654).

[50] *Lettres spirituelles*, i. 2, 5.

[51] Ibid. ii. 19.

[52] Ibid. i. 93.

& non pas triste comme les hypocrites. Car Dieu veut que l'on se réiouïsse en luy, & que l'on se diuertisse les vnes auec les autres, auec douceur & charité.'[53] Among the many possible intertextual comparisons, Pascal's *Provinciales*, Antoine Arnauld's *De la fréquente communion* (1643) (more or less directly contradicted in i. 30), and Molière's *Tartuffe* come to mind.

Some of the letters amount to treatises or tracts, notably iii. 25–27: 'Discours de la theologie mystique', 'Les neuf degrez de l'amour Seraphique', and 'Sur l'horrible aueuglement des personnes du Monde'.[54] Others seem more personal: ii. 3, for instance, 'Que la recreation des Religieuses ne doit pas estre d'vne seule auec vne seule'. 'Qu'il ne faut aimer les creatures qu'en Dieu, & pour l'amour de Dieu', ii. 5, brings out the supernatural nature of grace—a doctrine pertinent to Desmarets's position on the Christian marvellous. It is argued in this letter that God's will is to be loved

surnaturellement, auec sa grace, laquelle est vn moyen surnaturel; parce que Dieu estant infiniment au dessus de nostre nature, il faut vn moyen surnaturel pour nous éleuer à son amour; & ce moyen surnaturel, est la grace par Nostre Seigneur IESUS-CHRIST, qui seul a le pouuoir de nous éleuer à Dieu; parce qu'il est seul Homme & Dieu, & qu'il est la seule voye de l'homme à Dieu.[55]

Similar assumptions underlie many a secular literary text of the century of Louis XIV.

A final example involves, as the following discussion will show, themes recurrent in this book, personalities in Cardinal Richelieu's entourage, and Molière's *L'École des femmes* (1662), a comedy in which the naïve Agnès, brought up in a 'petit couvent loin de toute pratique', is reported as having asked 'si les enfants qu'on fait se faisaient par l'oreille' (i. 1). Her question involves a notion which a bright teenager might have picked up from any number of allusions to the Annunciation. Consider *De partu Virginis* by Iacopo Sannazzaro (1456–1530), author of the *Arcadia*. One of the finest neo-Latin poems of the Renaissance, *De partu Virginis* was republished in Paris in 1646 by the Jesuit scholar Philippe Labbe (1607–67). A year earlier Labbe had republished the French prose translation of *Les Couches sacrées de la Vierge, poëme héroïque de Sannazar* (1634), which

[53] *Lettres spirituelles*, i. 100, 169–75, and 189, respectively.
[54] Ibid. iii. 113–49, 150–72, and 174–251, respectively.
[55] Ibid. ii. 32.

Guillaume Colletet had dedicated to Mme de Combalet, the future Duchesse d'Aiguillon. In this poem Mary, who has taken a vow of chastity, makes the angelic messenger a party to her doubts about the sexual implications of the Annunciation. He assures her, in Colletet's words, that

le Saint Esprit descendra du Ciel en terre, & entrant par vôtre oreille dedans vostre cœur, remplira vos chastes flancs de cet Enfant imcomparable. Vous vous estonnerez de sentir vostre ventre s'enfler peu à peu. Mystere qui vous causera d'abord quelque apprehension . . .[56]

Lettres spirituelles ii. 7, 'Sur les Liures où les fictions Payennes sont meslées aux veritez Euangeliques', indicates that around 1660 *Les Couches sacrées de la Vierge* was read in at least one provincial convent, because when apprised of that fact Desmarets writes that a prudent Mother Superior would banish such books 'encore plus seuerement que les Comedies & les Romans, qui ne sont pas mesme si dangereux, parce que l'on sçait qu'ils ne sont composez que de feintes'.[57] He is particularly concerned about Sannazzaro's ornamental incorporation of the pagan marvellous into such a central event of the Christian marvellous, something that might 'remplir de vaines chimeres nostre esprit'.[58] This letter—and Molière's comic line— illustrate the extent to which fashions in the literary marvellous had altered between Richelieu's early literary patronage and the beginning of Louis XIV's personal reign. The Christian marvellous was (and still is) fraught with difficulties. Times, tastes, and interests were changing. In 1660–2 Guillaume Colletet's son François (1628–80) produced more than a dozen publications relating not the Annunication but the marvellous triumphal entry of Louis XIV and his new queen into Paris.

La Vie et les Œuvres de Sainte Catherine de Gênes

The work which Desmarets himself was editing for republication in 1661 indicates that, for part of the public, literary fashion changed little in these years: *La Vie et les Œuvres de Sainte Catherine de*

---

[56] Sannazzaro, *Les Couches sacrées de la Vierge* (1634 and 1645), pp. 25 and 16 respectively. In association with French the Latin text makes an unfortunate bilingual pun (my italics): 'At venter . . . / . . . *sine vi*, sine labe pudoris, / Arcano intumuit verbo'. Compare Molière, *La Comtesse d'Escarbagnas*, I, VII.

[57] *Lettres spirituelles*, ii. 51.   [58] Ibid. 48.

Gênes. His 'nouvelle édition plus nette et plus correcte' was published by Florentin Lambert with a new 'Approbation' signed 3 April 1661 by M. Grandin and a *privilège* for seven years dated 5 April, 'achevé d'imprimer' on 22 June 1661. Lambert reprints earlier 'Approbations'. One by the Apostolicus Inquisitor Hieronymus de Genis is dated 25 April 1597. Another on 20 September 1597 dates the first French translation.

The life and works—essentially a dialogue of the Soul, the Body, and Christ, and a treatise on purgatory—of Catherine Adorni, known as Saint Catherine of Genoa (1447–1510), are an important source for Desmarets's own writings on mysticism, union with God, and the dangers of self-love, which she considers an instrument of the Devil and prefers to call self-hate.[59] Her analysis of self-love, rather more than her erotic metaphors for mystic union, seems to be echoed in secular literary works of the century of Louis XIV, although Desmarets appreciates both. Particularly striking is her reaffirmation of the tradition by which

l'amour propre spirituel est bien plus dangereux, & plus difficile à connoistre que le charnel: parce qu'il est vn poison tres-subtil & penetrant, duquel peu se garantissent, estant bien plus couuert sous beaucoup de subtilitez, à sçauoir, sous pretexte de santé, de necessité; & quelquefois de charité, de compassion, & sous d'autres couuertures presque infinies.[60]

One could scarcely ask for a better contemporary key to the pretexts advanced by dominant characters in Molière's major comedies (Orgon in *Tartuffe*, Argan in *Le Malade imaginaire*, etc.) than 'l'amour propre spirituel' as presented in this passage.

De la Vita mirabile [attributed to C. Marabotto and E. Vernazza] *e Dottrina santa de la Beata Caterinetta da Genova*, first published by Capuchins (Genoa, 1551), was followed by a better edition (Florence, 1568). *La Vie & les Œuvres spirituelles de S. Catherine d'Adorny de Gennes, reueuës & corrigez* was published in a translation by 'les Venerables Peres Religieux de la Chartreuse de Bourg-Fontaine' (Lyons, 1616). Both because the 'Approbation' dates from 1597 and because it is presented as a corrected edition, this is unlikely to have been the first French edition, although it is the earliest in

---

[59] 'De l'amour propre, & de l'amour diuin', in *La Vie et les Œuvres de Sainte Catherine de Gênes*, i (1661), 125–30.
[60] Ibid., 127–8.

the Bibliothèque Nationale, which holds other editions, dated 1627 and 1646. In a sympathetic study of Catherine's religious experience, the Capuchin Teodosio da Voltri mentions an edition (Lyons, 1610) as 'revès et corrigés' (*sic*).[61] H.-J. Martin includes Saint Catherine of Genoa among mystics who retained or gained readership in France in the early seventeenth century, observes that the Bourgfontaine translation was often reprinted, and states that 'le chartreux M. Thanner en donna une nouvelle version'—that of Freiburg, 1626.[62]

Desmarets's revised edition was reprinted at least three times between 1661 and 1667 and was followed by posthumous editions in 1695-7 and 1743.

Le Chemin de la paix et celuy de l'inquiétude

Some time in 1664 Desmarets wrote to Henry-Marie Boudon (1624-1702), Archdeacon of Evreux and author of numerous devotional works, in an attempt to interest him in a 'Société de Paris pour les intérêts de Dieu', closing with a request to be associated with Carmelites of Boudon's acquaintance 'à la Société des victimes unies à Jésus'.[63] *Le Chemin de la paix et celuy de l'inquiétude* reads something like a manual for such a society, developing themes now familiar in Desmarets's spiritual writings. This time he presents a dual imaginary progress of the soul that is more abstractly allegorical: either the way of anxiety to hell or the way of peace, through the acceptance of grace within, to a great temple in which the soul is united in love with God. The spiritual captivity of excessive activity is contrasted with the spiritual freedom, peace, and quietude of mystic contemplation and union. The reader is provided with a curious extensible map charting the two ways: on the one hand the path of active anxiety, leading back towards the spiritual captivity of Egypt, undoing the progress toward the promised land narrated in Exodus (traditionally signifying not only freedom from enslavement but freedom of the soul from sin, of the immortal soul from the perishable body, and of mankind from original sin—the promised

---

[61] T. da Voltri, *Santa Caterina da Genova. La Gran Dama dell'amore* (Genoa, 1929), p. 259. See also the praise of her orthodoxy and sanctity in F. von Hügel, *The Mystical Element of Religion as Studied in Saint Catherine of Genoa and her Friends*, new edn., (2 vols.; London, 1923).

[62] Martin, *Livre, pouvoirs et société*, i. 130-1.

[63] Letter to H.-M. Boudon, quoted in Bremond, *Histoire littéraire*, vi. 492-4.

redemption); and on the other hand a path through the stages of quietude—something of a spiritual *Carte de Tendre*.

The 'Approbation' of the Sorbonne was obtained on 14 July 1665. Desmarets's general *privilège* (used here for the last time) was transferred for this work to Audinet on 19 July, and the first volume was 'achevé d'imprimer' on 31 July. The *Seconde Partie contenant l'exode ou sortie des ames de la captivité spirituelle de l'Egypte* was not 'achevé d'imprimer' until 30 April 1666, during the Quarrel of the *Imaginaires*. The first volume was reprinted 'à la sphère' in 1680.

The thirty-eight chapters of this book are in many places more austere than Desmarets's earlier devotional writing, particularly ch. 11, 'Suite du chemin de la Conversion par vanité', which mentions a 'Palais du Mépris des ames simples' and a 'Chasteau élevé . . . qui est l'Amour des visions & des revelations', as if sumptuous habitations of *Les Délices de l'esprit* were sketched more succinctly and more critically.[64] Some chapters are more moralist than mystical: ch. 14, for example, 'Du déguisement de la Nature, sous le masque de la Prudence'. The swimming metaphor recurs in ch. 32, 'De diverses manieres de ceux qui se lavent ou qui nagent dans le grand fleuve de l'Abandon à Dieu, & de ceux qui le passent à nage'. Space permits mention of scarcely more than the titles of the progressively more mystical final chapters, where the Devil still finds a place—further evidence of a firm belief in the Devil, character-istic enough of the century of Louis XIV but particularly pertinent (*a*) to Desmarets's socio-political activities around this time and (*b*) to his illustration and defence of the Christian marvellous. The last six chapters respectively treat: (33) 'Que la Nature, le Monde & les Demons taschent à tirer l'Ame de la Presence de Dieu, & de l'Abandon à Dieu'; (34) 'Du Chasteau de la Charité, & du pur Amour increé, qui détruit l'impur amour creé'; (35) 'La consommation de l'Amour creé dans la chambre du pur Amour'; (36) 'Le Détroit des Epreuves & de la totale Destruction de tout ce qui n'est point Dieu en l'Ame'; (37) 'Du calme divin. Rapport d'une Ame avec un vaisseau agité de la Mer'; and (38) 'L'Adoration perpetuelle du Saint-Sacrement', in which Grace and Hope bring the faithful Soul, instructed by Charity, to the 'port de la Tranquillité pour continuer son chemin de la Paix'. Supported by Faith and Charity, the Soul enters a great temple on which is inscribed the title of this final

---

[64] *Le Chemin de la paix* (n.p. 'à la sphère', 1680), 17.

chapter and where they find 'la Majesté de Dieu sous l'espece du pain consacré':

Aussi-tost l'Ame s'y prosterne avec elles devant la Majesté de ce Dieu caché, & se sent tressaillir de respect, de joye & d'amour, voyant devant elle son Dieu vivant en l'état d'un aneantissement inconcevable.

Faith presents the Soul's God, Charity the Soul's spouse. 'A ces mots l'Ame se pasme & tombe dans un doux ravissement . . . sans avoir aucun usage de ses sens'. Faith and Charity explain that every communicant soul is separately and individually embraced by God, 'chacune selon le degré de son amour':

L'Ame émuë par ces considerations que la Foy et la Charité luy representent en son interieur, embrasse son unique Epoux encore plus ardemment; & sent en l'embrassant que rien n'est capable de la separer jamais de luy, ny de luy faire perdre cette paix si profonde dont elle joüit par sa grace.[65]

[65] Ibid. 54–5.

14

Clovis, ou la France Chrestienne

Il n'y a rien de si simple, ni de si doux, il n'y a rien de plus *beau*
ni de plus *fort*, que la passion naturellement exprimée

Jean Desmarets to his brother Roland on the
composition of *Clovis*.[1]

Heroic or epic poems celebrating Christian, biblical, national, and
other historical heroes were a Renaissance aspiration inherited by
French writers who became prominent during Cardinal Richelieu's
ministry. Their most important epics, however, were not published
until the 1650s: Pierre Le Moyne's *Saint Louys, ou le héros chrestien*
(1653), Saint-Amant's *Moyse sauvé, idyle heroïque* (1653), Georges
de Scudéry's *Alaric, ou Rome vaincue* (1654), Chapelain's *Pucelle,
ou la France délivrée* (1656), Desmarets's *Clovis, ou la France
chrestienne* (1657), and so on. Whatever the later reputation of these
poems, *Clovis* clearly belongs to that mainstream of French heroic
poetry, once prestigious. It occupies a central position, particularly
in the efforts of mid-century poets to develop a French national and
Christian epic, anticipated by *Saint Louys* and *La Pucelle*, followed
by Louis Le Laboureur's *Charlemagne, poëme héroïque* (1664) and
Carel de Saint-Garde's epic on Charles Martel, *Les Sarrazins chassez
de France* (1667).

This now somewhat despised literary activity is discussed in books
by Richard Sayce and David Maskell.[2] If the neo-Latin *Turciad* by
the Capuchin Père Joseph de Paris (1577–1638), Richelieu's *éminence
grise*, is added to their evidence, the theme of a new Crusade in
Clovis, in Court ballet, in other verse, dedications, and 'Avis' by
Desmarets is better understood in terms of the political and religious
preoccupations of Richelieu's entourage. According to Aldous Huxley,

---

[1] Letter from the château de Richelieu, 1652, Bibliothèque de l'Arsenal, Mss. 3135.
The italicized words were first written in reverse order and crossed out.
[2] R. A. Sayce, *The French Biblical epic in the Seventeenth Century* (Oxford, 1955);
D. Maskell, *The Historical Epic in France (1500–1700)* (Oxford, 1973); and *Clovis*,
ed. F. R. Freudmann (Louvain and Paris, 1972).

a Crusade against the Turks remained one of Father Joseph's principal concerns; and the *Turciad* delighted Pope Urban VIII, who called it 'the Christian *Aeneid*'.[3]

Clovis is Desmarets's most substantial contribution to heroic poetry. It is his longest, most carefully crafted, best produced, and most successful non-dramatic poem. It is also the literary work with which he was concerned for the longest time, over forty years from *c*.1634 until his last volumes written in its defence in 1674–5. In the 'Epistre' rededicating *Clovis* to Louis XIV in 1673 he calls it 'le plus riche Poëme que j'entreprendrai jamais'. In terms of editions in the decade after first publication, the success of *Clovis* is comparable to that of Desmarets's best-received plays. Altogether there were five editions and a selection of extracts between 1657 and 1673—a reception roughly similar to that of *Saint Louys*, *Alaric*, and *La Pucelle*, or indeed of *Paradise Lost*. The first edition of Milton's epic (London, 1667) was, like *Clovis*, reissued in altered states and followed by four further editions in a comparable period. The gap between the literary fortunes of the more noteworthy mid-century French epics and *Paradise Lost* developed later.

The exemplary subject

Clovis, 'poëme héroïque' which might equally well be described as an allegorical romance in verse after Ariosto and Torquato Tasso, is a celebration of the life, conversion, and deeds of Clovis I, King of the Francs (465–511).[4] The baptism of Clovis at Rheims by Saint Remy on 25 December 506?, some thirty years after the collapse of the Roman Empire in the west, made him the first barbarian Christian king in western Europe as well as the first of the Louis,

---

[3] A. Huxley, *Grey Eminence: A Study in Religion and Politics* (London, 1949), 114–15.

[4] Writing to his brother from Richelieu between 4 June and 6 July 1652, Desmarets states: 'Le Roman & le Poëme, ne diffèrent d'vne chose, sinon que l'vn est en prose & l'autre en vers. Ainsi le Tasse est vn Roman. Croyez-vous que tout ce qu'il y a d'Armide & de Renaud dans le Tasse soit à rejetter pour ce qu'il est tout romanesque?', Bibliothèque de l'Arsenal, Mss. 3135. However, in the 'Discours pour prouver que les sujets Chrestiens sont les seuls propres à la poësie Heroïque' published with the 1673 edition of *Clovis* Desmarets argues various differences related to unity of form, elevation of diction, status of the hero, and the marvellous (see Freudmann edn., 735–6).

kings of France.[5] Victorious over 'les Romains, les Bourguignons, les Germains, & les Goths', Clovis is said by Desmarets in the epistle 'Au Roy' to have become 'maistre de tout l'Occident; & le Prince le plus redoutable de la Terre', considered an excellent model for a prince:

> L'histoire dit des merveilles de ses grandes qualitez. Il estoit valeureux en guerre, doux en paix, aimé des bons, terrible aux méchans, ne laissant aucun crime sans châtiment, & toutefois ayant vne telle veneration pour les personnes saintes, que mesme dès le temps qu'il estoit Payen, il ne pouvoit refuser à sainte Genevieve les criminels que sa charité luy demandoit.

By 'l'histoire' Desmarets means virtually any traditional written testimony, including hagiography, legend, and myth. As a literary concept, 'l'histoire' is an accepted story, which he embellishes, normally taking care to limit ornamental reference to the pagan gods to pagans, including sorcerers who summon up demons in the guise of pagan gods.[6]

The storms, enchantments, pictorial histories, apparitions, prophecies, illusions, reversals, flashbacks, tales-within-tales, and resurrections of *Clovis* are related to traditions of epic and romance as well as to the historic subject and associated legends. Such aspects of Desmarets's narration are now more easily studied with the help of the Freudmann edition, which includes much of Desmarets's own commentary and a reprint of M. Petit's detailed *Étude sur le Clovis de Desmarets* (Le Mans, 1868). I differ somewhat from Freudmann, however, over the extent to which *Clovis* should be considered an allegorical poem.

Freudmann hesitates between Archimède Marni's view (1936) that the religious and moral importance of Desmarets's subject 'excluded from his mind any possible idea of allegorizing his *Clovis*' and the

---

[5] For a twentieth-century perspective on one of the '30 journées qui ont fait la France', see G. Tessier, *Le Baptême de Clovis* (1964). The chronology of the poem is somewhat more faithful to history if the evidence for 506, not for 496 etc., is accepted.

[6] What is not clear is the extent to which 'l'histoire' is intended here as a literary concept involved with stories accepted only as 'images' useful in image-making. Would Clovis have been idealized as 'aimé des bons, terrible aux méchans' without the precedent of Machiavelli's *Il Principe* 17, 2? In answer to the question of whether it is better for the Prince to be loved or to be feared, Machiavelli states with unusual precision that (ideally) he should be both loved and feared. On the question of ornamental mythology, metonymy based on the names of pagan divinities—a frequent poetic trope at the time—does occasionally occur in the 'voice' of the narrator.

allegorical interpretation advanced in 1966 by William A. Goodman, for whom Albione represents England and Agilane embodies 'the one true and orthodox Church, the Church Visible', etc.[7] Goodman suggests, for instance, that the name Agilane is invented from Greek words meaning 'holy' and 'amphora' (or 'ampulla'?) in allusion to the miracle of the 'sainte Ampoulle' associated with Clovis's anointment with an ampulla of oil delivered by the Holy Ghost in the form of a white dove. While Goodman's analysis sometimes leads to debatable interpretations, Marni's negative assertion is difficult to reconcile either with convincing aspects of Goodman's analysis or with Desmarets's general practice as a writer, whether in *Aspasie*, *Mirame*, and *Europe*, or *Les Promenades de Richelieu*, *Le Combat spirituel*, *Les Délices de l'esprit*, and *Marie-Madeleine*. Many aspects of *Clovis* make better sense, and the poem as a whole becomes more complex and more coherent, if a sometimes multiple allegorical dimension is admitted. In particular, the allegory of *Clovis* is associated with flights of invention reminiscent of the symbolic fantasy of Court ballet, machine plays, and opera—aspects of the poem generally disliked by critics whose approach to imaginative literature is circumscribed by rationalist considerations, beginning with Chapelain's 'Observations sur le *Clovis*'.[8]

The Christian marvellous is an integral part of the subject: the miracles associated with the conversion and baptism of Clovis are the first associated with the miraculous Kings of France, anticipating the miraculous birth of Louis XIV himself.[9] What some readers find difficult is the extent to which Desmarets defends the marvellous as verisimilar in terms of Christian 'truths', linking it to current events and policies: witch-hunting, for instance.

The sorcerer Auberon who invokes a storm in *Clovis* I (in imitation of the storm aroused by Æolus at Juno's behest in *Aeneid* i) is based on the same thirteenth-century *chanson de geste*, *Huon de Bordeaux*,

---

[7] A. Marni, *Allegory in the French Heroic Poem of the Seventeenth Century* (Princeton, 1936), 167; W. A. Goodman, 'The Heroic Poems of Jean Desmarets de Saint-Sorlin' (Univ. of N. Carolina Ph.D. thesis (1966)), in *Dissertation Abstracts* (1967), 2530–1, 80 ff.

[8] Chapelain, *Opuscules critiques*, 321–39.

[9] For the association of the French and English kings with the most widely attested miracle in European history, see M. Bloch, *Les Rois thaumaturges, étude sur le caractère surnaturel attribué à la puissance royale particulièrement en France et en Angleterre* (1961), or *The Royal Touch: Sacred Monarchy and Scrofula in England and France*, transl. J. E. Anderson (London and Montreal, 1973).

as the eponymous sorcerer in C. M. von Weber's opera *Oberon*
(1826), the Nibelung Alberich in Richard Wagner's *Der Ring des
Nibelungen*, and Oberon the fairy king in *A Midsummer Night's
Dream*. Pagan gods as Christian demons feature not only in the
Christian marvellous of *Paradise Lost* but also in the Venusberg music
which Wagner added to *Tannhäuser* for the production at the Paris
Opéra in 1861.[10] The symbolic dove bringing the ampulla in *Clovis*
XXIV is no more ridiculous than the white dove of the Grail which
draws away the hero's boat in Wagner's *Lohengrin* III, except that
Desmarets's emphasis on the miraculous was, understandably, judged
dangerous by threatened contemporaries.

It is a problem of sincerity. Desmarets really believed in miracles
as evidence of the political authority of divine-right monarchy; and
he really believed in sorcery, not only in the Old and New Testaments
and other former times but in the Paris of his century. Not that he
accepted every accusation of witchcraft; Joan of Arc, for instance,
treated as a witch by Shakespeare in *The First Part of King Henry
VI*, is already referred to as 'la Sainte' in *Clovis* IX. These were
sensitive issues, particularly in a prominent publication by 'une des
plus belles plumes de la cour'.[11]

The illustrated quarto

Publication of *Clovis* in a richly illustrated quarto by Augustin
Courbé, Henry Le Gras, and (unusually) the printer Jacques Roger
(to the three of whom Desmarets had transferred his general *privilège*
the day before the 'achevé d'imprimer' on 6 April 1657) is an event
of consequence in the history of the French book, because none had
been produced previously with engraved illustrations set on the same
page between separate ornamental headbands and tailpieces. *Saint
Louys*, *Alaric*, and *La Pucelle* especially had been published in
sumptuous folio editions. It may be that, with *Les Délices de l'esprit*

---

[10] The important differences between Wagner's operas and *Clovis* need not
obscure the similar ways in which the medieval Christian marvellous is exploited for
symbolic works rooted in nationalist cultural aspirations. *Tannhäuser* only required
translation into French and the addition of a ballet because they were demanded by
traditions of the Paris Opéra originating in French Court ballet, in which dance,
symbolism, nationalism, and a commitment to 'total theatre' all feature prominently.

[11] Corneille's reference to Desmarets in the 'Au lecteur' of his version of *L'Imitation
de Jésus-Christ* (1656), quoted in Corneille, *Œuvres*, viii. 13.

in prospect, Desmarets and/or his publishers wished to reserve publication in folio for the devotional book and make it the first folio illustrated in the new style. In any case, what David Bland writes of *Les Délices de l'esprit*, published a year later, must be true *a fortiori* of *Clovis*; for *Clovis* too 'must have been startling when it appeared because of the amazingly elaborate ornamentation above and below the pictures and on the title-pages'.[12] The frontispiece depicting the conversion of Clovis is engraved by Nicolas Pitau after Charles Le Brun; and the equestrian portrait of Louis XIV is by Jean Couvay after Sébastien Bourdon. According to Diane Canivet, Abraham Bosse engraved the pictorial plates for Livres XII, XV, XXIII, and XXIV after François Chauveau and Bourdon; and Chauveau engraved the other twenty-two after his own drawings.[13] More recently, John Harthan attributes the design of the illustrations generally to Chauveau and the engraving to Bosse and to Jean Le Pautre (1618–82).[14] Le Pautre was a specialist in woodcuts. Chauveau's designs, states Harthan, are 'among the most remarkable' in the French epics of the 1650s (see Fig. 13):

The first plate of the text shows a highly dramatic scene . . . The gesture of the riders as they shelter beneath raised cloaks is a convention of the period for depicting storm scenes. Chauveau introduced a highly original decorative motif in the form of interlacing letters at the top and bottom of the page. The 'plumed initials' . . . appear to be based on pattern-books of cyphers but resemble also ornamental ironwork of the period.[15]

---

[12] D. Bland, *A History of Book Illustration*, 2nd edn. (London, 1959), 180. H.-J. Martin, who notes the growing interest in the early seventeenth century in 'l'histoire nationale et l'histoire de la monarchie', contrasts the illustration of *Clovis* and other mid-century epics with the poorly produced editions of plays and novels in the 1650s, *Livre, pouvoirs et société*, i. 205; ii. 637–8.

[13] D. Canivet, *L'Illustration de la poésie et du roman français au XVIIe siècle* (1957), after R.-A. Weigert, *Inventaire du fonds français de Cabinet des Estampes* [*de la Bibliothèque Nationale*] (1939–   ), i. 507; ii. 459–61.

[14] Harthan, *The History of the Illustrated Book*, 114.

[15] Ibid. 114–15. There is clearly some disagreement about the origins of the highly original designs for *Clovis* and *Les Délices de l'esprit*. I am the more sceptical about the attribution of the ornamentation to François Chauveau as Bland appears to have been unaware of its use in *Clovis*. Not just the illustration but the storm itself is a topos of epic narration, as Maskell shows, *The Historical Epic*, 214–29. He remarks: 'What is striking about Desmarets' narration of this episode is the intricate interweaving of the description of the storm with the reactions of the characters concerned', as the supernatural storm arises without such warnings as swallows and/or swifts ('ces vistes oyseaux / Qui rasent de leur aile & les champs & les eaux'), Clotilde is frightened by the ominous sky, the lovers' clothes are drenched, Clotilde puts her arm

FIG. 13. The tauriform sea monster from *Clovis* (1657 quarto), Livre V.
Plate engraved by François Chauveau from his own drawing. Headband
and tailpiece cut by (?) Jean Le Pautre after (?) Armand Desmarets de Saint-
Sorlin (*Phot. Bib. Nat. Paris*)

Whether or not Chauveau designed or helped design the headbands and tailpieces, they are clearly related to the similar work of Armand-Jean Desmarets, to whom the British Library (correctly, in my view) attributes the ornamental initials of *Clovis*, as noted in Chapter 2. The placing, particularly of the large monogram crowned redoubled interlacing *L*, varies in different copies.

The first books

Desmarets had begun work on *Clovis* more than twenty years before its publication. According to Paul Pellisson, he had already written two books when, after the performance of *Aspasie* on 19 February 1636, he sought to avoid Cardinal Richelieu's request for a new play annually 'sur le travail de son Poëme héroïque de Clovis, dont il avoit déjà fait deux livres, & qui regardoit la gloire de la France, & celle du Cardinal même'.[16] Pellisson's account, first published in 1653, is confirmed by Desmarets himself in 1666; it is also corroborated by a letter from Chapelain to Guez de Balzac in November 1637:

> Au reste je vous déclare que j'ay un rival dans la Poësie héroïque. Mr Desmarests a entrepris la conversion de Clovis et l'établissement du Christianisme en France qui sera un fort bel ouvrage, son autheur ayant toutes les conditions requises pour le conduire à la perfection.[17]

In November 1637 Chapelain had been associated with Desmarets for some months in evaluating *Le Cid*, but his news may reflect discussion in the Académie-Française.

Composition during the Fronde

By the end of 1652, when Pellisson must have completed his *Histoire de l'Académie-Françoise*, nine of the twenty-six books of *Clovis* had been written.[18] Chapelain's letter implies that Desmarets had

around Clovis, the horses' hooves trample the rising water, Clovis heads for high ground, reaches a summit, and sees Auberon's enchanted palace . . . Among the 'clichés' of epic storm-narration, features like the 'vistes oyseaux' seem to reflect a genuine feeling for nature as well as the poetics, more bucolic than epic, of *Les Promenades de Richelieu*.

[16] Pellisson and d'Olivet, *Histoire de l'Académie-Françoise*, i. 89–90, quoted at greater length in Chapter 6.

[17] Chapelain, *Lettres*, i. 174. Desmarets confirms Pellisson's account in *Seconde Partie de la Response*, 86.

[18] Pellisson and d'Olivet, *Histoire de l'Académie-Françoise*, i. 283.

continued to work on the poem until November 1637; but he can have made little progress between 1636 and 1649. Between 4 June and 6 July 1652 he wrote to Roland Desmarets from Richelieu: 'pendant le siège de Paris, je faisois cent vers tous les jours, et j'achevay ainsi le Second Livre et fis le 3ᵉ entier'.[19] That must have been in the two months between 7 January 1649, when—the day after the royal Court fled to Saint-Germain-En-Laye—the Prince de Condé laid siege to Paris, and the treaty of Rueil, which ended the siege on 11 March. If Jean wrote the books more or less in the order in which they were first published, he probably added to Livre II during revision. His commentary in the same letter indicates, however, that the published Livre X must have been among the nine books completed by the end of 1652; and it seems likely that during composition some episodes may have been moved about within the poem. Desmarets did redistribute episodes in revision for the 1673 edition, introducing new episodes related to the deeds of Louis XIV between 1657 and 1672 and reducing the number of books from twenty-six to twenty, without noticeably reducing the overall length of the poem (11,052 lines).

Writing a hundred lines a day during the siege of Paris, Jean must have reported the completion of four books in two months to Roland, who replies: 'Quòd verò duobus mensibus qvatuor libros composueris'—progress perhaps too rapid, for in commenting on the five books he had been sent earlier, Roland recalls that Virgil is said to have spent eleven years on the *Aeneid*, 'qvam tamen inemendatam reliquit'.[20] In reply, Jean describes his methods of writing and revision, defending the 'romanesque' in heroic poetry on the example of Tasso and criticizing the length of Aeneas' narration in *Aeneid* ii and iii (more than 1,600 lines), contrasted with his own narration of the 'combat des jeunes prieurs' in *Clovis* X, 'bien fondée' in the writings of the sixth-century historian of France St Gregory of Tours and only requiring some 400 lines. For, he observes, 'il faut que nous ayons mille fois plus de circonspection que les anciens, lesquels nous avons pour modeles, mais en ce qu'ils ont de bon seulement'.[21] As for his facility in writing, he assures Roland that he always works 'avec un soin égal':

---

[19] Bibliothèque de l'Arsenal, Mss. 3135.

[20] *Rolandi Maresii Epistolarum philologicarum Libri II*, ii. 449.

[21] Bibliothèque de l'Arsenal, Mss. 3135. Later in the same letter he repeats: 'Il faut suivre les anciens en ce qu'ils ont fait de mieux, & ne pas s'attacher

Vous serez étonné des vers que j'abandonne, pour ceux que je fays en leur place. Mais je ne me contente point que je ne sois dans la plus belle expression, & ayant travaillé un jour entier à la composition j'employe tout le jour suivant à la correction, à remplir & à fortifier tout ce qui est de moins fort. J'ay fait les premiers Livres avec pareilles facilité & promptitude, y gardant le mesme ordre . . .

In a second letter from Richelieu dated 6 July 1652 Jean gives Roland this further reassurance, which I quote at length because it is unusual to find such a detailed firsthand account of the habits of composition of writers of the century of Louis XIV:

Il ne faut pas que ma grande facilité donne de mauvaises impressions. Il est impossible que je me retienne quand ma veine est eschauffée, & je ne passe pas un seul vers que je ne l'aye mis au point le plus fort que je puis. Si l'on voyoit mes grandes corrections, & comme le lendemain je fortifie, ou je change tout ce que j'ay fait le jour précédent, on verroit bien que je ne travaille pas à la légère. Ce qui est de plus fort, est ce que je fays le plus viste, pource que la matiere me porte; & ainsi si l'on condamnoit ma diligence, on condamneroit ce qu'il y a de plus beau. Je travaille par trois diverses fois, & mesme par quatre, sur chaque chose. La premiere fois quand je compose, le lendemain quand je m'employ à la correction; quand le livre est fait je l'escris tout entier, & je m'arreste encore sur chaque vers, pour le fortifier, ou le corriger. J'ajoute des comparaisons, & autres choses, aux lieux que l'on passe dans la composition; & j'ay rescrit, & par conséquent corrigé, tous les livres 2 [ou] trois fois; mais la grande facilité que j'ay, soit à la production, soit à la correction, fait que je ne laisse pas d'avancer beaucoup. Ce n'est pas encore que j'en veüille demeurer-là, ni précipiter l'édition, estant résolu de consulter sur chaque chose les plus savans que je pouray, & de laisser reposer l'ouvrage autant qu'il faudra. Il n'y a personne qui ayme tant que moy à recevoir les auis, & plus je corrige facilement, plus volontiers je les reçois . . .[22]

Livre VIII, he continues is 'le plus beau, le plus fort, & le plus plein' of the books completed:

& de ce qu'il y a de plus beau dans ce livre-là, j'en ay fait en un seul jour 134. vers. Il est certain que les plus beaux vers sont faits par la Nature mesme, par la grace & par le grand vol que l'on a pris. Je vous remarquerois des tirades de plusieurs vers en plusieurs endroits, que j'ay faits sans aucune peine, & comme par Inspiration, & il n'y a rien de plus beau en tout l'ouvrage . . .[23]

servilement à toutes choses. On est bien plus délicat que l'on n'estoit mesme du temps d'Auguste'.

[22] Ibid. 35–6.   [23] Ibid. 36.

Livre VIII is thoroughly 'romanesque'. In the midst of a passionate affair with Albione (who through black magic has taken the form of his Christian wife Clotilde) Clovis is challenged to a joust by the jealous Yolond, whom he fails to recognize, defeats, and spares. His councillor Aurèle (already Christian) is distressed that the false Clotilde seems to be turning Clovis away from Christianity. On the advice of St Marcel, Aurèle seeks guidance from St Genevieve, who discloses Albione's imposture and Clotilde's location in Vienne (Isère). St Genevieve also predicts illustrious descendants, not only for Clovis and Clotilde but for Aurèle himself, ancestor of the Richelieu family. He is sent to the forest of St-Germain-en-Laye to receive a gift for Clovis from a hermit . . .

By 1649 when Desmarets resumed work on *Clovis*, he was almost certainly aware not only of the *Aeneid* as a model of the genre but of other ancient epics and other poems mentioned in correspondence with Roland in 1652 and elsewhere: Tasso's *Gerusalemme liberata*, other Renaissance Italian epics, and the *Lusiads* by the Portuguese poet Luiz de Camoëns (1524–80)—perhaps the most strikingly modern epic of the Renaissance in terms of the contrasts it makes between the extent of Portuguese explorations and the far more circumscribed navigations of the ancients.[24] Contrary to the assumption that it remained unknown in Paris until publication of the first edition of Moréri's *Dictionnaire* (1674), in a letter to Félibien dated 17 July 1648 Conrart mentions the *Lusiads* 'dont on parle comme d'un chef d'œuvre'.[25] Scarcely anyone in Conrart's circle on the eve of the Fronde can have been more interested in the work, its themes, and its confidence than Desmarets.

Desmarets renews a legend central to Ronsard's *Franciade*, which opens with the legendary *reditus regni Francorum ad stirpem Gallicam* through which the French monarchy is traced to Francion

[24] However, the modern position, anticipated in some respects by Du Bellay's *La Deffense et illustration de la langue françoyse* (1549), is also explicit in the third of Tasso's *Discorsi del poema eroico*: 'Credono molti . . . che de le scienze e de l'arti più nobili sia avvenuto come de' popoli, e de le provincie, e delle terre, e de' mari, molti de' quali non erano ben conosciuti da gli antichi, ma di nuovo son ritrovati oltre le Colonne d'Ercole verso Occidente . . . e rassimigliano costoro gli ammaestramenti de l'arte poetica e de la rettorica a le mete ed a' segni i quali son posti per termini a' timidi naviganti.' The currency of modern attitudes among poets associated with Court ballet in the 1620s is noted in Chapter 3.

[25] V. Conrart, quoted in Kerviler and Barthélemy, *Valentin Conrart*, 471. In his reference to Moréri, B. Coutinho, 'Camoens en France au XVIIᵉ siècle', *Revue de littérature comparée*, 18 (1938), 175, appears to have overlooked this evidence.

or Francus, alias Astyanax, son of the Trojan worthy Hector and
of Andromache: *translatio imperii.*[26] He must also have known
Jean Heudon's *Conversion du Roy Clovis*, dedicated to Jean Davy,
Sieur Du Perron et de La Guette, Archbishop of Sens and Conseiller
au Conseil privé du Roi, and posthumously to Cardinal Jacques Davy
Du Perron (1556–1618). That earlier *Clovis*, with its fierce attack
on the pagan marvellous, appeared with an 'Approbation' of the
Theology Faculty of Paris (1619):

> Arriere maintenant les fureurs Castalides
> Du profane Apollon, & des Sœurs Pierides:
> Arriere maintenant ces termes vicieux
> De fortune, de sort, de destins, & de Dieux.[27]

After release from prison, at some time in 1650–1, for his part in
the clandestine marriage of the Duc de Richelieu and for unpaid debts,
Desmarets continued to work on *Clovis* in Saintonge, doubtless in the
household of the Duc de Richelieu, who escaped at that time from
house arrest in Sainte-Mesme and sought refuge in Brouage (Charente-
Maritime). In his letter on *Clovis* Roland refers to Jean's comment that
much of the nine books completed by the summer of 1652 had been
written under siege in Paris and, presumably, Brouage 'opido tuto':

cujus magnam partem inter arma composuisse dicêris: nempe Lutetiae cùm
obsideretur, & in Santonici littoris opido tuto qvidem, se tamen hostilibus
copiis undique cincto.[28]

Combat in the third phase of the Fronde, between the Prince de
Condé's troops and royalist forces, took place near Brouage in the

---

[26] In his *Lettre . . . à M.* [*Pierre*] *de La Chambre* (1673), Desmarets objects to
Marolles's comparison of this legend to the ' "Livres de chevalerie qui furent condamnez
au feu par ceux qui voulurent guerir la cervelle blessée du Chevalier de la Manche"
. . . particulierement sur le sujet de mon second Livre où il n'y a que l'origine des
François, que nos Historiens-mesmes disent estre venus de Troye', 4 (Freudmann edn.,
750). The legend, usually traced to the fourth-century pseudo-chronicles of Dictys
of Crete and Dares the Phrygian revived in the twelfth-century *Roman de Troie* by
Benoît de Saint-Maure, is generally supposed to have been discarded by historians
before the mid-seventeenth century. It survived in the theatre: in Racine's *Andromaque*
and in a spectacular lost machine-play for the Hôtel de Bourgogne in the autumn
of 1656—*Le Grand Astyanax ou le Héros de la France*—detailed documents concerning
the spectacular allegorical staging of which are published by Jurgens and Maxfield-
Miller in *Cent ans de recherches*, 401–3.

[27] J. Heudon, *La Conversion du Roy Clovis. 6ᵉ Liure des aduentures de la France*
(1619), 12.

[28] R. Desmarets, *Epistolarum philologicarum Libri II*, ii. 449.

autumn of 1651, despite the proclamation on 7 September of
Louis XIV's majority. The siege of Cognac (Charente) was lifted on
18 November 1651 by forces loyal to Mazarin and commanded by
the Comte d'Harcourt.[29] After taking Saintes (between Brouage and
Cognac), frondeurs under Henri, Seigneur de La Trémoille, third
Duc de Thouars (1598–1674), had joined troops brought up from
Bordeaux by François VI, Duc de La Rochefoucauld. A flood swept
away the bridge of boats over the Charente by which the two
frondeur armies were linked. Harcourt's army was therefore able
to attack and destroy La Trémoille's army on the right bank, lift
the siege, and successfully race Condé (who had arrived from
Bordeaux to lead the attack on Cognac, but could only watch
helplessly from the left bank while the siege was lifted) to La Rochelle,
occupied for Mazarin just over a week later.

In *Clovis* XXV three bridges over the Charente allude to the family
of the Duchesse de Richelieu's first husband, François-Alexandre
d'Albret, Sire de Pons, etc.:

> Puis vient le brave Pons, qui d'vn bras sans repos
> Sur trois ponts de Charente arresta tous les Goths,
> Renviant pour sa gloire, & celle de sa race,
> L'exploit si renommé du valeureux Horace . . .
> Il porte le beau nom de ce fait memorable,
> Pour en rendre à jamais le souvenir durable:
> Et pour vn fier vainqueur, encore que vaincu,
> Il ose de trois ponts enrichir son écu.

A typical shoulder-note confirms that 'Ceux de la maison de Pons,
portent trois ponts en leurs armes.' This parallel, the substitution
of French legend for the Roman heroism of Horatius Cocles, and
the metamorphosis not of the site but of the warrior's arms is a
translatio studii. It is also an idealization of the actual fighting at
Pons, a fortified town near Cognac captured for Condé by Henri-
Charles de La Trémoille, Prince de Tarente (1621–72). In Condé's
absence the Chevalier d'Albret de Miossans led a revolt and executed
Condé's garrison despite a safe conduct. When the Prince de Tarente
retook Pons on 21 March 1652, 'on passa au fil de l'espée une grande
partie de ceux qui se trouvèrent sous les armes'—except d'Albret,
who was imprisoned in the château de Pons.[30] Beyond *translatio*

[29] P.-G. Lorris, *La Fronde* (1961), 272.

[30] J. Pellisson, *La Fronde à Cognac 1650–57* (Pons, 1884), 36–7, after a pamphlet,

studii, this heroic allusion—and there are many like it in the poem—is almost certainly intended not only to celebrate the royal and noble connections of the Duchesse de Richelieu's first husband but also to disguise, idealize, or efface the squalor of such recent events. The Freudmann edition is helpful on allusions through which legendary French national events, often selected as parallels to events in the legends and epics of antiquity, are narrated to provide an idealized allegory in which the politics and personalities of the century of Louis XIV are often evident.

Predictions

After suggesting in the 'Au Roy' how Louis XIV may '*acquérir le nom de* **Louïs le Grand**', Desmarets predicts that he will indeed acquire 'ce beau titre', explaining that 'les Poëtes prophetisent quelquefois'. In *Clovis* IX St Daniel Stylite elaborates:

> Ce Roy donne à l'Europe & ses loix & la paix.
> Puis seul & digne Chef des Chrestiennes armées,
> Va délivrer du joug les terres Idumées.
> Voy qu'au port de Marseille il a l'œil menaçant,
> Allant trancher l'orgueil des cornes du Croissant.
> Voy qu'il couvre de nefs l'Egée & le Bosphore:
> Que de Bysance il vole aux beaux champs de l'Aurore.

In short Louis XIV

> Ne void nulle grandeur que sa valeur n'abbate;
> Et triomphe des bords du Tigre & de l'Euphrate.

This prophecy devised by the Secrétaire général de la Marine de Levant supposes that Louis XIV may re-enact the exploits of Saint Louis and of Alexander the Great—an ambition worth recalling in the context of Le Brun's *Batailles d'Alexandre* and of Racine's dedication of *Alexandre le Grand* to Louis XIV.[31]

La Prise de la ville de Pons par les troupes de M. le Prince de Condé, sous la conduitte du Prince de Tarante (Bordeaux, 1652).

[31] The Alexander paintings, tapestries, and engravings are anticipated by the imaginary Alexander decorations in *Les Délices de l'esprit* and, as 'peinture ordonnée à des desseins politiques', by the Galerie des Hommes illustres in the Palais-Cardinal: 'A cet égard', observes Dorival, 'comme à tant d'autres, Richelieu avait donné l'exemple au Roi-Soleil'. *Bulletin de la Société de l'histoire de l'art fran*çais (1973), 43–67.

As time passed, Desmarets clearly felt the need to incorporate into the text of *Clovis* new predictions related to the King's actual deeds in the years 1657–72; and in the 'Au Roy' of the 1673 edition, he commends predictions as a link between a poetically distanced subject and its current significance:

> Il faut . . . que le sujet du Poëme soit antique, pour donner lieu par l'éloignement du temps aux fictions necessaires à la poësie, & pour faire annoncer dés ce temps-là, par des predictions vray-semblables, le Prince à qui l'on consacre l'ouvrage, & ses grandes actions de guerre & de paix: car il n'y a rien de si ingenieux, de si agreable, ni de si magnifique, que ces sortes de loüanges données par des personnes ou celestes, ou inspirées par le ciel.

Anchises' predictions in *Aeneid* vi, said to have charmed Augustus Caesar, are considered flawed by Desmarets because the pagan dead cannot foretell the future.

The prophecies in *Clovis* are based instead on the tradition of Old and New Testament prophecies, many of which have been fulfilled. Their verisimilitude is grounded for the poet in the belief that millenarian and apocalyptic biblical prophecies for a universal kingdom of latter-day saints are about to be fulfilled in the century of Louis XIV. Citing in the rededication of *Clovis* various prophecies

> qui ont annoncé les quatre grands Empires du monde distinctement; & que des Rois devoient venir ensuite, qui feroient tantost la guerre, & tantost alliance, comme il s'est fait depuis mille ans entre la France, l'Espagne, l'Angleterre, l'Allemagne, l'Italie, & les autres Etats; après lesquels doit estre enfin l'Empire universel des Fideles, qui regneront auec Jesus Christ, de qui vn grand Prince doit estre l'image precedente. Et ce Prince est representé dans Daniel par la pierre détachée de la montagne; dans Jeremie, par le Fils du Juste, qui seroit le vrai Roi & le Sage; & dans Saint Jean par ce Fils aisné de l'Eglise, si desiré d'elle, si long-temps attendu, & enfin obtenu . . . qui . . . doit réünir les Chrestiens, & rétablir la Religion en plusieurs lieux, d'où elle avoit esté bannie.[32]

---

[32] The 'Empire universel des Fideles' would appear to refer to such prophecies as Dan 7: 18—'But the saints of the most High shall take the kingdom, and possess the kingdom for ever'; 'la pierre détachée de la montagne' refers to Daniel's interpretation of Nebuchadnezzar's dream 2: 44–5—'And in the days of these kings shall the God of heaven set up a kingdom, which shall never be destroyed . . . Forasmuch as thou sawest that the stone was cut out of the mountain without hands, and that it brake in pieces the iron, the brass, the clay, the silver, and the gold; the great God hath made it known to the king what shall come to pass hereafter; and the dream is certain, and the interpretation thereof sure'; etc.

For Desmarets, that 'Roi si merveilleux' is Louis XIV, 'le fils de Louis le Juste . . . long-temps desiré, attendu, & enfin obtenu par les prieres de l'Eglise', chosen by God 'pour la felicité de tout le monde'. It is a prophecy which suggests both continued respect for Louis XIII, albeit as the father of his son, and an early end to history. Two years later, the following lines of Desmarets's 'Epistre à Monsieur Perrault', which may seem to open on to an indefinite future superior to any cyclic summit in the past would appear to be based instead on the assumption that the world would not last much longer:

> Un peuple a pour un temps & l'empire & les mots.
> Rome & sa langue enfin tomberent sous les Gots.
> Mais nostre langue regne, & doit estre immortelle.
> Nos Rois sont protecteurs de l'Eglise éternelle.
>   Cet estat & nos vers
> Dureront avec elle autant que l'Univers.[33]

Eighteen years earlier, in the first edition of *Clovis*, there are of course already prophecies, 'Qui d'vn glorieux siecle étalloient les mysteres'. Independently of any literary considerations, the implications of some of these prophecies are of historical interest. Borne in Livre IV to the Temple de la Vérité by the Virgin Mary, Clotilde

>   voit qu'vn Roy juste, vn treiziesme Louis,
> Doit en ses jours heureux, d'vn cœur infatigable,
> Esteindre en ses Etats vne secte indomptable,
> Dissiper la fureur des esprits factieux,
> Punir de tous costez les rois ambitieux,
> Et voir par sa valeur ses Provinces bornées
> Des Alpes, des deux mers, du Rhein, des Pyrenées . . .

It is a striking tribute and an early expression of French national aspiration to unity within natural frontiers. Clotilde is also shown

> Qu'vn sage & noble Armand, grand de cœur, de conseil,
> D'un esprit plus actif que le cours du Soleil,
> Intrepide vainqueur de cent ligues naissantes,
> Tousjours poussant le cours des armes triomphantes,
> Et fidele, & fecond en projets genereux,
> Prendroit part aux lauriers d'un Roy si valeureux.

---

[33] 'Epistre à Monsieur Perrault', in *La Defense de la Poësie* (1675), 26.

> Que d'vne sainte ardeur il auroit l'ame éprise,
> Pour seruir & son Prince, & la France & l'Eglise:
> Et qu'il sçauroit ranger sous sa fatale main,
> Le Rebelle, l'Erreur, l'Ibere & le Germain.
> Qu'avec vn tel éclat, sur terre & sur Neptune,
> Nul ne feroit briller la Françoise fortune;
> Et qu'il seroit enfin, dans les siecles suivans,
> Le regret eternel des bons & des Sçauans.

There is a remarkable continuity in Desmarets's tributes to Cardinal Richelieu, from the 'Discours de la poësie' of 1633, through the *Tombeau du Grand Cardinal Duc de Richelieu* to these lines of *Clovis*. Indeed, in the exordium of the poem Richelieu's spirit is invoked immediately after God and Louis XIV, for whom the pagan Muses are discarded. Compare the 'revelation' in *Clovis* of the 'future' policies of Louis XIII and Richelieu with these famous lines in the latter's *Testament politique*:

Je lui promis [à V. M.] d'employer toute mon industrie et toute l'autorité qu'il lui plaisait me donner pour ruiner le parti huguenot, rabaisser l'orgueil des Grands, réduire tous ses sujets en leur devoir et relever son nom dans les nations étrangeres au point où il devait être.[34]

These lines sum up what Desmarets admired in Richelieu's policies, recommended 'Au Roy' in *Clovis* with altered emphases which reflect socio-political changes in the intervening decades—especially the defeat of the Princes in the third Fronde, Desmarets's conviction that force of arms was no longer necessary for the conversion of the Huguenots,[35] and perceived increase in *libertinage*:

Ce sera, Sire, en suivant ces grands exemples de vertu heroïque [Clovis, Louis XIII, Saint Louis, etc.], que vous dompterez tous les vices de vostre Royaume: parce que les peuples se forment toûjours sur le modele de leur Prince . . . Ainsi l'exemple de vostre vie destruira les dangereuses pestes de vostre Estat, l'Impieté & l'Heresie, qui corrompent & divisent vos sujets, & qui empeschent vostre Majesté de porter ses armes contre les Infideles, d'exercer sa glorieuse charge de Deffenseur & de Vengeur de la Foy, & de remporter sur les Ennemis de Dieu des victoires dignes de la valeur de vostre

---

[34] Richelieu, quoted in V.-L. Tapié, *La France de Louis XIII et de Richelieu* (1967), 172. Tapié denounces a 'tradition pédagogique funeste' in oversimplified interpretation of these lines, written probably in 1638.

[35] 'Mais il n'est plus besoin ny de valeur ny de force, pour ramener au sein de l'Eglise ceux que l'Heresie a corrompus. Il ne faut plus d'armées . . . Il ne faut qu'vne vie exemplaire.'

Majesté, du titre qu'elle porte de Tres-chrestien, & de Fils aisné de l'Eglise, & qui par consequent doit estre le Chef des armées Chrestiennes, & les commander par tout où son Dieu & la Foy l'appellent. C'est là qu'vn si sage & vaillant Prince, apres avoir donné la paix à son Estat, fera voir son zele & son courage: & c'est là qu'il doit acquerir le nom de Louïs le Grand.

The inclusion of Louis XIII among the exemplary kings proposed to the young Louis XIV may surprise some readers, but only because historians usually ignore or marginalize the evidence of Desmarets's engraved sonnet on Louis XIII publicly displayed in the Place-Royale, his *Cartes des Rois de France*, and *Clovis*. On the death and succession of Louis XIII Hubert Méthivier writes:

Dernier roi pleuré de ses sujets, mais conspiration du silence après sa mort: sa veuve ne parlera jamais de leur père à ses fils, auxquels on donnera en exemple le grand-père 'Henri le Grand', ainsi dans son édifiante biographie le précepteur Hardouin de Péréfixe.[36]

I wonder. Contrast the lines above from *Clovis* IV and the following double parallel from the 1657 epistle 'Au Roy':

Non seulement vous avez succedé au grand Clovis, qui receût tant de dons du Ciel pour tous les Rois qui le devoient suivre, & qui dompta les ennemis de Iesus-Christ: mais encore vous auez esté donné de Dieu à l'Eglise & à la France, avec toutes sortes d'avantages de l'esprit & du corps, pour accomplir tout ce que l'on peut attendre de vostre miraculeuse naissance. Vous avez le mesme foudre que le feu Roy vostre Pere, de glorieuse memoire, lança sur l'Heresie: vous avez la mesme pureté de mœurs, qui attire les benedictions du Ciel; & la mesme grandeur de courage, qui brille dans tous vos exercices . . .

If Louis XIII did fall victim to a conspiracy of silence, the conspirators did not include Desmarets. Either he was courageously independent or else he published his conspicuous eulogies of Louis XIII with the consent of the Court. The political dimensions of the poet's encomium are explicit: the adolescent King is not simply praised but called upon to behave and formulate policies in keeping with ideal norms: 'Mais, Sire, plus les dons de Dieu sont grands, plus ils obligent à de devoirs, à de fidelitez, & à de reconnoissances.' Those norms include the policies and deportment of Louis XIII. The Louis le Grand envisaged by Desmarets is destined to fulfil millenarian prophecies.

---

[36] Méthivier, *Le Siècle de Louis XIII*, 49.

Completion and revision

In his poem *Au Roy, Sur Sa Conqueste de la Franche-Comté* (1668), Desmarets recalls:

> Tu n'auois pas quinze ans, lors qu'vn iour tu me dis,
> Hé bien, quand verrons-nous les grands faits de Clovis?
> Dans peu de mois, te dis-je, on les verra parrestre,
> Où parmy les Heros, ie parle de mon Maistre.
> Sur ton front s'épandit vne auguste rougeur.
> Tu repris, soupirant d'vn magnanime cœur,
> Ie n'ay rien fait encor qui marque du courage;
> Des mensonges flateurs feroient tort à l'Ouvrage.

Although the young King's age is expressed in terms of a figure associated with youthful heroism, this anecdote is datable to the summer of 1653, just before his fifteenth birthday.[37] By that time Desmarets must have returned from Richelieu to Paris; and his own published reminiscences imply that he continued work on *Clovis* while engaged on his major devotional poems, completing eight further books between the end of 1652 and his conversion some time in 1654.

During the Quarrel of the *Imaginaires* Desmarets states that before his 'separation des conversations du monde' he had completed *Les Promenades de Richelieu* and his translations of *L'Imitation de Jésus-Christ* and *Le Combat spirituel*,

desquels Dieu se servit pour m'émouvoir à changer de vie. Puis je quittay toute volontaire production d'esprit, & je demeuray quatre ou cinq ans ayant l'ame bien éloignée de penser de faire des livres.[38]

Clovis was at that time abandoned. In the 'Epistre aux Beaux Esprits' of *Les Délices de l'esprit*, Desmarets states that afterwards

---

[37] Compare these lines from Heudon's *La Conversion du Roy Clovis*:

> A peine auoit il lors les quinze ans accomplis
> Que le corps & l'esprit esgallement remplis
> De force & de sagesse esmeurent son courage (p. 13),

and the 'Au Roy' of *Clovis* (1673): 'Sire, comme vostre vie depuis l'âge de quinze ans est vne vie toute nouvelle, & qui a bien surpassé toutes nos esperances; ce Poëme paroistra aussi tout nouveau par les augmentations & par les changemens que j'y ai faits.' Desmarets and Louis XIII must have been about fourteen when Desmarets was first allowed to attend meetings of the Conseil.

[38] *Seconde Partie de la Response*, 76–7.

i'ay eu tant de mépris pour les vaines productions de l'esprit, que mesme j'auois sacrifié à Dieu dix-sept livres du Poëme de Clovis; quoy que ce fussent les plus chers enfants de mon esprit; & je luy auois promis de les brusler, si ses seruiteurs iugeoient que ce sacrifice luy deust estre agreable: parce que parmy plusieurs choses assez nobles & Chrestiennes qui y sont déduites, il y a aussi quantité de descriptions & de passions, qui portent plustost l'Imagination aux choses sensibles qu'aux spirituelles; & qui sont plustost pour le plaisir, que pour l'utilité.

Relegating the completed books of *Clovis* 'au rang des choses mortes', Desmarets continues, 'j'auois composé, auec le secours de Dieu, tout cét ouurage des Delices de l'Esprit'. However, while the new book was being examined by 'plusieurs pieuses & doctes personnes', the world which he had begun to reject approached him

par toutes sortes de machines, pour me faire achever le Poëme; tantost par des flatteries, & par la consideration de la gloire humaine; tantost par l'authorité de ceux qui ont du pouvoir sur moy, & par celle du Roy mesme.

Others tried to shame him with the suggestion that with devoutness he had 'perdu l'esprit' and become 'incapable de la Poësie Heroïque', so that

Enfin Dieu me fit connoistre, par la bouche de ceux qui luy sont les plus agreables, qu'il vouloit que i'achevasse le Poëme, & que j'en fisse present au Roy . . . pour honorer ma Patrie, & mon Prince: & pour la gloire de Dieu mesme; qui peut-estre a voulu faire voir aux esprits mondains, que ceux qui le veulent aimer, ne se donnent à luy par affoiblissement d'esprit. Aussi m'a-t-il assisté si sensiblement pour me faire finir ce grand ouurage de Poësie . . . que je n'ose dire en combien peu de temps i'ay achevé les neuf liures du Poëme qui restoient à faire, & repoly les autres.[39]

If we allow several months after Desmarets's conversion during which no work on *Clovis* was attempted and several more for illustrating and printing, the final spurt of composition and revision must have occurred in 1655–6.

Revision of *Clovis* for the 1673 edition is unlikely to have been undertaken before the text was reprinted, almost unchanged, for the

---

[39] In reply to Nicole's 'impertinente & malicieuse pensée' that *Clovis* was inspired by the Devil, Desmarets reaffirms that he completed the poem at the request of the King and of 'personnes de la plus grande pieté & doctrine', adding: 'Ie fis . . . les neuf derniers livres par obeïssance & par conseil, & d'une telle sorte, que les delicats du Monde ont jugé que j'y avois mis trop de devotion; & je supprimay plusieurs choses des premiers livres, qui y estoient exprimées en paroles un peu sensibles', ibid. 82–4.

second legitimate edition in 1665.[40] The new edition was probably prompted by French successes in the War of Devolution and once more appears to have been requested by the King himself. The poem *Au Roy, Sur Sa Conqueste de la Franche-Comté*, 'achevé d'imprimer' on 14 March 1668, ends with Desmarets's assurance that the heroic destiny predicted in *Clovis* has been fulfilled and that 'Le Ciel . . . [le] rendra vainqueur de l'un à l'autre Pole.' Additions in praise of Louis XIV must have been effected during the six years or so from 1667 to 1672 between the War of Devolution and early successes in the War with the Netherlands.

A few themes and lines

One may conclude that in *Clovis* Desmarets fails to reconcile various contradictions. In the 1673 'Au Roy', he explains that he wishes to depict his hero with 'toute la politesse, & tous les avantages que peut desirer la delicatesse du goust de nostre siècle'. However, the ferocity of a king capable of carrying out his own executions and of cutting his unborn bastard from the belly of a woman warrior whom he had just killed in battle without recognizing requires some special pleading from a poet who wishes to idealize his hero. When *Clovis* was published, European monarchs carried out executions through interposed persons, though some still retained the controversial authority to order summary executions. For example, only a few months after the publication of *Clovis* Christina of Sweden personally ordered that of her grand equerry, and the Marquis of Monaldeschi was executed (or murdered) at Fontainebleau on 10 November 1657. Even the most barbarous episodes of *Clovis* bear some imaginative relationship to such 'gothic' events of the century of Louis XIV; and Desmarets develops ingenious arguments to reconcile verisimilitude with the ideal and with the marvellous. He cannot entirely avoid the implication that the pen which admits having embellished the record of a monarch past may be assumed to have similarly enhanced the image of the reigning king, not only to propose an ideal of kingship but to cover up personal and political mistakes.

---

[40] *Clovis* was officially 'achevé d'imprimer pour la seconde fois' in 12mo on 29 Aug. 1665. Each of the twenty-six Livres is illustrated with a reduced copy from a single plate of the three-part original illustration, signed 'Le Doyen'—another engraver who escaped the notice of M. Grivel, *Le Commerce de l'estampe à Paris* (Geneva, 1986).

The themes of this book—Richelieu and the century of Louis XIV —have led me to emphasize aspects of *Clovis* which bring literary expression close to the methods and aims of propaganda and other forms of advertising. Numerous unresolved tensions exist in the poem between poetics and politics, between Desmarets's conflicting desires to ground his epic in history and also make his hero's actions exemplary, between the eroticism of his love-stories and the limits to the literary expression of sexuality imposed by his own conversion and by the stricter literary proprieties of the mid-seventeenth century, between the freedom with which he depicts his numerous female heroines and the restrictive social norms of his times, and between his unusually sensitive response to the natural world and his strong taste for the marvellous.

On the other hand, the tears of masculine sensibility met in Desmarets's tragicomedies also feature in *Clovis*, e.g. Aurèle's in Livre XI:

> Le sensible Guerrier, au triste souvenir,
> Laisse couler les pleurs qu'il ne peut retenir.

Such tears, reminiscent perhaps of Aeneas 'lacrimans' in *Aeneid* i, of magnanimous tears in Plutarch, and of Jesus weeping, anticipate the tears of magnanimity in tragedies by Racine, Otway, and their admirers. There are few tears in the tragedies of Corneille; and they are likely to be off-stage, feminine, and/or private, like those of Chimène in *Le Cid* III. IV: 'Je cherche le silence et la nuit pour pleurer.' According to Plutarch, when Pompey's severed head was delivered to Julius Caesar, Caesar 'se prit à pleurer'; but in *La Mort de Pompée* II. II, Corneille only permits Achorée to voice the opinion that César 'Ne pourra refuser des soupirs et des pleurs'.[41] Any account of fashions in sensibility should take note of *Clovis*.

---

[41] Plutarch, *Les Vies des hommes illustres*, transl. J. Amyot, ed. G. Walter, ii. 463. Other illustrious weepers in Plutarch include Pompey himself at the sight of the Roman dead following his last victory, when he 'se couvrit le visage et s'en alla pleurant' (ii. 417); M. F. Camillus, who at the sight of the sack of the city of the Veii 's'en prit à pleurer de pitié' (i. 289); Manlius Capitolinus accused of tyrannical ambition 'pleurant à chaudes larmes' (i. 323); Pericles 'pleurant à chaudes larmes' when defending Aspasia against charges of atheism (i. 370); Cornelius Lentulus on leaving the Consul Paullus I Lucius Aemilius to die at Cannae; and Alexander the Great, who spent a whole night and day after the death of Clitus 'à pleurer amèrement' (ii. 386). In the Gospels, moreover, Jesus wept (Luke 19: 41; John 2: 35).

In a preliminary 'Advis' Desmarets discusses the rhetoric of *Clovis*, which Maskell's study also treats in detail. Heroic similes and such tropes as inversion ('Des grands temples Romains les antiques images'), oxymoron, anacoluthon, and spun metaphors (e.g., 'voûte azurée' for 'blue sky') abound. Architectural descriptions are numerous: Auberon's enchanted palace and the depiction of Francion's new Troy (II), the Temple de la Vérité (IV), the prophesied aqueduct at Arcueil (VII) and gardens at Rueil (VIII), the cathedral at Rheims (XXIV), and so on. Silent readers of *Clovis* may miss the imitative harmony of verses like 'La scie aux dents d'acier, long suplice des arbres' (II).

In quiet moments narrator and characters are no less responsive to nature than the poet of *Les Promenades de Richelieu*: the melancholy Aurèle alone with his horse by the Seine near Suresne, for example: 'O! beau desert, dit-il, ô! bois delicieux' (VIII), or the vengeful Yoland guiding her horse through the Vosges after her defeat in battle (XXI):

> Elle monte à pas lents ces croupes si fecondes
> En chesnes verdoyans, en murmurantes ondes.

The ethos of the epic and a certain feeling for nature can even lead the poet to prettify without irony Viridomare's death in battle (XIX):

> Dans vn sommeil paisible il semble qu'il s'endort.
> Il conserve sa grace encore dans la mort:
> Comme vne belle fleur que la faux a tranchée,
> Qui languit & se meurt, sur les herbes couchée.

Nor is involvement with nature always passive. Riding to the beach for a swim in Livre V, Clodion glimpses the ship bringing his bride, rides into the sea to meet her, and is about to go under

> quand la belle Ildegonde,
> Dés ses plus tendres ans docte en l'art de nager,
> Dans les vagues s'élance, & le veut dégager.

As others dive or ride to help the couple, a sea monster suddenly appears, terrifying horses and men. Reminiscent of sea monsters in *Orlando furioso* and of the myth of Perseus and Andromeda—in Corneille's *Andromède*, for instance—this 'taureau marin' anticipates the monster associated with Hippolyte's death in Racine's *Phèdre* V. VI. The monster seems to symbolize irrational obstacles to ideal love. The Danish Ildegonde,

> dont la noble beauté,
> Les charmes du discours, l'agreable fierté,
> Et l'addresse, & la force en ses forests acquise

even anticipates the 'noble savage' topos—a free spirit on deck as her ship comes in,

> sa tresse au vent;
> Et sa juppe ondoyante, aux Zephirs s'émouvant.

As an image of woman, contrast her dive to the assistance of Clodion with the symbolic dependence of the naked and bound Andromeda in the myth—whether adapted to other names in *Orlando furioso* or dramatized in Corneille's *Andromède*—or with the passive role invented by Racine for Aricie in *Phèdre*, or with the heroine of a novel hugely successful at the end of the *ancien régime*, Bernadin de Saint-Pierre's *Paul et Virginie* (1787). In sight of the land where Paul is waiting, Virginie goes down with a sinking ship rather than let sailors see her underwear.

Finally, neglecting numerous features of this complex epic, it is strange that the critics have had so little to say in praise of verse like this apostrophe on the distress of Clotilde, abandoned in Livre I:

> Quelle voix rediroit, Princesse infortunée,
> A quel excés d'ennuis tu fus abandonnée?

Among less distinguished lines, some, such as the 'nox erat' topos in Livre III, are nevertheless quite striking:

> Le silence & la nuit regnent aux environs.
> Le Ciel sembloit dormir, & tout ce qu'il enserre,
> Et les feüilles des bois, & les eaux, & la terre.

15

The Late Biblical and Heroic Poems

Between 1669 and 1671 Desmarets published two biblical poems—
Marie-Madeleine, ou le Triomphe de la Grace (1669) and *Esther*
(1670)—and a short historical 'poème héroïque', *Regulus, ou le vray
genereux* (1671). Two of these poems have been studied in the
context of the French epic in books by Richard Sayce and David
Maskell.[1] They reflect Desmarets's last literary preoccupations.
Although his defence of the Christian marvellous and of heroic poetry
in late polemical works relates largely to *Clovis*, it stems also from
these new poems and from the grand literary design of his last years.
In 1673 he republished *Esther* in a revised edition with changes to
Livre IV, three further books, and a preface announcing (1) 'la plus
grande & la plus hardie entreprise qui se fera jamais en Vers, qui
est de faire des Poëmes de tous les plus grands Sujets de l'Ancien
Testament', (2) completion of poems on the Creation, on Abel, on
Abraham, and on Joseph, and (3) the intention to write poems
on Moses, on David, and on Judith (a heroine of the Catholic
Old Testament). Of the four unpublished epics on Old Testament
subjects mentioned as completed in 1673, only one survives, printed
posthumously 'à la sphère': *Abraham, ou la Vie parfaite* (1678).

The plan to retell the great Old Testament stories in French verse
may have been suggested by Louis XIV, to whom the first edition
of *Esther* is dedicated. The suggestion may date from *c.*1667–8.
Neither revision of *Clovis* nor any other late work corresponds so
well to the 'grand ouvrage' mentioned as having been requested by
the King in Desmarets's 'Ode' to Colbert, probably written after
11 August 1667 but before 29 August 1668 (dates of examination
successes of Colbert's sons, to one of which the ode alludes):

> Pour avancer vn grand ouvrage
> Selon les desirs de Louïs,
> Je fais des efforts inouïs . . .[2]

---

[1] Sayce, *The French Biblical Epic*, and Maskell, *The Historical Epic*.
[2] Bibliothèque de l'Arsenal, Mss. 5418. For the full poem, see my article (superseded
on this point) in *Studi francesi*, 21 (1977), 40–9.

There is nothing implausible about such an invitation to the senior Academician from whom Louis XIV accepted more dedications between 1657 and 1674 than he did from any other writer. Desmarets was a cousin of and protected by the Première Dame d'honneur de la Reine and probably the only Conseiller with first-hand experience of meetings of the Conseil going back more than fifty years.[3] The derogatory polemics of Nicole's *Visionnaires* had not been accepted as literary history, least of all by Louis XIV; and Boileau's *Art Poétique* had not yet been published.

Marie-Madeleine, ou le Triomphe de la Grace

The longest and most curious of Desmarets's late narrative poems is *Marie-Madeleine, ou le Triomphe de la Grace*.[4] In the preface Desmarets argues that as a 'Femme illustre' Marie is a worthy heroine; but because the hero is Christ, he distinguishes this poem in ten stanzaic 'chants' from heroic poems proper:

> Voicy une sorte de Poëme dont il n'y a ny preceptes ny exemples dans l'Antiquité; & ceux qui voudront en juger sur les regles d'Aristote, ou sur les Poëmes d'Homere & de Virgile, se tromperont, ou voudront en tromper d'autres . . . Il y a bien de la difference entre un sujet heroïque, dont le principal personnage n'est qu'un homme d'une valeur & d'une force extraordinaires, & où le merveilleux & le surnaturel ne paroist qu'en des assistances ou en des contrarietez du Ciel & de l'Enfer, ce que l'on appelle des machines inventées par le Poëte; Et un sujet dont le principal personnage est un Homme-Dieu, & qui fait par luy-mesme les choses merveilleuses & surnaturelles, & si grandes, que le Poëte n'a qu'à les bien representer selon la vérité, avec de riches figures, pour attirer l'admiration; mais il ne doit pas y mesler des machines de son invention, qui ne pourroient jamais paroistre si admirables.

Pagan heroes, he continues, pale in comparison with a man-God who walks on water, commands the winds and the waves, drives out

---

[3] Desmarets's dedications to Louis XIV include *Clovis* with a new epistle for the revised version (1657–66 and 1673); the lost 'Avis du Saint-Esprit au Roi' (1662); the four separately dedicated parts of *Response à l'insolente Apologie des Religieuses de Port-Royal* (1666–8); poems on the first and second conquests of Franche-Comté (1668, 1674) and on the capture of Maastricht (1673); *Esther* (1670); and *Le Triomphe de Louis et de son siècle* (1674).

[4] *Marie-Madeleine* was published in 12mo by Denys Thierry with a *privilège* for ten years dated 11 Oct. 1669 and a frontispiece engraved by Pierre Landry (?–1701).

devils, resurrects and is resurrected from the dead, ascends into heaven through his own miraculous power. 'Jamais,' he remarks, 'Hercule ny Achille n'ont fait rien de semblable'. Nor in Desmarets's view was any of the monsters defeated by Hercules equal to the monster pride, vanquished by the humility of God's assumption of humanity.

Just as Christ is superior to pagan heroes, Christian subjects are superior to those drawn from pagan traditions: firstly because their authenticity is guaranteed by the blood of martyrs, secondly because Christian morals and sentiments are superior to those of pagans, and finally because Christian diction, grounded in the rhetorical figures of the Bible, is richer than that of pagans. The respect owed to Christ precludes the inclusion of 'aucune chose dont on puisse douter, ny dont l'invention puisse pretendre de passer pour merveilleuse'.[5]

Rhetoric emanates from the Holy Spirit, who, as the inventor of nature, from which rhetorical figures are drawn, is the master of the art, imitated by the Devil in disguise for the inspiration of pagan poets, whose works thus reflect only distant and dangerous images of the Bible's true light. Desmarets, however, still claims guidance from the rules of heroic poetry related to subject, *mœurs*, sentiments, and diction, discussed in some detail. Since biblical stories are true, he concludes, biblical subjects bear more relation to reality than pagan subjects, which no Christian can accept as verisimilar:

On peut seulement alleguer des choses qui peuvent estre historiques parmy les fables, comme Hercule qui a peu estre un homme fort, & comme Medée, qui a peu estre une Magicienne, parce que la Magie n'est pas une chose fabuleuse, & que nous croyons qu'il y a des Magiciens qui ont eu pact avec les Demons, comme il y en a encore.

Desmarets's viewpoint is controversial but entirely coherent in terms of legal realities of his time. Around 1670 there was a resurgence of witch-hunting, particularly in provincial France, with numerous denunciations, trials, and sentences to death. In 1672, following various appeals to the Conseil against judgements by the Parlement of Rouen, Colbert finally excluded accusations of witchcraft from

---

[5] On the fifth day of *Les Délices de l'esprit* Philédon comments: 'Pour moi, tout m'est également fabuleux, & ce que l'on dit des dieux des païens, & ce que l'on dit de Iesus-Christ', to which Eusebe replies: 'Toutefois, nul Poëte n'a souffert le martyre pour soutenir la vérité de ses contes.'

the jurisdiction of the courts.[6] The nature of the marvellous was literally a burning question.

As a 'Femme illustre', Desmarets argues, Mary Magdalene (hereafter Marie, as a character in the poem) is a worthy heroine, invoked in Chant I after the Holy Spirit. He then describes pride, enumerates the deadly sins, recalls the record of pride in the Old Testament (Cain, the Tower of Babel, etc.), describes grace and relates it to such Old Testament stories as Noah and the Flood, Lot, the infant Moses, David and Goliath, Judith and Holophernes, and so on. In Chant II he invokes Christ, describes a great imaginary 'Fort de Magdal', Marie's beauty, her lovers, wealth, possession by demons, and distress at preference for Orcade by Abner, whom she loves (characterization after Alcina/Armida). In Chant III Marie is tempted by demons, including Asmodée, demon of gluttony:

> Cependant sept Demons en elle ont leur demeure;
>   Sans cesse allument sa fureur.
> Trois sont dans son esprit, & quatre dans son cœur.

She conspires with Herodiade to destroy Abner, organizes a great hunt in which it is intended Abner should be ambushed; but both Abner and Herod's son Agrippa are saved by Crispe and the Romans. Chant IV relates Marie's feigned regret for the conspiracy, demonic convulsions, the intervention of Christ summoned by Eucharie, and Marie's conversion. Consider this prayer *De profundis*:

> Sur l'abyme profond de ma grande misere,
>   Sur toutes mes iniquitez,
> De l'abyme infiny de tes grandes bontez
> Fay tomber, ô mon Dieu, le secours salutaire.
>   Lave les traces de Demons,
>   Comme un torrent tombant des monts;
> Verse sur moy les flots d'vn deluge propice.
>   Par douceur sur ce cœur pervers,
>   Fay ce que tu fis par justice
> Lorsque ton grand courroux lava tout l'Univers.

In Chant V Marie frees her estate staff to follow Jesus, finds her brother Lazare and sister Marthe, attempts with Eucharie to convert them, and has been told about Christ's miracles (the marriage at

---

[6] R. Mandrou, *Magistrats et sorciers en France au XVIIe siècle, une analyse de psychologie historique* (1968), 447, 449–58.

Cana, the miraculous loaves and fishes) when Christ appears, converts Lazare, walks on water. In Chant VI Jesus calms a storm, Marie anoints his feet. Chant VII is based on the story of Mary and Martha and the resurrection of Lazarus. In Chant VIII comes the report: 'A Delphes, dans Ephese, on n'entend plus d'oracles'; but demons conspire, and the powerful Demon de l'argent enters the body of Judas. The Crucifixion occurs in Chant IX:

> De l'horreur de sa mort toute la Terre tremble,
> Et demeure en obscurité . . .

Desmarets remarks in the preface:

La fin de ce Poëme est la plus noble & la plus utile qu'un Poëte se puisse proposer, qui est d'aider avec la Grace à la conversion des ames, particulierement des belles personnes, dont la conversion attireroit celle de tant d'autres.

Celles qui ont beaucoup de vanité verront icy dans la premiere vie de Marie Madeleine, l'image de ce qu'elles sont, & de ce qu'elles font; & dans la seconde, l'image de ce qu'elles doivent estre, & de ce qu'elles doivent faire.

As an edifying narrative poem, *Marie-Madeleine* fits easily into the *Corpus maresianum* not only with *Clovis* and *Esther* but with *Rosane* and *La Vérité des fables* (exemplary novels) and the devotional works. Desmarets was anticipated in his choice of subject, notably by Louis Le Laboureur's *La Magdelaine penitente* (1643), a poem in five 'livres' by a poet well aware of the tradition by which Mary Magdalene 'la premiere a planté la Croix dans la Provence'. The *privilège* for five years is dated 9 December 1642, just five days after Cardinal Richelieu's death. Referring to plays on Christian subjects encouraged in Richelieu's last years, Le Laboureur anticipates several of the arguments on the Christian marvellous later advanced by Desmarets. In an essay published with the poem, 'Sentimens de l'Autheur, sur la Poesie Chrestienne & Profane', for example, Le Laboureur suggests

c'est outrager sensiblement les Histoires sacrées que de les laisser pour courir après des desbauchées & des profanes; lesquelles avec toutes leurs licences ne contiennent point encor des auantures si diuerses & si merueilleuses.

Le Laboureur is anticipated in turn by the *Art poëtique* (1605) of Jean Vauquelin de la Fresnaye, an early seventeenth-century champion of the Pléiade poetics of the mid-sixteenth century. Vauquelin's ideal tragedy was 'païenne de forme, chrétienne de sujet et d'inspiration'. Long before the exordium of *Clovis* Desmarets may have been mindful of Vauquelin de la Fresnaye's injunction:

Pleust au ciel que tout bon, tout Chrestien et tout Saint
Le François ne prist plus de sujet qui fust faint.[7]

Esther

Desmarets is one of a dozen seventeenth-century French writers who derived a French literary work from the Old Testament book of Esther before the Moreau and Racine oratorio *Esther*, performed at Saint-Cyr in 1689. Sayce finds Desmarets's *Esther* interesting for its 'grotesque originality'.[8] Dedicated to Louis XIV, it was published pseudonymously in Paris in four 'chants', in quarto, by Pierre Le Petit, with a *privilège* for seven years dated 6 February 1670. Why Desmarets chose to publish *Esther* under the pseudonym 'de Boisval', which he had abandoned since the first edition of *Ariane* in 1632, is not clear. An allusion to *Ariane* for the novelistic technique by which he fuses historical, biblical, and fictional episodes in the embellishment of *Esther* cannot be ruled out; and the choice may be nostalgic for the early success of *Ariane*. His decision is unlikely not to be related to disappointment with the critical reception of *Clovis* and of *Marie-Madeleine*. However, the revised *Esther* (1673) appeared under Desmarets's own name, dedicated to the Duchesse de Richelieu.[9] There are two important differences between the texts of the two editions. The duodecimo extends the narrative from four to seven books; and Livre IV is sufficiently modified to allow for the continuation, in which the poet's creative urge seems to give way to moralist concerns.

Sayce is struck by 'the complete absence of even feigned modesty' in Desmarets's presentation of *Esther*. His immodesty may compensate for disappointments late in life but may be understood in relation

---

[7] Vauquelin de la Fresnaye, *Art poëtique* (iii. 33), quoted in H. Gillot, *La Querelle des Anciens et des Modernes* (1914), 427. Gillot also quotes from the same work these ironic lines (III. 845):

> Si les Grecs, comme vous, Chrestiens, eussent escrit,
> Ils eussent les hauts faits chanté de Jésus-Christ.

[8] Sayce, *The French Biblical Epic*, 1.

[9] Sayce suggests that the headband depicting Esther before Ahasuerus in the 4to edn. is based on Poussin's painting of that subject in the Hermitage, Leningrad; and he shows its general similarity to the unsigned engraving of the same subject—doubtless also by Chauveau—in the *Bible de Royaumont*, also published by Pierre Le Petit in 1670, ibid. 229–30 and Pl. iv.

to personal identification with his royal and religious subject. In a striking illustration of what mid-twentieth-century 'new criticism' labelled 'intentional fallacy', the literary work is valued in terms of authorial intention and of doctrine concerning the value of the subject. Perspectives have changed; but in 1670–3 Desmarets, like Chapelain, was a literary 'official', with strong political backing for his plans and works. The frequency with which humility is treated as a theme of Desmarets's devotional writings suggests that, quite apart from contradictions involved in celebrating the Incarnation itself as a worshipful event, he writes immodestly not so much for himself as for the idea of an imaginative royal and religious poetry in which the reader could actually believe. Sayce's detailed account of the action, calling attention to the syncretism by which Desmarets blends reminiscences of Plutarch and Xenophon with Josephus and the Old Testament, need not be repeated.[10]

Paying special attention to Desmarets's frequent, apparently arbitrary use of recitals, Sayce considers that Iasbel's story is 'introduced abruptly and without any real justification' while Pharsandate's narrative is 'involved and very difficult to follow' with 'no appreciable connexion with the fortunes of Esther'.[11] It seems to me less interesting, however, that these recitals are 'irregular' in terms of epic theory than that they are provocative and used in the same imaginative way as similar recitals in *Ariane*. Sayce notices that Pharsandate's narrative in Livre III, for example,

appears to be fictitious, not only in relation to absolute truth but in relation to the truth of the poem. Artemis, who tells it, is really Pharsandate and lies in order to impress Vashti [the rival queen to Esther]. So far the pattern is complex but not very surprising: parallels can be found in classical epic. Closer examination reveals, however, that all is not fictitious, that Aman's Macedonian origin is derived from the Bible, that the revolt of Cyrus is an historical fact; in brief that much of the recital was intended to recount the early history of Aman . . . It is thus impossible for the reader to decide where truth ends and fiction begins. The grafting of the story of Artemis on the main recital means that the narrator's personality is doubled and another element of confusion is added . . . The whole formal structure is changed: instead of a clearly defined path which winds backwards and forwards to a fixed object, we are suddenly confronted with a prospect receding into infinity.

---

[10] Sayce, *The French Biblical Epic*, 122–31.   [11] Ibid. 204.

This technique of narration, as Sayce observes, may be compared with the *trompe-l'œil* employed in baroque architecture; and he finds similarities between Desmarets's chronological manipulations as narrator and 'the tortured masses of baroque architecture'.[12] It is a matter of style, of aesthetic preferences; and he might have cited the *trompe-l'œil* decoration and perspectives of the Grand'Salle de spectacle of the Palais-Cardinal. More frequently perhaps than any of his contemporaries, Desmarets describes architectural features, such as Vashti's palace in *Esther* II, as opulent 'peintures parlantes'.

Abraham, ou la Vie parfaite

Perhaps the most curious thing about *Abraham, ou la Vie parfaite* (1678) is the confirmation it provides for Desmarets's grand plan announced in the preface to the 1673 *Esther*. The poet's declaration about completed books settles, as Sayce notes, any doubts about the attribution of this posthumous poem, published anonymously: 'Le troisiéme est Abraham, ou l'estat de la vie parfaite, par une vive foi de la presence de Dieu.'[13] For Sayce, 'it is merely a narrative framework for a series of moral and theological reflections and is of little importance from the point of view of epic'.[14] Similar in that respect to *Regulus*, it may also be compared with the last three books of *Esther*, which are more severe and less figured in poetic expression than the first four. The didacticism ever present in Desmarets's imaginative works has gained at the expense of poetic invention. Indeed, this short narrative poem resembles in more ways than one the moralist verse of the *Maximes chrestiennes* and other late devotional poems with which it was printed (?) at Richelieu.

Regulus ou le vray genereux

Desmarets's only 'poëme héroïque' from Roman history, *Regulus ou le vray genereux*, comprises three hundred and eighty-eight alexandrines in five 'chants' retelling the traditional story of the consul Marcus Atilius Regulus' successful invasion of Africa in 256 BC, his

---

[12] Ibid. 241–2. Sayce mentions 'the treatment of the pediment in baroque architecture, where the simple classical form, triangle or segment of a circle, is broken, inverted (two halves of a triangle back to back), or convoluted'.

[13] Ibid. 122.   [14] Ibid. 122–3.

subsequent capture by the Carthaginians, his return to Rome on parole, and his heroic decision to return to Carthage rather than betray Rome or break his word. Printed with the 'permission' of Gabriel Nicolas de La Reynie (1625–1709), who in 1667 became the first Lieutenant de police in Paris, *Regulus* was dedicated to the no less 'généreux' M. de Bartillat, 'Conseiller du Roy en tous ses Conseils, Garde du tresor Royal, & cy-devant Tresorier general de la feu Reyne Mere de sa Majesté'. David Maskell deals effectively both with the place of this poem in the trend towards brevity in the epic after 1658 and with the attribution to Desmarets, which the signature J. D. M. (used also for various poems and the 1664 reprint of the *Jeux de Cartes des Roys de France*) confirms.[15] As in so many of Desmarets's poems, the verse is uneven but is often pleasant to read aloud. Consider the abrupt transition from Chant I, which closes like an act of a play with this heroic couplet:

> Il assiége Cartage, & prépare ses fers,
> Et son nom éclattant fait trembler l'univers,

with the contrasting opening of Chant II:

> Qu'est-ce que la fortune? elle est une inconstante,
> Qui promet tout aux grands, & frustre leur attente;
> Qui renverse & qui change à son gré les humains . . .

For Maskell the brevity of *Regulus* makes it readable, while 'its intensity, its emphasis on dialogue are more appropriate to tragedy than epic'.

---

[15] Maskell, *The Historical Epic*, 110–12.

16

The Quarrel of the Imaginaires

In December 1665 Desmarets engaged the Jansenist apologist Pierre Nicole in a doctrinal controversy, which Nicole turned into a personal *ad hominem* attack on Desmarets: the Quarrel of the *Imaginaires*. After the Peace of the Church temporarily ended public disputes over doctrine and morals among French Catholics in 1668, doctrinal and personal differences resurfaced in other forms, notably in disputes over the Christian marvellous and the French national epic. Although these controversies may be separated for the purpose of study, interconnections are strong. Desmarets's earlier prosecutions of Charpy de Sainte-Croix and Simon Morin, his spiritual direction, Catholic organizational work, and writings—sacred and profane— became issues in the Quarrel of the *Imaginaires*, which soon involved public theatre as a whole and later led directly to the arrest of Isaac Le Maistre de Sacy and other fugitive Port-Royalists.

Attitudes and antagonisms evident in the Quarrel of the *Imaginaires* were carried forward into the literary quarrels of the 1670s from which the Quarrel of the ancients and moderns is said to have developed in 1687, although as early as 1671 the literary controversies in and around the Académie-Française are described in terms of metaphoric war by Gabriel Guéret in *La guerre des auteurs anciens et modernes*. Between 1665 and 1675 these phases of two continuing quarrels prompted a number of new works and poems by Desmarets, including the polemical anthology mentioned in Chapter 11 and the prefaces to *Clovis* and to other poems discussed in Chapters 14 and 15. *Le Triomphe de Louis et de son siècle*, three other late poems expressing the modern position, a letter addressed to the Abbé Pierre de la Chambre in answer to reservations on the French epic expressed by Michel de Marolles, Abbé de Villeloin, and a volume of dialogues critical of Boileau's *Œuvres diverses* belong to the quarrel of ancients and moderns and will be discussed in the Conclusion. This chapter deals with the circumstances and implications of the four book-length pamphlets against an apology for the recalcitrant nuns at Port-Royal between December 1665 and June 1668.

The Quarrel of the *Imaginaires* and the literary quarrels to which it led involve substantial issues: the politics and administration of France at the beginning of Louis XIV's personal reign, the nature and limits of royal and papal authority, the relation of a national literature to religious beliefs and to the State, that of verisimilitude and the imaginary to faith, the restructuring of institutions, revisionism, reversed alliances, and changing fashions in Catholic doctrine and in the historiography of the century of Louis XIV.

Pascal's Lettres provinciales

The doctrinal quarrels which prompted the publication in 1656–7 of Pascal's clandestine *Lettres provinciales* are generally better known than the somewhat later quarrels involving Desmarets directly. First with Socratic irony and later with indignation, Pascal's voice in the *Provinciales* mocks the doctrine of Jesuit theologians. He satirizes moral laxness and corrupt casuistry in such matters as the direction of intention, mental restrictions, and 'probabalism'—the uncritical acceptance of opinion from the most convenient 'authority'. Although sixteenth-century Spanish Jesuits are sometimes targeted in the letters, Pascal's French Jesuit contemporaries are not spared: for instance the remark about the 'manière si profane et si coquette dont votre Père Le Moyne a parlé de la piété dans sa *Dévotion aisée*' (1652) in the eleventh *Provinciale*. For readers who look beyond that reference, Le Moyne proves to be rather more than a moralist accused of laxism. Significantly, as author of such works as *Les Triomphes de Louis le Juste en la réduction des Rochelois et des autres rebelles de son royaume* (1629), *La Galerie des femmes fortes* (1647), and the epic *Saint Louys, ou le héros chrestien* (1653), Le Moyne typifies Court culture in the period of Louis XIII and Anne of Austria. Like Desmarets, he was very much involved with the magnification of the monarchy, in the production of literature offering positive images of woman, and in the poetics of the Christian marvellous associated with the national experience of France.

The Inquisition put the *Provinciales* on the Index on 6 September 1657, and in 1660 the letters were condemned by the French Conseil d'État to be shredded and burnt by the public executioner.

As a devout man with strong royalist sympathies, Desmarets was suspected in Jansenist circles of having written the *Response generale à l'autheur des Lettres qui se publient depuis quelque temps contre la Doctrine des Jesuites* (Lyons, 1656).[1] Indeed, there is evidence that he was at least receiving complaints about Jansenists around that time. Desmarets soon afterwards passed on to Henry-Marie Boudon, Archdeacon of Evreux and member of the *Aa* or inner council of the Compagnie du Saint-Sacrement, three anti-Jansenist letters from one of the penitent girls with whom he was in correspondence.[2] In any case, as Léon Brunschvicg observes, Pascal had Desmarets in mind when, closing the fifteenth *Provinciale*, dated 25 November 1656, he replies to the following 'Imposture', or alleged misrepresentation, contained in the *Response generale*:

'Que je suis aussi pensionnaire de Port-Royal: et que je faisois des Romans avant mes Lettres', moy qui n'en ay jamais leü aucun, et qui ne sçay pas seulement le nom de ceux qu'a faits vostre Apologiste.[3]

Clarification followed. Ten days later Pascal closes the sixteenth *Provinciale* with a postscript, addressed to the Jesuit Fathers:

Je viens d'apprendre que celuy que tout le monde faisoit Auteur de vos Apologies, les desavoüe, et se fâche qu'on les luy attribue. Il a raison, et j'ay eü tort de l'en avoir soupçonné. Car quelque assurance qu'on m'en eust donnée, je devois penser qu'il avoit trop de jugement pour croire vos impostures, et trop d'honneur pour les publier sans les croire . . . Je m'en repens, je la desavoüe, et je souhaite que vous profitiez de mon exemple.[4]

The testimonial is worthwhile.

---

[1] Leading Jansenists, critical of the Christian marvellous in the French epic, accepted the miraculous in support of their own beliefs and interests. The miracle of the Holy Thorn by which Pascal's niece Marguerite Périer is said to have been cured of an eye infection on 24 Mar. 1656 was followed by a suspicious number of further 'miracles' among Port-Royal *pensionnaires*. Another famous Jansenist miracle was the recovery on 6 Jan. 1662 of Catherine de Champaigne, niece of Philippe de Champaigne (1602–74), the subject of one of the artist's paintings in the Louvre.

[2] A. Auguste, *Les Sociétés secrètes catholiques du XVIIᵉ siècle et H.-M. Boudon* (1913), 17, mentions finding in Boudon's correspondence 'trois lettres d'une sainte fille à son Père spirituel' dated 30 June, 21 July, and 20 Aug. 1657, unsigned, but in Desmarets's handwriting. 'Il avait dû les copier pour les envoyer,' states Auguste, adding: 'Elles sont anti-jansénistes, d'un mysticisme qui m'a paru tout à fait orthodoxe et fort curieux, en cela surtout qu'il y est souvent question de confidences, on dirait presque de révélations . . . du Cœur de Jésus', quoted by Bremond, *Histoire littéraire*, vi. 482–3.

[3] B. Pascal, *Œuvres*, vi, ed. L. Brunschvicg (1914), 209–10.

[4] Ibid. 293.

The formulary

Or so thought Jean Racine. For when, almost a decade later, Desmarets intervened in the Jansenist controversy, Nicole attacked Desmarets in the first of the *Lettres visionnaires*, or eleventh *Imaginaire*, declaring that Desmarets's 'première profession' had been 'de faire des romans et des pièces de théâtre' and that 'un faiseur de romans et un poète de théâtre est un empoisonneur public, non des corps, mais des âmes des fidèles', Racine himself took umbrage, as well a young playwright might, and reminded Nicole of Pascal's praise.[5]

Racine's intervention plunges us *in medias res*. Whether or not prompted by the new Archbishop of Paris, Hardouin de Péréfixe, Racine must have known that Louis XIV chose to affirm his personal authority soon after Cardinal Mazarin's death through a decree of the Conseil d'État, promulgated on 23 April 1661, and a 'lettre de cachet' requiring even the *pensionnaires* and postulants of religious houses to sign a formulary condemning as heretical five propositions on the grace of God said to be contained in the *Augustinus* (Louvain, 1640) of Cornelius Jansenius; the decree also stated that unreserved acceptance of the formulary was demanded by Pope Alexander VII. At Port-Royal these propositions were disputed both as to fact (Are the propositions actually stated or implicit in the *Augustinus*?) and in law (On what authority are the alleged propositions condemned?), raising basic questions about the nature of authority, both ecclesiastical and political. Inherited from a period in which Anne of Austria and Mazarin still governed in Louis XIV's name, this issue is perhaps the first to manifest the totalitarian tendencies of a monarch who was sometimes more than simply authoritarian.

[5] See J. Racine, *Lettre à l'auteur des 'Hérésies imaginaires' et des deux 'Visionnaires'* and *Lettre aux deux apologistes de l'auteur des 'Hérésies imaginaires'*, in his *Œuvres complètes*, ed. R. Picard, ii. 18–31. Picard's presentation of the two letters which Racine published on this occasion is grossly misleading, not only on the serious general issues of the relation of theatre to Church and Crown but on the most ordinary matters of bibliographical fact easily verified. For instance, Port-Royal is not attacked in the comedy *Les Visionnaires*; and *Aspasie* is not a novel, as asserted on pp. 13, 1000; nor had Desmarets been mentioned in Nicole's ten *Lettres sur l'hérésie imaginaire* (1664–5) inspired by the *Provinciales*, as asserted by Picard in *Carrière de Racine* (1956), 119. How, one wonders, did Picard interpret Racine's comment in the first letter to Nicole: 'Vous, Monsieur, qui entrez *maintenant* en lice contre Desmarets' (p. 24, my italics)? Desmarets and the young Racine deserve more sympathetic historiography.

According to Louis Cognet, Louis XIV himself further politicized the doctrinal quarrel:

Très hostile aux jansénistes, dont le loyalisme monarchique lui semblait au moins douteux et en qui parfois il n'était pas loin de voir des républicains, hanté par le souvenir de la guerre civile, il craignait qu'il n'y eût là les germes d'une nouvelle Fronde.[6]

Louis XIV can scarcely have been reassured in this respect by the Jansenist sympathies of such eminent former frondeurs as the Duc de La Rochefoucauld, the Duchesse de Longueville, and especially Cardinal de Retz.[7]

The *Mémoires de Louis XIV écrits par lui-même, composés pour le Grand Dauphin, son fils*, published in two volumes in 1806 by J. L. M. de Gain-Montagnac, assert that in 1661 disorder reigned everywhere, that schism was threatened not only by theologians in hiding but by influential bishops in their sees, that Cardinal de Retz (Archbishop of Paris at the beginning of his personal reign) was inclined to Jansenism and found support in it—later adding that he dedicated himself to destroying Jansenism and to breaking up the communities where 'this spirit of novelty was developing, well-intentioned perhaps, but which seemed to want to ignore the dangerous consequences that it could have'.[8] Academician, Conseiller, and Secrétaire du Roi, Desmarets was particularly sympathetic to this aspect of royal policy.

The Apologie des religieuses de Port-Royal

Since well before the *Provinciales* Nicole, Antoine Arnauld, and Le Maistre de Sacy had been engaged in public polemics over the five

---

[6] L. Cognet, *Le Jansénisme* (1960), 76. At that time, moreover, the monarchy in England was only recently restored; and memories of the beheading of King Charles I, Louis XIV's uncle by marriage, were still strong.

[7] Jansenists were not the only devout enemies of Court culture suspect to the Crown for similar reasons. One of Nicole's allies in attacks on theatre in the 1660s, the Prince de Conti, sometime patron of Molière's company and author of the hostile *Traité de la comédie et des spectacles* (1666), not only had been a *frondeur* but was governor of Languedoc, a province associated with sedition since before the siege of Montpellier in 1622. As cousins of the King, however, Conti and Mme de Longueville are thought to have been able to offer some protection to Jansenists.

[8] Louise XIV, *Mémoires de Louis XIV, écrits par lui-même, composés pour Le Grand Dauphin, son fils*, quoted in English in A. Sedgwick, *Jansenism in Seventeenth-century France: Voices from the Wilderness* (Charlottesville, 1977), 107.

propositions and the formulary propagated to condemn them, when in 1665, with Arnauld and Claude de Sainte-Marthe (1620–98), Nicole published an *Apologie des religieuses de Port-Royal du Saint-Sacrement, contre les injustices et les violences du procédé dont on a usé envers ce monastère.*[9] Some of the nuns had signed the formulary, and steps had been taken to coerce the others. Some of the nuns who had signed then retracted. Others still refused to sign, even after a visit to Port-Royal de Paris by the new Archbishop, who interviewed recalcitrant nuns individually before dispersing them to other convents, withdrawing the sacraments of the Church, and later returning the nuns—still without the sacraments—to Port-Royal des Champs. The ordeal of the nuns is relatively well known: it will suffice simply to quote the account by Charles A. Sainte-Beuve's in his *Port-Royal* (1840–59) and Henri de Montherlant's historical drama *Port-Royal* (1954). The latter has as its basis an irreconcilable conflict of conscience with authority similar to that which underlies Sophocles' *Antigone*, the subject of which Racine adapted for his first tragedy, *La Thébaïde*, performed by Molière's troupe in 1664.

It was to Nicole's *Apologie* for these nuns that Desmarets replied in a series of four *Responses* dedicated to Louis XIV. Desmarets's intervention is generally not well documented in secondary accounts of the ensuing quarrel.[10] Nor do Nicole's quarrels with Pascal and with Martin de Barcos, Abbé de Saint-Cyran, over the proper response to the formulary often figure in accounts of these troubles sympathetic to Jansenism.[11] The formulary did, however, open deep divisions among the partisans of Port-Royal. An anonymous contemporary Jansenist account of Nicole's quarrel with Barcos *c.*1658–9 records that Barcos and others were convinced that

---

[9] The *Apologie* is in four parts and fits into 'toute une série de Défenses, Déclarations, Requêtes, rédigées pour la plupart par Claude de Sainte-Marthe, de 1664 à 1667', as noted by Bourgeois and André, *Les Sources de l'histoire de France.* iv. 318. With Arnauld, Nicole had in 1654 published their *Response au P. Annat, provincial des jésuites, touchant les cinq propositions attribuées à M. l'évêque d'Ipres* (Jansenius); and Le Maistre de Sacy, *Les Enluminures du fameux Almanach des PP. Iesuistes, intitulé, La Deroute et al confusion des Iansenistes ou Triomphe de Molina Iesuiste sur S. Augustin* (1654).

[10] A. Sedgwick, *Jansenism in Seventeenth-century France*, devotes a useful chapter to '*Droit et fait*, 1661–69', 107–38, without mentioning Desmarets. Nor is it clear that he grasps the extent to which the political situation in 1661 differs from the later contexts in which Jansenist memoirists revised their memoirs and Racine wrote his *Abrégé de l'histoire de Port-Royal.*

[11] B. Pascal, *Œuvres complètes*, ed. J. Mesnard, i (1964), 1006, 1037–47.

'M. Arnauld et M. Nicole s'étaient gâté l'esprit par la scolastique' and that Nicole 'demeura odieux à plusieurs personnes, et il ne s'en est jamais relevé à leur égard'.[12]

The Lettres visionnaires

Some months before the *Apologie* appeared, Nicole had already begun to publish a fresh appeal to public opinion in imitation of the *Provinciales*: the new series of open letters known as the *Imaginaires*, from the author's argument that the heresy of which Jansenists stood accused is imaginary. Ten of the letters had appeared in 1664–5 before Desmarets's *Response*; and another eight followed, until the eighth *Visionnaire* or eighteenth *Imaginaire* appeared on 1 May 1666, after which the controversy took other forms. Nicole did not wish his letters to be more numerous than the *Provinciales*.

Desmarets's Response

'Achevé d'imprimer' on 12 December 1665, Desmarets's *Response à l'insolente Apologie des religieuses de Port-Royal. Avec la découverte de la fausse Eglise des Iansenistes, et de leur fausse Eloquence* seeks to refute the *Apologie*, to prove that the Jansenist movement did amount to an heretical sect within the Church inspired by hell and sustained by pride, to discredit the rhetoric through which their case is argued, and to link their reservations concerning papal infallibility to political disloyalty.[13]

The Jesuit memoirist René Rapin notes the shock produced by Desmarets's intervention:

le début seul qu'il fit par le titre . . . les déconcerta; il portoit: *la Response à l'insolente Apologie des religieuses de Port-Royal. Avec la découverte de la fausse Eglise des Iansenistes, et de leur fausse Eloquence.* C'était les

---

[12] Ibid. 1043.
[13] *Response à l'insolente Apologie . . . Presentée au Roy. Par le Sieur de S. Sorlin, Conseiller de sa Maiesté, & Controlleur general de l'Extraordinaire des Guerres,* an 8vo volume of xxix + 340 pp. for which a five-year *privilège* was issued to Saint-Sorlin on 3 Dec. 1665 and transferred three days later to the publishers. The volume exists in two states: 'Chez Nicolas Le Gras . . . Et . . . Claude Audinet . . . 1666' and 'J. Couterot, 1666'. One copy is held by the Univ. of Minnesota and three by the Bibliothèque Nationale, including a copy from Louis XIV's own library. Alone of the polemicists Desmarets signed his publications.

prendre par leur sensible, eux, qui faisoient profession de mépriser tête levée tous ceux qui se mêloient d'écrire . . .[14]

Hence Nicole's reply in the eleventh *Imaginaire*, or first *Visionnaire*, with its personal attack on Desmarets, clandestinely published on 31 December 1665 and followed by the second and third *Visionnaires* on 8 and 15 January 1666, the fourth on 20 February, the fifth on 9 March, and the sixth on 28 March.

A new Compagnie du Saint-Sacrement?

Desmarets's intervention is all the more interesting because he had written to Henry-Marie Boudon in 1664 seeking to interest him in a devout society to replace the Compagnie du Saint-Sacrement, formally dissolved at that time. Perhaps he had in mind an extension of the prayer-circle founded in 1657 and mentioned in *Le Chemin de la paix et celuy de l'inquiétude*, but it may have been more sinister.

In this letter to Boudon Desmarets recalls that in the five years past 'il a plu à Dieu me faire connaître plusieurs des plus abominables de ses ennemis . . . et il a fallu que seul j'aie soutenu les frais' of prosecution.[15] The reference must include both Charpy de Sainte-Croix and Simon Morin, whose prosecutions are discussed in Chapter 4. Indeed, he names Morin before reporting other, more recent cases:

Vous avez su ce qui s'est passé contre le grand ennemi de Jésus-Christ, Morin, qui fut brûlé vif l'année dernière. Depuis cela, Dieu m'a fait connaître trois prêtres magiciens, et deux séculiers, lesquels, s'étant entièrement découverts à moi et m'ayant donné leurs écrits abominables, pour se donner au diable, pour l'invoquer, pour l'encenser, pour faire mourir des personnes . . . et ayant toutes preuves . . . je les ai fait prendre, et ils ont été vingt mois en prison; et le démon ayant fait passer l'un d'eux, nommé Saint-Marc [Pierre Costard] pour un grand opérateur et guérisseur de maladies incurables, lui a fait avoir tant d'amis qu'ils ont été mis en liberté comme absous, faute de personnes qui voulussent fournir aux frais du procès . . . Vous voyez donc la nécessité de l'établissement de la Société de Paris pour les intérêts de Dieu.

Clearly, much depended on the outcome of Desmarets's late quarrels. Doubts over witch-hunts were growing, especially in the jurisdiction

---

[14] Rapin, *Mémoires*, iii. 360.
[15] Letter to H.-M. Boudon, quoted in Bremond, *Histoire littéraire*, vi. 492–4.

of the Parlement de Paris. Yet they still occurred, not only in France but throughout Europe and such European colonies as Salem, Massachusetts, since Protestants could be as intolerant as Catholics. In particular the French Court was involved with cases no less horrendous than that of Morin and his associates from Desmarets's adolescence until after his death. The cases of Concini's widow and of Urbain Grandier, and the famous 'affaire des poisons' in which Racine became implicated in 1677 are but a few examples.[16] Mental illness was not yet a defence in cases such as that of Morin, which raised fears of regicide. Desmarets's personal investigations antedate the establishment of a police department in Paris. Indeed the appointment of La Reynie as Lieutenant de police in 1667 may well have been to some extent prompted by questions raised during the Quarrel of the *Imaginaires*. Finally, Louis XIV himself is well known to have insisted—unsuccessfully, as it happened—on the death penalty for Nicolas Fouquet, whose trial took place at much the same time as Morin's. Courts able to resist the King's wishes with regard to Fouquet's sentence could certainly have returned a different sentence for Morin had that been desired by the judges. The dehumanizing metaphors which Desmarets uses for the execution of Morin in the *Seconde Partie de la Response*—'Morin fut . . . un grand dragon que j'écrasay . . . avec les autres serpens de sa secte, par le mesme zele, qui est le baston que Dieu m'a donné'— could have been inspired by distant memories of allegorical Court ballet or of serpent-dragons smitten by St Michael the Archangel in paintings such as the one on that subject which Raphael painted for François Ier. On the other hand, Desmarets's metaphor may echo the language of Pope Alexander VII's encyclical *Regiminis apostolici* of February 1665, which compares the Jansenist heresy to a serpent whose head had been crushed but whose body still thrashed about.

The tone of Desmarets's letter to Boudon and its concluding request to be associated in prayer with Carmelites of his acquaintance 'à la Société des victimes unies à Jésus' leave Bremond in no doubt as to his sincerity.[17] In replying to Port-Royal Desmarets must have thought—as the Jansenist apologists for their part also evidently thought—that he was acting in God's interest.

---

[16] See Mandrou, *Magistrats et sorciers*; Chapters 3 and 4 of the present work (for the earlier convictions); and F. Funck-Brentano, *Le Drame des poisons* (1906).

[17] Bremond, *Histoire littéraire*, vi. 494.

Racine's Lettres à l'Auteur des Imaginaires

Whatever the sympathies expressed in the *Abrégé de l'histoire de Port-Royal* written after Desmarets's death, the young Racine certainly realized that there was something rather odd about Nicole's polemics. In his *Lettre à l'Auteur des Imaginaires et des deux Visionnaires*, Racine reminds Nicole:

> Mais, Monsieur, si je m'en souviens, on a loué Desmarets dans ces lettres [*Provinciales*]. D'abord l'auteur en avait parlé avec mépris, sur le bruit qui courait qu'il travaillait aux apologies des jésuites. Il vous fit savoir qu'il n'y avait point de part. Aussitôt il fut loué comme un homme d'honneur, et comme un homme d'esprit.
>
> Tout de bon, Monsieur, ne vous semble-t-il pas qu'on pourrait faire sur ce procédé les mêmes réflexions que vous avez faites tant de fois sur le procédé des jésuites?[18]

It is a trivialization of literary history to suppose that Racine intervened as he did simply through ingratitude or ambition. Picard himself recognizes the perspicacity with which the young Racine turns against Pascal and Nicole the reproach to Jesuits in the fifteenth *Provinciale*, 'de ne mesurer la foi et la vertu des hommes que par les sentiments qu'ils ont pour eux'.[19] In any case, as a reader of novels and author of plays, Racine was insulted. He also had cause for alarm.

The more recent of Racine's first two tragedies was about to be dedicated to Louis XIV: *Alexandre le Grand*; and the future Historiographe du Roi was well versed in the political symbolism of parallels of ancients and moderns. He can scarcely have failed to know about the 'petite académie' set up in 1663 to supervise royal image-making through inscriptions, medallions, sculpture, painting, tapestries, etc., since the theme of Alexander's victories is shared by Le Brun's depictions of Alexander with the features of Louis XIV and the series of tapestries on Alexander's victories made around that time in the Gobelins factory, established by Colbert in 1662. He probably knew Desmarets's similar parallel of Alexander and Cardinal Richelieu, that Desmarets's plays had been performed in theatres built by a great prince of the Church, with bishops and priests as ushers, that *Mirame* had opened in the presence of

---

[18] Racine, *Œuvres complètes*, ii. 21.
[19] Ibid. 1000.

Anne of Austria and Louis XIII, that Cardinal Richelieu and
Louis XIII had accepted the dedication of his plays, and that
Anne of Austria—renowned for piety in her own style and dying of
cancer when the Quarrel of the *Imaginaires* began—had accepted
dedications of Desmarets's *Office de la Vierge Marie* and of his third
novel.

An attack on Court culture

Far more was involved than the personal reputation of Desmarets
or the career of Jean Racine. Consider the political implications of
reference in the first *Visionnaire* to *Clovis* as 'un Roman en vers plein
de fables scandaleuses' in the context of (*a*) the *fêtes galantes* of *Les
Plaisirs de l'île enchantée* produced on a theme from Ariosto's
Orlando furioso at Versailles in 1664 and (*b*) the publication of
Clovis with a portrait of and dedication to Louis XIV, a parallel
of Clovis and Louis, and its rededication to the King in 1666. The
reference to theatre as a corrupting influence further implicates the
King himself through *Les Plaisirs de l'île enchantée*, festivities in
which the theatrical *divertissements* included the first version of
Molière's *Tartuffe*. Nicole and his associates wanted to introduce
censorship of imaginative literature and theatre different from, but
no less severe than, the censorship which Church and State attempted
to impose on the apologists of Jansenism—beginning with Molière's
Tartuffe and continuing with his *Dom Juan*, performances of which
were discontinued in 1665, probably in response to pressures similar
to those which generally prevented public performances of *Tartuffe*
from 1664 to 1669. Some Port-Royalists wanted to close the theatres,
severely restricting the pastimes and pleasures of Court and nation.
Indeed Nicole seems not so much concerned at the fate of Morin
as disappointed that Desmarets himself was not burnt at the stake.
Well aware of the implications of Nicole's attempt to link his activities
with those of Charpy and Morin as a third visionary fanatic,
Desmarets denounces Nicole's apparent wish 'de faire mon procès
. . . & me faire brûler tout vif plus justement que . . . [Morin]'.[20]

---

[20] *Seconde Partie de la Response*, 52–3. P. Roullé, Curé of the church of
St-Barthélemy on the Île de la Cité in Paris, had celebrated the banning of public
performances of *Tartuffe* in a pamphlet entitled *Le Roi glorieux au monde, ou
Louis XIV le plus glorieux de tous les rois du monde* (1664). In that pamphlet Roulé
states that, for intending to perform *Tartuffe* publicly, Molière 'méritait, par cet attentat

Desmarets's 'Avis du Saint Esprit au Roy'

In his *Visionnaires* Nicole either ignores the 'Approbations' of Desmarets's publications or else minimizes them, as with the lost 'Avis du Saint Esprit au Roy, sur la création des chevaliers du Saint-Esprit', published on 1 January 1662 with the 'Approbation' of Henri de La Mothe-Houdancourt, Grand Aumônier de France, Bishop of Rennes, and a member of the Conseil de Conscience who that day became a Chevalier de l'Ordre du Saint-Esprit.[21] Desmarets appears to have exhorted King and Chevaliers, in terms not greatly different from those he used in other 'Avis' and dedications to Louis XIV in this period, to lead a spiritual and military crusade. Desmarets's idea is not unlike the Christian Militia which Father Joseph and Charles I de Gonzague-Clèves, Duc de Nevers, began to organize around 1620 as a new order of chivalry and the nucleus of an international army for a crusade against the Turks, opposed by Philip IV of Spain but sanctioned by Pope Urban VIII in 1625.[22] The Port-Royalist Godefroi Hermant transcribes a letter written by

---

sacrilège et impie, un dernier supplice exemplaire et public, et le feu même, avant-coureur de celui de l'Enfer, pour expier un crime si grief de lèse-majesté divine', quoted in Molière, *Œuvres complètes* (1971), i. 1143. Molière and Desmarets were luckier in this respect than Morin, who was formally tried, convicted, and executed with the full rigour of law. Tactful about performance of *Tartuffe* at Versailles, Roullé appears to allude approvingly to the execution of Morin and other repressive measures when stating that Louis XIV is 'sourd pour les médiateurs de ces impies et abominables athées, de ces innovateurs de religion, inventeurs de magie et sortilèges, et tels autres criminels de lèse-majesté divine', ibid. 1143.

[21] G. Hermant, *Mémoires sur l'histoire ecclésiastique*, v, ed. A. Gazier (1905–10), 412–3. In the first two *Visionnaires* Nicole makes much of the fact that the Archbishop of Paris—still Cardinal de Retz until later in 1662—had declined to give the pamphlet an 'Approbation'; he shows no such respect for Retz's successor. There was a great ceremony at the Grands-Augustins on 1 Jan. 1662 for the installation of the new Chevaliers de l'Ordre du Saint-Esprit, who included not only La Mothe-Houdancourt but also François de Harlay, Archbishop of Rouen, Hardouin de Péréfixe's successor as Archbishop of Paris in 1671. Details of the ceremony are given in Loret, *La Muze historique*, iii. 445: grandstands for twenty thousand spectators etc.

[22] Huxley, *Grey Eminence*, 114. Tapié, *La France de Louis XIII*, 138, notes that Bérulle too was involved in that plan. In the late seventeenth century the philosopher Baron G. W. von Leibniz (1646–1716) called for such a crusade while first minister of Mainz, as noted by G. Clark, *War and Society in the Seventeenth Century* (Cambridge, 1952), 16. Clark notes sceptics nearer the throne of France, but Bremond is certainly correct in linking the 'Avis' to a long series of pious 'Dieu le veut' since the first Crusade, *Histoire littéraire*, vi. 490. The date of the 'Avis' makes it unnecessary to suppose that Desmarets could have intended the new army to replace the Compagnie du Saint-Sacrement, not dissolved until 1664.

a Jansenist, probably Nicole or Sainte-Marthe, accusing Desmarets of madness for having written this 'Avis', as does Nicole in the first two *Visionnaires*.[23] The letter was probably written after 1665, under the influence of Nicole's *Imaginaires*. The pioneering work of Henri Bremond, the positive appraisal of Desmarets's spirituality by André Dodin, and the recovery of Desmarets's *Lettres spirituelles* make further discussion of his sanity unnecessary.[24]

Seconde Partie de la Response

In the *Seconde Partie de la Response à l'insolente Apologie de Port-Royal* Desmarets himself accounts for his intervention in the Quarrel of the *Imaginaires* as follows:

Dieu le sçait, & un bon Ecclesiastique avec qui je demeure, qui au mois de Iuin ou Iuillet 1665, me voyant de retour d'un voyage de sept ou huit mois, voulut me faire voir par nouveauté les deux premieres parties de l'Apologie, lesquelles je refusay longtemps de regarder, luy disant que Dieu m'avoit toûjours preservé d'entrer dans les questions des Iansenistes, & de lire un seul de leurs écrits. Enfin il me força d'en voir quelques endroits, où estoient des invectives contre le Roy, & contre M. de Paris [Hardouin de Péréfixe]. Sur quoy je luy dis que cela n'estoit point d'un esprit Chrestien, mais orgueilleux, malicieux, & heretique.[25]

The 'bon Ecclesiastique' with whom Desmarets was living in 1665 is Jacques Testu. Later admired for a volume of *Stances chrétiennes* (1669), in 1665 Testu was, like Desmarets, a member of the Duc de Richelieu's household, having earlier spent some time with Armand-Jean de Bouthillier de Rancé, Abbé de la Trappe (1626–1700), who had recently taken orders in the monastery for

[23] J. Dryhurst, who drew my attention to Hermant's *Mémoires*, once thought that the accusation of madness might date from 1662 (letter dated 9 Feb. 1962).

[24] Bremond, *Histoire littéraire*, and A. Dodin, 'Desmarets de Saint-Sorlin', in *Dictionnaire de spiritualité ascétique et mystique*, iv (1957). The medical thesis by M.-A. Caillet, *Un Visionnaire du XVIIe siècle*, ignores Bremond's research, takes Nicole's accusations at face value, confuses Desmarets's fictional characters with autobiography, and, like Nicole, fails to distinguish between what Desmarets describes as his own experience and what he derives from the mystic tradition (Daniel, Revelation, St Augustine, St Bernard of Clairvaux, Blosius, Gerson, St Catherine of Genoa, *et al.*). No doctor in Molière's comedies of 1666–73 achieves such a triumph of rhetoric over experimental diagnosis.

[25] *Seconde Partie de la Response*, 21. Desmarets's *privilège* of 3 Dec. 1665 was transferred to F. Muguet on 30 Mar. 1666 for this volume, 'achevé d'imprimer' on 2 Apr.

the reform of which he is remembered. Desmarets denies that his *Response* had been inspired by Hardouin de Péréfixe, whom he had not seen for about two years and who heard about it from unnamed theologians whom Desmarets had asked to read it. Only when he met the Archbishop in the city did the latter invite him, Desmarets continues,

d'aller chez luy, où il me retint quelques jours, pendant lesquels je luy lüs quelques endroits de mon livre qui luy furent assez agreables. J'allay deux fois à Port-Royal, où je parlay aux Religieuses soumises à l'Eglise, qui depuis m'ont envoyé les billets que j'ay fait imprimer.[26]

He spoke only twice, he states, with Sister Flavie Passart (who had signed the formulary), did not see her in private, spoke only once about silent prayer, and after the *Response* returned only once to Port-Royal.[27]

The *Seconde Partie de la Response* replies generally to the first *Visionnaires*, accusing the author of misrepresenting and falsifying passages quoted from Desmarets's works:

Il n'y a presque pas un seul article en ces Lettres visionnaires, qui ne porte un mensonge & une calomnie inventée par la seule imagination furieuse de l'Auteur, sans raison ny preuve quelconque; & dont la refutation ne soit facile . . .[28]

As for being called a 'visionnaire', Desmarets suggests, as noted in Chapter 1, that 'par la mesme raison l'on pourroit donner le nom d'Avare, à celuy qui auroit fait une Comedie où il auroit rendu les auares ridicules', that the term is more suited to the author of the letters, and that

s'il estoit permis de traiter en Comedie les fausses & extravangantes Religions . . . il me seroit facile de composer une seconde Comedie des Visionnaires, dont les personnages seroient des Iansenistes.[29]

---

[26] *Seconde Partie de la Response*, 22. The Archbishop seems to have sent to Port-Royal whoever might have helped his cause. According to Cardinal L.-F. de Bausset, *Histoire de Bossuet, évèque de Meaux*, i. 3rd edn. (1821), 157: 'Fatigué de ne pouvoir vaincre l'opiniâtreté de ces religieuses, après avoir inutilement employé tous les moyens de douceur et de patience que la modération naturelle de son caractère lui avoit fait mettre en usage, M. de *Péréfixe* imagina d'employer l'intervention de [Jacques-Bénigne] Bossuet [1627–1704, then Chanoine de Metz and a fashionable preacher in Paris] pour les ramener à leur devoir.'

[27] *Seconde Partie de la Response*, 29.

[28] Ibid. 20.

[29] Ibid. 16–8.

No wonder Racine opens his letter to Nicole without taking sides: 'Je laisse à juger au monde quel est le visionnaire de vous deux.'[30] He was certainly aware that in the first *Visionnaires* Nicole, knowing nothing of Desmarets's private life and declaring that 'je n'ai nul dessein de m'informer', constructs a 'character' largely from Christian polemics written long before the seventeenth century.[31] Hence Racine's ironic advice to Nicole: 'Employez l'autorité de saint Augustin et de saint Bernard, pour le déclarer visionnaire.'[32] It is not only on the King's side of the quarrel that the notion of authority was abused.

A *wall-poster campaign against the* Visionnaires

The last *Visionnaires* appeared on 10 April and 1 May 1666; but the quarrel continued. Around that time Desmarets seems to have challenged the Port-Royalists through a wall-poster campaign. In an 'Avis sur le Placart du Sr Desmarets', issued after publication of Desmarets's *Seconde Partie de la Response* on 2 April 1666, the author (probably Nicole or Sainte-Marthe) complains that the Archbishop has endorsed Desmarets's *Response*, that he

souffre qu'il prenne le titre de son deffenseur; il le presente au Roy; il le retire dans sa maison; il le fait manger à sa table . . . On imprisonne des Imprimeurs, M. le Lieutenant Civil est obligé de rendre compte au Sr Desmarets de ce qu'il trouve chez eux . . .[33]

According to Rapin, it was the arrest on 10 February 1666 of Villars, an agent of Louis Fouquet, Bishop and Comte d'Agde—the exiled brother of the imprisoned Surintendant des Finances—which had provoked new hostility at Court towards Port-Royal, implicated

---

[30] Racine, *Œuvres complètes*, ii. 18.

[31] P. Nicole, *Les Imaginaires ou Lettres sur l'hérésie imaginaire*, ii (Liège, 1667), 51–2.

[32] Racine, *Œuvres complètes*, ii. 24.

[33] For the 'Avis sur le Placart du Sr Desmarets', see my article in *Papers on French Seventeenth Century Literature*, 9 (16/2) (1982), 305–11. I now realize that the author of the 'Avis' draws upon the *Seconde Partie de la Response* for his complaint that posters had been displayed with the sole permission of the Archbishop, whose approbation seems to count for less with Port-Royalists than when the same office was held by Retz. In the 'Avis' Péréfixe's emissary to Rome, a certain Father Mulard, is called 'un Moine renegat & vagabond, diffamé dans toute la France par ses insignes fripponeries'. Some two years elapsed between Retz's resignation in 1662 and final confirmation of Péréfixe in 1664.

in Villars's schemes.[34] Papers were found on his person considered injurious to Louis XIV and which implicated Louis Fouquet and other Port-Royalists.

The arrest of Le Maistre de Sacy

The 'Avis' is answered in ch. 17 of the *Troisiesme Partie de la Response à l'insolente Apologie de Port-Royal, et aux lettres et libelles des Iansenistes, avec la découverte de leur arsenal sur le grand chemin de Charenton*, 'achevé d'imprimer' by Muguet on 30 August 1666. The 'arsenal' was a bookish one, mainly scholarly papers related to a translation of the New Testament; and 'sur le grand chemin de Charenton' is suggestive beyond its literal meaning, since it was in that town at the confluence of the Seine and the Marne that Protestants were allowed to preach and that lunatics were housed in infamous 'petites maisons'. As noted in Chapter 2, in following up implications of Villars's papers, Desmarets had located Le Maistre de Sacy's hide-out in the Faubourg St-Antoine. The account in Rapin's *Mémoires* is more detailed than that of Desmarets, who appears to have thought that a certain Le Brun mentioned in Villars's papers might be Arnauld. A friend accustomed to argue with Protestants on the way to Charenton was asked to investigate and reported a suspicious household. Desmarets posted his valet to keep it under observation and traced the occupants to the home of Pierre Le Petit, 'imprimeur ordinaire des jansénistes'.[35] Le Maistre de Sacy, Pierre and Augustin Thomas ('fils du maître des comptes de Rouen, fort attaché au party'), Nicolas Fontaine (1625–1709), and other Jansenist publicists were arrested.[36] Le Maistre de Sacy was held prisoner in the Bastille 'près de deux ans avec bien de la rigueur, sur de certains papiers qu'on trouva dans sa cassette'.[37] Papers in his 'cassette' implicated him with Villars, Louis Fouquet, and the Duchesse de Longueville, all of whom appear to have been interested at that time in Le Maistre de Sacy's French translation of the

---

[34] Rapin, *Mémoires*, iii. 341. See also X. Azema, *Un prélat janséniste, Louis Foucquet, évêque et comte d'Agde (1656–1702)* (The Hague, 1963).

[35] Rapin, *Mémoires*, iii. 361–2. Pierre Le Petit also published for Louis XIV, the Académie française, and exceptionally for Desmarets, e.g. *L'Imitation* (1654).

[36] Rapin, *Mémoires*, iii. 362.

[37] Ibid. 364. Le Maistre de Sacy and Fontaine were released from prison under the terms of the Peace of the Church early in 1669, when Arnauld and others came out of hiding.

New Testament, published at Mons in 1667 and an important concern of the *Quatriesme Partie de la Response aux insolentes Apologies de Port-Royal*, 'achevé d'imprimer' by J. Hénault on 18 June 1668.

Desmarets's dedicatory epistle in the *Troisiesme Partie*, addressed 'Au Roy', makes a number of points relating to the question of the responsibility for the arrests. The Jansenists, he repeats, are inspired by the Devil, who

leur inspire de semer des libelles iniurieux, par lesquels ils ne se contentent pas d'attribuer à des animositez particulieres, & de faire passer pour des violences, & pour d'horribles excès, les emprisonnements qui se font des principaux de leur Secte, comme s'ils se faisoient sans le sceu de Vostre Majesté; mais encore ils osent asseurer qu'elle est bien éloignée de les authoriser.

The evidence does not support Nicole's assertions: Louis XIV must have been pleased with the arrests. It is not clear why in this affair Desmarets was less than forthcoming with Le Tellier, whose last important act as Chancelier de France was drafting the Revocation of the Edict of Nantes. However, the Jansenists had some powerful supporters in the Parlement, at Court, and in the Church—notably four bishops who refused to sign the formulary without qualification, so closely involving the liberties of the Gallican Church with the questions of 'droit' and 'fait' that a major schism in the Church was feared.

Historiography of the Quarrel

The Quarrel of the *Imaginaires* is not edifying, with intolerance and fanaticism on all sides. If this account seems to favour Desmarets, this simply redresses the balance, following three centuries dominated by Jansenist historiography. Desmarets cast himself as a David against Goliaths; but reversals in alliances after his death allowed the Goliaths to do more lasting damage. As a polemicist, Desmarets was figuratively decapitated by neglect of his earlier fame. Yet the tragic situation of the nuns of Port-Royal and other dissidents, the quarrel of the *Imaginaires*, the Peace of the Church, all make better sense if Desmarets is considered as a 'mighty opposite' to the Port-Royalists. So do subsequent reversals of alliances and revisionism in the Church and in the academies around the time of the Revocation of the Edict of Nantes in 1685. Bossuet, for instance, was eager, like Desmarets, to argue against the distinction of 'fait' and 'droit' when attempting to persuade the dissident nuns of Port-Royal to sign the formulary in 1664–5; but by 1674 he was meeting with Arnauld, Le Maistre de Sacy, Nicole, and Abel de La Lane, Abbé de Val-Croissant, at the Hôtel de Longueville to revise the New Testament of Mons.[38] By way of contrast, even before Chapelain's death in 1674 religious and political differences appear to have destroyed the friendly relations which Desmarets evidently enjoyed with the Duchesse de Longueville before the Fronde des Princes. Finally, Bossuet's *Maximes et réflexions sur la comédie* (1694), no less intolerant of theatre than the cited texts of Roullé, Nicole, and Conti between 1664 and 1666, has made it difficult for historians to recall how much theatre—especially Court ballet—had meant to Cardinal ministers, Queens Regent, Louis XIII, and the young Louis XIV.[39]

Doubtless under the influence of Testu, *La Deffense du poëme héroïque*, published jointly in 1674 by the Abbé Testu, Philippe-Julien Mancini-Mazarini, Duc de Nevers, and Desmarets, included criticism of the rhetoric of Port-Royal. As a founder-member of the Académie française, established thirty years earlier to promote eloquence in the national interest, Desmarets must have felt well qualified to attack their 'art de persuader'. Indeed, to some degree the controversy over rhetoric and religion between the Hôtel de Richelieu and Port-Royal continues hostilities begun during Cardinal Richelieu's ministry between writers in his service and Port-Royalists and anticipating the literary quarrels—also involving rhetoric and religion—between such rival groupings as the Hôtel de Richelieu and the Hôtel de Lamoignon. The Premier Président au Parlement de Paris from 1658, Guillaume de Lamoignon, later Marquis de Baville etc. (1617–77), resisted royal pressure for the death penalty during the trial of Fouquet and, less successfully, further pressure from the same source to increase the use of torture generally to extract confessions. Now perhaps best known for having banned public performances of Molière's *Tartuffe* in 1667, he was also a patron

---

[38] De Bausset, *Histoire de Bossuet*, i. 157–80.

[39] It is especially ironic that classical ballet is traced to the end of the century of Louis XIV, when he had ceased to dance, not because traditions originate at that time but because a system for noting steps was devised—admittedly an important development but also a useful illustration of the way in which historiography is influenced by the availability and promotion of select documentation.

of letters. Boileau and Baillet were both associated with the Hôtel de Lamoignon; and both were hostile to Desmarets for reasons evidently related as much to religion and politics as to the rhetoric of heroic poetry, different as it was from that of Port-Royal.

Revolutionary implications of Jansenism

The copious literature on Jansenism deals with most of the main religious, political, and intellectual implications of the acrimonious public debate on 'droit' and 'fait'.[40] It is perhaps difficult to imagine just how much support there was for absolutism as expressed by Desmarets in the preface to the first volume of his *Response*:

Dieu a establý dans le Monde un ordre certain & infaillible, qui est d'avoir recours au Chef de son Eglise en chose qui regarde la Religion, & au Roy en chose qui regarde l'authorité temporelle, ou le soustien de l'authorité spirituelle; & Dieu veut que l'on obeisse à l'un & à l'autre . . .

Nor has the Church invariably followed the Jansenists' lead in matters of doctrine. For instance, Desmarets complains not only that the Jansenist apologists resist the doctrine of papal infallibility but that in the fourth part of the *Apologie* they treat 'l'opinion de la Conception immaculée, comme *une devotion superstitieuse, & une honteuse hypocrisie*'.[41]

Desmarets clearly perceives the revolutionary implications of Jansenist doctrine. If they could, he argues in ch. 10, they would do

ce que les Demons voudroient pouvoir faire: Ils destruiroient Dieu, la Vierge, les Papes, les Roys . . . la Religion, l'Eglise. Puis comme Dieux nouveaux ils feroient un autre Monde, d'autres Papes, d'autres Roys, d'autres Prelats, d'autres constitutions, d'autres loix, une autre Religion, & une autre Eglise . . .[42]

Authority, 'droit', 'fait', and progress

Nicole, Arnauld, and other Jansenists assemble powerful arguments on the limits to royal and papal authority, which cannot of themselves

---

[40] *Divers actes, lettres, et relations des religieuses de Port-Royal du Saint-Sacrement touchant au sujet de la signature du formulaire* (3 vols.; Utrecht, 1735), is an important primary source.

[41] *Response* (1666), 19.

[42] Ibid. 126.

determine matters of fact. As the work of Pascal illustrates, new methods of calculating, improved observations with telescopes and microscopes, experiments on atmospheric pressure, on fluids under pressure, were establishing areas of experience no longer subject to the authority of discredited dogma, such as the scholastic assumption that 'nature abhors a vacuum', valid until experiment showed otherwise.[43] For an increasing proportion of people, the Creator was revealed not only through Scripture and the Church but through creation itself. Nature instructs mankind through intelligence, Pascal argues. In contrast with animal instinct, it allows any man to advance 'de jour en jour dans les sciences' and mankind to make 'un continuel progrès à mesure que l'univers vieillit'. However, revelation through intelligent experiment did not commend itself at once to all sections of opinion; and debates over precedents and progress in a wide range of subjects suggest anything but uniform and straightforward change.

Cartesians and animal intelligence

Descartes, for instance, is also associated with the idea of progress, especially perhaps the 'progrès que j'ai espérance de faire à l'avenir dans les sciences' mentioned towards the end of his *Discours de la méthode* (Leiden, 1637). In the *Discours* and other texts, Descartes also seeks to establish a unique status for human intelligence by separating it from the material body (old dogma with new rigour) and from any signs of intelligence apparent in other animals.[44] Thus Christian doctrine on the immortality of the human soul is reaffirmed with new rigour, Western man's image of himself as master of Creation is enhanced, and at the same time ethical objections to vivisection are removed. The vivisection practiced by Cartesian Jansenists on crucified dogs reflects, along with curiosity and perhaps a latent sadism shared with witch-hunters, new dogma partly propagated in defence of old. From contempt of the body,

---

[43] B. Pascal, 'Préface sur le Traité du vide', in *Opuscules et lettres de Pascal*, ed. L. Lafuma (1955), 48–56.

[44] At the end of pt. V of the *Discours* Descartes denounces as an error second only to atheism 'que d'imaginer que l'âme des bêtes soit de même nature que la nôtre, et que, par conséquent, nous n'avons rien à craindre, ni à espérer, après cette vie'.

particularly in its sexuality, the path is short to cruelty to animals as reminders of the animality of mankind.[45]

While sharing many of Descartes's—and indeed Jansenist—assumptions, Desmarets seems, like La Fontaine, to have avoided the worst of that particular counter-current. Government depended far more then than now on the horse in agriculture, transport, and war. In France it used more horses than desks, at least at the beginning of Desmarets's life if not at the end. So this is not a matter on which wrong theory is trivial.[46] Desmarets was probably trained in horsemanship—perhaps he learnt with Louis XIII himself as a teenaged favourite admitted even to the Conseil—according to the methods of Antoine de Pluvinel (1525–1620), Écuyer principal, Chambellan, Sous-gouverneur de sa Majesté, and Conseiller in the Conseil d'État. Unlike Descartes, Pluvinel recognizes horse sense and sensibility. Indeed, Pluvinel's system of horsemanship, recorded in his posthumous *Maneige royal* and lately still in use at the Spanish Riding School in Vienna, is based on a sympathetic understanding of animal intelligence and feeling as well as on instinct.[47] The Cartesian logic of Port-Royal has been disastrous to the animal populations of France.

Implications of science for royal image-making

Mid-century progress in the natural sciences has implications not only for the limits of authority but for images and perceptions of the monarchy in France. Here are two illustrations. In his 'Ode' to

[45] Compare B. Pascal, *Pensées sur la religion*, ed. L. Lafuma (1951), i. 362: 'La vraie et unique vertu est donc de se haïr, car on est haïssable par sa concupiscence.' Several times Pascal contrasts the beast in man with angelic aspirations, a 'contrariété' both parts of which must be acknowledged: ibid., 81, for instance, where human animality is only acknowledged to be overcome. There is no effort to understand animals, no willingness to participate in animal acceptance of instinct. Contrast the courtly values reflected in the 'Prologue' to Molière's *Amphitryon* (1668):

> Et, dans les mouvemens de leurs tendres ardeurs,
> Les Bestes ne sont pas si Bestes, que l'on pense.

[46] In pt. VI of the *Discours* Descarts himself acknowledges that a battle for truth is lost in accepting 'quelque fausse opinion touchant une matière un peu générale et importante', because it is harder to make up ground so lost than 'à faire de grands progrès, lorqu'on a déjà des principes qui sont assurés'.

[47] See A. de Pluvinel, *Maneige royal, où l'on peut remarquer le défaut et la perfection du chevalier en tous les exercices de cet art digne des princes* (1623) and H. de Terrebasse, *A. de Pluvinel, Dauphinois, écuyer des trois rois Henri III, Henri IV et Louis XIII* (Lyons, 1911).

Colbert, written towards the end of the Quarrel of the *Imaginaires* and already reflecting some of the difficulties which it caused him, Desmarets compares himself to 'le Roy des abeilles' which, disturbed by sheep, may abandon his work and lead his hive to a calmer place. Similarly, in lines of *Les Promenades de Richelieu* reprinted in *La Comparaison de la langue et de la poësie Françoise avec la Grecque & la Latine* (1670), Demarets evokes (after Virgil's *Georgics*)

> un jeune Roy, dans une cour sans nombre,
> Quand de la ruche il sort, pour mener au Printemps,
> Jouër parmy les airs ses sujets voletans . . .[48]

The hive presents an image of the State governed by a king, as writers had assumed at least since compilation of the elder Pliny's 'De apibus' (*Naturalis Historia*, xi) in the first century AD—an image supportive of the monarchy based on Salic law in France, as perhaps it had been for the Caesars of imperial (as opposed to republican) Rome. But in his *Historia insectorum generalis* (Utrecht, 1668), Jan Swammerdam showed that the 'king' is in fact a queen.[49] With the advance of science and the liberation of the French language from the limiting example of Latin offered by the French translator—advances fully consonant with the modern positions adopted by Desmarets for technology and literature, but not for religion and politics—this support for the French monarchy in natural history disappeared.

Cosmological changes and the Sun King

Changes in cosmology involving the sun must alter perceptions of a Sun King—a conceit central to the image-makers of the French monarchy under Louis XIII and XIV but far less stable than absolutists might have wished. For perception of the sun itself was changing. Consider two texts published the year before the birth of Louis XIV, both reacting to Galileo's abjuration in 1633: *Le Discours de la méthode* and *Les Visionnaires*. Explaining in Part vi of the *Discours* his failure to publish the major work of physics on which he had been working, Descartes cautiously explains that persons

dont l'autorité ne peut guère moins sur mes actions que ma propre raison sur mes pensées, avaient désapprouvé une opinion de physique, publiée

---

[48] *La Comparaison*, 119.

[49] The French translation (Utrecht, 1682) attacks the dependence of the French language on Latin precedent: 'nous en gardons le *Roi* (Rex), qui est femelle', 'la *Reine* (à qui on donne mal à propos le nom de *Roi*', 'la femelle que l'on nomme d'ordinaire le *Roy*', p. 96.

un peu auparavant par quelque autre, de laquelle je ne veux pas dire que je fusse, mais bien que je n'y avais rien remarqué, avant leur censure, que je pusse imaginer être préjudiciable ni à la religion ni à l'Etat.

No one doubts that Descartes refers to Galileo or that Church and State were still very much concerned with authority over fact.

In the first scene of the comedy *Les Visionnaires*, the braggart soldier boasts

> Voyant que le soleil courait incessamment,
> J'arrêtai pour jamais sa course vagabonde,
> Et le voulus placer dans le centre du monde;
> J'ordonnai qu'en repos il nous donnât le jour,
> Que la terre et les cieux roulassent à l'entour;
> Et c'est par mon pouvoir, et par cette aventure,
> Qu'en nos jours s'est changé l'ordre de la nature . . .
> De là vient le sujet de ces grands dialogues . . .[50]

As Molière might have put it in *Tartuffe*, 'c'est un visionnaire qui parle'. But Desmarets's 'visionnaires' are generally mad, not so much in what they express so eloquently but in how they relate to valour, lovers, wealth, etc. Lines on such a delicate subject at such a time are remarkable for the stage of a great French prince of the Church.

Perception of the order of nature was indeed changing, and the new cosmology brought difficulties. Not only had earth and sun changed places, observation of variable spots on the sun suggested imperfections previously unsuspected beyond the moon's sphere. More seriously, heliocentrism seems scarcely to have survived geocentrism. A famous fragment of what in 1670 became Pascal's *Pensées* hesitates, like Milton in *Paradise Lost* VIII, between a Ptolemaic and a Copernican cosmology: 'la nature entière dans sa haute et pleine majesté . . . objets bas . . . cette éclatante lumière mise (*au*) comme une lampe éternelle (*au centre de*) pour éclairer l'univers'.[51] But already Pascal imagines (for the sake of argument?) 'l'univers muet et l'homme sans lumière abandonné à lui-même, et comme égaré dans ce canton détourné de l'univers'.[52] Either 'égaré dans ce canton détourné' suggests a sun vastly remote from the

---

[50] Artabaze in *Les Visionnaires*, I. I, quoted from Scherer and Truchet, (eds.), *Théâtre du XVIIe siècle*, ii. 409. I agree with the editors that, with some audacity, the last word 'semble faire particulièrement allusion aux *Quatre dialogues sur les systèmes du monde de Ptolémée et de Copernic* de Galilée' (ibid., 1363–5).

[51] Pascal, *Pensées*, i. 134.

[52] Ibid. 133.

earth or else it already implies the post-heliocentric demotion of the sun to the rank of vulgar star. Compare 'un coin de cette vaste étendue'.[53] In any case, 'l'univers muet' implies, like 'le silence éternel de ces espaces infinis m'effraie', that the music of the spheres is no longer heard.[54]

Sun symbolism may, through perception of a heliocentric cosmos, have been briefly enhanced as an image of royal majesty around the middle of the century when Louis XIV danced Apollo.[55] By 1670, when Louis XIV ceased to dance in Court ballets, courtiers celebrating the cult of the King's majesty could no longer suppose that the harmony of the now displaced spheres was symbolized by their dance, as their elders had evidently done before the people of Paris half a century earlier. Indeed, like the sun in Pascal's perception, the King at Versailles was becoming more remote. As the reign lengthened, fewer thinking people can have seriously connected sun-king symbolism either with the silent cosmos or heliocentric cosmology. Apollo had become a dominant theme: an ornamental mythology, drawn from religion universally regarded as invalid, false, even diabolical. Unlike Catholic doctrine, moreover, its main appeal must have been to the privileged élites for whom Renaissance humanism was meaningful without posing awkward questions on such matters as the nature of grace. The Sun King as Apollo in royal image-making in the late seventeenth century has an exact parallel in the near exclusion of Christian doctrine and the reliance on classical mythology as a source of 'ornements reçus' in serious French literature after the publication of Boileau's *Œuvres diverses* in 1674. Boileau actually uses that phrase in *L'Art poétique* iii—with all the intellectual limitations and none of the irony associated two centuries later with the *Dictionnaire des idées reçues* of Gustave Flaubert (1821–80). Beyond the dangers of sterility inherent in any closed system of received ideas, those particular 'ornements reçus' had the specific disadvantage of separating important aspects of royal image-making and of high culture both from contemporary developments in experimental science and from the fundamental doctrines of the Church, which, within arbitrary limits, Louis XIV still sought to protect through the savage repression of Huguenots and other dissidents in the decades after Desmarets's death.

[53] Pascal, *Pensées*, i. 247.
[54] Ibid. 142.
[55] N. Mitford, *The Sun King; Louis XIV at Versailles* (London, 1966), beautifully illustrates the imagery.

Conclusion

> Quand on fait voir des beautez qui n'ont jamais esté connuës,
> on surpasse les regles connuës, & l'on en fait de nouvelles
> pour les autres Poëtes, par de nouveaux modeles qu'on leur
> donne, bien plus raisonnables & plus parfaits que ceux des
> Anciens.[1]

The epigraph expresses a conception of creative writing and art constant in Desmarets's career even before his entry into Cardinal Richelieu's personal service and already common among Court poets during the Regency of Marie de Médicis: the modern position. His attitude towards the rules is not perhaps the first to come to mind when dealing with literary creation in the 'century of Louis XIV'. Nor does it characterize historiography of the Académie-Française, which Desmarets served for longer than any other founder-member.[2] Beyond its limited immediate application in context, however, it does provide a focus for this Conclusion, which will not re-develop arguments brought forward to the Introduction and Chapter 1.

The Quarrel of the *Imaginaires* and the Quarrel of the ancients and moderns ushered in by Desmarets's quarrel with Boileau were decisive not only for Desmarets's reputation but for French cultural developments to the end of the *ancien régime* and for their historiography. The issues are so important that it is tempting to expand this Conclusion to add—tentatively and subject to further research—a little speculation on their implications. The concept 'modern' used in the Quarrel has subsequently evolved—not only with the passage of time but also because the creation of a French classicism also created a realigned set of French 'ancients'. The classics of the century of Louis XIV are now ancients just as easy to contrast with

---

[1] 'Discours pour prouver que les sujets Chrestiens sont les seuls propres à la poësie Heroïque', in *Clovis*, ed. F. R. Freudmann (Louvain and Paris, 1972), 744.

[2] Perception of the 'freedom of French classicism' is, however, greater than it once was, thanks partly to E. B. O. Borgerhoff, *The Freedom of French Classicism* (Princeton 1950).

'les gens de maintenant' as the ancient Romans, in Angélique's retort in Molière's *Le Malade imaginaire* (II, VI), performed in the year the epigraph above was published.

Epic and Tragedy

It seems reasonable to conclude that perception of Desmarets's literary originality was doubly lost in the Quarrel with Boileau, through demotion of epic as the highest form of literary expression and promotion of tragedy to take its place. When writing for the stage, the poet of *Clovis* had been more interested in comedy and in modern forms of theatre—Court ballet, tragicomedy, and heroic comedy—forms which he had ceased to practise almost two decades before the death of Mazarin. The example of Molière shows that a great literary reputation may be based on comedy; but most of Desmarets's literary efforts went into genres even less favoured by literary histories of the century of Louis XIV.

In the rising tide of rationalism—so positive for the development of a philosophy of science, but sometimes narrowly literal-minded with regard to theatre and imaginative literature—Desmarets's suggestion that the creative writer develops rather than follows rules was often forgotten. The contemporary importance of Chapelain, like that of Boileau before the death of Desmarets, has been exaggerated at the latter's expense. It is an irony of the literary history of French theatre that *La Pratique du théâtre*, finally published in 1657 by the Abbé d'Aubignac (whose practical contribution to the evolution of French stagecraft under Richelieu was less appreciated and far less inventive than Desmarets's) came to be so magnified by literary historians—as if the practice of theatre were more what an unsuccessful playwright prescribes and proscribes than what a favoured dancer, actor, choreographer, and playwright invented, performed, and wrote. Critical judgement of theatre, especially tragedy, by the rules tended to overlook that verisimilitude as understood by Aristotle—and by Desmarets—includes idealism: 'things as they ought to be'.

The creative writer

It is important to conclude also that creative writing for Desmarets is a religious notion, based on belief firstly in the Holy Spirit as the ideal rhetorician and secondly in man as an image of God. As the work of the Holy Spirit, the Bible in Desmarets's view is the best guide to eloquence; but to be faithful to himself as an image of God, the writer must not simply imitate what he sees according to rules but must invent fresh forms and new rules in imitation of the Creator. To conform to God's image man must create.

There is a biblical inspiration for Desmarets's lines on the inventive Muse already quoted from 'L'Art de la poësie', which he wrote for Cardinal Richelieu:

> Mais alors qu'elle invente vne belle aventure
> Glorieuse elle suit l'autheur de la Nature;
> Et produisant au jour ce qui ne fut jamais,
> Imite du grand Dieu les admirables faits.

Contrast these lines from Boileau's *L'Art poétique* III:

> L'Evangile à l'Esprit n'offre de tous côtés,
> Que pénitence à faire, et tourmens mérités:
> Et de vos fictions le mélange coupable
> Même à ses vérités donne l'air de la Fable.

In this passage Boileau attacks Desmarets, the French epic, and the Christian marvellous. His 'ne . . . que' leaves little room for miracles, devils, or redemption.

Desmarets's quarrel with Boileau

It is an aberration to suppose that Jansenism is unrelated to Boileau's hostility to the Christian marvellous, as Antoine Adam remarks in his commentary on the passage just cited from *L'Art poétique*.[3] Boileau objects to many of the same aspects of Desmarets's writing as Nicole; he first mentions Desmarets in a satire in relation to Jansenism; and both of his two witty epigrams mocking Desmarets refer to Port-Royal: 'Racine, plain ma destinée', written in anticipation of *La Deffense du poëme héroïque*, and 'Dans le Palais hier Bilain'.[4]

Two other points are worth making about 'Racine, plain ma destinée'. Firstly, Racine is known to have owned a copy of the

---

[3] Adam, *Histoire de la littérature française au XVIIᵉ siècle*, iii. 242.
[4] N. Boileau, *Œuvres complètes*, ed. A. Adam (1966), 254, 256.

quarto *Clovis*, to reread which Boileau finds repugnant; but Boileau possibly did not.[5] Secondly, Boileau's rime 'Armé de cette même poudre / Qui mit le Port-Royal en poudre' seems to echo Boisrobert's reference to his disgrace at the first performance of *Mirame*: 'Je r'entré dans ma gloire, apres ce coup de foudre / Qui devoit en tombant m'avoir reduit en poudre'.[6] It is not well known that 'Dans le Palais hier Bilain', which Adam suggests was written *c.* twenty years after Desmarets's *Response à l'insolente Apologie*, thus *c.* ten years after Desmarets's death, adapts an epigram written in fact many years earlier against Nicolas Boileau's brother Gilles:

> Hier un certain Personnage
> Au Palais me voulut nier
> Qu'autrefois Boileau le rentier
> Sur Costar eût fait un Ouvrage . . .[7]

Both epigrams are clever, but misleading as literary history.

Of *La Deffense du poëme héroïque* Antoine Adam observes:

Si elle frappe fort, elle n'en frappe pas moins juste, et fait apparaître au grand jour les erreurs et les paralogismes de Despréaux, les défaillances de son style, la pauvreté de sa versification.[8]

In *La Deffense* Desmarets, the Abbé Testu, and the Duc de Nevers make a good case against the aspects of Boileau's *Œuvres diverses* which they deplore, particularly his lack of imagination.[9] Religious and political differences underlie incompatible aesthetics, as I have argued elsewhere without reference to Desmarets's co-authors.[10] Like Cardinal Richelieu, but unlike leading Jansenist publicists

---

[5] See P. Bonnefon, 'La Bibliothèque de Racine', *Revue d'histoire littéraire de la France*, 5 (1898), 169–219, and D. Atkinson, *The Libraries of Olivier Patru (1604–81) and Nicolas Boileau-Despréaux (1636–1711)* (Oxford, 1981). Patru owned a 4to *Clovis* and also Desmarets's *L'Imitation*.

[6] F. Le Métel de Boisrobert, *Epistres en vers*, ed. M. Cauchie (1921). i. 59.

[7] See Boileau-Despréaux, *Œuvres*, ed. C. -A. Lefebvre de Saint-Marc (1747), iii. 121 n.

[8] Adam, *Histoire de la littérature française au XVIIᵉ siècle*, iii. 144.

[9] W. Bornemann, *Boileau-Despréaux im Urtheile seines Zeitgenossen Jean Desmarets de Saint-Sorlin* (Heilbronn, 1883) somewhat conceals in his title the important difference in generations but brings out the main points.

[10] 'Aspects esthétiques et religieux de la Querelle des Anciens et des Modernes', in M. Fumaroli (ed.), *Critique et création littéraire en France au XVIIᵉ siècle*, (1977), 213–20. Testu's association with Rancé, founder of the Trappists, is mentioned above; this Duc de Nevers, brother of the Marie Mancini whom Louis XIV wanted to marry in 1658, had held his train at the coronation in 1654.

before 1668, Desmarets and his allies demand absolute loyalty to the Crown. Finally, both Boileau and his three opponents appeal to 'le bon sens', without agreeing what it is.

Of course Jansenism is not the whole story. The disagreement over 'bon sens' implies philosophical differences, divergent conceptions of the role of rationalism in faith and in literature. 'Aimez donc la Raison', writes Boileau near the beginning of L'Art poétique. Desmarets invokes a different, less Cartesian order of reason, a different style of rhetoric. His Neoplatonism supposes radically different valuations of many aspects of life.

Boileau fits more easily than Desmarets into the revolution taking place in cultural values evoked by Nussbaum as Cartesianism. The decline of poetry in France in the last century of the ancien régime— whether poetry is understood as a preference of verse forms to prose or as an imaginative rather than purely rational response to existence— is often associated with Cartesianism. A master of versification, the Boileau of L'Art poétique, 'Satires', and epigrams is more a wit than a poet. By way of brief contrast, the Fables of La Fontaine, steeped in the imaginative experience of early seventeenth-century poets whom Boileau despised, contains explicit rejections of key Cartesian doctrine.

Note too that the two volumes of Malebranche's De la recherche de la vérité (1674-5) are as exactly contemporary with Boileau's Œuvres diverses, Desmarets's Le Triomphe de Louis et de son siècle, La Deffense du poëme héroïque, and La Defense de la Poësie as they are with An Attempt to Prove the Annual Motion of the Earth from Observations by Robert Hooke (1635-1703). Opinion on the greater systems had come a long way from Desmarets's playful evocation of Copernicanism on Cardinal Richelieu's private stage in 1637.[11] Malebranche, who 'more than any other individual symbolized the achievements by Cartesianism as the form of the European mind', helped to undermine the imaginary framework of Desmarets's world.[12] Desmarets remained more literary, moral, and mystic than metaphysical or scientific, although even after his conversion he refers to joy in scientific knowledge and to new

[11] The freedom of expression in Artabaze's lines on the sun in Les Visionnaires I. 1, is compatible with Redondi's view that Galileo was tried not so much for Copernicanism as for atomism, with its implicit rejection of transubstantiation. See P. Redondi. Galileo: Heretic, transl. R. Rosenthal (London, 1988). In the century of Louis XIV the eucharist was a matter not only for celebration in every sense but also of controversy.

[12] Nussbaum. The Triumph of Science, 4.

scientific advances cited in support of the modern position. Like Malebranche, Boileau and Jansenist publicists were in their own various ways attempting to reconcile Christianity with Cartesianism. Desmarets, who understood the search after truth more in the Neoplatonic tradition represented by Cardinal Bellarmini, was not.

A fundamentalist modernism

Perhaps the most striking thing about Desmarets's modernism is the extent to which it is grounded in 'medieval' historiographical traditions of the miraculous and of royal and ecclesiastical authority. He is one of many statesmen and writers, not all of them his contemporaries, whose innovations in certain areas coexist with or depend upon a high degree of fundamentalism elsewhere. It is scarcely paradoxical to include Desmarets's Jansenist adversaries in that category, which would also include Pierre Bayle, whose rationalist historiography often serves a Protestant fundamentalism. Desmarets is innovative in defence of Church and Crown without questioning the ancient bases of their authority. He is sometimes most creatively modern in defence of valued aspects of the past.

Desmarets strikingly illustrates an aspect of French seventeenth-century literature often neglected by current critical trends: even in his secular works he is a deeply religious writer. As an apologist to *libertins* in *Les Délices de l'esprit* he resembles Pascal. Again, he makes a sharp distinction between matters considered subject to established authority and matters subject to invention and progress, just as Pascal does in his 'Préface sur le Traité du vide'. They differ in regard to *belles-lettres* and the arts, which Pascal scarcely considers and which Desmarets considers subject to progress, like science and technology. Pascal and Desmarets differ from the Protestant Bayle in the uncritical attitude they share toward the historiography of the Old Testament, miraculous aspects of which were increasingly difficult to reconcile with new chronologies and new cosmologies. Scripture apart, Desmarets seems a good deal less naïve towards historiography than the Pascal of the cited preface.

The historiography of Desmarets

Here, I am not so much concerned with Desmarets's historiography as with the historiography of Desmarets, which has been too strange to want significance. Consider the question whether progress is possible in *belles-lettres* and the arts—a central issue of the literary and linguistic Quarrel of the ancients and moderns. Desmarets maintains that it is, but Boileau seems to deny it with respect to such select masterpieces of Graeco-Roman antiquity as the *Iliad* and the *Aeneid*. Perfect works representative of privileged centuries is an appealing notion.[13] Yet in *L'Art poétique* i, 'Enfin Malherbe vint, et le premier en France', Boileau supposes a cyclic progress towards such works and such a century. In that respect he is working within the humanist cyclic conception of history long propagated by Desmarets, for whom the century of Louis XIV was bringing not only the return of a privileged cycle but progress to a higher level. It was Desmarets's misfortune to be largely written out of accounts of the preparation of the cyclic summit.

Jansenism, Cartesianism, and elements of Protestantism assimilated by the Enlightenment reacted in different ways against the eroticism, feminism, idealism, and apocalyptic millinarianism variously characteristic of Desmarets's imaginative works. The millinarianism of *Clovis*, which already contrasts with the absence of millinarianism in Milton's mid-century quarrel over regicide and republicanism with Claude Saumaise (1588–1653), lost credibility in the last quarter of the century. As noted in Chapter 3, the Church in France also turned its back on Cardinal Bellarmini, whose style of Neoplatonism permeates Desmarets's writings. The Académie française also changed. Founder members include several poets and performers of Court ballet besides Desmarets, but it did not elect Molière. Instead it elected some notable classicists, including Huet and Marolles, scarcely committed to French *belles-lettres*. In the changing fashions of literature and of royal image-making, Desmarets may also have lost more than he gained through his opposition around 1675 to the resurgence of Latin as an official language of the French Court. In *La Defense de la Poësie* he criticizes Latin poems by Jean-Baptiste Santeul (1630–97) and Jean Commire (1625–1702), Latinists influential after Desmarets's death.

Desmarets's reputation has suffered also through the specialization beginning to displace Renaissance aspirations to universal knowledge and competence. The 'virtuoso' certainly persists into the century

[13] The failure of 'perfect' works to sustain the cultures in which they occur may seem contradictory to anyone who has considered the implications of the concept of perfection as treated by Descartes in *Discours de la méthode* iv.

of Louis XIV as redefined from 1661 by Perrault; but in Thomas Shadwell's comedy *The Virtuoso*, performed a few months before Desmarets died, the virtuoso (even one interested in the sciences) is a figure of fun. Specialist academies were being established in France as well as England: Inscriptions et Belles-Lettres in 1663, Sciences in 1666, Music in 1672, etc. Desmarets did not belong to these new academies, and in the last quarter of the seventeenth century the Académie des Inscriptions et Belles-Lettres turned hostile to his memory. Narrow specialisms in literary history or criticism and in institutional history have neglected music, dance, theatre in performance, and unfashionable aspects of religious experience in relation to Desmarets's contemporary successes and literary works.

A more imaginative tradition of French literary history and criticism might have taken note of Desmarets's repeated insistence on the difference between the opinions expressed by a character in a literary work and the opinions of the author.

Towards a new perspective

However fragmentary the evidence remains, a more informed perspective on Desmarets's rich career makes a difference to perception of the cultural and political history of France in the seventeenth century. It matters, for instance, to understand that Desmarets evidently frequented the Hôtel de Rambouillet and sang his own madrigals there for 'La Guirlande de Julie', before entering Richelieu's personal service. It matters that *Aspasie* preceded Corneille's *L'Illusion comique* and may have opened the first theatre in the Palais-Cardinal, with its capacity for the newest effects of theatrical illusionism. It also matters that those effects were only surpassed five years later by effects designed for *Mirame* and *La Prospérité* by Bernini on a commission from Mazarin, who had seen the première of *L'Illusion comique*. From February 1636 Richelieu possessed a theatre whose style and equipment rivalled more closely than hitherto supposed the new court theatres of Parma, Venice, Whitehall, Madrid, and so on.[14] In this light, Richelieu's patronage

---

[14] Richelieu's château at Rueil also had, if not a theatre, a 'salle des fêtes', a playing place for Court theatre on which I can offer no new evidence—and no evidence at all that it was any less modern than the small theatre in the Palais-Cardinal.

seems more plausible, more conscious of new fashions, more aware of Court tastes, more alert to Court connections, and more intelligent than it does in previous accounts. His selection and use of 'creatures' seems more perceptive, less arbitrary, and politically much more astute than hitherto proposed.

Some of the evidence advanced in this study—from Tallemant des Réaux's *Historiettes*, for example—remains anecdotal. Yet once I had identified Desmarets, the Contrôleur général de l'Extraordinaire des guerres, the writer, and Academician, with Marets, the actor-dancer-musician and 'bouffon du Roi', no new problems arose and many unsatisfactory aspects of earlier accounts of Desmarets disappeared. Nor is Tallemant des Réaux the only source of anecdotes. As late as 1666 the Abbé Charles Cotin (1603–81)—the Conseiller and Aumônier du Roi, member of the Académie française, mocked as Trissotin in Molière's *Les Femmes savantes*—recalls that Marais had mocked the Duc d'Épernon in the presence of Louis XIII.[15] Since either of the two possible Ducs d'Épernon was a powerful governor and military leader, such mockery must have had a political dimension; and it matters that the King's jester was also his Député Surintendant des fortifications.[16]

Because discovery of the pamphlet identifying Desmarets as Député Surintendant des fortifications in 1620 and the notorized document confirming his borrowing 10,000 *livres* to purchase that office in 1634 came late in my research, I may well have understated the implications of Desmarets's career in that commission during the siege warfare of the 1620s: Montauban, Montpellier, La Rochelle, etc.

[15] C. Cotin, in *La Critique désintéressée ou les Satyres du temps*, ed. Bibliophile Jacob (1883), 75–6. It is not entirely clear whether Cotin means Jean-Louis de Nogaret et de la Valette (1554–1642), the picturesque governor of Provence, of Guyenne, and of Metz, or (using the title retrospectively) his son Bernard (1592–1661), a patron of Molière's troupe. The former sided with Marie de Médicis in 1619 and was not always in favour with Louis XIII and Richelieu after 1624; and the incidents recalled (including Richelieu's mockery of the Duc) probably relate to that period. However, Bernard was disgraced in 1638–9 and fled from France until after Richelieu's death.

[16] Desmarets may be queried as the last 'bouffon du Roi' without materially affecting the interest of the identification if a certain L'Angély is regarded as still within the jester tradition under Louis XIV, and not as a postscript to it. By the early years of the personal reign of Louis XIV, when Molière played 'plaisants de Cour' in *La Princesse d'Élide* and *Les Amants magnifiques*, the vanished office is recalled as a theatrical convention, later romanticized in the Triboulet of Victor Hugo's *Le Roi s'amuse* and the counterpart in Verdi's *Rigoletto*. See J. Emelina, *Les Valets et les servantes dans le théâtre comique en France de 1610 à 1700* (Cannes and Grenoble, 1975), 27.

Finally, in any attempt to understand the operation of the French government at the beginning of the personal reign of Louis XIV, it must also matter that Desmarets's prosecution of Simon Morin was not a private affair but conducted in close consultation with the Conseil de Conscience.

To the historiography of Desmarets, Jansenist hostility was crucial, because Jansenist condemnation of Desmarets in relation to Morin and theatre distorted the record. Not the least astonishing aspect of Nicole's *Visionnaires* is the image of Desmarets it imposed as a writer whose novels and plays, written to entertain and edify, poison souls. Richelieu's 'creatures' are seldom remembered as edifying. 'Les Beaux esprits auroient suivi leurs exemples, si ce n'etoit qu'ils ne sont pas grands édificateurs,' writes La Fontaine, somewhat unfairly, of Richelieu's secretaries of state, paraphrasing a letter from Costar to Voiture.[17] Contrast *Aspasie*, *Scipion*, and the preface to *Rosane*, exemplary works written when Desmarets was most in favour with the Cardinal. All reflect the idealism of the Député Surintendant des fortifications whose 'Discours de la poësie' challenged Cardinal Richelieu in 1633: 'Rends nostre siecle illustre en lettres comme en armes.'

Arguably, as early as the end of the century of Louis XIV the privileged perspective in which the Latin and Greek civilizations were perceived by the ancients promoted the interests of all those of any descent who learned Latin and Greek. Relegation to the literary scrap-heap of national epics like *Clovis*, which celebrate the 'medieval' origins of the monarchy and of great noble families of France, must have helped to undermine the cultural prestige of the monarchy and of the celebrated families.

In the eighteenth century Voltaire had no interest in redeeming perception of Desmarets's career, aspects of which conflict with his purposes in *Siècle de Louis XIV*. After the revolution of 1789, historians of the *ancien régime* continued to neglect an office-holder who was not a minister of state, while literary history focused on the period of Louis XIV's early patronage *c*.1660–85. Later, in the nineteenth century, nothing in the politics of French education under the Third Republic made Desmarets's career an attractive subject of

---

[17] Costar had written: 'Nous autres beaux esprits nous ne sommes pas grands édificateurs', quoted by M. J. Pretina, Jr., 'Vincent Voiture, Creation and Reality: a Study of his Prose', (Yale Ph.D. thesis, 1967), 14.

serious research. On the contrary, separation of Church and State fostered academic neglect of French religious experience. The literary *license-ès-lettres* taken in French, Latin, and Greek under the Third Republic clearly favoured the ancients in the Quarrel of the ancients and moderns, consecrating the notion of a French classicism.

In *Le Triomphe de Louis et de son siècle* [Fig. 14], however, Desmarets was the first to celebrate the century of Louis XIV as the beginning of French cultural hegemony in Europe:

> Nos voisins n'ont plus de Genies
> Dont leurs Etats soient glorieux.
> Toutes clartez y sont ternies,
> Ou viennent reluire en ces lieux.
> Tous cherchent ta splendeur, voyant que tu ramasses
> Le sçavoir et les Arts, les vertus & les graces,
> Radoucissant pour tous l'éclat que nous voyons.[18]

Of course, Desmarets underestimates genius foreign to France: Sir Isaac Newton (1642–1727), for instance, whose researches were already reported in the then-new *Journal des savants*, or John Dryden. In other important areas of cultural and military activity, however, Desmarets's boast is not unsound. The French language was learnt, French fashions copied, French manners studied, and French neo-classical theatre imitated throughout Europe for over a century. Anticipated in now almost forgotten ways by the château de Richelieu, Versailles became the most prestigious seat of government, architecturally and politically. Until the end of Louis XIV's reign French armies were matched only by great alliances.

It is scarcely necessary to repeat Nussbaum's judgement that 'the intellectualism with which the Europeans [of this period] undertook the mastery of the rest of their world was not extended to the problem of their relations as Europeans with each other'.[19] Desmarets's *Europe* had at least addressed that unresolved problem. Desmarets is no less and no more guilty than Boileau or Racine in celebrating French military victories; but from *Le Ballet de la Félicité* to *Le Triomphe de Louis et de son siècle* he also celebrates self-mastery, peace, and two themes later associated with the eighteenth-century—the pursuit of happiness and enlightened despotism:

---

[18] *Le Triomphe de Louis*, 29.
[19] Nussbaum, *The Triumph of Science*, p. xiii.

LE TRIOMPHE
DE LOUIS
ET
DE SON SIECLE.
POEME LYRIQVE,
Dedié
AU ROY.
J. DES-MARESTS.

A PARIS,
Chez JACQUES LE GRAS, au Palais.
NICOLAS LE GRAS, au troisiéme Pilier de la grande Salle
du Palais, à L. Couronnée.
AUGUSTIN BESOIGNE, dans la grande Salle du Palais, vis-à-vis
la Cour des Aydes.
Et CLAUDE AUDINET, ruë de Amandiers, à la Verité Royale,
devant le College des Graffins.

M. DC. LXXIV.
AVEC PERMISSION.

Figure 14 *Le Triomphe de Louis*

Faire l'heur des mortels est le bonheur supréme:
La plus grande victoire est se vaincre soy-mesme:
Sans une longue paix nul Siecle n'est fameux.
         Si pour le repos de la Terre
         La Paix triomphe de la Guerre.
Par de plus doux rayons tu seras lumineux.[20]

Here enlightenment is still a religious notion: the Sun King luminous because illuminated by the invisible light of God. How differently the eighteenth-century enlightenment might have begun had the old poet managed to persuade with this conditional prophecy.

----

[20] *Le Triomphe de Louis*, 32.

Bibliography

In both Bibliography and Notes, the place of publication is Paris unless otherwise stated.

A. Corpus Maresianum

Separately printed titles (including ballet verse) in order of first publication, followed by posthumous works and manuscript writings. For anthologized pieces, inscriptions, notarized documents, and lost works, see Introduction (15–17) and text, *passim*.

LIST OF ABBREVIATIONS

achevé	'achevé d'imprimer'
BA	Bibliothèque de l'Arsenal, Paris
BL	British Library, London
BN	Bibliothèque Nationale, Paris
Brunet	J.-C. Brunet, *Manuel du Libraire*, 5th edn. (1860–6)
CF	Bibliothèque de la Comédie-Française, Paris
ded.	dedicated (to)
edn. (edns.)	edition(s)/separate printing(s)
engr.	engraved (by)
ex lib.	ex-libris
Folger	Folger Shakespeare Library, Washington
front.	frontispiece
illus.	illustrations/illustrated (by)
l. (ll.)	leaf (leaves)
LC	Library of Congress, Washington
Mazarine	Bibliothèque Mazarine, Paris
n.d.	no date
n.p.	no place
NUC	USA *National Union Catalog*
NL	Newberry Library, Chicago
d'Olivet	Pellisson and d'Olivet, *Histoire de l'Académie-Françoise* (1729)
priv.	*privilège*
TI	Taylor Institution, Oxford
Tchemerzine	A. Tchemerzine, *Bibliographie des éditions originales et rares d'auteurs français des XVe, XVIe, XVIIe et XVIIIe siècles* (1927–34)

tit.   title-page
UL   University Library
vol. (vols.)   volume(s)

1. SEPARATELY PRINTED TITLES

Descriptions simplified; titles normally omitted and entries stylized for reprints and unseen translations; entries expanded for 'bibliothèque elsevirienne' and owners of exceptional interest; locations in parentheses following each entry.

1.01 *Articles accordez par la Clemence du Roy. A Monsieur Prudent Lieutenant du Chateau de Caen. Et ceux qui ont esté refusez pour le regard de Monsieur le Cheualier de Vendosme . . . Le tout Recueilli par le Sieur Des-marests deputé pour les fortifications de l'Armée du Roy, present en ladicte affaire*, Isaac Mesnier (1620), 8vo, 16 pp. (BN)

2.01 *Le Voyage de Fontainebleau, faict par Monsieur Bautru & Desmarets. Par Dialogue* (n.p. 1623), 8vo, 21 pp. Probably by Bautru and Desmarets. (BN)

3.01 *L'Entreprise des Rochelois descouuerte . . . Ensemble vn recit veritable de ce qui s'est passé pres la ville de Bourdeaux, à l'encontre de quelques Espagnols. L'execution à mort d'vn marchand Bourdelois, pour auoir traficqué auec lesdits Espagnols contre les Ordonnances de sa Majesté. Le tout suiuant le memoire envoyé par le Sieur des Marests, à Monsieur de la Tisardiere, Gentilhomme ordinaire de la Chambre de sa Maiesté, le 26. Aoust 1625*. Veuve du Carroÿ (1625), 8vo, 12 pp. (BN)

4.00 Ariane

4.01 *Ariane premiere* [*seconde*] *partie . . . chez la veufe Mathiteu* [*sic*] *Guillemot* (1632), 2 vols., 8vo. i: engr. tit., [16 minus 1–4], 523 pp.; ii: engr. tit., 423 [3] pp. 'Epistre' sig. DE BOISVAL. Ded. 'Aux Dames'. *Priv.* 10 years 21 Jan. 1632, achevé 10 Mar. 1632. (Folger, ex lib. David Garrick; J. G. Aspin cat. no. 72 (1984), 14). This edn. evidently escaped the notice of Tchemerzine and of M. Lever, *La Fiction narrative en prose au XVII*e *siècle* (1976), 71.

4.02/?03 Another edn. with same engr. tit., 2 vols., 8vo. i: engr. tit., 574 pp.; ii: 4 ll., 438 pp. (BL, BN, Sorbonne; a second BL 8vo part-copy may represent a third edn.)

4.04 *L'Ariane de Monsieur Des Marets, Conseiller du Roy, et Controlleur general de l'Extraordinaire des guerres. De nouueau reueuë ęt augmentée de plusieurs figures*. Chez Matthieu Guillemot (1639), 4to. Engr. front., 4 ll., 775 pp., 16 illus. General *priv.* 20 years 14 Mar. 1639. Front. and plates engr. A. Bosse after C. Vignon. (BL, BA, BN)

4.05 *L'Ariane de Monsieur Des Marets, Conseiller du Roy, et Controlleur general de l'Extraordinaire des guerres. De nouueau reueuë, et augmentée de plusieurs Histoires par l'Autheur, Et enrichie de plusieurs figures.* Chez Matthieu Guillemot (1643), 4to. Engr. front., 4 ll., 774 pp. including 16 illus. from plates for 4.04. (TI, BA, BN, Princeton UL, *ex meis*)

4.06 Rouen, I. Boulley (1644), 2 vols., 12 mo. (NL)

4.07 Leiden, F. de Hegher (1644), 2 vols., 12 mo. Plates copied from 4.04 or 4.05. '[Edn.] que quelques curieux placent dans la collection elsevirienne', Brunet. (BL, Manchester UL, BN)

4.08 Rouen, I. Besongne or I. Calloue (1651), 2, 12mo. Two states of one edn. (Chicago UL, Columbia UL)

4.09 Lyons, C. La Rivière (1661), 2 vols., 12mo. (Brown UL, Harvard UL)

4.10 Rouen, et se vend à Paris par la Cie des marchands libraires du Palais (1666), 2 vols., 12mo. (BA, LC)

4.11 Cie des Libraires (1724), 3 vols., 12mo. (BA, BN, Yale UL)

4.12 *Ariana, as it was Translated out of French and Presented to my Lord Chamberlain* (London, 1636), folio. (BL, *NUC* (3))

4.13 New edn. (London, 1641). (BL, Manchester UL, *NUC* (11))

4.14 *Von der schönen Ariana . . . erstlich von dem französischen Herren Des Marets . . . in hoch teutsche Sprach übersetzet* (Frankfurt am Main, 1643), 8vo, illus. (BN)

4.15 Flemish translation (1644). (Brunet)

4.16 *Ariana, in frantzösischen Spraach beschreiben, und aus derselben in Teusch gegeben durch G. A. Richter* (Leiden, 1644), 8vo. (Bodley, Princeton UL)

4.17 Dutch translation. Amsterdam, Elzevier (1658), 2 vols., 12mo. Plates from Leiden edn., 1644 [4.15 and/or 4.16]. (Brunet)

4.18 German translation. Amsterdam, Elzevier (1659). Same plates as 4.17. (Brunet)

4.19 *Ariana, Staats-u.-Liebes-Geschichte* (Frankfurt am Main, 1705), 8vo. (*Gesamtverzeichnis des deutsch-Sprachigen Schriftums (GV) 1700–1910*, vol. 28)

4.20 *Der schönen Ariana anmutige Staats und Liebesgeschicte des Herrn des Marets, übersetzt von Talandern* (Frankfurt am Main, 1708). (Brunet)

4.21 *D'Onvergelijkelijke Ariane. Vertaalt door J. J. Schipper* (Amsterdam, 1714), illus. (*NUC*)

5.00 Aspasie

5.01 *Aspasie, comedie*, Iean Camusat (1636), 4to, 2 ll., 94 pp., 1 l. *Priv.* 14 Feb. 1636. (BL, BA (3), BN (4), CF)

5.02 Henry Le Gras (1640), 4to. Reprinted for 14.01.

5.03 In *Théâtre françois*, vii (1737), 245–350.

6.01 *Les Amours du Compas & de la Regle, & ceux du Soleil & de l'Ombre*: 'piéce d'environ 200 vers' (1637), 4to. (d'Olivet)

7.00 Les Visionnaires

7.01 *Les Visionnaires, comedie*, Iean Camusat (1637), 4to. 6 ll., 125 pp., [1 p]. *Priv.* 7 years 20 July 1637. (BA (2), Harvard UL, Yale UL)

7.02 *Seconde Edn.*, Camusat (1639) 12mo. Front. engr. A. Bosse dated 1638. Issued also in *Theatre françois des sieurs de Scudéry, Tristan, Desmarets et autres*, A. Courbé (1648)—a collected edn. (BA, BN (2))

7.03 '*Sur l'imprimé à Paris*' [pirated from 7.02]. (BA)

7.04 Henry Le Gras (1640), 4to. Reprinted for 14.01. Locations include three modified states: (*a*) with full tit. (1640), (*b*) with half-title in *Œuvres poëtiques*, and (*c*) with full tit. as reissued by Le Gras in 1644. (BL, BA (4), BN (4), CF, *NUC* (4))

7.05 Rouen, Iacques Herault (1646), 12mo. (ex lib. R. Lebègue)

7.06 '*Dernière Edn / Suiuant la Copie imprimée*' . . . (1648), 12mo. [Leiden, Elzeviers, according to Brunet: apparently pirated from 7.04]. (BA)

7.07 Toulouse, Arnaud Colomiez and Jean Brocour (1652), 12mo. (U California at Los Angeles)

7.08 '*Seconde Edn*'. Lyons, Claude La Rivière (1653), 8vo. Apparently reprinted from 7.02. (CF)

7.09 'Par Mr. Corneille'. / *Sur l'imprimé* [pirated from 7.05] (1659), 12mo. (BL)

7.10 Nicolas Bessin (1663), 12mo. (BN (2), Mazarine, Harvard UL)

7.11 Claude Audinet (1676), 12mo. (CF, *ex meis*)

7.12 In *Théâtre françois* (1705).

7.13 In *Voyage de MM. Bachaumont et La Chapelle* (Amsterdam, 1708).

7.14 In *Recueil de pièces choisies* (The Hague, 1714).

7.15 In *Nouveau Théâtre françois* (Utrecht, 1735).

7.17 In *Théâtre françois*, vii (1737), 103–243.

7.18 In *Recueil de pièces galantes* [*de la Comtesse de la Suze*] (Trévoux, 1748).

7.19 In *Recueil de pièces galantes* (Trévoux, 1750).

7.20 Separate edn. Didot jeune (1800).

7.21 In E. Fournier (ed.), *Le Théâtre français au XVIᵉ et XVIIᵉ siècles*, ii (1871), 353–432; based on 7.04.

7.22 In T. Martel (ed.), *Comédies du XVIIᵉ siècle* (1888), pp. 1–86; based on 7.13.

7.23 Ed. H. G. Hall, Société des Textes Français Modernes (1963); based on 7.01.

7.24 In *Théâtre du XVIIᵉ siècle*, ed. J. Scherer and J. Truchet, (2 vols.; 1975–86), ii, 405–92, 1354–77; based on 7.23.

7.25 *Bly-spel van der Grillagers, naa de franse Visionnaires* (Amsterdam, 1658), 4to. (BN)

7.26 *I Visionarj*, transl. P. Rossi. (Venice, 1737). (G. S. Santangelo and C. Vinti, *Le Traduzioni italiane del teatro comico francese* (Rome, 1981), p. 100.)

8.00 Scipion

8.01 *Scipion, tragicomedie*, Henry Le Gras (1639), 4to, 4 ll., 90 pp., 1 l. Front. engr. A. Bosse after C. Vignon. Ded. Cardinal Richelieu. General *priv.* 20 years 14 March 1639, achevé 18 March 1638. (BL, BA (2), BN, *NUC* (4)) Collected in 14.01; the 4to edn. (1641) mentioned by Brunet and the copy Antoine de Sommaville (1641) (*NUC* for UL Southern California) would appear to be states of this edn.

8.02 Another edn. (1644), 12mo. (CF)

8.03/04 Dutch translations (1651, 1657). (J. Bauwens, *La Tragédie française et le théâtre hollandais* (Amsterdam, 1921), 262.)

9.01 *Ballet de la Félicité sur le suiet de l'heureuse naissance de Monseigneur le Dauphin. Dansé à S. Germain, à l'Hôtel de Richelieu, & à la Maison de Ville, Gazette* no. 30, 12 March 1639, 137–47. Partly by Desmarets. (BN)

9.02 Libretto. May have preceded 9.01. Poems by Desmarets included in 14.01. (BN)

10.00 Rosane

10.01 *Rosane, histoire tirée de celle des Romains et des Perses*. Dédiée à Madame la Duchesse d'Esguillon. Par Mr Desmaretz. Con[seill]er du Roy . . . Premiere partie, Henry Le Gras 1639, 8vo. Engr. tit., 13 ll., 541 pp., [1 p.]. General *priv*. 14 March 1639, achevé 17 Sept. 1639. Tit. engr. A. Bosse after C. Vignon. (BA, BN, Duke UL)

10.02 *La Rosana, istoria cavata dalle romane e persiane del sig. de'Marassi, algarizata dal francese per F. F. D. B.* (Venice, 1650). (BA)

11.00 Roxane

11.01 *Roxane, tragicomedie*, Henry Le Gras (1640). 4to, 4 ll., 88 pp. Ded. Cardinal Richelieu. General *priv*. 14 Mar. 1639, transferred to Le Gras 12 June 1640. Tit. vignette A. Bosse after C. Vignon. Collected in 14.01. The '4to edn. 1641' listed by Brunet may be another state of this edn. (BN. LC, Harvard UL)

11.02 Henry Le Gras (1640), 12mo, 4 ll., 83 pp., 1 p. Achevé 20 July 1640. Tit. vignette as in 11.01, which it may have preceded. (*ex meis*)

11.03 Henry Le Gras (1647), 4to. Text somewhat revised; tit. vignette absent in Yale UL copy. Replaces 11.01 in some copies of 14.01. (BN, Yale UL)

11.04 '*Sur l'imprimé à Paris chez Henry Le Gras*' (1648), 8vo. Probably the 1648 '4to' listed by Brunet. (BA)

11.05 *Roxane, tragicomedie.* (n.p., n.d.), 12mo. Listed by BN as '1639 . . . 8vo', 1639 perhaps a misprint for 1659. (BN)

12.01 *Psaumes de Davide paraphrasés, et accommodés au Regne de Louis le Juste*, Henry Le Gras (1640), 4to. May have been issued separately from 14.01. Reprinted in 27.01–27.03. (Goujet, *Bibliothèque françoise* (1741–56).)

13.01 *Pour une Mascarade des Graces et des Amours s'adressans à Mme la Duchesse d'Aiguillon sous le nom de Sylvie. En présence de Mme la Princesse* [*de Condé*] *et Mlle de Bourbon* (n.p., n.d. [1640?]). Poems, pp. 67 ff., some also in 14.01. (McGowan, *L'Art du ballet de cour en France (1581–1643)* (1963), 307.)

14.00 Œuvres poëtiques

14.01 *Œuvres poëtiques du Sieur Desmarets, Con*[*seill*]*er du Roy et Controlleur gen*[*er*]*al de l'extraordinaire des guerres*, Henry Le Gras (1641),

4to. Partly a collected edn. of four (later five) verse plays: 11.01 (later 11.03), 8.01, 7.04, 5.02, and later 19.01 (5.02 and perhaps 7.04 specially reprinted for 14.01), together with 'Autres Œuvres poëtiques' (including 12.01 and part of 13.01) (pp. [75]–80, 5–20, 6 (sometimes 7) ll., 21–109) and later 23.01. General *priv.* 14 Mar. 1639, achevé 20 Nov. 1640. Tit. engr. Stefano della Bella. Extracollational ll. on death of Marquis de Fors appear to be a stop-press addition. Some copies also contain 19.01 and/or 24.01. (BA (2), BN (3), *NUC* (4))

15.00 Mirame

15.01 *Ouverture du Theatre de la Grande Salle du Palais-Cardinal: Mirame, tragicomedie*, Henry Le Gras (1641), folio. Engr. tit., 1 l., 110 pp., 5 plates. Ded. Louis XIII. General *priv.* 14 Mar. 1639, transferred to Le Gras 16 Mar. 1639 (*sic*). Tit. and plates engr. Stefano della Bella. (BA (3), BN)

15.02 Another edn. (1641), 12mo, no illus. (BA, Harvard U). Brunet, Tchemerzine, *et al.* list a 4to edn. (1641), doubtless after d'Olivet, who must mean 15.01. *Mirame* occurs in no known copy of 14.01.

15.03 Another edn. (1642), 12mo. (BL)

15.04 '*Jouxte la copie imprimée à Paris*' (1642), 12mo. 'Elseviers de Leyde', according to Brunet. (Brunet)

15.05 *Die Heldenreiche Mirame, oder: die Unglückseelig-verliebte Printzessin aux Bythinien. Trauer-Freuden-Spiel aus dem Französischen des Herrn des Marets* (Görlitz [Zgorzelec], 1662), 8vo. (BL)

16.01 *Ballet de la Prospérité des armes de la France* (n.p., [1641]), 4to. (BN)

17.00 Érigone

17.01 *Erigone, tragicomedie*, Henry Le Gras (1642), 12mo, 127 pp., [1 p.]. General *priv.* 14 Mar. 1639, transferred to Le Gras 16 Mar. 1642. (BL, BA, BN, *ex meis*)

18.01 *Sur la Maladie de Monseigneur le Cardinal. Elegie.* (n.p., n.d. [1642]), 4to, 4 pp. (BN)

18.02 *Récit des vers présentez à Monseigneur le Cardinal sur sa Maladie.* (n.p., n.d. [1642]), 4to. 18.01 set as prose. Reprint as verse in 23.01. (BN)

19.00 Europe

19.01 *Europe. Comedie heroique*, Henry Le Gras (1643), 4to. Engr. front., 4 ll., 101 pp., [3 pp.]. *Priv.* to Le Gras for 20 years 2 Dec. 1642, achevé

13 Jan. 1643. Added to some copies of 14.01. The '4to edn. 1648' listed by Brunet not found. (BL, BA (2), BN (2), Yale UL)

19.02 Henry Le Gras (1643), 12mo, 4 ll., 82 pp. (73–4 omitted), 2 ll. (BL, BA, BN, Columbia UL)

19.03 'A Leyde, par Severin Matthiev, *Iouxte la Copie de Paris*. Chez Gualtier de Haes, anno 1643', 8vo, pp. 1–94, 1 l. (BA)

19.04 '*Sur l'imprimé* [18.01 or 18.02]' [1643?]. 4 ll., pp. 1–93, 2 ll. (BN)

19.05 Charles de Sercy (1661), 12mo. (BA)

19.06? The edn. 'New York, Institute of French Studies' announced as 'republished with an introduction by M. H. Kelley' in *The Year's Work in Modern Language Studies* for 1935/6 could (in 1957) not be located either by LC or by the late Justin O'Brien of that Institute. No copy known.

20.01 *Sonnet* (n.p., n.d. [1643]), 4to, 1 l. 'Armand si tu pouuois hors du plomb qui t'enserre'. Reprinted in 23.01 etc. (BN)

21.01 *Tombeau du grand Cardinal Duc de Richelieu*, Henry Le Gras (1643), 4to, 16 pp. Reprinted in 23.01 etc. (BN)

21.02 Another edn. (1677), 4to, 16 pp. (BN)

22.01 *A la Reyne Régente, sur la Bataille de Rocroy gagnée par Monseigneur le Duc d'Enghien. Ode*, Henry Le Gras (1643), 4to, 8 pp. Reprinted in 23.01. (BN)

23.01 *Odes, poëmes et autres œuvres*. [Henry Le Gras (1643)], 4to, 28 pp. Added to 14.01. (BN, Yale UL)

24.01 *A son Altesse Royale Monseigneur le Duc d'Orleans, sur la Prise de Graueline. Poëme* (n.p., n.d. [1644]), 4 pp. Added to some copies of 23.01 and 14.01. (Yale UL)

25.00 Cartes des Rois de France

25.01 *Cartes des Rois de France. Jeu des Reynes renommées. Géographie* . . . Henry Le Gras (n.d. [1644–5]). Ded. Anne of Austria. 'Cartes avec texte divisées en 3 parties, montées en 1 vol. in 8vo'. May contain first issues of the *Cartes des Rois* and *Jeu des Reynes* (1644) and of the *Jeu de la Géographie* (1645); wants *Jeu des Fables* (1645). Captions by Desmarets, engr. Stefano della Bella. (BN)

25.02 *Les Jeux de cartes des Roys de France, des Reines renommées, de la Géographie et des Fables* . . . *par J. D. M.*, Florentin Lambert (1664),

8vo. Engr. tit., ? ll., 60 pp., 195 plates. Text includes 26.01. Tit. and full set of 195 plates after 25.01. (BN; LC, incomplete)

25.03 *Jeux historiques des Rois de France, des Reines renommées, de la Géographie et de la Métamorphose, par feu M. J. Desmarets . . . et gravé par do la Bella (sic)*, N. Le Clerc and F. Le Comte (1698), 12mo, 4 vols. (BN; LC, incomplete)

26.01 *Lettre d'une Dame de Rennes à M. des Marests sur le Jeu des Reines renommées, avec la réponse de M. des Marests* (1645), 8vo, 60 pp. (Re?) printed in 25.02. (d'Olivet)

27.00 Office de la Vierge Marie

27.01 *Office de la Vierge Marie, mis en vers auec plusieurs autres prieres par I. Desmarests*, Henry Le Gras (1645), 12mo, 5 ll., 218 pp., 7 ll. Ded. Anne of Austria. 'Approbation' 26 Mar. 1645. (BA)

27.02 Another edn. (1647), 12mo. (LC)

27.03 *Prieres et Œuvres Chrestiennes. Dédiées à la Reine [Marie-Thérèse] par Jean Des-Marests, Seigneur de Saint-Sorlin, Conseilleur du Roy et Controoleur general de l'extraordinaire des guerres*, Denys Thierry (1669), 8vo (Tchemerzine gives '18mo'), 5 ll., 335 pp., [1 p.]. 27.01 with corrections and additions. (TI, BA)

28.01 *La Vérité des Fables, ou l'Histoire des dieux de l'antiquité*, Henry Le Gras (1648), 2 vols., 8vo. i: engr. tit., 17 ll., 640 pp., 7 ll.; ii: engr. tit., 675 (for 735) pp. (pp. 461–521 repeated), 8 ll. Ded. Anne of Austria. Engr. tit. signed 'C. Mellan inu[enit]'. General *priv.* 14 Mar. 1639, transferred to Le Gras 14 Nov. 1647, achevé 16 Nov. 1647. (BA, BN, Princeton U) Note: edn. reissued in two other states: (*a*) Florentin Lambert (1661) (BN) and (*b*) *L'Histoire des dieux, ou les Fables moralisées*, E. Loyson (1667). Neither (*pace* Tchemerzine) a new edn. nor a 12mo. (BA, BN)

29.01 *Les Promenades de Richelieu, ou les Vertus chrestiennes. Dediées à Madame la Duchesse de Richelieu. Par I. Desmarests Conseiller du Roy, Controolleur general de l'extraordinaire des guerres, Secretaire general de la Marine de Leuant, & Intendant de la Maison & affaires de M. le Duc de Richelieu*, Henry Le Gras (1653), 8vo, 1 l., 63 pp. General *priv.* 14 Mar. 1639, transferred n.d. to Henry Le Gras. 'De l'Imprimerie d'Antoine Vitré'. (TI, BA, BN, LC) Note: Substantial extracts reprinted as 'Les Beautez et les douceurs de la campagne. ou la Journée du solitaire' in 47.01 and as 'Les Sept Vertus chrestiennes' in 57.01.

30.00 L'Imitation de Jésus-Christ

30.01 *Les Quatre liures de l'Imitation de Jesus Christ traduits en vers par I. Des Marests*, Pierre Le Petit and Henry Le Gras [1654], 12mo. Engr. tit., 2 ll., pp. 1–275, [5 pp.], 1 l., 4 plates. General *priv.* 14 Mar. 1639 transferred to Le Petit and Le Gras on 2 June 1654, 'Approbation des docteurs' 2 July 1654, achevé 6 July 1654. (BA (2), BN, LC, *ex meis*)

30.02 Reprinted with 31.02 at Richelieu. Le Gras and Le Petit [1654], 12mo. Achevé 6 Oct. 1654. (BA)

30.03 '*Seconde édn*', Florentin Lambert (1661), 12mo. (BN)

30.04 Another edn. (1662), 12mo. (BL, BA)

31.00 Le Combat Spirituel

31.01 *Le Combat Spirituel ou de la perfection de la Vie Chrestienne; Traduction faite en vers. Par I. Desmarests. Imprimé, Au Chasteau de Richelieu*, Pierre le Petit and Henry Le Gras (1654), 12mo, 4 ll., 57 pp., [1 p.], achevé 24 Aug. 1654. (BL, BA, BN)

31.02 Reprinted with 30.02, q. v.

31.03 Another edn. (n.p. [Richelieu?], 'à la sphère', 1680), 12mo, 2 ll., 44 pp. (*ex meis*)

32.01 *Le Cantique des Cantiques, représentant le Mystére des Mystéres. Dialogue amoureux de Jésus-Christ avec la Volonté son Epouse, qui s'unit à lui en la réception du Saint Sacrement* (1656). 'Approbation' 18 Mar. 1656. Reprinted in 35.01. (d'Olivet = (?) BA 8o T.7068)

33.01 *Le Cantique de degrez, ou les quinze Psaumes Graduels, contenant les quinze degrez par lesquels l'Ame s'élève à Dieu* (1657), 12mo. 'Approbation' 5 July 1657. Reprinted in 35.01. (d'Olivet)

34.00 Clovis

34.01 *Clovis, ou la France chrestienne. Poëme heroique. Par I. Desmarests*, Augustin Courbé, Henry Le Gras, and Iacques Roger (1657), 4to. Engr. tit., front., 17 ll., 464 pp., 27 further plates. General *priv.* 14 Mar. 1639 transferred 5 Apr. 1657 to Courbé, Le Gras, and Roger, who transferred it with copies in stock to Florentin Lambert on 12 Sept. 1659, achevé 6 Apr. 1657. Ded. Louis XIV. For illus. see text. (BL, TI, BA (3), BN (2), *NUC* (8), ex lib. F. R. Freudmann) Note: edn. reissued in two other states: (*a*) Florentin Lambert (1661). (BN, Yale UL); (*b*) Louis de Heuqueville (1681). (Bibliothèque Municipale, Marseilles).

34.02 'A LEYDE, Par les ELZEVIRS' (1657), 12mo. Reprints text of 34.01. Considered a pirated edn.: Grenoble, according to Kerviler, *Jean Desmaretz*, 88; Rouen, according to R. Toinet, *Quelques Recherches autour des poëmes héroïques-épiques du XVIIe siècle* (2 vols.; Tulle, 1899–1907), i, 180. I wonder. (BL, TI, BN, ex lib. R. A. Sayce)

34.03 '*Sur l'imprimé . . . A LEYDE. Par les ELZEVIRS . . . Auec Permission & Approbation*' (1658), 8vo. Probably the same pirated edn. as the 'small 12mo' mentioned by Toinet (op. cit., i, 180), as printed perhaps at Avignon. Contains neither 'Permission' nor 'Approbation'. (TI)

34.04 *Clovis, ou la France chrestienne. Poëme Heroïque. Enrichy de plusieurs figures. Par I. Desmarests.* Issued in two states: (*a*) Théodore Girard (1666), 12mo. Front., 17 ll., pp. 1–347, 24 plates. Illus. copied for Livres I–XXIV only onto single small plates from 34.01 by Le Doyen. General *priv.* 14 Mar. 1639 transferred 5 Apr. 1657 to M. Bobin, N. Le Gras, and T. Girard. This edn. achevé 29 Aug. 1665. (*NUC* (8), J. G. Aspin catalogue no. 29 (1970)); (*b*) Michel Bobin & Nicolas Le Gras (1666). (BA, ex lib. R. J. Hayhurst)

34.05 *Clovis ou la France chrestienne. Poëme, Reveu exactement, & augmenté d'inventions, & des actions merveilleuses du Roi. Dédié à Sa Majesté pour la seconde fois. Par I. Desmarests, Controlleur General de l'Extraordinaire des Guerres. Troisiéme édition,* Claude Cramoisy (1673), 8vo, 24 ll., pp. 1–413, 1–102, 1 l. For front matter of 34.01 substitutes a new epistle 'Au Roy' and 'Discours pour prouver que les sujets Chrestiens sont les seuls propres à la poësie Héroïque', rearranges narrative in twenty instead of twenty-six Livres, updates royal allusions, and adds a 'Traité pour juger des Poëtes Grecs, Latins, et François' largely reprinted from 48.01. General *priv.* 14 Mar. 1639 and (for 'Traité') *priv.* 7 years 13 Apr. 1670. 'De l'imprimerie de la Veuve Edme Martin'. (Advocates Library Edinburgh, BA (3), BN (2), *NUC* (2))

34.06 Ed. F. R. Freudmann. Louvain, Nauwelaerts, and Paris, Béatrice-Nauwelaerts (1972). Facsimile of 34.01 with introduction, notes, arguments, glossary, index, bibliography, and a 'Notice bibliographique' by H. G. Hall. Reprints tit., 'Epistre', and 'Discours pour prouver que les sujets chrétiens' from 34.05, 50.01, and M. Petit, *Étude sur le Clovis de Desmarets* (Le Mans, 1868).

35.00 Les Délices de L'Esprit

35.01 *Les Delices de l'Esprit: Dialogues dediez aux Beaux Esprits du Monde. Enrichis de Plusieurs Figures, et divisez en quatre parties. Par I. Desmarests,* Augustin Courbé, Henry Le Gras, and Iacques Roger (1658), folio. 5 vols.

in one. i: engr. tit., 9 ll., 125 [for 123] pp., [8 pp.], 8 plates; ii: engr. tit., 63 pp., [6 pp.], 5 plates; iii: engr. tit., 8 ll., 195 pp., [13 pp.], 2 plates; iv: engr. tit., 8 ll., 153 pp., [4 pp.], pp. 161–241, [26 pp.], 1 plate; [v]: 75 [for 83] pp., [8 pp.], 4 plates. Also ded. Cardinal Mazarin. Parts i–iv comprise thirty dialogues; [v] contains 33.01, 32.01, 'Instructions pour l'Oraison', and may contain 'Moyen pour s'élever à la Connoissance des Perfections de Dieu'. 'Approbations' 18 Mar. 1656 (for 32.01), 5 July 1657 (for 33.01), and 10 Apr. 1658 for parts i–iv. General *priv.* 14 Mar. 1639 transferred 12 Apr. 1658 to Courbé, Le Gras, and Roger, who transferred it with copies in stock to Florentin Lambert on 12 Sept. 1659, achevé 15 Apr. 1658. For illus. and ornamentation see text. (Glasgow UL, BA, BN, Abbaye de Royaumont, Columbia UL, Louisiana State UL, Berès catalogue 1977). Note: edn. reissued in two other states: (*a*) Florentin Lambert (1659). (BN, *NUC* (3)); (*b*) Florentin Lambert (1661). (BA, BN, *NUC* (8))

35.02 4to edn., tit. wanting: thirty dialogues only. pp. 1–34, 33–123, 1–112, 1–88 (84 for 88), 1–63. (BA)

35.03 Dialogues only. Augustin Besoigne and Claude Audinet (1675), 2 vols., 8vo. Vignettes as fold-outs (without headbands and tailpieces) from 35.01. (Manchester UL, BN (2), LC).

35.04 Dialogues. A. Besoigne (1676), 2 vols., 8vo. Vignettes as in 35.03. (Cornell UL, Rutgers UL)

35.05 Dialogues. C. Audinet (1677), 2 vols., 8vo. (BN)

35.06 Dialogues (n.p. [Richelieu?] 'à la sphère', 1680), 12mo. (Brunet)

35.07 *Les Délices de l'esprit. Entretiens sur la divinité, sur la religion et autres sujets*, A. Besoigne (1686), 8vo. (BA, *NUC* (3))

35.08 Another edn. (1687), 12mo. (Sorbonne)

35.09 Another edn. (1689), 12mo. (Edinburgh UL, Stanford UL)

35.10 *Les Délices de l'esprit, entretiens d'un chrétien et d'un athée sur la divinité, la religion, l'immortalité de l'âme, et autres sujets, par M. Des Marests*, A. Besoigne (1691), 12mo. (BN)

35.11 Spanish translation (not seen). (39.01, p. 31).

36.01 *Examen du livre, intitulé, L'Ancienne Nouveauté de l'Ecriture Sainte, ou, L'Eglise triomphante en terre* (n.p., n.d. [1661]). 'Bibliotecae Colbertinae'. (Mazarine)

37.00 Lettres Spirituelles

37.01 *Lettres spirituelles, recueillies par vn Ecclesiastique* [Jean de Lessot],

Florentin Lambert (1660–3), 12mo, 6 vols.: i–iii (1660), iv–v (1661), vi (1663). *c.* three hundred letters. 'Approbation' 17 Dec. 1659, *priv.* 10 years to Lambert 19 Dec. 1659, achevé 20 Dec. 1659 to 15 Sept. 1663. (BN: D 41552)

38.01 *La Vie et les Œuvres de Sainte Catherine de Gênes. Nouvelle édition plus nette et plus correcte*, Florentin Lambert (1661), 8vo, 2 vols., i: 8 ll., 300 pp.; ii: 5 ll., pp. 3–228. Contains biography of Catherine Adorni and her 'Dialogue'. 'Approbations' 25 Apr. and 20 Sept. 1597 and 3 Apr. 1661, *priv.* to Lambert 7 years 5 Apr. 1661, achevé 22 June 1661. New 'Approbation' and *priv.* attribute edn. to 'Iean Desmarests'. Issued in two states: (*a*) without name of editor (BN); (*b*) with mention 'Par Iean Desmarets'. (BN)

38.02 Another edn. (1661–2), 8vo, 2 vols. (BN)

38.03 Another edn. (1666–7), 8vo, 2 vols. (BN)

38.04 Another edn. (1667–1666), 12mo, 2 vols. (BL)

38.05 '*Troisiéme édition*', E. Michallet (1695–7), 8vo, 2 vols. (BN)

38.06 Valleyre (1743), 8vo, 2 vols. (BN)

39.00 Le Chemin de la Paix

39.01 *Le Chemin de la paix et celuy de l'inquiétude. Premiere Partie*, Claude Audinet (1665), 12mo, 22 ll., 266 pp., 1 plate. General *priv.* 20 years 14 Mar. 1639, transferred to Audinet 19 July 1665, achevé 31 July 1665. (BN)

39.02? Another edn. (1666). (Tchemerzine)

39.03 *Le Chemin de la paix et celuy de l'inquiétude. Seconde Partie contenant l'exode ou sortie des ames de la captivité spirituelle de l'Egypte*, Claude Audinet (1666), 12mo, 24 ll., 284 pp., 1 plate. *Priv.* as for 39.01, last used for this vol., achevé 30 Apr. 1666. (BN)

39.04 Another edn. (n.p. [Richelieu?] 'à la sphère', 1680). (*ex meis*)

40.01 *Response à l'insolente Apologie des religieuses de Port-Royal. Avec la découverte de la fausse Eglise des Iansenistes, et de leur fausse Eloquence. Presentée au Roy. Par le Sieur de S. Sorlin, Conseiller de sa Maiesté, & Controlleur general de l'Extraordinaire des Guerres.* Issued in two states: (*a*) Nicolas Le Gras and Claude Audinet (1666), 8vo, 29 ll., 340 pp. *Priv.* 5 years to 'Sieur de S. Sorlin' 3 Dec. 1665, transferred to the *libraires* 6 Dec. 1665, achevé 12 Dec. 1665. (BN (2) (one copy ex lib. Louis XIV), Minnesota UL); (*b*) Jean Couterot (1666). (BN)

41.01 *Seconde Partie de la Response à l'insolente Apologie de Port Royal avec la découverte de la fausse Eloquence des Iansenistes, et de leur fausse église nouvelle, et la response aux Lettres visionnaires. Presentée au Roy par le Sieur de S. Sorlin. Desmarests* . . . F. Muguet (1666), 12mo, 5 ll., 188 pp., 30 pp., 1 l. Achevé 2 Apr. 1666. (BN)

42.01 *Troisiesme Partie de la Response à l'insolente Apologie de Port-Royal, et aux lettres et libelles des Iansenistes, avec la découverte de leur arsenal sur le grand chemin de Charenton*, F. Muguet (1666), 12mo, 6 ll., 186 pp. Achevé 30 Aug. 1666. (BN)

43.01 *Au Roy sur sa Conqueste de la Franche-Comté.* Poëme, Claude Audinet (1668), 4to, 6 pp. Permis et achevé, 14 Mar. 1668. (BN)

44.01 *Quatriesme Partie de la Response aux insolentes Apologies de Port-Royal, contenant l'histoire et les dialogues présentés au Roi avec les remarques generales et particulieres sur la traduction du Nouveau Testament imprimé à Mons, par le Sieur de S. Sorlin Des-Marets*, J. Hénault (1668), 12mo, 12 ll., 228 pp. Achevé 18 June 1668. (BN)

45.01 *Marie-Madeleine, ou le Triomphe de la Grace. Poëme. Composé par Jean Des-Marets, Seigneur de S. Sorlin, Conseiller du Roy, & Controoleur General de l'Extraordinaire des Guerres*, Denys Thierry (1669), 12mo. Engr. front., 14 ll., 197 pp., [1 p]. *Priv.* 10 years 11 Oct. 1669. (BA (2), BN (2), NUC (4))

45.02 Reprinted in 57.01

46.01 *Esther. Poëme heroïque composé et dedié au Roy par le Sieur de Boisval*, Pierre Le Petit (1670), 4to, 90 pp. Contains verse preface 'L'Excellence et les plaintes de la Poësie Héroïque' and chants i–iv. Headbands by François Chauveau. *Priv.* 7 years 'au Sieur de Boisval' 6 Feb. 1670. (BN, NUC (3))

46.02 *Esther. Poëme. Dedié à Madame la Duchesse de Richelieu, Dame d'honneur de la Reyne. Par. I. Des-Marests, Conseiller du Roy, & Controlleur General de l'Extraordinaire des Guerres*, Iean Guignard (1673), 12mo, 96 pp. Contains chants i–vii with modifications, especially to chant iv, and 49.01. (BA)

47.01 *La Comparaison de la langue et de la poësie Françoise, avec la Grecque & la Latine, Et des Poëtes Grecs, Latins & François. Et les Amours de Protée et de Physis. Dediez aux beaux Esprits de France. Par le Sieur Des-Marests, Seigneur de Saint Sorlin, Conseiller du Roy, & Controlleur general de l'extraordinaire des guerres.* Issued in two states; (*a*) Thomas Jolly (1670), 12mo, 9 ll., 328 pp. *Priv.* 10 years 13 Apr. 1670, achevé 14 June 1670. (BN, NUC (3)); (*b*) Louis Billaine, as reprint in 47.03.

47.02 *Traité pour juger des Poëtes Grecs, Latins, et François.* Revised version issued in two states: (*a*) in 34.05, q.v.; (*b*) *Traité pour juger des Poëtes Grecs, Latins, et François*, Claude Cramoisy (1673), 8vo, 104 pp. (BN)

47.03 Facsimile of 47.01 (*b*) (Geneva, 1972).

48.01 *Regulus, ou le vray genereux. Poëme heroïque. Dedié à monsieur de Bartillat*, Laurent Rondet (1671), 4to, 42 pp. 'Avec permission'. 'Epistre' signed 'J. D. M.'. (BN, LC)

49.01 *Au Roy, sur la prise de Mastrich. Ode*, Sebastien Martin (1673), 8vo, 11 pp. Reprint in 46.02. (BN)

50.01 *Lettre de Monsieur Des-Marests, à Monsieur l'abbé de la Chambre. Sur le suiet d'un Discours Apologetique de Monsieur l'Abbé de Villeloin* [*Michel de Marolles*], *pour Virgile. Et de ses observations sur le Poëme de Clovis*, Sebastien Martin (1673), 12mo, 23 pp. 'Avec permission'. Reprint in 34.06. (BN)

51.01 *Indignation. A Monseigneur le Duc de Richelieu. Ode.* (n.p., n.d., [1673]), 8vo, 16 pp. (BN)

52.01 *La Deffense du Poëme heroïque, avec quelques remarques sur les Œuvres satyriques du Sieur D***. Dialogues en Vers & en Prose*, Jacques Le Gras, Nicolas Le Gras, Augustin Besoigne, and Claude Audinet (1674), 4to, 5 ll., 136 pp. Priv. 25 July 1674, achevé 18 Aug. 1674. (Written in collaboration with Abbé Jacques Testu and Duc de Nevers.) (BA (4), BN (3), NUC (4))

52.02 Another edn. Jacques Le Gras *et al.* (1675), 4to, 8 ll., 141 pp., [1 p]. (BL, BN, NUC)

52.03 Reprint with 47.01 (*b*) in 47.03.

53.01 *Le Triomphe de Louis et de son siècle. Poëme Lyrique, Dedié au Roy. Par J. Des-Marests*, Jacques Le Gras, Nicolas Le Gras, Augustin Besoigne, and Claude Audinet (1674), 4to, 3 ll., 32 pp. (BA, BN)

54.01 *Au Roy sur sa seconde conqueste de la Franche-Comté. Stances* (n.p., n.d. [1674]), 4to, 6 pp. Signed 'Des-Marests'. (BN)

55.01 *Traduction. Du mépris injuste qu'on fait des Poëtes Latins. Elegie* [by Jean de Santeul] (n.p., n.d. [1674?]), 8vo, [4 pp]. Addressed to Charles Perrault. Reprinted in 56.01 and 47.03. (BN)

56.01 *La Defense de la Poësie, et de la Langue Françoise. Addressée à Monsieur Perrault*, Nicholas Le Gras and Claude Audinet (1675), 8vo, 30 pp. (BN (2))

2. POSTHUMOUS WORKS

57.01 *Poëmes sacrés* (n.p., [Richelieu?] 'à la sphère', 1678), 12mo, 11 ll., 137 pp. Publishes 57.02. Reprints 47.01 and part of 29.01 as revised for 45.01.

57.02 *Abraham, ou la vie parfaite. Poëme* (n.p. [Richelieu?] 'à la sphère', 1680), 12mo, 34 pp. (LC)

58.01 *Vertus, maximes, instructions, & meditations Chrestiennes* (n.p. 'à la sphère', 1678), 12mo, 22 pp. (Tchemerzine, who gives the place as Paris)

59.01 *Maximes Chrestiennes* (n.p. [Richelieu?] 'à la sphère', 1680), 12mo, 2 ll., 65 pp. (*ex meis*)

59.02 *Maximes Chrestiennes* (additional to 59.01) (n.p. [Richelieu?] 'à la sphère', 1687), 12mo, 22 pp. (*ex meis*)

60.01 'Relation de la découverte du faux Christ nommé Morin, chef des Illuminés', ed. F. Ravaisson, in *'Archives de la Bastille': Règne de Louis XIV (1661–1664)*, 1227–91.

61.01 'Ode [à Colbert]', ed. H. G. Hall, *Studi Francesi*, 21 (1977), 40–9.

62.01 MS notes on N. Faret, *Projet de l'Académie, pour servir à ses statuts*, ed. J. Rousselot (St-Etienne, 1983).

63.01 'Art de la poësie', ed. H. G. Hall, 'Desmarets de Saint-Sorlin's "Art de la poësie": Poetics or Politics?', forthcoming in D. L. Rubin (ed.), *Convergences: Rhetoric and Poetic in Seventeenth Century France* (Columbus, Ohio).

3. MANUSCRIPTS

Ballet and theatre

64.01 *Ballet de la Prospérité des armes de la France.* BN, Mss. fr. 24,375.

65.01 *Mirame.* BN, Mss. fr. n.a. 4724.

Verse manuscripts in alphabetical order

66.01 'A Monseigneur le Chancelier [Séguier], sur le retour du Roy à Paris en l'année 1649. Ode'. BN, Mss. fr. 20,035.

67.01 'L'Art de la poësie à Monseigneur le Cardinal-Duc de Richelieu', BA Mss. 4116.

68.01 'Au Roy sur sa seconde conqueste de la Franche Comté'. BN, Mss. fr. 13,647.

69.01 'Desmarets'. BN, Mss. fr. 19,145.

70.01 'Indignation à Monseigneur le Duc de Richlelieu. Ode'. BN, Mélanges des Mss. de Colbert, no. 37.

71.01 'Ode à Colbert'. BA, Mss. 5418.

72.01 'Vers de Monsieur des Marestz'. BA, Mss. 4129.

Correspondence

73.01 Avis de Desmarests à l'Académie-Françoise touchant le prix fondé par Balzac, BA, Mss. 5422.

74.01 Lettres à M. Desmarets d'une Dame de Rennes sur son Jeu des Reines renommées, avec la réponse de M. Desmarets [1644–5]. BA, Mss. 4119.

75.01 Lettres datées de Richelieu, 1652. BA, Mss. 3135.

Documents concerning Simon Morin

76.01 Déposition du Sr Jean Desmarests de S.-Sorlin contre Simon Morin, Déclaration de Morin, Arrêt de la Cour de Parlement, BA, Mss. 5758.

76.02 Déposition contre Simon Morin, BN, Mss. fr. n.a. 22,140.

77.01 Relation de la découverte du faux Christ nommé Morin, par Desmarets, l'aisné; Examen du livre imprimé intitulé *Les Pensées de Morin*; extraits de ces lettres; Abrégé du Procès. BA, Mss. 5421.

78.01 Desmarets, *Examen du livre intitulé 'L'Ancienne Nouveauté de l'Escriture Sainte'*. BN, Mss. fr. 2436.

B. Select Secondary Sources

The criteria adopted generally give preference to four categories of publication: (*a*) works specifically on Jean Desmarets and his family, (*b*) select memoirs and contemporary works with extensive or multiple reference to Desmarets, (*c*) works frequently consulted, e.g. those of Cioranescu and Moréri, and (*d*) works considered particularly useful for further reference. Literary works are generally cited to facilitate reference to any edition. Items of occasional reference are acknowledged in the notes and indexed.

ABRAHAM, C. K., *Gaston d'Orléans et sa cour* (Chapel Hill, 1964).

ADAM, A., *Histoire de la littérature française au XVIIe siècle* (5 vols.; 1956) (first publ. 1949–56).

APOSTOLIDÈS, J. M., *Le Roi-Machine: Spectacle et politique au temps de Louis XIV* (1981).

AUGUSTE, A., *Les Sociétés secrètes catholiques du* XVII*ᵉ siècle et H. M. Boudon* (1913).

BAYLE, P., 'Marests', in his *Dictionnaire historique et critique*, iv, 5th edn. (Amsterdam, 1734).

BEAUCHAMPS, P.-F. Godard de, *Recherches sur les theatres de France*, ii, (1735), 148–55.

BEIJER, A., 'Une maquette de décor récemment retrouvée pour le "Ballet de la Prospérité des armes de France" dansé à Paris, le 7 fevrier 1641', J. Jacquot (ed.), *Le Lieu théâtral à la Renaissance* (1964), 377–403.

BEIK, W. H., *Absolutism and Society in Seventeenth-century France: State Power and Provincial Aristocracy in Languedoc* (Cambridge, 1985).

BERGIN, J., *Cardinal Richelieu: Power and the Pursuit of Wealth* (New Haven and London, 1985).

BJURSTRÖM, P., *Giacomo Torelli and Baroque Stage Design* (Stockholm, 1961).

BLAND, D., *A History of Book Illustration*, 2nd edn. (London, 1959).

BONNEY, R. J., *Political Change in France under Richelieu and Mazarin, 1624–1661* (Oxford, 1978).

—— *The King's Debts. Finance and Politics in France, 1589–1661* (Oxford, 1981).

—— *Society and Government in France under Richelieu and Mazarin, 1624–61* (London, 1988).

BORNEMANN, W., *Boileau-Despréaux in Urtheile seines Zeitgenossen Jean Desmarets de Saint-Sorlin* (Heilbronn, 1883).

BREMOND, H., *Histoire littéraire du sentiment religieux en France*, vi (1922), 445–581.

BRIAND, R., 'Sur la découverte des *Lettres spirituelles de* Desmarets de Saint-Sorlin', XVII*ᵉ siècle*, 112 (1976), 41–6.

BRUN, P., 'La Critique littéraire et pédagogique: Roland Desmarets', in his *Autour du Dix-Septième siècle* (1901), 73–103.

CAILLET, M.-A., *Un Visionnaire du* XVII*ᵉ siècle* (1935).

CANOVA-GREEN, M.-C., 'Créatures et créateurs: les écrivains patronnés et le ballet de cour sous Louis XIII', *Papers on French Seventeenth Century Literature*, 15 (1988), 101–13.

CHAPELAIN, J., *Lettres*, ed. P. Tamizey de Larroque (3 vols.; 1883).

—— *Opuscules critiques*, ed. A. C. Hunter (1936).

CHURCH, W. F., *Richelieu and the Reason of State* (Princeton, 1972).

CIORANESCU, A., *Bibliographie de la littérature française du Dix-septième siècle* (3 vols.; 1965–6).

COGNET, L., *Le Jansénisme* (1960).

COULET, H., *Le Roman jusqu'à la Révolution* (2 vols.; 1967–8).

COUTON, G., *Richelieu et le théâtre* (Lyons, 1986).

DELAPORTE, P. V., *Du merveilleux dans la littérature française sous le règne de Louis XIV* (1891).

DELASSAULT, G. (ed.), *La Pensée janséniste en dehors de Pascal* (1963).

DESMARETS, R., *Epistolarum philologicarum Libri II* (1655).

—— 'Lettres philologiques *i* (1650)', transl. and ed. L. Sigaux (3 vols.; thèse de 3ᵉ cycle; Sorbonne, 1978).

DESMARETS DE SAINT-SORLIN, A., *Livre de touttes sortes de chyffres par alphabets redoublés* (1695).

DESSERT, D., *Argent, pouvoir et société au Grand Siècle* (1985).

DORIVAL, B., 'Art et politique en France au XVIIᵉ siècle: La Galerie des hommes illustres du Palais-Cardinal', *Bulletin de la Société de l'histoire de l'art française* (1973), 43–67.

DRYHURST, J., 'Les Idées de Jean des Marests, Sieur de Saint-Sorlin (1595–1676)' (Ph.D. thesis, Liverpool, 1963).

—— 'Evhémère ressuscité: *La Vérité des fables* de Desmarets', *Cahiers de l'Association internationale des études françaises*, 25 (1973), 281–93.

—— 'Des Marests, *Le Tartuffe* et l'ombre de Molière', *Revue d'Histoire littéraire de la France*, 74 (1974), 20–8.

DUBUISSON-AUBENAY, F.-N. Baudot de, *Journal des guerres civiles (1648–1652)*, ed. G. Saige (2 vols.; 1883–5).

DUCHESNE, J., *Histoire des poëmes épiques français du XVIIᵉ siècle* (1870).

ELLIOTT, J. H., *Richelieu and Olivares* (Cambridge, 1984).

FERRIER, N., *L'Image de Louis XIV dans la littérature française de 1660 à 1715* (1981).

FOUCAULT, M., *Histoire de la folie à l'âge classique* (1972).

FUMAROLI, M., *L'Age de l'éloquence* (Geneva, 1980).

GEBHARDT, R., *Jean Desmarets, Sieur de Saint-Sorlin, als Dramatischer Dichter* (Leipzig, 1912).

GILLOT, H., *La Querelle des Anciens et des Modernes en France* (1914).

GOODMAN, W. A., 'The Heroic Poems of Jean Desmarets de Saint-Sorlin', (Univ. of N. Carolina Ph.D. thesis, 1966).

GOUJET, C.-P., *Bibliothèque françoise ou Histoire de la littérature françoise*, xvii (1756).

GRIVEL, M., *Le Commerce de l'estampe à Paris au XVIIᵉ siècle* (Geneva and Paris, 1986).

HALL, H. G., 'Three Illustrated Works of Desmarets de Saint-Sorlin', *Yale University Library Gazette*, 33 (1958), 18–28.

—— 'Jean Desmarets de Saint-Sorlin: His Background and Reception in the Seventeenth Century' (Ph.D. thesis, Yale, 1958).

—— 'Racine, Desmarets de Saint-Sorlin and the 'Querelle des *Imaginaires*', *Modern Language Review*, 55 (1960), 181–5.

—— Desmarets de Saint-Sorlin's Ennoblement and Conversion Reconsidered', *French Studies*, 27 (1973), 151–64.

—— 'Aspects esthétiques et religieux de la Querelle des Anciens et des Modernes: Boileau et Desmarets de Saint-Sorlin', in M. Fumaroli (ed.), *Critique et création littéraire en France au XVIIᵉ siècle* (1977), 213–20.

HALL, H. G.,'From Extravagant Poet to the Writer as Hero', *Studies on Voltaire and the Eighteenth Century*, 183 (1980), 117–32.

—— 'A Polemical Parisian Wall Poster in 1666: Desmarets de Saint-Sorlin *vs*. Port-Royal', *Papers on French Seventeenth Century Literature*, 9 (16/ 2) (1982), 305–11.

—— (ed.), *A Critical Bibliography of French Literature, III A, The Seventeenth Century, Supplement* (Syracuse, NY, 1983).

—— '*Europe*, allégorie théâtrale de propagande politique', in J. Mesnard and R. Mousnier (eds.), *L'Age d'or du mécénat, 1598–1661* (1985), 319–27.

—— 'Desmarets de Saint-Sorlin's *Le Triomphe de Louis et de son siècle*: The Modern Position', in S. A. Zebouni (ed.), *Actes de Baton Rouge* (Biblio. 17, no. 25; Tübingen, Paris, and Seattle, 1986), 243–53.

—— 'Le Siècle de Louis le Grand: L'Evolution d'une idée', in L. Godard de Donville (ed.), *D'un siècle à l'autre: Anciens et Modernes* (Marseilles, 1987), 43–52.

HARTHAN, J., *The History of the Illustrated Book: The Western Tradition* (London, 1981).

HUET, P.-D., *Memoirs*, transl. J. Aiken (2 vols; London. 1810).

HUPPERT, G., *Les Bourgeois Gentilshommes: An Essay on the Definition of Elites in Renaissance France* (Chicago and London, 1977).

HUXLEY, A., *Grey Eminence: A Study in Religion and Politics* (London, 1949).

JAMES, E. D., *Pierre Nicole, Jansenist and Humanist: A Study of his Thought* (The Hague, 1972).

JANSEN, P., *Le Cardinal Mazarin et le mouvement janséniste français 1653–1659* (1967).

JAUSS, H. R., 'Asthetische Normen und geschichtliche Reflexion in der "Querelle des Anciens et des Modernes"', in Charles Perrault, *Parallèles des Anciens et des Modernes* (Munich, 1964), 8–64.

KERVILER, R., *Jean Desmaretz, Sieur de Saint-Sorlin, un des quarante fondateurs de l'Académie-Française* (1879).

KLEINMAN, R., *Anne of Austria: Queen of France* (Columbus, 1985).

LACHÈVRE, F., *Bibliographie des recueils collectifs de poésie publiés de 1597 à 1700* (5 vols.; 1901–22).

—— *Le Libertinage devant le Parlement de Paris; le procès du poète Théophile de Viau* (2 vols.; 1909).

—— *Les Recueils collectifs de poésies libres et satiriques publiées depuis 1600 jusqu'à la mort de Théophile* (1922).

LACOUR, L., *Richelieu dramaturge et ses collaborateurs* (1926).

LANCASTER, H. C., *A History of French Dramatic Literature in the Seventeenth Century* (9 vols.; New York, 1966) (first publ. Baltimore, 1929–42).

—— 'Le Château de Richelieu and Desmaretz's Visionnaires', *Modern Language Notes*, 60/3 (Mar. 1945), 167–72.

LASSALLE, J.-P., 'Un Esprit supérieur passionné d'architecture: Jean Desmarets de Saint-Sorlin . . .', *Cahiers de la Grande Loge provinciale d'Occitanie*, NS 3 (Feb., 1986), 23-7.

LAURAIN-PORTEMER, M., *Études mazarines* (1981).

LAWRENSON, T. E., *The French Stage & Playhouse in the XVIIth Century: A Study in the Advent of the Italian Order*, 2nd edn. (New York, 1986).

LEBLANC, P., *Les Paraphrases françaises des psaumes à la fin de la période baroque, 1610-1660* (Clermont-Ferrand, 1961).

LEINER, W., *Der Widmungsbrief in der französischen Literatur (1580-1715)* (Heidelberg, 1965).

LUBLINSKAYA, A. D., *French Absolutism: The Crucial Phase, 1620-29*, transl. B. Pearce (Cambridge, 1968).

MᶜGOWAN, M. M., *L'Art du ballet de cour en France (1581-1643)* (1963).

—— *The Court Ballet of Louis XIII: A Collection of Working Designs for Costumes 1615-33* (London, [1986]).

MANDROU, R., *Magistrats et sorciers en France au XVIIᵉ siècle, une analyse de psychologie historique* (1968).

MARTIN, H.-J., *Livre, pouvoirs et société à Paris au XVIIᵉ siècle (1598-1701)* (2 vols.; Geneva, 1969).

MASKELL, D., *The Historical Epic in France 1500-1700* (Oxford, 1973).

MÉTHIVIER, H., *Le Siècle de Louis XIV*, 6th edn. (1971) (first publ. 1950).

—— *L'Ancien Régime*, 3rd edn. (1966) (first publ. 1961).

—— *Le Siècle de Louis XIII*, 3rd edn. (1971) (first publ. 1964).

—— *La France de Louis XIV; Un grand règne?* (1975).

MONGRÉDIEN, G., 'Une Précieuse: Madame du Vigean (1600-1682)', *Revue de France*, 8, 4 (15 Feb., 1928), 666-91.

—— *La Journée des Dupes* (1961).

MORÉRI, L., *Le Grand Dictionnaire historique* (10 vols.; 1759).

MOUSNIER, R., *Les Institutions de la France sous la monarchie absolue* (2 vols.; 1974-80).

NAJAM, E. W., '*Europe*: Richelieu's Blueprint for Unity and Peace', *Studies in Philology*, 53 (1956), 25-34.

NICERON, J.-P., *Mémoires pour servir à l'histoire des hommes illustres dans la République des lettres* (43 vols.; 1727-45), xxxv, 135-8.

NICOLE, P., *Les Imaginaires ou Lettres sur l'hérésie imaginaire* (2 vols.; Liège, 1667).

NIDERST, A., *Madeleine du Scudéry, Paul Pellisson et leur monde* (1976).

NUSSBAUM, F. L., *The Triumph of Science and Reason 1660-1685* (New York, 1953).

PARROT, D., 'French Military Organization in the 1630s: The Failure of Richelieu's Ministry', *Seventeenth-Century French Studies*, 9 (1987), 151-67.

PATIN, G., *Lettres*, ed. J.-H. Reveillé-Parise (3 vols.; 1846).

PELLISSON and D'OLIVET, *Histoire de l'Académie-Françoise* (2 vols.; 1729) (first publ. by P. Pellisson [-Fontanier], 1653).

PINTARD, R., *Le Libertinage érudit dans la première moitié du* XVIIe *siècle* (2 vols.; 1943).

PRETINA, M. J. JR., 'Vincent Voiture, Creation and Reality: a Study of his Prose' (Ph.D. thesis, Yale, 1967).

RANUM, O., *Richelieu and the Councillors of Louis XIII* (Oxford, 1963).

—— *Artisans of Glory. Writers and Historical Thought in Seventeenth-century France* (Chapel Hill, 1980).

—— 'Jeux de cartes, pédagogie et enfance de Louis XIV', in *Les Jeux à la Renaissance* (Tours, 1982), 553–62.

RANUM, O. and P., *The Century of Louis XIV* (New York, 1972).

RAPIN, R., *Mémoires, 1644–1669*, ed. L. Aubineau (3 vols.; 1865).

REIBETANZ, A., *Jean Desmarets de Saint-Sorlin, Sein Leben und Seine Werke* (Leipzig, 1910).

RULE, J. C. (ed.), *Louis XIV and the Craft of Kingship* (Columbus, 1969).

SAUVAL, H., *Histoire et recherches des antiquités de Paris* (3 vols.; 1733).

SAYCE, R. A., *The French Biblical Epic in the Seventeenth Century* (Oxford, 1955).

SEDGWICK, A., *Jansenism in Seventeenth-century France: Voices in the Wilderness* (Charlottesville, 1977).

SIMONE, F., 'Gli schemi umanistici nella storiografia francese del secolo XVII' and 'Il Rinascimento nelle concezioni storiografiche del Fleury e del Bayle', in his *Il Rinascimento francese* (Turin, 1961), 297–360.

—— *Storia della storiografia letteraria francese* (Turin, 1969).

SOREL, C., *La Bibliothèque françoise* (1664).

STELLWAGEN, J. H., *The Drama of Jean Desmarets de Saint-Sorlin* (Chicago, 1944).

TALLEMANT DES RÉAUX, G., *Historiettes*, ed. A. Adam and G. Delassault (2 vols.; 1960–1).

TAPIÉ, V. L., *La France de Louis XIII et de Richelieu* (1967). (First publ. 1952).

—— *France in the Age of Louis XIII*, trans. D. M. Lockie (London, 1974).

TAVENEAUX, R., *Le Catholicisme dans la France classique 1610–1715* (2 vols.; 1980).

VIGNIER, *Le Chasteau de Richelieu ou l'Histoire des Dieux et des Héros de l'antiquité avec des Réflexions morales* (Saumur, 1676).

VULSON DE LA COLOMBIÈRE, M., *Les Portraits des hommes illustres françois qui sont peints dans la galerie du Palais Cardinal de Richelieu* (1650).

Index

Abraham, Claude K.   85 n.
Abraham, ou la Vie parfaite   310, 317, 372
Abrégé de la science universelle   16, 234, 277–8
Académie de Caen   87
Académie des Inscriptions et Belles-lettres   328, 350
Académie des Sciences   259, 350
Académie-Française, *see also* ancients and moderns: activities 1670–76   28–9, 34–5, 106, 124, 293, 319, 349, 351; Chancelier 1, 84; *Cid*   162, 185, 293; Desmarets recruited   81, 83, 120–1; early Neoplatonism   72, 146, 148–50; early objectives   14, 16, 72, 142–3, 236; *Europe*   194, 199; foundation/founder members   8, 20, 21, 36, 40, 88, 97, 118–21, 343, 349, 351; other references   48, 153, 166, 170, 254, 274
Académie-Royale de musique   71, 350
Adam, Antoine   3, 46 n., 68 n., 91 n., 119 n., 131, 137–8, 142 n., 157 n., 171, 187 n., 217, 262, 345–6
Ado of Vienne   128
Adorni, Catherine, known as Saint Catherine of Genoa (1447–1510)   27, 28, 281–3, 265, 281–3, 331 n.
Agrippina the younger (15?–59)   118
Ahasuerus   315 n.
Aiguillon, Marie-Madeleine de Vignerot, Duchesse d' (*c*.1604–75); appreciates *Roxane*   170; dedications to   1, 14, 47, 124–7, 280–1; Lambert's marriage   71; relations with Desmarets   4, 48, 243–49, with Mme du Vigean   46–7, 48, 243–4; Richelieu's executrix   47, 107, 243–4, 255, 262; *Sylvie*   201; *Uranie*   125
Aiguillon, Magdalène-Thérèse Vignerot, second Duchess d'   48

A la Reyne Régente, sur la bataille de Rocroy   209 n., 224, 237, 364
Albret, François-Alexandre d', Sire de Pons   298–9
Albret de Miossens, Chevalier d'   298
Alexander III of Macedon ('the Great') (356–323 BC)   35–7, 115, 128, 134 n., 154, 156, 169, 170–8, 234, 250, 271, 299, 307 n., 328
Alexander VII, Pope (Fabio Chigi) (1599–1667)   322, 327
Aligre, Etienne II d', Seigneur de la Rivière (1592–1677)   91, 92
'Amours'   214
'Amours de Protée et de Physis'   130, 223
Amours du compas et de la règle, Les   6, 87, 214, 220–4, 228, 360
Amyot, Jacques (1513–93)   94, 148, 163 n., 171, 174 n., 231
ancients and moderns   5, 8, 24, 30, 34, 37, 39, 66, 115, 118, 168–9, 173, 176–8, 217–24, 296–7, 307 n., 319–20, 343–55; see also *Comparaison de la langue*, etc.
Ancre, Maréchal d', *see* Concini
Anderson, J. E.   289 n.
André, L.   100 n., 324 n.
Angennes, Julie d' (later Duchesse de Montausier)   119, 215–6, 350
Anguittard, Anne Arnould de Saint-Simon, Mme d'   155 n.
Annat, François (1590–1670)   100, 324 n.
Anne of Austria: dances   20, 76, 78, 336; death   33; dedications to   1, 2, 24, 33, 66, 128, 186, 224, 227, 230–6, 240–3; entertained in Grande Salle   183–4, 207, 328–9, in Petite Salle   137, 139, 204; ladies in waiting   79–80; loved (?) by Buckingham   152, 187, Montmorency   68, 152, Richelieu   152, 185–7; marriage   46, 59, 89, 152; *Mirame*   183–9; miscarriage   70; *Orfeo*   143–4; pregnancy   238; Regency Court   47, 48, 97–9, 197, 212, 236, 320, 322;

Anne of Austria *(cont.)*
'sainte' 235–6; symbolized by
goddesses 203; by moon 22, 67,
187–8
Anne of Brittany (1477–1514) 232
Annibal 134
Apollo 28, 39, 55, 60, 63–7, 71,
128–30, 189, 297, 342
Arbessier, L. 116 n.
Ariane 2, 6, 12, 14, 16, 23, 27, 28,
72, 87, 109–18, 120, 121–4, 129,
132, 134, 146, 147, 148, 152, 158,
159, 163, 173, 181, 197, 214, 315,
358–60
Ariosto, Ludovico (1474–1533) 123,
249 n., 287, 308–9, 329
Aristotle (384–322 BC) 127, 219,
311, 344
Armani, A. S. 157 n.
Armida/Armide 60, 313
Arnauld, Antoine (1612–94) 15,
280, 324, 325, 334, 336
Arnauld, Henri (1597–1692) 137,
180, 194
Arnauld d'Andilly, Robert
(1585–1674) 216 n.
Arnauld de Pomponne, Antoine
(1616–98) 180 n., 185
Arrian, Flavius 263
Artabazus 156, 172
Artaxerxes I, King of Persia (465–424
BC) 148 n.
'Art de la poësie, L'' 219–20, 345,
372
*Articles accordez par la Clemence du
Roy* 86–7, 94, 168, 358
*A Son Altesse Royale Monseigneur le
Duc d'Orléans, sur la prise de
Graveline* 90, 364
Aspasia (mother of Darius II) 148 n.
Aspasia (mistress of Pericles) 148,
149, 151, 307 n.
Aspasie 28, 77, 79, 82, 134, 136,
142–53, 157, 158, 159, 162 n.,
181, 185, 188, 237, 247, 289, 293,
322 n., 350, 352, 360
Atkinson, F. 346 n.
Aubignac, François Hédelin, Abbé d'
(1604–76) 141, 161, 169, 170,
179, 344
Aubray, François Dreux d' 57
Audinet, Claude 325 n.
Auguste, Alphonse 44 n., 321 n.

Augustine of Hippo, Saint (354–430)
66–7, 204 n., 322, 324 n., 331 n.,
333
Augustus Caesar (63 BC–AD 14) 35,
37, 40, 295 n., 300
Au Roy, sur la prise de Mastrich
205 n., 311 n., 371
*Au Roy, sur sa conqueste de la
Franche-Comté* 2, 209 n., 304,
306, 311 n., 370
*Au Roy sur sa seconde conqueste e la
Franche-Comté* 371
'Autres ŒEuvres poëtiques' 200, 206,
213–19, 200–6, 363
Auvray (playwright) 151
Aveugle de Smyrne, L' 138, 157
'Avis du Saint-Esprit au Roi' 311 n.,
330–1
Azema, Xavier 334 n.

Baïf, Jean-Antoine de (1532–89)
72
Bailbé, Jacques 80 n.
Baillet, Adrien (1649–1706)
31–2, 337
Ballet at Château-Trompette 62–3
Ballet comique de la Reine 161
Ballet d'Apollon 63–6, 128
Ballet de la Blanque 58
Ballet de la Boutade des comédiens
161
*Ballet de la Courtisane appelée La
Ronde* 58
Ballet de la délivrance de Renaud 8,
59–61, 62, 271
Ballet de la Douairière de Billebahaut
62, 73–4, 82, 157
Ballet de la Félicité de l'âge doré 59
*Ballet de la Félicité sur l'heureuse
naissance de Monseigneur le
Dauphin* 8, 20, 35, 36–7, 47,
134, 159, 187, 193–4, 200–11,
214, 271, 353
Ballet de l'Harmonie 66, 72, 82
Ballet de la Merlaizon 79
*Ballet de la Prospérité des armes de la
France, Le* 16, 49, 63, 83, 131,
134–7, 140, 182, 185, 193, 195,
200–11, 227, 350, 363
Ballet de la Reine, see *Grand Ballet de
la Reyne*
Ballet de la vieille Cour, see *Ballet du
Roy*

Ballet de Madame, see *Ballet du Triomphe de Minerve*

Ballet des Bacchanales 68, 158

Ballet des Cinq sens 72, 82

Ballet des Effets de la nature 72, 82

Ballet des Improvistes 79

Ballet des Nymphes bocagères de la forêt sacrée 82

Ballet du Château de Bicêtre 75–7, 82, 118

Ballet du Rhinocéros 210

Ballet du Roy 59, 67, 77–8, 82, 150 n.

Ballet du Soleil 63–7, 77–8, 82, 89, 128

Ballet du Triomphe de la beauté 215

Ballet du Triomphe de Minerve 59, 210

Ballet royal de la nuit 28, 71

Balzac, Honoré de (1799–1850) 32

Balzac, Jean-Louis Guez de (1595–1654) 61–2, 119–21, 124–5, 169, 170–1, 293

Barcos, Martin de (1600–78), Abbé de Saint-Cyran 107 n., 324

Baro, Balthasar (1590–1650) 82 n., 109, 121, 135, 136, 139–40, 162

Barthélemy, E. de 212 n.

Bartillat, M. de 318

Bassompierre, François de (1579–1646) 58, 62, 92, 120

Baudeau de Somaize, Antoine 55–6

Baudoin, Jean (1564–1650) 236, 264

Bausset, Cardinal L. F. de 332, 336 n.

Bautet, Pierre, Seigneur de Marivatz 52

Bautru, Guillaume I, Comte de Serrant 88

Bautru, Guillaume II, Comte de Serrant (1588–1665): Académie-Françoise 40, 119–21; Court hedonist 68; death 33; dedication to 214; friendship with Desmarets 45–6, 79, 85 n., 88–94, 96, 261; suggests *Les Visionnaires* 154; see also *Voyage de Fontainebleau, Le*

Bayle, Pierre (1647–1706) 19 n., 32, 278, 348

Beauchamps, P. F. de 19 n., 181

Beauchet-Fillet, H. 101 n., 229 n.

Beaufort, François de Bourbon, Duc de (1616–69) 77, 255 n.

Beaumarchais, Vincent Bouhier, Seigneur de 92–3

Beijer, Agne 16, 22 n., 135, 182 n., 208–9

Beik, W. H. 104 n.

Béjart, Madeleine (1618–72) 123

Bella, Stefano della (1610–64) 22, 182–3, 189, 213, 230–6

Bellarmini, Cardinal Roberto (1541–1621) 72, 188, 254, 265, 348, 349

Belleau, Rémy (1528–77). 77

Bellemore (actor) 154, 156, 160

Bellerose, Pierre Le Messier, known as 80, 139

Belleville, Jacques de 60

Bellier, Catherine-Henriette 48

Bellièvre, Nicolas de (1583–1650) 46, 91

Bellièvre, Pomponne de 46

Bembo, Pietro (1470–1547) 72

Benedetti 140–1

Benoît de Sainte-Maure 297 n.

Benserade, Isaac de (1612?–91) 28–9, 66, 71, 106, 212

Bergin, Joseph 104–5

Bernard of Clairvaux, Saint (1090?–1153) 240 n., 331 n., 333

Bernard of Saxony, Duke of Weimar (1604–39) 206

Bernardin de Saint-Pierre, Henri (1737–1814) 309

Bernini, Giovani (1598–1680) 22, 140–1, 182, 187, 208–11, 350

Bertaut, F., see Motteville

Berthelot (libertine poet) 69

Bérulle, Cardinal Pierre de (1575–1628) 62, 330 n.

Besmaux or Baismaux 100

Beugnot, Bernard 253 n.

Beuil, Sieur de 255 n.

Beys, Charles (1610?–59) 36, 155

Bibas, H., 62n.

Binet, Estienne (1569–1639) 6, 72, 159

Blanche of Castille (1188–1252) 236

Bland, David 291

Bloch, Marc 289 n.

Blosius, Louis de Blois (1506–66?), known as 265, 331 n.

Blum, André 170 n., 275 n.

Blunt, Anthony 159 n., 245
Boccaccio, Giovanni (1313–75) 116, 128
Bochart, Jean V, Seigneur de Champigny 87, 90
Bochart, Samuel (1599–1667) 87
Boësset, Antoine de (1585–1643) 59, 64
Boësset, Jean-Baptiste de (1614–85) 59
Boileau, Gilles (1631–69) 346
Boileau-Despréaux, Nicolas (1636–1711) 6 n., 8, 29–31, 33–41, 125, 217, 277, 319, 337, 342–9, 353
Boisrobert, François Le Metel de (1592–1662) 5, 62, 80, 81, 83 n., 87, 89, 96–7, 119–21, 139–40, 142, 166, 200
Boissat, Pierre de 15, 149–50
Bonnaffé, Edmond 244 n.
Bonneau-Avenant, Alfred 47 n., 144 n.
Bonnefon, Paul 346 n.
Bonney, Richard 7 n., 90–1, 92 n, 93, 95, 98 n., 103, 120 n.
book illustration 12–14, 54–5, 122, 264, 275–7, 290–3
Bordier, René (died 1658?) 59, 63–7, 73, 82, 128
Borgerhoff, E. B. O. 343 n.
Bornemann, Wilhelm 346 n.
Bosse, Abraham (1602–76) 9, 12, 112, 114, 117, 122, 127 n., 169, 170 n., 199, 269 n., 291
Bossuet, Jacques-Bénigne (1627–1704) 32–3, 197, 332, 335–6
Bouchard, Jean-Jacques (1606–41) 166
Boudon, Henry-Marie (1624–1702) 44 n., 283, 321, 326–7
'bouffon du Roi' 1, 2–3, 68, 84–5, 351
Bouillon, Ducs de, alive in 1623 93 n.
Bourbon, Mlle de, see Longueville, Duchesse de (1619–79)
Bourbon, Nicolas 20, 50
Bourdon, Sébastien 26, 291
Bourgeois, Emile 100 n., 324 n.
Bourzeis, Amable de (1606–72) 162, 262 n.

Bouthillier, Léon, Comte de Chavigny 170
Boyer, J.-B. de 263
Brantes, Duc de 62–3, 64
Bréda, Antoine de 257
Bremond, Henri 13, 51 n., 271, 277, 321 n., 326–7, 330–1
Brézé, Nicole du Plessis-Richelieu, Marquise de 155 n., 204
Brézé, Urbain du Maillé, Marquis de (1597–1650) 44 n., 102, 204, 205 n., 207, 214 n.
Briand, René 15 n., 27, 278
Brigstock, H. 159 n.
Briggs, Robin 32
Brion, François-Christophe de Levis-Ventadour, Comte de (later Duc de Damville) (1603–61) 77, 208 n.
Brosse (playwright) 151
Brûlart family 46, 88–94, 89, 201 n.; see also Puisieux and Sillery
Brûlart, Claude 46, 91
Brûlart, Jeanne-Isabelle 46, 89
Brun, Pierre 49 n.
Brunet, Jacques-Charles 263 n.
Brunschvicg, Léon 321
Bry, Theodore de 115
Buckingham, George Villiers, Duke of (1592–1628) 152, 187
Buisseret, David 45 n.
Bullion, Claude, Seigneur de Bonnelles (c.1580–1640) 93, 99, 103–4
Bunyan, John (1628–88) 110, 266
Burckhardt, C. J. 86 n., 97 n.
Butler, K.-T. 62 n.

Cabinet satyrique 70
Cadenet 62, 64
Caesar, Gaius Julius (102 or 100–44 BC) 35, 36, 307
Caillet, M.-A. 33 n., 331 n.
Calderón de la Barca, Pedro (1600–81) 65, 164
Caldicott, C. E. J. 167 n., 216 n.
Camillus, Marcus Furius 307 n.
Camoëns, Luiz Vaz de (1524–80) 296
Campion, Henri de (1613–63) 180
Camus, Jean-Pierre (1584–1652), Bishop of Belley 110
Camusat, Jean 153, 160
Candale, Duc de 75
Candaux, Jean-Daniel 197 n.

Canivet, Diane 291
Canova-Green, M.-C. 83
Cardelin (dancer) 210
Carel de Sainte-Garde, Jacques (died 1684) 38–9, 286
Carpentariana 277
Cartes des Rois de France, etc. 24, 27, 124, 133, 174–5, 186, 212, 230–6, 237, 278, 303, 318, 364–5
Cartesianism 10, 12, 35, 41, 56, 338–9, 347–50
Castagniza, Juan de 257
Castiglione, Conte Baldassare (1478–1529) 72
Castille, Nicolas Jeannin de, Baron de Montjeu 91
Cassander 128
Castille, Pierre de 91
Catherine de Médicis (1519–89) 152, 236
Catherine of Aragon (1485–1536) 152
Catherine of Genoa, *see* Adorni
Caumartin, Louis le Fèvre, Seigneur de 90–1
Caumont family 209 n.
Cérisy, Abbé de, *see* Habert, Germain
Cervantes Saavedra, Miguel de (1547–1616) 32, 80; *see also* Don Quixote
Chamaillard, Edmond 47
Champaigne, Catherine de 32 n.
Champaigne, Philippe de (1602–74) 321 n.
Chancy, François de 200 n., 212 n., 216
Chantérac, Marquis de 92 n.
Chapelain, Jean (1595–1674): Academician 5, 20, 28, 96, 119–21, 149, 162, 166, 170, 316; contemporary importance 344; Graziani's *Cromwell* 145; 'Guirlande de Julie' 215; *Liste de quelques gens de lettres* 27; mentioned (?) by Desmarets 53; *Nouvelles Muses* 83 n., 121, 219; patronage 255; politics 30; *Pucelle* 39, 286–7, 290; remarks on Desmarets 46, 95, 124–5, 127, 133, 162, 166, 170–1, 193–4, 289, 293, 336; satirized 39; *Sentiments de l'Académie-Française* 8, 162 n.,

185, 293; theory of *vraisemblance* 193
Chappuzeau, Samuel (1625–1701) 142–3, 196–7
Charlemagne (768–814) 286
Charles I, King of England (1600–49) 89, 173, 323 n.
Charles II, King of England (1630–85) 52
Charles V, Emperor (and King of Spain) (1500–58) 90
Charles Martel (*c*.685–781) 38, 286
Charmeur charmé, Le 134
Charnacé, Hercule-Girard, Baron de (died 1637) 214
Charpentier (engraver) 31 n., 54
Charpy de Sainte-Croix (1610–70) 99–100, 105, 319, 326, 329–30
Chateaubriand, François-René Vicomte de (1768–1848) 14
Chauveau, François (1613–76) 275–6, 291, 315 n.
Chavigny, *see* Bouthillier
Chemin de la paix et celuy de l'inquiétude, Le 30, 283–5, 326, 369
Chéruel, A. 31 n.
Chevalley, Sylvie 82 n.
Chevreau, Urbain (1613–1701) 123, 163
Chevreuse, Duchesse de, *see* Rohan, Marie de
Cheze, René de la 78 n.
Childebrand 38
Christ 116, 147, 150, 185, 239–40, 300, 307, 311–14; see also *Imitation de Jésus-Christ*
Christian marvellous 14, 65–7, 281, 284, 288–90, 300–1, 310–17, 319, 320, 321 n., 344–8
Christina of Sweden (1626–89) 277, 306
Church, W. F. 17 n., 87 n., 95
Cicero, Marcus Tullius (106–43 BC) 128, 164
Cinq-Mars, Marquis de (1620–42) 99, 194
Cioranescu, Alexandre 15, 197 n.
Clark, Sir George 330 n.
Clarke, Janet 169
Clement of Alexandria, Saint (150?–220?) 240 n.
Clitus 172–4, 250, 307 n.

Clotaire (497–561) 234

Clovis I (465?–511) 38, 287–8, 289, 291, 302

Clovis 1 n., 2, 6, 11–14, 25, 26, 27, 28, 39, 48, 54, 55, 67, 72, 76, 96, 102, 128, 142, 146, 149, 150, 166, 177, 213, 219, 237, 240 n., 258, 274, 275, 277, 286–309, 310, 311 n., 314, 315, 329, 344, 346, 349, 352, 366–7

Cognet, Louis 323

Cohen, J. M. 115

Cohortanus 171

Colbert, Jacques-Nicolas, Archbishop of Rouen 31 n.

Colbert, Jean-Baptiste (1619–83) 1, 27, 30–1, 34, 44, 53, 228, 328, 339–40

Colbert, Jean-Baptiste II, Marquis de Seigneley 31 n.

Colbert, Marie 44

Collège de Clermont 49

College of Propaganda 241 n.

Colletet, François (1628–80) 281

Colletet, Guillaume (1598–1659) 61, 66, 69–70, 72, 81, 157, 216 n., 264, 280–1

Collinet, Jean-Pierre 119 n.

Combalet, Antoine de Roure, Sieur de 47

Combalet, Mme de 47

Combat spirituel, Le 25, 146, 237, 254, 257–8, 264, 271, 289, 304, 366

Comédie des Tuileries, La 78, 80

Commire, Jean (1625–172) 349

Compagnie du Saint-Sacrement 229, 254, 321, 326

Comparaison de la langue et de la poësie françoise avec la grecque & la latine, La 2, 16, 130, 213, 219, 223, 225, 227, 246, 251 n., 340, 370–1

Concini, Concino, Maréchal d'Ancre 46, 60, 61, 66

Condé, Henri II de Bourbon, Prince de (1588–1646) 62–3, 204

Condé, Prince de, known as 'le Grand Condé' (1621–86) 5, 24, 49, 51–2, 125, 177–8, 200–1, 207, 209, 224, 225 n., 294, 297–9

Condé, Princesse de (Louis XIV's godmother) 125–7

Conrart, Valentin (1603–75) 9, 12, 30, 84, 119–21, 170, 212, 216 n., 296; *see also* 'Recueils Conrart'

Conseil de Conscience 99–101, 352

Conseiler du Roi 7–8, 21, 52, 88, 96–101, 108, 122

Conti, Prince de (1629–66) 5, 8, 24, 51–2, 188, 255, 323 n., 336

Contreveritez de la cour 85

Copernicanism 347–8

Corneille, Pierre (1606–84): see also *Ballet du Château du Bicêtre*; *Andromède* 79 n., 308–9; birth 20; *Cid* 8, 14, 37, 159, 162–3, 169, 177, 185, 307; *Cinna* 14, 111, 185; *Clitandre* 75; early comedies 180; Five authors 81, 140, 142, 187; *Galerie du Palais* 78; *Horace* 14, 169, 185; *Illusion comique* 136, 139–40, 141, 156, 350; *Imitation de Jésus-Christ* 254–7, 290 n.; *Mélite* 80, 139 n.; *Menteur* 155; *Mirame* 76, 142, 187; *Mort de Pompée* 307; *Office de la Sainte Vierge* 258; *Pertharite* 166; piety 259; *Place Royale* 78; 'Poésie à la peinture' 255; *Polyeucte* 14; psychology 279; reputation 153; tears 177, 307; *Théâtre* (1660) 258, (1663) 22; *Triomphes de Louis le Juste* 36

Corneille, Thomas (1625–1701) 151, 185

Corpus maresianum 15–17, 121, 169, 314, 357–73

Cortés, Hernando (1485–1547) 115–16

Cossé-Brissac, P. de 216 n.

Costar, Pierre (1603–60) 25, 97, 121, 352

Coste, P. 107 n.

Cotin, Charles (1603–81) 351

Council of Trent 239

coup d'état of January 1623 93; of 24 April 1617 60, 89, 177; of 13 August 1624 70, 91–2

Courbé, Augustin 275, 290

Cousin, Victor 47 n., 49, 78 n.

Couterot, J. 325 n.

Coutinho, B. 296 n.

Couton, Georges 22, 135, 234

Coutura, J. 25 n.

Couvay, Jean 26, 291
creative writer 219–20, 344–5
crusade(s) 38, 59–61, 62–3, 73–5, 202–4, 206–7, 227, 234, 330–1
Cureau de la Chambre, Pierre 149
Curtius, Ernst Robert 65 n
Cyril, Saint (827–69) 240 n.
Cyrus 'the Great', King of Persia (600?–529 BC) 36, 127, 169 n., 271

Daniel 300, 331 n.
Dares the Phrygian 297
Dalziel, M. 110 n.
Damville, see Brion
Darius II, King of Persia (died 404 BC) 148 n.
Darius III, King of Persia (died 330 BC) 156, 169, 173
Dauvet, Charlotte 45
Dauvet, Claude (or Douet), Chevalier Des Maretz 45
Dauvet, Gaspard, Seigneur des Marets 45, 46, 89
Dauvet-Desmarets family 45–6
David (c.1015–c.970 BC) 33, 238, 246–7, 272–3, 310, 335
Davies, John, of Kidwelley 213
Day of Dupes 119–20
Decharme, P. 128 n.
décolletage 229
Defense de la poësie, La 8, 16, 34, 41, 42, 301, 347, 349, 371
Deffense du Poëme héroïque, La 8, 16, 40–1, 371
Delassault, Geneviève 3 n., 91 n.
Delfau, François 154–5 n.
Délices de l'esprit, Les 1, 4, 6, 11–14, 21, 25, 38, 54, 70, 72–3, 99, 107–8, 158, 223, 234, 240, 259, 264–78, 289, 291, 299 n., 312 n., 348, 367–8
Deloche, Maximin 15 n., 262–3
Demay, Henri 196
Demetrius 151
Denise, L. 219 n.
Denys of Alexandria, Saint 240 n.
Deprechains, A. 121 n.
Desargues, G. (1593–1662) 269 n.
Des Barreaux, Jacques Vallée, Seigneur (1599–1673) 68
Descartes, René (1596–1650) 56, 68, 236, 338–9, 349 n.; see also Cartesianism

Descrières, G. 161 n.
Desfontaines, Nicolas-Marc 122–3
Desmares 15
Des Marets (? son of Mme des Loges) 45, 69
Desmarets, Charles (1602–75) 45
Desmarets's daughters 53, 55–6
Desmarets, Henri 15
Desmarets, Jehan (father of Clément Marot) 42
Desmarets, Marguerite 50, 51–2, 53, 56
Desmarets, Nicolas, Seigneur de Maillebois (1648–1721) 5, 44–5
Desmarets, Roland (1593 or 1594–1653) 6, 42, 49–51, 53, 54, 56, 88, 123, 134 n., 231, 256, 258, 286, 287 n., 294–5, 297
Desmarets, Samuel (1559–1673) 45
Desmarets de Saint-Sorlin, Armand-Jean 4, 15, 19 n., 31 n., 52, 53, 54–5, 56, 275, 293
Desmaretz, Jean (father of Nicolas Desmarets) 5, 44
De Thou, François (1607–42) 176, 194
Dhéran, B. 161 n.
Díaz del Castillo, Bernal (1492–1581) 115–16
Diodorus Siculus 128–9
'Discours de la poësie' 83, 149, 214, 302, 352
'Discours pour prouver que les sujets Chrestiens' 343, 367
Dodin, André 331
Don Quixote 80, 157, 297 n.
Dorival, Bernard 50 n., 299 n.
Dryden, John (1631–1700) 353
Dryhurst, James 128 n., 331 n.
Du Bartas, Guillaume de Salluste, Seigneur (1544–90) 246
Du Bellay, Joachim (1522–60) 246, 251
Dubois, Elfrieda 151
Dubois, Guillaume (poet mason) 87
Du Bosc, Jacques 234–6
Dubuisson-Aubenay, F.-N. Baudot de 4, 24 n., 46, 53 n., 107 n., 243–4
Du Fayot, L. 151
Du Périer, François 257
Du Perron, Cardinal Jacques Davy (1556–1618) 297
Du Perron, Jean Davy, Sieur 297

Duportail, Jeanne   275 n.
Dupré, Guillaume   51–2, 255 n.
Dupré, Marguerite, *see* Desmarets,
　Marguerite
Dupré, Marie   52, 56–7
Dupuy, Geneviève   71
Durand, Etienne
　(1585–1618)   59–61, 212
Du Ryer, Pierre (1606–58)
　171
Du Vair, Guillaume (1556–1621)
　17 n., 85
Du Vergier de Hauranne, Jean
　(1581–1643)   107 n.
Du Vigean, Anne de Neubourg,
　Baronne   1, 46–7, 48, 89
Du Vigean, François Poussart, Baron
　de Fors, Sieur   75–6, 155 n.
Du Vigean, Marthe (Soeur Marthe de
　Jésus)   49

Edict of Nantes, Revocation of   335
Eine, Simon   161 n.
Elbeuf, Charles I de Lorraine, Duc d'
　(1556–1605)   208 n.
Eleanor of Aquitaine (1122?–1204)
　236
Eliade, Mircea   37 n.
Elizabeth I, Queen of England
　(1533–1603)   234
Elliott, J. H.   148, 155 n.
Emard, Paul   100
Emelina, Jean   351 n.
Enghien, Duc d', *see* Condé, Prince de
　(1621–86)
enlightenment   67, 353–5
*Entreprise des Rochellois descouuerte,
　L'*   94–5, 173, 358
Epernon, Bernard de Nogaret, Duc d'
　(1592–1661)   351
Epernon, Jean-Louis Nogaret de La
　Valette, Duc d' (1554–1642)   61,
　62, 351
Epictetus   15, 262–5
Erasmus, Desiderius (*c.*1469–1536)
　177, 265
Erigone   14, 125, 127, 132, 133,
　134, 189–93, 363
Erlanger, P.   155 n.
Esprit, Jacques (1611–78)   225
Esther   175, 219, 315, 316
Esther   6, 14, 38, 48, 99, 102, 310,
　311 n., 314, 315–17, 370

Estrées, François Annibal, Marquis de
　Cœuvres (1573–1670)   95–6
Estrées, Gabrielle d'   86
euhemerism   65–6, 128–30
Euhermerus of Messene   128–30
Europe   23, 27, 179, 193–9, 200–3,
　210, 220, 227, 289, 353, 363–4
Eusebius   128
Eustis, Alvin   61 n.
Evelyn, John (1620–1706)   252 n.
*Examen du livre, intitutlé, L'Ancienne
　Nouveauté de l'Ecriture Sainte*
　15–16, 99–100, 368
Extraordinaire des guerres   7, 21, 42,
　44, 96, 97, 99, 101–5, 108, 122, 351

Faret, Nicolas (1596–1646)   16, 72,
　119–20, 148–9
Félibien, André (1619–95)   212, 296
Female Quixotes   110, 156
Ficini, Marsilio (1433–99)   72
Finta Pazza, La   22
Flaubert, Gustave (1821–80)   342
Fleuret, Fernand   88 n.
Fleury, Anne   43, 52–3, 86
Fleury, René   43, 44, 52–3, 86
Fontaine, Nicolas (1625–1709)   334
Fontenelle, Bernard Le Bouvier de
　(1657–1757)   248
Forestier, Georges   167
Fors, Marquis de (died 1640)   47,
　201 n., 205 n., 214
Fors, Marquis de (younger brother of
　preceding)   47 n., 243–4
Fortifications de France (Député)
　Surintendant des   7, 21, 45, 85–7,
　95–6, 164, 236, 351
Fouquet, François (died 1656)   213
Fouquet, Louis, Bishop of Agde
　333–4
Fouquet, Nicolas (1615–80)   1, 29,
　82, 91, 253, 327, 333, 336
'France à la Reine régente, lors de la
　Guerre de Paris, La'   2
Francini, Tomaso (machinist)   59
François I (1494–1547)   327
Frank, Grace   59
Freemasons   6
Frénicle, Nicolas (1600–62?)   69
Freudmann, Felix R.   16, 78 n.,
　286 n., 287 n., 297 n., 343 n.
Fronde, La   8, 24, 30, 243–4, 294,
　296, 297–9, 302, 336

Fumaroli, Marc 6 n., 346 n.
Funck-Brentano, F. 327 n.

Gagliardo, A. 257
Gain-Montagnac, J. L. M. de 323
Galigai, Léonora, Maréchale d'Ancre 61, 327
Galilei, Galileo (1564–1642) 340–1, 347 n.
Garasse, François (1584–1631) 69–70, 273 n.
Garber, P. M. 160
Garnier, C. G. T. 49 n.
Gascar, Henri (c.1634–1701) ii, 31
Gassion, Jean de (1609–47) 87
Gaudeau, Y. 161 n.
Geneviève, Saint 296
Genis, Hieronymus de 282
Gerson, Jean Charlier, known as (1363–1429) 254–5, 331 n.
Giffre de Rechac, Jean de 228 n.
Gillet de la Tessonnerie 151
Gillot, Hubert 315
Girard, Antoine (1603–79) 265 n.
Giry, Louis (1596–1666) 119
Godeau, Antoine (1605–54) 6, 83 n., 119–21, 149, 193–4, 216 n., 219
Godet des Marais, Paul (1648–1709) 45
Gombauld, Jean Ogier de (1590–1666) 96, 119, 162, 216 n.
Gomberville, Marin Le Roy, Sieur de (1600–74) 109, 122–4, 149, 231
Goodman, William A. 289
Gosset, I. and/or Nicolas 279 n.
Goujet, C.-P. 238
Gournay, Marie Le Jars de (1566–1645) 56, 218–19
Gramont, Antoine III, Duc de (1604–78) 31 n.
Grand Bal de la Douairière de Billebahaut, see Ballet de la Douairière de Billebahaut
Grand Balet des Bachanales, see Ballet des Baccanales
Grand Ballet de la Reyne représentant le Soleil, see Ballet du Soleil
Grande Pastorale, La 138
Grandier, Urbain 61, 327
Grandin, M. 282
Gravier, G. 161 n.
Graziani, Girolamo 145

Gregory of Nazianzus, Saint (c.330–c.390) 239–40
Gregory of Tours, Saint (c.538–c.594) 294
Grenaille, François de (1616–80?) 23, 166
Grijalva, Juan de (c.1489–1527) 115
Grimm, Jürgen 178 n.
Grivel, Marianne 31, 306 n.
Guédron, Pierre (musician) 59
Guéret, Gabriel (1641–88) 124, 319
Guérin de Bouscal, Daniel (died 1657) 167 n.
Guiche, Comte de 80
'Guirlande de Julie, La' 8, 119, 215–16, 350
Guise, Charles de Lorraine, Duc de (1571–1640) 106, 118
Guise, Henri II, Duc de (1614–64) 212 n.
Guyon, André 19 n., 44 n., 52 n., 53 n., 96 n., 102

Habert, Germain (1614–54), Abbé de Cérisy 119, 162
Habert, Philippe (1605–37) 83 n., 119–21
Hagen, Victor Wolfgang von 115
Hallé, Pierre (Petrus Hallaeus) 50, 51, 56
Hamlet 80
Hanley, S., 98 n.
Hannibal (247–182 BC) 134, 162–3, 170
Harcourt, Henri de Lorraine, Comte d' (1601–66) 77, 208, 298
Harlay, François de 330
Harlay de Sancy, Achille de (1581–1646) 171
Harlequin 80
Harthan, John 25 n., 291
Hartle, Robert W. 178 n.
Hay, Denys 197 n.
Hay du Châtelet, Daniel (1596–1671) 149, 159
Heinsius, Nicolas (1620–81) 51
Henri II (1519–59) 77, 152
Henri III (1551–89) 339 n.
Henri IV (1553–1610) 21, 44, 49, 59, 86, 105, 118, 121, 152, 303, 339 n.

Henriette d'Angleterre, see Orléans,
  Henrietta Anne Stuart, Duchesse d'
Henriette-Marie de France (1609–69)
  89
Henry VIII, King of England
  (1491–1547) 152
Herbault, Seigneur de, see Phélypeaux
Hermant, Godefroi 330–1
Heudon, Jean 297, 304 n.
Hilary, Saint (c.315–c.367) 240 n.
Hippeau, C. 189 n.
Homer 311, 349
Hooke, Robert (1635–1703) 347
Horace (65–8 BC) 125, 246, 268
Horatius Cocles 298
Hôtel de Bourgogne 133, 161
Hoy, B. 68 n.
Huet, Pierre-Daniel (1630–1721) 87,
  215, 349
Hügel, F. von 283 n.
Hugo, Victor (1802–85) 6 n., 251,
  351 n.
Hugues Capet (c.941–96) 38
Hunter, A. C. 27 n.
Huppert, George 42
Huxley, Aldous 286–7, 330 n.

Imitation de Jésus-Christ, Les Quatre
  livres de l' 25, 27, 254–5, 258,
  260, 264, 304, 346 n., 366
Indignation. A Monseigneur le Duc de
  Richelieu 20, 228, 371, 373
Isidore of Seville (Isidorus Hispalensis)
  128

Jacquot, Jean 22 n., 135 n., 182 n.
Jal, Auguste 24 n., 44, 52, 106, 108
Jansenism 4, 8, 9, 10, 12, 29–35,
  107–8, 124, 319–42, 348, 349,
  352; see also Response à l'insolente
  Apologie
Jansenius, Cornelius (1585–1638)
  322 n.
Jarry, Nicolas 215
Jeanne de France (1464–1505) 152
Jeannin, Pierre, Baron de Montjeu
  91
Jeremiah 300
Jerome, Saint (c.347–420) 33, 128
Jesuits 6, 49, 69–70, 73, 100,
  202–4, 319–42
Jeux de cartes, see Cartes des Rois de
  France

Joan of Arc (1412–31) 290; see also
  Chapelain, Pucelle
Jodelle, Etienne (1532–73) 77
John the Evangelist, Saint 300,
  307 n.
Jombert (poet) 73
Jombert, C.-A. 133 n., 230
Jones, Inigo (1573–1652) 211
Joseph de Paris, François Le Clerc du
  Tremblay, known as ('l'Eminence
  grise') (1577–1638) 286–7, 330
Josephus, Flavius (c.37–c.100) 316
Jurgens, Madeleine 82, 138 n.,
  297 n.
Justice (musician) 70
Juvernay, Pierre 229

Kerviler, René 25 n., 29 n., 42, 51,
  53 n., 56, 89 n., 118, 214 n.,
  257 n., 262
Kleinman, Ruth 68 n., 70 n., 186–7
Kochno, Boris 60, 73

Labatut, J.-P. 48 n.
Labbe, Philippe (1607–67) 280–1
Labrousse, Elisabeth 259 n.
La Calprenède, Gautier de Coste,
  Sieur de (1614?–63) 110, 124,
  135, 174, 179, 185
La Chambre, Pierre de 319, 371
Lachèvre, Frédéric 69, 200 n., 212 n.
Lacour, Léopold 125, 166–7,
  168 n., 175–6
Lacroix, Paul 7 n.
Lactantius (250?–317?) 128
La Faye, Antoine de 160
Lafayette, Marie-Madeleine Pioche de
  la Vergne, Comtesse de (1634–93)
  113, 279
La Flèche, Collège de 49
La Fontaine, Jean de (1621–95) 45,
  47 n., 54, 124, 125, 243, 253, 339,
  347, 352
La Force, Armand Nompar de
  Caumont, Duc de 209
Lafuma, Louis 159 n., 338 n., 339 n.
Lagrange, Charles Varlet de (1635–92)
  34 n., 153, 161
Lair, J. A. 213 n.
La Lane, Abel de 336
Lambert, Florentin 27, 54, 275–6,
  278, 282
Lambert, Madeleine (Mme Lully) 71

Lambert, Michel (1611–96) 70–2, 215

La Mesnardière, Jules de (1610–63) 145, 171

Lamoignon, Guillaume de, Marquis de Baville (1617–77) 336–7

Lamoignon, Hôtel de 31, 40, 336–7

La Mothe-Houdancourt, Henri de 100, 330

Lancaster, Henry Carrington 15 n., 79 n., 81, 122–3, 132 n., 133, 164, 172, 175–6, 180–1, 184–5, 187, 189

Landry, Pierre 331 n.

Lannel, Jean de 109

La Pelouze, E. de 101 n.

La Porte, Pierre de (1603–80) 187, 234

Lapp, John C. 150 n.

La Reynie, Gabriel Nicolas (1625–1709) 318, 327

La Rochefoucauld, Cardinal François de (1558–1645) 62

La Rochefoucauld, François, VI Duc de (1613–80) 201 n., 225, 263, 279, 298, 323

La Rochefoucauld, Marie-Catherine, Marquise de Sillery 201 n.

Lassalle, Jean-Pierre 6, 87 n.

La Tisardiere, M. de 94

La Trémoille, Henri, Seigneur de (1598–1674) 298

La Trémoille, Henri-Charles, Prince de Tarante (1621–72) 298–9

Laugier de Porchères, Honorat (1572–1653) 149, 201

Launoy, Jean de 254 n.

Laurain-Portemer, Madeleine 22 n., 140–1, 182, 211

L'Ausbespine, Charles de, Marquis de Châteauneuf (1580–1653), Abbé de Préaux 93

La Valette, Duc de 77, 80

La Vieuville, Charles, Duc de (1582–1653) 70, 90–3

La Vigne, Marie-Anne de (1634–84) 56

Lavisse, Ernest 168

Lawrenson, T. E. 135–6, 137 n.

Le Bailly (musician) 59

Leblanc, Paulette 239

Le Bouthillier, Claude 93

Le Brun, Charles (1619–90) 291, 299, 328

Lecouvreur, Adrienne (1692–1730) 197

Le Doyen (engraver) 306 n.

Lefebvre, Denis 19 n.

Le Febvre, Marie 19, 42

Lefèvre, Louis, see Caumartin

Lefèvre d'Ormesson, André 91 n.

Lefèvre d'Ormesson, Olivier (1616–86) 31 n.

Lefort de la Morinière 24 n., 251 n.

Le Gascon (bookbinder) 215–16

Le Gras, Henri 169, 170, 187, 193, 196, 213, 225, 254, 257, 263, 275, 290

Le Gras, Nicolas 325 n.

Leiner, Wolfgang 1 n., 2, 122 n., 202 n.

Le Laboureur, Louis (died 1679) 286, 314

Lemaire, Jean (1598–1655) 132

Le Maire, Nicolas 240

Le Maistre de Sacy, Isaac 8, 29, 30, 56–7, 255, 319, 324 n., 334–5, 336

Lemercier, Jacques (1585–1654) 131–2

Le Moyne, Pierre (1602–71) 216 n., 286–7, 290, 320

Le Mur, P. 229 n.

Lenglet du Frenoy, N. 255 n.

Lennox, Charlotte (1720–1804) 110

Lentulus, Lucius Cornelius 307 n.

Léon, Don Pedro de 183

Le Pautre, Jean (1618–82) 291

Le Petit, Pierre 254, 257, 315

Lesclache, Louis de (1620?–82) 274

Lescot, Jacques 107, 261–2

L'Escuyer, A. 240

Lessot, Jean de 15, 27, 278–9

Lestocq, Nicolas (died 1662) 279 n.

Lestoile, Claude de (1597–1652) 73, 81, 82, 83 n., 121, 162

Le Tellier, Michel (1603–85) 57, 100, 335

Lettres spirituelles 15, 27, 278–81, 331

libertinage 68–70, 203, 264–75, 348

Livy, Titus (59 BC–AD 17) 164

Loges, Marie Bruneau, Dame des (c.1585–1641) 45, 69

Lombart, Pierre (1612?–82) ii, 31

Longueville, Henri II d'Orléans, Duc de 1, 5, 24, 46 n., 75–7, 78, 255
Longueville, Duchesse de, first wife of Duc Henri II 78
Longueville, Duchesse de (1619–79) 1, 5, 24, 30, 47, 49 n., 51–2, 78, 101, 200, 214, 255, 259, 323, 334, 336
Loret, Jean 101, 330 n.
Lorraine, Charles IV (really III), Duc de (1604–75) 207
Lorris, P.-G. 298 n.
Louis IX, known as Saint-Louis (1214–70) 11, 234, 236, 299, 302
Louis XII (1462–1515) 152, 232
Louis XIII (1601–43): birth 21; campaigns 62, 86–7; century of 61 n.; confidence 77; cult figure 72, 254; dances 60, 64–7, 68, 79, 83, 204, 336; death 4, 23–4, 227; declares war 55; dedications to 1, 21, 33, 69, 172 n., 179, 182, 186, 207, 237, 238–9; Duc d'Epernon 351 n.; enlightenment 67; entertained in Grande Salle 183–4, 207, 328–9, in Petite Salle 139, 142–4; exemplary king 302–3; Gallic Hercules 208–9; half-brothers 86; horsemanship 339 n.; La Rochelle 94–5; *lits de justice* 86, 98, 120; Louis le Juste 36, 60, 67, 177, 225, 227, 301, 320; majesty 60, 63–7; majority 59; marriage 46, 152; *oraison funèbre* 257; policies 302; reign 23, 25, 90, 200, 217, 223; relations with Desmarets 3, 20, 58–9, 60, 70, 83, 89, 93, 97, 200, 304 n.; revels 85; song composed for 200; statues of 11, 24, 77–8, 227, 303; sun king 22, 65–7, 86, 116, 187–8, 340–2; theatre policy 21–2, 141–3; Thunderer 64; triumphs 8, 36, 62–3, 77, 78 n., 86, 179, 202, 320; 'voeu' 238; war-wounded 76–7
Louis XIV (1638–1715): Alexander the Great 236; anticipation of 238; attitude toward Richelieu; Bernini's bust 140; birth 8, 21, 23, 36, 125, 187–8, 199, 200–7, 237, 289, 340; century of 1, 9,
10, 11, 19–41, 34–9, 110, 199, 207, 223, 246, 256, 261, 271, 278, 280, 284, 295, 299, 300, 302, 306, 307, 320, 343–4, 349–50, 352–5; coronation 346; dances 28, 71, 336, 342; dedications to 1–2, 19, 177–8, 205 n., 209 n., 231, 253, 287, 299, 304 n., 310–11, 315, 328–9, 330, 335; education 125–7, 230–6, 302–3; executions 99–101, 177, 327; exploits 39, 294, 300, 306; Hôtel des Invalides 77; intolerance 30, 322–3, 334–5, 342; library 2, 325 n.; Louis le Grand 2, 34, 36, 66, 178, 279; majority 24; Marie Mancini 346 n.; marriages 25, 33, 45; *Mémoires* 323; patronage 40, 352; portrait 25, 26, 291, 329; reign 3, 11, 30, 35, 41, 48, 61, 66, 82, 99, 116, 139, 177–8, 197, 254, 281, 320, 351–3; relations with Desmarets 20, 212, 304–5; Roi très-chrétien 116; style 54; sun king 39, 65–7, 71, 116, 202, 340–2, 355; theatre 136–7, 142–3; triumphal entry 281; victories 205 n., 228
Loyson, Jean-Baptiste 263
Lublinskaya, A. D. 92 n., 102–3
Lucius, Henriette 160
Luke, Saint 307 n.
Lully, Jean-Baptiste (1632–87) 28, 71
Luynes, Charles d'Albert, Duc de (1578–1621) 20, 60, 62–8
Luynes, Duchesse de, *see* Rohan, Marie de
Luz, Maria 60, 73

Mabillon, Jean (1632–1707) 255 n.
Macandrew, H. 159 n.
Machiavelli, Niccolo (1469–1527) 288 n.
Magendie, Maurice 123
Magne, Emile 49 n., 85 n., 119, 133 n., 167, 189 n.
Maillé-Brézé, Clémence de 49, 207
Maillé-Brézé, Jeanne de 214 n.
Maillé-Brézé, Marquis and Marquise de, *see* Brézé
Maintenon, Françoise d'Aubigné, Marquise de (1635–1719) 45

Mairet, Jean (1604–86) 81, 151
Malebranche, Nicolas de (1638–1715)
 160, 347–8,
Malherbe, François de (1555–1626)
 6 n., 58, 87, 212, 217–18, 243,
 257, 263, 349
Mallet, Daniel (dancer) 82
Mallet (historian) 103
Malleville, Claude
 (1597–1647) 83 n., 119–21,
 158 n., 216 n.
Mancini, Marie (later Princess
 Colonna) 346 n.
Mandat, Gallion 96
Mandrou, Robert 313 n., 327 n.
Manlius Capitolinus 207 n.
Manse (lieutenant, dancer) 201 n.,
 216 n.
Mantegna, Andrea (1431–1506) 245
Marabotto, C. 282
Marais, Louis 45
Marais, Mathieu (1664–1737) 45
Marais, Théâtre du 80, 133, 154,
 166–7
Marbeuf, Pierre de (1596?–1645)
 121
Marcou, F. L. 274
Mareschal, André 79, 135, 140 n.,
 156
Marestz, Jean 19, 42
Margarita de' Medici 144
Marguerite de Lorraine 152
Marie de Médicis (1573–1642) 3,
 44, 58–62, 86, 88–9, 90–1, 97,
 118, 120, 152, 336, 343, 351 n.
Marie-Madeleine 6, 14, 38, 124,
 127, 289, 310–15, 370
Marie-Thérèse d'Autriche 1, 25, 33,
 48, 99
Marillac, Michel de (1562–1632)
 93, 102–3
Marine de Levant 7, 23–4, 33–4,
 45, 48, 53, 105–8, 299
Marino or Morini, Giambattista
 (1569–1625) 69, 197
Marni, Archimède 288–9
Marolles, Michel de, Abbé de Villeloin
 (1600–81) 50, 132, 180, 183–4,
 211, 253, 297 n., 319, 349, 371
Marot, Clément (1496–1544) 42
Martilière, Pinel de la 15 n.
Martellotti, G. 164 n.
Martin, Henri-J. 25 n., 95, 240 n.,

254, 259, 265 n., 275 n., 283,
 291 n.
Martina, Saint 55
Martinelli, Tristano (1557?–1630)
 80
Martino, Pierre 141 n.
Marty-Lavaux, C. 257 n.
Mary Magdalene, Saint 311–13
Mary the Virgin, Saint 147, 203,
 209, 237–8, 280–1, 301, 337; see
 also Office de la Vierge Marie
Mary, wife of Louis XII 152
Masaniello (1624–47) 212 n.
Maskell, David 286 n., 291 n., 308,
 310, 318
Masons, see Freemasons
Massar, P. D. 230 n.
Mathieu or Matthieu, Pierre 260
Maxfield-Miller, Elizabeth 138 n.,
 297 n.
Maximes chrestiennes 16, 237,
 259–60, 317, 372
Mayenne, Duc de 63
Maynard, François
 (1582–1640) 83 n., 121
Mazarin, Cardinal Jules (1602–61):
 Charpy de Sainte-Croix 99;
 collections 254; death 25, 100,
 322, 344; dedications to 1, 70,
 226, 231, 264; diplomatic activity
 208; entertained in Petite
 Salle 136, 137, 139–40; Finta
 Pazza 22; Fronde 298;
 ministry 322; Mirame 140–2,
 182, 187–8, 190; Morin 99–100;
 Orfeo 137, 143–4; 'Plainte' to
 266
McCallin, Gary 45 n.
McGowan, Margaret M. 58, 59 n.,
 60, 66, 71, 200–1, 207 n.,
 210–11
Medea 312
Medici family 35, 144, 152
Ménabrès, A. 107 n.
Ménage, Gilles (1613–92) 49, 50,
 88, 154, 216
Menestrier, Claude-François
 (1631–1705) 66
Menghini, Nicolò 141
Mercœur, Duc de 77
Méré, Antoine Gombauld, Chevalier
 de (1610?–84) 47 n.
Mesmes, Jean-Jacques I de 84

Mesmes, Jean-Jacques III de 28, 84, 106

Mesnard, Jean 135, 179 n., 324 n.

Méthivier, Hubert 10 n., 61 n., 78 n., 238, 303

Mézerai, François Eudes de (1610–83) 231

Michel, G. 161 n.

millenarianism 259, 299–301, 349

Milton, John (1608–74) 66, 248, 251, 287, 290, 341, 349

Mirame 12, 14, 21–3, 67, 76, 131–42, 179–89, 208, 211, 220, 230, 247, 289, 328, 350, 363, 372

Mitford, Nancy 342 n.

Mitton, Damien (1618?–90) 68

Molé, Mathieu (1584–1656) 69

Molière, Jean-Baptiste Poquelin, known as (1622–73): *Amants magnifiques* 351 n.; *Amphitryon* 243, 339 n.; *Avare* 151, 153, 192; *Bourgeois Gentilhomme* 73–5; burial 197; *comédies-ballets* 71, 82; *Comtesse d'Escarbagnas* 281 n.; Conti 323 n.; decides on stage career 141; *Dom Juan* 138 n., 329; *Ecole des femmes* 153, 161, 193, 240, 280–1; Epernon, Duc d' 351 nn.; *Fâcheux* 82, 153; *Femmes savantes* 50, 161, 351; *Malade imaginaire* 153, 282, 344; *Misanthrope* 54, 153, 154, 247, 263; ghost 41; *Précieuses ridicules* 161, 266, 268; *Princesse d'Elide* 351 n.; publications 22 n.; repertory, *Alexandre le Grand* 178, *Aspasie* (?) 146, 153, *Belle Esclave* 82, *Thébaïde* 324, *Les Visionnaires* 29, 153, 161; reputation 23, 28 n., 29, 32, 344, 349; Richelieu family patrons 34; *Sganarelle* 161; signature 82; *Tartuffe* 67, 153, 280, 282, 329–30, 336, 341; theatres 22, 82, 97

Molière d'Essertines, François (1600?–24) 119

Molina, Luis (1636?–1701) 324 n.

Molinier, *see* Moulinier

Monaldeschi, Marquis of (died 1657) 306

Mongrédien, Georges 47 n.

Montaigne, Michel Eyquem de (1533–92) 218

Montausier, Charles de Sainte-Maure, Duc de (1610–90) 215–16

Montausier, Duchesse de, *see* Angennes, Julie d'

Montbazon, Duc de 88

Montchal, Charles de (1589–1651) 180 n., 186

Montdory, Guillaume Desguilbert, known as (1594–1651) 80, 133, 139, 154, 160

Monteverdi, Claudio (1567?–1643) 152, 195

Montezuma II (1480?–1520) 115–16

Montglat, François de Paule de Clermont, Marquis de (1620–75) 24 n., 180 n., 211, 255 n.

Montherlant, Henri de 324

Montmorency, Henri II, Duc de (1595–1632) 68–9

Montpensier, Marie-Louise d'Orléans, Duchesse de (1627–93) 204, 211

Montpouillon, Jean de Caumont de 209 n.

Montrésor, Comte de 176

Morales d'Epictète, de Socrate, de Plutarque et de Sénèque 15, 262–4

Moreau, J.-B. (musician) 315

Moreau, M.-J. 147 n., 265 n.

Moréri, Louis 19 n., 32, 90–1, 150 n., 206, 296

Morgues, Mathieu de 104, 195

Morin, Simon 8, 9, 25, 29, 61, 99–101, 105, 180–1, 279, 319, 326–7, 329–30, 352, 372, 373

Mortemar, Marquis de 77

Moses 310

Mother and Son Wars 61–2, 91

Motteville, Françoise Bertaut, Dame Langlois de (1621–89) 24 n., 137, 255 n.

Moulinier (musician) 70–1, 77, 206

Mousnier, Roland 87 n., 92, 102 n., 104, 120 n., 179 n.

Mozart, Wolfgang Amadeus (1756–91) 153

Mulard, Father 333 n.

Murillo, C. 161 n.

Najam, E. W. 196 n.

Napoleon Bonaparte (1769–1821) 11

Naudé, Gabriel (1600–53)   254
Nebuchadnezzar   300 n.
Nelson, Horatio (1758–1805),
  Viscount   11
Neoplatonism   13, 72–3, 146–51,
  157–8, 187–9, 218–20, 230–1,
  265–75, 347–9
Neostoicism   263–4
Nero Claudius Caesar (37–68)   110
Neufgermain, Louis de (1574–1662).
  85, 119, 228
Nevers, Charles I de Gonzague-Clèves,
  Duc de   330
Nevers, Philippe-Julien Mazarini-
  Mancini, Duc de (1639–1707)
  40–1, 336, 346, 371
Newton, Sir Isaac (1642–1727)   353
Niceron, J.-P.   19 n., 49, 57
Nicole, Pierre (1625–95): *Apologie*
  324; 'Avis sur le Placard du Sr
  Desmarets'   15; *Imaginaires*   2, 29,
  124, 160 n., 277, 304, 319–42,
  343; *Visionnaires*   12, 14, 29,
  31–3, 35, 41, 160 n., 197, 253,
  277, 305, 319–42, 352
Nicoll, Allardyce   80
Nies, Fritz   217 n.
Noëlle, P.   161 n.
Nouvelles Muses, Les   83 n., 218–19
Nussbaum, F. L.   9, 347, 353
Nyères, Sieur de   77

'Ode à Colbert'   30–1, 53, 339–40,
  372, 373
Odes, poëmes et autres œuvres   23,
  224–6, 364
Œuvres chrestiennes   216, 237–40
Œuvres poëtiques   16, 18, 22 n., 23,
  71–2, 78, 83 n., 88, 90, 96, 125,
  134 n., 187, 200, 206, 213–19,
  220–6, 228, 230, 262–3
Office de la Vierge Marie   24, 33,
  186, 237, 240–3, 258, 365
Olivar, Alexandre   67 n.
Olivares, Gaspar de Gusmàn, Count-
  Duke of (1587–1645)   148, 155 n.,
  167
Olivet, Pierre-J. d'   120 n., 134 n.,
  142 n., 194 n., 214, 232 n., 293 n.
Orléans, Gaston, Duc d'
  ('Monseigneur', later 'Monsieur')
  (1608–60)   1, 63, 70–1, 77, 80,
  85, 90–1, 119–20, 143, 150 n.,

152, 176, 183, 204, 207, 209 n.,
  216, 224, 228, 243 n.
Orléans, Henrietta Anne Stuart,
  Duchesse d' (1644–70)   52
Orléans, Philippe, Duc d' ('Monsieur')
  (1640–1701)   52, 187
Orosius, Paulus   128
Otway, Thomas (1652–85)   307
Ovid (43 BC–c.18 AD)   25, 129, 146,
  246, 249, 270

Palais-Cardinal, later Palais-Royal:
  Chapel   207; Galerie des hommes
  illustres   50, 176, 231, 299 n.;
  Garden   236; Grand'Salle de
  spectacle   8, 12, 21–2, 76, 81,
  125, 131–9, 143–5, 179–99, 200,
  207–11, 269 n., 350; Petite Salle de
  spectacle   81–3, 131–9, 143–5,
  156, 157, 167–8, 200, 204, 350
Paris, Claude   53
Parker, R. A.   81
Parlement de Paris   7, 45, 49, 50,
  69–70, 88, 96, 120, 336
Parlement de Rouen   86
Parma, Odoardo Farnese (1612–46),
  Duke of   142–4
Parma, Ranuccio I Farnese, Duke
  of   144
Parnasse des poëtes satyriques, Le
  69–70
Parrot, David   7 n., 104
Pascal, Blaise (1623–62): experimental
  work   338; historiography   334;
  Lettres provinciales   13, 264 n.,
  280, 320–3, 328, 348; libertine
  friends   68; 'Mémorial'   259;
  Pensées   13, 159, 341–2;
  reputations   32
Passart, Sister Flavie   332
Patin, Gui (1601–72)   24, 46, 51,
  52 n., 106, 255 n.
Patru, Olivier (1604–81)   346 n.
Paulet, Charles (inventor of *la paulette*)
  103, 162 n.
Paulet, Mlle (above's daughter, 'la
  lionne')   162 n.
Paullus I Lucius Aemilius   307 n.
Peace of the Church   41, 319, 334 n.
Pearce, B.   92 n.
Pellevé, Cardinal Nicolas de (1518–94)
  121
Pellisson, J.   298 n.

394 INDEX

Pellisson, Paul (1624–93) 119–21,
134, 142–3, 148–9, 162 n., 214 n.,
230, 234 n., 274 n., 277–8, 293
Perceau, Louis 88 n.
Péréfixe, Hardouin de Beaumont de
(1605–70) 33, 100, 303, 322,
330 n., 331–2
Pericles (died 429 BC) 35, 37, 148,
307 n.
Périer, Marguerite 321 n.
Perrault, Charles: Court ballet 66;
dedications to 1, 8, 41, 301, 371;
Eloges de Messieurs Arnauld et
Pascal 32; Mémoires 7; Parallèles
des Anciens et des
Modernes 35–6, 41; Siècle de
Louis le Grand, Le 9, 10 n., 34–6,
350
Perrault, Claude (1613–88) 56, 140
Peruginom, Pietro Vannucci, known
as Il (1446–1523) 245
Petau, Denis 49, 128
Petit, M. (or J.-F.?) 288
Petit-Bourbon, le 56, 63
Petit de Julleville, L. 249
Petitot, A. 24 n., 255 n.
Petrarch, Francesco (1304–74) 164
Petrarchism 61 n., 75, 157–8
Phélypeux, Raymond, Seigneur
d'Herbault 93
Philip, Saint (Apostle) 237
Philip II of Macedon (c.382–336 BC)
173
Philip IV, King of Spain (1605–65)
89–90, 199, 330
Phradates 171
Pibrac, Guy Du Faur, Seigneur de
(1529–84) 54, 260
Picard, Raymond 34, 322 n.
Pico della Mirandola, Giovanni
(1463–94) 72
Pintard, René 219 n.
Piron, Alexis (1689–1773) 161
Pitau, Nicolas 291
Plato (428–348/7 BC), see also
Neoplatonism; dialogues 125, 127,
189, 263; Laws 230–1; Lysis
147–8; Menexenus 148; Phaedo
150; Symposium 265; Timaeus
72
Pléiade 77–8, 150 n., 158, 217–20
Pliny the Elder (23/4–79) 128, 340
Plutarch (c.50–c.125) 15, 94, 127,

128, 148, 151, 163–4, 169, 171–2,
174, 177, 231, 262–4, 307, 316
Pluvinel, Antoine de (1525–1620)
339
Poe, Edgar Allen (1809–49) 251
Pompey the Great (106–48 BC) 307
Pont-de-Cé 62, 91
Pont-de-Courlai, François de Vignerot,
Marquis du (died 1646) 47, 106
Pontus de Tyard (1521–1605) 150
Poquelin, Jean-Baptiste, see Molière
Port-Royal 4, 9, 319–39; see also
Jansenism and Response . . .
Poussin, Nicolas
(1594–1665) 158–9, 245, 249,
263, 315 n.
Pradon, Nicolas (1632–98) 169–70
Pralon, A. 161 n.
Préaux, Abbé de, see L'Aubespine
Pretina, Michael J., Jr. 352 n.
Prières et OEuvres chrestiennes 33,
238, 242, 258, 365
Priézac, Salomon de 169 n., 252
progress, idea of 338–9, 349
Promenades de Richelieu, Les 6, 11,
76, 213, 237, 243–53, 258, 265–6,
272, 289, 304, 308, 340, 365
Protestantism 9, 32, 35, 62, 66, 73,
87, 94–5, 172–3, 348–9
Prudent (lieutenant of the Château de
Caen) 86
Psaumes de Davide
paraphrasés 238–41, 362
Puget de la Serre, Jean 168, 176,
177–8, 179, 196–7, 274
Puisieux, Pierre Brûlart, Marquis
de 46, 89, 93
Puisieux, Charlotte d'Estampes-
Vançençay, Marquise de 46, 88–94
Puisieux, Madeleine de Neufville-
Villeroi, Marquise de (died 1613)
89
Puylaurens, Antoine de Lage, Sieur
(later Duc) de 80

Quatremaires, Robert 254 n.
Quatrhommes 257
Quinault, Philippe (1635–88) 151
Quintus Curtius 156, 172–4, 177

Racan, Honorat de Bueil, Seigneur de
(1589–1670) 68, 83 n., 121, 243,
251

Racine, Jean-Baptiste (1639–99):
 *Abrégé de l'histoire de Port-
 Royal* 324 n.; *Alexandre le
 Grand* 175 n., 178, 299, 328;
 Andromaque 123, 166, 175 n.,
 184, 297 n.; *Athalie* 37;
 Bérénice 177; Boileau and
 Clovis 345–6; celebrates military
 victories 353; dramatic formula
 171; *Esther* 315; *Mithridate* 151,
 153; *Paysage, ou Promenades de
 Port-Royal* 253; *petites lettres*
 31, 34 n., 322, 328–9, 333;
 Phèdre 2, 67, 308–9;
 Plaideurs 161; poetic
 diction 251; tears 177, 307;
 Thébaïde 324
Rambaud, Alfred 168
Rambouillet, Catherine de Vivonne,
 Marquise de (1588–1665) 8, 33,
 125–7, 133, 189, 215
Rambouillet, Charles d'Angennes,
 Marquis de (c.1577–1652)
 119–20
Rambouillet, Hôtel de 30, 46, 49 n.,
 133, 167, 215–16, 350
Rambures, Charles ('le brave') (died
 1633) 214 n.
Rambures, Jean V, Sire de (died
 1637) 214 n.
Rampalle, Daniel (1603?–60?) 197
Rancé, Armand-Jean Bouthillier de
 (1626–1700) 331, 346 n.
Ranum, Orest 3, 10 n.
Ranum, Patricia 10 n.
Raphael (1483–1520) 327
Rapin, René (1621–87) 30 n., 51,
 325–6, 333–4
Ravaillac, François (1578–1610) 121
Ravaisson, F. 29 n., 100–1
Ravenel, J. 101 n.
Rayssiguier (playwright) 252
Recueil des plus beaux vers
 (1661) 134 n., 200, 212 n.
'Recueils Conrart' 119, 212,
 215–16, 229, 274
Recueils de Sercy 78 n., 215 n.
Redondi, P. 347 n.
Regulus, Marcus Atilius 317–18
Regulus, ou le vray genereux 310,
 317–18, 371
Rembrandt van Rijn (1606–69) 160
Remus, King of the ancient Gauls 77

Remy, Saint (c.437–c.533) 287–8
Renaudot, Théophraste (1584–1653)
 211
Renty, Gaston-Jean-Baptiste, Baron de
 (1611–48) 272 n.
*Response à l'insolente Apologie de
 Port-Royal* 4, 32, 99–100, 107–8,
 143, 277, 278, 293 n., 311 n., 319,
 324–37, 346, 369–70
Retz, Henri de Gondi, Duc de
 (1590–1659) 106
Retz, Jean-François-Paul de Gondi,
 Cardinal de (1614–79) 255 n.,
 323, 330 n., 333 n.
Richard III, King of England
 (1452–85) 234
Richelet, Pierre-César (1631–98) 160
Richelieu, Cardinal Alphonse de 15,
 152, 155 n., 262–4
Richelieu, Anne Poussart de Pons (née
 du Vigean) (1622–84) Duchesse de:
 celebrated in *Clovis* 48, 298–9;
 dedications to 1, 14, 150 n., 315;
 marriages 5, 8, 24, 78, 243–4,
 298–9; salon 274; section
 on 47–9
Richelieu, Armand-Jean du Plessis,
 Cardinal-Duc de (1585–1642):
 Académie-Française 118–21;
 addresses Estates General 59;
 Alexander parallel 328; ambitions
 for theatre 197–9; appreciates
 Mirame 180, *Roxane* 171;
 cardinalship 62; collections
 158–9, 245–6; commissions *Cartes
 des Rois de France* 230; Corneille
 rewarded for *Le Cid* 162 n.;
 created Duke 168; 'creatures' 83,
 352; death 23, 106, 127, 134,
 243, 263, 314, 351 n.; dedications
 to 1, 37, 87, 119–21, 146, 168,
 170, 214, 263, 328–9, 352;
 Desmarets's tributes to 224–6,
 302; Epernon, Duc d' 351 n.;
 estate 84; exile 61;
 finance 101–4; Five Authors 78,
 79–83, 135, 157, 187; Général des
 Galères 106; godfather 54;
 Grand Maître du Commerce
 105–6; heritage 39–41;
 illnesses 224; Inventaire après
 décès 136–7; La Rochelle 94–5;
 loves (?) Anne of Austria 152,

Richelieu, Armand-Jean du Pleissis
(*cont.*)
186–7; mediator 62;
Mémoires 88–90, 107; military
strategy 168–9; ministry 8, 36,
83, 286; Montrésor affair 176;
passion for verse 220;
patronage 21–3, 32, 34, 40,
72–3, 79–83, 104, 125 n.,
131–211, 227, 280–1, 293, 314,
350–1; *Perfection du
chrestien* 107, 261–2; policies 9,
125, 193–9, 302, 346; reason of
state 18 n., 95, 151, 163. 172;
relations with Desmarets 3–5, 24,
39, 44, 61, 79–83, 84, 93, 96–7,
104, 118, 131–211, 217–26, 293,
343; returns to Conseil (1624) 68,
91; Rueil 204, 216, 269 n., 294,
308, 350; Scipio parallel *see
Scipion*; situation in 1623 46, 88;
Testament politique 302;
Tombeau 224–6, 302; *see also*
Palais-Cardinal *and* Richelieu,
château de
Richelieu, Armand-Jean du Plessis,
second Duc de (1629–1715):
dedications to 1, 20, 39, 163 n.,
228; Général de la Marine de
Levant 33, 48, 84, 106–8;
household 331–2; marriage, first
5, 8, 24, 47, 78, 243–4, 255, 297;
relations with Desmarets 5, 6, 20,
24–5, 106–7, 234, 243–4, 255–6,
277–8, 297, 331; victory at Naples
48
Richelieu, Armand de Vignerot du
Plessis, third Duc de (1696–1788)
48
Richelieu, château de 50, 51, 53,
55, 56, 76, 158–9, 163 n., 220 n.,
257, 259, 262, 265, 286, 294, 353
Richelieu, Emmanuel-Joseph Vignerot,
Comte de (1640–65), (Abbé de
Marmoutier, etc.) 34, 48
Richelieu, Jean-Baptiste, Marquis de
(1632–62) 34, 48, 244
Ripa, Cesare 236
Roannez, Artus Gouffier, Duc de
(died 1696) 68
Robert, Nicolas 215–16
Robin, L. 147 n., 265 n.
Roger, Jacques (printer) 275, 290

Rogers, H. 61 n.
Rohan, Duc de 94
Rohan, Marie de 20–1
Ronsard, Pierre de (1524–85) 6 n.,
77, 158 n., 219–20
Roquelaure, Gaston, Duc de
(1615–83) 205 n.
Rosane 14, 47, 72, 109, 124–7,
129, 150, 165, 170, 219, 230, 314,
352, 352
Rosenstein, R. 61 n.
Rosenthal, R. 347 n.
Rossillion de Bernex, Charles Amédée
205 n.
Rossillion de Bernex, Michel-Gabriel
205 n.
Rotrou, Jean de (1609–50) 81, 82, 153
Roullé, Pierre 329–30, 336
Rousseau, Jean-Baptiste (1671–1741)
15
Rousseau, Jean-Jacques (1712–78)
253
Rousseau, Marie 43, 52, 86
Roussel, Placide 254 n.
Rousselot, Jean 16
Roxana 171–8, 236
Roxane 1, 14, 25, 37, 134, 165,
167, 170–8, 250, 362
Rubin, David L. 61 n., 220 n.
Rule, John C. 39 n. 234 n.

Saige, G. 4 n.
Saint-Aignan, François VII de
Beauvillier, Comte (later Duc) de
224
Saint-Amant, Marc-Antoine de
Gérard, known as (1594–1661)
69, 273 n.
Saint-Cyran, Abbé de 107–8; *see
also* Barcos *and* Duvergier Du
Hauranne
Sainte-Beuve, Charles Augustin
(1804–69) 324
Sainte-Marthe, Claude de (1620–98)
15, 324, 331, 333
Sainte-Mesme, Anne-Alexandre de
l'Hôpital, Comte de (1624–1701)
243 n.
Saint-Germain Beau-Pré, Comte
de 75
Saint-Marc, Pierre Costard 326
Saint-Réal, César Vichard de
(1629–92) 94

Saint-Simon, Claude de Rouvroy, first Duc de 3, 77

Saint-Simon, Louis de Rouvroy, Duc de (1675–1755) 3

Salomon, Herman Prins 229 n.

Sannazzaro, Iacopo (1456–1530) 280–1

Santeuil *or* Santeul, Jean-Baptiste (1630–97) 15, 349

Saumaise, Claude (1588–1653) 349

Sauval, Henri (1623–76) 5, 131–2, 136

Sayce, Richard A. 286, 310, 315–17

Scarron, Paul (1610–60) 153, 155, 213

Scève, Maurice (1501?–60?) 157

Scherer, Jacques 135, 137–9, 144 n., 341 n.

Schomberg, Charles, Duc d'Hallewin (1601–56) 91 n.

Schomberg, Henri, Comte de Nanteuil (1575–1632) 90–3

Schomberg, Marie de Hautefort, Maréchale de 200

Schwarzenberg, E. 178 n.

Scipio Africanus (*c*.235–*c*.183 BC) 37, 134, 162–4, 168–9

Scipion 25, 37, 134, 162–70, 352, 361

Scudéry, Georges de (1601–67) 80–1, 139 n., 159, 162, 171, 215, 216 n., 286–7, 290

Scudéry, Madeleine de (1608–1701) 56, 123–4, 253, 284

Scupoli, Lorenzo (born 1610) 25, 257–8

Sedgwick, A. 323 n., 324 n.

Segraisiana 154 n.

Seguier, Nicolas 172 n., 174

Séguier, Pierre 1, 17, 227–8

Séguirant, Père 70

Seneca, Lucius Annaeus (4 BC–65 AD) 15, 127, 262–4

Sérisay, Jacques de (1598–1654) 119

Sessions, B. 128 n.

Sévigné, Marie de Rabutin-Chantal, Marquise de (1626–96) 161

Seznec, Jean 128 n.

Shadwell, Thomas (*c*.1642–92) 350

Shakespeare, William (1564–1616) 80, 166, 184–5, 290

Sigaux, Lucette 49, 50

Siguret, François 202 n.

Sillery, Louis Brûlart de (1619–91) 201 n.

Sillery, Nicolas Brûlart, Marquis de (1544–1624) 46, 88–94

Smith, John, of Christ's College, Cambridge 123

Snaith, Guy 135 n.

Socrates (470?–399 BC) 15, 189, 262–4

Soir, Le 135–6, 195, 211

Soissons, Louis de Bourbon, Comte de (1604–41) 76, 77, 176

Somaize, *see* Baudeau de Somaize

Sorel, Charles (1600–74): ballets 72, 73; *Bibliothèque françoise* 109, 123–4, 219, 257, 277, 278–9; *De la perfection de l'homme* 232; reputation 32; situation at Court 3

Soubise, Benjamin de (1583–1642) 94

Soulfour, Nicolas de (1549–1624) 172 n.

Stellwagen, J. H. 189 n., 193

Stendhal, Henri Beyle, known as (1783–1842) 161, 253

Strauss, Richard (1864–1949) 32

Streicher, Jeanne 64 n.

Sublet des Noyers, François 6, 87, 96, 97

Sully, Hôtel de 46

Sully, Maximilien de Béthune (1560–1641), Duc de 21, 45, 103

'Sur le retour de Roy à Paris en l'année 1649' 17, 372

Swammerdam, Jan (1637–80) 340

Tallemant des Réaux, Gédéon (1610–92) 3, 4, 6, 58–9, 68 n., 70–1, 85, 91, 104, 107, 121, 142 n., 152, 155 n., 160, 180, 185–6, 194–5, 200–1, 207, 214 n., 261, 351

Tamerlane *or* Tamburlaine (1336?–1405) 36

Tamizey de Larroque, P. 5 n.

Tapié, Verdun-Louis 302 n., 330 n.

Tasso, Torquato (1544–95) 59–61, 229, 287, 294, 296

Tchemerzine, Avenir 15, 259–60

Terrebasse, H. de 339 n.

Tertullian (160?–230?) 67, 128

Tessier, Georges 288 n.

Testelette, Philbert 255 n.
Testu, Jacques (1626–1706) 40–1, 331–2, 336, 346, 371
Thanner, M. 283
Théophile, see Viau
Thibaud, Roger de 203
Thierry, Denys 311 n.
Thomas à Kempis, Thomas Merken, known as (1380?–1471) 254–7
Thomas, Augustin and Pierre 334
Tirso de Molina (or Gabriel Téllez) (c.1584–1648) 167 n.
Tomlinson, Philip 81, 153
Torelli, Giacomo (1608–78) 211
Tornell, R. Vera 164–5 n.
Traité pour juger des Poëtes Grecs, Latins, et François 240 n., 371
Trask, Willard 65 n.
Trier, Elector of 95–6
Triomphe de Louis et de son siècle, Le 19, 36, 39, 94, 223, 311 n., 319, 347, 353–5, 371
Tristan L'Hermite, François Du Solier, known as (1601–65) 123
Truchet, Jacques 144, 209 n., 341 n.
Tulip mania 160
Turenne, Henri de la Tour d'Auvergne, Vicomte de (1611–75) 209 n.

Urban VIII, Pope (from 1623 to 1644) 241, 287, 330
Urfé, Honoré d' (1567–1625) 72, 109–10, 123–4, 129
Ursins, François Jouvenel des 53

Valençai, Léonor d'Estampes, Seigneur de (1588–1651) 183
Valgrave, François 254 n.
Vallée, Elisabeth 68–9
Vallée, Jacques, see Des Barreaux
Vauquelin de la Fresnaye, Jean (1536–1606) 314–15
Vautray, see Vautrel
Vautrel, François 85
Vega Carpio, Lope Felix de (1562–1635) 110, 155, 167 n., 192, 274
Vendôme, Alexandre de, Grand Prieur 86
Vendôme, César de Bourbon, Duc de (1594–1665) 86

Verdi, Giuseppe (1813–1901) 351 n.
Vérité des fables, La 6, 24, 66–7, 109, 128–30, 165, 186, 236, 237, 314, 365
Vernazza, E. 282
Verpré (musician) 200
Vertus, maximes, instructions, & meditations Chrestiennes 260, 372
Vial, F. 219 n.
Viau, Théophile de (1590–1626) 61, 62, 64–6, 146, 212, 273
Vie et les OEuvres de Sainte Catherine de Gênes, La 27, 28, 281–3, 369
Vigneul-Marvilliana 49, 277
Vignier, Benjamin (Capitaine of the château de Richelieu 1662–84) 150 n., 163 n.
Vignon, Claude (1593–1670) 112, 114–15, 117, 122, 127 n., 132, 169
Villars (Louis Fouquet's agent) 333–4
Ville, Antoine de (1596–1656) 96, 214
Villeloin, Abbé de, see Marolles, Michel de
Vincent de Paul, Saint (1581–1660) 99, 107–8, 264 n.
Virgil (c.70–19 BC) 50, 157, 246, 249 n., 287, 294, 296, 300, 307, 311, 340, 349
Visionnaires, Les 2, 16, 17, 25, 27, 28, 31–3, 59, 63, 64, 72, 75, 76, 130, 133–4, 144–5, 150 n., 152, 154–61, 162, 171, 179, 218, 220 n., 228, 244, 322, 340–1, 360–1
Voisin, André-Clément de 68, 70
Voiture, Vincent (1597–1648) 49 n., 85 n., 170–1, 212, 352
Voltaire, François-Marie Arouet, known as (1694–1778) 10 n., 28, 35–9, 48, 352
Von Lochon (engraver) 135–6
Voyage de Fontainebleau, Le 7–8, 16, 44–5, 68, 85 n., 87–94, 97, 358
Voyer de Paulmy, René II de, Seigneur d'Argenson (1620–1700) 229 n., 254
Vulson de la Colombière, M. 50 n.

Wagert, F. 30 n.
Wagner, Richard (1813–83) 290

Walter, G.   148 n., 174 n., 307 n.
War of Devolution   306
War of the Spanish Succession   205
War with the Netherlands   306
Weber, Carl Maria von (1786–1826)
    290
Weigert, R.-A.   291 n.
Werth, Johann von (Bavarian general)
    183
Whitman, N. T.   39 n.
Wolf, J. B.   2

Xenophon (c.430–c.354 BC)   127,
    169 n., 263, 316

Young, Bert Edward and Grace
    Philputt   34 n.
Yvan, Antoine (1574–1653)   272 n.

Zaga Christ (died 1638)   228, 237–8
Zamet, Jean and Sébastien   214
Zenobia   124